'For Diane, simply the best'

Brief Table of Contents

Preface   xiv
Guided tour   xvii
Acknowledgements   xxii

Part 1:   The firm and the creation of value

1   Economic organizations and efficiency   3
2   A strategic approach to the firm   31
3   Vertical and virtual boundaries   64
4   Horizontal boundaries and diversification   99
5   Growth and entrepreneurship   134
6   Corporate control and organizational design   170
7   Wages, incentives and human resources   209

Part 2:   Capturing value from the market

8   Market structure and the strategic environment   249
9   Imperfect competition and government intervention   284
10   The dominant firm and predation   324
11   Price discrimination and bundling   363
12   Reputation and vertical restraints   398
13   Product differentiation and advertising   442
14   Competitive advantage, invention and innovation   480

Glossary   511
Index   553

Detailed Table of Contents

Preface		xiv
Guided tour		xvii
Acknowledgements		xxii

Part I	**The firm and the creation of value**	**1**
	1 Economic organizations and efficiency	3
	Introduction	3
	Profit, revenue and costs	5
	What's in a name?	8
	The strategic environment	9
	A dramatic change of environment	12
	Game theory	13
	Competition or collusion?	15
	Creating value	16
	European exuberance	20
	Capturing value	21
	Market disciplines	24
	Competition policy	25
	Critical articles	27
	Concluding thoughts	28
	Key learning points	29
	Exercises	29
	References	30
	2 A strategic approach to the firm	31
	Introduction	31
	The neo-classical paradigm	32
	Three steps to heaven	35
	Towards a model of the firm	36
	Transaction costs	39
	Organizational architecture	39
	Organizational change at General Motors	42
	An historical perspective	43
	The pursuit of excellence	47
	The firm as a governance structure	47
	Marks and Spencer	51
	A competence approach	52
	An evolutionary firm	56
	An integrated approach to the firm	57

Concluding thoughts   60
    Key learning points   61
    Exercises   62
    Problems   62
References   62

3 Vertical and virtual boundaries   64
Introduction   64
Vertical integration   66
    Vertically expanding farmers   69
Private information and uncertainty   70
    Fashion to go   73
Transaction costs   74
    Cosworth   75
    Hold-up   79
Governance approach   79
    Power in more than one sense   83
A competency approach   83
    Vivendi   85
Alternatives to vertical integration   86
    Dell computers   92
Concluding thoughts   93
    Key learning points   94
    Exercises   95
    Problems   95
References   96
Appendix   97

4 Horizontal boundaries and diversification   99
Introduction   99
Scale effects   101
    Minimum Efficient Scale   104
Learning by doing   104
    A threatened species   108
Multi-plant economies   109
Economies of scope   112
    Changing the focus   115
Diversification   116
    A tale of two multiples   122
Boundaries, coherence and uncertainty   122
    Boredom or exuberance   126
Virtual boundaries   127
    Joined-up wireless   129
Concluding thoughts   130
    Key learning points   131
    Exercises   132

Problems	132
References	133
5 Growth and entrepreneurship	**134**
Introduction	134
An agenda for growth	136
Sales maximization	136
Sales forces	138
Growth and demand	139
Out with the old	143
Growth of supply	143
Microsoft's core competency	148
Entrepreneurship	149
Biotechnology	152
A managerial model of growth	153
From smells to fragrances	160
Mergers and acquisitions	160
LloydsTSB marries a widow	163
Concluding thoughts	164
Key learning points	165
Exercises	166
Problems	166
References	166
Appendix	168
6 Corporate control and organizational design	**170**
Introduction	170
Management costs	172
Explaining the gap	176
Organizational architecture	177
From predator to quarry	184
Non-profit-maximizing behaviour	185
Will a leprechaun bring success?	189
Principal–agent theory	190
Farmer controlled	195
Stakeholder capitalism	196
A phoenix snuffed out	199
Concluding thoughts	200
Key learning points	201
Exercises	202
Problems	202
References	203
Appendices	204

7 Wages, incentives and human resources   209
  Introduction   209
  The supply of labour   211
    Trade union power   215
  The demand for labour   215
    The death of orthodoxy   217
  Imperfect markets   218
    Reversing roles   221
  Employment contracts   222
    Team work   224
  Motivating effort   224
  Attracting and retaining employees   232
    Planning for succession   236
  Concluding thoughts   237
    Key learning points   238
    Exercises   239
    Problems   239
  References   240
  Appendices   241

Part II   Capturing value from the market   247

8 Market structure and the strategic environment   249
  Introduction   249
  Competition or rivalry?   250
    EU competition policy   253
  The structure–conduct–performance paradigm   254
    Seeking compatibility between NACE and NAICS   256
  Seller concentration   256
    Food retailing   259
  Industry or strategic groups?   260
    Going Dutch   263
  Conduct and performance   264
    Structural change   268
  Porter's Five Forces Model   269
    Interpreting competition   274
  Clusters and networks   275
    The Community, clusters and competitiveness   279
  Concluding thoughts   279
    Key learning points   281
    Exercises   281
    Problems   282
  References   282

9 Imperfect competition and government intervention 284
Introduction 284
Mutual interdependence 286
Simultaneous quantity setting 288
Market sharing in the Belgian beer market 294
Price-setting models 294
Eurotunnel 297
Dynamics and uncertainty 298
Testing market power 302
A game theoretic approach 302
Vitamins and healthy competition 306
Cartels and industrial policies 307
Airbus Industries 313
Concluding thoughts 314
Key learning points 315
Exercises 316
Problems 316
References 317
Appendices 318

10 The dominant firm and predation 324
Introduction 324
Dominance and entry barriers 326
Competing for market 330
Quantity leadership 330
Through a glass darkly 334
Price leadership 335
Taking the lead 338
Strategic deterrence 339
Locking-in 347
Predatory pricing 347
The practice of dominance 354
Competition law and predation 355
Newspaper price wars 357
Concluding thoughts 357
Key learning points 358
Exercises 359
Problems 359
References 360
Appendix 361

11 Price discrimination and bundling 363
Introduction 363
Price discrimination 365
Parallel imports 367

First-degree price discrimination 369
  Road sense 372
Second-degree price discrimination 373
  Turning the screw 376
Third-degree price discrimination 377
  Low-cost airlines 380
Differentiation and discrimination 381
  Lessening the noise 387
Bundling 387
  Micro bundling 390
Competition policy and price discrimination 391
Concluding thoughts 393
  Key learning points 394
  Exercises 394
  Problems 394
References 395
Appendix 396

12 Reputation and vertical restraints 398
Introduction 398
Pricing with imperfect information 400
  Vanishing variety 405
Pricing quality 406
  Cows and confusion 412
Vertical exchange relationships 413
  A tale of two auction houses 418
Vertical restraints 419
  A chip off the old block 428
Vertical restraints and competition policy 429
Concluding thoughts 432
  Key learning points 434
  Exercises 435
  Problems 435
References 436
Appendices 437

13 Production differentiation and advertising 442
Introduction 442
Product differentiation and consumers' preference 444
  Conspicuous consumption 452
Optimal advertising 452
  Fatal attraction 457
Advertising as a source of information 458
  Frightfully British 462
Persuasion or signalling? 462

Monopolizing merchandising 467

Advertising and market structure 467

Concluding thoughts 472

Key learning points 473

Exercises 474

Problems 475

References 475

Appendix 478

14 Competitive advantage, invention and innovation 480

Introduction 480

Competitive advantage 482

Recording a competitive advantage 487

Market structure and pay-off 488

Innovation or imitation? 492

Strategic innovation behaviour 492

Racing for a prize 496

Patents and diffusion 497

Delayed diffusion 501

Organizing for innovation 501

Concluding thoughts 506

Key learning points 508

Exercises 508

Problems 509

References 509

Glossary 511

Index 553

Preface

What is it that business students need to learn from a course in economics? Some will go on to become professional economists, but the vast majority will seek careers in management of functional specialisms such as marketing, finance or information systems. Yet, to operate successfully in such positions requires a clear focus on efficiency, and an understanding of the working of markets and exchange transactions. Whether the concern is the co-ordination and motivation of subordinates and colleagues or devising a strategic response to competitors' rivalry, successfully carrying out these activities benefits from a knowledge of economics – specifically, the application of economic thought to the inner workings of organizations and their interaction with rival firms in a business environment. This book is focused very clearly on providing business students with an economics textbook whose subject matter is directly relevant to the real world and therefore aiding a better understanding of business behaviour and solving the problems of modern business life. This book seeks to capture the interest of business students by bringing together the twin pillars of business life – strategy and organizational structure – within an economics framework.

Economics in a Business Environment

All managers, whatever their level of seniority, must have the ability to not only successfully formulate and implement plans, but also to co-ordinate and motivate those they lead. In a world of increasing global integration and rapid technological change, firms have to be responsive to a continuously changing business environment. This necessitates not only an ability to think and act strategically, but also the building of organizational structures that are highly motivated, very knowledgeable and flexible. For this reason strategic flair and organizational efficiency are the backbone of a successful business, and in both cases a thorough understanding necessitates familiarity with the concepts and tools of industrial economics. Where this book differs from the traditional business or management microeconomics textbook is that it is less focused on economics as a subject in its own right and primarily concerned with the application of economic concepts and methodologies to strategic and organizational issues.

In this author's experience most economic textbooks, even when titled business or management economies, are not sufficiently focused on the realities of business life to catch the imagination of students planning a career in business. The traditional approach is to slavishly set out highly theoretical models, which assume away many of the problems and issues that those working in business encounter in practice. In such books competitive strategy is frequently confined to the comparative statics of equilibrium models and the inner working of the firm is treated as a 'black box'. In reality, competitive strategy is undertaken in an environment of imperfect and asymmetric information and encompasses a wide variety of strategic and tactical decision making. As regards the firm, the day-to-day reality is striving to overcome efficiency-constraining behaviour such as the pursuit by individuals of personal goals and a failure to balance motivation with rewards. The learning needs of future managers demand a closer study of these matters and, in particular, the contribution of economics to their understanding.

Strategic management textbooks generally make the implicit assumption that readers have a detailed knowledge of the economic theories and concepts that underpin much of the analysis of strategic behaviour. Such books are replete with the jargon of strategy, such as outsourcing, core competencies and alliances, all of which are founded on older economic theories. If students lack the appropriate grounding in economics, then knowledge of these strategic concepts can only be superficial. Most importantly, it is still rare to find other than a cursory acknowledgement of game theory – the analysis of strategic behaviour – in strategic management textbooks. Similarly, when it comes to the internal structure and behaviour of firms, very few textbooks draw on economic theories and concepts to explain management hierarchies, physical boundaries, diversification and inter-firm co-operation.

Change is gathering pace and within business schools economics is increasingly being taught from the perspective of business needs. There are now a few textbooks that explicitly place the teaching of strategy and organizational efficiency within the framework of industrial economics. But, they primarily focus on either strategy or organizational efficiency: bringing the two pillars of competitive advantage together within an industrial economics framework is rare. In the view of this author, it is not sensible to separate an examination of strategic behaviour from an examination of the way firms develop and utilize their resources. In addition to explicitly combining the study of strategy and organizational efficiency within an industrial economics framework, there is also a need to present the learning in ways that are accessible. For students lacking a degree in economics, this requires an emphasis on narrative and diagrams to augment a modest resort to formulae.

Why Adopt This Book?

This book has evolved from my experience here at Cranfield of teaching graduate students from many different backgrounds the relevance of economics to business life. It does this by applying an economist's perspective to strategic behaviour and organizational efficiency. Although the subject matter is pitched above the standard economics textbook, it assumes only a basic knowledge of economics, and from my experience of teaching MBA students, much of the text is accessible without any previous knowledge of economics. The book devotes space and care to developing the reader's understanding of more advanced concepts and methodologies so as to impart a much greater depth of knowledge of strategic and organizational behaviour. Although the text resorts occasionally to formulae, it does not assume an advanced level of mathematics and care is taken to explain and demonstrate all concepts and methodologies.

The opening chapter sets the framework for the book by exploring the explicit link between the achievement of a firm's strategic goals and the simultaneous achievement of external and internal efficiency. It goes on to show how concepts of efficiency underpin both the creation of value within the firm and also its ability to capture the value created from the market. The opening chapter also introduces two themes that run throughout the book; namely, the use of game theory to study strategic interactions and the role of competition policy in encouraging higher levels of business efficiency. The book is then separated into two parts: the first focuses on the contribution of a firm's organizational structure – or as described in this book, its organizational architecture – to its competitive positioning and profitability. The second part of the book places the firm within its external environment and examines alternative strategic behaviours that can be employed to maximize the value of its position within different market structures. In a little more detail, the main subject areas covered by the two sections are:

- **Part I: The firm and the creation of value** The neo-classical approach to the firm is augmented by the addition of two complementary approaches: an examination of the firm as a governance structure and as a creator of heterogeneous competencies. In this part of the book, these approaches are employed to examine the contribution a firm's organizational architecture and resources make to the creation of strategic opportunities and competitive advantage. The governance and competency explanations of the primary functions of firms are explored in order to explain variations in the structure and capabilities of firms. Topics dealt with include *inter alia*: internal control and reward systems; production scale and scope; vertical integration and vertical relationships; diversification; mergers and acquisitions, strategic alliances; entrepreneurship; growth; and organizational forms. The purpose is not only to demonstrate the importance of motivating and co-ordinating a firm's workforce so that its capabilities are internally consistent and aligned with the firm's strategic objectives, but also to explore the policies and procedures that might be employed to achieve this objective.

- **Part II: Capturing value from the market** Building on the importance of an internally consistent set of capabilities and their alignment with strategic objectives, this part of the book examines how a firm's proximate market environment and its strategic interactions influence its financial performance and the behaviour of rivals. In essence, the chapters that comprise this part explore how a firm's capabilities can be positioned for maximum competitive advantage in varying external environments. Topics dealt with include *inter alia*: market structures; strategic groups; price leadership; price discrimination and predation; communicating and capturing the value of quality; non-price strategies; and the role of invention and innovation in determining competitive advantage. The approach uses a combination of economic models of market structures and game theory to provide an understanding of strategic behaviour and the contribution such interactions make to competitive advantage and the capture of value.

This book is differentiated by its range and treatment of topics. Its value to business students is that, within its covers a very wide range of key business topics of direct relevance to organizational efficiency and strategy are explained and demonstrated. I have striven to write in a style that is both capable of being understood by someone with a limited knowledge of economics while also representing a challenge to a more advanced student. The text contains many illustrations and examples drawn primarily from the European business environment, including mini case studies that relate the learning to real-world examples. Key concepts are highlighted in bold and are explained in more detail in a glossary. Each chapter includes a summary of key learning points, student exercises and references.

Guided Tour

Example Boxes

The book includes example boxes throughout, to apply the chapter material to real-world situations.

Figures and Tables

Each chapter provides a number of figures and tables to help you to visualize the various economic models, and to illustrate and summarize important concepts.

Key Learning Points

Each chapter ends with a list of key points, summarizing what readers should have learnt from each chapter.

Concluding Thoughts

This briefly reviews and reinforces the main topics you will have covered in each chapter to ensure you have acquired a solid understanding of the key topics.

Exercises and Problems

These end-of-chapter features are the perfect way to practice the techniques you have been taught and apply the methodology to real-world situations.

Technology to enhance learning and teaching

Visit www.mcgraw-hill.co.uk/textbooks/rickard today

Online Learning Centre (OLC)

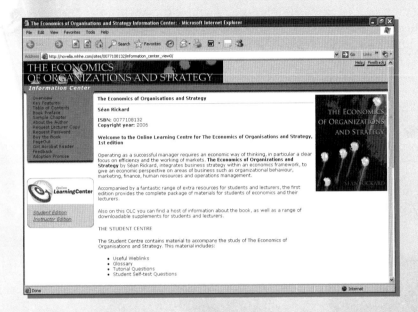

After completing each chapter, log on to the supporting Online Learning Centre website. Take advantage of the study tools offered to reinforce the material you have read in the text, and to develop your knowledge of marketing in a fun and effective way.

Resources for students include:

- Chapter summaries
- Weblinks
- Glossary
- Self-assessment exercises

Also available for lecturers:

- Power Point Slides
- Lecturer's manual
- Tutorial questions

Lecturers: Customize Content for your Courses using the McGraw-Hill Primis Content Centre

Now it's incredibly easy to create a flexible, customized solution for your course, using content from both US and European McGraw-Hill Education textbooks, content from our Professional list including Harvard Business Press titles, as well as a selection of over 9,000 cases from Harvard, Insead and Darden. In addition, we can incorporate your own material and course notes.

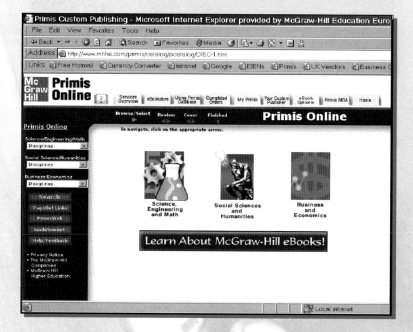

For more information, please contact your local rep who will discuss the right delivery options for your custom publication – including printed readers, e-Books and CDROMs. To see what McGraw-Hill content you can choose from, visit **www.primisonline.com**.

Study Skills

Open University Press publishes guides to study, research and exam skills to help undergraduate and postgraduate students through their university studies.

Visit www.openup.co.uk/ss to see the full selection of study skills titles, and get a £2 discount by entering the promotional code study when buying online!

Acknowledgements

This book has evolved over several years of teaching economics to MBA students at the Cranfield School of Management. Their classroom challenges, debates and insights based on wide-ranging business experiences have been invaluable in helping me to collect my thoughts. I want to thank them and my colleagues at Cranfield for all their support and encouragement. Very special thanks go to Dawn Richardson, who suffered through the typing of many drafts and my illegible adjustments with good cheer and professionalism. She spent many hours preparing the illustrations, working at great speed and with uncanny accuracy, for which I am extremely grateful.

Séan Rickard

The publishers would like to thank the following reviewers for their comments at various stages of the text's development.

Bob Rothschild, Lancaster University
Todd Kaplan, University of Exeter
Guglielmo Volpe, London Metropolitan University
Carlo Morelli, Dundee University
Ola Sholarin, Westminster University
Martin Robson, Durham University
Claudio Piga, Loughborough University
Phil Bowers, University of Edinburgh
James Wilson, Glasgow Caledonian University
Catherine Heyes, Royal Holloway University of London
John Chard, University of Exeter
Staffan Hulten, Stockholm School of Economics
Jorn Rothe, London School of Economics
Bruce Rayton, University of Bath
Romano Dyerson, Royal Holloway, University of London

PART I

THE FIRM AND THE CREATION OF VALUE

CHAPTER 1

ECONOMIC ORGANIZATIONS AND EFFICIENCY

Introduction

We all spend our lives as members of a variety of groupings. Whenever people come together in a group they form an organization. The family is an organization, as is a school and a hospital. The particular type of organization we are concerned with in this book is an economic or business organization, which is more frequently described as a *firm*. A firm produces goods or services. Throughout this book we will use the word *product* to represent either a good or a service. A firm is a productive organization, within which people interact and co-operate to achieve the firm's collective goals and also their own individual goals. An organization's goals and the goals of those who are paid an income or dividend by the organization are espoused values shaped by economic, institutional and cultural factors. For the moment, we will make the simplifying assumption that a firm's collective goal is to make a *profit*. Even a not-for-profit organization must have a profit objective; namely, to avoid a negative profit, i.e. a loss by breaking even.

The profit goal for a commercial firm owned by members of the public is to maximize the value of its shareholders' investment, i.e. profits over the life of the firm. For a non-profit organization the goal will be to maximize some other variable, e.g. the quality of advice or the distribution of aid. In all cases, the achievement of a firm's goals are subject to the quality of the *resources* that the firm has at its disposal, and in particular the quality of its management resources. If organizations are successfully to meet their goals – successfully, in the sense that it would not be possible with fewer resources to achieve their goals – they must achieve *productive efficiency*. This means not only avoiding the waste inherent in not fully employing their existing resources, but also ensuring that individual resources are utilized in ways that maximize their contribution. Idle or under-utilized resources add unnecessarily to costs, preventing the firm from minimizing its production costs. Although productive efficiency is a necessary condition for success, it is rarely sufficient. In practice, a firm is unlikely to achieve its goals solely by minimizing production costs.

Productive efficiency does not guarantee that a firm's target customers will be prepared to pay a price for its output that covers the costs of production; indeed, they might not be prepared to buy its products at any price. A successful firm is therefore one that is capable of producing products for which not only is demand sufficient to ensure that revenue exceeds production costs, but also there is no alternative allocation of the firm's resources capable of delivering a greater excess of revenue over costs. A firm is defined as having achieved ***allocative efficiency*** when its resources are aligned with the markets in which demand for its products is highest. Productive and allocative efficiency is therefore necessary for the creation of maximum value, but it is not sufficient. A successful firm must also succeed in capturing its full share of the value it creates by means of effective marketing and pricing strategies. In essence, a successful firm manages to combine *productive and allocative efficiency with the ability to capture the value created.*

The marshalling of a firm's pool of resources efficiently to produce and sell products that are viewed by customers as competitively meeting their specific demands is the domain of strategy. The nature and scope of strategy varies according to the level under consideration. For a large, multibusiness firm – more generally known as a corporation – ***corporate strategy*** is concerned with determining the markets that will maximize the corporation's profits. For specialist firms or business units within corporations, ***business strategy*** is directed at efficiently meeting the demands of existing and potential customers in individual markets. A feature of contemporary business life is the widespread use of collaborative relationships between firms and this has given rise to ***network strategy*** where the focus is the co-ordination of the separate firms' resources better to achieve productive and allocative efficiency.

The prime purpose of this book is to set out, analyse and explore the contribution of economic principles to the design and conduct of strategy. Its aim is to integrate economic theory and the foundations of strategy in a manner that will emphasize the economic underpinnings of sustained ***competitive advantage***. A careful study of this book will provide the reader with an in-depth understanding of relevant economic theories and concepts that can help a firm to successfully achieve its strategic goals. The prime learning outcome from reading this book will be the ability to apply relevant economic theories and concepts to determine:

- How the structure and management of a firm's organizational architecture can enable it to achieve the highest levels of efficiency, leading to the creation of value and competitive advantage.
- How knowledge of its customers and business rivals helps a firm choose more profitable markets in which to sell and within these markets how to capture the value inherent in its competitive advantage.
- How a firm's scale, scope, capabilities and reputation help it adapt to a changing external ***business environment*** and evolve to new scales and capabilities.

This opening chapter utilizes our simplifying assumption, that firms exist to maximize profit in order to outline what is the underlying theme of this book; namely, that the economic concepts of productive and allocative efficiency are the foundations of business strategy. At its broadest level, we can think of productive efficiency as being determined by factors internal to the firm, such as its ability to attract, motivate and co-ordinate people with the right balance of skills and knowledge. Again at the broadest level, we can view allocative efficiency as a response to the firm's external environment. The choice of markets, the quality and variety of its products – in essence the positioning of the firm relative to its competitors – are crucial to strategic success. As these twin pillars of internal productive efficiency and external allocative efficiency provide the platform upon which this book rests, it is appropriate to devote this opening chapter to showing how a firm's external environment conditions both external and internal behaviour. Having read this chapter you will:

- Appreciate the importance of the business environment in determining the strategic context in which a firm chooses the balance of co-operation and competition with rivals.
- Understand how the way in which a firm manages its resources determines not only its internal efficiency but also its formulation of strategy.
- Be aware of the role of economic models and in particular **game theory** in analysing interactions within the firm and externally with rivals.

What follows is divided into six sections. The first section links the most fundamental of all business relationships – the profit equation – to a firm's internal and external environment. Each chapter in this book deals with a different element of a firm's internal or external behaviour but every element links back to the profit equation, and to drive home the point this section contains a brief case study on Richard Branson's Virgin that draws out a number of the issues that are dealt with in the following chapters. The second section provides a broad introduction to the business environment by identifying three distinct layers: the markets in which the firm competes; the macroeconomic environment; and the global economic environment. For this book, the external environment is largely confined to a firm's proximate market environment. However, it is appropriate at this early stage to acknowledge the influence of government and **European Union** (EU) policies as well as the growing influence of international bodies such as the World Trade Organization (WTO) and global economic activity in general.

The third section introduces an important tool for analysing strategic behaviour that we will feature prominently. Game theory provides many valuable insights into behaviour in situations of interdependence and is as relevant when considering behaviour within the firm as strategic interactions with rivals. The fourth section examines in more detail the relationship between efficiency and the impact on both production costs and revenue. The minimization of costs and the maximization of the gap between revenue and costs determine the success of a profit-maximization strategy and in the fifth section the concept of **organizational architecture** is introduced to show how firms seek the efficiencies that create value at minimum cost. The sixth section shows how game theory sheds light on the efficient capture, via revenue, of the value created. In particular, how the adoption of a co-operative stance can generate a higher revenue than aggressive competition. A co-operative stance does not necessitate explicit collusion with rivals; indeed, such relationships are generally outlawed. The final section provides a brief overview of **competition policy** in order to emphasize the limits to co-operation amongst rivals and also to establish a key determinant of the business environment.

Profits, Revenue and Costs

Although non-profit economic organizations make an important contribution to economic activity, overwhelmingly in a **capitalist system** it is profit-making firms that dominate the **supply side** of economic activity. This fact, together with the knowledge that it is easier to demonstrate the principles of productive and allocative efficiency if we concentrate on profit-making organizations, justifies the focus on profit-making firms for much of this book. The prime objective of a profit-making organization is to maximize the value it delivers to its owners over its lifetime. The reference to 'over its lifetime' is important. It would have made very little sense to assess the profitability of Eurotunnel solely on one or even all of the years it took to construct the channel tunnel. Again, the profits of a firm that is currently undergoing a programme of restructuring to better align its resources with anticipated market conditions is unlikely to provide a reliable guide to future profits. What is beyond dispute is that for a firm to have a value in excess of the sale value of its assets, there must be an expectation that in the future revenue will exceed costs. A firm that is prone to incurring losses will, sooner or later, cease to exist or it will be taken over by another firm. Notwithstanding the importance of taking a perspective that is longer than a year, in practice, profit performance is normally measured on an annual basis, e.g. by company accounts. For the moment, we can demonstrate the relationship between business strategy and economic concepts by confining attention to a discrete period of time, say, one year, and by so doing we can sum up profitability with the following fundamental equation:

$$\pi = TR - TC \tag{1.1}$$

where TR is the total revenue generated by the firm from its sales over the year, TC is the total cost of resources employed by the firm in generating this revenue and π is the profit achieved.

One way to capture the essence of this book is to appreciate that all that follows is concerned with the expansion, in words and diagrams, of the economics lying behind the right-hand side of Equation (1.1) and in particular to examine in what way productive and allocative efficiencies reduce TC and boost TR. Each of the following chapters examines in some detail strategic economic concepts that directly influence costs or revenues or both. But in contrast to traditional economic approaches to the firm, this book will provide a much greater focus on the firm as an organization and as a player in a strategic game. The traditional economic approach to the firm treats the inner workings of economic organizations as a 'black box' and the markets they sell into as approaching **perfect competition**. Yet reality is very different. The way in which a firm organizes itself and the fact that most sell into markets that would more correctly be defined as examples of **imperfect competition** are the very essence of business life. As Herbert Simon (1991, p. 27) observed, 'a mythical Martian equipped with a telescope that reveals social structures and approaches earth from space would recognise organizations rather than connecting markets as the dominant feature of the landscape.' Why economic organizations exist, how they are constructed and the ways in which they interact in pursuit of competitive advantage and profits is what this book is about.

An important empirical observation is that the profitability of firms within the same industry differs and these differences tend to persist over long periods. One of the tenets of **neo-classical economics** is that competition erodes such differences. In part, explanations can be found in **industrial organization** economics and game theory. The former offers concepts such as **entry barriers**, learning and **first-mover advantage** and the latter concepts such as **pre-emption**, **reputation** and **co-operation** to explain the persistence of differing profit rates for firms in the same industry. To these essentially external explanations can be added **transaction costs** and **resource-based** economics. These concepts lead to an internal focus on the way decision-making authority is delegated, performance is motivated and people rewarded. They also stress the importance of accumulated knowledge and its embeddedness in organizational systems and routines. All these concepts can be linked to the right-hand side of Equation (1.1), though they tend to be dynamic rather than static concepts.

Ultimately, for a profit-making organization, its measure of success must be profit but this calls for a broader strategy than aligning a firm's resources with its external environment. It also necessitates the elimination of waste, including impediments to the accumulation and application of new knowledge. Although the elements set out in Equation (1.1) are merely the tip of an iceberg they do rest on the twin pillars of efficiency. Despite Pigou's (1922, p. 463) rather lofty claim, 'it is not the business of economists to teach woollen manufacturers to make and sell wool', economic theory has a great deal to contribute towards an understanding of the efficient operation and market behaviour of an economic organization. Economic relationships are the bedrock of both the internal workings of the firm and its external behaviour. The key to efficiency and profitability is the nature of relationships and interactions. Within the firm, employees interact to achieve their own and the firm's goals and, externally, firms interact with suppliers, customers and business rivals to achieve their goals. Before looking in more detail at the relationship between these interactions and strategy, the mini case study below, outlining the rise of Virgin from an unsuccessful publisher of the *Student* magazine to a global brand, provides some insights into the economic principles and behaviours that underlie the building of a successful profitable organization.

Virgin succeeded because the entrepreneurial Richard Branson, despite an initial failure, had the vision to identify market segments where consumer demand was not being fully met and then had the energy and sufficient skill to focus Virgin's resources on meeting this demand. Richard Branson named his company Virgin and whether by design or default this was an appropriate description of the young entrepreneur's business experience. But he learnt quickly and by applying his accumulated knowledge, Virgin very quickly began to profitably exploit the market segments identified by Branson. But success breeds its own problems and as Virgin rapidly grew in size so it had to rapidly accumulate the managerial skills necessary to run a large-scale business efficiently. Building, co-ordinating and motivating a large-scale workforce efficiently necessitated building an organizational architecture with the flexibility to grow with the firm and accommodate its leader's passion for **diversification**. As Virgin diversified into new **market segments**, so systems of control and co-ordination had to become more sophisticated, providing Virgin's managers with new opportunities to apply their learning and to accumulate more knowledge. Virgin's persistent profitability reflected not only a focused and motivated workforce, but also the maintenance by its managers of a shared vision and values. The identification of profitable demands and the organizational ability to meet them competitively are, as observed above, the basic necessities of success. But it would be incorrect to assume that meeting these objectives guarantees success. In the real world, success is not so easily won.

Virgin did not have the markets it entered to itself. It had to compete with other suppliers and in so doing it had to engage in competitive rivalry. An important, but by no means exclusive, influence on the nature of competitive rivalry is the structure of the market. The structure of the airline market which Virgin entered in 1984 was an **oligopoly**. Essentially, Branson faced only three direct business rivals on the transatlantic route: British Airways, Pan Am and People Express (a similar operation to Branson's). Oligopolistic markets are characterized by interdependence: a competitive move by one firm, say a reduction in price, will have a dramatic impact on the profits of rivals. In addition, all firms have to adjust to random events, i.e. shocks that disturb the external environment's underlying trends. Thus, whether the focus is the internal operation of a firm or its external relationships, the Virgin story offers many valuable insights.

What's in a Name?

Consider the situation back in 1967, as the 17-year-old Richard Branson, a fledgling entrepreneur, contemplated the launch of his brainchild, *Student* magazine. Branson had invested money and time in developing *Student*. He had built up a small workforce, from his fellow students, and he used a nearby public payphone as his office. But launching any new product is a risk and despite parting company earlier than anticipated with the exclusive Stowe School to devote all his attention to the *Student* magazine, it was not a runaway success. Undaunted by the lack of profits and in the true spirit of an entrepreneur, Branson turned his attention to a new enterprise: the retailing of records. He saw an opportunity to profitably undercut traditional record retailers and he used the last issue of *Student* to advertise records of bands and singers on the fringe of the rock scene at a 15 per cent discount. Casting around for a name for his new business, he came up with Virgin, a name that certainly reflected his commercial innocence.

By luck or design, Branson had struck gold. He had identified a market in which demand was growing rapidly and as a mail order business Virgin did not incur the costs of traditional retail outlets. So rapid was the growth of sales – in excess of 20 per cent per year – that within a few years Virgin Records had become a large-scale business and despite Branson's somewhat 'less rigid' management style, it was being transformed into an organization with a command and control architecture.

As time passed and demand continued to grow, so Virgin Records began to reap the benefits of a large-scale organization. One

consequence of the growth of sales was the economies that arise from the cost-reducing effects of large scale and the benefits were reinforced as Virgin's management and employees gained experience and accumulated knowledge that enabled them to improve the efficiency of their operations. But as an entrepreneur, Branson could not rest on his laurels. He used Virgin's profits to invest in its own record stores, thereby expanding Virgin's horizontal boundaries from a mail order business to a high street retailer.

Despite the company's phenomenal rate of growth during the 1970s, the 1980s started badly for Virgin Records. The UK entered a period of severe recession and demand for records fell sharply, causing Virgin to register a loss of about £1m in 1981. This 'shock' to Virgin's business environment had not been anticipated, but again, Branson's entrepreneurial flair came to the rescue. In the 1970s, in addition to expanding its horizontal boundaries, Virgin had also expanded its vertical boundaries by moving 'upstream' to produce its own records. The punk rock band, the Sex Pistols, were one of the first groups to be signed. Virgin also extended its vertical boundaries 'downstream' by purchasing two London nightclubs. The risks paid off. Just as demand for records in the UK suffered in a deep recession, so Virgin's revenue started to benefit as some of the bands signed in the 1970s became globally successful. Between 1982 and 1983, turnover doubled to £94m and profits soared to £11m.

Branson's entrepreneurial instincts continued to drive the business and in an abrupt change of direction, in 1984 he launched the airline, Virgin Atlantic. Thus, by the mid-1980s the

continued

Virgin brand had extended into artistic management, films, nightclubs, computer games and an airline. A diverse range of activities inevitably places great pressures on a company's senior managers to develop a corporate strategy that ensures a coherent organization. Branson responded to the pressures of diversity by organizing Virgin into a number of separate business units, each charged with developing their own strategies; the common link being the brand name Virgin, which by the 1980s was one of the world's best-known brands. The strategic development of Branson's burgeoning empire continued with the sale in 1993 of the record side of the business – Virgin Music Group – to Thorn EMI. Two years later, Virgin Direct Financial Services and Virgin Cola were launched and in 1997 Virgin won the franchise to operate West Coast rail services in Great Britain. By the end of the 1990s, Virgin had not only grown vertically and horizontally, but also it had diversified into a conglomerate business with a turnover of more than a billion pounds per year.

The Strategic Environment

Firms do not exist in isolation. At the level of the business unit, firms are players within an industry and, with the exception of a ***monopoly***, firms compete with industry rivals for a share of the value created by consumers' demand. Although government statisticians allocate firms to an industry grouping, the practice is not particularly helpful to a study of strategic behaviour. In part, this is due to the fact that the boundaries of an industry are frequently unclear and at the level of a specialized firm or business unit the focus for strategy is one or more market segments. A market is a set of products that may be thought of as sharing similar uses and/or ***attributes***. Most importantly, markets frequently span the officially delineated industry boundaries. For example, the producers of butter are officially located in the manufacture of dairy products industry, but they compete with the producers of margarine, who are classified by government statisticians as part of the manufacture of vegetable oils industry. The size of an individual market is determined by demand and within each market a firm's share of demand depends not only on consumers' perceptions of the relative value of its products, but also on the extent of the information possessed by consumers and the behaviour of rivals.

One of the first steps towards understanding the strategic interaction between firms was the recognition by Mason (1939) that the size and number of firms competing for market share influences their behaviour. A few years earlier, Chamberlain (1933), with his model of ***monopolistic competition***, had sought to demonstrate how the characteristics of the products being offered for sale also influenced behaviour. Some markets are characterized by great volatility, e.g. fashion goods, others by rapid technological change. In volatile markets, strategic uncertainty is high and it is rational for firms to seek to reduce their exposure to risk and uncertainty by attempting to influence the behaviour of rival firms. The technique for analyzing market situations of interdependence was invented by von Neumann and Morgenstern (1944), but it was not until the 1970s that game theory started to make its mark. And in the 1980s, Michael Porter (1980) revolutionized the study of strategy with his ***Five Forces Model***, which provides a systematic way of studying how competitive forces work at an industry level.

A key influence on the nature of competition between market rivals is government policy. Governments not only determine the underlying legislative framework by means of ***competition policies***, but also they frequently directly influence the competitive process with ***industrial policies***. Their fiscal, monetary and trade policies influence overall demand and cost inflation. Thus, individual firms may deal on a daily basis with their proximate markets but the framework in which they compete and coexist with rivals has been determined beyond their industries' boundaries by regional, national, EU and international policies, e.g. multilateral trade agreements. In democratic countries we assume that the political system ensures that (on the whole) government policies are consistent with majority opinion regarding the scope and role of government involvement in the working of the economy. We rely on the political system to resolve conflicts such as demands for economic growth and a comprehensive welfare system. The latter necessitate high rates of taxation, whereas the former appears more likely to be achieved – particularly as global competition increases – with the motivation imparted by lower rates of taxation.

As implied by the reference to global competition, the external business environment stretches beyond national boundaries to the wider world. Both economic organizations and governments are influenced in their respective strategies and policies by global developments. The trend towards *free trade*, the existence of a global financial market and 'shocks' such as the collapse of the Soviet Union all influence the business environment, even for firms that do not directly compete with overseas rivals. The liberalizing and deepening of international economic relationships are a manifestation of what has become known as *globalization* (Williamson, 1998). Globalization has a direct influence on the business environment by opening up markets to overseas competitors and an indirect influence via the response of government policies and legislation to the process of globalization. Finally, we should also acknowledge that a growing external pressure is for firms to conduct their business in ways that limit environmental damage. We might think therefore of an individual firm's strategic environment as being determined by essentially three factors: the nature of the products it sells and the behaviour of its competitors; the national economic system within which it operates, including relevant EU policies; and the 'openness' of its markets to the influence of global economic and political events. These three factors represent the firm's external business environment and are summarized by the three outer concentric circles in Figure 1.1.

What Figure 1.1 represents is a multi-layer environment of constant change, driven in large measure over recent years as much by the rapid development of *information and communication technology* (ICT) as by the process of globalization. Globalization is a process underpinned by the ascendancy of *economic liberalization* and greatly reinforced by ICT, which has exponentially improved global communications by removing many of the constraints imposed by time and distance. Hence the direction of the arrows in the figure pointing from global economic and political events towards the firm. Globalization has also encouraged, and is encouraging, nation states to divest aspects of sovereignty to international organizations such as the European Union, the World Trade Organization (WTO) and the United Nations. In the case of the EU, membership automatically results in many decisions concerning the business environment being taken at the level of the European Community; most notably competition policy. Thus, globalization is blurring the boundaries between the influence of national governments and that of regional blocs and global groupings. And straddling the industry, national and global environments are transnational corporations who by their scale of operation have a major influence on the business environment of nations where they locate.

The forces outlined above determine the business environment and individual firms have no choice but to respond to these forces when formulating their strategies. The nature of their strategic responses will be influenced by many factors – e.g. a multilateral trade agreement – but the greatest influence is likely to be the proximate strategic behaviour of rivals. We can think of the strategic behaviour of all firms as being a weighting of co-operation and competition with rivals. The strategic position that results will determine not only the variety, quality and prices of the products offered for sale – and hence the welfare of their customers – but also the firm's demand for employees and its reliance on other firms for the supply of key inputs. Finally, the more effectively firms can meet the demands of the domestic population, the more likely that they will be internationally competitive with benefits for the balance of payments. The consequences of the response of firms to their business environment is represented by the arrows pointing down from the firm in Figure 1.1.

This book is primarily concerned with the firm and its proximate competitive environment, i.e. the two inner rings in Figure 1.1. This is the subject area of **microeconomics** and, as its name implies, it is an area of study that is focused on explaining the behaviour of individual elements of the economic system, such as consumers, firms and markets. It seeks to explain why the volume, variety and prices of the products produced in an economy are constantly undergoing change. Its explanations are based on theories and empirical studies that reach back more than 200 years, over which time theories have been introduced, improved or discarded so that the discipline has a broad and empirically robust stock of models to explain the behaviour of individual elements such as firms. The two outer rings are more the concern of **macroeconomics**, which is concerned with aggregate forces such as total consumers' expenditure and unemployment and beyond the nation state with trade flows and exchange rates. Macroeconomics seeks to explain what happens to the system when there is change in aggregate behaviour, for example households collectively decide to save more of their incomes, and the policies governments employ to influence the workings of the system. This area of economics is not generally the subject of this book; though some aspects of policy, notably competition and industrial policies, are directly of relevance to strategy and are therefore included.

In fact, the bulk of this book draws its inspiration from a specialist area of microeconomics known as industrial organization. A comprehensive, if advanced, overview of industrial organization can be found in Schmalensee and Willig (1998). In this book we will draw heavily on industrial organization theories and models to answer fundamental questions such as how do firms organize and motivate

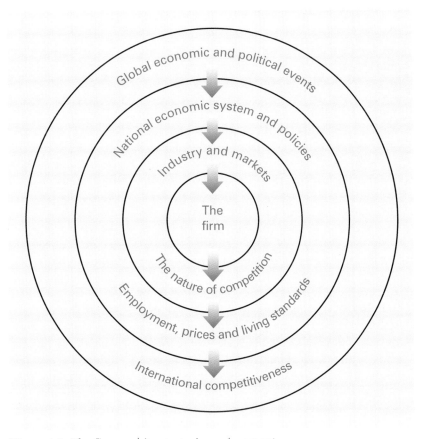

Figure 1.1: The firm and its strategic environment

their resources; how are the prices they pay for their inputs and the prices they receive for their outputs determined; how does market structure influence the nature of competition, including the 'games' that rivals engage in; and how do these factors influence the development and growth of firms. In short, industrial organization theories and empirical studies provide rich insights into firms as strategic organizations, operating in strategic environments and taking decisions in situations of uncertainty.

A Dramatic Change of Environment

On 10 November 1989, the world awoke to the news that the Berlin Wall was being demolished. This was the most visible manifestation of the collapse of the Soviet Union and as Eastern European Communism collapsed, so the business environment for firms in Central and Eastern European Countries (CEECs) changed dramatically. Once free to determine their own political and economic systems, the CEECs immediately expressed an interest in joining the European Union (EU). But a prime condition for membership of the EU is a functioning market economy and guaranteed human rights secured by democratic institutions.

Before the demise of the Soviet Union, the CEECs were all centrally planned economies; that is, decisions about what to produce and what prices to charge were taken by a central planning authority. In a market economy individual businesses make these decisions, thus membership of the EU necessitated the transition to market economies, replacing state-run enterprises with privately owned businesses focused on profits rather than output targets. The transition involved the replacement of one social framework of norms, values and acceptable economic behaviour with a completely new, and for most of the population, an alien framework. The dismantling of the Communist social, political and economic institutions created uncertainty, upheaval and widespread hardship. In retrospect, what the CEECs achieved in becoming EU members by 2004 was amazing and due in

large measure to an overwhelming desire to reinforce their new-found freedoms within the protection of the EU.

The transition to a market economy involves more than changes at the state level. At the level of firms, managers had to learn a whole new way of conducting their businesses. Under central planning managers were accustomed, when vital inputs were in short supply, to meet their needs via unofficial channels. So inefficient was central planning that finding ways to beat the system was viewed as a sign of resourcefulness, if not ingenuity. Thus, part of the transition to a market economy involved the adoption by managers of new legal and ethical standards, as well as a new focus on competing with rival firms for consumers' expenditure. Under central planning, managers needed a production mentality – output targets not profits were the prime goal. The transition to a market-based system necessitates a new skill set for managers. The arbitrary decisions on levels of output and prices that characterized central planning had to be replaced by independent decisions of individual managers. Most importantly, managers had to understand the concept of consumers' demands and then set about meeting them. This involved aligning their firm's resources to these demands and learning how to respond to price signals in their production decisions. They also had to learn to control production costs by seeking competitively priced inputs and utilizing their resources efficiently.

Game Theory

The foregoing has referred frequently to the interdependence of firms and the implications for strategic behaviour. Situations of interdependence are strategic settings and throughout this book we will resort to game theory to analyse such situations. Game theory is a relatively modern discipline, the seminal work, as observed above, being John von Neumann and Oskar Morgenstern's (1944) densely mathematical tome, *Theory of Games and Economic Behaviour*. Game theory's initial applications, in the early 1950s, were the study of war, but it has found a fruitful and receptive home in the sphere of economics, particularly with respect to business strategy. Coping with uncertainty is an inescapable feature of business life and strategic decision-making and this insight prompted Carl Shapiro (1989) to argue that, 'game theory has emerged as the predominant methodology for analysing business strategy' (p. 125). Others would no doubt take issue with such a forceful statement, but game theory is ideally suited to understanding behaviour in a world characterized by **imperfect information, asymmetric information** and **bounded rationality**, where decisions are typically made without full knowledge of their consequences.

Decision-makers must not only decide what risks are acceptable to them but also how the uncertainties of others affect their decision-making. Game theory attempts to deal with these uncertainties by helping to predict what course of action others will choose. It is based on the simple, but important, assumption that decision-makers are rational in the sense that they are concerned to do the best they can, i.e. they are self-interested. In situations of interdependence a rational decision is therefore one that includes a prediction of the responses of those affected. And rationality also implies that decision-makers are not going to consistently make the same mistake; they learn from the reactions of others and adjust their behaviour accordingly.

Game theory is separated into two branches: **non-cooperative game theory** and **co-operative game theory**. In non-cooperative game theory the focus of analysis is an individual participant's decision-making, for example a firm. It seeks to analyse how the individual participant can maximize the return or pay-off from participating in the 'game' subject to the behaviour of other participants. Non-cooperative game theory is suitable for modelling strategic situations where rivals are either unable or unwilling to enter into enforceable agreements and must choose between adopting co-operative or rivalrous modes of behaviour. But many strategic situations do involve contractual relationships and analysing models with joint actions is the province of co-operative game theory. Joint actions imply agreement by the participants on the terms of their contractual relationship. In some cases contracts are explicit, such as between a firm and an employee, in other cases the contract is tacit.

The fact that individual firms are unable – due to competition laws – or unwilling to enter into enforceable agreements with rivals does not mean that non-cooperative game theory is only concerned with conflict. Game theory throws light on profit-seeking behaviour and in strategic settings, the success of one firm does not automatically mean that another must fail. As will be shown, oligopolists frequently have the incentive to co-operate or 'collude', but to do so each player must overcome the fear of **opportunistic behaviour** by rivals if the co-operation is not genuine or liable to break down. In some situations, the best way to achieve a profit goal is to tacitly co-operate with other firms and in others – subject to the law – to formally co-operate. In fact, most strategic settings contain elements of rivalry as well as elements of potential co-operation.

Throughout this book, whether we are focusing on the behaviour of individuals within the firm or on the strategic behaviour of firms within their business environment, we will resort, wherever appropriate, to the use of game theory to help explain and analyse situations of interdependence. We will use game theory to demonstrate why co-operation between managers within a firm is more likely than rivalry to deliver productive and allocative efficiencies. And when analysing markets, we will use game theory to indicate when co-operation is likely to generate higher profits for individual firms and when 'war' is the best course of action. The concept of interdependence can be demonstrated with the aid of one of the most important contributions to game theory, namely, the game of **Prisoners' Dilemma**, which is credited to the mathematician Albert Tucker (2001) and is reproduced (slightly modified) in Figure 1.2.

The story that gives this game its name runs broadly as follows. The police apprehend two people for committing a minor crime, but they strongly suspect that the couple have together committed a far more serious crime for which the normal sentence is ten years in jail. But the police lack the evidence to mount a prosecution for the more serious crime and both prisoners know that if they do not confess they will be prosecuted only for the minor offence, for which the maximum sentence is two years in jail. The police know their only hope is to obtain a confession and they set about obtaining one in the following manner. They hold the prisoners *incommunicado* in separate cells and to each in turn they make the following offer: 'Confess and be prepared to give evidence against your partner in crime and we will prevail upon the judge to release you in view of your co-operation. If both you and your partner in crime confess, we will lessen the charges so that the maximum years in jail will be five. If you do not confess but your partner does, we will ensure that you receive the maximum sentence of ten years in jail.'

The pay-offs shown in Figure 1.2 are in years in jail. By far the best joint pay-off is for the prisoners to co-operate and agree that neither will confess. The problem here is that the game is non-negotiable; the prisoners cannot share information on their preferred course of action or determine a joint course of action. In the absence of a co-ordinated response or more correctly absolute trust, both prisoners, being rational, will confess. Once the prisoners are locked in their cells at the police station, even if there was an agreement between the two prisoners not to confess, it now becomes a question of how much each trusts the other. If absolute trust is lacking, it is rational for each prisoner to choose the confess strategy and thereby limit their years in jail.

The game of Prisoners' Dilemma succinctly demonstrates one of the major tensions facing firms in a strategic setting. Both parties are likely to receive a better pay-off if they co-operate. Yet, each party has the incentive to cheat. In terms of our earlier discussions, the decision to co-operate is more efficient for both prisoners – though perhaps not for society – as the outcome is preferred by both prisoners. If we position the game of prisoners' dilemma in terms of efficiency, we would define a particular strategy as being efficient if

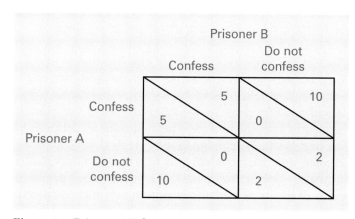

Figure 1.2: Prisoners' Dilemma

no feasible alternative strategy is likely to deliver a greater pay-off. In the case of business rivalry, it is possible that an individual firm or player could earn a larger profit if in pursuing their own self-interest they recognise that they will achieve the best pay-off if they co-operate with rivals rather than declare war.

The underlying problem brought to the fore by the Prisoners' Dilemma is the players' incentive to cheat, with or without an agreement. If we are to find a solution, it must be one where player(s) are able to deter cheating. The Prisoners' Dilemma may be resolved if the game is repeated. Repetition itself does not alter the game's paradox, but it can modify behaviour. A prisoner who confesses and implicates his partner in crime may avoid a jail sentence this time, but what happens next time. Mutual trust is unlikely to exist. In short, the gain from cheating may be short-lived if there are likely to be similar situations in the future. In terms of the business world, what the Prisoners' Dilemma highlights is that there is no solution that achieves reciprocal co-operation in a one-time game. A collapse of co-operation must carry a future cost and only in an ongoing relationship is there the opportunity to punish, and thereby to encourage co-operation. For example, when two firms are competing for market share, if one firm says to the other, 'I will not lower my price during the next four weeks, but whatever you do to your price during this period I will do in the subsequent period,' this is a credible threat. It is credible because if the first firm lowers its price, the second firm will have to follow. Repeated experiments using Prisoners' Dilemma have demonstrated that in such situations people normally reach co-operative solutions.

The logic of the foregoing translates to the real world where we find many examples of successful co-operation. One reason may be that in practice players fear the longer-term costs of being punished by rivals for cheating. Another explanation is that the real world contains people who attach great utility to behaving decently, i.e. reputation. The problem in the classic Prisoners' Dilemma is one of imperfect information, an inability, given the lack of communication and trust, to know for sure how the other player(s) will behave. The lesson is that co-operation is much more likely to emerge between oligopolists if rival managers build trust by keeping one another informed of their plans and activities. Explicit co-operation, or as Anglo-Americans would phrase it, collusion, is technically outlawed in most developed nations if it has the purpose of reducing competition. But as free agents, firms can independently choose and publicize a course of action by making judicious use of the business press, conferences and transparent behaviour as the means of communicating intentions.

Competition or Collusion?

Prisoners' Dilemma brings to the fore the issue of collusion. Most economic textbooks follow the Anglo-American philosophy that collusion between firms is a crime. Collusion according to this view is bad for consumers and therefore bad for the country. Yet, globally, this is a minority view. Only a small number of the world's 192 nations have anti-collusion laws that are rigorously enforced. In the majority of countries, the prevailing view appears to be that whatever is good for businesses must be good for the country.

continued

The European Union provides a good example. Under its competition policy all 'agreements' between companies to predetermine market share, fix prices or constrain investment and technological developments are in theory void and unenforceable. However, the authorities also recognize that such agreements may, in some circumstances, be in the public interest. The EU approach therefore permits explicit collusion if, in the view of the authorities, it promotes 'efficiency' in production, distribution or technical progress and provides consumers with a fair share of the benefits.

With the exception of the UK, most EU member states would not recognize the word collusion, but would instead talk of 'agreements' and 'understandings'. For firms, the attraction of collaboration is that it avoids, or delays, the inevitable downward pressure on profits of unbridled competition and hence protects returns to those engaged in or investing in the business. Indeed, the game of Prisoners' Dilemma demonstrates that, depending on the situation, collusion or co-operation can yield higher joint profits for the firms concerned than rigorous competition.

Creating Value

Returning to Equation (1.1), let us first consider the link between productive efficiency and the total costs (TC) of production. The traditional microeconomic approach views a productively efficient firm as one whose use of the resources at its disposal enables it to achieve its goals at minimum cost. All firms are endowed with, or for a price, have the use of, a wide range of resources. These will include all the people who are members of its labour force and depending on the firm's business, natural resources – e.g. livestock, land, forests, water, minerals and fish; man-made physical resources – e.g. buildings, machines and vehicles; and finally intangible resources such as the knowledge and experience it has accumulated from its history of producing. All these resources are economic goods; that is, they are **scarce** in the sense that their quantities are finite and consequently the volumes of goods or services that are produced using these resources are also finite.

Because scarcity exists, **choices** must be made. For the individual firm the volume, and quality, of productive resources at its disposal during the current production period depends in part on its **investment** behaviour and access to financial resources, but also in part to the efficiency with which it captured the learning inherent in previous production and embodied it in its labour force and in its routines and systems. The prime source of cash for a firm is its revenue flow: even when starting up, the firm will only be able to borrow or persuade shareholders to invest funds on expectations of future revenue. Cash generated by sales provides the means to pay for the hire or purchase of resources, including interest, the repayment of borrowed capital and the payment of dividends to shareholders.

Having obtained **property rights** over a set of resources, the firm's managers must select from the possible range of outputs that the firm's resources could produce, that sub-set of outputs that will best meet its goals. As scarcity ensures there is a physical limit to the outputs that could be produced, it follows that, in making decisions as to how their scarce resources will be employed, managers must explicitly forgo the opportunity of producing an alternative set of outputs. More formally, given a firm and its set of resources, the economic cost of producing a set of products is what might it might have produced instead. Given the objective of maximizing profits, the most highly preferred opportunity forgone is that set of outputs that yields the second-highest profit. The forgone opportunity is known as the **opportunity cost** and rational managers will only incur such an opportunity cost when compensated with the expectation of higher profits or required by legislation to do so. These three concepts – scarcity, choice and opportunity cost – are the foundations of economic efficiency and as such underpin **organizational strategy**. It is because a firm's resources are finite that in formulating strategy it has to make choices, and the more efficient its choices, the more likely that in achieving its strategic goals it will be fully compensated for any opportunity costs.

We need to be a little careful in blandly accepting the foregoing as a succinct description of **strategy formulation**. The idea that an individual or a firm when choosing between alternatives will happily switch providing they expect to be compensated in full for any opportunity cost needs qualification. Responsible managers would dismiss, despite the likelihood of a large gain, an option that carries a high risk of death or serious injury for the firm's workforce. Ethical, even religious, considerations may rule out many choices. For example, Body Shop refuses to sell products that have been tested on animals, though we should not overlook the fact that this stance also serves to align Body Shop with the values of its target market. Despite these caveats, the idea that there is some monetary payment that would compensate for the acceptance of an opportunity cost – e.g. increased wages for more effort – holds for the vast majority of business decisions. We can therefore proceed on the basis that, in general, providing managers are rational and have both the information and freedom to choose between alternatives, they will tend to choose strategies with efficient outcomes, i.e. those that minimize resource costs and involve non-negative opportunity costs. The concepts of choice, opportunity costs and efficiency are illustrated in Figure 1.3.

Figure 1.3 is a highly simplified representation of an individual firm, which, at a point in time, has property rights over a set of productive resources, e.g. its workforce, physical capital, raw materials and organizational knowledge. As a profit-maximizing organization, the firm will want to employ all of its resources efficiently. Let us assume that our representative firm with the resources available to it can produce only two products, say, x and y. The vertical axis measures the quantity of x produced and the horizontal axis the quantity of y produced and the curved line is a schematic representation of the firm's **production-possibility frontier** (*PPF*). The *PPF* shows all the combined volumes of x and y represented by Q_x and Q_y that the firm can make in a production period, say one month, if it uses *all of the resources at its disposal efficiently*. Efficiently utilizing resources means not just using resources, but using them in ways that maximize their contribution to the firm's goals. Scarcity is represented by points outside the frontier, such as D, which show combinations of Q_x and Q_y that cannot be produced with the resources currently available to the

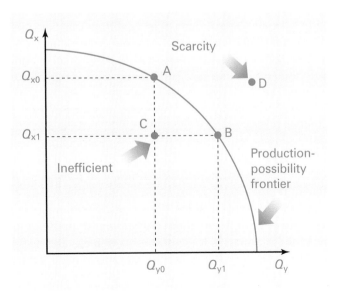

Figure 1.3: A production-possibility frontier

firm. Points inside the *PPF* – such as C – represent combinations of Q_x and Q_y that are inefficient. They are inefficient in the sense that they involve waste; the firm could produce more of either *x* or *y* for zero opportunity costs. For example, given Q_{x1} – where the second subscript refers to a particular quantity – it could increase Q_{y0} to Q_{y1}, i.e. move from C to B without giving up any of its output of *x*. At points A and B, the firm is full utilizing all of its resources. If it is currently producing the output bundle represented by point A but wishes to move to point B, it can only do so if it reduces its production of *x*, moving from Q_{x0} to Q_{x1}; i.e. it incurs a positive opportunity cost.

The foregoing is typical, albeit simplified, of the theoretic principles that populate the higher reaches of economic theory (Machlup, 1967). Of more relevance here is how the firm brings about a movement from, say, C to the *PPF*. Or put more generally, how does an organization become efficient and avoid the waste implied by point C? In essence, a firm's efficiency depends on the mechanisms by which it allocates its resources between different uses and then motivates them to high levels of **productivity** in conditions where it cannot observe all the actions of its workforce. It was some years after Ronald Coase (1937) investigated the nature of the firm that economists turned their attention to the internal organization of the firm. Just how firms co-ordinate and motivate their resources raises many very complex issues and a comprehensive answer must involve a range of disciplines including *inter alia* organizational behaviour, human resource management and operations management: in short, the range of courses taught on a good MBA programme. The important point is that if the firm is to achieve productive and allocative efficiency it must ensure that individual members of its workforce are putting effort into employing their skills and co-operating with their fellow employees, both formally and informally, to achieve the firm's goals.

The framework in which the efforts of individuals are co-ordinated, focused and motivated is known as the firm's organizational architecture. It is a firm's organizational architecture that determines how value is created from the pool of resources over which it has property rights. The attitudes and behaviour of people who are nurtured within a particular organizational architecture give rise to the concept of **organizational culture**: in essence, how it treats its workforce; how it aligns its resources to the business environment; and how it *gets things done* (Kay, 1993). Figure 1.4 shows the relationship between the external environment, a firm's organizational architecture and its strategy. The firm absorbs information from the external environment via its organizational architecture – its authority hierarchy; its methods of evaluating performance; and its incentive systems – where in response it reformulates its strategies.

The authority structure is a key element for any firm; namely, the ways in which decision-making rights are assigned and the way in which they are carried out. The firm, as pointed out by Alchian and Demsetz (1972), is a nexus of contracts where overwhelmingly a command-and-control hierarchy co-ordinates decision-making. How the decision hierarchy chooses to exercise control largely determines the organization's culture. The more centralized its system of control, the less the scope for individuals to exercise discretion and the greater the need for large-scale information flows up and down the organization. The more discretion and control over their activities is delegated to individuals or groups, the more complex and challenging must be the systems used to measure and reward performance. If people are to be motivated to reach their full potential and to co-operate efficiently with their fellow workers, the firm must have in place systems that equitably measure and evaluate performance and also motivate and reward individuals and groups for their contribution (Brickley *et al.*, 2001).

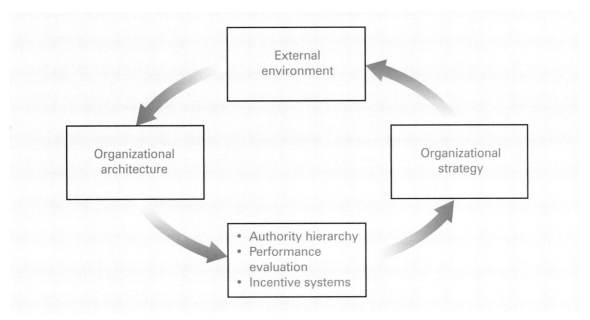

Figure 1.4: Organizational architecture and strategy

In order to maximize the performance of its pool of resources, the organization must train and develop its people to co-operate in capturing and sharing the value inherent in information flowing in to the firm from the external environment. As new ideas and knowledge are generated they must be defused throughout the organization to reach the parts where they can be employed to maximum advantage. It should be clear that if we are to understand why efficiency varies from firm to firm, indeed why firms are heterogeneous, we must start with the firm's organizational architecture. As we shall see, the creation and exploitation of heterogeneity are key elements in a successful strategy. The scale and scope of a firm's operations, the number and mix of the markets it serves and its ability to anticipate and respond to new situations and opportunities are all the product of, and in turn likely to directly influence, its organizational architecture.

In addition to the accumulation of skills and knowledge, an efficient firm requires an organizational architecture that reveals and discourages waste and a culture that rewards managers and employees for effort. What Figure 1.4 implies is the danger, *à la* company accounts, of measuring a firm's efficiency in terms of its production costs for an isolated product period. In contrast to Figure 1.3, which related efficiency solely to the bundle of outputs produced by the firm's resources, Figure 1.4 implies a dynamic concept of efficiency. It implies the need over successive production periods to capture new information and from it to generate and disseminate new knowledge amongst a co-operative workforce. It is in this way that a firm learns how to respond to a changing external environment and to modify its systems and routines to achieve its strategic goals. Put simply, a profit-maximizing firm must constantly be developing and allocating its resources so that over successive production periods not only will waste be minimized but also the firm is in position to capture maximum value from the external environment. This brings us to the second element on the right-hand side of Equation (1.1), namely, total revenue.

European Exuberance

In 2000, at their summit in Lisbon, European Union (EU) leaders demonstrated they were not immune to *irrational exuberance*. They issued a ringing pledge to turn the EU into the most competitive and dynamic, knowledge-based economy in the world by 2010. Tony Blair, the British prime minister, hailed the announcement as a *sea of change* in EU economic thinking. Lacking any real power in the area of creating a knowledge-based economy, the EU leaders issued a shower of targets all designed to help firms – particularly small and medium-sized enterprises (SMEs) – create value by becoming more entrepreneurial, more innovative and consequently more competitive.

Five years on, and EU leaders are busy trying to play down their exuberance. The Lisbon agenda preceded by only a matter of months the puncturing of the dot.com bubble. There have been other extenuating circumstances – terrorism, the war in Iraq and crashing stock markets – but the Lisbon agenda has become synonymous with missed targets and a failure of political will. Undeterred, the new Commission president, Jose Manual Barroso, is urging member states to breathe new life into the initiative by moving away from the welfare-based capitalism that was the hallmark of the EU, towards a more *neo-liberal* economic agenda. According to Barroso, the Lisbon goals were right and remain relevant, what failed was the implementation by member states.

But where governments are moving too slowly, corporate Europe is taking up the challenge. Firms are dramatically restructuring in order to cut wage bills, improve market responsive-ness and increase profits. In Germany, Siemens, Daimler-Chrysler and Volkswagen are among those who have extracted longer hours or pay freezes from their workforces. Helping to drive these changes is the increased competition from the new central and eastern European countries that joined the EU in May 2004. Their relatively high rates of economic growth, their lower wage and tax rates and most importantly their hunger to succeed are forcing businesses in the 'old' EU to rethink their attitudes towards the way they organize and conduct their businesses.

Corporate Europe can boast many leading companies: Nestlé in food, Vodafone in telecommunication services, Nokia in mobile handsets, SAP in enterprise software, Airbus in aircraft manufacture, Novartis in pharmaceuti-cals, BP in oil and HSBC in banking. But these global leaders are followed by a long tail of businesses whose performance is below that of US and Asian competitors. European business leaders put the blame on the regulatory envi-ronment within which they have to operate. Red tape and labour market rules are far more constraining in the EU than in the US and even the cost of patenting a new invention is about four times more expensive in the EU than in the US. The message is very clear – the 'old' approach of state involvement and the shield-ing of 'national champions' from competition are going. In the future the ability to create value will depend to a much greater extent on the capabilities of individual firms and their willingness to adopt new organizational struc-tures, to seek new market opportunities and to embrace the increasing competition from Asia.

Capturing Value

The previous section has argued that a key element in formulating and conducting strategy is the possession of an efficient organizational architecture to create value. We now turn to the capture of the value created. Although a firm's organizational architecture will influence how it approaches and responds to its external environment, for a commercial firm capturing value ultimately comes down to setting the correct price for its products. If the goal is to maximize total value, the firm must choose a price for each product that maximizes the difference between revenue and costs. The price decision is not only the most important determinant of revenue, but also of profits and, hence, for a public company, shareholder value. Optimal decisions regarding the prices of products cannot be taken in ignorance of the value potential consumers place on their products or the likely response of rivals. If the firm is to maximize its profits, it can only do so if it understands its customers' needs and the value they place on the products that it sells and, unless it is a **monopolist**, it must also understand how its rivals will react to the prices it sets.

For some firms, namely those operating under a market structure that approaches perfect competition, e.g. cereal farms, producers have very limited influence over the price at which they sell their output. Such markets are commodity markets and the business environments in which commodities are sold force individual firms into the position of being **price takers**. More generally, firms operate in markets characterized by imperfect competition. In this business environment firms retain some control over the prices they charge derived from their scale and/or the selling of differentiated products. The size and numbers of competitors, as well as the characterization of the products being offered for sale, are the key influences on the behaviour of competitors. As noted previously, obtaining the best outcome from a strategic setting may not always be achieved by aggressive competition and the ability to curb the intensity of rivalry can improve the scope for capturing value. The lesson from game theory is that in many instances a better outcome in terms of profits will be obtained by engaging in co-operation rather than ruthless competition. Nalebuff and Brandenburger (1996) have coined a word for this behaviour, **co-opetition**. For example, co-operating in the provision of information to provide consumers with details of new product developments, e.g. 3G mobile telephones, can increase demand for all firms in the market, thereby creating more scope to capture value. Co-operative behaviour is an example of strategic interaction and by lessening the likelihood of aggressive behaviour by rival firms it can allow firms to retain more of the value they create.

Understanding and influencing consumers' needs and preferences is the essence of marketing. By learning from its experience and engaging in market research a firm can build knowledge and understanding of its current and potential customers and by advertising it can make customers aware of how its products' attributes align with their demands. It can also use advertising to invest in building a reputation that will help the firm maintain demand for its products over the long term. The increase in demand that a firm expects to follow from its expenditure on advertising is often achieved at the expense of competing firms. From this perspective, the outcome of advertising could be viewed as a **zero-sum game**, where an increased market share for one firm equals the share lost by rivals. In terms of game theory, such advertising would amount to an aggressive competitive tool and is likely to bring forward an equally aggressive response from rivals. In the absence of co-operation, competing firms will spend excessively on advertising, largely with the effect of curtailing the impact of rivals' advertising and, in the process, reducing the amount of value retained.

As observed above, of all the marketing tools available to a firm the price it charges for its products is the most important. By definition, total revenue, *TR*, is the product of the volume sold and the price charged. As there is an inverse relationship between the price charged and the quantity sold, setting a price impacts directly on the quantity sold and unit production costs. Setting the price also involves risks for the firm: a high price will result in modest sales and hence a small market share; whereas a low price will threaten rivals' market share and thereby provoke an aggressive response, e.g. a **price war**. Setting the price therefore influences both productive efficiency and allocative efficiency. But for a firm capable of producing more than one product, the issue of allocative efficiency is more complicated. Sticking with our simple two-product firm represented in Figure 1.3 and writing *P* for the price and *Q* for the volume sold, total revenue is given by:

$$TR = P_x Q_x + P_y Q_y \tag{1.2}$$

where subscripts *x* and *y* refer to two products and *Q* is an inverse function of *P*, i.e. $Q = f(P)$ where $\Delta Q/\Delta P < 0$. Now say our firm is producing the quantities of *x* and *y* shown at point A in Figure 1.3. This implies that the prices set, and therefore the quantities sold, are sufficient to achieve a point of productive efficiency on the *PPF*. But this is not sufficient to maximize profits. To achieve this, the firm must be both productively and allocatively efficient in the bundle of outputs that it sells. In terms of Figure 1.3, a profit-maximizing firm must choose between productively efficient points – i.e. points that lie on the *PPF* – on the basis of total value captured.

This can be demonstrated by referring back to points A and B in Figure 1.3. To keep matters simple, we will assume that only the output bundles represented by points A and B are available to the firm. Point A involves a high price for *y* and a low price for *x* and point B a low price for *y* and a high price for *x*. In formulating strategy, the firm needs to calculate the pay-offs from its choices and in doing this it will need to incorporate the expected responses of its rivals. If we assume that the firm and its rivals will each make their decisions simultaneously, we can represent the strategic setting with a **normal form game**, as shown in Figure 1.5. The pay-offs are shown as profits in €m and on the assumption that all the players in the game are profit maximizers, we can rank their preferences in order of their pay-offs. An efficient strategy for the firm is the one that maximizes the expected pay-off, which is dependent on the decisions of rivals. The firm has only imperfect information on its rivals' behaviour; it may know the choices and outcomes, but can only reason which choice is likely to be made. Viewed through the framework of the normal form game, it would appear that the firm has a **dominant strategy**; namely, whatever the rivals' response, bundle B delivers the largest pay-off.

Rivals, being rational, will expect strategy B to be chosen and will therefore choose to be aggressive. Thus, we have identified, in this simple example, a solution to this non-cooperative game; namely, the strategy profile (B, aggressive). This solution is known as a **Nash equilibrium**, after the Nobel Laureate, John Nash (1950). A

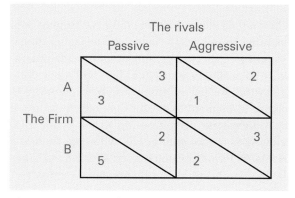

Figure 1.5: A normal form game

strategy profile is a Nash equilibrium if, and only if, each player's chosen strategy is the best response to the expected strategies of others. In short, *each player is doing the best they can given that their rivals are doing the best they can.* But note a better solution is possible if the firm and its rivals are prepared to co-operate to achieve the strategy profile (A, passive); indeed, this solution will be the outcome if the game is played sequentially; that is, rivals can observe the firm's decision before choosing a response. A sequential game can be modelled using the **extensive form game** tree, shown in Figure 1.6.

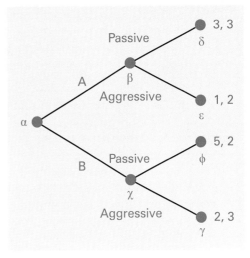

Figure 1.6: An extensive form game

The game shown in Figure 1.6 starts at node α with the firm's decision regarding output bundles A and B. Once the decision is made the action moves to nodes β or χ, where rivals have to decide how to respond. In this simple representation of a strategic setting we will assume that the firm's rivals act as one. The rivals can either passively accommodate the prices implied by bundles A and B or they can respond aggressively, possibly with a price cut of their own. The terminal notes δ, ε, φ and γ show the expected outcomes of the game and each corresponds to a unique path through the tree. The pay-offs are shown as profits in €m and arranged in vectors at each node. The first number is the pay-off to the firm and the second the (average) pay-off to its rivals. The extensive form game shown in Figure 1.6 is solved by **backward induction**. Going to the pay-off nodes, it is clear that if strategy A is chosen the best response for the rivals is to be passive; hence, if the game is played sequentially, an alternative Nash equilibrium is generated with the strategy profile (A, passive).

In demonstrating that the concept of allocative efficiency and strategic efficiency are congruent we have also demonstrated a mechanism for bringing it about; namely, strategic interaction. However, the outcome arrived at by adjusting behaviour to take account of the responses of rivals was not necessarily the best outcome for consumers. The solution does not guarantee that prices are as low as they could be, nor that the products x and y are produced in the quantities desired by consumers. This is only likely to happen if there is unfettered competition, which means no one firm, or a group of firms acting collectively, has the power to influence the quantity supplied to a market and/or the market price. Hence, the use of legislation by all developed economies to prevent one firm, or group of firms acting in concert, from dominating a particular market. The result of the strategic interaction discussed above is therefore a bit disconcerting until allowance is made for the realities of business life. Given the uncertainty surrounding the development of new products and processes, the cost efficiencies associated with **economies of scale** and the longer-term damage inflicted by price wars, it is rational for firms to manage risk. This raises something of a paradox for legislators, who can reason the potential benefits of co-operative outcomes but also the potential costs in terms of social welfare if the disciplines of the market are smothered by collusive practices.

Market Disciplines

The creation of the National Health Service (NHS) on 5 July 1948 was the pride of the UK's post-war Labour Government. Doctors working as General Practitioners (GPs) in the community and hospitals serving the community became non-profit-making, publicly funded organizations with the goal of efficiently and effectively improving the health of the nation. Accordingly in the ensuing years, they built their organizational architectures to control and align their resources to meet this objective.

By the 1980s, it was clear to the then Conservative Government that after 35 years of national funding significant inefficiencies existed in the NHS treatment of patients. Kenneth Clark, the cigar-smoking, beer-drinking Secretary of State for Health, believed the introduction of an internal market within the NHS would improve matters. The idea was to attempt to combine the co-operation that must exist between medical staff with the disciplines of the market in order to encourage the monolithic bureaucracy of the NHS to utilize and allocate its resources more efficiently. The idea was that 'purchasers' – health authorities and some fundholding GPs – would be given budgets to buy health care from 'providers' – hospitals and organizations caring for the mentally ill and elderly. Providers were to become independent organizations – NHS Trusts – and allowed the freedom, within NHS guidelines, to determine their own strategies for competing with other trusts to secure the expenditure of the purchasers. In principle, like their private sector counterparts, the more closely trust managers aligned their resources with the demands of providers, and the more efficiently they used their resources, so they could hope to capture a larger share of providers' expendi-

ture. Similarly, fundholder GPs were encouraged to more efficiently manage their budgets as they would be allowed to retain surpluses to invest in their practices.

By 1985, all health care was provided by NHS Trusts and the internal market was credited with improving efficiency in the use of NHS resources – waiting times were reduced, access to services such as radiology improved and there was better communication between hospitals and GPs. But many observers believed that the reforms created a 'two-tier system' of health care, where patients of fundholding GPs received hospital care more quickly than those at non-fundholding practices. Some went further, arguing that the internal market gave GPs the incentive to under-refer and under-treat patients and in the extreme not to accept potentially high-cost patients into their practice.

After coming to power in 1997, the New Labour Government declared its intention to lessen the emphasis on competition and return to co-operation as the means of providing health care. The new government described its approach as the 'third way', defined as steering a course between the centralized command-and-control systems of the 1948 NHS and the 'divisive' internal market reforms of 1985. Despite New Labour's criticisms that the internal market achieved greater efficiencies at the cost of equity, in 2003 the by now established Labour Government reinforced the two-tier nature of health care with the introduction of foundation hospitals who are required to compete more forcibly for patients. In so doing, they demonstrated a preference for efficiency over equity.

Competition Policy

We demonstrated above that where possible a profit-maximizing firm will engage in strategic behaviour to increase its profits and such behaviour would have a more certain outcome if firms could enter into collusive agreements with rivals to restrict competition. However, rivals are generally prevented from entering into collusive agreements because such behaviour is proscribed by the existence of competition laws. Such legislation is the product of competition policy, whose purpose is to ensure that, within reason, firms are subject to the disciplines of free and fair competition when it comes to selling their products and setting prices. Competition policy endeavours to maintain effective competition by preventing firms from colluding to divide up markets and using such powers to raise prices with adverse consequences for consumers' welfare.

Competition policy is one of a number of ways that governments intervene to influence or regulate the behaviour and performance of firms and industries. Indeed, competition policy in attempting to influence the behaviour and performance of firms might properly be viewed as an element in the set of policies falling under the heading of industrial policy. Other elements in the set of industrial policies include direct financial support, the provision of a regional infrastructure and agricultural policies, all of which seek to influence the performance, location and size of specific industries. At one level, competition and industrial policy can be viewed as having the same objective; namely, sustained efficiency improvements. At another level, the two policies are in conflict. The provision of **state aids** to industries and the facilitation of market power through the encouragement of **mergers and acquisitions** have the potential, if not the intention, of creating scope for firms to abuse their market power, with adverse consequences for consumers' welfare and overall economic performance.

Competition policy in the UK and other EU member states is subject to Community legislation. The founders of the Community were seized with the necessity of encouraging trade between member states and therefore the need to legislate to prevent (restrictive) practices likely to frustrate this objective. The Community's founding treaty – the **Treaty of Rome** – makes explicit reference to competition and the belief that encouraging intra-Community competition is the best way to ensure efficiency and social wellbeing. Although renumbered, Articles 81 and 82 constitute the core of EU competition policy. These two Articles have direct effect throughout the EU, indeed throughout the **European Economic Area**. In contrast, industrial policy remains predominately the province of member states and its operation is frequently in conflict with the aims and objectives of EU competition policy. However, EU competition policy is slowly gaining at the expense of direct intervention by member states; a trend that is reinforced by a world shift towards economic liberalization, freer trade and global capital markets.

Uniquely, competition policy in the EU also has to address the actions of governments, as they affect competition and these are limited under Article 31, which deals with state monopolies, Article 86, which deals with companies to whom their governments have granted special or exclusive rights; and Articles 87–88, which deal with state aids. The **European Commission** alone has the power to select cases and impose fines but its lack of transparency in carrying out this function is the subject of much criticism. Conscious of the need to avoid conflict with the Council, from its earliest days the Commission took a pragmatic approach to competition issues. In 1962, when it called for firms to provide information on agreements that might fall within the provisions of Article 81 it was swamped with more than 35,000 applications for clearance. Using its discretion, most of these were dealt with by **block exemptions**. The Commission's pragmatic approach was very much in evidence as economic conditions worsened in the 1970s. As European industries attempted to come to terms with a quadrupling in oil prices, rapid inflation and rising unemployment, so member states sought to protect their industrial bases by aiding and encouraging restructuring. Such behaviour constituted an aggressive industrial policy and as such was in direct conflict with the aims of competition policy. The Commission, sensitive to the harsh economic climate of the 1970s, chose to exercise the political discretion granted to it under Article 81. The swing back to a pre-eminent position for competition policy came with the preparations for the **single market** programme in the mid-1980s and with it – or because of it – a revival of the Community's dynamism.

The earlier discussion of game theory demonstrated the potential benefits of a co-operative attitude, but policy makers are concerned to prevent co-operation developing into restrictive agreements. Whereas a monopoly might be defended as yielding advantages such as economies of scale to offset the exploitation of market power, agreements between firms to restrict competition are, in the view of policy makers, difficult to justify and are, in principle, prohibited under Article 81. The Commission does not, however, treat all restrictive agreements in the same manner. The Commission considers secret agreements the most destructive. It has wide powers of investigation and if it finds evidence of a secret agreement or a concerted practice, the agreement is automatically void under Article 81 and fines of up to 10 per cent of a company's (worldwide) turnover may be imposed. For example, in 1999, the Commission imposed fines totalling €99m on seven producers – four European and three Japanese producers of seamless steel tubes who had secretly colluded until 1995 to protect their respective domestic markets.

In order to avoid discovery and possible punitive action, the parties to an agreement may apply to the Commission for either 'negative clearance' i.e. it falls outside the scope of Article 81, or exemption. A 'letter of comfort' from the Commission saying that it does not intend to challenge a notified agreement does not imply immunity from legal action in the future if the agreement were subsequently found to have anti-competitive effects. The logic that an agreement to restrict competition cannot have significant anti-competitive effects if the parties to it have an insignificant market share is reflected in the *de minimis* doctrine, which is manifested in the general derogation or 'block exemption' for 'all agreements or concerted practices between two or more undertakings, each of which operates at a different level of production or distribution chain … providing the share of the single market is less than 30 per cent.' Above the 30 per cent threshold, agreements are not presumed to be illegal, but require investigation.

The increasing pace and cost of technological advance presents a challenge to a competition policy designed to encourage productive and allocative efficiency. Co-operative agreements are a proven method of helping firms keep pace and this calls for the authorities to not only exercise judgement in carrying out policy but also to come to their decisions speedily and deliver them with clarity. In response, EU competition legislation is being simplified and is shifting from its traditional *per se* formalistic approach towards a focus that incorporates potential wider benefits of agreements; for example, the development of industry standards. In this respect, EU competition law is moving towards the US model where, under the Sherman Act, courts hear evidence as to the effect of an agreement before reaching a judgement as to whether the law has been infringed. Courts adopting this approach are said to adopt a '**rule of reason**', in essence weighing up the pro- and anti-competitive effects of an agreement. Advocates of a 'rule of reason' point out that co-operation in areas such as R&D, joint ventures and distribution can all have pro-competitive effects. In particular, agreements of this type can help reduce the substantial investment costs and considerable risks involved. Figure 1.7 attempts to summarize the essence of EU competition policy and its transition from *per se* rule to the rule of reason.

	Per se rule	Rule of reason
Restrictive agreements	Only necessary for the authorities to be convinced that a proscribed agreement occurred regardless of effects	Agreements are considered in their market context and anti- and pro-competitive effects balanced
Market dominance	Emphasis on establishing relevant market and the extent of market power by consideration of potential competition	An assessment of market power important, but greater emphasis on the longer-term impact on competitiveness

Figure 1.7: Alternative approaches to competition policy

Critical Articles

Article 81

Article 81 focuses on anti-competitive agreements. It treats as being '... inconsistent with the common market ... all agreements between undertakings, decisions by associates of undertakings and concerted practices which may have as their objective or effect the prevention or distortion of competition within the common market.' For an agreement to fall under Article 81 it must both involve competitors and have an impact on the commercial conduct of *either* party. Such agreements include the acquisition of legal or *de facto* control over a competitor; provision for commercial co-operation; creation of a specific structure likely to be used for such co-operation; the possibility of the investing company increasing its influence over its competitor and perhaps to take control later; relationships between parties outside the community (global co-operation); rights of representation on the board of the company; special voting rights; and pre-emption and option rights.

Article 82

Article 82 states that '... any abuse by one or more undertakings of a dominant position within the common market or in a substantial part of it shall be prohibited as incompatible with the common market in so far as it may affect trade between member states.' The meaning of 'dominant position' is defined as, 'a position of economic strength enjoyed by an undertaking which enables it to prevent effective competition being maintained in the relevant market by giving to it the power to behave to an appreciable extent independently of its competitors, customers and ultimately of its consumers.' In assessing a dominant position, the Commission must define the relevant market (product and geographic),

continued

measure market share and take account of both actual and potential competition, i.e. barriers to entry, technological superiority, potential entrants, substitute products, pricing behaviour, and ownership of important vertical assets. A market share of more than 80 per cent is taken as sufficient proof of a dominant position. Market shares in excess of 25 per cent justify an initial presumption of dominance. Demonstrating actual abuse of a dominant position is more difficult to prove. Abuse, it is held, occurs when the behaviour of companies remaining in the market depends on the dominant company.

Concluding Thoughts

Our focus in this book is primarily the firm and, in particular, how it meets its strategic objectives while simultaneously meeting the needs of society's demands for higher living standards. Society wants productive efficiency – scarce resources should not be used wastefully – and allocative efficiency – production decisions should be responsive, in terms of quality and price, to consumer demands. In addition, society (generally) wants its firms to be progressive, taking advantage of science and technology to increase productivity whilst adopting a responsible attitude towards its stakeholders and the natural environment.

A firm is an economic organization and it is within firms that the resources available to an economy, e.g. human capital, physical capital, materials and knowledge, are generally brought together for the purpose of production. A capitalist society relies overwhelmingly on the market mechanism to ensure that firms strive to achieve efficiency in their use and allocation of scarce resources. The market mechanism punishes those who are wasteful and rewards those who most accurately meet customers' demands. Underlying the paradigm of the market is the belief that firms – or rather their managers – will, given a free choice and sufficient information, seek out and settle upon efficient choices. Yet, within firms market exchange is replaced by hierarchal governance, paradoxically a direct response to the general desire by the owners of firms and their employees to behave economically; that is, to make their economic activities and the organization they work for efficient rather than wasteful.

Within firms, it is a management hierarchy rather than markets that allocates, co-ordinates and motivates resources. This leads to the inescapable conclusion that management hierarchies are better at allocating resources efficiently to productive tasks *within* firms than the alternative of leaving the market to bring about the necessary co-operation and motivation. Within firms, the market mechanism is replaced by an organizational architecture: decentralized decisions by individuals in response to their self-interest are replaced by the outcome of conscious and enforceable decisions of managers. To use Dennis Robertson's (Robertson and Dennison, 1960) vivid metaphor, firms are 'islands of conscious power in an ocean of unconscious co-operation' (quoted by Coase (1937), p. 35). Just why it is more efficient within the firm to replace the market mechanism with a management-controlled and directed organizational architecture and, externally, to seek to restrain unbridled market competition with co-operative outcomes, will be addressed in later chapters.

The idea of market competition as a battlefield in which there are only winners and losers is far from reality. Markets are places of interaction. A successful strategy must take account of the responses of rivals if firms are to capture as much as possible of the value they have created. From the perspective of firms, markets are places where value is captured and if greater value can be delivered and captured by the adoption of a co-operative stance, rational firms are likely to build it into their strategies. This raises a paradox for the operation of competition policy: if co-operation is a potential source of higher value, judgement must be exercised in order to balance the disciplines of the market with the beneficial outcomes of co-operation.

Key Learning Points

- Firms are created entities that function as economic organizations within which, and through which, people interact to achieve individual and collective goals.
- The achievement of a firm's goal – normally the maximization of its value – is subject to its ability to maximize productive and allocative efficiencies.
- A firm is defined as productively efficient if there is an absence of waste and resources are co-ordinated and motivated to achieve optimal productivity.
- In reality, firms operate in conditions of asymmetric information and bounded rationality and they therefore create organizations, and engage in behaviours that limit risk.
- Within the firm, productive and allocative efficiency is determined by its organizational architecture; that is, its authority control hierarchy, its methods of evaluating performance and its incentive and rewards systems.

- A firm achieves allocative efficiency if the bundle of products produced is aligned with the preferences of customers, thereby offering the firm the opportunity to capture the highest possible market value.
- Most firms have some discretion over the prices they charge and/or the way in which they market their products and in making these decisions they must be mindful of the response of rivals.
- The interaction with market rivals raises the possibility of a co-operative rather than a competitive solution to the firm's goal of maximizing its value.
- Competition policy is designed to prevent co-operation developing into collusive market-fixing agreements that result in adverse welfare consequences for consumers.

Exercises

1.1 Why are concepts such as globalization and economic liberalization relevant to understanding the strategic behaviour of firms?

1.2 In what way do corporate, business and network strategies differ?

1.3 How does game theory inform firm behaviour in situations of strategic interaction?

1.4 Explain why productive and allocative efficiencies are critical to business success.

1.5 What are the objectives of competition and industrial policy? Is there a conflict?

References

Alchian, A. and Demsetz, H. (1972) 'Production, information costs and economic organization', *American Economic Review*, vol. 62, pp. 777–795.

Brickley, J., Smith, C. Jr. and Zimmerman, J. (2001) *Managerial Economics and Organizational Architecture*, 2nd edn, McGraw-Hill International, London.

Chamberlin, E. (1933) *The Theory of Monopolistic Competition*, Harvard University Press, Boston.

Coase, R. (1937) 'The nature of the firm', *Economica*, vol. 4, pp. 386–405.

Kay, J. (1993) *Foundations of Corporate Success*, OUP, Oxford.

Machlup, F. (1967) 'Theories of the firm, marginalist, managerial and behaviour', *American Economic Review*, vol. 57, pp. 1–33.

Mason, E. (1939) 'Price and production policies of large scale enterprises', *American Economic Review*, vol. 29, pp. 61–74.

Nalebuff, B. and Brandenburger, A. (1996) Co-opetition, Profile Books, London.

Nash, J. (1950) 'The bargaining problem', *Econometrica*, vol. 18, pp. 155–162.

Pigou, A. (1922) 'Empty economic boxes: a reply', *Economic Journal*, vol. 32, p. 463.

Porter, M. (1980) *Competitive Strategy, Techniques for Analyzing Industries and Competition*, Free Press, New York.

Robertson, D. and Dennison, S. (1960) *The control of industry*, Cambridge University Press, Cambridge.

Schmalensee, R. and Willig, R. (1998) *Handbook of Industrial Organization, Vol I and II*, North Holland, Netherlands.

Shapiro, C. (1989) 'The theory of business strategy', *Rand Journal of Economics*, vol. 20, pp. 125–137.

Simon, H. (1991) 'Organizations and markets', *Journal of Economic Perspectives*, vol. 5, pp. 25–44.

Tucker, A. (2001) 'A two-person dilemma: unpublished notes, Stanford 1950' in *Readings in Games and Information*, E. Rasmusen (ed.), Blackwell, MA.

Von Neumann, J. and Morgenstern, O. (1944) *The Theory of Games and Economic Behaviour*, Wiley, New York.

Williamson, J. (1998) *Globalisation and the Labour Market: Using History to Inform Policy in Growth, Inequality and Globalisation*, Cambridge, England.

Introduction

In the opening chapter we presented business strategy as comprising an internal organizational dimension and an external market-focused dimension. In this chapter we turn in more depth to an analysis of the economic organization itself. At its most basic, a firm exists to transform the services of the **factors of production** into outputs of goods and services. It does this through the process of **production**. With the exception of primitive societies, the firm through its dominance of the production process is at the heart of economic activity. Yet, despite the importance of the firm, the traditional microeconomic textbook has very little to say about the nature of the firm. This is partly the legacy of the founding fathers' obsession with perfect competition and it is also, in part, a consequence of the fact that a firm is not an easy economic concept to fully explain.

Many people have a tendency to define a firm as a factory. Giants such as Microsoft, General Motors and Sony tend to be viewed as global organizations rather than firms. Major retailing chains are viewed as shops or stores and companies offering services, such as insurance, are more likely to be described as an office rather than a place of production. Yet the underlying principles of a firm apply to all these organizations just as they also apply to the local grocer's shop, a family farm and a charity such as Oxfam. From an organizational perspective, a global giant such as Microsoft and a family-run sheep farm nestling on the slopes of a Welsh valley would appear to have very little in common. Yet both exist to transform inputs into outputs and this provides us with a starting point for a strategic approach to the firm; namely, the firm as a production unit.

But this view of the firm is far from sufficient. Firms are living organizations, they consist of human and non-human resources and within their boundaries individuals develop relationships, identities and strive to achieve personal goals. The firm achieves its objectives – with varying degrees of success – according to the quality and quantity of the resources over which it has **property rights** and also its ability to co-ordinate, direct and motivate their efforts. It follows that the internal structure of the firm – the way in which it organizes and develops its resources – is a key influence on its **strategy formulation** and **competitive advantage**. For students of business economics, the neo-classical focus on what firms should do has to be augmented with a knowledge of how they do what they do. In this and subsequent chapters we will seek to explain the purpose of an internal structure and how it relates to the economic concepts of efficiency and incentives. We will start by looking more closely at the role of firms as the prime means of allocating productive resources in a market economy. By reading this chapter you will gain:

- Knowledge of the main alternative approaches to explaining the nature of the firm as a strategic player.
- An understanding of **transaction costs** and the function of organizational hierarchies in countering such costs.
- An appreciation of the relationship between intangible, internally generated knowledge resources and **competitive advantage**.

What follows is divided into seven sections. The first serves to establish the **neo-classical approach** to the firm as the base upon which the subsequent approaches to the firm will be compared. The second section relaxes the neo-classical assumptions of **perfect information** and **hyper-rationality** to introduce the concept of transaction costs and their role in explaining the existence of hierarchical internal structures for firms. The third section analyses the concept of **organizational architecture** as the means by which hierarchical control is made efficient and effective. The fourth section provides an historical perspective in order to reinforce the contribution of a firm's organizational structure to strategic formulation and competitive advantage. The fifth section explains how transaction costs and organizational architecture are combined in the **governance approach** to a strategic theory of the firm which, as the name implies, is concerned with the way resources are co-ordinated, motivated and rewarded. The sixth section focuses on an alternative and more recent view of the firm, which has become known as the **competency approach**. In essence, this approach reflects a number of influences that have in common a view of the firm as not so much a collection of resources, but rather as an organization with the capability of developing productive resources, particularly tacit knowledge resources. The final section attempts a synthesis of these alternative approaches in order to produce an integrated strategic theory of the firm.

The Neo-Classical Paradigm

The traditional or neo-classical approach is to represent the firm as a **production function** and (implicitly) as a single-plant, single-product firm. This approach allows the firm to be represented by a mathematical formula that determines the maximum quantity that can be produced by the resources over which the firm has property rights. This approach to the firm can be formally represented thus:

$$Q = f(X_1, X_2, X_3, X_4, \ldots\ldots\ldots\ldots X_n) \tag{2.1}$$

where Q represents the maximum quantity of a particular output that (implicitly purchased) volumes of the input resources (X_is) can produce over a given production period when combined together within the constraints of the prevailing technology as represented by the production function, i.e. $f(\ )$. As Q is defined as the maximum possible output, the resources must be combined in their most efficient proportions and motivated to maximize their productivity. The precise way in which the X_i's are combined is determined by their relative prices, the services of the more costly inputs being substituted by cheaper alternatives, so that production costs are minimized. Implicitly, all the management issues that arise in organizing the team production inherent in the production function – where the productivity of one resource depends on the presence and interaction with the production function's other resources – are deemed in the standard neo-classical approach to have been solved by resort to the price mechanism. Managers are gifted with perfect information and hyper-rationality and thereby are fully aware of the particular combination of the X_is that will minimize costs. As such, the neo-classical production function amounts to a disregard of the two key hallmarks of a successful firm: firstly, the contribution of its own organizational capabilities to lowering costs; and secondly, its ability to discover and develop new processes and products.

It is because in practice managers are not all-knowing and their organizational capabilities are influenced by intellect, education and experience, that the volumes of inputs X_i in Equation (2.1) will vary from firm to firm, even when producing exactly the same output volume. It is therefore more realistic to think of the X_is being multiplied by a *scalar* θ where $\theta \geq 1$. If we think of θ as taking the value of unity when the inputs are combined in their most efficient combination, then $\theta > 1$ represents a degree of inefficiency. We can visually demonstrate this inefficiency with the aid of a highly simplified production function:

$$Q_X = f(\theta_N N, \theta_K K) \tag{2.2}$$

which is displayed in the following ***isoquant*** diagram (see Figure 2.1).

Points A and B on the isoquant are both productively efficient; that is, in producing quantity Q_x and fixing one of the inputs, say K, it is not possible to use a smaller amount of N than shown by points A and B on the isoquant. The allocatively efficient combination of K and N is the least-cost combination capable of producing Q_x. This is the mirror image of profit maximization. Profits can only be maximized when costs are minimized. The least-cost combination depends on the relative prices of K and N, which are represented by the ***isocost line***. At point A, the isocost line is tangential to the isoquant and this represents the least-cost combination, or, to be a little more technical, the point at which production of Q_x is optimized given the constraints of the prices of K and N. In contrast, if the combination of K and N represented by point C is used to produce the same volume of output, i.e. Q_x, resources are being wasted and production costs are not being

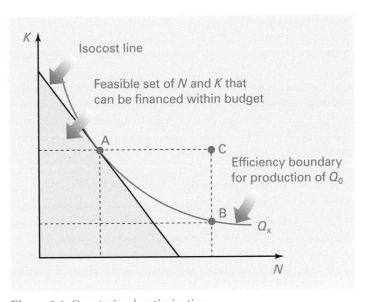

Figure 2.1: Constrained optimization

minimized. In terms of Equation (2.2), θ_K would take the value of unity, but θ_N takes a value > 1, implying that the firm is not using its labour input efficiently. This simple example demonstrates that efficiency requires more than knowledge of relative prices and technically feasible minimum input combinations. In practice, the workforce must be organized and motivated to high levels of co-operation and effort so that both physical and intangible resources are utilized efficiently to meet the firm's goals. It follows that one of the key functions of a firm – or more correctly its managers – is to create within the firm an environment that will help secure the efficient use of its resources.

For the neo-classical approach, the assumption of maximum efficiency was justified on the grounds that the theory was primarily concerned with understanding the determinants of maximum efficiency rather than actual performance. The assumption of hyper-rationality was equated with long-term adjustment, whereby all firms within an industry have gained perfect knowledge of the prevailing technology and production system thereby causing a convergence over the longer term to the lowest cost option available: i.e. where $\theta = 1$. Although this represents a process of discovery and learning, it assumes away the likelihood that over time such a process would enable firms to find individual ways to improve the **productivity** gains associated with the **division of labour**. It also implies that all resources are purchased when in fact firms necessarily create intangible organizational resources – e.g. production routines – that may have zero opportunity costs and can therefore only be fully exploited by the firm to achieve a cost advantage and/or the scope to differentiate its products from rivals. It would therefore be formally more correct to represent the neo-classical firm, even a specialist firm producing only one product for sale, as a combination of inputs and outputs that are available to the firm under the technology it employs. Hence, for a given production period, if T is the technology set we have:

$$T = \{(X_1, X_2, \ldots X_n, Q_1, Q_2, \ldots Q_m): Q_i \leq f(X_1, X_2 \ldots X_n, Q_1, Q_2, \ldots Q_m)\} \tag{2.3}$$

where X_i represents the services of specialist inputs purchased by the firm and Q_i the outputs produced by the firm, which include not only products for sale but also waste products and importantly tangible and intangible organizational resources for use by the firm, e.g. a design capability. The neo-classical approach is therefore deficient in that it is silent on the internal mechanisms that contribute to improving efficiency by the deployment and developing of its organizational resources.

The foregoing neo-classical representation of the firm reduces management decision making to **constrained optimization**. The production and sale of products is constrained by the costs of production and given the assumption of **perfect competition**, the profit-maximizing output is determined by achieving the minimum cost combination of inputs available to the firm. This approach has the advantage of generating 'laws' or rules regarding behaviour based on highly restrictive assumptions regarding knowledge and intent. For the neo-classical school, knowledge of the prices of the factors of production, their productivity and alternative technologies is not clouded by uncertainty. And in order to avoid conflicts between owners and managers, the firm is assumed to be owner-managed by someone normally called an **entrepreneur**, who acts rationally and with the single purpose of maximizing profits. This neo-classical approach has given us elegant mathematical models of the firm, but as a basis for understanding the firm it can only be justified on the basis of explaining what firms *should* do, rather than what they *actually* do, in order to maximize profits.

Arguably, the neo-classical approach was easier to justify in the early nineteenth century, when the typical firm was a sole trader, or a workshop owned and managed by one individual. In this world there existed a prevailing technology for producing individual products and hired labour provided only innate strength and/or dexterity and was literally viewed as 'a pair of hands'. But it is not a satisfactory or sufficient approach, particularly for larger-scale enterprises. In a large-scale firm, ownership and management is likely to be split between shareholders and professionals and as an organization it has more in common with the behaviour of an economy (albeit small) than an individual. In a firm, performance and profits are the outcome of the interaction of those employed in a web of complex relationships that are defined by, and developed within, the firm's organizational architecture. Moreover, in contrast to the neo-classical paradigm, in practice all firms, regardless of size, operate in conditions of uncertainty and limited information. No manager has the breadth of knowledge that would be required to evaluate all alternative production processes. Managers may be well informed as to the market prices for inputs, but it is unlikely that they know for certain the productivity of all resources – particularly labour and intangible resources – as assumed by the neo-classical school. In short, the neo-classical approach assumes away many of the issues that are of key importance when analysing the strategic behaviour of managers.

Three Steps to Heaven

The UK's manufacturing sector has the unenviable reputation of a poor performer in terms of productivity. In part this is blamed on too great a reliance on 'old' economy industries such as food processing, paper and textiles. But this is not a sufficient explanation. During the 1990s, the gap between total productivity in UK manufacturing and its more productive counterparts in Europe and North America widened to historically high proportions.

Some observers suggested that the solution would be higher levels of capital investment to improve the capital–labour ratio. But a close look at the figures suggests that capital investment is not the major problem. At around 14 per cent of the value of output, the UK's capital expenditure is close to the levels typical in Europe and North America. However, studies do show that the contribution to total output from the capital–labour ratio remains relatively low in the UK. Put simply, UK manufacturing may invest in the capital, but it does not appear to use it as efficiently as its rivals.

But the problem is not confined to manufacturing. According to McKinsey & Company, arguably the world's leading firm of business consultants, who were appointed by the incoming Labour government in 1997 to report on the UK's lacklustre productivity, the problem of low labour productivity is the scourge of non-manufacturing as well. The difference is that many non-manufacturing businesses are currently not facing the intense competition from global rivals that is the lot of manufacturers.

The problem, according to McKinsey, is that UK businesses have failed to adopt three key practices that have proved themselves elsewhere. The three are: lean manufacturing techniques that result in less waste; setting goals and rewarding their achievement; and attracting high-calibre managerial talent.

Towards a Model of the Firm

Despite its lack of focus on specific organizational capabilities, the neo-classical theory of the firm provided many insights into the economics of production that remain highly relevant and ensure that to this date the neo-classical model remains the dominant economic paradigm. It is, however, subject to a range of criticisms as an all-embracing theory of the firm; indeed, it might more correctly be described as a short-run theory of production in a setting in which, given the prevailing technology, nothing but the prices of inputs and outputs need be known. In essence, the neo-classical approach explained the existence of firms as being necessary to achieve the productivity gains arising from combining together labour of various skills with physical assets. This approach focused on the flow of tangible resources such as manual labour and introduced the concept of the entrepreneur as the co-ordinator of these tangible flows.

The significance of the neo-classical assumption of hyper-rationality cannot be over-emphasized. In entering into transactions, all parties were assumed to have perfect knowledge as to the alternatives on offer and certainty regarding the outcome of their transactions. But these assumptions – convenient for developing elegant mathematical models – also undermine the neo-classical approach to the firm. If transactions between individuals are deemed to be undertaken in conditions of certainty, then subject to the purchase price all exchange transactions are costless. In such a world there would still be merit in firms producing outputs where team production delivered the productive benefits of the division of labour, e.g. iron making, but there would be little advantage in bringing *the separate stages of production under one roof*, e.g. iron and steel production. If we are to understand the firm, then we must start with the recognition that exchange transactions are not costless when agents lack perfect information. Overwhelmingly, decisions concerning the allocation of productive resources are taken within firms, whereby exchange transactions – e.g. the supply of products at one stage to production to the next – are controlled and co-ordinated by means of hierarchical governance structures. The nature of decision making within the firm is of a different kind than the exercise of choice in markets. Employees act as agents for their superiors rather than themselves. A comprehensive theory of the firm must therefore be able to explain why decision makers in firms replace the 'invisible hand' of the market mechanism with the very visible hand of an authority hierarchy.

Such an explanation – or perhaps the foundation of a more complete explanation – was provided by Ronald Coase (1937), in his classic article on the nature of the firm. In order to explain why firms exist, Coase eschewed the production function approach of the neo-classical school and focused instead on contrasting 'the firm' and 'the market' as alternative modes of governance. For Coase, the choice between using the market to exchange products at different stages of production and bringing successive stages of production under one roof was principally decided by transaction costs. According to Coase, the main reason why it is profitable to produce within a firm – i.e. under conditions of command and control – is that, in contrast to a key assumption of the neo-classical approach, the world is characterized by **incomplete information** and **imperfect information**. Limited and **asymmetric information** gives rise to uncertainty and in such a world, market exchange involves additional costs. In principle, a budding entrepreneur could go out into the market at the start of a production period, and negotiate separate contracts with specialist suppliers for individual goods and services in exchange for a fee. Some individuals would manufacture parts and others would assemble them, the whole process being co-ordinated by the entrepreneur via a nexus of specific contracts. But this method of organizing production is expensive because there are transaction costs associated with drawing up the contracts for market exchange. Ultimately, these costs are positively related to a lack of information and informational asymmetries.

Let us explore some of these problems. The first problem encountered by a budding entrepreneur is uncertainty regarding the price to pay for someone to carry out a production process. When contracting with an individual for the first time, ascertaining the likely contribution – in terms of both productivity and quality – requires the time and effort necessary to search for the information. The problem here is one of asymmetric information; the individual specialist (the supplier) is better informed as to his or her skills and experience than the buyer. Owing to the lack of information and the positive cost of acquiring information, the people with whom our entrepreneur contracts would have **hidden characteristics** and the entrepreneur may end up paying a higher price than is justified by the skills and experience of the seller because continued search is too expensive. Alternatively, if the wage offered is lower than a skilled supplier expects, the end result may then be that only second-class suppliers will be prepared to enter into a contract to supply. Thus, the existence of asymmetric information can result in the market price being too high or too low, and in the former buyers will leave the market and in the latter sellers will leave the market. These are examples of **adverse selection**.

Imperfect and asymmetric information presents our budding entrepreneur with a second problem. Having reached agreements with individual suppliers, uncertainty still exists regarding the manner in which they fulfil their obligations. This is a **hidden action** problem, whereby the seller chooses how much effort to put into the contracted work. The supplier may put in little effort, resulting in poor quality, or alternatively, the price agreed allowed for unnecessarily expensive equipment to be used. These are examples of **moral hazard** which arise where the probability of a satisfactory outcome is directly influenced by the behaviour of the party contracted to supply, but whose behaviour cannot easily be observed. The contract to supply may seek to minimize moral hazard by including costly supervision by the entrepreneur, a promise of future work or some form of incentive payment, e.g. for timely delivery. But again, these are all additional costs.

Reasonably acceptable contracts are frequently drawn up despite information asymmetries, but a third concern for our budding entrepreneur would be to ensure that the work of each contracted specialist is co-ordinated, so that not only do all specialists work together in a logical order but also they will be able to adjust their contributions should contingencies arise. Experience will help our entrepreneur to plan and allow for the more likely contingencies, but it would be impossible for anyone to imagine all possible future contingencies and then process the information so that all possible outcomes are incorporated in the contracts of each specialist hired. In this respect our entrepreneur faces a problem known as **bounded rationality**. This concept, credited to Herbert Simon (1961, p. xxiv), views economic actions as 'intendedly rational, but only limitedly so'.

A good example of bounded rationality is provided by the game of chess. As the movement of each piece is governed by a set of rules, it ought, in principle, to be possible to construct a list of all possible legal moves in a game following an opening move. But this would produce a **decision tree** of such complexity that it would be impossible for any chess player to make a decision based on it. Even grand masters must make their decisions in the absence of a complete list of all future contingencies that might flow from them. Our budding entrepreneur is in a similar situation. In all but the simplest situations a complete list of all the possible outcomes arising from a particular action cannot be known. The more complex a process of production, the more certain it is that decisions will need to be taken under conditions of uncertainty. Our entrepreneur may be completely rational but this rationality is bounded by the sheer impossibility of accounting for all possible future contingencies.

Bounded rationality arises whenever a contract is being drawn up. The more complex and uncertain the product or service in question, the more the impossibility of drawing up a contract that can anticipate all possible contingencies. Put more simply, enacting and enforcing a **complete contract** is in all but the very simplest cases a fiction. As explained, in practice it is rarely possible in business relationships to allow for all possible contingencies that might alter the outcomes initially contracted for; indeed it may not be possible to ascertain who is at fault if outcomes are not as expected, and hence what businesses enter into with external sellers and buyers are more correctly described as **incomplete contracts**. Because individuals are boundedly rational, contingencies will arise that have not been anticipated and when they do, the parties must find ways to adapt. However, in adapting to an unforeseen circumstance, scope is introduced for **opportunistic behaviour**. For example, a toy manufacturer having entered into an agreement with a buyer finds that following a fatal accident with a similar toy changes must be made to the product being supplied. In order to meet the cost of these changes, the supplier would like to raise the price, but the buyer, knowing that the supplier has little option, may refuse to pay a higher price. The seller, having incurred the costs of setting up a plant to manufacture toys, is now at a disadvantage owing to the inability to anticipate the need to make expensive changes and opportunistic behaviour on the part of the buyer. Hidden characteristics and hidden actions also provide scope for opportunistic behaviour. In essence, opportunistic behaviour amounts to self-interest-seeking behaviour, which is frequently disguised with guile. Calculated efforts to mislead, obfuscate and confuse are all examples. Fear of opportunistic behaviour may even prevent contracting between parties, e.g. the tendency on the part of a buyer to distrust the quality of an almost brand-new car that is offered for sale. It is the existence of these transaction costs that Ronald Coase brought to the fore in explaining why the firm was generally preferred to the market for organizing production. Figure 2.2 sums up transaction costs.

These Coasian insights have been developed to provide a theory of the existence of firms based on transaction costs. In essence, when the transaction costs of exchange outweigh the benefits of using the market mechanism it is profitable to establish a firm as an alternative mode of governance to undertake co-operative exchange. In the absence of a firm, each contractor would need to contract with every other contractor whose co-operation is required in the production of some product. Not only would this require enormous time and effort in searching for suitable suppliers, but also the existence of bounded rationality implies that contracts with suppliers – of whom there would generally be a large number – must be incomplete.

Adverse selection	Moral hazard
Fear that prior to a contract a seller's private information will prove adverse to the buyer	Fear that post the contract, lack of adequate information exposes buyer to seller's self-interest
Bounded rationality	Opportunistic behaviour
Fear that the inability to anticipate all possible contingencies will produce an incomplete contract	Fear that an incomplete contract will create scope for the exploitation of unforeseen circumstances

Figure 2.2: Transaction costs

Transaction Costs

When Charlie Green retired at the age of 55 from his office-bound job, he decided to set up as a contract builder. It was not long before he won his first contract to build a house. Charlie had always taken a keen interest in building, but he lacked many of the skills needed in building a house and he therefore set about sub-contracting the more specialist tasks. In his ignorance, Charlie believed he could go out into the market and purchase the required hours of specialist help from bricklayers, plumbers, electricians and so forth. But as Charlie was soon to realize, matters are not so simple.

Charlie was confident he could lay the foundations, so the first skill he required was a bricklayer. But having located a bricklayer, a number of problems arose. Before agreeing a rate of pay Charlie needed to know how productive the bricklayer was. As the 'bricky' was unknown to Charlie, it was going to take time and effort to obtain this information. The next stage was to draw up a contract. But again, this was not straightforward. The building of the house would require the services of the bricklayer for many weeks and involve many details that are rarely clear at the start of such a project. For example, the order of the bricklaying would, to some extent, depend on the contracts Charlie had yet to settle with other specialists, e.g. carpenters, and aspects of the design may have needed to be changed as the work proceeded.

Overcoming the difficulties of formulating enforceable contracts with each specialist was only the first complication. If Charlie was to keep within budget he needed to co-ordinate the activities of all the specialists employed. But in organizing the work flow so that specialists completed their tasks in time for the next specialist, Charlie knew there would be unforeseen contingencies and these created scope for the specialists to take advantage. Moreover, Charlie had not worked with specialist craftspeople before and he was therefore subject to the effort and care that the craftspeople chose to put into their work. In short, while Charlie had no choice but to rely on the market mechanism to supply the necessary specialists, Charlie was beginning to realize that, in practice, for many types of specialist the transaction costs associated with his first project as a builder were going to be high.

Organizational Architecture

The replacement of perfect information and hyper-rationality with transaction costs provides an explanation as to why technologically separate stages of production are integrated with a firm, but it also opens the door to a strategic theory of the firm. The existence of transaction costs directs attention to the firm as an organization that exists in contrast to the market as a mode of governance for co-operative exchange transactions. This in turn focuses attention on governance structures and the likelihood of heterogeneous organizational capabilities. Having arrived at this point, it is but a small step to recognize that a firm's internal organization may be a source of competitive advantage and hence a strategic variable.

In a modern firm, the variety of tasks that are carried out are widespread and complex. Somehow, each of these tasks must be accomplished in ways that use the appropriate amounts of resources, fully utilize the workforces' skills and knowledge and aligns this effort with the firm's goals. This co-ordination of the firm's resources necessarily generates organizational routines and relationships and hence the production of intangible resources. It is these internally generated resources that have a powerful influence, arguably a decisive influence, on efficiency, as well as influencing strategic choices and competitive advantage. Failure on the part of managers to build and develop routines and relationships that have the potential to fully utilize the firm's resources gives rise to inefficiencies and lost opportunities. Thus, the way in which a firm organizes and co-ordinates its resources is a key determinant when analysing the conduct and formulation of strategy. In contrast to the neo-classical approach, which in effect assumed all firms within an industry had discovered – by virtue of perfect information – and were applying the most efficient organizational systems, in practice, even within the same industry, individual firms display heterogeneity in their organizational structures and capabilities.

It is the task of senior managers to build an organizational architecture that has a hierarchical authority structure that is both supportive of the firm's current strategy and capable of adapting to future strategic opportunities. Strategic business decisions are characterized by infrequency, they are complicated by the fact that they have to be taken on the basis of imperfect and incomplete information and they may be irreversible, e.g. the adoption of a new technology. A firm's organizational architecture is an internally produced resource whose prime purpose is to control decision making, but in a strategic context can go much wider. For example, by putting in place and developing routines and systems that encourage learning, risk taking and flexibility, the firm is capable of creating value as the strategic goals of the organization vary with a changing external environment. No two organizational architectures will be identical; each will follow a path determined in large measure by past experience and the actions and views of its current senior managers and shareholders. Organizational architecture therefore imparts heterogeneity to a firm. An individual firm's organizational architecture inevitably becomes a major influence on the shaping of strategy. The selection of goals, the choice of products and the positioning of the firm to compete in the market are all strategic issues that are influenced by the firm's organizational architecture.

Although architectures vary from firm to firm, they all face the challenge of maximizing the likelihood that when individuals make decisions they have the best available information and also the incentive to make decisions that benefit the firm. An inefficient architecture increases the risk that decisions will be taken on the basis of inadequate information and to meet personal rather than organizational goals. As an internally generated resource, a firm's organizational architecture is of critical importance not only to the pursuit of efficiency, but also to the success of the firm in meeting its strategic goals. An organizational architecture is also an information system that permits better decisions. And better decision making is reinforced by the architecture's supervisory and incentive structures.

A firm's organizational architecture starts with its legal statutes. The firm may be a publicly owned company, a mutual or a partnership. The legal status of these organizational forms may vary, but in terms of overall performance is unlikely *per se*, to be a major influence. Much more influential are the other elements of a firm's organizational architecture, which are summarized in Figure 2.3. The point to note is that, with the exception of the legal statutes, all the elements shown in Figure 2.3 are concerned with the gathering, control and use of information. In any organization, individuals will differ with regard to their knowledge and cognitive capabilities and it is therefore important that the organization itself builds common information and knowledge that can be accessed to support coherent and efficient decision making. This is not to imply that all information and knowledge is held centrally. On the contrary, the larger the organization, the more likely that sub-groups will have their own architectures. When parts of an organization, e.g. business units, have their own architectures, the corporate architecture has the objective of co-ordinating these sub-groups.

A second point to note is that, although organizational architectures are created for individual firms by their senior managers, they take on a life of their own. Senior managers will fashion the hierarchical authority structures, assign decision-making powers and map out the routines and systems. But over time these elements will develop their own cultures – many of which will be tacit – that will also impart their influence on the architecture's way of utilizing and developing the firm's resources. Thus, a firm's organizational architecture evolves in response to myriad influences and consequently is unique. Tacit information and knowledge are extremely difficult to replicate and once it is understood that these resources are integral to a unique organizational culture, it becomes understandable as to why firms, even those operating in the same industry, display very different levels of efficiency.

Figure 2.3 shows six influences that separately and jointly comprise a firm's organizational architecture. The importance of these organizational features has been recognized by a number of authors, but in distilling these six elements into three areas of analysis we follow Brickley *et al.* (2001). The key elements of a firm's organizational architecture are the:

- Hierarchy for assigning and authorizing decision-making powers.
- Systems for co-ordinating, monitoring and evaluating performance.
- Reward and incentive systems.

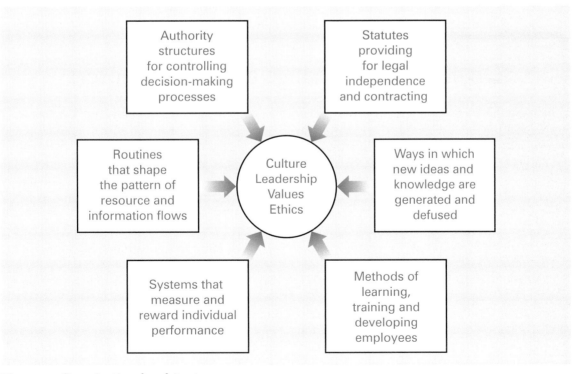

Figure 2.3: Organizational architecture

The larger an organization, the more its senior management team is constrained by an increasing inability to absorb and react to the enormous volume of information relating to aspects of the firm's efficiency. To cope with this problem, senior managers must delegate many decisions to lower-level staff. This raises issues such as what decisions should be delegated, on what basis can individuals make relevant decisions and how will senior managers ensure that the process is working efficiently, i.e. decisions are timely and being made in a manner designed to benefit the organization's strategic goals. It follows that accompanying the delegation of decision-making powers must be comprehensive systems for co-ordinating, monitoring and evaluating performance at each decision level. These systems will themselves generate information, not only on current activities, but also on the way ideas and knowledge are generated and diffused throughout the organization. A comprehensive monitoring system will also inform on training and development needs, as well as providing information on the firm's stock of human, physical and intangible resources.

What the monitoring and evaluating systems will record are the outcomes of the firm's success in co-ordinating and motivating its workforce. Thus, the third critical element of an organizational architecture is its reward and incentive system that encourage both co-ordination and co-operation of individual effort. Efficient reward and incentives systems are ones that cause individuals to make decisions that benefit the organization. At all levels, the ideal is individuals motivated to engage in appropriate levels of co-operation – including the sharing of new information and knowledge – and applying effort to achieving the best outcome. Given the varying skills and knowledge embodied in the workforce, reward and incentive systems need to be augmented by adequate training and development of human resources. In short, the organizational architecture's prime purpose is to maximize the efficiency benefits of **specialization** by enabling specialists to co-operate in achieving **goal congruence**, i.e. the alignment and motivation of resources towards the organization's goals.

Organizational Change at General Motors

In 1920, the US economy slipped into recession and the demand for cars fell sharply. In response, the Ford Motor Company took advantage of the huge cost advantage it enjoyed as a result of its one-car strategy. By producing very large volumes of the Model T it was able to reduce its price by about 25 per cent. General Motors (GM) was unable to match Ford's price cut and over the course of the year saw its sales fall by a staggering 75 per cent. Ford's market share rose to 55 per cent, while GM's shrank back to 11 per cent. GM could not match Ford's price cut because it was organized into divisions. Each division produced a different make of car – Cadillac,

Buick, Oakland, Oldsmobile and Chevrolet. These divisions were in direct competition with each other and made no attempt to co-ordinate their activities. Each division designed its own parts, thereby forgoing the economies that would have resulted from common parts.

In 1921, Alfred Sloan was appointed as GM's CEO. He introduced a strategy that involved segmenting the car market and requiring each division to focus on a particular market segment. The Cadillac division would make luxury cars for the highest-income segment and other divisions would focus on successively lower-income segments. To succeed,

continued

this strategy necessitated co-operation between the separate divisions. Each division would need to design, produce and market cars for a specific market sector whilst avoiding direct competition with other divisions. This new approach involved the sharing of information not only between division, but also with suppliers so that duplication could be removed from production systems and R&D. Compared to Ford's one-car strategy, GM's product market segmented strategy involved much more co-ordination throughout the company. But the result was significant cost reductions.

To achieve this heightened level of co-ordination, Sloan introduced a multi-divisional structure under a powerful central HQ. Unlike other business organizations, GM's HQ would not be responsible for day-to-day operations. Each division would have the autonomy to design, produce and market its own cars. The role of the HQ would be to audit each division's performance and to plan and co-ordinate overall strategy. Sloan's new organization, which had been ridiculed by Henry Ford, rapidly transformed GM's fortunes. GM became highly profitable and its market share increased to 45 per cent by 1940, whereas Ford's once dominant market share shrank to 16 per cent. The creation of a new multi-divisional structure not only provided a framework upon which the company could profitably expand its product line, but it also provided GM with a strategy that allowed it to compete successfully.

An Historical Perspective

Although economic organizations existed before the industrial revolution, it was the 'revolution' that laid the foundations for the modern economic organization. Prior to the mechanization of production in factories, production was largely organized by systems of sub-contractors. Cottage workers, i.e. families, converted raw materials, such as wool, into basic products such as cloth. These were then sold to other households, or small workshops, who added another stage of production, e.g. dyeing, before selling the product on for a further stage in the production process. The development of steam power in the late eighteenth century, together with a series of inventions such as the spinning jenny and the mechanical loom, led to the bringing together, under one roof – i.e. in a factory – of a number of stages of production. These early factories of the industrial revolution were relatively small and labour intensive. Nevertheless, their establishment required an entrepreneur who not only possessed the drive to organize people in factories, but also put up the funds to establish the business. The combining of labour with steam-driven machines and the division of the production process into a number of discrete stages produced enormous improvements in productivity. Consequently, the factory as a means of organizing production flourished because 'cottage' workers could not match the levels of productivity achieved by factory workers.

The idea that firms involve the co-ordination of people to achieve the benefits of specialization was clearly understood by the founding fathers of economics. Adam Smith (1776) explained in some detail, using the example of a pin factory, the boost to productivity arising from specialization, or in his words, the division of labour. Smith's classic 'cost of production' approach was superseded around the 1850s with the development of what is now known as the neo-classical economic theory of the firm. This, as noted previously, provided an elegant theory but one that focused on the firm's ideal state rather than the process of getting there. It rested on a single-product firm operating in a perfectly competitive environment. The firm was small relative to the market – justifying a single-plant firm – and had to compete with very large numbers of firms. Not surprisingly, the neo-classical model reflected the prevailing industrial conditions.

The industrial revolution had given rise to the owner-managed factory and the model's central assumption was that the firm's owner/manager – the entrepreneur – strove only to maximize profits. Technology was relatively simple and new developments, e.g. weaving machines, spread rapidly throughout the industry. The way in which factories organized their systems of production was also relatively straightforward. Populated mainly by women and teenagers, factory production involved very long hours, the drudgery of repeated actions and severe penalties for transgression. In the first half of the nineteenth century it was not therefore so outlandish to assume that within an industry all firms had much the same organizational knowledge and would all be organized in much the same way. And as employees were viewed as a commodity, whose time was purchased solely for the services of their physical labour – hence the expression 'factory hands' – there was little interest in matters other than punctuality and obedience.

During the latter half of the nineteenth century, a number of major innovations transformed the organization of production. Technological advances greatly increased the potential scale of production and also the capital needed to establish an individual plant or firm. The need for large-scale funding gave rise to the joint stock or public company with limited liability, providing an outlet for the savings of the growing ranks of the middle class. The growing scale and complexity of economic organizations necessitated professional management and the ascendancy of the professional manager was assured by the advent of the joint stock company, which separated the owners of the firm's capital from its day-to-day management.

Technological developments and mass transport systems – the coming of the railways in the second half of the nineteenth century was a particularly powerful driving force – helped deliver lower unit costs, but this was not the only reason for the emergence of very large-scale firms towards the end of the nineteenth century. A large-scale firm might dominate the market it served and as a result 'manage' the market to restrict competitive pressures and thereby secure an ***economic rent***. This in turn gave rise to concerns relating to the consequences for economic performance and welfare if these giant firms could avoid or control the disciplines of competition. Figure 2.4 is an attempt to sum up the key drivers, and the implications, of the growing scale of economic organizations over the last 150 years.

The mass-production methods, pioneered in the United States, are now known as the ***Fordist model*** of production. As the Fordest model spread to Europe and other parts of the world, each country adapted it to reflect national attitudes and conditions. Until the middle of the twentieth century, family ownership remained dominant in the UK. Many reasons have been advanced: the smaller size of UK companies; the greater importance of foreign trade; the historical fact that Britain had industrialized before the coming of the railways; and so on. In contrast to the US and Britain, where shareholder capital was becoming pre-eminent at the turn of the century, a distinctive feature of German industrial organization was the Kreditbank – a financial institution focused on the financing of large-scale industrial enterprises. These banks, through their extensive staffs, developed in-depth knowledge of specific industries and companies. In return for seats on supervising boards, these banks provided enough capital to build large-scale firms and the supporting transportation and communications infrastructure.

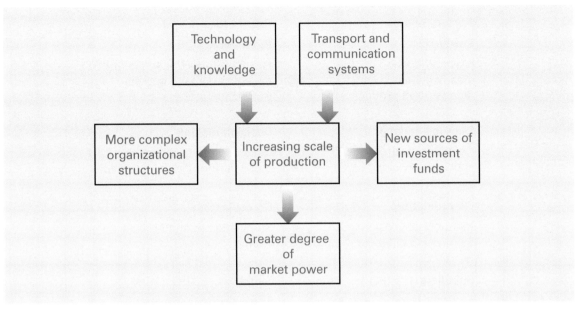

Figure 2.4: Drivers and implications of scale

As the twentieth century entered its last quarter it was the Japanese production model that seized the initiative. Like the Germans, Japanese firms relied on long-term relationships with powerful banks to supply investment capital. But in contrast to the Fordists approach to manufacturing, they developed the *lean production model*, which has since come to dominate manufacturing systems across the world. The key element of this model was the building of long-term relationships with suppliers based on mutual trust so as to improve the quality of inputs and reduce inventories by *Just-in-Time* and *Kanban* systems. The Japanese model encouraged amongst its employees a wide knowledge of its operations, a culture of learning on the job and a willingness to act flexibly and co-operatively. The Japanese model gave much greater control to those performing the operations; consequently it was characterized by a much greater degree of horizontal co-ordination in contrast to the traditional Western approach of co-ordination through vertical systems of hierarchical control.

Over the past 25 years the Japanese model has spread throughout the globe. Directly in the form of Japanese transplants, i.e. establishment of subsidiaries in various countries, and indirectly by the widespread attempts to copy the lean and 'flexible' production systems. It would, however, be a mistake to assume Japanese firms all have the same organizational architectures. Different industries display marked variation in the lean production model. The Toyota model – with its emphasis on *Kaizen*, i.e. continuous improvement – appears to have confirmed its superiority in assembly line industries such as cars and consumer electronics, though not in other sectors such as chemicals and pharmaceuticals. The claimed advantages of the Japanese model owed something to the institutional architecture, e.g. banks as the suppliers of capital, as much as to the firm-level organization. The combination of new organizational and institutional architectures established a pattern of relationships with firms and between firms that were not only complex and subtle but also, in many instances, difficult to clearly define and therefore to precisely replicate. Figure 2.5 attempts to contrast some of the key organizational changes that mark the transition from the Fordist model to the Japanese-inspired Post-Fordist model. A simple diagram can do no more than indicate some of the

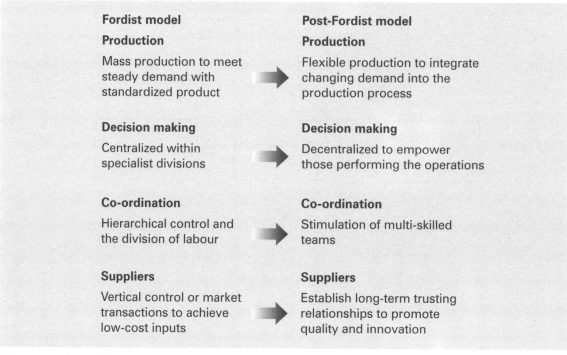

Figure 2.5: The Fordist and Post-Fordist models

key elements, but it serves once again to emphasize how interrelated are organizational changes and the nature of the firm.

Even as the industrial world absorbed with varying degrees of success these organizational changes, so they were being augmented by new forms of inter-firm relationships. Over the latter years of the twentieth century, firms increasingly entered into alliances and joint ventures with other firms to **outsource** key activities. This gave rise to the concept of the hollowed-out firm, a process aided by the explosive growth of digital technology, the creation of global markets by the removal of trade barriers and the reality of a global financial market. Many leading firms now rely very heavily on other lower-cost firms located in other parts of the world to carry out a large part of their operations. For example, the Boeing 767 is produced in co-operation with Mitsubishi and Apple's Notebook is made by Sony. Perhaps the best example of these new organizational structures is the Dell Computer Corporation, which has outsourced all but the assembly of its computers. In contrast to the industrial giants at the start of the twentieth century, Dell has not invested in large-scale production but it has invested heavily in the organizational structures necessary to run outsourced production.

A key implication of digital technology is that the benefits do not reside solely within the firm. It also has the effect of providing consumers with much greater information than in the past on prices and the choice of alternatives. In turn, this has brought to the fore the need for organizations to respond rapidly and flexibly to changing market conditions. This can more easily be accomplished if the firm's organizational architecture is such that it enables the firm's resources to be swiftly redeployed and motivated so as to meet the changing circumstances. These developments over some 200 years of industrial development serve to emphasize that a firm's organizational architecture is a key element in achieving and maintaining competitive advantage.

The Pursuit of Excellence

Quality is now a key competitive advantage, so ensuring that the quality of output is of the standard planned is of key importance. There was a time when businesses checked the quality of their output by means of random checks at the end of the production process. This method reflected a product-orientated approach, but over the last 20 years there has been a remarkable change in the way businesses operate. Part of the change has been driven by Total Quality Management (TQM), which has resulted in changing the thinking about the way business is conducted. Sometimes labelled 'market led' or 'market orientated', the focus is very squarely on the needs of the customer or consumer.

TQM is, as the name implies, related to the monitoring of quality throughout the organization. This means that wherever in the organization a problem is identified, it is the responsibility of those that have identified the problem to solve it. In this way, it is hoped that problems will be solved before they turn up at the end of the production process, or even worse, with the customer. The use of the CE mark to indicate that products conform to all relevant EU directives and the International Standards Organization (ISO) 'badges' send signals to all concerned that the delivery of quality, indeed the pursuit of excellence, is now a prime focus for all organizations.

The Firm as a Governance Structure

As explained above, Coase's seminal work on transaction costs has been developed – most notably by Oliver Williamson (1975) – into what has become known as the governance approach to the firm. Coase's perceptive insight and Williamson's many additions provide a basis for a strategic theory of the firm: a theory that provides an understanding of and explanation as to how firms make choices that are central to their existence and survivability. The governance approach eschews the neo-classical hyper-rationality in favour of bounded rationality and it places information, or rather the lack of it, at the heart of organizational architectures. The lack of information – i.e. uncertainty – as an influence on firms cannot be over-emphasized. At the heart of the way in which a firm organizes and incentivizes its resources is imperfect and asymmetrically held information.

The adoption of a governance perspective provides insights into key strategic issues. By providing an explanation for the existence of firms, it also explicitly sheds light on the scale of firms. Scale is generally associated with the volume of output, but it is also a function of the number of transaction undertaken in-house. As will be explained in the next two chapters, the governance approach helps explain why some transactions are more efficiently undertaken within a firm's governance hierarchy and others more efficiently concluded using market exchange. It therefore provides a theory as to the limits on the size of firms; that is, a theory of firm boundaries. In addition to providing a means of determining a firm's boundaries, the theory also explains why organizational architectures are heterogeneous and how both scale and organizational capabilities contribute to competitive advantage; namely, the creation of value and its capture as economic rent. For example, it is with the aid of a governance perspective that we can compare the strategies of firms such as Dell and IBM. Michael Dell has obviously found a way of reducing the uncertainties associated with greater reliance on the market to supply much of the hardware and the software inside Dell's computers, whereas traditionally IBM relied much more on sourcing such inputs from within their own resources.

As observed by Milgrom and Roberts (1992), markets and hierarchies are just two alternatives for organizing economic activity and both involve contracts. Markets are characterized by voluntary bargaining, whereas hierarchies are characterized by authority relationships. The firm exists as a legal entity that enters into the former type of contract with suppliers and customers and the latter with employees. In a world of imperfect and incomplete information, boundedly rational individuals will seek to mitigate their contracting risks. A contract for market exchange is vulnerable to unanticipated events and in the event of a dispute resort to the courts can result in a lengthy and uncertain outcome. The more important the exchange, the greater the safeguards provided by a governance hierarchy to resolve disputes. A contract for labour services provides a first-class example and is set out as an extensive form game in Figure 2.6. The pay-offs to the firm and the individual are set out, respectively, in the parentheses.

Viewed from the perspective of a firm, at node α the firm has to choose between hiring an employee to carry out a service or using the market to engage a consultant. Viewed from the perspective of an employee, there is a decision to be made regarding accepting paid employment or becoming a consultant. Assuming these services are of an ongoing nature, say the collection and analysis of market data, if the firm contracts with the individual as a consultant, over time the consultant will develop specific knowledge but the benefit of this learning may not accrue to the firm. If now a dispute arises between the firm and the consultant, there is a high probability that the firm will not receive the service contracted for and it may resort to the courts. In this situation there is a risk that the consultant will not be paid. The inability to write a complete contract with the consultant increases the probability of a dispute when contingencies arise.

The firm may judge that it can lessen these risks if it chooses to employ someone to provide the same services and from the individual's perspective an employment contract may increase welfare by the provision of a regular income. The essential difference here is that the firm will enter into a ***relational contract*** with the employee. Such contracts do not attempt the impossible task of complete contracts, but instead settle for an agreement that frames the relationship. Rather than attempt to agree detailed plans of actions for all contingencies, the parties agree on goals and objectives. Most importantly, a firm's contract with its employees

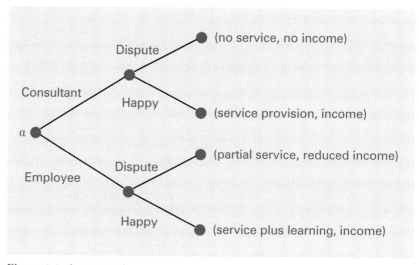

Figure 2.6: A contracting game

involves a grant of authority by the latter to the former. Employees agree, within understood or specified limits, to carry out activities as directed and, if there is a dispute, to settle it (at least in the first instance) by means of an agreed procedure. The incentive for individuals to concede some freedoms and accept direction is that through the firm's co-ordination mechanism individuals achieve higher levels of productivity, which enables the firm to pay higher wages.

Whether purchased from the market or produced within the firm, a product or service will involve a contract. Each contract will involve negotiation of the terms, and its implementation and enforcement. Each contract must specify the service that will be performed, the time of delivery and the circumstances under which delivery will be made. The problem with using the market is that the more complex the product and the longer the time period over which the contract is to run, the higher will be the transaction costs of agreeing a contract. The alternative of bringing production within the firm also involves a contract – indeed, as famously declared by Alchian and Demsetz (1972), the firm is a **nexus of contracts**, but these can be of a relational nature. A relational employment contract avoids the costs of bargaining over what is to be done and on what precise terms it takes place, and implementation is much easier to enforce. Within the firm, individuals work as a part of a team and jointly use the firm's assets. In such situations it is difficult to precisely identify individual contributions and relational contracts avoid the costs of attempting to do so. By bringing the activity within the firm's authority hierarchy, its systems of control and co-ordination economize on bounded rationality, curtail the scope for opportunistic behaviour and thereby lower the transaction costs of production. We will return to these issues in Chapter 7.

Thus, for Williamson, a firm is distinguished from market transactions not in terms of a price co-ordinated production function but in organizational terms. As a governance structure, the firm employs an authoritarian hierarchy to co-ordinate and economize on transactions costs. This is very different from the implied neo-classical view that the market mechanism operates within – as well as without – the firm to allocate the use of resources, particularly labour. Under the neo-classical model's assumption of perfect information and hyper-rationality, both the owners and employees of firms were blessed with perfect foresight and reasoning regarding their decisions and actions. Once this assumption is relaxed, then imperfect and asymmetric information generate transaction costs that a firm seeking productive and allocative efficiency has an incentive to lower and this can be done by replacing the market mechanism with a command-and-control system. By emphasizing that a key characteristic of business life is uncertainty and that a firm's organizational architecture is a means of accumulating information over time, the transaction costs approach brings us to a more practical understanding of why firms exist and why they develop heterogeneous organizational architectures. As we shall see in the following two chapters, by providing a basis for determining what activities a firm will undertake and what goods and services it will buy from the market, transaction costs also provide a guide to the boundaries, i.e. the size, of a firm.

At its most basic the transaction cost theory explains why firms with **property rights** – the right within reason to determine the use to which a productive resource will be put – are more efficient at allocating resources than the market costs of bargaining and negotiating in a world characterized by uncertainty. Viewed as a 'nexus of relational contracts', the firm achieves flexibility in the face of unpredictable events. Today, when a large proportion of a firm's resources are knowledge-based, we might hesitate to go as far as Coase and argue that within the firm employees undertake activities only as directed. A more modern approach would recognize that employees increasingly have discretion in their work, and reward systems frequently include incentives tied to outcomes. Nevertheless, the purpose of a relational employment contract is to allow the firm to override the market mechanism for the purpose of allocating and motivating its resources. In order to determine how rewards will be allocated among the firm's resources, individual property rights must be specified. People cannot be bought or sold like an item of equipment, but the firm's owner(s) can enter into an employment contract whereby an individual is incentivized to agree to some degree of control over the development of their skills and experience. It is the specification of property rights through contracts that sets the framework within which individuals will work and co-operate within organizations.

The foregoing has outlined the governance approach to the firm as a strategic theory of the firm. Competitive advantage and thereby the capture of economic rent is, *ceteris paribus*, positively related to the efficiencies achieved by the firm in the employment of the resources at its disposal. The causation runs from the organizational architecture through the use of incentive contracts to secure property rights, to determine the scale, co-ordination and motivation of resources. The more efficiently these organizational functions are performed, the lower will be the firm's transaction costs and the more accurate its flow of information and knowledge on the performance characteristics of its resources. To quote Alchian and Demsetz (1972, p. 783) efficiency differences between firms are 'a result of not having better resources but in knowing more accurately the relative productive performances of those resources'. It follows that a firm's governance structure is a major influence on its strategy and success in meeting its goals. Transaction costs, incentive contracts and property rights are central to a host of management-related issues such as the make-or-buy decision and much else of direct relevance for strategy. Figure 2.7 attempts to summarize the governance approach as a strategic theory of the firm.

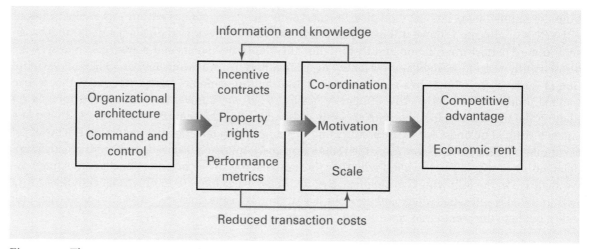

Figure 2.7: The governance approach

Marks and Spencer

The sustained success of Marks and Spencer over many years – the best brand on the high street – provided a clear demonstration of an organizational architecture capable of extracting exceptional performances from ordinary people. The external architecture of M&S's organization was built around an almost Japanese type relationship with suppliers; a long-term trusting relationship that allowed M&S detailed influence on product specification and design. Its internal architecture was centred on permanent employment relationships, strong organizational routines and a shared sense that there was a M&S way of doing things. Rivals found it difficult to duplicate M&S's performance, though in creating its competitive advantage M&S had to strike a balance between short-run profits and reaping the long-term profits that result from developing a heterogeneous and effective organizational architecture. At M&S the focus on improvement was ingrained: employees were effective at making incremental changes and did not see such change as a threat.

However, when companies such as M&S are faced with discontinuous change they find it much harder to adapt because the resources that have been developed may not be consistent with the new environment and organizational consensus may be lacking. In the 1990s, the business paradigm was for companies to become leaner, meaner and more aggressive. Adopting these traits will always result in increased profits for a successful retailer like M&S. By taking full advantage of its strong customer franchise in prices, by putting pressure on suppliers, by diversifying supply relationships, by reducing staff numbers and employment security, M&S could increase profits in the short run but only by eroding the things that made it different from its competitors – the things that were the source of its enviable record of longer-term profits.

On 3 November 1998, M&S reported its first profits fall – not a loss – in 30 years. But the profits fall provided a catalyst and analysts were quick to point out some of the company's deficiencies. For years the company was content to run itself behind closed doors, an autocratic management style seeking to tightly control the organization from the centre. As long as the company's formula was successful it was unquestioned within and without the company. However, following the profit fall it all started to go wrong. The M&S culture came under criticism from City analysers and within a year the then chairman and chief executive, Sir Richard Greenbury, had departed. As far as the City was concerned, M&S had been too slow to change.

There is, however, an alternative view; namely, that M&S changed too much. Its lacklustre performance since 1998 is perhaps the price it is paying for becoming leaner, meaner and more aggressive in the 1990s. If so, it defines a dilemma: does it meet City expectations for earnings today and tomorrow by pushing these processes so that M&S becomes more like its competitors? The logic of such behaviour is that in the long run it will lead to M&S earning the same returns as its competitors.

A Competence Approach

The governance approach has made a significant contribution to understanding how a firm's internal structure contributes to competitive advantage. Indeed, it is now inconceivable that an explanation of the firm can avoid augmenting the neo-classical production function with discussion of transaction costs, incentives and contracts as part of the process of efficiently allocating resources. And yet, the governance approach is deficient as a comprehensive strategic theory of the firm. As demonstrated by its lacklustre performance over recent years, despite the creation of an identifiable organizational architecture M&S found it very difficult to adapt when market conditions changed unexpectedly. A basic requirement for a strategic theory of the firm is the ability to explain market effectiveness in the generation or seeking of economic rent. This involves not only the development of products that are closely aligned with existing consumer demands, but also the ability to adapt to unexpected changes in these demands. The experience of M&S serves to caution an acceptance that the governance approach amounts to a comprehensive strategy theory of the firm. The governance focus on the internal working of the firm underplays, if not overlooks, the need to anticipate and respond to changing market demands. Rather than a concentration on *how* a firm co-ordinates, incentivizes and motivates its workforce, an alternative approach would be to analyse *what* a firm does particularly well.

Such an approach would emphasize the building of competitive advantage through the firm's possession of a particular **capability**. In some cases, the 'capability' may arise from the possession of a physical asset such as a uranium mine, but more generally we should view a capability as arising from the large number of activities carried out by firms. These activities relate not only to the process of physical transformation, but also to areas such as research and development, design and the discovery of future customer demands. The concept of a capability can be traced back to George Richardson (1972), who pointed out that in order to carry out these activities the firm must possess the appropriate capabilities, i.e. the relevant knowledge, skill and experience. From this perspective, sources of competitive advantage and therefore economic rent are derived from firm-specific capabilities or competencies. These capabilities can be deployed and developed to build and protect market effectiveness. In principle, the governance approach can build competitive advantage through the capability of a superior organizational efficiency; but, as pointed out in the opening chapter, firms need to be both productively and allocatively efficient. A firm with a particular capability must therefore be able to allocate its resources so as to capture the opportunities and competitive advantages offered by the capability. And like organizational efficiency, a competitive capability can only endure if rivals find it difficult, if not impossible, to replicate it.

From both the governance and the capability perspectives, competitive advantage lies upstream of product markets and rests on the firm's idiosyncratic and difficult-to-imitate resources. In the case of a firm-specific capability, sustained competitive advantage, and hence the generation of an economic rent, results from resource heterogeneity. As noted above, this will normally be achieved by the accumulation of internally generated knowledge resources, such as intellectual property and routines, that are unique to the firm and also value creating. These heterogeneous resources will be capable of sustained value creation if they not only contribute to meeting a market demand but also by their very nature, other firms find it difficult, if not impossible, to precisely replicate their value-creating properties. Only in this situation will the firm that has property rights over these heterogeneous resources be able to sustain an economic rent from its competitive advantage. Within the firm's organizational architecture, heterogeneity may be created by the form of hierarchical control, the nature of incentives or strategic relationships with suppliers. But rent-generating capabilities are more broadly based than organizational relationships: they include unique resources such as brands, new processes, new products and new channels to market. The governance approach has little to say on how such resources are developed and exploited.

What is lacking from the governance approach to the firm is an appreciation of the firm as an organization for facilitating learning: an organization that generates knowledge capable of capturing value. This suggests a different strategic theory of the firm, one that does not view the firm as a *locus of co-ordination*, but rather as a *locus of creation* (Winter, 1982). As observed above, a theory worth its salt must be able to explain why firms exist, how they are internally organized, what determines their size and how they achieve competitive advantage. The governance approach can fairly claim to offer such a theory, but it is not without challenge. An alternative theory of the firm is known as the **competence approach**. This approach is relatively young – dating from the early 1980s – though its antecedents are the much older concerns with corporate strengths and weaknesses. The approach spawns a number of theories of the firm, but all have in common a resource-based firm-specific capabilities approach to the firm.

The competence-based approach draws much of its inspiration from influential books by Edith Penrose (1959) and Joseph Schumpeter (1942). Penrose is credited with being the first to define the firm as a collection of human and non-human resources whose services are combined in unique ways within the individual firm's organizational architectures. Penrose was concerned to discuss a theory of the growth of the firm, but in so doing she argued that knowledge most suitable for production-related activities is better generated within than without firms. Firms use this knowledge resource to produce products for sale, but the process of **learning by doing** means that it is always adding to its stock of knowledge. Over time, the firm is likely to own an excess of knowledge resources and this motivates entrepreneurial managers to seek profitable outlets for these assets. The incentive to exploit this knowledge is all the greater as in doing so the firm will not incur positive **opportunity costs**. Thus, for Penrose, the essential characteristic of a firm is a bundle of resources, of which the most important are the internally accumulated knowledge-based, heterogeneous resources, e.g. **patents** that can be co-ordinated with other resources to yield competitive advantage and economic rents. We will return to Penrose and the growth of the firm in Chapter 5.

The competence school, in seizing on the concept of heterogeneous knowledge resources, has focused in particular on routines and processes as embodying the skills of the organization (Nelson and Winter, 1982). This provides a strategic theory of the firm based on the proposition that only within firms can heterogeneous knowledge routines and processes be developed, co-ordinated and exploited. Consequently, a firm delivers higher value than could be obtained from market transactions. This approach also suggests limits to the size of the firm as the process of learning and accumulating knowledge resources is time-consuming. The competitive advantage embodied in heterogeneous resources can only be delivered via superior products and/or processes and again the time and management resources devoted to discovering value-added outlets places limits on the size of the firm. These heterogeneous resources or capabilities embody subtle relationships that depend on the way information and knowledge is exchanged via routines and processes throughout the organization. Over time, the firm accumulates a stock of internally generated resources whose services rivals find difficult to replicate because to varying degrees the information and knowledge they are based on is tacit, that is, not capable of being codified. The reliance on **tacit knowledge** will also set limits to the size of a firm and as such it is primarily an immobile resource and a strategic asset of the firm.

To understand the importance of resource heterogeneity, consider a firm operating in an industry where each resource category consists of homogeneous and perfectly mobile resources, e.g. unskilled labour and shovels. Whatever strategy one firm adopts, as other firms have identical resources it is easy for them to copy a successful strategy. Thus, it is impossible for a firm in such a situation to generate an economic rent as other firms will easily duplicate its strategy, thereby reducing the return to all firms. It is therefore the existence of internally generated resources that are difficult, if not impossible, for other firms to replicate that impart a distinctive competence to a firm; a concept given prominence by Prahalad and Hamel's (1990) notion of a firm's **core competency**. Prahalad and Hamel ascribed greater core competencies to Japanese rather than American corporations during the 1980s. That is, on the basis of previous investments in knowledge resources Japanese firms gained a distinctive capability allowing them to conceive of and engage in strategies that American firms found impossible to replicate.

Whereas the governance approach is concerned to link competitive advantage to heterogeneous organizational capabilities, the competency approach focuses on the knowledge resource and in particular how new knowledge is created and developed in a dynamic organization. As such, it is a dynamic strategic theory of the firm that views the firm as an evolving organization whose prime purpose is to develop knowledge-based resources. The theory is at its strongest when linking a hard-to-imitate knowledge capability to a sustained competitive advantage in dynamic environments. But, as noted above, a theory of the firm must also be able to explain not only its existence and size, but also how its internal organization leads to competitive advantage. The competency approach lacks microeconomic foundations for the generation of new knowledge. Nor is the link between competency and competitive advantage unassailable. As with the governance approach, the competence approach is vulnerable to the criticism that building a stock of heterogeneous knowledge resources may be a disadvantage if market conditions change unexpectedly.

Doubts as to the longer-term value of a focus on building or exploiting a stock of heterogeneous resources – doubts fostered by the rapid changes in global economic relationships and the exponential growth of information and communication technologies – have given rise to a number of variant formulations of the competence approach. During the 1990s, successful companies demonstrated a management capability to rapidly and effectively redeploy and co-ordinate core competencies. This ability to rapidly achieve new forms of competitive advantage has been described by Teece *et al.* (1997) as a **dynamic capability**. This refers to the capacity to renew and thereby align competencies with a changing external environment. Dynamic capabilities emphasizes the managerial ability to adapt, reconfigure and integrate organizational resources. The dynamic capabilities approach owes much to Nelson and Winter's (1982) **evolutionary firm**. The evolutionary approach to the firm views it as primarily a processor of knowledge resources whose value is to provide the firm with the flexibility and rapidity necessary to respond successfully to changes in the external environment, e.g. a change in consumer tastes. Both of these dynamic approaches view the firm as being primarily concerned with the co-ordination and development of two specific capabilities – routines and learning – that are central to the process of generating new and appropriable knowledge. Routines have a strong cohesive function as they largely survive the replacement of people who created them and they keep the organization together by conferring on it an individuality that is partly independent of human resources. Like the governance approach to the firm, evolutionary and dynamic capability models are an attempt to explain the behaviour of firms in the absence of the neo-classical assumption of hyper-rationality. The faster a firm can collectively adapt to an unexpected new market environment, the more likely it is to survive and prosper.

What these various 'competency' approaches have in common is the notion that it is the process of striving for a superior profit performance that creates diversity. The contrast with the neo-classical approach to the firm is again extreme. Central to the neo-classical model is homogeneity, which in turn implies – within an industry – identical knowledge known by all firms. The very essence of the competency approach is that knowledge by its nature is heterogeneous, being frequently tacit and hard to communicate. Within the cohesive shell of a firm, entrepreneurial managers can control the development and use of knowledge in a way that would be impossible if reliance was placed on market exchange. Once it is accepted that in order to understand the nature of the firm we need to be able to explain heterogeneity in the behaviour and performance of firms, the competence approach represents an important addition to the attempt to explain the economics of production. From the competence perspective, the firm must do more than combine resources in productively and allocatively efficient ways, it must also develop heterogeneous resources and find new ways of capturing their inherent value that rivals find difficult to imitate. Only in this way can firms generate greater value from their resources than the market would deliver and in the process gain competitive advantage.

The idea that a firm can build competitive advantage from the development of heterogeneous resources has a lot of adherents. Successful organizations tend to have a 'distinctiveness' – contrast the 'softer' corporate culture of Marks and Spencer in the 1970s and 1980s with the more robust culture of Hanson in its heyday. But as these two examples demonstrate, whether firms can build enduring advantage through the development of firm-specific capabilities is open to question. According to Simon (1993), a firm's 'niche' or competitive advantage typically has a half life that can be counted in years not decades. The task of senior managers is to ensure a stream of new ideas that will allow the firm to continue to adapt to an uncertain world. The management capabilities and patterns of relationships and communication that will deliver these resources within firms are complex, subtle and hard to define precisely. Financial building blocks are investments in organizational and human capital, with the objective of developing heterogeneous resources, but such investment is in many instances a **sunk cost**. Thus, the capabilities perspective not only offers an explanation as to why firms are different, but also it offers an explanation as to why they are frequently unresponsive to even major shifts in their competitive environments.

It is important to stress that the competence-based approach to the firm – so beloved by strategic management academics – is not a self-contained theory; indeed, compared to the neo-classical and governance approach to the firm, the theory has been criticized for lacking rigour, refutable implications and predictive ability. The claim by leading proponents of the competency approach that at the end of the 1980s Japanese corporations had greater core competencies than their US counterparts was a claim that did not survive into the 1990s. The concept of a capability cannot be precisely defined and there is a tendency by the competency school to rationalize a competitive capability *ex post*. Nevertheless, the competence perspective does serve to augment the narrow view of the firm as a production function by focusing on management and organizational features as an explanation of inter-firm heterogeneity and competitive advantage, and we will return to its concepts and insights in the following chapters. Figure 2.8 is an attempt to summarize the competency approach. It is an approach that is still relatively young – after all, it took more than 30 years for economists to start taking seriously Coase's transaction costs approach to the firm – and one that attracts much research and analysis.

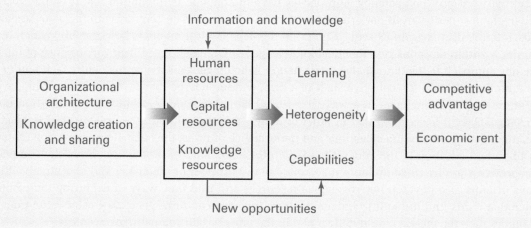

Figure 2.8: The competency approach

An Evolutionary Firm

Celltech is arguably Europe's leading biotechnology company, whose growth and very existence depends on the creation and exploitation of knowledge. Founded in 1980 as the UK's first biotechnology company, it initially had a broad research programme in such diverse areas as food processing and antibody engineering, but by the mid-1990s its focus was primarily the discovery of novel drugs. In 1990, the company was divided into two operating divisions – Celltech Therapeutics and Celltech Biologics – responsible for drug discovery and manufacturing, respectively. In 1996, after a listing on the London Stock Exchange, Celltech Biologics was sold, leaving Celltech to concentrate on the discovery of novel drugs.

It would be hard to imagine a more knowledge-based company. Biology is the new physics; genes, proteins and nanotubes have replaced dark matter and quarks as the intellectual challenges. The growing mastery of genes and molecules promises to provide not only medicines but also materials and microorganisms that will transform the economics of many industries. And Celltech's very success depends critically on its 'genes'. Its very survival depends on the efficiency with which knowledge is created, selected and distributed. The cognitive mechanisms by which its employees discover and develop new drugs involve not only individual intellect but also the utilization of accumulated knowledge encompassing routines and learning.

Central to the creation of new drugs is the core competency of processing new knowledge. For Celltech's managers, governance amounts to the capability to co-ordinate the many diverse pieces of knowledge drawn from a variety of learning processes. Moreover, this capability must be dynamic as the company has to have the flexibility to respond to new scientific discoveries and changing market expectations, e.g. cheaper drugs. In order to

continued

develop a dynamic capability, Celltech has formed a range of strategic partnerships with universities and biotechnology companies. These partnerships represent an evolving process of learning and Celltech's contribution is the capability of adapting knowledge created in diverse forms to the discovery of novel drugs. This capability is its strategic core competency and it is potentially the source of value creation for Celltech.

Despite its core competency, Celltech has yet to produce a blockbuster. Novel drug development is a long-term process and Celltech's big hope – a drug called CDP870 that partner Pfizer has in phase-three clinical trials for rheumatology applications – is still some three years from market. But the company continues to develop in an evolutionary manner. The knowledge created by its learning and captured within its routines is in many respects unique and capable of being applied to a wide range of uses, from drugs to new products. Whether or not it succeeds in the long run, what Celltech clearly demonstrates is the need, in an uncertain and rapidly changing world, to build management capabilities that encourage not only learning but also the entrepreneurial flair to exploit the new knowledge.

An Integrated Approach to the Firm

The neo-classical, governance and competence approaches to the firm are frequently viewed as being in conflict. Scholars seek nuances and contradictions, but in large measure the three approaches are complementary. Although the neo-classical approach assumed away many of the issues that are of interest and relevance to those faced with the task of managing economic organizations, it is founded on the principle that by co-ordinating the varying skills and experience of individual employees within a production process, the firm gains the benefit of higher productivity and therefore greater efficiency. Moreover, the neo-classical theory provides predictive outcomes for a firm faced by external change, e.g. a fall in demand. Implicitly, the neo-classical firm had an organizational architecture and strategy, but in a world of perfect information and hyper-rationality neither would be a source of competitive advantage as the more successful routines and systems would soon be adopted by all firms. In such a world it is permissible to talk of the 'representative firm', but the assumptions of perfect information and hyper-rationality obscured more than they reveal. Once these twin assumptions are relaxed we have a world of uncertainty and bounded rationality, and in response the existence of firms with heterogeneous governance structures and strategies to exploit heterogeneity, rendering the concept of the representative firm as meaningless. In such a world, to quote Williamson (1991, p. 75) 'strategy, like charity, begins at home'.

The governance approach to a strategic theory of the firm, with its emphasis on contracts, authority structures and incentives, is a direct response to the transaction costs arising from asymmetrically held information and bounded rationality. Transaction costs not only explain the existence of firms, but also the control, co-ordination and incentive functions of their organizational architectures. The competence approach to a strategic theory of the firm, with its emphasis on the dynamic development of heterogeneous knowledge resources, is also an attempt to come to terms with a world of uncertainty and bounded rationality. This approach puts less emphasis on the control and co-ordination functions of firms and instead focuses on the role the organizational architecture plays in the creation, development and sharing of knowledge. It is, therefore, with the concept of an organizational architecture, that the governance and competence approaches to the firm come together in an integrated approach to the firm. Figure 2.9 attempts such a synthesis. In the centre of the figure, lies the organizational architecture; that is, the firm's authority hierarchy, with its assignment of decision-making rights, its systems for monitoring and evaluating performance and its methods of rewarding and incentivizing individuals.

At the top of Figure 2.9 is the one influence which the firm's senior managers know for certain and must take as given – its history and experience. The performance of the firm, the markets it currently serves and its culture are all path dependent. New technologies and the external environment serve to remind us that firms operate in situations of constant change, and reducing vulnerability to the uncertainty this begets is a prime objective for a firm's organizational architecture. Working round the left of Figure 2.9, the firm's tangible resources – human and physical – are both shaped by, and will in turn shape, the firm's organizational architecture. The way in which these resources are managed and developed will create firm-specific synergies and knowledge resources ranging from intellectual property to routines capable of reacting rapidly to change. Exploiting the potential value of these internally generated resources calls for entrepreneurial skills and strategies. Moving to the right-hand side of the diagram, the firm's resources define its feasible set of strategies. The sub-set of strategies that the firm pursues will reflect its history, experience, culture and the entrepreneurial flair of its senior managers. Its strategies are likely to provoke responses from its market competitors, though whether these are co-operative or aggressively competitive depends in part on the skill of the firm's senior managers as game players. Finally, the diagram seeks to effect a synthesis of the two approaches by making it clear that the architecture's role is to align the firm's resources with its strategy and then to achieve high levels of co-operation and motivation, which are necessary if the firm is to be efficient and focused on its goals of competitive advantage.

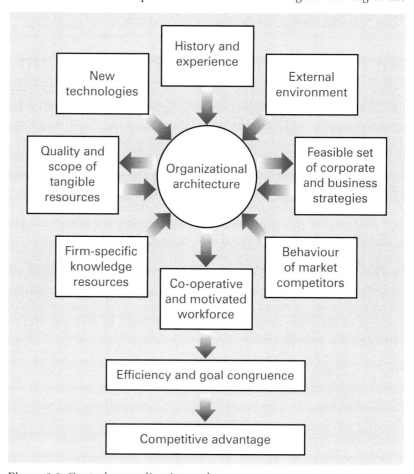

Figure 2.9: Control, co-ordination and congruence

Figure 2.9 attempts to make clear that neither the governance approach nor the competence approach are sufficient to provide a comprehensive theory of the firm in a world of imperfect information and bounded rationality. The governance approach to the firm can fairly claim to contribute to an understanding of the development of strategy. Virtually all aspects of business strategy involve issues such as what should be produced and how the firm should be organized to meet its goals. But strategy also involves the entrepreneurial skill to recognize and select productive opportunities and also the energy and drive to develop the appropriate level and mix of resources to meet the challenge. Thus, the dynamic capability to respond to new, unforeseen events is every bit as important, possibly more important, than the adoption of internal behaviours to achieve co-operation and efficiency. Learning, adapting and responding is a core capability that all firms must strive to achieve. Taken together, the three approaches all contribute to a comprehensive understanding of the role, organization and behaviour of firms. Figure 2.10 attempts to capture the essence of these alternative approaches to the firm.

One diagram cannot hope to do justice to the complexities and subtleties of the different approaches. Its purpose is to present the alternative theories of the firm as being complementary. The neo-classical, production-focused approach highlights the technological determinants of the firm and – using highly restrictive assumptions – provides refutable hypotheses and predictions. The governance approach is very much in the formal, deductive approach of microeconomics, with an emphasis on hypothesis testing. Its starting position is the recognition that firms operate in an uncertain world,

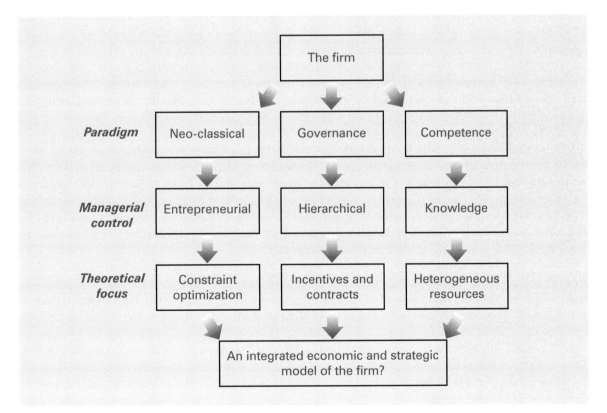

Figure 2.10: An integrated approach to the firm

where the existence of bounded rationality and opportunistic behaviour create positive costs when using the market mechanism to organize production. The competence approach has developed from the study of strategy and organizations in business schools. It is more focused on explaining how firms develop their resources – and in particular their internally generated knowledge resources – to achieve sustained competitive advantage. However, it lacks the microeconomic foundations of the other two approaches and is characterized by case studies and non-formal discourse. On their own, none of these theories provide all the answers, but together they do indicate the future direction of research if a comprehensive theory of the firm is to be advanced; namely, an integration of these approaches that will *perforce* integrate the economic bedrock of constrained optimization with the efficient organization of the resources that are controlled and developed within the firm.

Concluding Thoughts

For the founding fathers of economics, the focus was on what firms should do rather than what they did do. By assuming that firms operated as sellers and purchasers in perfectly competitive markets, the neo-classical theory of the firm could set down precise laws regarding cost minimization and the efficient allocation of resources. The firm's perfectly informed and hyper-rational owner – the entrepreneur – was assumed to be solely motivated by the desire to maximize profits; similarly gifted employees were assumed to be solely motivated by the desire to maximize their earnings; and the firm sold its output to consumers whose objective of maximizing **utility** was secured by the possession of perfect information and hyper-rationality. In such a world, the way in which the entrepreneur organized and co-ordinated the workforce was of little importance. Perfect information ensured that all employees worked hard and efficiently and the underlying assumptions implied that all firms in an industry would sooner or later adopt the same technology, organizational architecture, products and prices.

For students of business strategy, the neo-classical approach is deficient. As business managers they will operate in a world characterized by uncertainty and bounded rationality. In co-ordinating and motivating their workforces they will need systems to motivate and measure performance. And in achieving competitive advantage they will seek to create heterogeneity. The neo-classical approach is silent on these issues. It fails to shed light on why firms are different and what they might do to create competitive advantage. A paradigm that is concerned with a world in which all firms within an industry are identical, not only in terms of the product produced, but also in terms of their internal organization, has assumed away the very essence of business strategy and competitive advantage. The fact that firms, as social communities, are likely to develop distinctive organizational architectures that influence the way they achieve productive and allocative efficiencies are ignored in the neo-classical world of perfect information and hyper-rationality.

Ronald Coase sought to address this deficiency with his concept of transaction costs: a direct consequence of uncertainty and bounded rationality. From this perspective, firms exist where a management hierarchy is more efficient at co-ordinating and motivating productive resources than the price signals inherent in the market mechanism. Coase's insights gave birth to the governance school, whose disciples have developed a body of theory that broadens our understanding of how firms organize themselves, why they grow to different sizes and why they have different cultures. Building on the benefits of specialization and co-ordination identified by the neo-classical approach, the transaction cost approach has developed into a study of the role of governance structures, incentives and contracts in delivering efficiency and competitive advantage.

A comprehensive theory of the firm must also be able to explain the rent-seeking behaviour of firms manifested in the desire to utilize firm-specific knowledge to exploit new products, new markets and new processes. The governance approach does not deal adequately with the generation and exploitation of knowledge within the firm and this deficiency has given rise to the competency approach. This approach to a strategic theory of the firm focuses on how firms strive to develop new knowledge-based resources that yield to the firm heterogeneity and thereby the scope for competitive advantage. This approach, along with the governance approach, is founded on the acceptance of imperfect information and bounded rationality, but is distinguished by the focus on the creation and development of heterogeneous capabilities rather than the management of an accumulated stock of knowledge. The competency approach is therefore dynamic or evolutionary and focused on the routines that encourage and capture learning. The view advanced here is that all three approaches to the firm are complementary and a greater understanding of the workings of a firm is achieved if all three approaches are taken into account.

Key Learning Points

- At its most basic, a firm is an economic organization whose primary purpose is to facilitate the division of labour within a co-operative environment so as to capture the productivity inherent in specialization.
- Firms not only produce outputs for sale, but also tangible and intangible resources that are then available to the firm to exploit in ways it judges will best enable it to achieve its goals.
- In a world of asymmetrically held information and bounded rationality, firms exist because their replacement of market exchange with an authority hierarchy avoids the transaction costs associated with the allocation, co-ordination and motivation of resources.
- As a governance structure, firms co-ordinate, motivate and develop their resources within firm-specific organizational architectures that determine decision rights, evaluate and monitor performance and establish reward systems.

- Lacking perfect information, it is impossible to write complete contracts. Hence firms settle for incomplete contracts with suppliers and customers and relational contracts with their employees.
- The governance approach as a strategic theory of the firm is, however, deficient in key areas; in particular, it does not explain why or how firms choose and develop the heterogeneous resources that open up new opportunities to capture competitive advantage.
- The competency approach to the firm attempts to address these issues by defining a firm as an organization for creating, storing and utilizing knowledge resources, many of which are based on tacit rather than codified knowledge and hence cannot be replicated by rivals.
- None of these approaches to the firm amounts to a complete theory of the firm. But combining the three approaches points to future success in developing a comprehensive theory of the firm.

Exercises

2.1 In what way does the traditional presentation of a firm as producing a single output for sale seriously underplay the outputs that a firm generates?

2.2 Outline the ways in which transaction costs increase the costs of market exchange.

2.3 A firm's organizational architecture may be summarized as the 'way it gets things done'. What are the key elements of a firm's organizational architecture?

2.4 Explain why relational contracts, property rights and incentives lie at the heart of the governance approach to the firm.

2.5 According to the competence approach, firms are an efficient means of developing new knowledge resources. Why is the emphasis on development rather than accumulation relevant?

Problems

2.1 Speed Fix is a small company involved in car body repairs. The company is owned by Jim Johnson, who employs nine people: four carry out the repairs, two paint the repaired bodies and three reassemble the cars. Jim takes care of the marketing, bookkeeping and general management. A rival co-operative has recently set up, involving ten people. In the co-operative, all decisions are taken jointly by the 10 worker-members of the co-operative:

(a) How would you characterize Speed Fix in the language of transaction cost economics?

(b) Compare the organizational form of Speed Fix with the co-operative in terms of advantages and disadvantages.

(c) If competition in the car body repair industry becomes intense, who is best placed to survive?

References

Alchian, A. and Demsetz, H. (1972) 'Production, information and economic organization', *American Economic Review*, vol. 62 pp. 777–795.

Brickley, J., Smith, C., Jr. and Zimmerman, J. (2001) *Managerial Economics and Organizational Architecture*, 2nd edn, McGraw-Hill Irwin, New York.

Coase, R. (1937) 'The Nature of the Firm', *Economica*, vol. IV, pp. 386–405.

Milgrom, P. and Roberts, J. (1992) *Economics Organizations and Management*, Prentice Hall, Englewood Cliffs, NJ.

Nelson, R. and Winter, S. (1982) *An Evolutionary Theory of Economic Change*, Belknap Press, Harvard University Press, Cambridge, MA.

Penrose, E. (1959) *The Theory of the Growth of the Firm*, Basil Blackwell, Oxford.

~d, C. and Hamel, G. (1990) 'The core compelencies of the organization', *Harvard Business Review*, May–June, 79–91.

Richardson, G. (1972) 'The organization of industry', *Economic Journal*, vol. 82, pp. 83–96.

Schumpeter, J. (1942) *Capitalism, Socialism and Democracy,* Harper & Row, New York.

Simon, H. (1961) *Administrative Behavior*, 2nd edn, Macmillan, New York.

Simon, H. (1993) 'Strategy and organizational evolution', *Strategic Management Journal*, vol. 14, pp. 131–142.

Smith, A. (1776) *An Enquiry into the Nature and Causes of the Wealth of Nations*, 1976 Bicentenary Edition, Clarendon Press, Oxford.

Teece, D., Pisano, G. and Shuen, A. (1997) 'Dynamic capabilities and strategic management', *Strategic Management Journal*, vol. 18.7, pp. 509–533.

Williamson, O. (1975) *Markets and Hierarchies: Analyses and Antitrust Implications*, Free Press, New York.

Williamson, O. (1991) 'Strategising, economising and economic organization', *Strategic Management Journal*, vol. 12, pp. 75–94.

Winter, S. (1982) 'An essay on the theory of production' in *Economics and the World Around It* (pp. 55–93), H. Hymans (ed.), University of Michigan Press, Ann Arbor, MI.

Introduction

We have seen, following Ronald Coase, that it is profitable to establish a firm when the **transaction costs** of using the market outweigh the benefits of market exchange. Viewed from a Coasian perspective, the firm consists of a supply chain where a product is exchanged between a number of discrete, sequential activities. It is these activities that create or add the value inherent in the good or service being produced and it is for this reason that supply chains are now frequently known as **value chains**. This approach to the firm immediately raises a key strategic question; namely, how many separable production activities should a firm undertake? A firm's **vertical boundary** is determined by the number of technologically separable intermediate production stages that are controlled by one hierarchical governance structure. This chapter implicitly focuses on the value chain for a single product; in the next chapter we will focus on multi-product firms and thereby a firm's **horizontal boundary**. This chapter builds on the concepts introduced in Chapter 2 to provide understanding of the factors that determine how many separable production stages it is productively and allocatively efficient for an individual firm to undertake. The decisions a firm takes as to what it produces or 'makes' for itself and what it chooses to purchase or 'buy' from the market are fundamental to its strategy at both the corporate and business unit level. Put succinctly, at the heart of all business strategy is the 'make-or-buy' decision.

If a firm's vertical boundary encompasses two or more separable, sequential production stages, the firm is described as being vertically integrated. The term **vertical integration** describes a situation where a governing hierarchy has replaced the market as the means of exchange between successive stages of production. We observed above that all firms are value chains, but most firms are embedded within a longer industry value chain incorporating the firm's suppliers and customers. Focusing on a firm in the middle of an industry's value chain, if it acts to produce some or all of the intermediate goods or services that it would otherwise purchase from suppliers it is described as having vertically integrated *upstream*. If the firm acts to utilize its output as an input to another value-adding activity, it is described as having vertically integrated *downstream*. Thus, a vertically integrated firm not only has **property rights** over the means of producing one or more separable stages of the production of an output, but also it has complete discretion as to how the intermediate product will be exchanged between the successive stages. Put another way, a vertically integrated firm controls by management authority the flow of production between two or more stages of the industry value chain.

Vertical integration may occur when a firm is set up – this is known as vertical formation. Alternatively, vertical integration that occurs as a result of organic growth is known as vertical expansion and vertical merger describes vertical integration that occurs through a merger or acquisition. Since the 1980s, two new words have entered the business language – 'downsizing' and '**outsourcing**' – reflecting a move away from vertical integration: their use is perhaps understandable given the alternative of 'disintegration'. In many cases, the internal governance of value exchange has been replaced with procurement via spot market transactions, but equally likely is outsourcing that takes the form of a vertical relationship lying somewhere between the polar extremes of a spot market transaction and vertical integration. One consequence of these vertical relationships is that firms build inter-organizational structures with suppliers and/or customers, the effect of which is to blur the boundaries of the firms involved. As governance in such arrangements is shared between two or more separate entities, there are no clearly defined boundaries and it is more realistic to think of the firms involved in such relationships as having virtual boundaries.

The theme underlying this chapter's focus on vertical and virtual boundaries is how the issue of vertical co-operation is influenced by the existence of **incomplete** knowledge, **imperfect** and **asymmetric information**. In later chapters, we will return to vertical integration and vertical relationships as a means of engaging in or resolving strategic conflict. Here our focus is within the firm and, in particular, how the presence of uncertainty can determine whether a firm chooses to produce its inputs in-house, or buy them from the market, or produce them jointly in partnership with other entities. These issues are key strategic elements and address the fundamental difference between a subsidiary and a supplier, an employee and a sub-contractor, an acquaintance and a partner. By reading this chapter you will:

- Appreciate how a firm's vertical boundaries determine its influence within its value chain.
- Understand how the efficiency criterion can explain the number of separable production stages within a firm's boundaries.
- Know why outsourcing frequently involves the creation of a new type of vertical relationship rather than spot market procurement.

This chapter is divided into six sections. In the first, we will start by defining and measuring vertical integration. We will then go on in the second section to explore how imperfect and asymmetric information can encourage vertical integration, and in the third section we will examine the role of transaction costs in the 'make-or-buy' decision. In the fourth section we will analyse the **governance approach** to vertical integration, and in particular how Oliver Williamson's development of Ronald Coase's perceptive insight into the nature of the firm has yielded a theory of vertical boundaries that explains why they are not fixed and are likely to wax and wane over time. As discussed in the previous chapter, despite the many valuable insights of the governance approach to the firm it is not a complete theory and needs to be complemented with the **competence approach**, which provides further insights as to why some firms grow by expanding their vertical boundaries. In the fifth section we will briefly outline the competences approach to vertical boundaries, before turning in the last section to investigate vertical relationships, and in particular joint ventures and partnership alliances, as alternatives to vertical integration.

Vertical Integration

We noted above that a firm can be described as vertically integrated if it encompasses two, or more, technologically separable, sequential production processes whereby the output from the upstream process is an intermediate product that becomes an input to the downstream process. Inherent in this definition is the substitution of market exchange, either a planned or spot transaction, with internal governance to procure the intermediate product. This definition implies ownership of the property rights in the resources utilized in the separable, but neighbouring, production stages and complete control over the production and exchange decisions at each stage.

In the rather special case of a new, functionally unique, product, e.g. the light bulb at the end of the nineteenth century, there may be no suppliers of key inputs. This may reflect a lack of technological knowledge or it may reflect incomplete knowledge as to the likely volume of sales. In such circumstances, the innovating firm may have no alternative but to produce these inputs itself as a vertically integrated business. To quote Adam Smith, (1776), the division of labour is 'limited by the extent of the market'. If the new product is successful, demand will grow and as it does so, this will create opportunities for the development of specialist producers of key inputs and, hence, procurement via market exchange. All other factors remaining equal, the outcome of a number of specialist producers competing to supply an intermediate input should result in the lowest possible unit price. But for the firm producing a highly specialized product it may never be economic to source key intermediate inputs from the market. It is not the price, but the total cost of the exchange that is critical to the decision. Before exploring the costs of exchange and their influence on a firm's vertical boundaries, we need to be clear as to how a firm's internal value chain relates to an industry or sector value chain. A highly simplified representation of a firm's internal value chain involving only one production stage before assembly of the product is shown in Figure 3.1

Say, for example, that Figure 3.1 represented a food processor who makes cheese flans. The processor purchases key inputs from the market, e.g. butter, cheese and flour, and then at the production stage prepares the flan base and fillings before baking the flan (assembly) to produce the finished product. Before packaging and despatching (sales) the product to customers, samples are likely to be tested. Figure 3.2 shows how our highly simplified, internal value chain (i.e. our food processor) sits within a greatly simplified value chain. All value chains start with raw materials, i.e. primary inputs or raw materials, which are then processed at successive stages in the chain into a finished product. In the

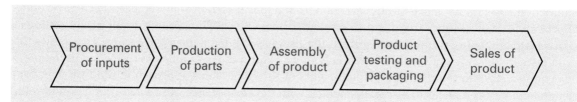

Figure 3.1: An internal value chain

example shown, inorganic fertilizers made from nitrogen become inputs into agricultural production. Note that some of the cereal output from arable farms is the raw material for animal feed processors (a separate value chain). Continuing down the chain, these agricultural commodities are then processed into flour, butter and cheese before being utilized by the food processor in the manufacture of its food products. These products are then packaged and distributed to the point where they are sold to consumers for consumption.

In Figure 3.2, starting with our representative firm – the food processor – moving back through its suppliers and its suppliers' suppliers is described as moving upstream. Alternatively, starting with the fertilizer manufacturer, the food processor is located downstream in the food value chain; that is, the flow of material inputs is described as moving down the chain. If we go downstream from our representative food processor, then we move to retailers and other outlets. It is the physical movement of resources down the chain that gives rise to the idea of vertical movement. Figure 3.2 is highly simplified; not shown are the merchants, wholesalers and distributors who move the intermediate products between each stage in the supply chain. Each stage in the value chain also purchases goods and services from other value chains, e.g. the purchase of machines. In practice, value chains are a highly complex web or network of exchange transactions. Figure 3.2 implies that each stage in the value chain deals only with firms that are immediately up- or down stream. Increasingly, this may not be the case; for example, in order to ensure safety and traceability, supermarkets and other final food sellers now routinely build links with farm businesses. Figure 3.2 also implies that our food processor only buys from one milk processor, one ingredient manufacturer and so on. In practice, unless the supplier has a monopoly, firms will usually trade with more than one supplier, though for reasons that will be discussed below, the trend is for firms to reduce the number of suppliers. By sourcing inputs from more than one supplier, the firm reduces the risk of a breakdown in supply and and also partly ensures the prices charged are competitive.

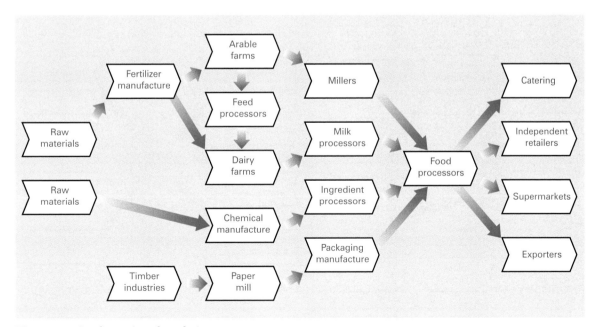

Figure 3.2: A schematic value chain

As illustrated, the food processor's vertical boundaries are clearly shown. If, however, the food processor decided to develop the in-house ability to undertake an upstream or downstream function, this would represent vertical expansion. To vertically expand the food processor could merge with, or acquire, a firm at the appropriate stage in the value chain or it could decide to develop the expertise itself. For example, if our food processor purchased a milk processor, or acquired the assets and the necessary skills to turn milk into butter and cheese, it would have added a separable production stage to its existing activities and in so doing the firm would have vertically expanded upstream. The effect of the processor's action would be not only to increase its vertical boundaries, but also to alter the structure of the food chain, as shown in Figure 3.3. Now the milk processor is missing from the value chain and dairy farms supply the food processor directly with milk. In the value chain shown, the range of activities that are co-ordinated within a governing hierarchy has increased and the number of transactions determining market exchanges has declined.

Vertical expansion will alter a firm's cost structure, as shown in Table 3.1, which continues the example of the food processor absorbing milk processing activities. The food processor sells products valued at €1,600m and to keep matters simple let us assume that before vertically expanding it purchased all €200m of the milk processor's output. These dairy products are then combined with €700m of other purchased inputs to total €900m of purchased inputs, generating a gross margin of €700m for the food processor. The annual cost of the food processor's labour and capital depreciation amounts to €300m, delivering a net margin – or profit before interest and tax – of €400m. Similarly, the milk processor, in producing milk products to the value of €200m, purchased intermediate inputs – mainly raw milk – to the value of €100m. After allowing for labour and capital costs of €90m, the milk processing company achieved a net margin of €10m. If now the milk processor is absorbed within the food processor, the situation is shown in the right-hand column of the table. In our simple example, the value of the food processor's output remains unchanged but the value of its purchased

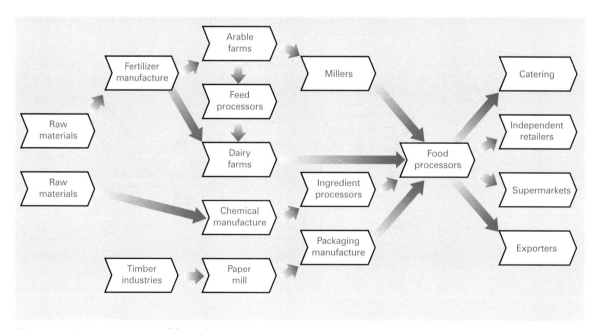

Figure 3.3: Increasing vertical boundaries

inputs falls. This follows because the food processor is now purchasing €100m of raw milk instead of milk products to the value of €200m. However, the vertically expanded food processor now incurs the cost of turning the milk into milk products. To do this, it must increase its labour force and add the necessary fixed assets to its stock of capital; hence, the increased costs of its labour and capital.

Table 3.1 Vertical integration and costs

All figures in €m	Milk processor	Food processor	Integrated food processor
Revenue	200	1,600	1,600
Less:			
Purchased inputs	100	900	800
Gross margin	100	700	800
Less:			
Wages and salaries	40	100	140
Capital costs	50	200	250
Net margin	10	400	410
Ratio: (*Inputs/gross margin*)	2.0	1.28	1.0

The foregoing is a very simple example, but it shows how moving from reliance on market exchange for inputs to making them in-house reduces the ratio of the firm's purchased inputs to its gross margin, and increases its labour and capital costs. As shown, the vertically integrated business makes no saving on the labour and capital costs of processing milk and hence the vertically integrated net margin is equivalent to the combined net margin prior to integration. The example has been prepared for heuristic reasons but if, in vertically expanding, our firm cannot generate a net margin that is greater than the combined net margin of the buyer and seller prior to vertical integration, then a rational justification for integrating the separate production stages must rest on less tangible cost savings, e.g. reducing uncertainty. Our food processor might believe that by vertically integrating it

Vertically Expanding Farmers

The 1990s were tough times for Britain's dairy farmers. As producers of a commodity product in over-supply, they were classic price takers and when the pound appreciated markedly against other European currencies they found their returns pushed to historically low levels. Even worse, in 1999 the Competition Commission (CC) determined that Milk Marque, the farmer-owned milk buying company, was a scale monopoly owing to its control of almost half of the country's sales of milk. The CC recommended, and the government implemented, the division of Milk Marque into three independent companies. One of these farmer-owned businesses is called Milk Link.

Milk Link realized that if it was to increase the returns to its 3,400 farmer members it had to capture more of the value that was added downstream to the 1.4 billion litres of milk that Milk Link's farmers produced each year. In order to achieve this objective Milk Link took the strategic decision to move into the processing of milk and set about raising sufficient funds to purchase processing capacity. In essence, the farmer members of Milk Link agreed to provide security for institutional financial support. Within a year Milk Link had sufficient funds to embark on a strategy to buy, merge or jointly produce with creameries, cheese and yoghurt businesses.

secures supplies of a key resource and thereby reduces the risk of a breakdown in supply or perhaps a reduction in quality. In fact, as we shall see, the desire to reduce uncertainty is a major determinant of vertical integration.

Before turning our attention to the main determinants of vertical integration, it is worth pointing out that merely measuring the ratio of the value of a firm's purchased inputs to its gross margin is not always an accurate measure of the degree of vertical integration. If we are comparing two firms at the same stage in the supply chain, then it may be a reasonable indicator, but not if we compare firms at different stages in the supply chain. Consider a coal mine and a retailer. The coal mine spends a relatively small proportion of its revenue purchasing inputs from other industries, but it incurs high labour and capital costs in bringing the primary input, coal, to the surface for sale. Typically, therefore, a coal mine – like other primary producers – will have a relatively low ratio of purchased inputs to gross margin. In contrast, a retailer who sells the products it purchases in a competitive market will have a purchased input–gross margin ratio that is relatively high – for UK supermarkets, it is typically around 1.8.

Private Information and Uncertainty

Vertical integration may arise from technological economies. For example, in the production of steel the blast furnace and the basic oxygen furnace are co-located within one firm on one site. In practice, the energy savings from not having to reheat the pig iron from cold are so large that only by co-locating the two stages can unit costs be minimized. The energy economies arising from the co-location of the two steel-making stages are not *per se* the subject of this chapter. What is the focus of this chapter is why the co-location of the two furnaces under separate management might result in a less efficient outcome than would be the case if the two production stages were under the control of the same governance hierarchy. As separate entities, the two firms would be highly dependent on each other, but on the basis of private information may make decisions that are adverse to the relationship. The downstream steel producer in attempting to profitably meet the demand for steel, seeks the certainty that the supply and price of pig iron will enable it to meet all variations in demand. For its part, the iron producer also seeks certainty in demand from the steel producer. The separate managements may, on the basis of private information, form different views as to the demand for steel in the next production period. As a result, the supply and demand for pig iron will be misaligned, causing either a fall or rise in its price. Let us examine the situation from the perspective of the buyer, i.e. the steel producer.

Being able to obtain the key input of iron in sufficient quantity and of the right quality, as and when needed, at a known cost, helps the steel firm in its planning and co-ordination. In principle, if the steel producer could source its iron from a competitive market this would provide greater certainty in respect of quantity and quality, but it would involve the additional cost of reheating the iron. The issue here is the extent to which the supplier of iron will exploit its quasi-**monopoly** position. If the upstream supplier behaves like a monopolist, this implies the downstream purchaser will have to pay a price in excess of **marginal cost** (*MC*). This might seem to suggest sufficient justification for vertical integration; namely, for the buyer to reduce and control the price of a key input and thereby to increase the purchasing firm's profit. But again, this is not a sufficient justification for vertical integration. To see this, consider the following, simplified example. Say firm (S) is our steel firm purchasing pig iron as an intermediate product from the upstream monopolist, firm (I) for which there is no scope for substitution. The annual profits for the upstream monopolist (I) can be represented thus:

$$\pi_I = P_I Q_I - c(Q_I) - \delta K_I \tag{3.1}$$

where $c(Q_I)$ represents annual variable costs, K_I capital costs and δ the depreciation rate. To keep matters simple, we will assume that firm S's only variable cost is the intermediate input – pig iron – purchased from firm I, and hence annual profits for firm S are:

$$\pi_S = P_S Q_S - P_I Q_I - \delta K_S \tag{3.2}$$

where K_S represents capital costs and δ the depreciation rate. The profit-maximizing condition for firm S is to set **marginal revenue** equal to marginal cost, i.e. $MR = MC$, and hence the profit-maximizing condition under the situation described can be written as:

$$P_S \left[1 + \frac{s_S}{\varepsilon_S} \right] = P_I \tag{3.3}$$

where s_s is firm S's market share and ε_S is the price elasticity of demand for its output. Appendix 3A explains the derivation of the left-hand side of Equation (3.3). In this example, P_I is the supply price for the pig iron, which is fixed for the production period and hence P_I is firm S's marginal cost. If S is a monopolist, then $s_s = 1$. If S operates under perfect competition, then $s_s \rightarrow 0$ and $s_s/\varepsilon_S \rightarrow 0$.

Given that $P_I > MC_I$, by vertically integrating, firm S could, in principle, source its pig iron (the key intermediate input) at marginal cost (MC_I) and from Equation (3.3) this would allow firm S to lower its price, thereby selling a greater volume of output and increasing its economic rent. In the process there would be the welfare gain for consumers of a lower price and increased supply. But, in fact, in this situation the two firms could come to a mutually beneficial arrangement involving a **two-part tariff** without resort to vertical integration. In essence, the upstream supplier, firm I, would provide pig iron at MC in return for a payment from the steel firm (the buyer) sufficient to restore I's economic rent. We will return to this issue in Chapter 12 when considering **vertical restraints**. Vertical integration could, however, be a rational response to uncertainty in the quantity or quality of a key input supplied by an imperfectly competitive market.

There are several important respects in which intermediate products, or rather their exchange, differs from final products. Unlike consumer products, a purchaser of an intermediate good will generally purchase a high volume, increasing the severity of the problem of **adverse selection**. In many instances intermediate products will possess complex bundles of attributes, increasing the risk of **moral hazard**. The downstream buyer's competitive advantage is likely to be heavily dependent on the private information and **hidden actions** of its suppliers. Kenneth Arrow (1975) pointed out that in a world of imperfect and asymmetric information, a justification for vertical integration could be the acquisition of valuable private information regarding effort and performance. We can demonstrate this observation with the extensive form game set out in Figure 3.4. The game represents a situation of asymmetric information involving a contract between an upstream supplier, firm A, who might be a **monopolist** or an **oligopolist**, and a downstream purchaser, firm B. The contract specifies the price and quality of the intermediate product, but only the upstream supplier knows at the time of supply whether the quality criteria have been met, and if the quality is represented by durability it may be some years before the buyer becomes aware of any problem.

At node a, buyer and seller agree a contract. If the seller, firm A, fulfils the contract the quality is high, generating total profits of π_A and π_B for firms A and B, respectively, over the lifetime of firm B's product. The probability of fulfilling the contract is ρ, where $0 < \rho < 1$ and the probability of failing to fulfil the contract is $(1 - \rho)$. In the situation of not fulfilling the contract, firm A's profit increases to $\mu\pi_A$, where $\mu > 1$ owing to reduced effort by firm A. In contrast, as the durability of firm B's products falls below expectations it suffers a loss of profits, i.e. $-\pi_B$, and must now decide whether to accept the situation or sues for compensation. There is a probability, λ, where $0 < \lambda < 1$ that firm B will sue, but if firm B resorts to litigation there is no guarantee of success and this is represented by φZ, where Z is the award of compensation and φ the probability of an award where $0 < \varphi < 1$. As set out and assuming no other influence on firm A, e.g. reputation, whether or not it puts effort into supplying firm B will depend on whether $[\lambda(\pi_A - \varphi Z) + (1 - \lambda)\mu\pi_A] < \pi_A$. Faced with this situation of asymmetric information, firm B may have a strong incentive to vertically integrate, either by acquiring firm A or setting up its own facilities.

The inability to monitor the behaviour of a supplier, and in particular behaviour relating to undertaking the necessary performance-enhancing investment, has given rise to a complementary theory of vertical integration. Grossman and Hart (1986) put forward the theory that vertical integration, by granting the vertically merged firm control of productive assets, allows it to exploit its property rights unencumbered by contract stipulations. Most importantly, ownership of assets allows the firm to capture the value created by performance-enhancing investment and hence increases the incentive to make the necessary investment. As demonstrated in Figure 3.4, without vertical control property rights are shared between buyer and seller, raising the possibility that joint profits are not maximized and consequently there is under-investment by both firms. Grossman and Hart point out that with vertical control the production decisions are vested in a single governing hierarchy which does not have to consider the probability, given **incomplete contracts**, of recontracting for the sale or purchase of the intermediate product.

Imperfect and asymmetric information can also justify downstream vertical integration. For example, consider a brewer who puts great effort and care into producing a quality beer. Whether or not the beer reaches consumers in perfect condition depends on the efforts of the owners of bars and restaurants who have a vested interest in attempting to negotiate a lower price with the brewer in order to offset the extra costs of serving 'perfect pints'. If the downstream buyers are imperfectly competitive, e.g. oligopolists, the brewer cannot rely on competition to drive out inferior performance. The extra effort is private information, which may only be revealed by the brewer vertically integrating downstream. If the brewer owns a number of retail outlets it will obtain private information that will help it to write a more **complete contract** with other publicans in order to minimize the probability of beer being sold in less than perfect condition. The gathering of private information at the retail level may also have the beneficial effect of helping the brewer remain competitive. The difficulty in evaluating performance is a significant factor in accounting for the fact that some manufacturers employ a direct sales force.

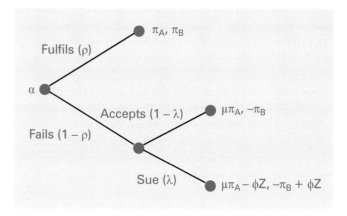

Figure 3.4: A contract to supply game

Fashion to Go

When Spain's Crown Prince Felipe and Letizia Ortiz Rocasolano announced their engagement in 2003, the bride-to-be wore a stylish white trouser suit. Within a matter of weeks, woman across the European Union were wearing what, to the untutored eye, looked like the same white trouser suit. The firm with the vision and capability to seize this opportunity was Inditex, a holding company of eight retail brands and one of Spain's biggest business success stories.

One of its brands, Zara, has built a global reputation for timely and relevant fashion designs. Not for Zara the catwalks of fashion houses or large advertising budgets. Zara's business success is built on its ability to reduce the informational uncertainties of the fashion world by monitoring the demands of its customers and fashion statements of public icons. Once it identifies a demand, the appropriate fashion design is sent to its outlets within a matter of weeks. While most Spaniards were rejoicing at the sight of the royal couple, Zara saw a very different picture, a fashion statement and an opportunity to be exploited.

Its ability to respond rapidly to such opportunities has raised Inditex from its humble beginnings in the 1960s to one of the world's fastest expanding makers of affordable fashion clothing. By 2004, it had more than 2,250 outlets and annual sales of more than €5 billion. Just as the European Union's textile industry was coming under pressure from cheap imports, Inditex was demonstrating how a modern European clothing company could counter the threat of cheap imports. Inditex, or rather Zara's, strategic response is based on the value of being fleet of foot. In contrast to many of its rivals, Zara is vertically integrated from design through just-in-time production to retail and this allows the company to respond very rapidly to market opportunities.

The production process starts with the 3,000 designers who work at the firm's head office in La Coruna in Galicia. Fabric is cut in-house and then sent to a cluster of local co-operatives for sewing. When the finished product returns it is ironed, wrapped and distributed to the firm's retail outlets in Europe and other parts of the world. In order to retain some exclusivity, production is deliberately carried out in small batches, Anyone buying a Zara design knows that only a limited number of people around the world will be wearing the same item. They also know that new designs arrive frequently and that they will reflect the latest in fashion thinking.

As a result of its vertically integrated organization, Zara's production cycles are much shorter than those of old rivals such as Sweden's Hennes and Mauritz or the US giant, GAP. In a typical year Zara launches more than 10,000 new designs. All Zara's shops use point-of-sale terminals to report directly to La Coruna and each evening store managers can check what designs are available and place their orders accordingly. In the case of Zara, vertical integration speeds the flow of information from the customer up to the organization for rapid decision making and it also speeds the product response, ensuring a close match between Zara's products and the demands of fashion-conscious customers.

So far we have focused on imperfectly competitive markets, but information can be lacking in competitive markets. Think of a milk processor whose need for a daily throughput of milk is supplied by a competitive dairy farm sector. The processor is dependent not only on a secure supply of milk, but also the assurance that the milk is safe to drink. However, because the dairy sector is an **atomistic industry**, the processor will be unable to monitor safety effort on the part of its farmer suppliers if it engages in spot market transactions. In this situation the need for assurance will encourage, at the very least, contractual arrangements between buyer and seller and in many cases these develop into longer-term relationships and even vertical integration in order to secure the desired degree of transparency and safety effort. It should be noted that the milk processor also faces uncertainty in the volume of milk supplied. Given the nature of an agricultural product, its quantity and quality are likely to vary according to the season. However, the uncertainty that arises from this potential source of instability cannot be avoided by vertical integration.

It might seem tempting to argue that, regardless of the extent of imperfect information a modern industrial organization will always gain from vertical integration because it avoids duplication of specialist support services such as human resource (HR) management, accounting and marketing. However, even if it is true that bringing successive production stages within a firm's boundaries economizes on specialist support activities, it does not follow that vertical integration results in an overall reduction in production costs. Indeed, if this were the case, we would need to explain why all firms are not vertically integrated. Any specialist support economies, e.g. HR management, arising from vertical integration must be set against the capital costs of acquiring the necessary assets, the costs of a lack of the specialization and the less tangible organizational costs associated with ensuring the activity is performed efficiently and in accordance with the goals of the vertically integrated organization. The organizational costs are known as **agency costs** and arise out of the need to co-ordinate, monitor and motivate a particular activity.

Transaction Costs

Information, or rather the lack of it, is central to the transaction cost approach to vertical integration, where the emphasis is to view value chain relationships from the perspective of exchange rather than production. All market transactions necessitate a human facilitator, but for the transaction cost school, the replacement of the neo-classical assumption of hyper-rationality with **bounded rationality** creates scope for **opportunistic behaviour**. Viewed from this perspective, the foregoing focus on market imperfections is incomplete because it ignores the transaction costs of exchange. If there is only one or a few suppliers of a particular input, uncertainty is created by the scope for opportunistic behaviour. Given the impossibility of writing a complete contract at some point in the future, an oligopolistic supplier might take advantage of an unforeseen contingency to charge an excessive price for a key intermediate product thereby capturing some or all of the buyer's economic rent and possibly making the final product more expensive and less competitive. Thus, a focus on imperfect competition is not sufficient because it does not explicitly take into account the implications of imperfect information and incomplete contracts. The attractiveness of the transaction cost approach is that it deals with these issues and in so doing it can explain a much wider range of motives for vertical integration.

The transaction costs approach is based on a straightforward proposition: if the transaction costs of market exchange outweigh the internal organizational costs of exchange, then vertical integration is to be preferred to market exchange. We can approach the transaction costs of exchange with a simple example. Think of the transaction involving the purchase of paperclips. For a firm this is a transaction that is probably undertaken frequently, the product is unlikely to be critical to the purchasing firm's achievement of its goals, and there is little doubt or uncertainty as to what will be received in return for the price paid. The paperclips' quality and performance will be very familiar and if paperclips are produced by a competitive industry, i.e. there are many suppliers, the price charged is likely to be competitive, i.e. close to *MC*. In this situation the problems of adverse selection and moral hazard are minimized. In short, the existence of competitors and knowledge based on experience of the product means that the transaction costs to the purchaser are minimal. In these circumstances paperclips will be sourced from the market.

But now consider the position of a firm contemplating the purchase of a highly specialized input that is critical to a new strategy, e.g. the launch of a new product. The existence of bounded rationality will ensure that uncertainty and risk are attached to the new strategy and both are greatly enhanced if the input is very complex and a potential supplier will only enter into a long-term contract. In this situation, the transaction costs of purchasing the input in the market are likely to be very high. For example, when developing a new model, the period from concept to mass-production is likely to be a complex three-to-four-year undertaking for a vehicle manufacturer. In such an environment key components are unlikely to be procured by simply announcing performance and design requirements and awaiting offers to supply. The risks of adverse selection and moral hazard are high as the buyer will have to trust the assurances of a potential supplier regarding price and performance. There is great uncertainty in such a transaction: is the price being charged too high? Will the part perform as required? Will it be produced in sufficient numbers? What happens if the supplier runs into financial difficulties? The more dependent a purchaser is on a particular supplier, the greater the purchaser's

Cosworth

In 1958, two young, very enthusiastic engineers, Keith Duckworth and Mike Costin, who worked for Lotus Cars, founded Cosworth Engineering, where they worked at night. At first, they worked in a small garage in Shaftesbury Mews, West London, but by 1964 Cosworth Engineering had established itself as a producer of high-performance engines and the company moved to Northampton. Both men were now working full time for the company and in 1966 they signed a contract with Ford to put their DFV engines in Ford's high performance cars. The deal turned Cosworth into a world leader and in the following years the DFV engine piled up Grand Prix victories.

Critical to the success of a high performance engine is the quality of the engine block casting. Only the highest-quality castings will allow the engine block to be machined to a width that will withstand the pressures of high performance whilst weighing less than a conventional engine. Grand Prix racing not only involves frequent changes in engine design, but also race track success demands that each new engine block casting be as near perfection as possible. In 1979, Cosworth Engineering decided that only by vertically integrating to produce their own castings could they achieve both the flexibility and the care and attention they demanded to remain amongst the leaders in engine design and Grand Prix racing.

vulnerability to opportunistic behaviour following an unexpected contingency. The situation is equally uncertain from the perspective of potential suppliers. The more specialized the intermediate input, the more likely that the supplier would need to invest in one or more specific assets in order to supply the product. In order to cover the risk, the supplier may want to charge a higher price for the intermediate product. In this situation, the transaction costs of market exchange might be so high that it would be more efficient for the buyer to produce its own intermediate component.

For the purchasing firm, the transaction costs associated with exchange are positively related to the importance of the intermediate product to the firm's final product and inversely proportional to the number of sellers of the intermediate product in the market and the frequency of transactions between buyers and sellers. If the intermediate input is not particularly specialized and the number of alternative suppliers is large, then it is likely that the market price is a 'sufficient statistic', i.e. decisions can be made on the basis of price information alone. However, in the case of a new technology, a highly specialized input or the likelihood of the exercise of upstream market power, the quoted market price is unlikely to be a 'sufficient statistic' and the alternative of making rather than buying the intermediate product might be the optimal solution.

We noted above, the technological economies of an integrated steel mill and the difficulties, even if the two furnaces are co-located, in aligning supply and demand for the intermediate pig iron. But transaction costs are also likely to rule out the separate ownership of a blast furnace and a basic oxygen furnace. If the blast furnace and basic oxygen furnace are separately owned, the scope exists for either the supplier or purchaser of pig iron to engage in opportunistic behaviour depending on whether demand for steel is high or low. Iron- and steel-making are linked via technology, but from a transaction cost perspective it is the scope for opportunistic behaviour that militates against market exchange and dictates the vertical integration of iron and steel production. We can represent this situation with the extensive form game set out in Figure 3.5.

Both the managers of the blast furnace and the managers of the steel furnace will have the incentive to draw up a contract that minimizes the scope for opportunistic behaviour. But both sets of managers will be boundedly rational and hence will not be able to contract for all possible contingencies.

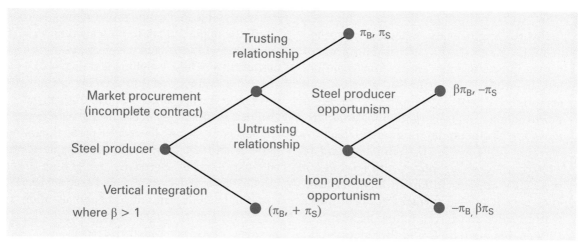

Figure 3.5: A relationship game

An unexpected change in demand for steel may provide the managers of the blast furnace with the opportunity to charge the highest possible price for the supply of pig iron, with the effect that the steel producer's margin or sales volume would be lower than anticipated. We can represent this situation as the steel furnace making a loss, $-\pi_S$, and the blast furnace enjoying an increased profit of $\beta\pi_B$, where $\beta > 1$ and the subscripts $_B$ and $_S$ refer to blast furnace and steel producer, respectively. But when the game is repeated in the next production period, the steel producer's management will not be prepared to trust the blast furnace managers and will be more disposed to engage in opportunistic behaviour should an unexpected contingency allow them to take advantage of their blast furnace suppliers. This is a situation of distrust and the net effect is that both supplier and purchaser run the risk that over a period of time both will make lower profits than need be. If the game is repeated, being rational, the managers of the blast furnace and the managers of the steel furnace will choose to co-operate in a trusting relationship, with the effect that average annual profits are π_B and π_S. That is, the outcome over a finite period will in fact be:

$$PV_B = \sum_{i=1}^{n} \pi_B/(1 + r)^i \ \text{ and } \ PV_S = \sum_{i=1}^{n} \pi_S/(1 + r)^i \tag{3.4}$$

where r is the cost of capital and $0 < r < 1$. Being rational, both players will realize that the outcome of distrusting each other and seeking 'advantage with guile' will be reduced profitability over n time periods. If, however, one of the parties cheats on the agreement to co-operate or if either for some reason feel unable to enter into a longer-term trusting relationship, vertical integration may offer a better outcome.

The foregoing highlights the importance of trust. As explained in the previous chapter, in practice contracts cannot adequately deal with situations where agents are boundedly rational and prone to opportunistic behaviour. The more infrequent the transaction and/or the more complex and specialized the product being exchanged, the greater the difficulty of writing, executing and policing a complete contract, i.e. a contract that covers all contingencies. The existence of incomplete contracts creates scope for opportunistic behaviour, particularly if potential suppliers are few in number. Once the contract comes into effect, *ex post* the contractual relationship between buyer and seller is transformed.

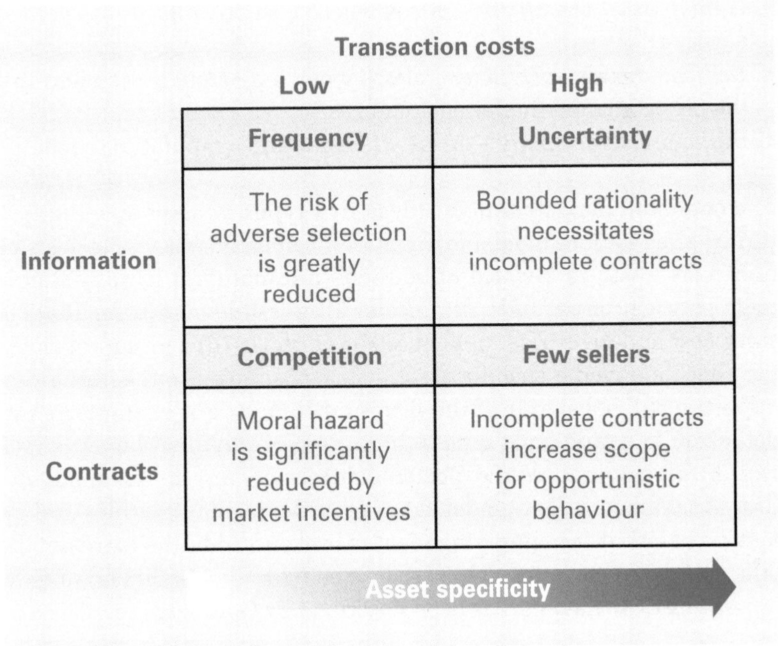

Any unexpected contingency gives one party the opportunity to exploit the situation. It is therefore the scope for opportunistic behaviour – as opposed to the lack of information – that from the perspective of transaction costs creates the conditions where it can be beneficial for

	Transaction costs	
	Low	**High**
	Frequency	**Uncertainty**
Information	The risk of adverse selection is greatly reduced	Bounded rationality necessitates incomplete contracts
	Competition	**Few sellers**
Contracts	Moral hazard is significantly reduced by market incentives	Incomplete contracts increase scope for opportunistic behaviour

Asset specificity →

Figure 3.6: Make or buy?

a firm to consider vertical integration rather than market procurement for a key input. In the presence of uncertainty and boundedly rational decision makers, the transaction costs associated with co-ordinating the flow of material inputs down the value chain may render market transactions inefficient. These points are summarized in Figure 3.6. The first column represents the situation when an intermediate input is purchased frequently in a competitive market. The second column represents the situation when the intermediate product is highly specialized. *Ex ante* there may be a number of potential suppliers, but once a contract is signed *ex post* there will be only one supplier of the specialized input.

The more specialized a particular intermediate input, the more likely that its production involves the employment of a highly specialized asset, i.e. an asset that either cannot be redeployed to alternative productive uses or can be redeployed only by incurring considerable additional expenditure or loss of productive value. In its intended use, a highly specialized asset is likely to yield economic gains in terms of productive efficiency, but being highly specialized has little or no value in any other uses. Williamson (1971) describes the extent of asset specialization as **asset specificity**. The greater asset specificity, the greater the scope, *ex post*, for opportunistic behaviour and the higher will be the transaction costs of products necessitating the use of a highly specialised asset. There has been a considerable amount of empirical work in this area and, as Shelanski and Klein (1995) report, it has tended to support this prediction. Put succinctly, there is a positive relationship between asset specificity and transaction costs, as indicated in Figure 3.6. Williamson defines five types of asset specificity:

- *Site specificity* – arises when there are cost advantages to locating the assets for successive production stages in close proximity, e.g. an iron foundry and steel mill.
- *Physical asset specificity* – arises when there are cost advantages associated with a customized asset, e.g. specialized dies.
- *Human asset specificity* – arises where cost advantages are gained from learning and tacit knowledge.
- *Dedicated asset specificity* – arises when a discrete investment in general purpose plant is made at the behest of a particular customer.
- *Brand asset specificity* – arises when a brand's reputation depends on its specific use.

The common characteristic of these five types of asset specificity is that in principle rents can be earned as a result of the deployment of the specific asset – e.g. a specialized machine reduces production costs – but, in a world of bounded rationality, it is not possible to specify the sharing of these rents between buyer and seller under all possible contingencies. The purchase of such an asset is a **sunk cost** and gives rise to what Klein *et al.* (1978) call appropriable **quasi-rents**. Once a supplying firm has deployed a specific asset, its *ex post* quasi-rent earning capacity becomes vulnerable to the opportunistic behaviour of the firm's customers. For example, a supplier that has invested in plant dedicated to supplying a unique input to an individual buyer is locked into the supply relationship and is vulnerable if an unexpected contingency arises. Alternatively, if individuals in the supplying firm accumulate a deep understanding of the buyer's routines and systems, the buyer's future profits may be at risk if the supplying team is broken up. In the extreme, the quasi-rent associated with specific assets may be reduced to zero (see below). The likelihood of either the buyer or seller engaging in opportunistic behaviour has been described by Goldberg (1976) as a problem of **hold-up**.

Hold-Up

Say a distributor has been offered a contract to supply a major multiple. This requires the distributor to invest in some highly specialised computer software. Not only would the software have to be specially developed and therefore very expensive, it would not be capable of being used for any other purpose. The multiple has offered a contract to pay the distributor a fixed price (p_0) for a minimum number of deliveries, Q per year, which, after allowing for the variable costs and a return on the cost of investing in the specialist software generates an acceptable economic rent (π) for the distributor, as shown:

$$\pi_t = p_0 Q_t - c(Q_t) - (r + \delta)K \qquad (1)$$

Where $p_0 Q_t$ is the expected revenue per year, $c(Q_t)$ is the variable costs and ignoring the distributor's other capital costs, K is the investment cost of the software and r and δ are the costs of capital and the depreciation rate, respectively, where $0 < r, \delta < 1$. Now consider the risk the distributor is taking. As the software is highly specialized, the capital costs are sunk. A contract has been entered into with the multiple regarding P_0 and Q, but the contract is necessarily incomplete and once the software has been purchased the distributor will be in a weak position if the multiple demands, owing to *force majeure*, a reduction in the price charged for each delivery. In considering the contract, *ex ante* the distributor faces uncertainty regarding future deliveries and would therefore need to charge a sufficiently high price to cover the risk associated with the purchase of a dedicated software program. Once the specialized software is installed, under *force majeure* or blatant opportunistic behaviour, the multiple could drive the price down, at the extreme to p_1 such that quasi-rent is reduced to zero:

$$p_1 Q_t = c(Q_t) \qquad (2)$$

That is, the price has been reduced to a level that allows the distributor to cover variable costs, but makes no contribution towards the investment cost of purchasing the specialized software. The actual outturn in the extreme is the failure to recoup $(r + \delta)K$ per period as opposed to the expected outturn of an economic rent of π. In this example, the difference between the expected rent and the quasi-rent measures the magnitude – the risk – of the hold-up problem. The (transaction) costs of market procurement are very high and the multiple may be forced to share the cost of the software or undertake its own distribution rather than using the market.

Governance Approach

We noted above, that if a firm is contemplating sourcing an intermediate input from the market it faces two costs: the price paid plus the transaction costs associated with the contract. However, if it is contemplating vertical integration it also faces two costs: the cost of physically making the good; and the internal organizational cost of ensuring production is carried out efficiently and in congruence with the firm's goals. We introduced the phrase agency costs above to represent the organizational costs that arise out of establishing appropriate incentives and monitoring performance within the vertically integrated firm. Depending on the degree of asset specificity associated with the production of an intermediate product, the transaction costs of using the market may or may not exceed the agency costs of organizing production in-house. Hence, highly relevant to a decision to vertically integrate will be a calculation of the agency costs of in-house production relative to the transaction costs of market procurement. We can demonstrate the relevance of asset specificity, agency costs and transaction costs using a heuristic model developed by Williamson (1998). If we define the agency costs of producing a fixed quantity of an intermediate product as $A(\bar{Q})$, where $\bar{Q}$ is the fixed quantity and the transaction costs (not the price paid) of obtaining the same quantity from the market as $T(\bar{Q})$, then we can define the net governance cost (*NGC*) as:

$$NGC = A(k, \bar{Q}) - T(k, \bar{Q}) \qquad (3.5)$$

where k is a measure of the degree of asset specificity. For an asset that can be used generally $k = 0$ and as the specialization of an asset becomes greater (i.e. its alternative uses become fewer), so $k > 0$. If $k = 0$ transaction costs are minimal and the agency costs of intermediate production outweigh the transaction costs of using the market, hence:

$$A(0, \bar{Q}) > T(0, \bar{Q}) \qquad (3.6)$$

but as the index of asset specificity increases above zero, so the change in the transaction costs, $T(\Delta k)$, is greater than the change in agency costs, $A(\Delta k)$, where Δ represents change. Hence the change in net governance costs, ΔNGC

$$\Delta NGC = A(\Delta k, \bar{Q}) - T(\Delta k, \bar{Q}) \qquad (3.7)$$

is an inverse function of Δk. Where asset specificity is slight $A(\Delta k) > T(\Delta k)$, but as the value of k increases so, at some point, $T(\Delta k) > A(\Delta k)$ and ΔNGC becomes negative, i.e. $\Delta NGC < 0$ and from this point on internal organization is progressively cheaper than the transaction costs of market exchange. This function is shown as curve AB in Figure 3.7 and the switchover point is shown as k_1.

Consider now how the relative physical costs of producing and procuring an intermediate product alter as the production process is increasingly subject to asset specificity. One of the benefits accruing to a firm that supplies a product to the market is the unit cost reductions arising from cumulative production, i.e. learning and more than likely **economies of scale**. It is reasonable, therefore, to expect that a firm specializing in the production of a standardized intermediate product is more likely than a vertically integrated firm to benefit from **productive** and **allocative efficiency**. Its learning enables it to enjoy relatively higher productivity and by supplying many customers it achieves economies of scale. Providing outside suppliers can find customers for the intermediate product, the ability to aggregate demands will impart cost benefits, e.g. fixed costs can be spread over a larger volume of output, and hence the cost of supplying the buying firm with any given volume, $\bar{Q}$, will benefit from learning and scale economies. We will represent the market price of market procurement as $P(\bar{Q})$. To simplify matters, we will continue with the assumption that the buying firm's demand for the intermediate product is fixed at $\bar{Q}$ and we will further assume its production does not yield **economies of scope**. If we now represent the physical costs – materials, labour and capital – of producing the intermediate product in-house, i.e. within a vertically integrated firm as $I(\bar{Q})$, we obtain the following expression for the relative advantage of market exchange over internal production:

$$NPC = I(k, \bar{Q}) - P(k, \bar{Q}) \qquad (3.8)$$

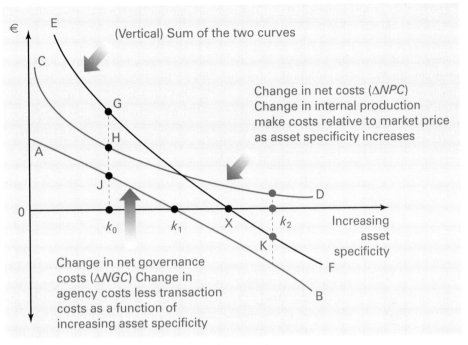

Figure 3.7: Asset specificity and vertical integration

where NPC is the net production cost of internally sourcing the intermediate input. Equation (3.8) expresses NPC as a function of the degree of asset specificity that influences relative 'make' costs in the following manner. A firm that decides to vertically integrate to produce a standardized product that utilizes assets that can be redeployed cheaply to other uses will incur relatively high production costs because, as explained above, an external supplier will enjoy the cost advantage of supplying other customers, i.e. economies of scale and cumulative learning. However, the NPC disadvantage of bringing production within the boundaries of the firm decreases as asset specificity increases. The more specialist the asset needed to produce the intermediate product – i.e. the greater the value of k – the less likely that it can be used by external suppliers to service other customers; by definition, the scope for economies of scale and specific cumulative learning will be diminishing. Put simply, as asset specificity increases, so the external advantages of economies of scale and learning diminish, i.e. as Δk increases in value, so ΔNPC declines towards zero:

$$\Delta NPC = f(\Delta k, \bar{Q}) \tag{3.9}$$

The function ΔNPC is an inverse function of asset specificity and is shown as the curve CD in Figure 3.7. As illustrated, although CD declines as k increases, it remains positive. This reflects the fact that despite the external supplier charging a higher price to compensate for the risk of hold-up, the specialist supplier's unit costs still benefit from experience. In an extreme case when the specific asset is unique and the specialist supplier has no experience to impart, the curve CD may touch or even fall below the horizontal axis. The strategic object for a cost-minimizing firm is not to minimize ΔNPC or ΔNGC separately, but given the optimal level of asset specificity to minimize the *sum* of net production and governance costs. In Figure 3.7, the vertical sum of $\Delta NPC + \Delta NGC$ is shown as curve EF and its crossover value – the point at which the sum of $\Delta NPC + \Delta NPG$ is equal to zero – given by point X.

Beyond this point, movements to the right along the horizontal axis reflect higher levels of asset specificity and result in $\Delta NPC + \Delta NGC$ becoming increasingly negative.

Figure 3.7 is interpreted in the following manner. Given a fixed demand, $\overline{Q}$, by the firm for the intermediate product, if its production involves only a limited degree of asset specificity the appropriate place on the horizontal axis might be k_0. At k_0, the sum of $\Delta NGC + \Delta NPC$ is represented by point G. That is, at k_0 the net physical cost is represented by point H and the net governance cost by point J. In contrast, at point k_2 production of the intermediate product involves a high degree of asset specificity and consequently the sum of ΔNGC and ΔNPC is negative, represented by point K. Thus at k_2, which is to the right of X, it would be more efficient for the firm to incur the physical and agency costs of producing the intermediate product rather than sourcing it from the market.

Figure 3.7 makes clear the importance of agency costs to a successful vertical integration. Whether or not a merger or acquisition between a buyer and a seller enhances efficiency depends critically on the buyer's **organizational architecture**. The success of a vertical integration depends not only on the ownership of the property rights associated with a specialized asset, but also on the synergies that can be achieved by co-ordinating the use of the specialized asset within the firm to better achieve its goals. This is particularly the case when the asset specificity that merits vertical integration is human. For example, if a firm purchases one of its suppliers to benefit from the supplier's employees' specialist knowledge, the vertically integrated firm will require careful and sensitive management if it is to continue to benefit from such knowledge – particularly if knowledge is tacit.

The foregoing has focused on backward integration, but forward or downstream integration can also be analysed using the forces summarized in Figure 3.7. Transaction costs increase when the actions of downstream firms directly affect the success of upstream suppliers, e.g. brand reputation. For example, a brand's reputation may be highly dependent on the quality of service at the point of sale. In these circumstances, the transaction costs of monitoring and motivating retailers may be so high that it is cheaper to exercise hierarchical control over the quality of service to consumers. This can be demonstrated by returning to the earlier example of draft beer. Draft beer has a relatively short shelf life; it also requires careful storage and tends to sell better in premises that provide comfortable, hospitable surroundings. The higher the reputation of a particular beer – a specific asset – the greater the transaction costs for the brewer of ensuring that independent publicans devote sufficient resources and care to the storage and serving of its beer. Traditionally, these transaction costs have encouraged brewers to vertically integrate downstream. However, we should add that when UK brewers were investigated by the competition authorities, vertical integration by breweries was viewed as a threat to the selling of beer at competitive prices.

There are market alternatives to downstream integration, e.g. **franchising** and **vertical restraints**, which we shall return to in Chapter 12. As the above reference to the competition authorities serves to indicate, there is another motive for vertical integration – to gain and exploit monopoly power. As the sole supplier of a key input, an aggressive motive would be the opportunity – subject to the competition authorities – to exploit the monopoly power by charging rivals using the same input a higher price than justified by production costs.

Power in More Than One Sense

Lignite is a low-quality, brownish-black coal. It is highly volatile and is used primarily to generate electricity. Its use does, however, attract criticism from environmentalists, who argue that its open mining techniques and the production of sulphur dioxide when it is burnt are damaging to the natural environment. In Greece, lignite accounts for more than 75 per cent of total electricity production and this is mostly supplied by two thermal power plants located at Ptolemais and Megatopolis.

In 2001, the state-controlled electricity generator Public Power Corporation (PPC) acquired the Greek lignite mines. As a consequence, PPC became responsible for 95 per cent of all lignite mined in Greece. The vertical integration was justified by the Greek government as a response to the EU's intention to create a single market in energy. In principle, the opening up of the Greek energy market to outside competition made it imperative that the Greek lignite mines improve efficiency. This involved large capital investment, which the Greek government was persuaded would only be forthcoming from PPC. One consequence of PPC's exclusive rights is that despite the signing by Greece of the Kyoto Protocol – which identifies lignite as one of the main sources of greenhouse gas emissions – under PPC's control, the extraction of lignite has increased over recent years.

The claims that PPC's vertical integration was a response to potential competitors did not impress the European Commission. In April 2004, it warned the Greek government that the exclusive rights granted to PPC to mine lignite may be in breach of European competition rules and in particular Article 86 of the EU Treaty in conjunction with Article 82. This, the Commission argued, follows because PPC is able to protect its dominance of the Greek electricity market due to its exclusive rights in the lignite sector. Put simply, the vertical power of PPC gives it an unfair competitive advantage and the Commission issued a Letter of Formal Notice, giving Greece two months to either provide a satisfactory explanation for the exclusive rights or to abolish them. PPC is still the country's only supplier of electricity.

A Competency Approach

The foregoing makes it clear that the decision to vertically integrate will always be a matter of judgement for senior managers who must weigh up the benefits of market exchange and the benefits of controlling exchange in-house. As we have seen, for the governance approach to the determination of a firm's vertical boundaries, the decision is based on the efficiency criterion of minimizing transaction costs. An alternative approach to determining a firm's vertical boundaries is provided by the competency school. From this perspective, it is not the exchange of products between stages in the value chain, but the exchange of knowledge between separate stages. The idea is that it is efficient to vertically integrate activities that benefit from a firm's **core competency**, i.e. activities that would benefit from a common repertoire of knowledge.

A firm, as we have previously noted, is a collection of resources – some of which, e.g. materials and physical assets are purchased from the market – that are controlled by a single strategic decision-making hierarchy. But other resources, in particular organizational and product knowledge, are internally generated and by definition are a potential source of heterogeneity for individual firms. Internally accumulated knowledge-based resources are rooted in the skills, experiences and co-operative routines that individuals and teams have developed within the firm. In this context, the knowledge may be largely tacit; that is, it cannot be codified and if so is not capable of market exchange. If a firm has developed a specific knowledge resource that can contribute to the generation of economic rents, this is equivalent to the firm acquiring a unique stock of a specific asset: in the language of strategic management, the firm has acquired a core competence. If this particular resource, e.g. a design skill, can be transferred across a firm's vertical boundaries to be used productively upstream or downstream, this may provide an alternative explanation of vertical integration.

This competency approach to vertical integration has a great many similarities with the governance approach. Indeed, the two approaches are complementary in explaining how a firm's vertical boundaries are determined. Both approaches recognize the existence of asymmetric information between stages in the value chain and the constraints imposed by bounded rationality. Both approaches view the heterogeneity of some assets as limiting or preventing market exchange. The divergence between the two schools arises from the way resources are acquired. For the competency approach, the boundaries of the firm are determined by the accumulation of internal resources, which in turn puts the focus on knowledge and learning. As such, resources have the potential to be firm specific and this limits the scope of beneficial vertical integration to those areas where the firm has a resource competency. That is, the competency approach suggests that the vertical expansion is limited to those areas where the firm can transfer its competencies along the value chain, i.e. the vertical growth of the firm is path dependent.

A firm's heterogeneity, i.e. tacit knowledge, can be confined to its procurement, production or marketing techniques and/or it can be embodied in the firm's organizational architecture. In both cases, a firm's accumulation of repertoires of such knowledge resources is equivalent to an investment, and efficiency demands that the firm strives to achieve the maximum return on its investments. In the previous chapter, we quoted Penrose (1959, p. 76): 'a firm's opportunities are necessarily widened when it develops a specialised knowledge'. If this knowledge offers economies of scope, these may be efficiently realized by expanding the firm's vertical boundaries. Economies of scope may arise from competencies in product design, production techniques, marketing campaigns or specific elements within the organizational architecture, e.g. strategy formulation. Alternatively, economies of scope may arise from the merging under a single governance hierarchy, complementary skills and knowledge. A buyer and a seller may be strong in complementary fields of, say, IT (e.g. software and databases) and a vertical merger could be justified in order to leverage rent from co-ordinating these two strengths.

It is the generation of specialized knowledge and the opportunities for economies of scope that such knowledge offers that provides a clear contrast to the asset specificity of the governance approach. If a specialized knowledge offers economies of scope, the knowledge cannot be specific to a particular product or firm. The logic of the competency approach to vertical integration is that the distribution of tasks along the value chain is not pre-ordained, but derives from knowledge accumulated by firms within the supply chain. Based on the extent to which a firm's knowledge can be applied to other stages in the supply chain, this would determine which inputs it will purchase from a specialist supplier and which are to be produced internally. In turn, the specialist supplier will, according to their competencies, decide what elements to purchase from upstream suppliers and which to produce themselves.

Vertical integration involves the ownership of productive assets and hence control. It also includes the right to exert control over the co-ordination of sequential activities in the value chain. And, significantly, it also confers the power to share tacit knowledge between sequential stages. A vertically integrated firm might better control the sharing of tacit knowledge and thereby realize the efficiency gains. That is, vertical integration is efficient if it minimizes the costs of transferring beneficial knowledge between the separate stages of the value chain. If vertically broadening the strategic use of heterogeneous knowledge under the control of a single hierarchy enables the firm to better capture the value inherent in the knowledge, then the firm has an incentive to vertically expand its boundaries.

So far in this section we have viewed the incentive for a firm to vertically integrate as arising from the desire to utilize and control specific knowledge. But an alternative incentive could be the desire to develop new knowledge, i.e. capabilities. Studies suggest (Conner and Prahalad, 1996) that a governance hierarchy has distinct advantages when it comes to developing new knowledge, particularly if the knowledge is tacit. Thus, if the capabilities a firm wants to develop are tacit, it may be necessary for the firm to use vertical integration in order to gain access to the opportunities and information deemed necessary to develop a specific capability. This competency approach to vertical integration elevates the importance of learning. Learning, innovation and knowledge are among the key issues for contemporary strategic decision makers. Rapid organizational learning and continuous innovation are perceived as important sources of competitive advantage and knowledge is the critical factor that underpins these capabilities. Rival firms are involved in a learning race and if vertical integration offers a rapid learning opportunity, then the need to enhance learning may dominate.

It would, however, be fair to observe that vertical integration poses difficulties for the competence perspective. Consider the vertically integrated oil companies. The capabilities to find and drill for oil are very different to those required to run a refinery and different again to those required to run a chain of retail service stations. Whereas the governance approach can explain why vertical integration may be pursued regardless of any similarity in capabilities at the separate stages in the supply chain, the competence approach is left to search for knowledge-sharing across vertical boundaries. Arguably, management is such a resource, but the competence school still needs to explain why a firm with such a skill would seek a vertical strategic direction rather than the opportunities afforded by a horizontal strategic direction.

Vivendi

By April 2002, Jean-Marie Messier, the chief executive of Vivendi, could feel rather pleased with himself. The French-based conglomerate had successfully completed a vertical integration with Seagram's Universal music and filmed entertainment businesses and Europe's largest pay-TV operator, Canal Plus. The French are extremely proud of Canal Plus, the channel is seen as epitomizing French culture and it spends vast sums investing in home-grown movies. After the merger, Vivendi, a company that started out as the water utility, Compagnie Générale des Eaux in 1853, became the world's second largest media company, after AOL Time Warner.

continued

The logic of the vertical merger was very straightforward. Seagram's Universal owned the world's second largest library of films and TV programmes, as well as the world's largest music library. The vertically merged conglomerate would therefore be in a very powerful position in the pay-TV market and also in a strong position to develop new services and markets for consumers. After an investigation by the European Commission, the vertical merger was cleared, in part because Vivendi gave an undertaking to grant open access to Universal's library and in part because the European Commission took into account the potential the merger offered for the development of new capabilities, ultimately benefiting consumers.

In the event, the market was less convinced as to the opportunities the merger would provide for creating value. By July 2002, Vivendi's share price had fallen 60 per cent over the year and the company posted the largest single loss in French corporate history – €12 billion. Messier's audacious move had landed the company with a €19 billion debt and under pressure from the board, he resigned. He successfully negotiated an €18 million severance package, which was ultimately rescinded due to his illegal activities. As a young man, the Total Oil Company had turned down his application for sponsorship through Harvard Business School. Mr Messier's handwriting, Total said, showed he lacked ambition.

Alternatives to Vertical Integration

The essence of a successful vertical integration is that the benefits of hierarchical co-ordination outweigh the benefits of market transactions when exchanging an intermediate product between successive, technologically separable stages in the value chain. If an integrated firm is to deliver better levels of efficiency than market exchange, it will incur the agency costs of monitoring performance and providing appropriate incentives. One way of reducing agency costs is to benchmark internal performance and this can be achieved by combining the internal production of an intermediate good with purchases of the same good from the market. This combination of market purchase and vertical integration is known as **tapered integration**, where some proportion of the total quantity of an intermediate product is purchased from an independent supplier(s) to augment the quantity produced within the vertically integrated firm. For example, Coca-Cola has its own bottling subsidiaries, but also relies on independent firms to bottle (and distribute) their drinks. Tapered integration has a number of advantages. Firstly, it serves as a check against **X-inefficiencies** in vertically integrated firms. Using independent suppliers (outlets) provides a check on costs and a source of motivation for its internal suppliers (outlets). Secondly, the firm can use information and knowledge gained from its own operations to negotiate contracts with independent suppliers (outlets). Thirdly, the use of independent suppliers (outlets) reduces the vertically integrated firm's capital outlays and it provides additional security in the supply of the particular input or outlets for the firm's products.

One of the main advantages accruing to the governance approach to vertical integration is that it offers an explanation for the trend towards 'downsizing' and 'outsourcing'. Since the 1980s, there has been a distinct shift away from vertical integration, in many cases replacing internal production with spot market procurement, but in many instances firms have turned to alternative forms of **vertical relationships** – that is, vertical inter-organizational structures that lie between the extremes of market procurement and vertical integration. Before considering the potential advantages of vertical relationships, it is instructive to consider how the governance approach helps explain the trend toward outsourcing. On the basis of the governance approach, the trend towards vertical relationships must reflect a change in the balance of costs between market exchange and the internal exchange of intermediate inputs. Over the past 15 or so years, two trends have come to dominate much of business life; namely, information and communication technology (ICT) and **globalization**. The use of computer-based systems to store, process and transmit data and information is now all-pervasive. Investment in ICT has grown rapidly since the 1980s, giving rise to new business models and facilitating global business relationships. Globalization is more difficult to define precisely, but broadly it sums up the growing openness of national markets to trade and investment and the increasing integration of global economic activities.

One of the consequences of the ICT revolution has been an exponential increase in information and its sources and it will be recalled that information, or rather its lack, plays a key role in the governance approach to vertical integration. The influence of imperfect and asymmetric information on transaction costs was captured in Figure 3.7 and this is now repeated in Figure 3.8. On the not unreasonable assumption that the increased flow of information has had a greater impact on reducing transaction costs than reducing agency costs, the effect of ICT would be to rotate curve AB – the net changes in agency and transaction costs – around point A to give a new curve, such as AB'. The competitive impact of globalization is likely to influence the position of curve CD – the net production cost of internal sourcing. The reduction in trade barriers, increased foreign direct investment by multinationals and the growth of export-orientated industries in low cost areas of the world have all combined to increase the scope for firms to source intermediate products from competitive overseas markets. The effect of this, *ceteris paribus*, is not only to lower the market price of competing intermediate inputs, but also to further reduce transaction costs associated with adverse selection and moral hazard. The price effect of heightened competition is reflected as an upward movement in curve CD to C'D' in Figure 3.8, as the physical costs of production within the firm rise relative to the cost of market procurement. The overall effect of these changes is captured in curve E'F', which has shifted to the right of EF. Consequently, the original point at which vertical integration made economic sense has shifted from X_1 to X_2. Put another way, a vertically-integrated firm operating at X_1 would – following the changes outlined above – find it beneficial to return to the

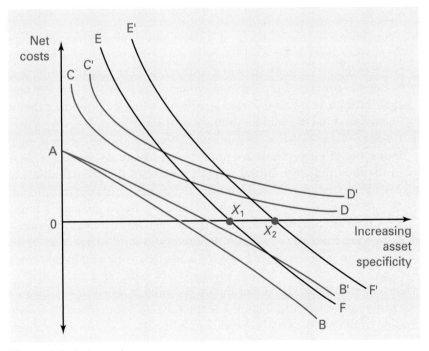

Figure 3.8: Outsourcing

market to source the intermediate input, involving a high degree of asset specificity, i.e. it would outsource its need.

Outsourcing does not, however, always involve a switch to pure market exchange. Many firms have chosen the intermediate solution of a vertical relationship, lying somewhere between vertical integration and a spot market transaction. A major influence on the attractiveness of a vertical relationship is the growing power of technology to improve communications and information. We noted above that ICT has reduced information asymmetrics and therefore in principle reduced transaction costs, but at the same time these new technologies have made it easier for firms to co-operate in innovative, inter-organizational arrangements that offer the prospect of combining the co-ordination benefits of vertical integration without sacrificing the cost advantages of specialist suppliers. Inter-organizational innovations that have been established or emerged over recent years all have one or more of the following purposes: to facilitate close planning between the co-operating firms; to protect specific investments from hold-ups; to develop and/or fully exploit heterogeneous knowledge; and to establish a better understanding of final consumers. Most importantly, these inter-organizational structures seek to achieve these aims without lessening the profit incentive for suppliers inherent in delivering a superior competitive performance when supplying a key intermediate input. The main inter-organizational innovations that have developed as alternatives to vertical integration are:

- A **partnership alliance** – where two or more firms formally agree to collaborate and share resources be they information, knowledge, human or physical assets. When first privatized, the Rover Car Company entered a strategic alliance with Honda to develop an engine for a new range of cars.
- A **joint venture** – where two or more firms create a new, jointly owned, independent organization. A prominent example is Coca-Cola's and Cadbury Schweppes' agreement to jointly set up a plant to bottle their products in the UK.
- **Franchising** – more common as a downstream alternative to vertical integration. Generally, the *franchisee* owns and runs a business using the *franchisor's* brand name and buying inputs from the franchisor, e.g. a McDonald's restaurant. This organizational arrangement takes advantage of the owner-operator's incentive to attract customers and care for the premises. At the same time, the control exerted by the franchisor adds value by providing the benefits of economies of scale and overcoming the hold-up problem of specific assets.
- **Co-operatives** – business organizations that are owned by their members. They take a number of forms, but of interest here are producer–processor co-operatives, which are particularly prevalent in the food industry. Of the world's largest 25 dairy companies, ten are producer–processors, where the farmers own and control the business. This organizational structure allows the benefits of economies of scale and value added to be shared amongst its members, who would otherwise have little alternative but to take a market-clearing commodity price.
- **Long-term contracts** – by definition involve a longer-term relationship and therefore the opportunity to gain information and develop knowledge that will benefit the relationship.

These alternatives to vertical integration lie within a spectrum between a spot market transaction and a vertically integrated firm. Figure 3.9 attempts, following Bart Nooteboom (1999), a schematic positioning of the more common vertical relationships within a spectrum bounded by organizational co-ordination and financial integration.

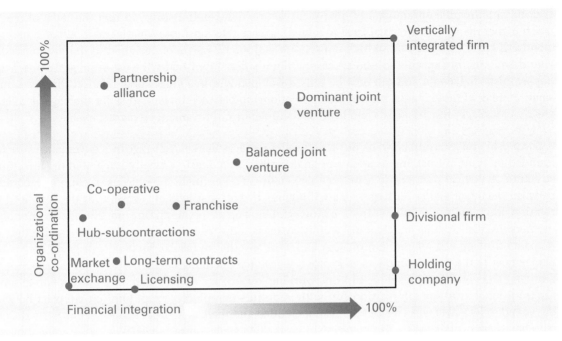

Figure 3.9: Degrees of vertical relationships

Our focus here is primarily on **strategic alliances** as alternatives to the polar extremes of vertical integration and spot market transactions. A joint venture is a particular type of strategic alliance involving the setting up of a firm under the shared ownership of two or more existing firms. Ownership may be shared equally or one firm may have a dominant stake, implying a distribution of decision rights and profits in favour of the dominant firm. A joint venture will normally result in the creation of a limited liability company, with its own legal identity and a clear strategic objective of creating value for the joint owners. The joint venture may serve as an outlet for products or knowledge produced by the owners or it may serve to provide the owners with intermediate products or knowledge, e.g. R&D. By definition, the relationship involved is expected to last over a number of time periods.

A superficial justification for a joint venture would be the sharing of capital costs, though with the existence of an **efficient capital market** this is a weak justification. More credible, in a world of imperfect and asymmetric information, is a joint venture which can facilitate the bringing together of private information and capabilities within a formal and controlled environment to the mutual benefit of the joint owners. A very common reason for a joint venture is as a vehicle for entering a national market. One partner has the product knowledge and the other knowledge of the particular market. We know from game theory that the prospect of a longer-term relationship – an infinitely repeated game – encourages a co-operative attitude on the part of rational players.

Another form of strategic alliance is a partnership alliance, which is defined as consisting of two or more firms who agree to co-operate closely, but the relationship does not involve the sharing of taking of equity and, most importantly, lacking a legal basis *it is based on a high level of trust and a high intensity of co-operation.* Thus, as defined here, a partnership alliance differs from a network of suppliers, hub sub-contractors and long-term contractual relationships, in that the level of trust is much higher than the contractual trust involved in these relationships. A partnership alliance involves 'goodwill trust' (Sako, 2003), which consists of actions by partners designed to deliver more than would be formally expected for the success of the relationship. Goodwill trust implies the absence of opportunistic behaviour and can only be fully developed within a longer-term relationship involving a small number of participants. A partnership relationship between buyer and seller therefore avoids, or greatly reduces, transaction costs and is thus an efficiency improvement on market exchange.

A partnership relationship between buyer and seller replaces market exchange by a governance structure founded on mutual trust and as such can be described as a quasi-vertically integrated organizational structure. A vertical partnership achieves the benefits of co-ordination by means of close collaboration between the buyer and seller based on a willingness by both participants to work for the benefit of the relationship. Such a relationship is a powerful means of economizing on bounded rationality. Partnership relationships are common within Japanese industry, where typically buyers and sellers are prepared to share confidential information and work together to resolve problems. In Japan, large companies refer to their SME suppliers as *kyoroku gaisha* (co-operating company) in order to highlight the mutually co-operative atmosphere of firms working towards a common goal. In a partnership alliance, the traditional arm's-length relationship with suppliers is replaced by an **implicit contract** between buyer and seller – that is, a contract that is not codified and there is no legal remedy if one party defaults or behaves opportunistically. The mechanism for making such contracts viable is loss of reputation and the prospect for the party that breaks the implicit contract of losing future business. This threat is more powerful than it at first appears. If two firms within a value chain have established a longstanding relationship that has enabled them through joint planning and monitoring to co-ordinate their activities, breaking the implicit contract means greater uncertainty and new contracts.

A partnership alliance can be explained and understood by either the more contractually focused governance approach to the firm, or the capabilities-orientated competency approach to the firm. A vertical relationship founded on trust reduces the potential for opportunistic behaviour and it also facilitates the combining of knowledge and capabilities in ways that will generate economic rents. Although the governance and competency approaches were originally developed to address different issues – exchange issues and competitive advantage, respectively – there is, as previously noted, a large element of overlap between the two. Both approaches are central to a strategy that seeks economic rents. This can be seen with the aid of the normal form game, set out in Figure 3.10.

The game is a 'simultaneous move' game in which both the buyer and seller have imperfect information, i.e. they do not observe some of the buyer's or seller's actions before engaging in exchange. In the absence of a trusting relationship, the buyer and seller enter into pre-play discussion before separately deciding their exchange strategies. If neither player trusts the other, they will withhold information and expect the other to engage in opportunistic behaviour if the scope

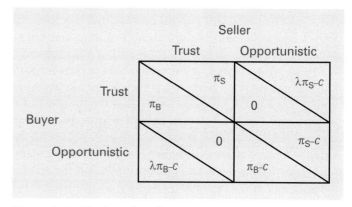

Figure 3.10: The benefits of trust

arises. In terms of pay-offs, both the buyer's and seller's potential rents, π_B and π_S respectively, are reduced by the transaction costs of minimizing the scope for opportunistic behaviour and/or the opportunity costs of not sharing information that could add value to the exchange; both costs are represented by c. If a player is trusting enough not to limit the scope for opportunistic behaviour or willing to share valuable information, but the other then takes advantage of this trust, the outcome is a much reduced rent for the trusting player – represented by 0 in Figure 3.10 – and an increased rent for the opportunistic player, where $\lambda > 1$. If the game is played once, the game has a unique Nash equilibrium: the dominant strategy for each player is to distrust the other and engage in opportunistic behaviour. If, however, the game is to be repeated over an unknowable number of time periods, the best strategy is for the players to trust each other and achieve a co-operative equilibrium.

Partnership alliances have the effect of extending the boundaries of the firm, but in a virtual manner. Under a vertical partnership, the vertical boundaries of the firm are based on:

- *Trust* – a highly efficient governance mechanism for minimizing transaction costs.
- *Shared knowledge and information* – in order to co-ordinate and increase the value of interdependent tasks.
- *Self-enforcement* – both partners have a vested interest in prolonging the relationship.

A successful application of this type of relationship is employed by Toyota. Over many years, the company has steadily developed long-term partnerships with first-tier suppliers who enter into implicit contracts regarding future business. In return, the suppliers are prepared to make asset-specific investments, which enhance the productivity and efficiency of the Toyota partnership. This virtual vertical integration has gained considerable support in the US and Europe over recent years. Firms are coming to see strategic advantages in such relationships and the process has been given an enormous boost with the development of the internet. This allows firms in a partnership relationship to share information in real time. In establishing partnership relationships, western firms have overcome the idea, long peddled in organizational theory, that a firm loses power when it increases its dependency on outside suppliers. They also have to overcome the western legal philosophy, which focuses on contractual, rather than trusting, relationships.

By their very nature, such partnership relationships will vary according to the culture of the firms involved and the strategic importance of the intermediate product being supplied. The closer the relationship, the greater the interaction between employees of both firms. Design engineers must co-ordinate with buying engineers, the buyer's marketing team must share information with the supplier's planners and so on. As these functional interrelationships multiply, so the boundaries between buyer and seller blur. The partners' destinies become ever more tightly intertwined and consequently both partners have a strong incentive to help the other. But partnerships may not last forever. Marks and Spencer had an enviable record as the best brand on the high street, a record that was in part built around partnership relationships with suppliers. However, in the 1990s, under pressure from shareholders, it started to exploit these supplier partnerships to improve short-term profits. Instead of improving matters, profits deteriorated. In eroding the very relationships that had made Marks and Spencer different, it appears the company also eroded the source of its higher profits.

The success of a partnership alliance depends not only on what resources are subject to joint decision making, but how this is accomplished. This starts with the partner selection process involving a search for partner compatibility in terms of vision, competencies and attitudes. The management of the alliance will involve an inter-firm organization architecture, involving a decision hierarchy, measurement systems and incentives. It must also be able to adapt to changing circumstances. The strength of a partnership alliance depends in part on the complementary knowledge that the partners bring to the alliance, but fundamentally the capture of value requires that the parties proactively and entrepreneurially engage in the relationship and make investments in relational specific assets. The important point is that the management of a partnership alliance requires a mindset that involves treating the relationship itself as a renewable asset (or resource) whose value-generating potential is enhanced by its management.

Dell computers

Michael Dell launched his computer company in 1984. It was not, however, just another computer company. By 2000, Dell had grown to a $20 billion company – a remarkable success story based on Michael's vision and confidence to develop a new business model. In contrast to the polar models of vertical integration and a value chain comprising arm's-length market transactions, he developed a compromise model which he described as *virtual integration*. The computer industry is about 50 years old and the founding companies had to build large vertically integrated firms to manufacture memory chips, disk drives, application software and so on. In short, they produced themselves everything a computer needed. As the industry grew, specialized companies developed to supply specific components, and it was Michael Dell's great achievement to realize that the computer industry did not have to develop into the traditional value chain.

As a small start-up, Dell was not going to survive if it merely attempted to replicate the 'engineering-centric' structure of IBM, HP and Compaq. Instead, it used ICT to integrate the value chain and make it very responsive to demand. Michael Dell's virtually integrated value chain involves the innovative use of technology to co-ordinate across company boundaries in order to achieve levels of productivity and efficiency that lead the industry. The Dell model of virtual integration harnesses the economic benefits of two separate business models. It offers the advantages of a tightly co-ordinated value chain that previously had only been achieved through vertical integration. And it also harnesses the benefits of focus and self-interest that traditionally had only been achieved by independent firms.

The virtual value chain pioneered by Dell has significant cost advantages. Firstly, Dell does not have to invest in the assets to manufacture components, hence its accounts boast a very high sales to assets ratio. Secondly, it has fewer operations to manage, including a smaller workforce. Thirdly, in the fast-moving computer industry Dell can rapidly respond to change. For example, it holds only a few days of inventory compared to three months of inventory for its rivals. In achieving these cost advantages Dell also incurs risk – for example, an interruption to supply as a result of a delivery failure by one of its first-tier suppliers. But in minimizing this risk, Dell has created another strength.

In order to minimize the adverse effects of a supply failure, Dell needs to understand very well the needs of its customers. Some have a

continued

priority for delivery, others are prepared to wait – in return for a lower price. To obtain this intimate knowledge of its customers – 90 per cent of Dell's sales go to organizations, not individuals – Dell has put enormous effort into looking inside its customers' businesses and understanding the growing, and separate, needs of the parts of the organization. By making it easy for individuals within large organizations to do business with them, Dell build up individual-specific information within organizations. In this way, the Dell value chain can truly be described as a demand chain: it is fully responsive to the needs of individuals who use its products, not the average needs of the organization.

The Dell model, formally described as virtual integration, represents an improvement on vertical integration in that all elements in the supply chain are focused on understanding and meeting the current and developing needs of its customers and all elements obtain a higher reward by performing better.

Concluding Thoughts

Vertical integration is only of benefit when a single organizational governing hierarchy is superior to the market as an exchange co-ordinating mechanism. We have set out above the main economic explanations as to the circumstances in which hierarchical organizations have advantages over market exchange. But, vertical integration is not without its costs; internal sourcing of an intermediate product will incur the agency costs associated with ensuring it is produced efficiently and managers keep abreast of related technological developments. These costs must be set against the transaction costs of sourcing from the market and/or the additional value that might be generated if the firm's capabilities are enhanced. From a strategic perspective, firms rarely compete on the basis of cost alone, but rather on the basis of value delivered. Value is manifested as the rent-earning capacity of an asset or resource, whether tangible or intangible. A single governance hierarchy might capture the available rent by lowering transaction costs or alternatively by co-ordinating initiatives that generate new knowledge.

By definition, vertical integration increases the size of the firm and it needs to be emphasized that as organizations grow in size so they are vulnerable to **control loss**. Given the limited span of control for any individual manager, increasing size implies either increasing hierarchical levels within the firm or innovative ways of circumventing control loss. As the number of hierarchies grows, so there is an inevitable loss of information as it is transmitted through the organization and this is paralleled by a reduction in the firm's ability to monitor. If vertical integration is an organizational form that developed purely as a result of senior managers seeking greater efficiencies in buyer–seller relationships, then we should expect new technologies and a changing business environment to alter senior managers' perceptions of the balance of forces.

This is precisely what has been happening since the 1980s. Just as at the end of the nineteenth century we witnessed the impact of new technology on industrial organizations – the coming of the railways and the telephone permitted the establishment of vertically integrated giants who dominated large sections of industry for most of the twentieth century – the 1990s witnessed the arrival of ICT, together with a concerted global drive to reduce trade barriers and increase competition. The increasing competitive pressures emanating from global competition have encouraged firms to view closer vertical relationships as an indispensable tool of strategy formulation and conduct. Advances in ICT are giving rise to new organizational structures and relationships. These new structures and relationships use the rapidly developing information and communications technologies to achieve the benefits of co-operation and co-ordination without sacrificing the efficiency benefits of the rent-seeking motive inherent in the independent firm.

One consequence of the focus on vertical relationships has been the outsourcing of many technologically separable activities that were formally co-ordinated by a single governance hierarchy. We now speak of the *hollowed out* firm, which relies on outside suppliers for the procurement of key inputs – in many cases, involving vertical collaboration such as joint ventures or alliances. The prevalence of vertical relationships demonstrates that the vertical co-ordination of value chain activities is no longer, if it ever was, solely about reducing the contractual costs of exchange. The opportunities such relationships offer for the pursuit of competitive advantage through the efficient and effective development of organizational capabilities is now central to strategy and the search for economic rent.

Key Learning Points

- Any good or service sold to a final consumer is the culmination of a value chain comprising a number of sequential processes and activities that convert raw materials into final goods or services.
- At one extreme, all sequential processes and activities involved in a value chain could, in principle, be carried out within one vertically integrated firm; at the other extreme, each step could be carried out by a separate, independent firm.
- As a general rule, individual firms are involved in one or a limited number of sequential stages relying on independent upstream suppliers for intermediate products and downstream independent outlets for sales.
- Once we depart from the ideal of perfectly competitive markets, the costs of using market exchange are positive. In a world of uncertainty and bounded rationality, the transaction costs of using the market are inversely related to the number of potential suppliers, the level of complexity and the degree of asset specificity.
- The governance approach to vertical integration elevates asset specificity and the scope this affords for opportunistic behaviour to a central role in explaining the incentive to organize and control production within a single governance hierarchy.

- Vertical integration avoids these transaction costs, but to be efficient the savings must outweigh the costs to the vertically integrated firm of a limited scale of production for the internally produced input, as well as the agency costs of achieving efficiency.
- Transaction costs emphasize the costs of imperfect and asymmetric information. The combination of globalization and ICT have increased competition and the flow of information, thereby reducing transaction costs and making outsourcing more attractive.
- The competency approach focuses on the importance of heterogeneous knowledge and capabilities. From this perspective, the motive for vertical integration is to develop and exploit knowledge assets so as to capture their full value.
- The competency approach to the firm can also provide an explanation for the trend toward vertical relationships over recent years. Driven by increasingly intensive competitive conditions, firms seek knowledge development opportunities inherent in joint ventures and partnership alliances.
- Alliances, joint ventures and other forms of vertical relationships extend, in a virtual manner, the vertical boundaries of the firm by reducing transaction costs, building new inter-firm organizational resources and retaining the benefits of market incentives.

Exercises

3.1 Can upstream vertical integration provide a solution to a stochastic pattern in the supply of a key commodity, intermediate input?

3.2 Why is vertical integration unlikely to be efficient if the target input is a frequent purchase and is supplied by a competitive industry?

3.3 The governance approach to vertical integration places emphasis on the scope for opportunistic behaviour by either the buyer or seller. How does asset specificity increase the scope for opportunistic behaviour?

3.4 The competency school focu... much on the stock of specific as... rather how they are acquired and t... What are these assets and how does v... integration help?

3.5 Using the governance framework, explain why globalization and ICT are encouraging many previously vertically integrated firms to outsource.

3.6 List the advantages of a trusting vertical relationship between buyer and seller of a key intermediate input relative to vertical integration and a spot market transaction.

Problems

3.1 Suppose the inverse market demand curve for Manchester United (MU) paperweights is $p = 100 - Q$. MU paperweights are exclusive to MU, who obtain them from a monopoly wholesaler (MW) *at price* w_0 per weight. MW in turn obtains the paperweights from a manufacturer (MM), who holds the patent for the technique and sells to MW at a price of w_M. MM incurs marginal costs of €10 per unit and MW and MU both incur marginal costs of €5 per unit in addition to the prices they have paid for the paperweights.

(a) Calculate the equilibrium price to consumers, the wholesaler and the manufacturer.

(b) What is the profit earned at each stage in the chain?

(c) Demonstrate that vertical integration by any two firms will increase profits and that integration by all three is even more beneficial.

3.2 An *avant garde* sculptor has been commissioned by the government to design the stage set for a one-off performance of *Waiting for Godot* to be performed for the president of the United States, who is expected to undertake a state visit within the year. The government offers the following contract: €500,000 when the stage set is erected. The sculptor, who normally uses items of organic rubbish in her work, calculates that, at most, materials will cost €20,000 and hired labour, at most, €150,000:

(a) Having built the set, but prior to acceptance by the government's Minister for the Arts that the stage is suitable, what is the sculptor's quasi-rent?

(b) In what circumstances might the sculptor find that she is out of pocket?

(c) At what point is the sculptor in a position to hold up the government?

References

Arrow, K. (1975) 'Vertical integration and communication', *Bell Journal of Economics*, vol. 6, pp. 173–183.

Conner, K. and Prahalad, C. (1996) 'A resource-based theory of the firm: knowledge versus opportunism', *Organizational Science*, vol. 7, pp. 477–501.

Goldberg, V. (1976) 'Regulation and administered contracts', *Bell Journal of Economics*, vol. 7, pp. 426–448.

Grossman, S. and Hart, O. (1986) 'The costs and benefits of ownership: a theory of vertical and lateral integration', *Journal of Political Economy*, vol. 94, pp. 691–719.

Klein, B., Crawford, R. and Alchian, A. (1978) 'Vertical integration, appropriable rents and the competitive contracting process', *Journal of Law and Economics*, vol. 21, pp. 297–326.

Nooteboom, B. (1999) *Inter-firm Alliances: Analysis and Design*, Routledge, London.

Penrose, E. (1959) *The Theory of the Growth of the Firm*, Basil Blackwell, Oxford.

Sako, M. (2003) *Prices, Quality and Trust: Inter-firm Relations in Britain and Japan*, Cambridge University Press, Cambridge.

Shelanski, H. and Klein, P. (1995) 'Empirical research in transaction cost economics: a review and assessment', *Journal of Law, Economics and Organization*, vol. 11, pp. 335–361.

Smith, A. (1776) *The Wealth of Nations*, Glasgow edition, R. Campbell and A. Skinner (eds), 1976 Bicentenary Edition, Clarendon Press, Oxford.

Williamson, O. (1971) 'The vertical integration of production: market failure considerations', *American Economic Review*, vol. 61, pp. 112–123.

Williamson, O. (1998) 'Transaction cost economics' in *Handbook of Industrial Organization*, 5th edn, pp. 135–182, R. Schmalensee and R. Willig (eds), North Holland, Netherlands.

APPENDIX 3A

Consider the diagram below showing an inverse relationship between the market demand for a product and its price, i.e. $P = f(Q)$.

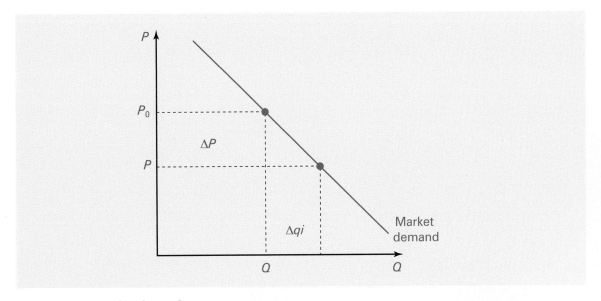

Figure 3A.1: A market demand curve

If the market is supplied by an oligopoly, we can define the output of each firm as q_i and total market supply as $Q = \Sigma q_i$. Assuming q_is are homogeneous products, the total revenue (*TR*) for the *i*th firm is:

$$TR_i = P_0 q_i \tag{3A.1}$$

as shown in the figure. Following a change (Δ) in the quantity supplied by the ith firm, the market price falls to P and, as shown in the figure, we have:

$$\Delta TR_i = P\Delta q_i + \Delta Pq_i \tag{3A.2}$$

Given that marginal revenue, $MR_i = TR_i/\Delta q_i$ we can divide through by Δq_i to get:

$$MR_i = P + \frac{\Delta P}{\Delta q_i} \cdot q_i \tag{3A.3}$$

and multiplying and dividing the right-hand side by Q/q_i yields

$$MR_i = P\left[1 + \frac{\Delta P}{Dq_i} \cdot \frac{Q}{P}\right]\frac{q_i}{Q} \tag{3A.4}$$

The second expression in parentheses is the inverse of the firm's price elasticity of demand ε_i and q_i/Q is its market share, s_i hence:

$$MR_i = P\left[1 + \frac{s_i}{\varepsilon_i}\right] \tag{3A.5}$$

CHAPTER 4

HORIZONTAL BOUNDARIES AND DIVERSIFICATION

Introduction

As explained in the previous chapter, the boundaries of a firm have traditionally been defined in terms of ownership. In this context, the phrase **horizontal boundary** refers to the mix and volume of products that a single firm produces from its resources in a given time period. Horizontal boundaries are therefore a measure of scale and it might seem that the best measure of horizontal scale is the volume of output produced by a firm per year. However, very few firms produce only one product and where multi-products are concerned, scale has to be measured indirectly in terms of turnover or **revenue**. This is not ideal as 'size' is then influenced by the level of the prices at which the firm's products are sold – but other indirect measures also have their limitations. Measures such as the numbers employed or the value of capital invested are not satisfactory measures of size because both will vary with the type of firm. For example, per €1m of sales, a supermarket will employ a relatively large number of people to provide services to its customers, whereas an oil refinery will employ relatively few people – but a great deal more capital – per €1m of output.

A more challenging issue is the dynamics of scale. There are very few examples of firms suddenly becoming big and in such cases government involvement in the creation of such enterprises is the norm. Generally, a firm can only grow in scale over a period of years and this is a dynamic process. The process might be accelerated by **mergers** and **acquisitions** but organic **growth**, that is, growth generated by increases in the firm's own resources, is the main engine for most firms – at least in their early years – developing an increasing scale of production. Mergers and acquisitions and the growth of firms are the subject of the next chapter. In this chapter, we continue the essentially static approach of the previous chapter in seeking to understand why a firm might choose to horizontally broaden the range of the activities controlled by its management hierarchy. We also examine why a firm might choose instead an intermediate form of horizontal collaboration such as an alliance or joint venture.

The field of corporate strategy focuses essentially on the question, what businesses should a firm be in? Put the other way round, what should be the horizontal boundaries of a firm? This was not a question likely to be posed by nineteenth-century economists, whose **neo-classical approach** was narrowly focused on a single product, single-plant firm and who viewed the firm's horizontal boundaries as being determined solely by production costs. The neo-classical school started with the likelihood that production processes displayed technologically determined **economies of scale** at low levels of output and that these became exhausted as the scale of output increased. From this perspective, scale economies determined optimal size and also provided an explanation for the observed tendency towards concentrated production. Similarly, the choice between single- and multi-plant operations was approached as an issue of cost minimization. As the neo-classical theory of the firm broadened to embrace multi-product firms, there remained a tendency to view them as more of a special case than the norm and, again, decisions as to the range of products produced and their relative proportions could all be reduced to the outcome of a search to minimize unit costs. However, the neo-classical bedrock of reducing inefficiencies and minimizing unit costs is not sufficient for a complete understanding of the relationship between a firm's corporate strategy and its horizontal boundaries.

The **governance approach** to the boundaries of the firm is, as we have seen, founded upon transaction costs and **incomplete contracts** giving an advantage to hierarchical management in directing and monitoring resources in the face of uncertainty. The concept of incomplete contracts throws light on when it is efficient for a firm to own productive assets and when it is efficient to purchase the output of such assets from the market. It may appear that the ownership of assets fixes the boundaries of a firm, but, again, a firm's horizontal boundaries cannot be fully explained by resort to the ownership of assets, its **organizational architecture** and its incentive contracts. Horizontal boundary choices relate also to issues such as location and **diversification** – what geographic regions to operate in and which products to offer – and the nature of participation in business networks. The essential focus on efficiency of both the neo-classical and governance approaches to the firm are somewhat lacking when it comes to fully explaining how firms make strategic decisions regarding diversification.

A full explanation augments the neo-classical and governance approaches with the insights furnished by the **competency approach** to the firm. To proponents of the competency school, a firm's horizontal boundaries have as much to do with entrepreneurial initiatives and rent seeking as reducing inefficiencies. From this perspective, firms seek to expand their horizontal boundaries in order to build or utilize surplus, heterogeneous, fungible capabilities to achieve **competitive advantage**. From the competency viewpoint, the boundaries of the firm are central to business strategy; they not only determine the firm's demand for resources, but also they provide opportunities for building and applying knowledge, as well as creating scope for appropriating rents. In the view of the competency school, many of the issues raised in seeking competitive advantage involve decisions as to where a firm should draw its horizontal boundaries.

From the perspective of practitioners, these alternative approaches would not be viewed as competing, but rather as complementary. In practice, a well-managed firm strives to be efficient, but also to accumulate and deploy rent-generating knowledge resources. We should also be mindful that horizontal expansion can generate problems and we will return to this issue in Chapter 6. This chapter focuses on answering the complementary questions of why and how firms might benefit from horizontal expansion. By reading this chapter not only will these questions be answered, but also we will clarify the issues raised by the alternative approaches outlined above in analysing and explaining a firm's horizontal boundaries. On completion you will:

- Understand the relationship between a firm's horizontal boundaries and unit *production* costs.
- Appreciate how horizontal boundaries relate to *business* and *corporate strategy*.
- Be aware of the intermediate forms of horizontal boundary and the benefits thereof.

This chapter is divided into six sections. In the first, we will start our analysis of horizontal boundaries by examining the relationship between unit production costs and scale, i.e. economies of scale for a single-plant, single-product firm. In the second section, we will extend the concept of economies of scale to include the effects of cumulative production on learning and lower unit costs. We will then augment the analysis of horizontal boundaries by considering in the third section the economics of multi-plant operations – which also raises the issue of location – before turning our attention in the fourth section to the multi-product firm and *economies of scope*. In the fifth section, we will look more closely at the nature of multi-product diversification and how firms choose between different types of diversification. In the sixth section, we will examine the issue of coherence and the influence of uncertainty on firms' diversification choices. In the final section, we introduce the concept of virtual horizontal boundaries; namely, how and why firms might use inter-firm collaborations to access many of the same benefits delivered by horizontal integration.

Scale Effects

We start our analysis of horizontal boundaries with the concept of economies of scale and the behaviour of unit costs as scale increases. The standard intuitive characterization is a single product produced by a single-plant firm, where a planned proportional increase in the scale of production involves a less-than-proportional increase in total production costs. Economies arising from increasing the scale of operations derive from the returns to scale embedded in the firm's production technology. If the technology displays increasing returns to scale, then increasing all factor inputs by a scalar λ results in output increasing by more than λ, by λ if there are constant returns to scale and by less than λ if there are decreasing returns to scale.

According to Koopermans (1957), this *proportionality postulate* implies that increasing returns to scale are impossible unless one or more of the technologically determined production inputs or fixed assets are lumpy or *indivisible*. If all inputs are perfectly divisible, then, in Koopman's words, any scale of production could always be sub-divided proportionately to produce the same level of efficiency at a smaller scale of production. In other words, in the presence of increasing returns it is impossible to reduce all of a firm's productive resources by the same proportion, $0 < \lambda < 1$, to achieve a similar proportional reduction in output. This can be seen more clearly if we consider the difficulty of reducing very different inputs – e.g. buildings, machines, materials, labour hours and knowledge – in equal proportion. Some of these inputs will be three-dimensional – buildings and machines – others, two-dimensional – sheets of materials – and some, one-dimensional – the flow of energy. So if a firm attempts to reduce all of its resources in the same proportion it will change their relative proportions and by assumption lower efficiency.

The geometrical relationships, governing three-dimensional resources or assets not only makes it difficult to reduce all resources in the same proportion, but it also ensures that costs do not change in proportion to capacity. This follows because the costs of materials used in buildings and plant increase – assuming constant prices – in proportion to the surface area, whereas capacity or output increase in proportion to the volume. In short, the capital costs of doubling the capacity of a steel mill, an oil refinery or a retail outlet are unlikely to be double, though this assumes the firm can obtain the land on which to expand at the same price. Viewed in terms of costs, we can express the degree of technological scale economies as an *elasticity*. Formally, the effect of a permanent percentage change (%Δ) in productive capacity on total costs, *TC*, can be expressed as:

$$S = \frac{\%\Delta TC}{\%\Delta q} = \frac{\Delta TC}{\Delta q} \cdot \frac{q}{TC} \tag{4.1}$$

where q is the volume of output that can be produced per period, and if:

$S < 1$ expansion involving economies of scale
$S = 0$ expansion involves **constant returns to scale**
$S > 1$ expansion involves **diseconomies of scale**

Total costs (*TC*) are summarized as:

$$TC = c(q) + \delta K \tag{4.2}$$

where c(*q*) is the variable costs function, *K* the value of the firm's fixed capital and δ the annual depreciation rate, where $0 < \delta < 1$. The importance of Equation (4.2) is that sources of scale economies can arise from variable costs, as well as the traditional characterization that they arise in large measure from the opportunities that the existing technology affords to specialize in both the use of fixed and human capital (Scherer and Ross, 1990). We have already explained that, in terms of cost per unit of output, larger production plants are inherently cheaper to build and run. Scale overcomes the problem of indivisibilities, but it also creates opportunities for human capital to utilize specific skills, thereby increasing specialization, with beneficial impacts on productivity and unit production costs. When analysing the influence of increasing scale on variable costs, the neo-classical resort to *ceteris paribus* is not appropriate. Larger scale increases a firm's bargaining power with suppliers, resulting in lower unit prices for materials and also greater scope for sharing some costs with customers, e.g. distribution. With more machines, the impact of a breakdown in one machine is less costly in terms of lost output – the so-called **economies of massed reserves**. Scale also allows the ratio of stocks to output to be reduced (Baumol, 1972), again with a beneficial impact on variable costs.

If a plant, or an office, producing a single product has the scope to exploit increasing returns, then, providing there is market demand for the extra output, its senior managers will plan for a permanent increase in the scale of production. Changing the scale of production may involve building new premises, or concentrating more machines or work stations within existing buildings. Whatever route is chosen, the firm's senior managers will need to commission plans, obtain permission from the relevant authorities and organize for a period of disruption while the additional productive capacity is put in place. By definition, this process takes time and hence the concept of economies of scale refers only to the **long run**. That is, an economy of scale can only be fully realized after allowing for a sufficient period of time to elapse to allow the firm to adjust all of its factor inputs to optional proportions for an increased scale of output. How long it takes a firm to achieve a particular scale of production will depend on many factors – e.g. the growth of demand, the behaviour of rivals – but it is likely that a firm will increase its scale over a number of discrete periods of expansion. Hence, Viner's (1932) familiar U-shaped **long-run average cost curve** (*LRAC*), as set out in Figure 4.1, represents the 'envelope' of potential unit costs at increasing scales of production. How long it takes to move along the curve is not defined and for some businesses could take several years, e.g. aircraft assembly.

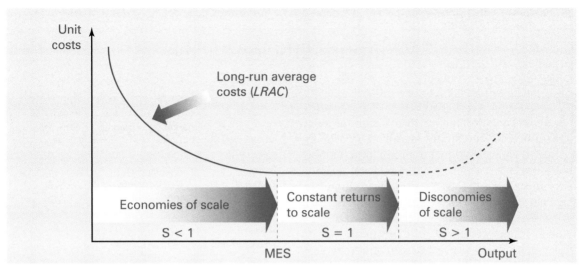

Figure 4.1: Long-run costs

By acknowledging that the *LRAC* is an intertemporal concept, it becomes more difficult to accept the *ceteris paribus* assumptions that underlly its construction. For example, over a period of time the prices of factor inputs may vary; indeed, the firm's increased scale may cause the prices of specialist inputs to rise. More significantly, the prevailing technology might be augmented or supplanted, changing the relationship between the volume of inputs, their relative proportions and output. Only by holding to the assumptions of a single plant, a single product and *ceteris paribus* can we define the concept of the **minimum efficient scale** (*MES*) of production: the point where economies of scale are exhausted.

Increasing scale beyond the *MES* results – according to the standard characterization – in total costs rising in proportion to output, thereby yielding constant returns to scale and eventually the onset of diseconomies of scale. The *MES* will vary with the technology employed and in terms of unit costs sets a boundary that – subject to sufficient demand – firms should strive to achieve over the long run. However, Figure 4.1 suggests that it is the onset of diseconomies of scale, rather than the *MES*, that sets the boundary for a single-plant firm. There is, however, a problem in using the concept of diseconomies of scale to provide an upper boundary for a single-product, single-plant firm. It is far from clear that the sources of economies of scale outlined above go into reverse at higher levels of production. There are some physical relationships that limit size. For example, the structural strength of any three-dimensional body diminishes as its dimensions are increased. Rather weakly, the intuitive justification for diseconomies of scale is based on the presumed difficulties of managing larger-scale production units. This can only be justified on the unrealistic assumption that over the long run it is beyond the ability of senior managers to change the firm's organizational architecture so that performance can continue to be monitored and appropriate action taken as the scale of production increases. Diseconomies of scale implicitly depend on the assumption that the firm's organizational architecture, along with technology, are fixed in the long run.

Minimum Efficient Scale

The table on the right shows estimates of the *MES* for a number of industries. The estimates were prepared for the European Commission in readiness for the single market. The *MES* is shown, not as a volume of production, but expressed as a percentage of the relevant market. By presenting the *MES* in this way, it shows whether a market – say, the UK market for cars – is big enough to support more than one or two firms operating at minimum cost. Depending on the prevailing technology and the size of the market, this can present the authorities with the difficulty of simultaneously achieving both lowest-cost production and competition for market share. One solution was offered by the European Union's single market programme. The creation of a European single market has turned the whole of the European Union into one market and, as shown in the table, greatly reduces the *MES* for individual industries as a proportion of the market.

	MES as % of UK market	MES as % of EU market	% increase in costs at 50% MES
Cars	200	20	6–9
Trucks	104	21	7–8
Aircraft	> 100	na	5–6
Computers	> 100	na	20
Refrigerators	85	11	4
Steel	72	9	6
Television sets	40	9	9

Source: Commission

The Commission supplemented the *MES* estimates with information on the extent to which sub-optimal plants suffered cost disadvantages compared with *MES* plants. As can be seen, although for some industries the UK market is too small to support more than one plant operating at *MES*, the cost disadvantages of sub-optimal plants are relatively small. It should also be added that free trade will allow a plant to reach *MES* even if the domestic market is small.

Learning By Doing

Another important issue raised by the concept of the long run is the impact of learning on unit costs. The benefit of knowledge acquisition by repetition was first widely revealed by Alchian's (1950) study of aircraft assembly. Alchian observed that with no changes in technology, labour productivity increased steadily year after year on the same production line. Alchian's observation has given rise to the expression **learning by doing** to describe a dynamic process whereby unit costs are reduced as a result of subtle changes being made to the routines employed by the firm's workforce on the basis of experience. Learning by doing must by definition be spread over successive production periods. As cumulative production increases, the firm's managers and workforce will add to their knowledge of the production process and seek to use this knowledge to reduce unit production costs. This organizational learning by experience adds new dimensions to an understanding of the behaviour of unit costs as scale increases.

By definition, if a firm takes advantage of the scope afforded by technologically determined increasing returns to scale for reducing unit costs it will only do so over a succession of production periods. This long-term process will inevitably be accompanied by learning spillover effects into areas such as simplifying production processes, improving the efficiency of routines and creating new specializations. It follows that as increases in the scale of production are achieved over a period of time as the *cumulative* volume of output increases, so it is extremely difficult to separate the effects of learning from economies of scale. The dynamic reduction in unit costs arising from learning by doing affects, is frequently represented by, the ***learning curve*** – see Figure 4.2. Note that the horizontal axis measures the cumulative output and the vertical axis the unit costs reflecting the knowledge gained as cumulative production increases.

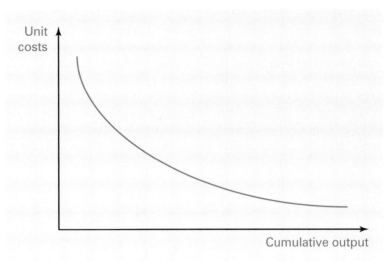

Figure 4.2: The effects of learning

This type of long-run reduction in production costs arising from learning by doing was at first believed to be *product-specific*, as it was originally observed in plants where intricate labour operations were performed, e.g. aircraft assembly. However, it is now realized that similar productivity improvements can be achieved in a wide range of industries. Every new plant has a 'start-up' period, when managers and workers are learning to operate it. The process of learning is enhanced when employees work together in teams, allowing knowledge acquisition to be shared for the benefit of team productivity. As the cumulative volume of output rises, team members learn how to co-operate more efficiently with each other, other teams and managers. The knowledge gained accumulates and improves not only manual and group skills, but also cognitive skills. This enhancement of the firm's human resources is manifested in the following cost-reducing improvements:

- The firm's human resources become more specialized in their contribution and hence more adept, faster working and less in need of supervision.
- Organizational routines are refined and improved, resulting in more efficient scheduling of the production process, from the inward flow of materials to the distribution of the final product.
- By creating a culture of learning – where employees continually update their knowledge base – the benefits spill over beyond a particular product to the organization and its ability to initiate and adapt to change.

In the case of human resources, progressive learning justifies the payment of ***efficiency wages***, which we will return to in Chapter 6. When it comes to intangible resources, e.g. routines, the effect of learning is to increase the value of these resources to the firm, *ceteris paribus*. If learning effects are judged to be significant, then it might be preferable for a firm to schedule the production of many smaller production runs rather than invest immediately in large-scale production. The learning curve effect can be particularly important for a firm deciding whether it is profitable to enter an industry. Senior managers faced with high initial labour requirements will obtain an overly pessimistic view of costs if allowance is not made for the lower production costs once learning begins to take effect.

As noted above, most firms will take a number of production periods to achieve the *MES* and consequently it is very difficult in practice to separate the effects of increasing scale and learning. Indeed, one of the major contributions to business strategy – the Boston Consulting Group's (BCG) **Growth–Share Matrix** – is based on the intertemporal benefits of combining economies of scale and learning by doing. In the 1960s, Bruce Henderson, president of BCG, noticed that learning effects went beyond labour costs and applied to all costs under the control of the firm. Further analysis by BCG suggested that each time the cumulative number of units produced doubled, costs declined by a given percentage. For example, in industries as diverse as integrated circuits and cement, BCG found that a doubling of cumulative production reduced unit costs by 30 per cent. In other industries, the impact of cumulative production on unit costs was much lower, indicating that learning curve advantages are industry-specific rather than economy-wide.

Based on its study of the effects of learning by doing, BCG developed one of the first, and arguably the best known, of what has become a long line of portfolio matrices as a means of analysing firms and the position of their products. The BCG's matrix, reproduced in Figure 4.3, separates a firm's products on two dimensions: the growth of market demand; and its market share relative to the next largest competitor.

In addition to the twin concepts of economies of scale and learning by doing, the BCG matrix is closely associated with another concept; namely, the **product life cycle**. When a product is first launched, average production costs are likely to be relatively high owing to the limited scale of production. If the product is successful and sales build up, over time the firm's unit production costs are likely to fall, partly in response to the exploitation of any economies of scale inherent in the production technology and partly in response to the absorption by its workforce of the learning embodied in cumulative production. A firm whose product commands a large market share is therefore, *ceteris paribus*, more likely to be benefiting from economies of scale and learning than a competitor with a smaller market share. It is these cost advantages that underpin the cash cow – a product that accounts for a large market share in a mature market – in the BCG matrix.

A product characterized as a rising star is in the early stages of its life, but has captured a high relative market share in a fast-growing market. Thus, in principle, a rising star offers potential unit cost gains from economies of scale and learning. A problem child has a low relative market share in a fast-growing market and, *ceteris paribus*, is at a potential unit cost disadvantage relative to a competitor with a larger market share. Strategy based on the BCG matrix suggests that funds generated by cash cows could be used to increase the production of stars and problem children in order to lower unit production costs – advice that is of little value if a problem child is the result of a bad design or a lower quality than offered by rivals. A dog is a product that may have enjoyed a long life but has a relatively low share in a declining market. A falling market share implies rising unit costs as the firm retreats back up the long-run average cost curve.

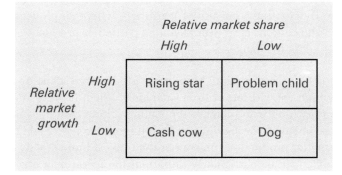

Figure 4.3: The BCG Growth-Share Matrix

The learning curve should be viewed as the means by which a firm capitalizes on the knowledge that its investment in higher volumes of output has generated. Learning by doing essentially involves two mechanisms. The first is simplification, whereby those involved in the production process learn to minimize interactions, spatial and temporal processes. The second mechanism is specialization, whereby the competency of those involved is enhanced by the narrow focus of attention on specific activities (Levinthal and March, 1993). Thus, the knowledge gained is specific and concerns fine-tuning in specific areas associated with the product in question, such as production scheduling, job layout and material flow control. As the knowledge embodied in the learning curve is generated in the process of producing specific goods or services, such knowledge may not be easily transferred to other products. This view of the learning curve might help explain why General Motors is not a major player in, say, coal mining. More generally, learning by doing may contribute very little to an understanding of the external business environment, particularly how to react to unanticipated 'shocks'.

Figure 4.4 attempts to summarize the linkage between learning-by-doing arising from cumulative production and a growing scale of production to long-run unit costs per production period. In the figure, $LRAC_0$ represents the technology-determined economies of scale in which learning is presumed unchanged. For example, say in the long run the firm's scale of production has increased from q_0 to q_1 per production period, the lower unit production costs owe nothing to any change arising from the knowledge and skills embodied in the firm's human capital and organizational routines. This economy of scale is illustrated by the move from point A to B. However, as the firm moves from A to B over successive production periods, it is also likely to benefit from the absorption by its man-

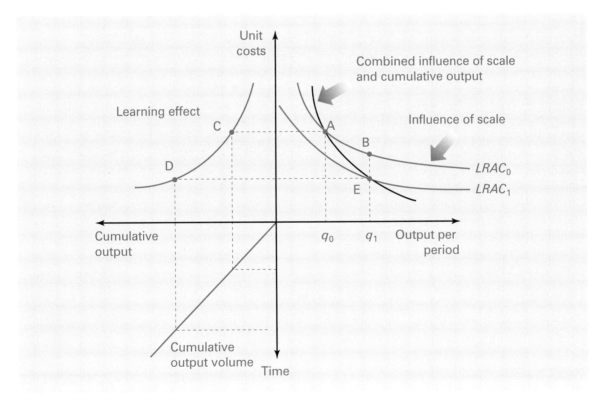

Figure 4.4: The effects of scale and learning

agers and workforce of the learning embodied in the cumulative output. Depending on the extent to which the firm's organizational architecture can apply this learning, so the unit costs of production at all scales of operation will tend to fall over successive production periods as cumulative output rises. This is represented by a move down the learning curve from point C to D and a corresponding, downward shift of the long-run average cost curve to, say, $LRAC_1$.

Thus, the combination of learning and a growing scale of operation will, over a period of time, enable the firm to push unit production costs to lower levels than indicated by economies of scale alone. This outcome is captured by the movement from point A to E in Figure 4.4. Note that learning by doing does not alter the technology determined *MES* of production for a single-product plant, but the potential for reducing unit costs at all scales of production makes knowledge accumulation an important strategic variable. Figure 4.4 implies that the rapid acquisition of knowledge can offset the cost disadvantage of smaller scale. In a competitive market, the cost advantage imparted by rapid and efficient learning are not only conducive to the earning of an **economic rent**, but also potentially an influence on an individual firm's market share and hence industry structure.

A Threatened Species

Traditionally, UK building societies were mutual institutions, restricted by statute to raising funds for mortgage lending. In 1986, the Building Societies Act enabled them to diversify, with some limits, into a much wider range of financial services. In 1997, all remaining restrictions were removed and building societies should now more correctly be viewed as mutual financial service organizations. Alongside the liberalizing legislation, some UK building societies merged and others converted to plc bank status. At the start of the 1990s, there were 86 UK building societies, but by 2004 the number had fallen to 63.

One of the key motivations for this consolidation and merger activity is economies of scale. Economies of scale is a difficult concept when applied to organizations with a branch network. The concept does not imply (or rule out) an increasing scale of branch outlets, but rather reduced unit costs arising from the management of a larger network. In part, this efficiency gain is attributable to the rationalization potential that mergers bring, but also relevant is new technology in banking and financial services that favours large scale. With the arrival of new delivery channels such as telephone and internet banking, many financial services are finding that the rationalization of branches, infrastructure and staff is more easily accomplished following a merger.

If there are economies of scale, what future is there for smaller building societies? There may be some scope for becoming highly focused and cultivating a local presence, but this assumes that there are X-inefficiencies that can be reduced by such a strategy. Much depends on the unit cost benefits of scale, and if, as the evidence suggests, they are significant, then smaller-scale, local building societies are a threatened species.

Multi-plant Economies

The foregoing representation of the neo-classical, single-plant, single-product approach to the horizontal boundaries of the firm is not representative of the real world. Industry studies show that single-plant operations are the exception. The magisterial study of industry structure by Scherer and Ross (1990) used data for US manufacturing industries to show that leading firms operated a single plant in only 5 per cent of the industries surveyed and a similar picture emerges for European industries. This suggests that the spreading of production across a number of smaller plants yields greater benefits than the economies of scale associated with concentrating production in a single plant. Or, as Scherer and Ross succinctly put it, how seriously disadvantaged are firms operating only a single *MES* plant compared to multi-plant enterprises? For the moment, we will retain the assumption of a single-product firm but now its horizontal boundaries are determined by the number and average size of the plants it controls. As both single plants and multiple plants are able to economize on central management functions such as accounting, marketing and HR, these are not a relevant consideration when comparing the economics of multi-plant and single-plant operations. More relevant would be whether the managers of smaller plants are in a position to learn more rapidly, to respond more speedily to shocks, to monitor more closely performance and to provide effective incentives. Multi-plant operations may also reduce risk. If plants are producing essentially the same products, multi-plant operations permit greater flexibility for firms in their operations. For example, a breakdown in one plant might be offset by increasing production at the other plants, or in periods of low demand the firm can reduce costs by closing or mothballing one plant.

This last point merits further attention. A multi-plant firm's response to external shocks can be very different to that of a single-plant firm. For example, multi-plant firms might be more inclined to shut down a plant whose production is less profitable, whereas a single-plant firm is more likely to strive to improve matters. For a multi-plant firm, closing down a less profitable plant allows it to continue operating and more closely focus on its other plants. Another implication of a multi-plant organizational structure is that it is better able to facilitate a programme of continuous improvement and restructuring. Although plants in the same firm may share common resources such as management, studies show that individual plants are likely to differ in terms of productivity (Scherer *et al.*, 1975). Senior managers can focus on less-productive plants using the knowledge gained in better-performing plants to replace vintage capital and improve team working and routines.

Multi-plant operations are likely to offer significant economies when the firm operates in spatial geographic markets and transport costs are significant. This can be demonstrated with the example of a manufacturer who wants to serve the national market and has to decide whether to do so from one location or two. Say these two locations are known as East and West and for simplicity let us assume the population is tightly concentrated around each location, i.e. not spread out between the two locations. This assumption allows us to simplify matters by setting the transport costs to zero for plants located within their local markets. Finally, owing to competition, the product is sold at the same price (p) in each location. Writing π_E and π_W as the profits in East and West, respectively, we have for each production period:

$$\pi_E = pq_E - c(q_E) - \delta K_E \tag{4.3}$$

$$\pi_W = pq_E - c(q_W) - \delta K_W \tag{4.4}$$

Where q_E and q_W are the quantities produced at the East and West plants, $c(q_E)$ and $c(q_W)$ are the variable production costs, which, without any loss of generality, we can assume on a unit-cost basis are identical in both locations; and K_E and K_W are the capital costs of building the plants in each location, respectively. These fixed costs are depreciated at the same rate, δ, spread over the life of the capital, where $0 < \delta < 1$. If, alternatively, production is located in a single plant, we have:

$$\pi = pq - c(q) - \delta K - T \tag{4.5}$$

where $q = q_E + q_W$, K is the capital costs associated with the larger plant and T is the cost of distributing the product to the combined East and West markets. From the foregoing it can be seen that, providing all plants have a common rate of depreciation, for it to be profitable to concentrate production at one location the following inequality must hold:

$$K + T < K_E + K_W \tag{4.6}$$

That is, the investment in a single location (K) plus the transport costs (T) of distributing the product must be less than the total investment costs of building two separate plants in East and West.

An alternative way to decide whether a firm's horizontal boundaries should be determined by a single plant or multi-plants is to recall that economies of scale are generally the outcome of a long-run process. Thus, providing demand is sufficient to warrant investment in new capacity, the firm's senior managers have to decide between replacing or extensively rebuilding an existing plant to gain economies of scale or adding a new plant in a new location. In practice, the firm's senior managers will need to take into account the disruption that will be caused to existing operations if the new capacity is installed at the existing site. Relevant to short-run disruption costs is the proportional increase in the capital stock and the speed at which it is installed (see, for example, Harisson, 1986). We can approach this decision by assuming that a firm is currently operating only in the East market. By assumption, the firm is currently producing the volume q_E and has incurred fixed capital costs of K_E. If now the firm chooses to also supply the West market, it needs to invest in additional production capacity and in making its investment decision, the firm's senior managers have essentially to decide between the additional capital and disruption costs of increasing scale at the current plant – ΔK_E and D, respectively – plus the transport costs, T, of delivering to the West market, or the alternative capital cost of building a second plant in the separate geographical market (K_W). On this basis, the decision as to how the firm expands its boundaries will depend on the following inequality:

$$(\Delta K_E + D) + T < K_W \tag{4.7}$$

If disruption costs and/or transport costs are high, the economies of scale associated with an addition to the existing plant or the building of one larger plant will need to be substantial to outweigh the building of a second plant in the West market. Figure 4.5 summarizes the relative costs of single-plant and multi-plant economics as an influence on a firm's horizontal boundaries. Ignoring transport costs, the technologically determined economies of scale are exhausted at *MES*. If there are economies of scale in transport, the firm could minimize its unit production and transport costs at a horizontal scale in excess of *MES*, say q_1, represented by *LRAC* + T_0. If, however, transport costs rise with distance and quantity, then a single-plant firm would face unit costs represented by the curve *LRAC* + T_1. As indicated, in this situation it would be more efficient for the firm to expand its horizontal boundaries by investing in multi-plant operations.

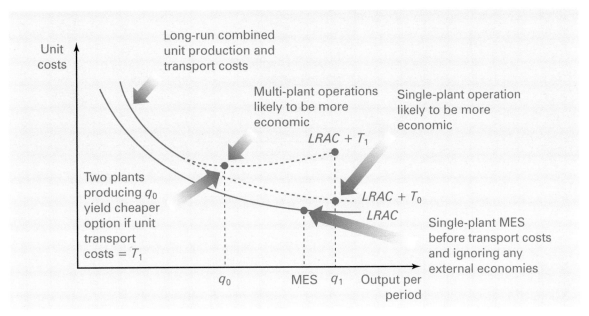

Figure 4.5: Multi-plant operations and transport costs

Another consideration when weighing the relative advantage of expanding a single-plant or investing in a multi-plant structure are external factors. By building a larger-scale plant in one location, the firm might benefit not only from economies of scale and learning, but also from positive ***externalities*** that further reduce unit production costs. Positive externalities arise from the infrastructure that surrounds the firm in its location. Two sources of positive externalities are ***agglomeration*** and ***clusters***. We will return in more detail to the benefits of clusters in Chapter 8; here we will briefly outline the influence of externalities arising from agglomeration – the loose grouping together of firms in a geographic location. Agglomeration is a feature of all developed and developing nations. Its effect is to concentrate industrial activity in a limited number of geographic regions. No matter which country of the European Union is selected, most of its industrial activity will be concentrated in specific areas. Why do firms tend to be located at a limited number of sites rather than spread evenly across a nation state?

In part, planning restrictions will limit the number of locations in which firms can locate, but by grouping together firms can benefit from the external infrastructure. If a firm is located in an area of industrial activity it is more likely that the surrounding infrastructure will be supportive, with beneficial consequences for unit production costs. For example, by locating within an area populated by other firms, the firm may be able to choose from a greater number of suppliers for specific inputs and services. As a result of competition between these suppliers, the firm is likely to pay lower prices for its materials and services. Also, an industrial location will attract labour and a plentiful supply will help to reduce search costs, moderate wages and provide a reserve pool of employees from which to recruit. An industrial area is also likely to have better transport and communication links and the firm's senior managers can join with the managers of other firms in the locality to lobby for an improved level of support from the local authorities. Agglomeration is not, however, always a benefit. If an industrial area becomes overcrowded, then bottlenecks, congestion and pollution are all likely to increase, with adverse consequences for the firm's cost base.

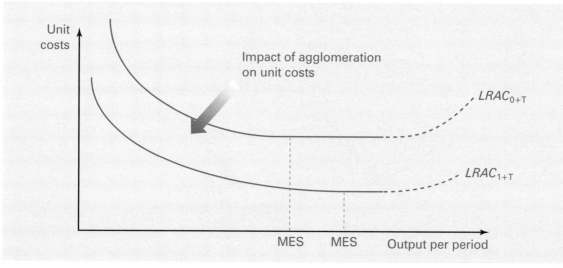

Figure 4.6: Impact of positive externalities

Figure 4.6 shows how the positive benefits of agglomeration combine to lower a firm's unit production costs. The advantage of a favourable location will have a beneficial effect not only on unit costs of production but also, with good road and rail links, transport costs are likely to be lower. In Figure 4.6, unit production and transport costs have been combined in the long-run average cost curve, represented by the subscript T. The impact of agglomeration on long-run unit costs is represented by the downward shift from $LRAC_{0 + T}$ to $LRAC_{1 + T}$. As illustrated, agglomeration allows the firm a larger horizontal scale before it reaches its *MES*. This would result if agglomeration yielded greater cost benefits for large-scale operations – for example, suppliers and distributors, who can offer lower prices by virtue of servicing other customers in the locality. If specialized services located within the area benefit from economies of scale and there is scope to share common amenities, agglomeration could contribute to a larger *MES* for a firm. If external benefits exist only at one location, then even if economies of scale are limited and transport costs are high, a firm may still have an incentive to locate production at one site.

Economies of Scope

The previous sections have concentrated on the relationship between unit production costs and the expansion of a firm's horizontal boundary for a single product. In practice, rather than steadily increasing the scale of production for a single product, firms are more likely to increase horizontal scale by widening the range of products produced. Intuitively, the production of a range of products implies an expanded horizontal boundary for a firm, but it can also result in lower unit production costs. When the production of two or more goods or services gives rise to savings in unit production costs, the firm is described as benefiting from economies of scope. The term economies of scope was defined and analysed by Panzar and Willig (1981). Formally, economies of scope exist when the costs of jointly producing two or more products is less than the cost of producing each product separately. The existence of economies of scope – actual or potential – forces senior managers to consider not only the revenue that might be generated by a new product, but also the cost implications across the firm's range of products.

A convenient and reasonable general demonstration of economies of scope is provided by the following simple example. To reduce complexity, we will assume only two products. The total cost (TC) of producing the two products – q_1 and q_2 – depends on whether they are produced at separate plants or jointly in one plant. If they are produced at separate plants, the total costs are:

$$TC(q_1, q_2) = [c_1(q_1) + \delta K_1] + [c_2(q_2) + \delta K_2] \tag{4.8}$$

where $c_1(q_1)$ and $c_2(q_2)$ are the variable costs and δK_1 and δK_2 the fixed capital costs – as previously defined – respectively. If the two products are produced jointly in one plant, the total costs are:

$$TC(q_1, q_2) = c_1(q_1) + c_2(q_2) + \delta K_J \tag{4.9}$$

where δK_J represents the capital costs of jointly producing q_1 and q_2. It follows that economies of scope exist if:

$$c_1(q_1) + c_2(q_2) + \delta K_J < c_1(q_1) + \delta K_1 + c_2(q_2) + \delta K_2 \tag{4.10}$$

Formally, if the inequality (Equation 4.10) holds, then the cost function is described as **subadditive**; that is, a single plant can supply the two outputs cheaper than two specialized plants, *ceteris paribus*. Equation (4.10) implies that economies of scope arise from the scope to share fixed capital expenditure but they could also arise from expenditure on variable inputs. Looking first at fixed capital, the inequality shown in Equation (4.10) could be satisfied if fixed capital embodied economies of scale arising from lumpiness or indivisibility. In this case, economies of scale would give rise to economies of scope resulting from the joint use of a production facility, say a building. In this situation, economies of scope arise if the prevailing technology allows joint production and the firm can fully exploit the fixed capital at one plant rather than operating with excess capacity at two plants. If we broaden K to include overheads, then economies of scope could result from: marketing programmes, administrative support or business knowledge. Perhaps the most intuitive examples of economies of scope arise when technology results in joint production. In this situation, both fixed and variable costs yield economies of scope. For example, it is cheaper to produce wheat and straw, wool and mutton, and beef and hides together than separately. Joint production may also allow learning accumulated by producing one product to be transferred costlessly, or at little cost, to another.

The common feature of the examples of economies of scope listed above is that one or more of the resources used in production has the nature of a **public good**. For example, having been acquired by a farm to produce wheat, fertilizer is then costlessly available for the production of straw as a by-product of wheat. While technologically determined joint production is an obvious example of a public good input, less obvious as sources of economies of scope are the services provided by resources that have excess capacity. Fixed capital such as an installed plant is a frequent source of scope economies. If a fixed capital asset is not fully utilized in the production of a particular product, then the spare capacity is costlessly available to produce another product. In this case, the spare capacity could be described as a quasi-public resource since the services of the fixed capital can be shared by two or more product lines at a lower cost than would be incurred if each were produced separately. But this answer only begs another question; namely, how did the spare capacity arise?

One answer would be the existence of economies of scale in the acquisition of a fixed resource. Alternatively, the spare capacity could result from the combination of indivisibilities and imperfect competition leading to a strategic decision to maintain the level of output below the firm's full capacity. We will return to the strategic benefits of maintaining spare productive capacity in later chapters; here our focus is on costs. Spare capacity is not confined to fixed capital. The firm might have a surplus of specialized human and intangible resources and, if so, these are also a source of economies of scope. For example, managerial expertise, business routines and even a good financial rating can all have the properties of a quasi-public resource. If a firm's accumulated knowledge is capable of being used in the production of a number of products without its value in any one application being impaired, this is an economy of scope. For example, a single management is often able to schedule and organize the production of more than one product without any loss of efficiency regarding the management of the original product.

The neo-classical theory of the firm had little interest in multi-product plants because it implicitly assumed zero **transaction costs**. In such a world, scope economies can be captured by using the market to share an under-utilized specialist resource that is indivisible. However, the existence in practice of transaction costs provides illumination and helps to explain the numerous examples of multi-product firms. These transaction costs can be demonstrated with the example of a capital asset that has some idle capacity. The more specialized the asset, the thinner the market for sharing its use, and the more certain an agreement for leasing a proportion of the asset's capacity will be an **incomplete contract**. **Asset specificity** poses the risk of **opportunistic behaviour** on the part of either the lessee or the lessor, resulting in the former in the loss of the **quasi-rent** that the leasor hoped to gain and in the latter the loss of the benefit expected by the lessee. Thus, the governance approach to the determination of a firm's horizontal boundaries would focus on the implications of incomplete contracts and asset specificity to help to explain multi-product production. From a governance perspective, the firm, in choosing to utilize spare capacity, seeks a way that avoids the potential transactional hazards: in effect, substituting the production of a new product for intra-firm trading of surplus capacity.

When it comes to an intangible asset such as knowledge, the transaction costs of market exchange to utilize spare capacity are likely to be prohibitively high. Take the example of proprietary knowledge of either a managerial or technological kind. Not only are there likely to be organizational and strategic obstacles to using the market for the transfer of excess capacity, but also the high transaction cost associated with obtaining the requisite information for an exchange is likely to render the transaction uneconomic. The very nature of competition encourages firms to conceal internally generated knowledge regarding the competitive benefits of a new technology or an organizational routine that generate cost advantages relative to competitors. But even if there were no impediments to sharing proprietary knowledge, in many cases such knowledge is tacit – particularly where it is shared within a team – and consequently it would be impossible to even consider a market exchange unless the firm was prepared to allow a transfer or sharing of its employees.

There is considerable overlap between economies of scope and scale. Both may arise from the shared purchase of raw materials; a shared production facility; or a fuller utilization of distribution systems. There is also a significant overlap between learning effects and economies of scope in the form of reusable knowledge. For example, software departments can reuse pieces of software codes for a number of applications. Perhaps the most important reuse of knowledge concerns managerial ability, which can be applied to the production of new products. These examples suggest that where learning is concerned, the boundary between economies of scale and scope are blurred. It is, however, frequently the case that economies of scope can be independent of economies of scale. A multi-product plant can enjoy economies of scope even if its production processes do not offer economies of scale.

For example, small-scale craft businesses frequently find that producing a number of products is cheaper than specializing in one product. This is a production process that will normally involve highly skilled labour and is most effective if undertaken on a small scale. In contrast, a multi-product manufacturer can have product-specific economies of scale for each individual product, yet enjoy little, if any, economies of scope.

It is difficult to demonstrate scope economies graphically, as it is not possible to precisely define a multi-product firm's horizontal minimum unit-cost boundary. In contrast to a single-product firm, the *MES* of multi-product production – the point at which economies of scale are exhausted – will vary with the composition of the firm's output bundle.

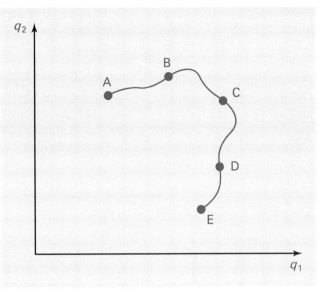

Figure 4.7: Loci of minimum efficient scales of multi-product production

In principle, a multi-product firm will have a locus of *MES* points as demonstrated in Figure 4.7. If the firm can produce q_1 and q_2 in varying proportions, and economies of scope exist, then points A, B, C, D and E could be points at which economies of scope are exhausted. Indeed, in the extreme, there could be a wide range of *MES* production represented by the AE boundary.

Changing the Focus

Prior to the coming into effect of the Single European Act on 1 January 1993, Multinational Enterprises (MNEs) operating in the European Union had adopted multi-domestic strategies, with individual subsidiaries focusing on supplying their host country. Such subsidiaries were often inefficient due to the lack of economies of scale inherent in supplying small markets. The process of European integration, particularly since 1993, with the removal of practically all restraints on trade between member states, threatened the survival of these national subsidiaries as their exposure to import substitution increased.

However, whereas free trade revealed the vulnerability of nationally focused subsidiaries, it also provided an alternative opportunity for MNEs. Slowly, MNEs' strategies have been evolving. The situation today is that instead of supplying a wide range of products from a subsidiary to a narrow national market, MNEs have now adopted the option of trade. Individual subsidiaries have been encouraged to take advantage of the potential for greater export orientation by restricting their operations to supply a much narrower range of products to a much wider regional market.

Before leaving this section, we can bring together the economics of multi-plant and multi-product production. Once we relax the assumption of a single product, an economic reason for multi-plant operations might be to achieve the cost benefits of specialization in different plants. If individual plants produce variations of a product, a potential cost benefit of multi-plant specialization is that it permits long production runs at each plant. This is particularly advantageous where the initial set-up costs are high. For example, in the car industry the tooling-up costs are substantial and a long production run helps reduce unit costs. Moreover, long production runs may permit the use of more specialist tools and generally greater automation. Finally, we should note that even if economies of scope do not exist, there can be revenue benefits for firms producing complementary products. We will return to this in Chapter 12.

Diversification

In our discussion of multi-product firms, we avoided discussion of the nature of the products produced. In a sense, all types of multi-product production can be described as diversification. However, from an analytical perspective, it is convenient to identify at least two types of diversification. **Related diversification** describes a multi-product firm that is producing a range of products with a high degree of commonality, e.g. home electronics, an arable farm. In practice, many firms produce a broad range of products that, as regards use, display little if any commonality. For example, at its height Hanson plc produced batteries, bricks and cigarettes. Firms such as Hanson are sometimes described as a **conglomerate**; we will, however, use the phrase **unrelated diversification** to describe multi-product firms whose product range displays little, if any, commonality. Generally related diversification is more likely at the level of an individual plant or business unit and this would form a key element of the plant's **business strategy**. Unrelated diversification is more likely to involve the distribution of products across a number of plants or business units, and hence it is more logical to think of unrelated diversification as being the province of **corporate strategy**.

Before looking at the factors that might encourage a firm to expand its horizontal boundaries by diversifying, we should consider how, in practice, we might measure the degree of diversification. Product line diversification can be measured in one of two ways. One method is simply to separate the firm's products according to standardized industry codes. The more product codes, the greater the degree of diversification. An alternative, somewhat more sophisticated, method is to derive a diversification index (_DI_), namely:

$$DI = 1 / \sum_{i=1}^{n} s_i^2 \tag{4.11}$$

where s_i is the proportion of the firm's output defined as belonging to the ith standardized industry code. This measure of diversification has the advantage of a minimum value of one when the firm produces one product. If each of the firm's products accounted for the same percentage of sales, the diversification index would have the same value as the number of lines. The more unequal the products in their share of total sales, the nearer the index to unity.

Diversity tends to be associated with large-scale firms and more frequently arises from mergers and acquisitions than from internal growth. But whereas concepts such as economies of scale and scope can intuitively be associated with related diversification, the benefits of unrelated diversification are not so obvious. Yet the examples of individual firms who have chosen a strategy of unrelated diversification are numerous, suggesting a rational motive. A rational starting point would be the belief by a firm's senior managers that specializing in one product or narrow range of related products may not allow the firm to achieve its longer-term profit objectives. These beliefs might be driven by demand or supply factors. On the demand side, if the longer-term prospects for the growth of demand for the firm's existing products appear limited, senior managers might be spurred into considering a strategy of unrelated diversification. Another widely accepted demand side justification for unrelated diversification is to reduce risk and/or cyclical or seasonal variations in cash flow. This can be demonstrated with the simple example of a firm that produces two products, A and B, and that in any production period A is produced for ρ of the time and B for $(1 - \rho)$ of the time where $0 < \rho < 1$. If the net cash flow associated with these two products – revenue less variable costs – varies from one production period to the next over a number of periods, we can define the mean expected net cash flow as π^e_A and π^e_B on products A and B, respectively. Formally, the total expected net cash flow, π^e, is:

$$\pi^e = [\rho \pi^e_A] + [(1 - \rho)\pi^e_B] \tag{4.12}$$

Say, $\pi^e_B = 90$ and $\pi^e_B = 110$ and A is produced for 60 per cent of the time, then Equation (4.12) becomes:

$$98 = (0.6*90) + (0.4*110) \tag{4.13}$$

If the **standard deviation** for both π_A and π_B is 10, this implies that for all practical purposes, the net cash flow for the two products will fluctuate within the bands shown in Figure 4.8.

The standard deviation associated with the total expected net cash flow, σ_{AB}, is the weighted average of the standard deviation for π^e_A and π^e_B. Writing σ_A and σ_B for the standard deviations, respectively, we have:

$$\sigma_{AB} = [\rho \sigma_A] + [(1 - \rho)\sigma_B] \text{ or} \tag{4.14}$$

$$10 = (0.6*10) + (0.4*10) \tag{4.15}$$

This suggests that as the net cash flow for both products has the same standard deviation, the risk is not reduced by joint production. However, this would be correct only if the two cash flows moved in

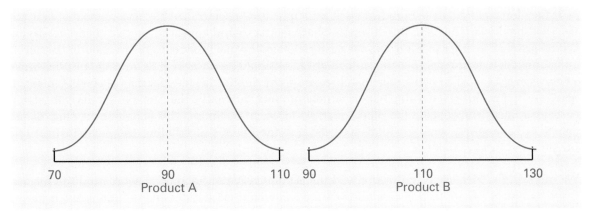

Figure 4.8: Variability of net cash flow

perfect lockstep. In any other case, diversification into multi-products will reduce the risk. The correct procedure for calculating the risk associated with π^e_A and π^e_B is – bearing in mind that the standard deviation is the square root of the variance, i.e. $\sigma = \sqrt{\sigma^2}$ – to calculate the variance of the two net cash flows thus:

$$\text{profit variance} = \rho^2\sigma_A^2 + (1-\rho)^2\sigma_B^2 + 2[\rho(1-\rho)r_{AB}\sigma_A\sigma_B] \tag{4.16}$$

The third expression on the right-hand side is the ***covariance*** – $r_{AB}\sigma_A\sigma_B$ – weighted by the product of the proportion of time devoted to both products. Of key importance is the ***correlation coefficient***, r_{AB}. If π^e_A and π^e_B are perfectly positively correlated, i.e. move in perfect lockstep, then $r_{AB} = 1$. If there is absolutely no correlation between π^e_A and π^e_B, $r_{AB} = 0$. If there is perfect negative correlation between π^e_A and π^e_B then $r_{AB} = -1$, which says that as π^e_A rises π^e_B falls. We observed above, that Equation (4.13) was only correct if π^e_A and π^e_B moved in perfect lockstep. Thus, letting r_{AB} take the value of unity, the total variance is:

$$\begin{aligned}\text{profit variance} &= (0.6)^2.10^2 + (0.4)^2.10^2 + 2(0.6(0.4).1.10.10)\\ &= 36 + 16 + 48\\ &= 100\end{aligned} \tag{4.17}$$

As the standard deviation is the square root of the variance, we have $\sqrt{100} = 10$, which is precisely as we obtained in Equation (4.15). But now consider the situation if there is absolutely no correlation between π^e_A and π^e_B. In this situation, $r_{AB} = 0$ and the product of Equation (4.16) is:

$$= 36 + 16 + 0 = 52 \tag{4.18}$$

which yields a standard deviation of 7.2. Again, if there is a perfect negative correlation between π^e_A and π^e_B then $r_{AB} = -1$ and the production of Equation (4.17) is:

$$= 36 + 16 - 48 = 4 \tag{4.19}$$

which yields a standard deviation of 2.

The idea that diversification can both boost and stabilize a firm's cash flow is appealing, but diversification for such a purpose does not create additional value. Earlier in this chapter we outlined the BCG Growth-Share matrix, which explicitly concerned a portfolio of diversified products where the cash flow from an established product is, in principle, used to subsidize the development of new, diversified products. Thus, the BCG Growth–Share matrix would appear to suggest that diversifying can be justified in order to allow surplus cash generated by one product to be invested in the development of another product. But this argument rests essentially on market failure. That is, the firm's senior managers must be better able to appreciate a new product's potential than specialist financial markets. By funding the development of a new product internally, the firm avoids the transaction costs associated with going to the capital markets for such a purpose. This is particularly the case in emerging economies, where capital markets lack the benefit of efficient financial institutions (Khanna and Palepu, 1999).

We can take the idea of diversification and the accumulation of financial resources a little further. Once imperfect capital markets are allowed for and combined with bounded rationality, it makes sense for a firm's senior managers – particularly if the firm is large and has a degree of market power

– to try to actively influence their business environment. By retaining control over the discretionary use of its financial resources, the objective may be the longer-term maximization of economic rent by increasing the power of discretion and reducing uncertainty in the short run. In practice, apart from technology and capability, a major constraint on diversification activities is the stock market via its impact on company valuation and the cost of funds. Whether or not the retention of funds for diversification is likely to create value must rest on the scope an internal flow of investment funds creates for greater experimentation and/or flexibility, including the power to respond more effectively to new trends and 'shocks' in its business environment.

A concern to offset the prospect of slow growing or even falling demand, or to counter cyclical profits, may provide a demand side spur, but it does not take us very far in understanding how a firm might choose the market for unrelated diversification. In the next chapter, we will examine in more detail how demand side factors, particularly the growth of demand, might influence a strategy of diversification. Here, our focus is the supply side. A supply-side motivation for unrelated diversification, as we have seen, is to achieve economies of scale and particularly economies of scope. These are likely to be forthcoming if unrelated diversified products are able to share some common production facilities, e.g. buildings, and/or common resources such as accounting, HR and marketing activities. These are all in principle logical justifications for unrelated diversification, but the very notion of diversification into a new, unrelated product line appears in conflict with the neo-classical justification for the firm; namely, an organization that benefits from allowing resources to specialize. Given the widespread incidence of unrelated diversification, a modern theory of the firm needs to explain how the benefits of specialization can be applied to a broad range of unrelated products and this calls for a closer examination of the concept of specialization.

Both the neo-classical and the governance approach to the firm make use of the concept of specialization and its influence on allocative and productive efficiency. The explicit recognition by the governance approach of the concept of asset specificity would at first sight appear to have little to offer in terms of explaining unrelated diversification. By definition, such assets are highly specialized and therefore apparently not capable of being used to produce an alternative unrelated product. But if we are to understand unrelated diversification, and in the next chapter the growth of firms, we need a more subtle definition of a specialized resource. Some resources – notably human – may be highly specialized, e.g. a designer or scientist, but their value to the firm depends on their ability to undertake a range of activities in which they can employ their specialization. This approach to a specialized resource focuses on the *abilities* of a specialized resource, i.e. the uses to which the resource can be put; whereas more generally the concept of asset specificity is associated with a restricted range of *outputs* arising from the use of a resource.

These alternative interpretations of specialization lead to fundamentally different perspectives on diversification. Some assets are highly specialized in their outputs, e.g. a steel mill, and as such represent a barrier to diversification as the potential for economies of scope is severely limited. But other specialized resources – particularly tacit knowledge – can be equally efficiently used to produce a range of outputs. Such specialized resources provide a theoretical basis for diversification as the value they are potentially capable of creating by their full deployment can only be appropriated within the firm. This view of diversification is at the heart of the competence approach to the firm: an approach, as explained in Chapter 2, that can be traced back to Penrose (1959) and her ***resource-based*** theory of the firm. As Penrose pointed out: 'a firm's opportunities are necessarily widened when it develops a specialised knowledge of a technology which is not in itself very specific to any particular kind of product' (1959, p. 76). In the Penrose sense, resource specialization is entirely consistent with diversification if it is focused on an under-utilized, fungible resource. This resource-based approach not only helps to explain why firms might expand their horizontal boundaries through unrelated diversification, but it also sheds light on the rate at which firms increase their scale of production, i.e. the speed at which they grow.

The competency school has built on Penrose's insight by putting a particular focus on the heterogeneous nature of specialized resources. Although by definition internally generated specialized heterogeneous resources are firm specific, for the competency school, inside the firm, such resources or, as they have become known, capabilities, are frequently fungible. In the view of many academics, the competency school's focus on capabilities has important implications for the boundaries of a firm (see, for example, Langlois and Robertson, 1995; Foss, 2002). Teece (1982), for example, has refined Penrose's approach to directly link the expansion of a firm's horizontal boundaries by diversification to the deployment of excess, heterogeneous, fungible capabilities. Following Penrose, Teece argues that opportunities for diversification will exist because the normal process of learning creates excess fungible resources. The process of learning means that over time a firm's established routines, together with its monitoring and reward systems, become less demanding of management time, thereby releasing managerial resources without any reduction in efficiency. We observed above, when considering multi-product firms, that the transaction costs of attempting to capture the value inherent in excess knowledge resources by market exchange are likely to be prohibitively high. The essence of Teece's argument is that, when a firm's heterogeneous capabilities are in excess to its needs, particularly capabilities that are based on tacit knowledge, the most efficient way of capturing the inherent value is to make use of this excess within the firm, if necessary by diversifying into new product areas.

Figure 4.9 attempts to capture the essence of the competency approach to diversification, and in particular its greater emphasis on economies of scope rather than economies of scale. A move away from the origin along either axis reflects the extent to which the firm has exploited the economies of scale and scope available to it. A move in the north-easterly direction implies that in the current production period, without any loss of efficiency, the firm has both increased its scale of production and widened its product range, thereby achieving both economies of scale and scope in utilizing spare productive capacity. Whether in expanding its horizontal boundary a firm moves in a northerly or more easterly direction depends in part on the perceived market opportunities, but primarily on the nature of the resources available to it.

A one-product firm whose production processes involve a very high degree of physical asset specificity is unlikely to view diversification as a strategic option. Its horizontal boundaries will be determined by the extent to which the firm has exploited available returns to scale – defined here to include constant returns to scale – inherent in its production technology. The obvious examples are steel mills, railway systems and airlines. More generally, a firm's assets might be thought of as having degrees of specialization; for example, a machine might be viewed as specialized in the sense that it can only press sheet metal into shapes, but such a machine can be used for producing a range of products. Take the example of a shoe company, which typically makes a range of styles and designs, but in essence is a highly specialized company. If physical assets have this characteristic and are also lumpy or indivisible, this implies that if capacity exceeds demand the firm will have at its disposal

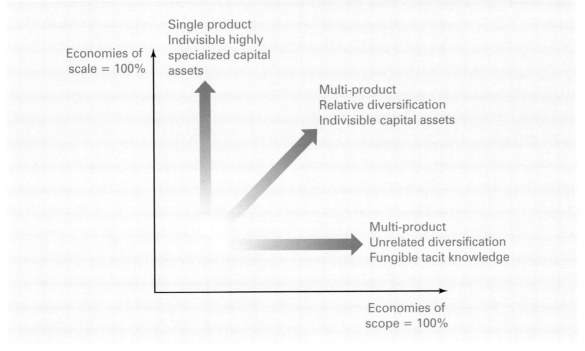

Figure 4.9: A competency approach to diversification

excess resources. As explained previously, these excess resources have the nature of a public good and can be used to produce another product without any loss of efficiency.

The foregoing would be in keeping with the neo-classical and governance approaches to the firm. As we move round in a more easterly direction in Figure 4.9, so the explanations of the competency school become of greater relevance. The key differentiator for the competency school is the emphasis it places on fungible knowledge resources. Knowledge, particularly managerial services, can be a common input to unrelated businesses and as learning increases the knowledge resources available to a firm, so the firm has at its disposal an excess of a resource that has the characteristics of a public good. As the *marginal cost* of employing surplus proprietary knowledge to the production of an unrelated product is likely to be much less than the transaction costs associated with attempting to bring about a market exchange, so the competency approach offers an explanation for unrelated diversification. In short, for the competency school, as firms carry out their normal business they will accumulate excess fungible knowledge resources. These resources are firm specific, that is heterogeneous and frequently tacit, but they have the characteristic of a public good in that they have the capability to be used across a range of unrelated products without loss of efficiency. By employing these excess knowledge resources, the firm achieves economies of scope; hence, for the competency school, excess heterogeneous capabilities can explain unrelated diversification. From a strategic perspective, a firm's horizontal boundaries will therefore be determined by the relative efficiency of acquiring knowledge, a process that is potentially enhanced and reinforced by unrelated diversification.

A Tale of Two Multiples

The trials and tribulations of Sir Ken Morrison, whose takeover of Safeway supermarket in 2003 has not turned out as planned, is a reminder that even hard-headed Yorkshire business folk are not infallible. Sir Ken's audacious acquisition catapulted the merged company to one of the top four supermarkets in the UK, with 600 stores, a staff of 135,000 and a turnover in excess of €19 billion. After a 14-month, €4.5 billion takeover battle, the 73-year-old Sir Ken walked into the west London head office of Safeway and told them that from now on things would be done his way. But within a year, the horizontal merger that was forecast to deliver profits of €900 million annually was going wrong and Sir Ken had to issue a succession of profit warnings.

Investor calls for boardroom changes, including a proper plan of succession to Sir Ken, started to grow as Morrison's financial crisis escalated. The problem, according to the City, was the lack of proper corporate governance at Morrison's – not something that was conspicuous in their enthusing about the potential merger. The final humiliation for Sir Ken was the City's demand that he appoint at least four non-executive board members to counter his dominant and acerbic style of governance. Sir Ken, for his part, viewed matters very differently. To his mind, the City's obsession with corporate governance was preventing him from getting to grips with the spiralling costs of integrating two distribution and IT systems, as well as the mammoth task of converting some 300 ex-Safeway stores. But beneath all the headlines regarding Sir Ken and his profit warnings, there remains the fact that the Morrison 'magic' has not (as yet anyway) worked for former Safeway stores. Whatever it was that Morrison's delivered in Yorkshire it was not working down South.

One major issue was the yawning gulf between the two cultures. Safeway staff quickly formed the view that if they did not have roots in the North, and preferably Yorkshire, then there was little future for them at Morrison's. And customers seem of the same view. In the first year, some 1.5 million shoppers – one in seven – deserted the company, forcing Morrison's to slash prices in response. In the end, Sir Ken had to bow to City pressure; like many before him, he discovered that it was not only Yorkshiremen who have had the charity squeezed out of them.

Boundaries, Coherence and Uncertainty

One might be forgiven, having read the previous section, for concluding that the competency school's emphasis on a firm's natural tendency to develop surplus knowledge resources provides the principled explanation for the existence of diversification, and in particular diversification into a wide range of unrelated products. But the competency approach is less impressive when it comes to explaining the limits to diversification and hence the limits to a firm's horizontal boundaries. Empiricism reveals a large degree of coherence in the way firms diversify. For example, BP has for more than 100 years been associated with all stages of the oil chain, from exploration to retailing petroleum products. Since its founding, BP has diversified into petrochemicals and other by-products of oil. More recently, it has carried out small-scale – by its standards – diversification into other sources of energy, e.g. solar power. BP has also developed its network of petrol stations so that many now incorporate mini supermarkets and, following its takeover of AMOCO, it also provides roadside assistance in the United States. But the striking aspect of BP's diversification is its coherence. All its product offerings – even the food and beverages offered in its petrol stations – can be traced to its core business of oil.

BP is not alone. Think of any large, transnational company, say Ford, IBM or Unilever, and we observe a coherence in that their constituent businesses are all, to a greater or lesser extent, related. The evidence is very strong – most companies over time add activities that relate to some aspect of their existing activities. New product lines share technological and/or market similarities with existing lines. In the words of Peters and Waterman (1982), firms appear to *stick to their knitting*. As observed by Rumelt (1974), it is the way that a firm's businesses are related that affects performance rather than the degree of diversification. It requires not just a new capability, but a superior capability to operate at a large scale in unrelated markets without sacrificing administrative coherence and hence performance.

An important rule for diversified horizontal expansion is that firms should seek to enter industries in which their heterogeneous resources will give them a competitive advantage and hence economic rents. In the 1960s, senior managers in many large corporations ignored this precept and attempted to buy their way into highly profitable industries, only to find that they did not have the resource capability to deliver a competitive advantage. Consequently, for many of these conglomerates profits declined, delivering lower returns than firms whose diversification had been constrained to products in which their heterogeneous capabilities yielded a competitive advantage (Montgomery and Wernerfelt, 1988).

The coherence of a diversified firm's evolution is the essence of corporate strategy. One explanation for observed coherence is organizational learning and knowledge. While individual human capital is a key element, its value to a firm depends on the organizational setting. It is a firm's organizational architecture that provides the setting within which individual and team learning takes place through repetition, imitation and reinforcement. Thus, the nature and depth of learning depends on the codes of communication and co-ordinated learning procedures embedded within the firm's organizational architecture.

The knowledge generated by such activity has been described as residing in organizational routines (Nelson and Winter, 1982). According to this view, organizations remember by doing; learning is reinforced through exercise and the knowledge gained can never be fully captured by attempts at codification. For Nelson and Winter, organizational architectures have two functions with regard to knowledge – namely, the ability to apply existing knowledge in the form of efficient routines, which includes knowing how and when to perform them; and also the encouragement of learning that adds to the firm's repertoire of routines. The organizational architecture must include mechanisms for the measurement and capture of performance so that efficiencies can be identified, supported and rewarded.

It follows that organizational knowledge, while not immune from external influences, will in large measure be driven by experience. On this reasoning, the nature of the diversification chosen by the firm to expand its horizontal boundaries will be path dependent. The perceived opportunities for successful diversification will to some extent be related to what it has done in the past. What is true at the operational level is also true at the strategic level. Bounded rationality and imperfect information limit the range of products that a firm's managers can seriously consider. Indeed, this is the basis of the concept of competency; namely, at any point in time there exists a set of organizational routines and capacities that provide the firm with its competitive position. It is these competencies that determine a firm's ability to compete successfully and a competence will typically be a combination of organizational and technical knowledge.

The foregoing has powerful implications for the nature and extent of a firm's diversification and hence horizontal boundaries. A firm engaged in an industry characterized by specialized assets and a fast-developing technology will have copious learning opportunities, i.e. learning is rapid within its existing industry. The outcome of a tight path dependency and rapid learning is that the firm is more likely to remain as a 'single'-product firm. A firm whose industry is rapidly developing, but whose production is based on a generic technology will have a weak or broad path dependency, but rapid learning opportunities. In this situation, a firm is likely to diversify into related products, i.e. engage in coherent diversification. A firm with a tight path dependency but whose industry is mature and offering only slow learning opportunities might sensibly consider expanding its vertical rather than horizontal boundaries. Finally, a firm in an industry whose production technology is generic and for whom learning is diffuse, i.e. slow, is most likely to engage in unrelated diversification. However, to succeed such firms must develop the strategic capability to maintain coherence across a broad range of products and markets. These perspectives are summarized in Figure 4.10.

So far we have placed great emphasis on the firm's learning and evolutionary path to help explain the nature and extent of diversification. But in expanding its horizontal boundaries by diversification the firm faces uncertainty, not only as to whether it has the necessary capability, i.e. knowledge and skills, to succeed in the new market, but also surrounding issues such as whether its organizational capabilities are sufficient to ensure that the new business can be managed without disrupting the firm's existing portfolio of products and the nature of the competitive environment for the new product. The firm's senior managers can only sensibly make a strategic decision regarding the rent-earning opportunity of a proposed diversification if it reduces the uncertainty and it can do this by seeking an optimal learning strategy. The option of sitting back and simply waiting until the uncertainties are sufficiently resolved is rarely a practical solution. Such an approach will almost certainly ensure that a competitor achieves ***first mover advantage***. At the very least, the firm will have to invest in gathering relevant information and this may involve making a small-scale entry to 'test the water' and thereby reduce the uncertainties.

The idea that firms might seek to build knowledge by engaging in small-scale diversification is very much in line with the competency perspective, which emphasizes that firms do not compete on the basis of unit costs alone. Rather, they compete on the basis of value creation. Value can be interpreted as the rent-earning capacity of the firm's resources, be they tangible or intangible. Rather than seeking efficiency

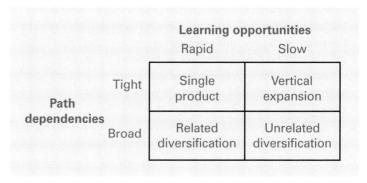

Figure 4.10: Diversification and coherence

through exploiting economies of scale and scope – important as these concepts are to the creation of value – the competency approach encourages a focus on a firm's horizontal boundaries in terms of the expansion of rent-earning capacity over the longer term (Madhok and Tallman, 1998). Hence, small-scale entry into a new market may, in time, translate into lower unit costs through scale and scope economies; but for the competency school, it is the opportunities such diversification opens up for revenue generation in the long run that are important. The learning from small-scale entry will enable a firm's senior managers to make a better informed decision as to whether its existing and developing competency is likely to give it a competitive advantage. It also provides information on the conditions of demand and the reaction of rivals that the firm is likely to face if it enters the market.

Unfortunately, in some industries – those whose technology is characterized by increasing returns to scale – a small investigating 'toe hold' may not be a feasible option. A similar conclusion might result from the conjecture that existing firms will adopt aggressive deterrence strategies if entry is attempted on any scale. Thus, in a world of uncertainty, a firm's horizontal boundaries are also influenced by the firm's ability to acquire the necessary knowledge to compete effectively in the market, as well as the desire to exploit a potential new source of economic rent before a rival. Only at a large scale of operation might a firm be in a position to exploit an opportunity to diversify. However, the large-scale entry creates an additional risk. While striving to achieve competitive advantage in its new market, the firm must also be mindful of the threat to its organizational coherence posed by large-scale entry.

The foregoing suggests that the expected behaviour of incumbents within the target market is a highly relevant consideration. We will return to these issues in Chapter 10; here, we will confine ourselves to noting that in understanding how a firm determines its horizontal boundaries, learning has a key role not only in building the scope for diversification, but also in reducing imperfect and incomplete information about the new market. A firm's boundaries are a dynamic process involving experimentation by firms as they attempt to build first knowledge that is embedded within their capabilities, and second knowledge of the pay-off potential of new products, as they seek to realize the potential of developing capabilities by diversifying.

We can represent the situation outlined above with the extensive form game set out in Figure 4.11. In deciding whether or not to diversify into a new market, a firm must first decide whether or not it has the capability, i.e. sufficient knowledge, to produce efficiently and profitably in the new market. If the firm's senior managers conclude that it lacks the necessary capabilities, the pay-off will be zero. If senior managers decide to enter the market, then they will need to invest. The pay-off consists of the present value of the net cash flow and this in turn depends

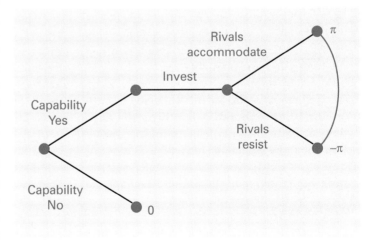

Figure 4.11: Diversification game

in large measure on the competitive conditions the firm faces. If incumbents choose to aggressively resist the new entrant, the pay-off could be negative. If the incumbents choose to accommodate the new entrant, the firm may earn an economic rent. The extent of the potential loss or gain is unknown and will lie on a continuum between the worst outcome, $-\pi$, and the best outcome, π. This range of pay-offs from the game is shown in Figure 4.11.

Boredom or Exuberance

In 1996, one of Britain's best-known industrialists, Lord Weinstock, after more than three decades as managing director of GEC, was forced by the City to step down. Under Weinstock's control, GEC had diversified from its electrical engineering base to embrace a number of diversified activities, but chiefly by the 1990s, in the area of defence. Weinstock's final years at GEC were not happy ones. He found himself increasingly out of favour with the prevailing City mood for investment in all things associated with computers and telecoms. GEC had been at the forefront of developing the silicon chip and cellular phone technology, but Weinstock had shown little interest in exploiting these commercially; a major mistake in the opinion of the City as the era of e-commerce and mobile phones dawned. In contrast to the irrational exuberance of the City, Lord Weinstock had adopted a very cautious approach. Nevertheless, the GEC that Weinstock bequeathed was not only strong in the defence industry but also had built-up a cash mountain of £2bn.

Lord Simpson, a former British Aerospace director, was appointed to succeed Lord Weinstock principally because of his knowledge of the defence industry. But Lord Simpson rapidly set about diversifying GEC into the more exciting area of telecoms. He sold GEC's defence operation for £7.7bn and armed with almost £10bn cash embarked on a telecoms spending spree. To reflect its new direction, GEC was renamed Marconi plc. The City loved it, pushing Marconi's shares to a peak of £12.50 and valuing Marconi at £35bn. Lord Simpson was feted by the City; he was an admired newcomer to the whiz world of telecoms and, most importantly, a complete contrast to his predecessor.

But Lord Simpson and the Marconi board were, like the City, suffering from irrational exuberance. The worldwide massive investment in telecoms during the 1990s had by the end of the decade resulted in chronic overcapacity. Matters were made worse by the colossal sums paid by telecoms operators for third-generation mobile phone licences. Short of cash, the telecom operators were forced to cut back on equipment expenditure, with adverse consequences for experienced telecom firms such as Nokia and Ericsson, and for newcomers such as Marconi, lacking the learning and knowledge of its rivals, disastrous consequences. Weinstock's penchant for consolidation rather than diversification may not have excited the City, but Lord Simpson's foray into telecoms turned a £2bn cash pile into a debt of £3bn and reduced the value of Marconi's share price to a few pence.

Virtual Boundaries

The above discussion of diversification has all been set in the context of a single firm. But empiricism reveals that collaboration between firms is an indispensable tool in the successful conduct of business today and this is manifested in the phenomenal increase in the number of collaborative ventures between firms in recent years (Madhok, 2000). As regards horizontal boundaries, there are increasingly alternatives to the polar extremes of large-scale specialism and unrelated diversification. Collaborations of all forms, whether strategic alliances, joint ventures, long-term contractual agreements and so on, offer new ways for firms to achieve many of the benefits of diversification, but inter-firm relationships blur the concept of the boundaries of a firm. Horizontal expansion by collaboration with another firm raises many of the issues discussed above. For example, collaborations can deliver economies of scale or scope and, in particular, the opportunity to develop and employ a capability. But they also bring with them additional demands. To be successful, all inter-firm collaborations call for the capability on the part of the firms involved in the collaboration to manage across traditional firm boundaries.

The object of every collaboration will vary; here, we are concerned with alliances or joint ventures that allow a firm to diversify, i.e. enter a new market. An alliance or joint venture offers the advantage of lower set-up costs, more flexibility and the sharing of risk. Most importantly, such collaborations provide a means of overcoming some of the constraints faced by an individual firm when contemplating diversification arising from the path-dependent nature of knowledge, the lack of appropriate capabilities and the stretching of organizational coherence. In the 1980s, a number of Japanese firms with high-quality products but lacking distribution and service networks in Europe entered into alliances with European companies to provide this capability. A collaboration in order to diversify does more than blur the participating firms' boundaries, it is also conceptually different than relying on internally generated knowledge. Diversification as part of an alliance, or a joint venture, means that the firm is no longer being co-ordinated from one centre of strategic decision making; indeed, non-integrated forms of horizontal expansion, such as alliances, create opportunities for opportunistic behaviour. By entering into an alliance or a joint venture, a firm may gain information on the partner's intangible assets which may be used to the partner's disadvantage in the future.

This raises once again the issue of coherence and organizational capability, only now the organizational architecture must be shared – a process that both demands and develops new knowledge-based capabilities for the partner firms. We have so far focused on horizontal boundaries from two perspectives: minimizing unit costs through the capture of scale and scope economies; and utilizing capabilities to capture and develop the rent-earning capacities inherent in knowledge-based intangible resources. The pursuit of an alliance or joint venture to achieve the potential to minimize unit costs inherent in economies of scale would not in itself provide sufficient justification. From a cost perspective, a horizontal collaboration is only justifiable if it results in lower unit costs than the firm could achieve on its own. For example, an alliance or joint venture between two firms to share their warehousing or distribution systems would mark an increase in efficiency if their respective market shares were such that each was constrained to operating below *MES* in warehousing or distribution. But even this does not justify a collaboration, as in principle one firm could build the larger warehouse or distribution system and sell spare capacity to a rival.

The problem here is the scope such an arrangement affords for opportunistic behaviour. If the asset is highly specific, this is a classic **hold-up** problem, and as demonstrated in the previous chapter neither firm is likely to undertake the investment. From a governance perspectives, such inter-organizational relationships bring with them transaction costs, and in particular the problem of bounded rationality. Unforeseen contingencies are bound to occur and over time the needs and aspirations of partners might change or even diverge. Whether or not this leads to opportunistic behaviour depends on loyalty and trust and both are vulnerable under conditions of fierce competition or unanticipated shocks. A decision to expand a firm's horizontal boundaries through some form of inter-organizational relationship comes down ultimately to the judgement that the inherent transaction costs are outweighed by the prospect of capturing value in the short run from economies of scope and in the longer run from new opportunities created by the new learning. Economies of scope will be the result of a collaboration that causes unit costs for one or both firms to be lower than the firms could achieve on their own within a reasonable time period. This implies that the alliance or joint venture results in the sharing of a highly specific asset or knowledge. One way of capturing the economies of scope inherent in sharing a specific asset would be for the firms to merge, but this would have the effect of reducing competition, particularly if both firms had a significant market share. Competition is itself a force for greater efficiency and consumers stand to reap the gains from competitive rivalry. Thus, in many cases the competition authorities would prevent a merger, but under the **rule of reason** might happily endorse the sharing of an otherwise inefficient use of an asset.

To the extent that collaborative ventures are means by which firms can expand their knowledge base, such inter-organizational relationships are of obvious interest to proponents of the competence-based approach to the firm. It is becoming increasingly common for firms to collaborate, rather than rely solely on internal accumulation, to achieve the knowledge and skills that will open up new opportunities for rent earning. Indeed, many academics would argue that the capability to manage external collaborative relationships is now a distinguishing feature of competitive advantage. How such collaborations are formed and developed depends on many factors, not only the history and experience of the firms and attitudes of its senior managers, but also the institutional and external business environment. Consequently, the boundaries of firms engaged in such relationships are never clear, as the processes of learning and knowledge accumulation are distributed across traditional firm boundaries and are no longer coterminous with one firm.

We noted above, that alliances and joint ventures are typical of such inter-firm relationships, but they are in fact just two – albeit the most important – of a spectrum of forms of horizontal collaborations between firms. According to Nooteboom (1999), these various inter-organizational forms of co-operation have at least two dimensions: financial integration entailing claims to profit; and organizational integration entailing decision rights. Figure 4.12 sets out the main co-operative arrangements – within and between firms – that might fairly be viewed as expanding in a virtual manner the horizontal boundaries of the firm.

It would be more correct to view horizontal collaboration as not so much a theory of the boundaries of the firm but rather a theory of firm learning and knowledge acquisition. As we have seen, we can relate a firm's horizontal boundaries to its capabilities, and within a firm's capabilities are embedded its knowledge resources. A trust-based alliance or joint venture is a vehicle for supporting the process of accumulating knowledge. The inherent repeated interaction with a partner firm will either directly or indirectly generate and transfer knowledge, from which the firm may in the future obtain

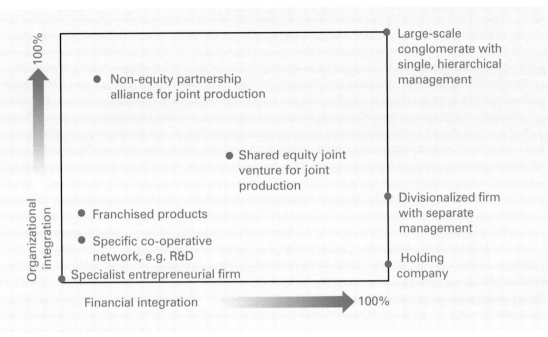

Figure 4.12: Spectrum of horizontal boundaries

the twin benefits of a lessening of uncertainty and increasing opportunities for diversification. As observed above, to the extent that a firm's boundary is a dynamic process involving experimentation, in order to learn about the potential pay-offs to new activities, collaborative ventures deserve to be considered as a significant influence.

Expansion through forms of horizontal relationships is now a widespread reality. The pursuit of technological and marketing linkages with other firms – which in many instances are located in other countries – raises a range of fundamental issues, many of which now form the agendas of research into the boundaries of the firm. One aspect of diversification by alliance is that the organizational resources employed cannot be firm specific. The competencies employed – at least initially before the relationship builds its own competencies – must have a value beyond the firm, but in accepting this we weaken the competency approach that is founded on the belief that heterogeneous resources are of greatest value to the firm that created them and are immobile.

Joined-Up Wireless

When Ericsson, Nokia and Psion decided to establish a joint venture company, Symbian, to develop and licence an operating system for use in wireless information devices, they had first to convince the European Commission that the joint venture's aim was to licence software to as many terminal manufacturers as possible and the joint venture's parents argued that they would not benefit from any preferential licensing terms.

continued

The relevant product market is the market for operating systems for wireless information devices, which was already supplied by a number of companies, including Microsoft, Sun Microsystems and Motorola. The proposed joint venture would not necessarily result in a dominant position, but at the time of the proposed joint venture in 1998, it was unclear how large the market might become for wireless information systems and whether one operating system would become the industry standard. Also relevant was the number of possible product categories downstream of the joint venture – e.g. mobile phones, wireless information devices, hand-held computers – that might be supplied.

A further consideration for the Commission was the cost of the operating system. This was judged to be only a small proportion of the overall cost of wireless information devices and hence unlikely to be capable of significantly influencing the price of the equipment in which it is used. The parties had also agreed to a confidentiality clause that forbade them from divulging confidential information to each other or the joint venture. The Commission duly decided not to oppose the joint venture and seven years on, the Symbian OS is now acknowledged as the market leader.

Concluding Thoughts

There are essentially two approaches to the determination of a firm's horizontal boundary: improved efficiency; and the creation of future competitive advantage. A single-plant, single-product firm must expand its horizontal boundary to the *MES* if it is to capture its technology-determined economies of scale. Economies of scale are the product of investment and normally the *MES* is only reached after a series of discrete investments spread over a number of production periods. Subject to the location of its markets, transport costs and external economies associated with particular locations, a firm might be more efficient by expanding its horizontal boundaries by multi-plant operations. However, as the firm expands its scale, cumulative production rises and consequently its workforce will be benefiting from learning by doing. Knowledge gained from experience of cumulative production is a proven method of reducing unit costs, thus the pursuit of increasing scale, augmented by the application of knowledge gained, provides a basis for determining the boundaries of a single product firm.

But rarely do we find firms that produce a single product. Multi-product firms are the norm, though in many cases the products are closely related, e.g. shoes, insurance policies and fuel oil. The efficiency justification for multi-product production is the achievement of economies of scope, whereby at least one of the firm's resources can be simultaneously utilized in the production of more than one product. This may be the consequence of a technology that yields joint products or a technology that involves lumpy or indivisible resources. Alternatively economies of scope may arise from the creation of spare resources as a result of the process of learning. What is important is that the resources used in production of more than one product have the nature of a public good; that is, they can be used in the production of a second product without any loss of efficiency for the first product. The existence of an economy of scope is not, however, sufficient to justify multi-product production. The link between economies of scope and multi-product production arises from the difficulties of trading spare resources. The lack of or thinness of a market gives rise to excessive transaction costs, particularly for intangible knowledge resources and hence the only way for firms to fully exploit the value of such resources is to utilize them to produce additional products.

Multi-product firms are perhaps intuitive where the products produced are closely related. But there are numerous examples where firms have diversified away from their core products to the production of a wide range of unrelated products. An explanation for this behaviour does not sit happily if solely reliant on economies of scope. A more satisfactory approach is the recognition that firms are the creators of much potentially valuable knowledge arising from the learning inherent in their activities. Learning is necessarily a dynamic process involving experimentation and reinforcement. By utilizing the firm's capabilities to enter new, unrelated product markets, the firm is broadening its learning and thereby the future opportunities for competitive advantage.

Increasingly, firms are expanding their boundaries in a virtual manner. In principle, alliances and joint ventures allow firms to jointly increase their scale of operations and to share an asset that would otherwise be under-utilized, e.g. a distribution system and both can generate economies of scope. Such inter-organizational relationships are also a means by which a firm can expand its knowledge base and hence widen its future opportunities for competitive advantage. However, by their very nature alliances and joint ventures bring with them transaction costs and in particular the problems associated with bounded rationality. When unforeseen contingencies occur there is scope for opportunistic behaviour.

Key Learning Points

- According to the neo-classical paradigm, the limits to a single-plant, single-product firm's horizontal scale boundary are determined by the onset of diseconomies of scale.
- As economies of scale are inherently a long-run concept, there is an overlap with the concept of learning-by-doing and the impact of accumulated knowledge on unit costs.
- One of the best-known contributions to strategy is the BCG matrix, which combines the twin concepts of economies of scale and learning-by-doing.
- Economies of scale are not decisive, even for a single-product firm. Multi-plant operations will be preferred if transport costs outweigh prevailing economies of scale and external economies arising from a particular location.
- Multi-product firms are more typical than single-product firms. The economic justification for multi-product firms is economies of scope.
- Economies of scope arise when a firm has a surplus of a particular resource whose services can be simultaneously employed in the production of a second product without any loss of efficiency in the production of the first product.
- In the neo-classical paradigm, any value embedded in surplus resources would be captured by trade, but in practice the transaction costs associated with market exchange, particularly if the surplus resource is proprietary or tacit knowledge, means that only the firm can capture the value by utilizing the surplus internally.
- Not so obvious is why firms diversify into unrelated products. The competency approach to the firm seems to offer the best explanation, where the pursuit of economies of scope is subservient to the desire to accumulate a stock of knowledge-based resources that widen the firm's future opportunities for competitive advantage.
- Increasingly, relationships between firms are providing an alternative means of increasing horizontal scale and in the process blurring the concept of a firm's horizontal boundaries.

Exercises

4.1 Explain why the concept of the minimum efficient scale of production is difficult to define for a multi-product firm.

4.2 What is the relationship between learning and knowledge accumulation and horizontal boundaries?

4.3 Why might economies of scope be potentially more important than economies of scale for a firm expanding its horizontal boundaries?

4.4 Distinguish between related and unrelated diversification and explain why the former might be more successful than the latter.

4.5 What limits the degree of diversification?

Problems

4.1 Suppose it costs €1,000 per month to rent a machine that can produce either uncooked or cooked meat pies. Let q_1 be the quantity of uncooked pies and q_2 the quantity of cooked pies, where the cost function is $c(q_1, q_2) = 1,000 + q_1 + 2q_2$:

(a) What are the marginal costs of producing q_1 and q_2?

(b) Calculate the measure of scale economies.

(c) Calculate the measure of economies of scope.

4.2 The following equation, using four explanatory variables, has been estimated for a manufacturer to calculate the effect of learning on unit production costs (AC):

$$lnAC = \alpha + \beta_0 lnCP + \beta_1 lnPS + \beta_2 lnCU + \beta_3 lnIP + \varepsilon$$

where CP = cumulative production
PS = plant scale
CU = capacity utilization
IP = an index of input prices
ε a random error term, with a mean = 0.

(a) Explain which of the equation's variables reflects the influence of learning and why.

(b) The data have been transformed into natural logarithms. Interpret the coefficients on the explanatory variables and consider whether they should take a value greater or less than zero.

(c) Why are the qualifications and experience of the workforce not entered as explanatory variables?

References

Alchian, A. (1950) 'Uncertainty, evolution and economic theory', *Journal of Political Economy,* vol. 58, pp. 211–221.

Baumol, W. (1972) *Economic Theory and Operations Analysis*, 3rd edn, Prentice Hall, Englewood Cliffs, NJ.

Harisson, I. (1986) 'Market adjustment and investment determination under rational expectations', *Economica*, vol. 53, pp. 505–514.

Khanna, T. and Palepu, K. (2000) 'Is group affiliation profitable in emerging markets? An analysis of diversified Indian business groups', *Journal of Finance*, vol. 55, pp. 867–891.

Koopermans, T. (1957) *Three Essays on the State of Economic Science*, McGraw-Hill, New York.

Langlois, R. and Robertson, P. (1995) *Firms Markets and Economic Change*, Routledge, London.

Levinthal, D. and March, J. (1993) 'The myopia of learning', *Strategic Management Journal*, vol. 14, pp. 95–112.

Madhok, A. (2000) 'Inter-firm collaboration: contractual and capabilities-based perspectives' in *Competence, Governance and Entrepreneurship: Advances in Economic Strategy Research*, N. Foss and V. Mahnke (eds), Oxford University Press.

Madhock, A. and Tallman, S. (1998) 'Resources, transactions and rents: managing value through interfirm collaborative relationships', *Organisational Science*, vol. 9, pp. 326–339.

Montgomery, C. and Wernerfelt, B. (1988) 'Diversification, Ricardian rents and Tobin's q', *Rand Journal of Economics*, vol. 19, pp. 623–632.

Nelson, R. and Winter, S. (1982) *An Evolutionary Theory of Economic Change*, Belknap, Cambridge, MA.

Nooteboom, B. (1999) *Inter-Firm Alliances: Analysis and Design*, Routledge, London.

Panzar, J. and Willig, R. (1981) 'Economies of scope', *American Economic Review*, vol. 71, no. 2, pp. 268–272.

Penrose, E. (1959) *The Theory of the Growth of the Firm*, Basil Blackwell, Oxford.

Peters, T. and Waterman, R. (1982) *In Search of Excellence*, Harper and Row, New York.

Rumelt, R. (1974) *Strategy, Structure and Economic Performance*, Harvard University Press, Cambridge, MA.

Scherer, F. and Ross, D. (1990) *Industrial Market Structure and Economic Performance*, Houghton Mifflin, Boston, MA.

Scherer, F., Beckenstein, A., Kaufer, E. and Murphy, R. (1975) *The Economies of Multi-plant Operations*, Harvard University Press, Cambridge, MA.

Teece, D. (1982) 'Towards an economic theory of the multi-product firm', *Journal of Economic Behaviour and Organization*, vol. 3, pp. 29–63.

Viner, J. (1932) 'Cost curves and supply curves', *Zeitschrift für National – ökonomie*, vol. 3, pp. 23–46.

CHAPTER 5

GROWTH AND ENTREPRENEURSHIP

Introduction

In her revolutionary book, *The Theory of the Growth of the Firm*, Penrose (1959) opened the black box of the firm and examined the internal processes that determine a firm's rate of growth. As set out in Chapter 2, the significance of her book was to refocus attention on the firm, not as a production function but as a coherent administrative organization, characterized by resources that are in some way specific to it. For Penrose, firms are 'flesh and blood' organizations, not points on cost curves. They consist of human and non-human resources co-ordinated within an ***organizational architecture***. A Penrosian perspective views the firm's managerial resources as being critical. It is the managers' entrepreneurial skills that provide both the inducement for the firm to expand and to place limits on the rate of expansion. To her mind, a firm is a 'managerial firm' run by a management assumed to be committed to the long-run interests of the firm. Back in 1959, stock options, golden handcuffs and the other paraphernalia of short termism had yet to materialize.

The crucial distinction between a Penrosian and neo-classical view of the firm is that, for Penrose, managers are not primarily interested in profitability *per se* but in the profitable expansion of the activities of their firms. In this paradigm, profits are treated as a necessary condition for growth and the more profits that can be retained within the firm, the better for growth. A growing firm needs additional resources including managerial resources, but in a Penrosian world, the firm's managerial resources must be largely built from within, so that the coherence of the firm's stock of firm-specific managerial knowledge is not weakened by absorbing managers from outside. It is the need for managerial learning and experience that necessarily limits the rate of expansion that can be planned and undertaken in any period of time. Thus, at any point in time, the value to the firm of its managerial resources depends on their inherited knowledge and the opportunities to apply this firm-specific management knowledge to new profitable ventures.

The notion of profitable opportunities brings two considerations into sharper focus. Firstly, managers have to make sense of the world in which their firms operate; they must have an external vision. This implies that managers must be able to comprehend and interpret the business environment so as to detect new possibilities, and anticipate mismatches between the firm's resources and future needs. Secondly, having detected external opportunities and threats, managers must also be able to align and motivate the firm's internal resources to take advantage of the expected business environment and this emphasizes the role of managers as **entrepreneurs**. To quote Penrose (1959, p. 137), 'in the long run the profitability, survival and growth of a firm does not depend so much on the efficiency with which it is able to organise the production of even a widely diversified range of products, as it does on the ability of the firm to establish one or more trade and relatively impregnable "bases" from which it can adapt and extend its operations in an uncertain, changing and competitive world.'

In this chapter, we seek to bring together the growth of firms and the entrepreneurial role of senior managers. We depart, albeit temporarily, from the single objective of profit maximizing heretofore and introduce an alternative approach whereby firms are characterized by behaviour that seeks to maximize their rate of growth. In this chapter, we will explore the behaviour of a firm's managerial resources in planning and executing the firm's expansion. In the next chapter, we will explore other aspects of senior managers' behaviour, in particular **satisficing** and **utility**-maximizing behaviour when the ownership and management of the firm are separate. Here, we focus on the growth of the firm and the twin roles of managers as co-ordinators and entrepreneurs. Within the boundaries of the firm, a management hierarchy co-ordinates and motivates the firm's resources so as to achieve the flow of services that will enable the firm to meet its objectives. But the very performance within firms of the activities that generate these services creates new knowledge and it requires entrepreneurial thinking on the part of managers to match the firm's new knowledge with opportunities emerging in the external business environment. By reading this chapter, you will:

- Appreciate why **diversification** provides the basis of growth for most firms.
- Be familiar with the constraints that limit the rate at which a firm can grow.
- Understand the role of the entrepreneur in the process of firm growth.

This chapter is divided into six sections. The first section examines a seminal step in moving from a profit to a growth objective for the firm; namely, a model of the firm whose objective is sales revenue maximization. In the second section, we turn to the issue of demand as a constraint on firm growth and as an incentive for diversification. This section introduces the notion of diversified growth and provides an explanation as to why most firms adopt this strategy in the pursuit of a faster rate of growth. The third section turns its attention to the **supply side**. It focuses on the role of managers in building the knowledge that will afford scope for growth and also for choosing the particular growth path. In the fourth section, we will examine in more detail the role of the entrepreneur. The analysis is directed at the need for a managerial skill that perceives and is prepared to act upon opportunities for growth. In the fifth section, we outline a formal model of firm growth, with the purpose of bringing out the three essential elements: the positive relationship between resource costs and growth; the necessity of matching the growth of demand to the growth of supply; and the adverse consequences of too rapid a rate of growth. The final section turns to the issue of mergers and acquisitions as a means of rapidly achieving firm growth. The advantages and disadvantages of this route to growth and the concerns of the competition authorities are discussed.

An Agenda for Growth

In the spring of 2000, EU leaders attending the Lisbon summit signed up to an ambitious economic reform programme. The underlying objective of the reform programme, quickly dubbed the Lisbon agenda, was to increase the EU's lacklustre rate of economic growth. At the heart of the Lisbon agenda was the desire to see the Community's businesses, particularly SMEs, increase their rates of growth. But five years on, the ambitious growth targets set in Lisbon have not been realized and there is little evidence that they are likely to be achieved in the near future.

The Lisbon agenda was a mixture of desired macro and micro economic reforms. At the micro level of the firm, EU leaders had set the goal of creating innovative, dynamic firms whose rate of growth would create jobs, raise incomes and improve living standards. But critics now point out that the EU does not sufficiently reward entrepreneurial success nor does it accommodate failure. Business managers are viewed as being averse to taking risk, but they in turn argue that they face obstacles to growth such as regulatory red tape.

Frustrated with the lack of progress, in early 2004 the European Commission presented an action plan for boosting entrepreneurship across the EU. It concluded that EU member states should take action in five key areas: encouraging more people to start their own businesses; offering better training; establishing a fair environment for risk taking; improving financial opportunities; and reducing the regulatory and administrative burden on SMEs. What the Commission is hoping to achieve is attitudes to enterprise and entrepreneurs that are prevalent in the United States and have been responsible for much better growth performance over recent years than the EU. Ultimately, economic growth can only come from business growth, a combination of new firm start-ups and expansion by existing firms.

Sales Maximization

The desire to increase the size of operations seems to be a very powerful one in virtually all forms of organization. A desire to increase size implies a desire for growth. Size is a static concept, but it is the product of a period of growth, which is a dynamic concept. In that growth is the objective, this implies that size in a succession of time periods is also an objective. We can therefore, by way of an introduction to understanding the behaviour of managers focused on a growth objective, examine the objective of sales revenue maximization. The seminal sales revenue-maximization model, and the most widely known, is that of Baumol (1958). His model was founded on the separation of ownership and management and a belief that managers have discretion in setting goals. In exercising this discretion, professional managers do not have the short-term objective of profit maximization, but rather they seek instead to maximize sales revenue. This objective is subject to a profit performance that shareholders find satisfactory – i.e. at least equivalent to a minimum level of profits – but in essence it comes down to a preference for larger scale.

Baumol's model focused on firms operating in ***oligopolistic markets***. He reasoned that in the short run sales revenue is a more practical goal than profit. Sales are measurable and can be used as specific targets for motivating staff. In contrast, profits are a residual and as such they are influenced by events beyond the firm's control. Moreover, it is more difficult to align a target profit with a specific team's or individual's performance. Baumol assumed that increasing the size of firm –

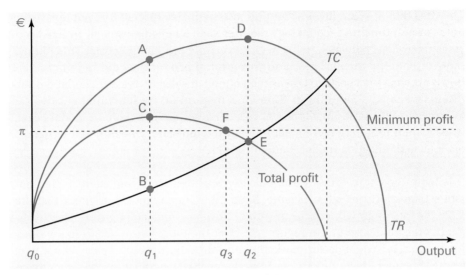

Figure 5.1: The Baumol sales-maximization model

as measured by sales revenue – would be viewed by the owners (i.e. shareholders) as a positive indicator of short-run increases in profits. Finally, he observed that increasing sales and hence the size of the firm make it easier to manage because it creates a positive environment in which employees believe the firm is successful.

Baumol's model is summarized in Figure 5.1. The figure captures the situation facing a single-product firm during one time period; that is, the short term, and consequently the shape of the total cost curve, *TC*, reflects **diminishing returns**. The firm as an **oligopolist** has a degree of market power and faces a downward-sloping **demand curve**. Hence, increasing the volume of sales in the current period necessitates a falling price, i.e. $p = f(q)$, and if unchecked this process would result at some point in prices falling to zero, yielding the shape of the total revenue curve, *TR*, shown in Figure 5.1 (see Appendix 5A for further explanation). At the level of output, q_0, revenue has grown to equal total costs. As output is increased beyond this point, both *TR* and *TC* are rising. However, given a downward-sloping demand curve beyond a certain level of sales, represented by q_2, total revenue will start to decline. Recalling that total profit equals the difference between total revenue and total cost:

$$\pi = TR - TC = pq - TC \tag{5.1}$$

the profit-maximizing manager would set output at q_1 – where the difference between revenue *A* and costs *B* is largest. Assuming **normal profits** are included in total costs, the firm is earning an **economic rent** measured by the vertical distance, Cq_1, which is equal to the vertical distance, *AB*. If instead of profit maximizing, managers were pursuing a sales revenue-maximizing objective, they would choose output q_2, which, given rising production costs, will always be to the right of q_1. At this level of output economic rent is shown as the vertical distance, Eq_2. The profit represented by the vertical distance, Eq_2, may not be sufficient to satisfy the owners of the firm, i.e. the shareholders. If they expect a profit greater than Eq_2 – say, at a minimum equal to Fq_3 – then the firm's sales revenue-maximizing managers are subject to this constraint. In order to achieve the profits expected by the shareholders, the volume of sales would need to be constrained to q_3.

The idea that at some level of output costs will rise to match revenue, as illustrated in Figure 5.1, holds even if the firm's technology requires such a large investment in fixed capital that declining average fixed costs outweigh rising average variable production costs. This follows because maximizing sales revenue (particularly for a **_differentiated product_**) would require marketing expenditure and this will cause total costs to rise as the volume of sales increases. The model set out in Figure 5.1 represents a snapshot, a point in time for a firm intent on maximizing sales revenue. Its purpose is to bring out the constraints inherent in such a policy. The Baumol model becomes more problematic if we switch to a long-run focus; indeed, Baumol later developed a dynamic version of this sales revenue-maximization model (Baumol, 1962).

It is more logical to think of the objectives of the firm's managers as being to maximize long-run rather than short-run sales revenue. Baumol's dynamic model assumes that the objective is to maximize the rate of growth of sales revenue. However, once a long-run objective is introduced, we must modify the model set out in Figure 5.1. Over the longer term, maximizing sales revenue implies that funds must be available for marketing and product development. Where would these funds come from? Ultimately they must come from the profits generated by the firm, hence, switching to a long-run sales revenue-maximization objective requires that profit in excess of the level expected by shareholders must be earned in order to fund expansion. Unlike his static model of sales revenue-maximization, where profit serves as a constraint to the desired level of output, Baumol's dynamic model views profits as the means of financing growth. This involves a second profit constraint; that is, firms set on long-run sales maximization must achieve sufficient profits to reward shareholders and leave a surplus for investing in growth.

Baumol's model has been subject to a number of criticisms. One regards the observation that large firm's are generally oligopolistic and hence the objective of maximizing sales revenue would be subject to the behaviour of rivals and possible co-operative behaviour on the part of rivals – we will return to these issues in Chapter 8. Another concern with Baumol's model is the testing of its predictions empirically. It is difficult for external observers to identify sales maximization; for example, excess advertising might be an attempt by risk-averse managers to reduce uncertainty. Much depends on the competitive environment within which the firm is operating, as in the longer term the requirement for profit performance may undermine the scope for discretionary managerial behaviour. A variation on Baumol's model is that firms attempt to maximize short-run profits subject to a minimum sales or market share constraint. Market share is viewed as important to long-run profits, hence reducing market share for the benefit of short-term profit is not viewed as rational.

Sales Forces

Audi is one of Europe's most successful car makers and this message is driven home by the company by informing the world that over the 11 years to 2005, the company increased sales every year. Audi is a global supplier, but it sells most of its cars in western Europe, which includes its home market of Germany.

A car maker has enormous fixed capital and therefore a good sales performance implies a

continued

reduced unit cost; though the effect on profits depends on the way in which the additional sales are secured. If prices are reduced to attract buyers, the net effect might be a lower profit. In Audi's case, the rise in sales was accompanied by rising profits. Nevertheless, the company thought it more appropriate to lead its press notices with the rise in sales rather than the rise in profits.

A similar approach is adopted by Audi's parent, Volkswagen. Over recent years, sales revenue growth for Volkswagen has been slow. But in reporting the company's results for 2004, Bernd Pischetsrieder, chairman of the board of management, observed that despite the weakness of sales revenue, the Volkswagen Group had delivered (not necessarily sold) 5.079 million vehicles to customers around the world, an increase on the previous year of 1.3 per cent. Herr Pischetsrieder went on to report that profits for the year had fallen €282 million below the previous year's level. But he closed on a positive note: Volkswagen were coming forward with new models and these would boost sales.

Growth and Demand

We observed in the previous chapter that diversification may improve profitability through *economies of scope*, though an alternative or perhaps more correctly, complementary, reason for diversification is to increase a firm's rate of growth. It is, however, important to analytically separate the twin concepts of diversification and growth because the two concepts are not inextricably linked. A firm may expand its *horizontal boundaries* by diversifying, but then not increase its scale further. In contrast, growth is a dynamic process by which firms build up their scale of operations over a period of years. European and US studies confirm that diversification into related or unrelated products is the main engine of company growth and this suggests that for most firms diversification allows a faster rate of growth than concentrating on a single market. Growth, as previously noted, requires investment, not only in physical assets, but also in human and organizational resources – but it also requires demand. The idea that the growth of demand is a major influence on a firm's rate and manner of growth is intuitive. Supply must balance demand and if it exceeds demand, *ceteris paribus*, the result will be a falling price.

In a *mature market*, characterized by little or no demand growth, a firm with a degree of market power, i.e. facing a downward-sloping demand curve, can achieve only a temporary growth of sales by reducing the price of its product as output expands to meet the new higher level of sales. Once the new scale of output is established, the firm reverts to a steady-state of zero growth. For a firm selling a single product, longer-term or steady-state positive growth requires growing demand, which has the effect of continuously shifting the firm's demand curve to the right. The rate at which demand for an individual firm's products increases will depend on two key factors: the rate at which overall demand within the geographic markets it serves is increasing; and the individual firm's share of sales in these markets. The growth of market demand is a function of many influences, though chiefly demographic change and rising *real incomes*. At the firm level, demand growth, i.e. market share, will be influenced – as discussed in relation to Baumol's sales revenue-maximizing model – by *endogenous* factors such as the level of demand-growth-generating expenditure, e.g. marketing. But a policy based on marketing expenditure has its limitations. As observed by Marris (2002), models of new product growth predict S-shaped paths. For a period of time the market's rate of growth may be reflected in the growth of demand for an individual firm's output, but the S-shaped life cycle for most products implies that sooner or later a product will reach the top of the S-curve as the market becomes saturated. Once the market has reached saturation, at best marketing expenditure can only serve to protect market share. Thus, if the firm's growth is to be sustained over the longer term, strategies other than a single product and high levels of expenditure on marketing must be enlisted.

From this perspective, Baumol's model of sales revenue-maximization fails as a steady-state model of growth. The idea that firms can continuously drive the location of their demand curves by spending money out of their profits when other demand-enhancing drivers are absent is erroneous. Once the growth rate of market demand has fallen to zero, at best by devoting a proportion of gross revenue to marketing, a single-product firm may be able to grow demand for a period of time by increasing its market share, though even this is conjectural as rivals' prices and marketing expenditure will have the effect of offsetting the growth of demand for an individual firm's output. Sooner or later, with few exceptions, growth-maximizing firms have to formulate diversification strategies. We can demonstrate this with the aid of Figure 5.2. The demand curve illustrated is the traditional representation of a static situation. Let us assume that the firm is a single-product, single-plant oligopolist and that the market in which the firm is established – after a period of positive growth – has now reached saturation point and growth has come to an end. Using returned profits to boost marketing expenditures could result in taking market share from competitors. This would allow a temporary period of growth but sooner or later the firm's growth rate is going to be limited by the growth of market demand.

As illustrated, our representative firm after a period of growth has increased its level of output, per period, to q_0. Given a price of p_0 and its production cost curves – including normal profits – it is earning a rent equivalent to AB on each unit sold. Operating in a saturated market, the firm may devote all or part of this rent to maintaining its market share. The figure makes clear the limited options open to the firm in this situation. If it has exhausted funds earmarked for outspending rivals on marketing, it could consider reducing the price of its product to the level represented by point C. But in the situation described, the effect of this on growth is problematic. In the short run, at point C zero rent would be earned and hence funds for marketing would be curtailed. Thus, a move to C might be accompanied by a leftward shift in the demand curve if rivals maintained their marketing expenditures. New entrants are unlikely to be an issue in the situation described, so a price reduction could not be justified on deterrence grounds. However, it might place rivals under greater pressure, so a price cut could be sufficient to maintain the position of the demand

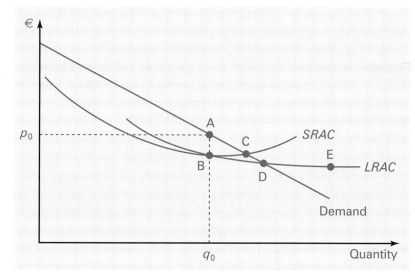

Figure 5.2: Demand and firm growth

curve. As illustrated, the firm has not achieved its **minimum efficient scale** (*MES*) represented by point E, so a price reduction to the level represented by point D might be judged appropriate if it encourages rivals to leave the market. If this is the intention of a strategic move to point E, we can better represent the situation underlying Figure 5.2 with the extensive game tree set out in Figure 5.3. To simplify matters we will assume just two firms: A and B.

The game shown in Figure 5.3 is a **zero-sum game** – apart from the pay-off to firm A if B leaves the market – and the pay-offs illustrated

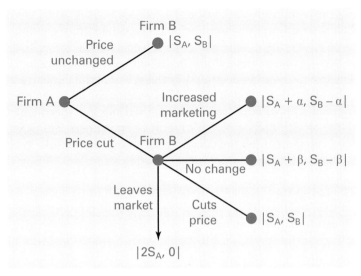

Figure 5.3: A game of market share

are in market shares. We lose none of the model's generality by assuming both firms currently have a 50 per cent market share and that Firm B is not proactive and will only make a strategic move in response to a change in firm A's behaviour. If A decides to leave its price unchanged, the pay-offs to both firms are a continued market share of 50 per cent, i.e. S_A and S_B, respectively. If now the price of A's product is reduced, B can choose from a set of options. It may decide to leave the market, in which case the pay-offs are $2S_A$ and 0, respectively. Firm B may choose to do nothing, in which case it would lose market share, yielding the pay-offs $S_A + \beta$, $S_B - \beta$, respectively where $0 < \alpha < \beta < 50$ percentage points. If B decides to increase its marketing expenditure in response, the addition to A's market share might be very small, α, and if B matches A's price cut there is no change in market shares – but both firms suffer lower profits so neither firm is indifferent between a strategy of leaving prices unchanged and cutting prices. We will return to the use of price as a deterrent strategy in Chapter 9, but the conclusion here is that neither an expenditure nor a pricing strategy can ensure continued growth for a single-product firm operating in a mature market.

Neither Figures 5.2 and 5.3 provide support for the view that a growth-maximizing firm will behave differently to a profit-maximizing firm. The logic of Figure 5.2 is that profits should be maximized in order to create the finance to fund diversification. From the dynamic perspective of growth, it is the rate of diversification that is of interest, the higher the rate of diversification, *ceteris paribus*, the faster the rate of growth of demand for a firm's products. Of course, all other factors are unlikely to remain equal as a firm diversifies. Firstly, the rate of diversification may influence the success of new products. A faster rate of diversification, given limited resources, implies less research, less development and hence a higher probability of failure. Secondly, the growth of demand for a product, at least initially, will depend not only on the price charged, by also on advertising and other types of promotion. Lower prices, advertising and promotion are all likely to reduce the firm's profit rate.

Whether or not a succession of new products can sustain a positive rate of demand growth for a firm's products over the longer term will depend on more than the prices charged and the level of marketing expenditure. Longer-term demand for a firm's product range will, as noted above, depend on a host of factors, including the behaviour of rivals, social and demographic factors. To the extent that advertising can also influence consumer needs and tastes, so in the context of diversification there will be a link between current levels of marketing expenditure and future demand growth. We will return to the issue of advertising expenditure and business strategy in Chapter 13; at this stage the point to be made is that a dynamic theory of firm growth appears to require a dynamic theory of consumer behaviour. The expansion of population translates to a simple quantitative increase in needs, but growing affluence and self-development produce qualitative change. The desire to explore and enjoy life becomes more complex and people are more willing to experiment with new demands. Most importantly, rising wealth and confidence result in consumers taking action to realise their demands, e.g. baby foods prepared from organically grown crops and meat. To the extent that consumers are successful, so they widen the **product space**, creating scope for business diversification.

The foregoing provides an explanation from the 'demand side' as to why diversification into multi-product businesses is the preferred model of growth for most firms. But placing the emphasis on a demand-side pull for diversification sits uncomfortably with the most elementary 'fact' about corporate growth thrown up by econometric studies on firms of all sizes; namely, the evidence from econometric studies showing that generally the growth of firms follows a **random walk** (Geroski, 2000). This can be illustrated by letting S represent a firm's size, i.e. sales revenue, at **constant prices**. The size of the firm in year t can then be denoted as S_t and its annual rate of growth is captured with the equation:

$$\Delta lnS_t = lnS_t - lnS_{t-1} = \varepsilon_t \tag{5.2}$$

where the prefix ln shows that the data have been transformed into natural logarithms and hence Δln is the annual growth. The variable ε_t is assumed to be a normally distributed random variable with a mean of zero and a fixed variance. Equation (5.2) can be rewritten to give:

$$lnS_t = lnS_{t-1} + \varepsilon_t \tag{5.3}$$

As Equation (5.3) makes clear, the size of the firm in period t depends solely on the size and sign of a succession of random 'shocks' represented by the random variable. This does not imply that growth is purely a matter of 'chance' or 'luck'. Rather, studies that suggest Equation (5.3) is a good representation of individual firm growth point to the fact that firms typically make large but infrequent changes in their scale of operations, e.g. investment in increased sales takes place in infrequent large lumps, rather than continuous smaller additions to the firm's capital stock. Unfortunately, Equation (5.3) does not result in long-term growth. As the variable ε is normally distributed with a mean of zero, the size of the firm, according to Equation (5.3), will meander up and down but never grow persistently for a significant period of time. To capture the impact of random shocks whilst allowing the size of the firm to increase over time, we need an equation of the form:

$$lnS_t = ln\alpha + lnS_{t-1} + \varepsilon_t \tag{5.4}$$

where $\alpha > 1$ serves to provide the random walk with an upward drift. What Equation (5.4) says is that random shocks have a permanent effect on the size of the firm, which means that the growth of a firm cannot be thought of as following an exponential trend, albeit with trend-reverting stochastic fluctuations. But Equation (5.4) is consistent with a pattern of sales that over a sufficient period of time has a high probability of resulting in larger-scale businesses.

The picture painted by Equation (5.4) is hardly consistent with firms smoothly diversifying to faster growing markets as growth in their existing markets slows. Nor is it consistent with life cycle theories of the firm, whereby firms go through a growth stage before declining. It suggests very differing behaviour; for example the existence of large adjustment costs causing firms to wait until the costs of diversifying are offset by the slowing growth of profits. In fact, empiricism supports the belief that firms typically make infrequent, but large, discrete changes in their operations, e.g. discrete large-scale investments rather than continuous small-scale investments (see, for example, Caballero *et al.*, 1995). It is possible that **exogenous** factors are in part responsible for the stochastic nature of the growth paths of firms, but the weight of academic study puts the emphasis on endogenous factors. Two conclusions follow: in a modern, growing economy, the pursuit of growth is the norm; and it is not possible to understand firm growth without paying attention to the supply side.

Out with the Old

It would appear that consumers in the European Union are infatuated with digital products, and Spain is no exception. Between 2003 and 2005, the demand for audio products declined slightly as demand for PCs and associated multimedia attachments increased. As demand for cassette and video players declines, demand for home 'cinemas' with DVD and flat screen technology has been soaring, as has demand for digital cameras and camcorders. In fact, the speed at which digital technology is rapidly replacing traditional analogue technology has taken Spanish retailers by surprise. The main television channels, such as RTVE, Antena 3, Tele 5 and Canalt, did not begin broadcasting digitally until 2002 and digital television and decoders did not come on the market until 2003.

Digital television involves a shift on the part of the consumer from passive to interactive viewing. It would be true to say that the Spanish are some way behind their northern European counterparts in this respect. But the same cannot be said of the Spanish demand for camcorders and digital cameras, where both the volume and value of demand continues to rise steadily. To say the Spanish are addicted to digital cameras would be an understatement. Sales almost doubled in 2004, aided by a general reduction in prices and a growing number of households with PCs. The digital revolution is still in its early stages, but so rapid are developments that not only is demand for analogue systems declining, but some early digital systems are now suffering falling demand as better systems, e.g. miniDVD camcorders, are coming on stream.

Growth of Supply

This brings us right back to Penrose's concept of the firm as an administrative organization capable of creating or recruiting new resources for expansion. This view of the firm as a growing entity can be traced back to Adam Smith's (1776) familiar account of the pin factory, chosen, as he explains, to reveal the power of the **division of labour**. But for Smith, this power was not so much the efficiency of co-ordinating specialist skills, but rather the power arising from the organization of specialisms to generate knowledge that would yield ways of producing existing products and new products. Smith and other classical economists, including Karl Marx, focused mainly on resources and wealth creation. It was their successors, the neo-classical school, that focused instead on co-ordination, the efficient allocation of resources and equilibrium.

For the neo-classical school, rational firms – or rather their senior managers – seek primarily to be efficient, which means reducing waste by fully utilizing in their most productive uses all the resources over which the firm has property rights. In such a world, unfettered competition and the pursuit of efficiency ultimately drive firms to the bottom of their U-shaped, short-run average cost curves. Growth of output was merely a matter of arriving at the equilibrium position of minimum cost. As the shapes of short-run cost curves and their envelope long-run cost curves were deemed to be set by factors beyond the control of the firm – technology and factor markets – the neo-classical school had nothing more to say about firm growth. The ability of firms with market power to choose their optimum size was only recognized in the special case of monopoly and for neo-classical economists this power could not pertain in the long run. Of course, the neo-classical model has been augmented and now allows for economies of scope, but the main criticism of the neo-classical approach is that it completely ignores internal organizational factors and the role of the firm's internally generated resources, which in the case of growth are more fundamental than economies of scale.

The gulf between Smith and the neo-classical school is a gulf between economic growth and equilibrium theory, respectively. Economic growth involves new products, new production processes and new industries. It is, at heart, a process of developing and applying new knowledge that can in the extreme result, in the much quoted words of Schumpeter (1942), in '**creative destruction**' as the new drives out the old. Diversified growth is a process that is necessarily disruptive of a firm's existing patterns of production, routines and organizational structure. No analysis of the forces making for equilibrium will shed much light on processes that are more concerned with movements away from an existing equilibrium – in essence, departures from what went before and installation of the new. The neo-classical school's penchant for comparing equilibrium position is not a method of analysis that helps an understanding of firms that are constantly in a state of disequilibrium; that is, involved in a dynamic process of growth.

For both Penrose and Schumpeter, the process of growth comes 'from within', from the firm's ability to perceive and act upon new possibilities: a failure to do so will sooner or later result in its own decline and destruction. A growing firm is therefore an organization that brings forth a process of resource accumulation that yields services that are surplus to the needs of current operations. Although Schumpeter's analysis of the firm came first, arguably it was Penrose's conceptualization of the firm as a unique collection of resources that marked a significant turning point in the theory of the growth of the firm. As Penrose (1959, p. 31) put it, echoing Adam Smith, 'a theory of the growth of the firm is essentially an examination of the changing productive opportunities of firms'. She defined a firm's productive opportunities as those possibilities for deploying resources that its managers perceive and are willing and able to act upon. But growth is accompanied by an increasing stock of accumulated resources and this taxes the ability of the firm's organizational architecture to maintain coherence. Opportunities are only of value to the firm if their pursuit does not threaten coherence; hence, the firm's set of possibilities will expand at a faster rate than the firm's realistic productive opportunities. The size of the disparity between its growth possibilities and the productive opportunities it chooses to exploit will depend on the organizational architecture; namely, its organizational ability to coherently deploy and develop new resources.

We argued in Chapter 2, that a firm's organizational architecture lies at the heart of the **governance approach** to the firm. However, the transaction cost approach is weak when it comes to explaining why diversification is a popular method of expanding a firm's horizontal boundaries. It tells us why it makes economic sense for a firm to adjust its boundaries in order to better utilize resources that are specific to a particular use and cannot be easily traded, but it sheds little light on the interaction between a firm's internally generated resources and the incentive to grow by diversification. This is not to overlook the fact that organizational governance is critical to the maintenance of **organizational coherence** in a growing firm. A firm whose organizational architecture is not adequately providing the means and motivation for growth will sooner or later cause a strategy of growth to fail.

In principle, the larger the firm, the greater its access to resources, and, *ceteris paribus*, the greater the range of possible growth paths, but as noted above, the larger the choice, the greater the need to ensure choices will maintain coherence. As acknowledged by Penrose, with increasing size the managerial function and the basic 'administrative structure' – essentially the firm's organizational architecture – must itself undergo re-organization to enable it to deal with increasing growth. A firm's organizational architecture is very influential in driving the use and productivity of resources, but before the firm's organizational architecture can carry out its function of marshalling and co-ordinating the resources under its control, a decision has to be made as to the direction in which the firm is going to expand. This is the difference between sustaining a growth path and determining the path in the first place.

We can safely assume that most, if not all of the firm's productive resources have alternative uses. How, then, does the firm choose from the set of 'productive opportunities' that the firm's accumulated knowledge makes possible? One way to attempt to answer this question is to resort to the **competency approach** to the firm – the approach whose antecedents reside in Penrose's resource-based approach to the firm. According to this school of thought, the growth of a firm is a process of developing, accumulating and productively utilizing the firm's internally generated resources. To the extent that some of the services of these accumulating resources are not needed or cannot be used to support current operations, they become available for adding to, and more importantly shaping, the set of possible directions for future diversified growth. A sub-group of these firm-specific specialist resources, which are commonly described as **capabilities** or **core competencies**, are perceived by the firm's senior managers as offering competitive advantage and it is their willingness to employ these resources that provides the motive for diversified growth.

Core competencies fall into a number of categories: superior technological know-how; organizational excellence; exceptional human resource management; longer-term trusting relationships with external parties; and financial expertise. To the extent that such resources are heterogeneous and cannot easily be copied by competitors, so they become sources of competitive advantage for the firm. By definition, if a firm's core competencies are capable of being simultaneously utilized in a variety of markets they are a source of economies of scope. The competency approach views growth as arising from the firm's ability to take advantage of new productive opportunities by deploying its core competencies, for which transaction costs impede a market exchange. Thus core competencies impart an important incentive for growth because these competencies are rarely fully utilized – they are continually expanding through the acquisition of new skills, information and knowledge – hence, their deployment in new projects offers the prospect of increased profits.

A firm's core competencies, particularly those embodied in the experience and skills of its workforce, are to varying degrees founded upon cumulative knowledge that is unique to the individual firm and as a result potentially highly valuable assets. To the extent that these valuable assets cannot be fully utilized to support current operations, or have the nature of a **public good**, so they are available for adding to and shaping the set of possibilities for future growth faced by the firm. One of the firm's internally generated resources with the potential to be a core competency is a firm's organizational architecture. This resource or capability plays a key role because it is only to the extent that the architecture maintains a coherent organizational structure within which diverse activities are co-ordinated in ways that reinforce complementarity and goal congruence that diversified growth can continue. In other words, part of the resource implications of growth is the ability of the firm to learn how to adjust its own organizational architecture to accommodate the direction of growth. No single firm can provide a context that sufficiently enables, motivates and stimulates the perception of more than a tiny fraction of the productive possibilities that are always within reach (Moran and Ghoshal, 1999). In other words, each firm, or rather its senior managers, favours a unique sub-set of growth opportunities. This sub-set will in part be determined by what the firm's management's perception of what its capabilities suggest it can do, but also – according to the entrepreneurial flair of its senior managers – what they believe it is possible to do.

The fact that a firm's capabilities as repositories of tacit knowledge are unique implies that firms are likely to grow idiosyncratically as they use and develop their knowledge base. This notion of firms possessing capabilities that are being constantly modified over time is very much in accord with the **evolutionary approach** to the firm (Nelson and Winter, 1982) and it means that each firm's development is likely to be path dependent. The notion of path dependencies recognizes that history matters. A firm's previous experience and its repertoire of routines constrains its future direction. Opportunities for successful diversified growth will tend to be close to previous activities in order to preserve complementarities and coherence. Entering a new market calls for new learning, which in turn places demands on the cognitive limits of managers, particularly if the firm is operating in dynamically competitive markets. This is because market evolution can be complex, making the capture of performance feedback for learning lengthy and costly.

To the extent that the pursuit of organizational coherence or 'what the firm can do' dominates management thinking, so growth will occur through diversification into areas that are related in some way to the firm's existing stock of knowledge. Such growth is likely to exploit complementarities that are inherent in the firm's existing stock of firm-specific heterogeneous resources. But the idea of long-term growth and the constraints of path dependencies and organizational coherence do not sit easily together. Sooner or later continued growth is likely to involve replacing some existing capabilities with new capabilities; that is, creative destruction within the firm is necessary to open up new opportunities for diversified growth. This is more a Schumpeterian than a Penrosian approach to the growth of a firm. For Schumpeter, diversified growth involves disturbing an existing equilibrium in order to bring about new productive and organizational capabilities (Langlois, 1995). From this perspective, 'what it might be possible to do' dominates management thinking on growth in order to create new knowledge, new resources and new complementarities.

Rumelt's (1974) finding that the way in which a firm's activities are related affects performance more than the degree of diversification and Teece *et al.*'s (1994) finding that a high degree of coherence is important for firm growth provide support for the view that diversified growth will be constrained to exploit existing complementarities in seeking growth opportunities. But this overlooks the entrepreneurial role of managers and the desire to develop new capabilities. For Schumpeter (1947), entrepreneurs 'get things done' and they have the ability to 'cope with the resistance and difficulties which action always meets when outside the rules of established practice' (p. 106). It is the entrepreneurial capability to change existing practices and routines that disturbs existing organizational coherence in a process of migrating to new capabilities and hence a wider set of diversified growth opportunities. From this perspective, as the firm will more rapidly add to its stock of cu-

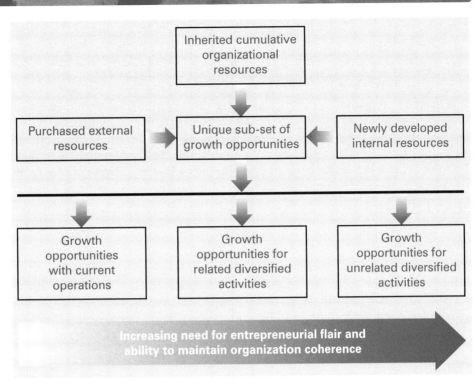

Figure 5.4: Diversified growth and organizational coherence

mulative capabilities if it pursues opportunities it believes it can learn to master, so it more rapidly increases its growth opportunities through the enlargement of its core competencies. However, this set of competencies cannot grow indefinitely. Because diversified growth by definition involves some restructuring of the firm's control and co-ordinating mechanisms, at some point the firm's organizational coherence will start to diminish. Increasing diversity beyond this point is likely to have an increasingly negative impact on performance. This approach to diversified growth is summarized in Figure 5.4.

The central role that the competency approach assumes in explaining the use and development of a firm's internally generated knowledge-based resources does not completely displace the governance approach. It is only to the extent that the firm's senior managers perceive new productive opportunities and are motivated to achieve them that the firm will grow. As is made clear in Figure 5.4, the more diversified the growth path, the more important the entrepreneurial role of senior managers in perceiving and seizing productive opportunities. But Figure 5.4 also makes clear that the more diversified the growth path, the greater the 'disturbance' created by the changes that must be made to the firm's existing systems and routines and this also demonstrates the important role of managers in maintaining coherence. In short, the more reliant the firm on diversified growth, the more important the traditional role of its organizational architecture in controlling, measuring and motivating the process of growth.

Unless the firm is able to adjust its organizational architecture to maintain coherence in the face of resource-based expanding possibilities, it cannot continue to grow, particularly if the accumulated resources make possible a widely diverse range of productive opportunities. Put simply, as large firms continue to grow the likelihood of sustaining the rate of growth lies less with the number of possibilities within the firm's reach and more with the firm's ability to maintain coherence. The more

Schumpeterian the productive opportunity, i.e. the more disruptive of existing complementarities, the greater the importance of the firm's organizational capability to change and adapt. The inability of a firm to undergo the organizational changes necessary to accommodate diversified growth can explain why some firms, after periods of growth, start to falter and eventually decline.

It is the entrepreneurial role of managers that comes to the fore when considering growth. According to Schumpeter, the entrepreneurial role of managers is that of **innovation** (as opposed to **invention**). Within the firm, entrepreneurs negotiate and manoeuvre to obtain command over the resources that will allow them to fulfil their ideas. To do this, they cultivate networks to increase their bargaining information and persuasiveness. In some instances 'getting things done' may involve the creation of new, knowledge-generating, organizational structures to redeploy the firm's existing resources. Thus, by moulding and shaping the firm's organizational architecture, entrepreneurial managers facilitate the accumulation of new resources, their co-ordination with existing resources, and create the basis upon which the firm grows.

This perspective on the growth of the firm elevates internal competition for the firm's resources as an influence on growth. To the extent that at any point in time a firm's productive resources have a range of alternative growth paths, so the greater the competition for resources within the firm and the greater the need for discipline to be exercised by managers over the firm's chosen growth paths. Competition for scarce, internally accumulated resources puts pressure on the firm's senior managers

Microsoft's Core Competency

Microsoft is the world's leading supplier of personal computer operating systems. It is estimated that some 80 per cent of the world's personal computers use Microsoft Windows to run Word, Excel and PowerPoint programs. Yet, many experts appear to question whether programming really is Microsoft's core competency. Many of its programs contain bugs and rival programs frequently contain better features and facilities.

Despite these shortcomings, Microsoft has come to dominate the market for PC software. The reason is that Microsoft's strength lies in its marketing and distribution competencies. It came from nowhere to rapidly dominate the market, not because of its MS-DOS operating system – in the event, this was purchased from a rival programming company – but because of Bill Gates' ability to negotiate a very favourable contract with IBM, who at the time was reeling from its lack of interest in the PC market and consequently was desperate to quickly catch up. IBM soon came to dominate the PC market, with the result that every IBM-compatible PC included a pre-installed MS-DOS, and later Windows, operating system. The existence of a Microsoft operating system greatly increased the likelihood that users would choose Microsoft products when seeking word-processing, spreadsheets and graphical programs. The identification of Microsoft with a range of PC software programs provided a competence that could be applied in a variety of markets – e.g. home or office use – and which other software manufacturers have, to date, found impossible to replicate.

to ensure that the firm's resources migrate to their most productive opportunities. It follows that the more resources available to the firm, the greater the set of opportunities at any time. Put another way, a small firm is more likely to be constrained in its growth opportunities than a large firm. This is not to say that small firms cannot grow as fast as large firms – indeed, the reverse is generally the case – rather that the opportunities for diversified growth are more limited in small firms. However, growth results in a firm accumulating an ever-increasing stock of resources, which in turn demands greater organizational resources if the firm's resources are to be co-ordinated efficiently and effectively.

A firm's internally generated resources, which will include unique capabilities, do not appear on the firm's balance sheet. The only way that the firm can capture their value is through use. Moreover, the scope to capture the value generated by the firm's internally accumulated knowledge resource base will develop idiosyncratically over time, depending on the firm's experiences and investments in its organizational structure. Thus, the ability to effectively exploit opportunities for growth through diversification will vary from firm to firm. This means each firm's growth will be path dependent and as firms accumulate a stock of heterogeneous knowledge-based resources, so this stock will determine the paths along which to push for expansion. From this perspective, no two firms' growth opportunities are the same; indeed, heterogeneity in resources both provides opportunities and places constraints on the opportunities for growth available to individual firms.

Entrepreneurship

In the previous section, we repeatedly referred to the importance of entrepreneurial flair to the process of diversified growth. It is now appropriate to delve a little more deeply into what role entrepreneurial skills play in management, and in particular in diversified growth. In fact, the word entrepreneur is not tightly defined and has a wide range of interpretations. Certain individuals, such as Richard Branson, Stelios Haji-Ioannou and Philip Green might, by common consent, be described as entrepreneurs, but the fact that these individuals have by their energy and drive created large-scale, successful businesses is not the defining definition of an entrepreneur. These attributes are important, but it is the search for, and discovery of, new knowledge that separates the entrepreneur from the workaholic or the manager who achieves 'efficiency' via a regime of brutality. Entrepreneurs, or rather entrepreneurial activity, is a learning process in the sense that there are incentives for individuals (and organizations) to discover new and better ways of doing things. Entrepreneurs use the knowledge they have acquired to co-ordinate and motivate resources over which they have **property rights** in order to capture the rewards inherent in the creation of new products and/or new processes.

The entrepreneur has existed as a factor of production since Adam Smith, but as the neo-classical school placed the emphasis on analysing equilibrium, or steady-state outcomes, its members naturally devoted less attention to the process of 'getting there' and the distinctive contribution of the entrepreneur. The idea of the entrepreneur as a person who perceives productive opportunities, and hence seeks to benefit from the knowledge, is implicitly a rejection of the neo-classical assumption of perfect knowledge. Within the neo-classical framework of competitive equilibrium, no opportunity remains unexploited. It is, to be fair, a caricature to label the neo-classical school as continuing to assume that the acquisition of knowledge is a costless process. As early as the 1920s, Frank Knight (1921) was writing about behaviour in an uncertain world and pointing out that in such a world: 'the actual execution of activity, becomes in a real sense a secondary part of life; the primary problem or function is deciding what to do and how to do it' (p. 268). A little later, Stigler's (1961) paper on the economics of information squarely positioned knowledge as a valuable good and in the process opened the way for the study of search behaviour and transaction costs.

There is, however, a major distinction between the neo-classical school and Schumpeter on the role of the entrepreneur. The former views the entrepreneur as a processor of information and a generator of new knowledge in an uncertain world, who acts as a catalyst for change by a desire to apply new knowledge and a willingness to take risks, together with the energy and drive to get things done. It is possible to view this entrepreneur as the progenitor of incremental change, someone who can spot advantages in a given situation, who creates a disturbance followed by a new path to equilibrium. In contrast, Schumpeter's entrepreneur is a disruptive, destabilizing force destroying

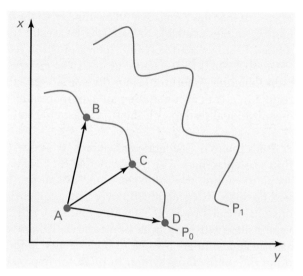

Figure 5.5: Entrepreneurs and knowledge

what has gone before and replacing it with completely new products or processes. Schumpeter's entrepreneur is also a processor of information and a generator of new knowledge, but this knowledge is used to promote radical innovation. A flavour of the difference between the two approaches is captured in Figure 5.5.

Confined to two dimensions, the production possibility curve p_0 shows the outer bounds of the possible attainable outcomes of products x and y. If point A represents a firm's position in the current time period, given prevailing knowledge, a north-easterly movement over time along one of the possible growth paths B, C and D is desired. The neo-classical entrepreneur seeks to discover how this might be achieved. Having detected an opportunity, and the means of achieving it, the entrepreneur will then marshal and co-ordinate the firm's resources to achieve the desired point on the production possibility curve. In contrast, Schumpeter's entrepreneur is engaged in shifting the production possibility curve to, say, p_1. This requires more fundamental innovation that has the effect of redefining the possible attainable outcomes. Schumpeter's entrepreneur may then determine the growth path or it may be left to others. The essential difference between these two approaches is that the former finds new uses for *existing* knowledge and the latter uses *new* knowledge. For example, in terms of PC operating systems, or more correctly, a graphical user interface, Steve Jobs was the Schumpeterian entrepreneur and Bill Gates the 'neo-classical' entrepreneur.

Having worked through the chapter to this point, the reader may be forgiven for believing we are only concerned with entrepreneurial activity in large firms. And it is the case that competition for internally generated resources, responsive organizational architectures and diversification are issues more likely to be encountered in larger-scale enterprises. Nevertheless, entrepreneurial activity is more generally associated with smaller firms. Indeed, EU member states now view the owner-managers of smaller enterprises as the primary generators of new business knowledge. Following publication of the 2000 Lisbon strategy (European Commission, 2004), it is now a commonly held view within the EU that achieving its objective of creating 'the most dynamic and competitive knowledge-based economy in the world' (p. 6), depends heavily on the entrepreneurial flair of the owner-managers of small and medium-sized enterprises (SMEs). This 'official' view of entrepreneurs is in the spirit of someone who possesses the characteristics of inquisitiveness, a willingness to learn, energy and drive and is prepared to take risks to get things done. The owner-manager's incentive is 'own advantage', but, as recognized in the Lisbon strategy, they are a breeding ground for business ideas that, if successful, will sooner or later spread and become and a key source of job creation.

It is clear that cultivating an entrepreneurial culture and fostering entrepreneurial attitudes has moved high on the EU agenda and the focus for much of this attention are SMEs. Lundström and Stevenson (2001) describe the EU's new policy direction as being: 'aimed at the pre-start, the start-up and post start-up phases of the entrepreneurial process' (p. 5). The route to growth for a start-up firm is shaped by the owner-manager's vision and ambition, an ability to secure the required resources and skills in co-ordinating and motivating productive resources. The concept of growth for a new start-up needs some explanation. Normally, the statistic used to measure the growth of firms is the rate of increase in sales measured in real terms. This statistic is fine for an enterprise that finds its sales growing soon after start-up, generating revenue and hence funding the building of internal resources. Other start-ups have a longer lead time before productive activity generates products for sale. These firms grow at first in terms of employment and assets and for these firms growth can only be measured in terms of resources. Biotechnology firms are a classic example; they can grow to a considerable size before their new knowledge is in a form that can be offered to the market. Firms that are in the process of growing, but have yet to generate revenues, are frequently referred to as **ventures**. Ventures have investors, while firms have revenues.

It is perhaps obvious that growth before revenues makes life difficult for a new venture and the faster the growth, the greater the potential organizational problems. Traditionally, it has been hard for start-ups to attract sufficient capital, though as regards ICT enterprises, the situation changed somewhat in the 1990s with the internet boom. Such firms were viewed as the vanguard of a longer-term paradigm change for business and society. When a longer time horizon is adopted, short-term profitability is likely to be viewed as an inadequate strategy. Caught up in the excitement of being in at the start of a **Kondratiev wave**, such firms attracted massive venture capital funding or experienced inflated share prices after an early stock market launch. The longer the time horizon, the greater the apparent justification for sacrificing rapid profitability for the costs of investing in the technology and customer base of the enterprise.

In many respects, a new growth path for an existing firm – a new growth venture – raises similar problems to those arising in a start-up venture. The key differences are that when an established firm incubates a new venture it may be managed by an entrepreneurial team rather than an individual, and generally there will almost certainly be more resources at its disposal. Within an established, successful firm a new venture is to some extent shielded from the risks associated with the preparatory and mobilization phases and it are therefore less vulnerable to 'infant mortality' (Garnsey, 2002). An interesting aspect of the launch of a new, diversified venture from within an existing firm is how the individual entrepreneur, or an entrepreneurial group, overcomes the tendency of organizations to favour the 'conventional', i.e. the adoption of the same behaviours and mindset. Conventional behaviour is approved of because it encourages stability and, hence, less uncertainty. In this environment, an individual with a different perspective, who may see opportunities of significance where others see none, is probably more likely to be suppressed and the opportunities missed. The danger for all firms, particularly those with a good track record, is that the *status quo* is entrenched. This does not conflict with the addition to knowledge arising from **learning by doing**, but this type of learning takes time and is linear.

The difficulty with this view of the firm, or rather its management hierarchy, is that unless individuals deviate from the accepted conventions in an attempt to rapidly accumulate new knowledge, it is not obvious what prompts endogenous change. One answer, provided by Choi (1999), is that opportunities neglected by conventionalists accumulate over time as individuals simultaneously (but unsystematically) learn from their daily experiences. That is, the gap between existing activities and

Biotechnology

In 1953, Francis Crick and James Watson discovered the double helix structure of DNA and set in train a series of advances in molecular biology out of which the modern biotechnology industry has been born. Two further developments in the 1970s, the first was the development of the recombinant DNA technique by Herbert Boyer, and the second, by Cesar Milstein and Georges Koehler, was discovering how to fuse two cells to form a clone, created a commercial opportunity.

But the established pharmaceutical companies were slow to recognize the commercial possibilities. Their expertise lay in synthetic organic chemistry and they saw no need to switch away from a technology that was delivering a steady stream of new drugs and high profits. It was left to scientific entrepreneurs to launch the new industry. One of the first was Genetech, which was founded by Herbert Boyer in partnership with the financial expertise of Robert Swanson. Founded in 1976, it focused in its early years on the development of proteins such as insulin and in 1978 signed a contract with Eli Lilly to supply a genetically engineered insulin. That marked the start of a commercial biotech industry.

Genetech's example was followed by several other firms all founded by scientists. Yet the growth of biotechnological firms has been uneven and punctuated by disappointments. The development of new drugs based on genetic engineering proved to be slower and more uncertain than protagonists had imagined. One of the main challenges facing the smaller-scale biotech start-ups was capital — not so much the cost of developing a genetic innovation, but rather their lack of skill and the enormous financial resources needed to bring new drugs to market.

What began to emerge in the 1980s was a division of labour between 'Big Pharma' and the new biotechnology firms. Increasingly, the newcomers chose to become suppliers of platform technologies or 'toolkits' to the pharmaceutical companies. Others continued to focus on developing innovative products but instead of taking the drug all the way to market they formed partnerships with pharmaceutical firms at the pre-clinical testing stage.

An example of the importance for biotech start-ups of building relationships with other industry players is provided by Amgen, who, after pursuing several technical paths with little success, hit upon a treatment for anaemia known as recombinant human erythropoietin. A partnership deal with Kirin, a Japanese brewer who was looking for a way to enter the pharmaceutical industry, provided much needed funds at a critical time. Once patented in 1989, Amgen's new treatment for anaemia, under the brand name Epogen, became the first blockbuster drug to emerge from biotechnology.

potential productive opportunities is growing over time. As the gap becomes bigger it becomes easier for the conventionalists to discover productivity opportunities. Put another way, the probability of an entrepreneur perceiving a productive opportunity that the management hierarchy can also be brought to appreciate increases with time. As the vision of what might be possible takes hold, the entrepreneur and the firm's senior managers enter a new period of learning, spanning the planning of the new venture through to the point at which the resources are in place to realize the productive opportunity. During this preparatory period, the entrepreneur, or entrepreneurial group, must discover how to bring the perceived opportunity to fruition. Necessary resources must be mobilized and motivated and the greater the departure from the firm's existing operations, the greater the learning involved in the new, diverse venture. It is during the preparatory stage that entrepreneurial energy and appropriate organizational support become important, driving the firm rapidly to be in a position to start production and generate revenue from the planned growth path of activity. Once the production stage commences, the entrepreneur (or group) enter yet another stage of learning: accumulating the knowledge to sustain viable production as the scale of operation increases. These processes are sequential; problems posed at each stage must be solved before moving onto the next stage.

Once the new venture has developed sufficient internal resources to provide a basis for viability, the danger is that the impetus to continue growing will weaken. This is certainly an issue for new start-ups. Empiricism shows that stability following early growth is a common pattern (Storey, 1994), as opportunities for continued growth are foregone as a desire to conserve outweighs the uncertainties associated with continued growth. Within established firms, resources essential to continued growth have to be secured and this means competing with the resource demands of others. The rate at which new resources can be mobilized may well be insufficient to maintain the impetus of growth. The cash flow crisis so common among growing SMEs is a classic example of this constraint (Garnsey, 1998). Once secured, the new resources must be integrated with existing resources to achieve efficient co-ordination and **goal congruence**. The logic for established firms or ventures that wish to continue exploiting growth opportunities is that their management hierarchy must be imbued with a true entrepreneurial bias. Echoing Nelson and Winter (1982), an entrepreneurial bias is necessary to counter the constraints that a conventional management place on the rate of growth of a firm. At least some members of the management team must from time to time engage in scrutiny of what the firm is doing and why it is doing it with the thought of revision or even radical change.

A Managerial Model of Growth

We introduced the subject of firm growth with a discussion of Baumol's sales revenue growth model. Baumol's model, you may recall, assumed that, subject to a profit distribution constraint, retained profits are used to finance growth and that the higher the proportion of profit retained, *ceteris paribus*, the higher the rate at which sales revenue is assumed to grow. We have also discussed many of the problems that such a model of firm growth gives rise to. Firstly, all other things may not be equal; sales growth may only be possible if expenditure on advertising is increased and/or the firm steadily reduces the price of its products. At some point, either of these actions will reduce profits, threatening the resource base on which growth is founded. Secondly, we have argued in this and the last chapter that diversification offers a way to reduce these profit-reducing effects, but diversification still requires resources – particularly managerial resources – though the additional costs are dependent on the economies of scope inherent in the firm's surplus capabilities. The larger the firm, the more likely it is to be diversified and also the greater the range of opportunities for growth made possible by its resource base. Thirdly, the larger the firm, the greater the likelihood that it will be run by professional managers on behalf of its owners, i.e. the shareholders. In this situation, the ability of senior managers to exercise discretion in the pursuit of objectives will depend on the effectiveness of the incentives put in place by the owners. We will explore in more detail in the next chapter how owners may seek to ensure that senior managers pursue profit-maximizing or value-maximizing objectives. It is against these considerations that we turn to a model of the growth of the firm put forward by Robin Marris (1964) that has become a standard theory for analysing the growth of managerially controlled firms.

The model developed by Marris is a coherent and integrated managerial theory of the growth of the firm. It is a managerial model in the sense that it assumes the firm's professional managers have the objective of maximizing the firm's rate of growth and the owners have the objective of maximizing profits. The model deals with both the demand and supply aspects of a firm's growth and, like all models, it includes a number of simplifying assumptions. The model is concerned with the underlying steady-state or long-run rate of growth, and hence the impact of random shocks is ignored. As noted above, in the real world, a random walk with positive drift appears a much better representation of firm growth, so the assumption of steady-state growth is a strong one. Once the firm has made its decisions concerning the relevant variables, the underlying rate of growth is presumed fixed until new decisions are made. Most importantly, steady-state growth implies that both demand and supply grow at the same rate. If the rate of growth of supply exceeds that of demand, then the result would be ever-growing stocks and/or spare capacity. If the rate of growth of demand exceeds that of supply, the outcome would be rising prices rising, profits and new entrants. We will return to the growth rate of supply – essentially the growth rate of the firm – below, but first we will identify the determinants of growing demand.

We have argued that sooner or later, for most firms, a steady-state rate of growth of demand for a firm's output will necessitate horizontal diversification into new products; indeed, a steady-state rate of growth necessitates successful diversification into new products. The launch of new products, whether related or unrelated to the firm's existing product portfolio, carries the risk of failure. Those that take off and establish a market share will follow an S-shaped, product life cycle curve. Thus the assumption of a steady rate of growth implies that the firm comes forward with sufficient new products to offset any failures and also to offset a slowing rate of growth as products reach the mature stage of their life cycles. The launch of new products and diversification implies that the firm will need to enter new markets and success here is greatly helped if incumbents are accommodating. Put simply, the growth of demand $\dot{g}_D$, where the dot represents a constant percentage annual increase, is a function of successful diversification in terms of both products and markets, that is:

$$\dot{g}_D = f(\dot{d}) \tag{5.5}$$

where is $\dot{d}$ the rate of successful diversification. Equation (5.5) is deceptively simple. An established firm's growth rate is, as noted above, normally measured by the growth of sales measured at constant prices. But a steady-state rate of growth implies that as new products – presumably at different prices – are added to the increasingly diversified portfolio, the weighting for each product will change. Only a proportion of new products will be successful and this implies that the firm must come forward with a faster rate of diversification than that represented by $\dot{d}$. Also the rate of growth for new products will vary, which makes the idea of a steady-state rate of growth easier to conceptualize than to deliver in practice.

Turning to the supply side, it is convenient to assume that the rate of growth of the firm's productive resources can be proxied by the rate of growth of the firm's fixed assets. The implication is that the firm's knowledge resources – so important to successful diversification – and human resources also grow at the same rate as the firm's fixed assets. We can further simplify matters by assuming a constant capital–output ratio α, such that:

$$K = \alpha q \tag{5.6}$$

where K is the firm's existing stock of fixed capital, q is the value of output (at constant prices) and $\alpha > 0$. As we are concerned here with the firm's rate of growth, we will write $\dot{g}_s$ for the rate of growth of q, and, letting $\dot{K}$ represent the rate of growth of the firm's fixed assets, we have:

$$\dot{g}_s = \dot{K} \tag{5.7}$$

which reflects the implication of a constant capital–labour ratio; namely, that the rate of growth of a firm's sales matches the rate of growth of its stock of assets, K. The growth of fixed assets involves **net investment**, i, and, hence, the growth rate of the capital stock is equal to the ratio of net investment to capital employed, i.e.:

$$\dot{K} = \frac{i}{K} \tag{5.8}$$

where $i = i^g - \delta K$, i.e. net investment is equivalent to gross investment, i^g, less the level of investment required to replace worn-out assets, δK, where $0 < \delta < 1$.

Investment requires funding and a robust theory of firm growth must explain how the firm generates the funds for the net investment necessary for a growing scale of production. In practice, successful firms can generally resort to financial markets for investment funds, i.e. borrowings or equity. However, whatever the immediate source of investment funds, they must ultimately be paid for out of earnings, hence we can demonstrate the basic principles if we confine ourselves to internally generated investment funds, i.e. retained profits. The ratio of retained profits to total profits is known as the **retention ratio**, but we need to be a careful in defining the retention ratio. If π^g represents gross profits, then net profits π^n are defined as:

$$\pi^n = \pi^g - \delta K \tag{5.9}$$

where δK is as defined above. Now harking back to Baumol's and Williamson's notion of a minimum profit constraint, and ignoring tax, we can define the funds available to senior managers for investment to increase the capital stock as:

$$\pi^i = \pi^n - \pi^e \tag{5.10}$$

where π^e is the minimum profit expected by shareholders for distribution as dividends. Hence, the amount of investment expenditure, i, available to senior managers to horizontally expand the firm's operations is equivalent to:

$$i = \beta[\pi^{n} - \pi^{e}] \tag{5.11}$$

where β is the retention ratio which for positive growth takes a value of $0 < \beta \leq 1$. If we now combine Equations (5.7), (5.8), (5.10) and (5.11), we have:

$$\dot{g}_{s} = i/K = \beta[\pi^{n}/K - \pi_{t}^{e}/K] = \beta[\pi^{g}/K - \mu] \tag{5.12}$$

where $\mu = \delta + \pi^{e}/K$. Raising the value of β lowers the proportion of profits distributed as current dividends and, according to Marris, shareholders might normally be expected to constrain the value of β to $\beta < 1$. In fact, the value of β will be the outcome of a non-co-operative game. There is no binding agreement between the firm's senior managers and its shareholders as to the value of β and from the perspective of senior managers, given the assumption that their objective is to maximize the rate of growth of the firm, they would like a value closer to unity, whereas the shareholders would, it is presumed, prefer a value nearer to zero. This suggests that the value of β will be the outcome of the balance between the power of shareholders and the power of senior managers to exercise discretion.

We now turn to the heart of the issue; namely, what determines the rate of successful horizontal diversification? A firm enjoying steady-state growth will be increasingly diversifying and *ceteris paribus* the faster its rate of growth the greater its need to seek new growth opportunities in an ever-widening horizontal range of products and to support these opportunities with the right mix and quality of resources. Penrose, it will be recalled, viewed the firm as an administrative organization that can always recruit new resources for expansion, but administratively the faster the firm hires new human resources, the greater the distraction of managers in training new human resources to the required levels of knowledge and co-operation. This notion of a constraint on the rate of growth is central to Marris' theory. Marris (1964) hypothesized that: 'there exists an inverse relationship between a widening range of diversification and the return on capital invested.' He argued that increasing the rate of growth by broadening the firm's product portfolio must eventually be accompanied by rising costs associated with a management more focused on inculcating new staff than applying existing resources to existing opportunities. In this, Marris adopts a subtly different approach to Penrose. Instead of saying the firm cannot effectively administratively expand faster than some fixed rate, he says that the faster a firm grows, the more likely that it will suffer a loss of efficiency. For Marris, the faster the rate of growth, the greater the pressures on the firm's organizational coherence, i.e. the ability of the firm to marshal and motivate the entrepreneurial abilities of its managers without sacrificing efficiency in its current operations.

As the firm attempts to apply its unique capabilities to an ever-wider diversity of product markets, its organizational coherence inevitably becomes stretched, with a consequential loss of organizational efficiency. Thus, one of the drivers of diversification – the incentive to use the firm's internally generated resources efficiently – is subject to diminishing returns, whereby the ability of the firm's unique capabilities to create value will, beyond some level of diversification, steadily be reduced and eventually exhausted. In short, as the firm adopts an ever-broader horizontal range of products, it is likely to suffer a loss of managerial efficiency. The impact of a loss of managerial efficiency will be manifested in the firm's profit performance. A growing firm, at least over some range of rates of growth, is likely to be accompanied by rising profits, but it is the profit rate rather than absolute profits that is relevant. As the firm grows, it is investing in additional assets; hence on the basis of the foregoing, the **profit rate**, π/K, will eventually start to decline in response to a growing loss of managerial efficiency as the rate of diversification increases. The decline in the profit rate will be exacerbated by the need for the horizontally expanding firm to engage in high levels of research and development and to incur high levels of expenditure on marketing and other promotional activities.

The idea advanced by Marris that there exists a trade-off between firm growth and profitability was not new. As we have seen, Baumol had come to the same conclusion. Nevertheless, Marris emphasized the tendency at higher rates of diversification to launch less successful products, pick the wrong markets and display poor judgement in executing market entry strategies. One or all of these inefficiencies reduce profits relative to the size of the firm (Marris, 2002). At low rates of growth, the firm finds it relatively easy to absorb new staff and, in the words of Marris, 'new blood is invigorating'. Put slightly differently, a zero growth environment is likely to be stultifying, i.e. offering managers only repetition of existing routines and practices and hence little scope for initiative. This is not an environment that is likely to create opportunities for managerial resources to utilize and develop their entrepreneurial abilities. It is the management of change that creates the scope to develop the firm's capabilities and scope for new challenges, hence a relatively low, manageable positive rate of growth can actually increase the profit rate. However, as the rate of growth increases, so the firm's rate of diversification must rise, leading eventually to a declining **profit margin** and hence a declining profit rate. The relationship between the profit margin and the profit rate can be more clearly seen with the following equation:

$$\frac{\pi^g}{K} = \frac{\pi^g}{q} \cdot \frac{q}{K} = \frac{m}{\alpha} \tag{5.13}$$

where m is the profit margin and α the capital–output ratio. It is the failure to maintain the profit margin that causes the profit rate to decline and this is due to the rate of diversification. Thus, from the demand side perspective, we have:

$$\pi^g/K = f(\dot{d}) \tag{5.14}$$

and by rearranging Equation (5.5) we have:

$$\pi^g/K = f(1/\dot{g}) \tag{5.15}$$

which says, as the rate of demand growth increases, so at some point the profit rate will start to decline. It is on the basis of this reasoning that we can account for the inverted U-shape relationship observed between the firm's rate of growth and its profit performance. This is illustrated in Figure 5.6 by the curve μABC. The stronger are exogenous demand forces, e.g. rising real incomes, the less the adverse effects of diversification on the firm's profit rate. This would be represented by point C moving out to the right in Figure 5.6.

Returning to the supply side, Equation (5.12) represents the internally generated funding for growth. By rearranging Equation (5.12), we have:

$$\pi^g/K = \frac{1}{s}(\dot{g}) + \mu \tag{5.16}$$

β

Equation (5.16) is a straight line intersecting with the vertical axis at point µ, as shown in Figure 5.6. The gradient of the line is given by 1/β: the closer β to unity, the flatter the line. Now let us hypothesize that for an individual firm there is some value of β, say β*, such that the rate of growth is just sufficient to achieve the maximum possible profit rate given the demands the firm faces in its diversified markets. This is shown as point A in Figure 5.6, where the straight line passing through point A is Equation (5.16) when β takes the value β*.

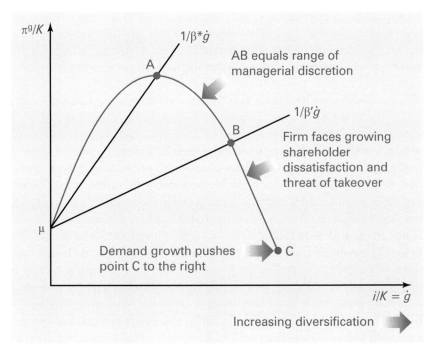

Figure 5.6: The Marris growth model

Figure 5.6 indicates that even if the firm's size is static, i.e. the growth rate is zero, it must generate a sufficient profit rate to replace worn-out capital and provide its shareholders with a minimum expected return on their capital. This is represented by µ on the vertical axis. The shape of curve µABC reflects the previous discussion; namely, between points µ and A, an increasing rate of growth is accompanied by a rising profit rate, as a modest rate of growth is hypothesized to have an invigorating effect on managerial efficiency. If senior managers wish to increase the growth rate beyond point A, they must first increase the retention ratio in order to raise the funds to increase the firm's rate of diversification. But given the inverse relationship between the profit rate and the rate of growth, there will be an upper limit on the rate at which the firm can grow. This limit is imposed by the expectations of shareholders and/or the threat of a takeover as predators realize that slowing the rate of growth would increase the profit rate. The managerial pursuit of growth is therefore restricted by the need to pay dividends.

If shareholders are unhappy with the company's dividend policy they may seek to change the company's policy or sell their shares, but compared to the firm's senior managers, shareholders will lack the information as to whether or not the firm is maximizing its profit rate. Given the asymmetry of information between the owners and the firm's senior managers, the shareholders are only likely to be aware of a profit rate that falls below their expectations. The existence of a minimum profit rate constrains the maximum rate of growth to, say, the rate represented by point B, which requires a retention rate of β' where β' > β*. We can then think of the area between points A and B as reflecting the range of managerial discretion regarding the firm's rate of growth. In part, this will reflect not only their objectives, but also their attitude towards risk. The more risk averse the senior managers, the nearer they will be to point A. We will return to the relationship between shareholders' objectives, managerial discretion and risk in the next chapter.

One implication of Marris' model – which overlaps with Baumol's sales revenue-maximization model – is that the firm must balance a trade-off between short-term profits and growth. The implication is that, in the short run growth-maximizing firms will not be profit-maximizing firms. But this depends on the extent of diversification and the rate of growth of demand. The firm may be fortunate to have a small, but fast-growing range of products. Moreover, the growth of demand for the firm's products will only partly be influenced by the actions of the firm's managers. Exogenous influences on demand are a rising population, rising affluence or the failure of a rival. Advertising and marketing expenditure is generally undertaken to boost demand, but the firm may be able to limit such expenditure if demand growth is being exogenously driven. The conclusion must be that profit-maximizing behaviour does not implicitly inhibit the growth of the firm. But in the absence of sufficiently rapid growth of demand, growth-orientated managers must take action that will stimulate demand for the firm's products. Whether this behaviour is described as discretionary and non-profit maximizing depends in large part on a definition of profits – and an adequate specification of the activities of an efficient and innovative management team.

The assumption that the firm's rate of growth is constrained by its retention ratio implies that too fast a rate of growth will be reflected in a depressed share price. This follows because, in principle, at any time the share price should represent the **present value** of the total dividend stream to infinity. With a constant retention ratio, current dividends are determined by current profits and the growth of dividends is determined by the growth of profits. Marris recognized that a theory of the growth of the firm requires a theory of stock market valuation. This issue is beyond the scope of this book, but we can briefly observe that in practice a firm's senior managers may be able to achieve both 'satisfactory' dividend payments and rapid growth by leverage, i.e. borrowing. This makes the firm's financial structure more risky and raises the cost of capital, but initially this is offset by the increased earnings the growth makes possible and the dividend benefits of a low retention ratio. But again, growth maximization occurs when leverage and the accompanying financial risk reach the maximum that shareholders are prepared to accept.

Finally, the Marris model, as explained above, is based on steady-state methodology. The idea that a firm fixes its decision variables for an indefinite period is, to say the least, heroic, even allowing for the general interpretation of steady-state as representing long-run 'normal' value around which considerable stochastic variation may occur. Following Nelson and Winter (1982), steady-state models have had to struggle against a completely new approach to growth, whereby firms are viewed as engaging in various search operations by which they discover, consider and evaluate changes. Very much within the competency paradigm, successful, i.e. profitable, growth within the Nelson and Winter 'evolutionary' model depends not only on the firm's capabilities, but also on its decision rules given its analysis of how the environment in which it operates is changing. In such a model there is no equilibrium, firms are in a constant state of disequilibrium and growth depends on the infinitely variable combinations of capabilities and decision rules. Despite the differences there is a link between the Marris and Nelson and Winter approaches. Research into, and the development of, new products are common to both models, and Marris' cost-of-growth function is embraced by Nelson and

From Smells to Fragrances

Today ICI can fairly claim to be a speciality products and paints company. It was the purchase of Unilever's Speciality Chemical business in 1997 that was the last critical step in transforming ICI from the bulk chemicals producer it started out as in 1926 into the speciality company it is today. ICI was formed from the merger of Britain's four largest chemical companies and in the following years not only did it enjoy rapid sales growth, but also a growing reputation for innovation in science and technology.

It is possible to chart ICI's growth as a succession of milestones, such as the launch of Perspex acrylic sheet in the 1930s, Paludrine, an anti-malarial treatment, in the 1940s, Procion fibre-reactive dyes in the 1950s, Paraquat weedkiller in the 1960s, Saffil inorganic fibre in the 1970s and Aquabase water-based paint in the 1980s. But despite 60 years of steady growth, the City was not sufficiently enamoured and when the corporate raiders Hanson Trust took an interest in ICI it reacted by demerging its bioscience business in 1993 to a publicly-listed company Zeneca (later AstraZeneca plc).

Since 1993, ICI has disinvested itself from 28 businesses, including agrochemicals, fertilizers, explosives and petrochemicals. Today, ICI has four main businesses: Starch and Chemicals; Paints; Flavours and Fragrances; and Oleochemistry. ICI is now a diversified technologically sophisticated producer of chemically based speciality products. Many of its products are household names, e.g. Dulux. If the chart of ICI's progress to date looks like a random walk, the company's achievements and reputation have grown steadily.

Winter's acceptance that beyond some point the lack of, or the rate of development of, new capabilities squeezes profitability. The steady-state approach of Marris has proved very helpful in providing a coherent framework for investigating the growth of firms and, as Nelson and Winter admit, their evolutionary model is both more complex and less transparent than neo-classical models.

Mergers and Acquisitions

So far we have considered the incentives underpinning growth, and in particular diversified growth, rather than the means. One of the main ways in which diversified growth is accomplished is by **merger** or **acquisition**, though there are a number of rationales other than diversified growth that might justify a merger or an acquisition. There are essentially two ways in which a firm might be merged into a larger-scale organization. The easiest is an agreed merger, whereby firm A acquires firm B in a bid recommended by the senior management of both companies and accepted by the shareholders. Alternatively, firm A may acquire firm B in a contested or hostile takeover, usually by means of a tender offer in which the senior managers of firm A make an offer directly to B's shareholders despite opposition from B's senior managers. In practice, even agreed mergers amount sooner or later to an acquisition as one of the merging firm's management team moves into the ascendancy. In addition to the means, there is also the type of merger. Textbooks like to define three types of merger: horizontal, conglomerate and vertical. We have dealt with **vertical integration** in Chapter 3;

here we are concerned with the first two types. A ***horizontal merger*** is one in which both firms are in the same product market and a ***conglomerate merger*** refers to a merger between two firms operating in different product markets. In fact, a conglomerate merger is a horizontal merger and one of the main incentives is likely to be firm growth.

Merger activity tends to follow a cyclical pattern, with periodic booms in merger activity. These merger 'waves' appear to be correlated with general economic activity and patterns in the behaviour of stock market prices. This suggests, if not wider motives, then wider influences than extending the boundaries of the firm to fully utilize a surplus capability. For example, the signing of the Single European Act in 1987 was followed by a merger boom in the European Community as firms prepared for the coming ***Single Market***. Ten years later, the imminent arrival of EMU and the euro produced another merger boom, this time involving banks and other financial sector businesses. More dramatically, the 1990s witnessed a 'merger mania' in the US in response to the arrival of the internet and a wave of 'irrational exuberance' that accompanied the coming of ICT. Other explanations for merger booms involve discrepancies in stock market valuations, whereby a perceptive management of company A realizes that company B is undervalued. Such discrepancies are more likely during periods of stock market volatility and have their causes in macroeconomic 'shocks'. Fascinating as these macroeconomic shocks might be, our concern here is with the firm and in particular, having explained why increasing the horizontal scale of a firm is a necessary counterpart of growth, we need to examine the advantages presumed to arise from merging two firms rather than growing organically.

This is not to overlook the fact that mergers are frequently justified by their participants as likely to produce cost savings. These most obviously arise in the sharing of an administrative structure (an economy of scope) and ***economies of scale*** may arise from the concentrating of production in fewer, larger facilities. The existence of a surplus intangible capability such as an organizational capability is another potential economy of scope. With one eye on the competition authorities, merging firms are bound to emphasize the efficiencies likely to arise, but the competition authorities – particularly in the case of horizontal mergers – are also mindful of the scope increasing scale might create for anticompetitive behaviour. A merger with a firm in the same product market is bound to increase market share and this may or may not result in an increase in market power. On the face of it, a horizontal merger eliminates a competitor, but much depends on the industry structure (see later chapters). There are at least grounds for adopting a rather sceptical approach to the efficiency claims, based on scale economies, that are frequently made in defence of a merger (Farrell and Shapiro, 2001).

As discussed in this and the previous chapter, diversification can have a number of benefits for a firm and mergers and acquisitions have a number of potential advantages in this respect. Diversification requires a firm to develop new products and/or to facilitate entry into new markets and both of these routes involve time and risk. Time is perhaps the most obvious trade-off from seeking growth by merger. We have discussed how a firm, in order to increases its growth opportunities, must grow and develop its resource base and in particular its knowledge-based intangible resources. This may take many years, whereas, by taking over a suitable firm, such resources may be acquired and in the process the acquiring firm's own resources may be developed and enhanced. Viewed from this perspective, a merger or acquisition offers not only a more rapid increase in scale, but also the prospect of more growth opportunities in the future.

A second advantage is that a firm that grows by merger does not face – or perhaps does not so obviously face – the trade-off between growth and profits. By engaging in a horizontal merger, the firm can expand its existing sales without the need to resort to costly advertising campaigns or price reductions. In principle, this should avoid a fall in the profit rate; indeed, if the firm acquires increased market power it could lead to a rise in the profit rate. By horizontally merging with a firm in an unrelated product market, i.e. engaging in a conglomerate merger, the firm can diversify without the expense and risk of investment in research and development that would be necessary before entering a new product area. In addition, it will potentially widen its set of productive growth opportunities for the future by exposing its managerial resources to new experiences and learning.

The rapid increase in scale associated with a merger or acquisition does bring with it the problems of maintaining organizational coherence. We have noted above that, as an organization becomes large and diversified, so it stretches its organizational coherence – and co-ordination and decision making begin to suffer. Senior managers may respond by decentralizing decision making – which raises the issue of incentives to maintain productivity and goal congruence – or employing more support staff, which increases costs. These problems are inherent in a firm that grows organically, but the complication factor in a merger is the likelihood of a merger between two different organizational architectures and cultures. Firms are social communities; employees become used to the environment and resistant to change.

The problems of conflicting cultures can arise when similar-sized organizations are brought together, but are at their most intense when a large hierarchically structured and controlled firm takes over a smaller entrepreneurial firm in the hope of taking advantage of its core competence. A smaller entrepreneurial firm is more likely to link rewards closely to performance. This is a way of avoiding the more costly sophisticated organizational architectures of larger firms. Putting such diverse cultures together is certain to cause resentment and jealousy. We have observed that, for individual firms core capabilities are generally embedded in the tacit knowledge of individuals and teams and are the outcomes of an evolutionary process, which has developed over time within the specific environment of the firm. It is the difficulty of sharing tacit knowledge that so often produces disappointing outcomes for mergers and acquisitions. A survey of post-merger performance by Pickering (1983), found that mergers do not on average 'have a favourable effect on the relative profitability of the merged company' (p. 267). Empirical studies of the long-run, post-merger effects for shareholders in the bidding firms show that generally they did not make gains in excess of what they might otherwise have gained (see, for example, Sudarsanam *et al.*, 1996; Gregory, 1997). These academic studies have been supported by consultant group reports. For example, KPMG (1999), taking a global perspective, showed that only 17 per cent of cross-border mergers had added to shareholder value, 30 per cent had made no discernable difference and 53 per cent had actually reduced shareholder value.

These rather negative conclusions for mergers and acquisitions are very much in line with the analysis set out above for organic growth. A desire to grow more rapidly by means of a merger to achieve horizontal expansions into a related or unrelated product area is likely to result in a lower profit rate if the expansion is over-ambitious. There is another dimension that senior managers contemplating a merger must consider; namely, the attention of the competition authorities. In 1989, spurred by the imminent arrival of the Single Market and a merger boom, the EU introduced a Merger Regulation. The Merger Regulation entered into force in 1990 and since that date more than 2,700 mergers have been notified to, and reviewed by, the European Commission. On 1 May 2004, the Regulation was revised, but its essential purpose remains; namely, to limit the use of mergers to either unilaterally or collusively exercise market power.

It is sometimes claimed that under the EU Merger Regulation there does not exist an efficiency defence. This is wrong and arises out of the EU's concern to exclude a defence based on ***industrial policy***. Some countries, notably France, wanted to allow mergers in order to create national champions. This view was successfully opposed by other member states and, so far, the European Commission in its decisions has not explicitly ruled out the possibility of using an efficiency defence; though it is also true to say that it has not shown much sympathy for this argument either. To the extent that a merger does facilitate faster growth for the merged firm, this is not sufficient to describe the merger as efficient. Efficiency would be manifested in lower unit production costs and/or better value products for consumers. The problem for the authorities – even when a merger involves firms producing products in separate markets – is that greater efficiency can have adverse effects for the number of competitors. A merged firm producing a wide range of products might – without any resort to anti-competitive practices – be too powerful, thus reducing the competition from rivals.

As noted above, the prevailing view is that generally mergers do not produce the expected gain in profitability. In part, this may be due to unrealistic expectations and/or the attention of the competition authorities. Interestingly, from the perspective of encouraging growth, Beiker *et al.* (2001) argued that mergers fail because too much attention is paid to cutting costs at the expense of encouraging revenue growth. It is also likely that too little attention is paid to the problem of integrating the two organizations. Cultural differences are an important constraint and as the dominant firm attempts to impose its culture, so managers will be distracted from the business of identifying and facilitating productive opportunities. The process of change itself at best creates uncertainty and at worse can

LloydsTSB Marries a Widow

In June 1999, Britain's largest bank, Lloyds TSB, purchased for £7bn the mutually owned Scottish Widows Life Assurance. The deal brought to an end 184 years of mutuality for one of the UK's biggest life and pensions groups and it changed the face of the UK financial services industry. Although Lloyds TSB paid a high price for Scottish Widows it gained arguably the strongest brand in the life and pensions business. It also gained a network of independent financial advisers that have recommended Scottish Widows products, and the ability to distribute Scottish Widows products through its 2,500 bank branches. The deal bears comparison with Lloyds' 1995 purchase of Cheltenham &

Gloucester, the former building society, which triggered a wave of demutualization among societies and led the Halifax, Woolwich, Alliance & Leicester and Northern Rock to convert to banks.

There are a number of reasons why we are likely to see more diversification by banks into insurance and vice versa. Firstly, there is the impact of low-cost stakeholder pensions in 2001. The prospect of stakeholder pensions is making many life assurance groups feel financially vulnerable. The government has capped consumer charges at just 1 per cent of funds under management – far below the 3 to 6 per cent charged by life companies

continued

on most current personal pensions – and at a time when life companies may have to spend up to £11bn to resolve earlier pensions mis-selling cases. Secondly, consumers are increasingly buying unit-linked policies rather than what are known as 'with profits' policies that offer lower margins to life companies. And thirdly, many overseas banks and insurers, such as Allianz and Generali, have entered the UK's long-term savings market. The sector is ripe for merger and acquisition activity because it is an extremely fragmented industry and life groups tend to be relatively small.

As regards banks, particularly former building societies such as the Halifax and Abbey National, the lure of diversified growth is the prospect of a growing 'long-term savings' market, in contrast to mature businesses such as mortgage lending. The UK long-term savings market is projected to grow 7 per cent a year, driven by an ageing population and government emphasis on private pension provision.

have a negative impact on morale and productivity. Despite the frequent failure of mergers and acquisitions, they continue to provide the main route to rapid growth. In addition to senior managers' beliefs that they can deal with the issues of governance, complementarity and efficiency that mergers and acquisitions give rise to, one must also suspect the private goals of management: prestige, status, power and income. We will return to these matters in the next chapter.

Concluding Thoughts

A comprehensive theory of the firm must be able to explain not only the incentive for firms to expand their horizontal boundaries, but also why firms within the same industry grow to different sizes and why, for some, growth is negative. Not all firms grow large and some firms having grown large then shrink and may eventually cease to exist. The pursuit of economies of scale and the stage a firm has reached in its life cycle do not explain the varying growth performances of individual firms. Although governance is critical to the organizational coherence of a growing firm, the governance approach to the firm sheds little light on sustained horizontal expansion and the incentive to grow by diversifying. We have therefore paid more attention to the competence or resource-based approach to the firm, and also within this perspective, to the role of the entrepreneur in driving firm growth.

The competency paradigm with its view that individual firms accumulate stocks of unique core capabilities that yield economies of scope provides a theoretical basis for the observed idiosyncratic nature of firm growth and the widely adopted means of growth – diversification. The competency approach places great emphasis on the entrepreneurial ability of the firm's senior managers to perceive new productive opportunities and to utilize the firm's internally accumulated knowledge resources to exploit them. Growth heightens the entrepreneurial role of senior managers and the more growth opportunities a firm perceives and exploits, the greater its stock of cumulative knowledge and hence the wider future potential growth opportunities.

There is considerable evidence that smaller firms grow faster than larger firms – not altogether surprising when you are growing from a small base. But company sizes, even within industries, do not converge. Far from growing at a steady annual rate, the evidence shows that firms tend to engage in infrequent large-scale bursts of net investment. This knowledge casts doubt on the ideal of an optimal size of firm and it dispenses with the idea that firms typically follow some life cycle. Indeed, empirical studies suggest that a firm's growth tends to follow a random walk; namely the way in which it grows, or declines, over the long run is stochastic, i.e. unpredictable.

The main way in which diversified growth is accomplished is by merger or acquisition. Such activity

Key Learning Points

- A modern theory of the firm must be able to explain why firms grow and why they grow at different rates and to different sizes.

- Baumol's sales revenue-maximization model was an early attempt to model firm growth, which gave priority to managerial objectives and a shareholder-imposed restraint.

- Baumol's model recognized the importance of growing demand and the need for firms to devote expenditure to advertising, sales promotion and new product design.

- Empirical evidence reveals that firms typically follow a random walk growth process, implying that growth results from infrequent but large discrete investments.

- As sales of individual products tend to follow an S-curve life cycle, the objective of sustaining growth will sooner or later force most firms to diversify, which focuses attention on capabilities.

- The starting point for a supply-side analysis of firm growth is Penrose's resource-based theory of the firm, which accords with the competency school's view that growth is a process of developing, accumulating and productively utilizing internally generated, particularly knowledge, resources.

- This perspective views a firm's growth opportunities as limited by its history and hence an additional benefit of diversified growth is to expand the firm's stock of knowledge resources.

- Sustained growth calls for an entrepreneurial managerial approach; namely, the ability to perceive new growth opportunities and the energy to secure and mobilize the resources necessary to make them happen.

- The model most generally associated with firm growth is that put forward by Marris more than 40 years ago. Despite differences with Nelson and Winter's evolutionary approach, both models embrace the notion that beyond some rate of growth, the development, or lack, of new capabilities squeezes profitability.

- One of the main ways in which diversified growth is accomplished is by mergers and acquisitions. These actions may have the advantages of facilitating rapid growth, but they are not immune from the problems of organizational coherence and the evidence for their success in terms of profits is on the whole disappointing.

Exercises

5.1 Is it necessarily the case that the objective of maximizing long-run firm growth is inconsistent with the goal of profit maximizing?

5.2 Contrast Penrose's managerial limits to growth with those of the competency school.

5.3 What role does an entrepreneurial management play in firm growth and what is the essential difference between an owner-manager entrepreneur and an entrepreneur operating in a large, diversified firm?

5.4 Explain, in broad terms, the demand and supply sides of the Marris growth model.

5.5 Why is the European Commission wary of efficiency claims made by firms notifying an intention to merge?

Problems

5.1 Total management services, m, needed by a firm at any point in time must be sufficient to run its current size , m_1 and also to carry out expansionary activities, m_2. where $m = m_1 + m_2$. If the firm's size is Q in period t and its rate of growth is g, then if the amount of management services required to run the firm is directly proportional to the size of the firm and the managerial services required for expansion are directly proportional to the size of the discrete expansion in each period:

(a) Show that the firm's growth rate will be constant in the absence of recruiting new managers.

(b) If new managers are recruited, why will the more rapid rate of growth be subject to diminishing returns?

(c) Graph your answer to (b) showing that there will be an optimum rate of firm growth and an optimum rate for the growth of management services.

5.2 Assume a firm achieves a fixed rate of growth, g, per year. Let R be the initial revenue, i.e. $R = pQ$, and r the cost of capital. Also $R = \alpha K$, where K is the value of the capital stock:

(a) Provide a formula converting the firm's revenue stream over years $0 \ldots \ldots \ldots T$, to its present value.

(b) If variable costs are a fixed proportion of revenue, formulate the present value of the net cash flow.

(c) If each year the firm must invest i, where i/K remains constant, provide a formula for the net present value of the investment.

may, in part, be motivated by the external business environment – such as government policy and stock market discrepancies – but it has some obvious advantages. A merger or an acquisition offers not only a more rapid increase in scale, but also a potentially wider range of growth opportunities in the future. By engaging in a horizontal merger, the firm can expand sales without resort to costly advertising campaigns or price reductions. And by engaging in a conglomerate merger, the firm avoids the cost and risk of research and development that would be necessary before entering a new product area.

References

Baumol, W. (1958) 'On the theory of oligopoly', *Economica*, vol. 25, pp. 187–198.

Baumol, W. (1962) 'On the theory of expansion of the firm', *American Economic Review*, vol. 52, pp. 1078–1087.

Beiker, M., Bogardus, A. and Oldham, T. (2001) 'Why mergers fail', *McKinsey Quarterly*, vol. 4, pp. 6–9.

Caballero, R., Engel, E. and Haltiwanger, J. (1995) 'Plant level adjustment and aggregate investment dynamics', *Brookings Papers on Economic Activity*, vol. 2, pp. 1–39.

Choi, Y. (1999) 'Conventions and learning: a perspective on the market process' in *Economic Organization and Economic Knowledge: Volume I*, S. Dow and P. Earl (eds), Edward Elgar, Cheltenham.

European Commission (2004) *Facing The Challenge: The Lisbon Strategy for Growth and Employment*, European Commission, Luxembourg.

Farrell, J. and Shapiro, C. (2001) 'Scale economies and synergies in horizontal merger analysis', *Antitrust Law Journal*, vol. 68, pp. 685–710.

Garnsey, E. (1998) 'A theory of the early growth of the firm', *Industrial and Corporate Change*, vol. 7, no. 3, pp. 523–556.

Garnsey, E. (2002) 'The growth of new ventures: analysis after Penrose', *The Growth of the Firm: The Legacy of Edith Penrose*, C. Pitelis (ed.), Oxford University Press, Oxford.

Geroski, P. (2000) 'The growth of firms in theory and in practice' in *Competence, Governance and Entrepreneurship*, N. Foss and V. Mahnke (eds), Oxford University Press, Oxford.

Gregory, A. (1997) 'An examination of the long run performance of UK acquiring firms', *Journal of Business, Finance and Accounting*, vol. 24, pp. 971–1002.

Knight, F. (1921) *Risk, Uncertainty and Profit*, Houghton Mifflin, Boston, MA.

KPMG (1999) *Unlocking Shareholder Value: The Key to Success*, KPMG, London.

Langlois, R. (1995) 'Capabilities and coherence in firms and markets' in *Resource Based and Evolutionary Theories of the Firm: Towards a Synthesis*, C. Montgomery (ed.), Kluwer Academic, Norwell, MA and Dordrecht, Netherlands.

Lundström, A. and Stevenson, L. (2001) *Entrepreneurship Policy for the Future*, Swedish Foundation for Small Business Research, Stockholm.

Marris, R. (1964) *The Economic Theory of Managerial Capitalism*, Macmillan, London.

Marris, R. (2002) 'Edith Penrose and economics' in *The Growth of the Firm: the Legacy of Edith Penrose*, C. Pitelis (ed.), Oxford University Press, Oxford.

Moran, P. and Ghoshal, S. (1999) 'Markets, firms and the process of economic development', *Academy of Management Review*, vol. 24, no. 3, pp. 390–412.

Nelson, R. and Winter, S. (1982) *An Evolutionary Theory of Economic Change*, Belknap-Harvard University Press, Cambridge, MA.

Penrose, E. (1959) *The Theory of the Growth of the Firm*, Oxford University Press, Oxford.

Pickering, F. (1983) 'The causes and consequences of abandoned mergers', *Journal of Industrial Economics*, vol. 31, pp. 267–281.

Rumelt, R. (1974) *Strategy, Structure and Economic Performance*, Harvard University Press, Cambridge MA.

Schumpeter, J. (1942) *Capitalism, Socialism and Democracy*, Harper, New York.

Smith, A. (1776) *An Inquiry into the Nature and Causes of Wealth of the Nations*, London.

Stigler, G. (1961) 'The economies of information', *Journal of Political Economy*, vol. 69, p. 213.

APPENDIX 5A

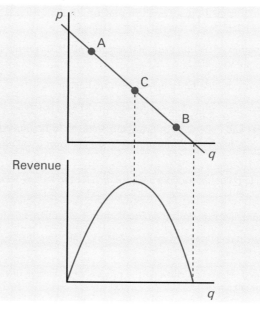

Figure 5A.1: Demand and revenue

Storey, D. (1994) *Understanding the Small Firm Sector*, Routledge, London.

Sudarsanam, S., Holl, P. and Salami, A. (1996) 'Shareholder wealth gains in mergers: effects of synergy and ownership structures', *Journal of Business, Finance and Accounting*, vol. 23, pp. 673–698.

Teece, D., Rumelt, R., Dosi, G. and Winter, S. (1994) 'Understanding corporate coherence: theory and evidence', *Journal of Economic Behaviour and Organization*, vol. 23, pp. 1–30.

The definition of total revenue, *TR*, is:

$$TR = pq \qquad (5A.1)$$

where p is the unit price and q the quantity sold. Given a downward-sloping demand curve in Figure 5A.1, if we let the price change to $p + \Delta p$, there will be an inverse change in the quantity sold, i.e. $q + \Delta q$, giving a new revenue of:

$$TR + \Delta R = (p + \Delta p)(q + \Delta q) \tag{5A.2}$$

which can be rewritten as:

$$TR + \Delta TR = pq + p\Delta q + q\Delta p + \Delta p\Delta q \tag{5A.3}$$

for a small change in p and q, the last term on the right-hand side can be safely neglected and by subtracting TR from both sides, we isolate the effect of a change in price on total revenue:

$$\Delta TR = p\Delta q + q\Delta p \tag{5A.4}$$

Referring back to the linear demand curve shown in Figure 5A.1, we know that the slope of the curve is given by $\Delta q/\Delta p$, hence a succession of equal price cuts Δp, will be accompanied by a succession of equal increases in the quantity sold, i.e. Δq. As we move down the demand curve, the second term on the right-hand side of Equation (5A.4) will always be negative, i.e. $q\Delta p < 0$. Thus, for a succession of equal price cuts, as long as $p\Delta q > q\Delta p$, total revenue will be rising and when $q\Delta p > p\Delta q$, total revenue will be falling.

Now consider point A on the demand curve. At this point, p is relatively high and q relatively small, hence at point A in Equation (5A.4), $p\Delta q + q\Delta p > 0$, and a price cut will result in an increase in revenue. At point B, p is relatively low and q relatively large, hence at B, $p\Delta q + q\Delta p < 0$ and a price cut will reduce total revenue. It follows that, when $p\Delta q = q\Delta p$, the effect of a small price cut on revenue is neutral; revenue remains constant, as represented by point C. The effect of successive price cuts on total revenue is shown in the lower half of Figure 5A.1. Starting at the extreme left of the demand curve, as $q = 0$, revenue equals zero. As price is reduced and q starts to increase, total revenue increases – but at a diminishing rate – until point C, after which successive price cuts now begin to reduce total revenue. The outcome is the revenue curve shown in Figure 5A.1.

Equation (5A.4) can be divided through by Δp to generate the change in total revenue resulting from a small change in price, i.e. the marginal revenue:

$$\frac{\Delta TR}{\Delta p} = q + \frac{\Delta q}{\Delta p}p \tag{5A.5}$$

which can be written as:

$$\frac{\Delta TR}{\Delta p} = q\left[1 + \frac{\Delta q}{\Delta p} \cdot \frac{p}{q}\right] \tag{5A.6}$$

The second expression in the parenthesis is the price elasticity of demand. The elasticity of demand is naturally negative, hence Equation (5A.6) can be rewritten as:

$$\Delta TR$$

CHAPTER 6

CORPORATE CONTROL AND ORGANIZATIONAL DESIGN

Introduction

The traditional, neo-classical theory of the firm viewed the roles of capitalist and manager as being undertaken by an individual **entrepreneur**. In the neo-classical firm, control is exercised unambiguously by the entrepreneur who, as the owner, is also the sole claimant on profits. This model of ownership and control was predominant for industrializing nations during the nineteenth century and it remains the dominant model today if attention is confined to the number rather than the output of firms. In a firm that is controlled by the owner, the problem of managerial incentives is by-passed. The assumption that a firm's behaviour can be understood as being determined solely by the owner-manager's desire to maximize profits is not unrealistic. Moreover, the relatively small scale of firms in the mid-nineteenth century conveniently avoids the necessity of examining the internal workings of the firm. The firm is represented by the individual entrepreneur, who is an integrated and indivisible decision-taking unit – a black box whose inner workings are of no interest, as the entrepreneur's **utility** is presumed to be determined solely by the achievement of maximum profits.

As industrialization gathered pace during the nineteenth century and successful firms experienced rapid rates of growth, the demand for resources to finance this growth began to exceed what could be retained from earnings or borrowed from banks. In response, the limited liability joint-stock company was born – a company with its own distinct legal entity, empowered to raise money from the public in return for a stake or shareholding in the company and whose liability would be limited to their investment. The limited liability joint-stock company was a British invention, but it was rapidly copied by other industrializing nations. As observed in Chapter 2, other countries made greater use of limited liability companies, most notably the United States and Germany. As late as the 1920s, many of Britain's largest firms were managed by members of the founding families. Publicly owned firms did eventually emerge and reached a dominant position in Britain when measured in terms of the share of total output – e.g. ICI, Unilever and Imperial Tobacco – and by the 1930s, a small group of economists, who became known as the **management school**, started to explore the implications for the governance of firms where ownership, through the holding of shares, had become highly dispersed. In such firms, professional managers exercised control over the day-to-day running of the business and the management school saw this separation of ownership from the control of decision making as giving the objectives of these professional managers ascendancy over the owner's objectives of profit or value maximization.

The management school's 'beliefs' have come in for considerable criticism in the ensuing years. Theories of voting behaviour have demonstrated that even when ownership is widely dispersed, effective control can remain with the **shareholders**. And the growth of shareholdings by financial institutions – in the UK, financial institutions, both domestic and foreign, account for more than 70 per cent of shareholdings – means that in practice ownership dispersion is now much less than in the 1930s. These considerations suggest there is in practice less scope for managerial discretion than hypothesized by the founders of the management school. Nevertheless, the separation of 'ownership' and 'control' does not preclude scope for professional managers to pursue priorities that are different from those who own the firm and the widespread use of senior management incentive schemes linked to some aspect of profitability suggests senior management discretion remains a reality.

In this chapter, we explore the implications of the separation of ownership from the control of decision making throughout a firm's management hierarchy. Our underlying interest is efficiency and in what follows we will attempt to understand and interpret the behaviour of both owners and managers in terms of efficiency choices. We start with the observation that the nature of decision making within firms is of a different kind to the choices made by individual consumers. Rational consumers make their choices so as to maximize expected utility, subject to their **income constraint**. In contrast, a firm's executive officers (i.e. senior managers) and directors act as agents (strictly fiduciaries) for the owners and lower down the hierarchy line managers act as agents for the firm's senior managers. Consequently, the behaviour of a publicly owned firm is the outcome of a complex joint decision-making process involving a network of interwoven human relationships. Once this is appreciated, the importance of the firm's **organizational architecture** is thrown into sharp relief. There is a direct and critical relationship between the performance of a firm – generally determined by some measure of current and expected profits – and the way in which decisions are made, its workforce is motivated and individual performance is measured.

By definition, firms that employ professional managers are large organizations and these organizations account for the bulk of economic activity in a modern industrial economy. It follows that in industrial nations a very substantial proportion of productive resources is allocated within firms rather than by competition between firms. We have explained in the previous chapters why it may be more efficient to allocate resources via the decisions of a management hierarchy than via market exchange and we have explored how the need for coherence in the management of the firm's resources places limits on vertical and horizontal expansion. In this chapter, we will focus on the external and internal mechanisms for exerting control and aligning objectives. The external controls discussed below are primarily executive compensation plans, designed to align the firm's strategic objectives – as well as motivating senior management to excel – with those of the shareholders. The internal mechanisms are the product of a hierarchical, authoritarian command structure, controlling how the resources over which the firm has **property rights** are allocated and motivated. The owners of a firm will wish to minimize the likelihood of senior managers pursuing their own objectives as this reduces or diverts effort from the achievement of the owner's objectives. Similarly, a firm's senior managers will seek to minimize the pursuit of private priorities by employees that are in conflict with the objectives of senior managers. It is the examination of these issues that sets the framework for this chapter. By reading this chapter, you will:

- Appreciate some of the reasons for, and the implications of, non-profit-maximizing theories of the firm.
- Understand the role of organizational architecture in the efficient flow within the organization of information for strategic and operation decision making.
- Recognize the relative power of shareholders and stakeholders in influencing the behaviour of executives.

This chapter is divided into five sections. In the first, we start by examining the impact on efficiency of imperfect monitoring and a lack of motivation within the firm. We will also explain why reliance on the objective of profit maximization is inadequate for understanding behaviours within the firm. In the second section, we explore the role of a firm's organizational architecture in co-ordinating effort and aligning goals. This section deals with a number of related issues including contracts, information flows and the design of organizations. In the third section, we examine alternative – non-profit-maximizing – theories of the firm. The purpose is to explore the objectives and behaviour of managers in exercising their discretion in **decision management rights**. In the fourth section, we turn to the issue of motivating senior executives so that their self-interest is aligned with the objectives of shareholders. This section draws heavily on the **principal–agent** model. Finally, in the fifth section we introduce the notion of stakeholder capitalism and the concept of corporate social responsibility.

Management Costs

The neo-classical approach to the firm is, as we have frequently remarked, founded upon **perfect information** and **hyper-rational** decision makers. In such a world, **cost minimization** – the counterpart to profit maximization – is not just the ideal, it is the norm. In practice, the world in which managers operate is characterized by **imperfect information** and also **incomplete information**, not only regarding market opportunities and the behaviour of rivals, but also as regards the efforts and capabilities of their workforces. Without the insights afforded by perfect information, it is not possible for managers to be sure that their subordinates are fully co-operating and applying the expected effort. Lacking perfect information, it is safe to conclude that few firms will routinely operate on their least cost efficiency frontier. Figure 6.1 represents this situation for a group of single-plant, single-product firms. This figure shows a technology-determined **isoquant** for a particular product. All points on the isoquant represent

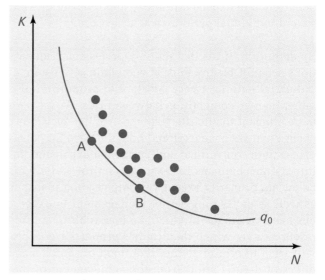

Figure 6.1: Relative production costs

technically efficient combinations of the services of capital, K, and an homogeneous labour force, N, that will produce the output, q_0, in a given period. Each of the individual firms making up the group are represented by a dot and are assumed to be producing the same level of output, q_0, per period. If we further assume that each is paying the same prices for their inputs, it is obvious that the further a dot is to the north-east of the isoquant, the higher are unit production costs.

Without further information on the unit prices of the K and N resource, we cannot know whether point A or B – or indeed some other point on the isoquant – is the lowest cost mix of inputs. But we do know that only a point on the isoquant can represent the most efficient cost combination of inputs to produce q_0 in the current period. Points to the north-east of the isoquant use more of at least one input than is technically necessary to produce q_0 and hence costs are higher than they need be. In practice, there could be many reasons why in a particular production period a firm's use of its inputs is technically inefficient. Machine breakdowns, unfavourable weather, industrial action and so on, create 'shocks' over which the firm's managers have only limited control – though managers do have influence over the firm's response and speed of recovery. Our concern here is not with random shocks, but with a persistent failure to operate on the efficiency frontier represented by the isoquant.

The implicit neo-classical assumption that, in the absence of such shocks, the firm will operate on the efficiency frontier was challenged in a seminal paper by Harvey Leibenstein (1966). On the basis of an analysis of empirical evidence, Leibenstein concluded that many plants persistently operated inefficiently. There are many reasons why, in practice, this might be the case. The most widely used measure of efficiency is **productivity** and in particular, **labour productivity**. In the UK, labour productivity is lower than the levels achieved by other industrial nations, most notably the US. A number of explanations have been put forward for the UK's lacklustre productivity performance, including low levels of investment, skill deficiencies and the lack of an enterprise culture. Efficiency involves learning and, by definition, this takes time. So, at any point in time, we would expect firms to be moving towards, if not actually achieving, complete efficiency. Leibenstein, however, postulated another cause of inefficiency; namely, the lack of internal monitoring and motivation, for which he coined the term **X-inefficiency**.

Figure 6.2 shows the effect of X-inefficiency on a plant's costs; it is the difference between actual and minimum unit cost performance. The short-run average total cost curve, $SRAC_0$, reflects the minimum attainable cost at different levels of output per production period and the plant shown is operating at output level q_0. Point A shows unit costs if the plant is operating efficiently, i.e. is on its least cost

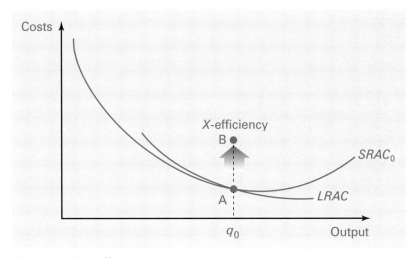

Figure 6.2: X-inefficiency

point on its production isoquant. The vertical difference between point A and B reflects the degree of X-inefficiency.

The problem identified by Leibenstein arises from the lack of perfect information. The essential function of a firm's management is to allocate and co-ordinate its productive resources so as to achieve the firm's objectives. This function starts with the allocation of resources among alternative uses. These allocations will be based on *a priori* information about the capabilities and past performance of individual resources. The co-ordination problem is to maximize productivity by encouraging effort and avoiding wasteful duplication. In principle, this would be achieved by the drawing up of a **complete contract** between the firm and each employee. Such a contract would specify precisely what each party would do in every possible circumstance. In practice, enacting and enforcing a complete contract is impossible because of information asymmetries regarding an individual's capabilities and **bounded rationality** in respect of future contingencies. The effect of this incompleteness is that self-interested behaviour is not completely controlled and motivation may be lacking. The larger and more centralized a firm, the greater the costs incurred in obtaining relevant information on team performance and individual effort. Milgrom (1988) offers an insight into the limits of the information that management can economically gather and assess with his concept of **influencing costs**. For Milgrom, influencing costs are undesired employee activities that are intended to change a superior's actions to the sole benefit of the employee.

Influencing costs is an important category of costs arising from **moral hazard**. This refers to any behaviour under a contract that is inefficient. It arises from the differing interests of the contracting parties and persists because **asymmetric information**. Within a firm it means that a manager cannot be certain whether an employee is fully honouring the contract terms. Thus, for Leibenstein, incomplete monitoring and a lack of internal motivation give rise to X-inefficiency. Insufficient or inadequate monitoring creates a situation where individuals essentially determine their own working practices and corresponding level of effort. In a hierarchical organization, decisions must be passed down to bring about changes in working practices at the various levels. But in hierarchical organizations, even if X-inefficiencies are recognized and instructions to improve productivity are given by senior managers, the decisions are likely to encounter resistance as they flow down the hierarchy because individuals will suffer disutility in changing from their familiar work routine. Such situations are the product of managerial failure.

X-inefficiency is sometimes mistakenly referred to as **organizational slack**. However, *slack* refers to the difference between an *acceptable* performance and minimum cost rather than *actual* performance, i.e. one that management is satisfied with, and minimum cost performance. In both cases, the organization is inefficient in its use of resources, i.e. resources are being wasted, and if they were fully utilized the effect would be an increase in profits. An astute investor who perceives the existence of X-inefficiencies or organizational slack in a company might profitably take over or merge with the company providing, having done so, the inefficiency is removed. Thus, the existence of X-inefficiencies and organizational slack are inconsistent with profit maximization. Before considering why X-inefficiencies are widespread, we will first examine the implications of a profit-maximizing goal.

The foregoing raises the issue as to how, in practice, firms should organize themselves to deal with the problems arising from both imperfect and incomplete information. This, as has been stated more than once above, was not a problem for the neo-classical firm. The entrepreneur held the dual role of owner-manager and under conditions of certainty had but one objective – the maximization of profits. Despite the fact that professional managers, rather than owners, generally run large firms, the assumption that firms pursue – to the exclusion of all other objectives – the goal of profit maximization was unchallenged until the 1930s. However, the profit-maximizing assumption should not be interpreted as implying that firms, or rather their managers, behave as though only motivated by maximizing profits. Economists of the neo-classical school were well aware that individual managers sought, like other individuals, to maximize their utility and that this might lead, at times, to behaviour that was inconsistent with profit maximization – e.g. the building of a lavish headquarters. Rather, the neo-classical model of profit maximization was an abstraction of a more complex model of the firm. The neo-classical school was more concerned with what firms *should do* rather than what they *actually did do* and in profit maximizing they believed they had isolated the primary long-run objective for profit-orientated organizations.

There are a number of reasons, both theoretical and pragmatic, for the resilience of the profit-maximization model. It has, for example, the advantage of being extremely well suited to mathematical modelling. A contemporary proponent of the neo-classical school, the renowned Milton Friedman, argued that the presumption that the 'firm' is a profit-maximizer is not to deny that its workers and managers have their own goals and motivations, but rather to accept that as a single entity the behaviour of individual firms should approximate to that which would occur if it was solely a profit-maximizing entity (Friedman, 1953). Friedman goes further and points out that as theories are abstractions, it makes little sense to judge them on the basis of their realism. The critical test for Friedman is whether the profit-maximizing model yields predictions that are more accurate than predictions from alternative models.

Friedman was writing in 1953, long before economists started to take an interest in the internal workings of organizations and some ten years before Leibenstein's empirical studies revealed the widespread existence of X-inefficiencies. For the neo-classical school, the firm was a 'black box' that acted as an indivisible decision-making unit, i.e. acting like an owner-manager regardless of its management structure. In fact, implicitly all members of the firm's workforce were behaving like individual profit-maximizers. Such a view is acceptable if attention is confined to questions such as the influence of a change in costs and prices on output and profits, but it is a wholly inadequate approach for answering some of the questions raised in preceding chapters, such as: why are some firms more diversified; and why do some firms grow at a faster rate? The neo-classical, profit-maximizing model of the firm is not designed to explain or predict behaviour within the firm. It offers only limited explanation for strategic issues

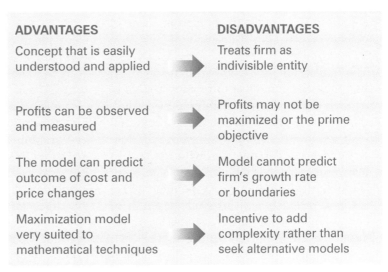

ADVANTAGES	DISADVANTAGES
Concept that is easily understood and applied	Treats firm as indivisible entity
Profits can be observed and measured	Profits may not be maximized or the prime objective
The model can predict outcome of cost and price changes	Model cannot predict firm's growth rate or boundaries
Maximization model very suited to mathematical techniques	Incentive to add complexity rather than seek alternative models

Figure 6.3: Profit-maximization model of the firm

such as the extent of horizontal and vertical boundaries, the rate of growth and how these affect decisions concerning R&D and investment. The neo-classical model is completely silent as to how conflicting objectives between owners, managers and workers are resolved.

If we are to understand how the organization known as the firm functions, then we require more than a model that is good at predicting the areas traditionally of interest to the economist. We need models that are not only based on real-world observations, but also can shed more light on the motivations and behaviour of the individuals within the firm. The profit-maximization model of the firm cannot explain or predict behaviour within the firm; what it does do is explain and predict the effects of changes in costs and prices on the behaviour of the firm's output. Predicting and explaining the behaviour of a firm's managers and workers presents a very different and more complex issue. The advantages and limitations of the profit-maximizing model are summarized in Figure 6.3.

Explaining the Gap

The election of the Labour Party in 1997 brought a heightened interest on the part of the government in improving the UK's relatively poor level, and rate of growth, of productivity. According to the OECD in 1999, the UK's labour productivity 'gap' with the US was 45 per cent, with France 18 per cent and with Germany 11 per cent. In the ensuing years, some studies have shown a modest improvement relative to France and Germany, but overwhelmingly the evidence at the firm level, with some notable exceptions, shows that productivity levels are significantly lower than competitor firms in other advanced industrial nations.

The Department of Trade and Industry (DTI) has published a number of reports seeking to explain the level and distribution of productivity among UK firms. The pattern revealed is of a group of leading firms whose productivity levels are comparable with the best in the world and a long tail of firms that are substantially less productive. In manufacturing, the most productive plants are between three and six times as productive as the least productive plants and, according to the DTI, there is evidence of an even wider productivity dispersion – as much as double that in manufacturing – in service sectors.

The DTI argue that at the level of the firm there are two main factors that account for productivity differences:

- Differences in the competitive environments they face; and
- Differences in the resources available to firms, e.g. physical and human capital, managerial and entrepreneurial capabilities.

The amount and quality (i.e. age) of the physical capital each unit of labour has to work with is a key determinant of labour productivity. The capital–labour ratio is the product of investment expenditure and there is a higher correlation between such expenditure and another important influence – namely, R&D and innovation. But expenditure on physical assets and new technologies is not sufficient; the skills and experience of the workforce are critical.

The DTI reports that about 60 per cent of the productivity gap with the US can be ex-

continued

plained by differences in human capital. More successful, faster growing firms spend more on training their workforces and managerial and entrepreneurial capabilities are higher in such firms. The DTI observes that managers, particularly entrepreneurial managers, are the key to a superior performance by firms. In addition to decisions regarding opportunities, investment, product design and production techniques, their managerial capabilities in motivating and organizing their workforces are of key importance. The DTI reports that the degree of managerial experience is positively associated with the growth rate of firms and productivity growth. Significantly, the report observes that plant level productivity is positively correlated to the productivity of the firm to which it belongs, both in levels and growth rates. This suggests that firms are frequently able to transfer key knowledge and skills between individual plants.

Organizational Architecture

Our purpose throughout has been to go beyond the neo-classical 'black box' representation of the firm as an indivisible decision-taking unit. A convenient starting point is to view the firm as comprising three distinct elements – owners, senior managers, e.g. the CEO and executive directors, and the workforce – and this brings into sharp relief the fact that issues of control, monitoring and incentives are at the heart of the firm. These issues exist between the firm's owners and its senior managers, and, in turn, the same issues arise between the firm's senior managers, their line managers and their subordinates. A firm's organizational architecture plays a critical role in co-ordinating the actions and efforts of individuals and groups within the firm. In this section, we will explore in some detail the issues the organizational architecture has to contend with and in the following sections we will consider related issues such as non-profit-maximizing behaviour on the part of senior managers and the design of executive compensation packages to minimize differences between the objectives of the owners and senior managers.

Ensuring that a firm's workforce is properly co-ordinated and motivated is a key responsibility for senior managers. The first stage in achieving this objective is the employment contract. A firm, as famously observed by Alchian and Demsetz (1972), is a hierarchy consisting of a nexus of contracts, indeed, a nexus of **relational contracts**. These employment contracts are incomplete, largely implicit and delegate authority – the residual decision-making authority – to the firm. Actual tasks and many decisions are carried out by individuals who, whether they work within teams or not, rely on other people. It would be costly and wasteful for every pair of workers to have their own bilateral contracts to co-ordinate activity. Instead, the firm as a separate legal entity enters into multilateral relational contracts with its employees that ultimately allows it, through its managers, to determine and enforce actions if the employees cannot agree amongst themselves.

Granting the firm the **residual decision rights** is the logical counterpart to **incomplete contracts** of employment as they are identified with the ownership of assets (Grossman and Hart, 1986). As contingencies arise, gaps in the contract would have to be filled through bargaining in the absence of a designated residual decision authority. Apart from economizing on information and the costs of contract, multilateral relational contracts serve another motivational purpose by emphasizing a broad commitment to all employees. Employment is a ***repeated game*** between the firm and its employees, and over successive periods a multilateral relational contract is self-enforcing. The firm will fear that deviations from the implied promises in the contract will lead to a breakdown in its relationship with its employees. Thus, an ongoing firm will wish to maintain a ***reputation*** for fairness because this will facilitate future dealings with its employees. The value of a reputation increases with the number of times it is displayed and as the firm can generally be presumed to have a longer time horizon than its employees, it will have a strong incentive to build and maintain its reputation by using its residual decision authority fairly.

Although all employment contracts are incomplete, they are supplemented by ***implicit contracts***. These implicit understandings govern many of the elements of the employment relationship, including work assignments, compensation and employees' duties to one another. Implicit contracts are intended to be self-enforcing. They are structures so that the parties have incentives to abide by them; in other words, any short-term gain from cheating will risk a long-term cost. We will return to these issues in the next chapter; here our focus is the firm's organizational architecture and its purpose in exerting control, promoting efficient communication and delivering incentives.

The next step in achieving co-ordination and motivation is the assignment of ***decision management*** rights, the setting up of monitoring routines and the creation of incentive and reward systems. This is the essence of a firm's organizational architecture and its crucial importance to the firm's efficiency, productivity and competitiveness elevates it to the status of a key capability. Like all capabilities, the nature and contribution of the organizational architecture is unique, as it is the product of accumulated knowledge. Moreover, in response to learning the architecture is constantly changing over time. To the extent that a firm's organizational architecture is the product of history, experience and learning, so optimal architectures will differ systematically across firms. The building of an organizational architecture starts with senior managers determining at what level in the organization decisions will be made. This determines which decision should be centralized, i.e. remain with the firm's senior managers, and which should be decentralized i.e. passed down the organization to the level at which the individual making the decision is best placed to do so. Decisions left at the senior manager level require further decisions about what information will be transmitted upwards to support centralized decision making and what information will flow back down to guide those charged with implementing the decision.

All jobs in a firm consist of both a task and a decision element. At the top of the decision hierarchy, the CEO's role is characterized by few tasks and many decisions and as the firm's senior manager there will be scope for discretion in making many decisions. In contrast, a shopfloor worker may have many tasks, but limited decision authority. Line managers and individual employees are likely to have more knowledge of their areas of responsibility and efficient organizations will seek to take advantage of the knowledge that exists at various levels in the organization. This may involve allowing individuals some autonomy in carrying out line managers' instructions and their own operations. However, decentralizing decision making can only be accommodated within clearly understood boundaries; it must be constrained so as to ensure that the pattern of decentralized decisions are coherent and complementary.

Pushing decision making down to lower levels may also have motivational benefits by imparting stronger incentives for local managers and workers to exert effort in meeting the objectives they themselves set. Decentralization also has the potential advantage of speeding up decision making, particularly in large-scale organizations, and freeing up senior management time to concentrate more on the external business environment and strategy. But decentralization also bears an ***opportunity cost***. Efficient decentralization necessitates a sufficient flow of information from the centre so that local decision makers can make coherent and complementary decisions. The need for coherence and complementarity becomes acute when decisions involve innovation, e.g. product innovation, that requires the collection and evaluation of all information relevant to the strategic choice. Also relevant here is Milgrom's concept of 'influencing costs', where organizational decisions affect the distribution of wealth or other benefits among members of the workforce. It is reasonable to assume that individuals, particularly local managers, are concerned with their careers and they may therefore make decisions on the basis of perceptions about how the outcome will affect their future career. Holmstrom (1982) shows that such career concerns have an impact because an organization learns (makes inferences) about an individual's capabilities on the basis of past performance.

The problem is one of information costs and incomplete contracts. In these circumstances, the firm, in designing its organizational architecture, has to find a balance between tight rules that necessarily involve bureaucratic inflexibility and devising an incentive system that will motivate the desired actions without involving excessive costs. We will be returning to the issue of employee rewards and incentive systems in the next chapter; it is sufficient here to note that the firm's organizational architecture, by influencing the efficiency of the firm's routines and systems, is a major influence on a firm's performance. And key to this is the use of information flows for decision making, at whatever level in the hierarchy. Strategic business decisions present particular complications. Good strategic decisions combine an understanding of the firm's external business environment with line managers' knowledge of operational capabilities. They may also involve access to new knowledge concerning untested technologies and new business partners. A strategic decision may also result in changes to the firm's organizational architecture.

Strategic decisions will normally have implications for the scale, scope and capabilities of the firm and these attributes tend to favour centralized strategic decision making. An anticipated increase in the scale of a firm's operations will have implications for many parts of the operation, for example the degree of capital, specialization, the number of distribution outlets and the recruitment and training of staff. Forecasting market growth, likely competitor reactions and resource availability calls for central co-ordination. A strategic decision may seek to benefit from ***economies of scope*** that arise from a capability that can be exploited across a range of activities. Again, this poses problems of co-ordination and decisions seeking to benefit from economies of scope need to be driven from the centre, e.g. applying knowledge accumulated in one part of the organization to a new venture. In a dynamic environment a firm's ability to introduce new products that align with changing demands – a ***dynamic capability*** – represents a strategic advantage that calls for centralized direction. Centralizing strategy decisions is logical because they depend on a large information flow from the firm's external business environment. But centralized decisions also call for large-scale information flows up and down the organization.

Information on capabilities and performance monitoring must flow up the organization and information must flow down the organization to ensure understanding and co-ordination. In contrast, operational decisions rely on less external information and relatively fewer instructions from senior managers. Senior managers need to be kept informed of performance, hence the need for a real time flow of information up the hierarchy. Figure 6.4 attempts to summarize the information flows associ-

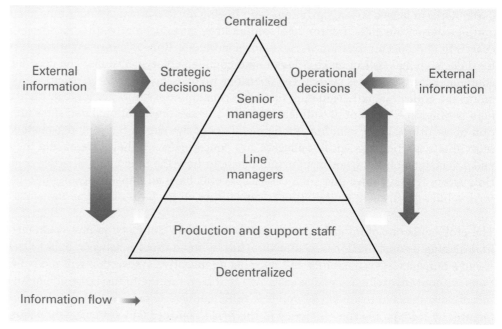

Figure 6.4: Decision assignment and information flows

ated with strategic and operational decision making. The width of the arrows indicates the relative values of the flows.

Figure 6.4 draws a crude distinction between strategic and operational decisions. The figure implies that operational decisions are more appropriate for decentralized decision making as information is largely gathered at a local level. Senior managers need to monitor performance, hence the two-way flow of information up and down the decision hierarchy. Strategic decisions, in contrast, require a lot of information on the external environment and the coherence and complementarities that can only be driven from the centre. When complementarities are present, the various aspects of the firm's strategy must be co-ordinated. But co-ordination may not be sufficient. As described in Chapter 2, Henry Ford effectively co-ordinated the production of the Model T, but Ford's strategy was eventually overtaken by Alfred Sloan's strategy at General Motors that involved redesigning General Motors' organizational architecture.

Within the firm, an organizational architecture replaces the market mechanism for allocating and motivating resources. Within the organizational architecture, the problem of co-ordination is transformed into a problem of management. By implication, in large, complex firms, neither complete centralization nor complete decentralization of decision making are likely to be optimal. Imperfect and incomplete information means that important information will reside with individuals and it is impossible to efficiently communicate all relevant information up to centralized decision makers. Attempts to centralize decision making improves co-ordination, but at the cost of information asymmetries. Leaving all decisions to the individuals involved in their execution risks these decisions being unco-ordinated and hence threatens a loss of coherence for the firm. The problem for the design of a firm's organizational architecture is to strike a balance between centralized and decentralized decision making, whereby optimal coherence and co-ordination is achieved by a clear decision as to what information should be communicated up and down the decision hierarchy and the form of incentives and rewards.

All firms, be they start-ups, SMEs or transnational corporations, have an organizational architecture, though like an iceberg, most of it is hidden from view, and much of the behaviours it engenders will be implicit and tacit. One aspect of the organizational architecture that is highly visible is the firm's ***organizational form***. All firms have an organizational form, but for a small-scale, owner-managed enterprise it will generally consist of a single workshop or office, with most managerial functions undertaken by the owner. This was the common 'form' at the start of the industrial revolution. But from the middle of the nineteenth century in both Europe and the United States, as the scale of business enterprise grew, so it proved increasingly impossible for one person to control and manage the business. Hence, from the mid-nineteenth century onwards, we see the emergence of an organizational form that Williamson (1971) has described as the ***unitary form*** (U-form) of organization.

The U-form gathers activities according to their function within the firm and the structure of a U-form enterprise is shown in Figure 6.5. It is the archetypical centralized hierarchy, with the CEO and board at the top of a structure divided into departments which specialize in function areas covering such activities as marketing, production and finance. These services serve the whole organization and report directly to the CEO. The U-form structure emerged during the development of the US railway system and is suited to the one-product firm that seeks to achieve economies arising from scale and learning. Managers specialize in a particular function and do not need, for the most part, to share much information or communicate regularly with other functional specialists. The U-form structure economizes on ***transaction costs*** by leaving managers within their functional 'silos' to concentrate on their areas of responsibility and in the process builds knowledge and expertise.

The U-form firm has distinct advantages for the development of functionalist specialisms and hence greater efficiency through the ***division of labour***. Specialization improves the performance of a function, increases managerial capacity and competency and thereby helps the firm to expand. The growth of functionalist specialists frees the CEO from undertaking these tasks and allows more time for formulating and implementing strategy. However, by the end of the nineteenth century, the desire to continue growing and the existence of economies of scope led many firms to embark on strategies of ***diversification*** and, in consequence, very large companies began to emerge, particularly in the US. The combination of product diversity and very large scale presented problems for the U-form organization. Horizontal expansion under a U-form structure requires each specialist function to contribute to a widening range of products. The competitive performance of a product, particularly a differenti-

ated product, depends on its design, the quality of its manufacture, marketing effort and post-sale service. As horizontal scale increases, each functional division becomes overloaded and it becomes increasingly difficult for senior managers to monitor and measure the performance of individual products. The ***control loss*** inherent in the growing difficulty of transferring accurate information horizontally across the functional division and vertically be-

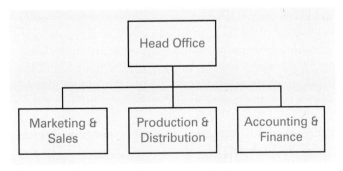

Figure 6.5: The unitary form of organization

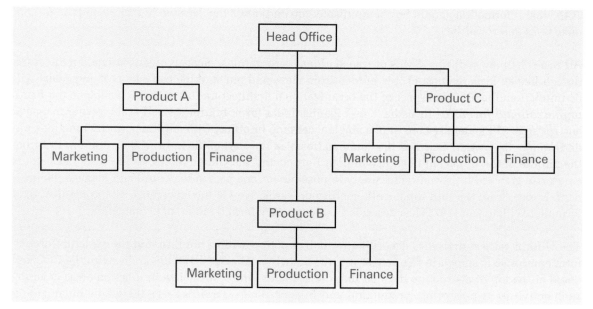

Figure 6.6: The multi-divisional structure

tween those at the sharp end and senior managers serves to increase transaction costs and in particular the scope for **opportunistic behaviour** on the part of line managers and individuals. Chandler
(1966) observed that the U-form collapsed with horizontal expansion and was replaced with what
Williamson (1971) termed the **M-form** (multi-divisional) organization. The M-form firm resembles a
set of scaled-down U-form structures. This organizational innovation consists of a set of operating
business units or 'divisions' or quasi-firms specializing in either a single product or a product range
or geographical areas. Within each business unit, management takes responsibility for both short-run
operational decisions and **business strategy.** Overseeing these business units are the firm's senior
managers, tasked with monitoring divisional performance, allocating resources between the division
and planning **corporate strategy**. Figure 6.6 shows a multi-divisional structure for a diversified firm.

The M-form of organization has a major advantage over the U-form organization. It reduces the 'inefficiency' associated with control loss and enables senior managers to more easily achieve corporate
objectives. The M-form structure allows the performance of each business unit to be measured and
compared. Divisions can also be added with little or no direct impact on the current operations of
other divisions, hence the M-form facilitates the growth of **conglomerate** companies as corporate
strategists pursue product diversification or geographically dispersed transnational business units. A
key feature of the M-form structure is that divisions remit financial surpluses to headquarters, who in
turn allocate resources to the business units on the basis of corporate strategy. Thus, the M-form business also performs as an internal capital market and the firm's longer-term development is therefore
to some degree dependent on the mechanism for allocating investment funds and the power of coali-
tions within the management hierarchy to influence the allocation of funds.

For large and diversified companies that now dominate industrial production in the developed
world, the M-form – or some variant – is the dominant organizational form. A number of hybrid organizational structures have emerged – most notably the **matrix organization**. The matrix organization

attempts to capture both functional and product specializations in one organization. A matrix organization is set out in Figure 6.7. It has functional departments reporting to a CEO, but employees within these functional departments are assigned to teams or sub-units organized around a particular product, product range or geographic area. As the name matrix implies, a matrix organization is characterized by horizontal and vertical lines of authority.

Matrix organizations are particularly suited to firms whose business is characterized by a succession of new products or projects and are found in organizations as diverse as consultancies, construction companies and defence contractors. Individuals are assigned to work in a team or sub-unit and the matrix structure is designed to facilitate the flow of information between all specialisms engaged on the project without compromising functional expertise. In practice, matrix organizations are vulnerable to the split loyalties of employees. Despite being assigned to a team or sub-unit, a functional specialist is likely to view their functional area as being the route to advancement and if so it will be the function rather than the project that dominates behaviour.

Another organizational form, or more correctly inter-organizational form, is the ***network organization***. Driven by the development of long-term relationships and ***alliances***, a network organization is characterized by a grouping of people drawn from separate, but co-operating firms. Like the matrix organization, the purpose and composition of the work groups is determined by the demands of a specific product or project. And like the matrix organization, information flows horizontally amongst the work group and also vertically within the separate organizations. The network organization in principle serves the need for skills and knowledge to be brought to bear on a particular project that do not exist within a single firm's capabilities. But as with the matrix organization, the priority for members of a work group is likely to be the assessment by their functional managers of their performance.

Whatever the claimed advantages of the M-form, matrix and network organizations, they all have in common the fact that the co-ordinating senior managers are heavily dependent on the information

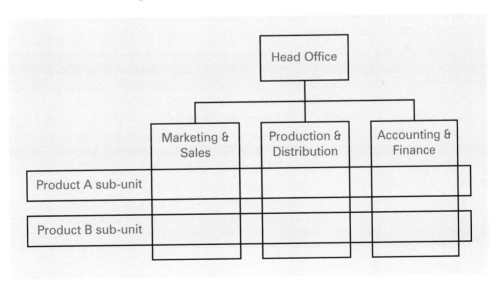

Figure 6.7: A matrix organization

they receive from the separate divisions. If information is inaccurate, untimely or opportunistically distorted, then senior managers will be compromised in their strategic decisions. Also, there is nothing in the organizational form that will guarantee profit-maximizing behaviour if the senior managers are composed of non-profit-orientated directors and it is to this issue we now turn.

From Predator to Quarry

If one company was associated with the phenomenon of Thatcherism in the 1980s, it was Hanson Trust plc. Created in the 1960s, Hanson became, by a process of high profile acquisitions, one of the world's largest companies, with annual profits of more than €2 billion. By the end of the 1980s, ruthless acquisitions and conglomerate growth had delivered spectacular gains to Hanson's shareholders as drastic downsizing and disinvestment in its acquisitions cut costs and boosted the return on capital. Hanson gave full meaning to the word conglomerate – its interests ranged from gold mines, chemicals, electricity generation, cranes, batteries, timber, cigarettes, cod liver oil capsules, toys, golf clubs and jacuzzis. But by the start of the 1980s, Hanson's performance had slipped markedly and it was substantially underperforming on the London stock market. In January 1996, the company was demerged into four separate companies: Imperial Tobacco, The Energy Group, Millennium Chemicals and Hanson. The demerged Hanson was to focus on heavy building materials, e.g. bricks and aggregates. In December 1997, Lord Hanson stepped down as chairperson and over the next three years the Hanson board set about selling off the remaining non-core businesses. By 1999, Hanson was a specialized company with four business units: Hanson Brick, Hanson Quarry Products Europe, Cornerstone-Hanson Building Materials America, and Hanson Pacific. Three years later, in 2002, Hanson Quarry Products and Hanson Brick were combined, and in 2004, Hanson announced further changes to its structure, organizing its business into four trading regions: the UK, US, Australia and Asia, and Continental Europe.

Despite the constant structural change the sparkle that was once associated with Hanson faded during the 1990s and the arch-predator is now itself the subject of much speculation as predators gathered. It would seem that as a focused business, Hanson found it more difficult to make money from its operations than it did when buying and selling businesses. The fate of Hanson has demonstrated a truth that many suspected; namely, those who deal in companies cannot grow companies, they have neither the patience nor the skills. Nor should the costs of such behaviour for the workforce be overlooked. The extensive downsizing has been at some cost to employee loyalty and commitment, particularly amongst white collar workers and also the disutility of increased workloads and stress for those remaining in employment.

Non-Profit-Maximizing Behaviour

We have expended considerable effort in demonstrating that a firm's organizational architecture is critical to its performance. The more accurate and timely the flow of information within the firm, the more likely that mistakes will be avoided and the more speedily can corrective action be taken. To this extent, an efficient organizational architecture will help the firm achieve its objectives. The question is, what are these objectives? If we return to the notion of a three-tier structure – owners, senior managers and the workforce – it might be presumed that it is the owner's objectives that the firm pursues and it is therefore the owners who ultimately influence and control the firm. This view is far from unchallenged. Even though the owners – the shareholders in a public company – have a formal channel of control through the firm's board of directors, there is considerable evidence to suggest that boards rarely take an active role in the running of the firm, and they are more often influenced by senior managers, e.g. the CEO, than shareholders. This raises two questions: in what way might the objectives of senior managers diverge from the objectives of the owners; and how might the owners constrain senior managers from pursuing their own objectives? We will return to the latter question in the next section; here we examine two theories of senior managers' behaviour that diverge from the assumption that the owners and senior managers of private firms both share a profit-maximization objective more normally expressed as maximizing the value of the firm.

In the last chapter, we examined Baumol's seminal non-profit-maximizing model of sales revenue maximizing. Here, we examine non-profit-maximizing behaviour more generally, and two models in particular. Theories offering an alternative to profit maximization as an explanation of the behaviour of firms usually involve the idea that managers pursue satisfactory rather than maximum profits. Evidence for this is provided by the observation that when firms are under pressure, whereby profits are deemed to be unsatisfactory by owners, managers normally succeed in cutting costs. Firms can improve profits in response to reducing costs only if organizational slack exists or X-inefficiencies are present. As observed above the concept of organizational slack is similar to, but not the same as, X-inefficiency, in that management is prepared, for reasons we will explore below, to operate with a degree of slack in the system, whereas they are unaware of X-inefficiencies, at least until they are forced to confront them. Whether senior managers are conscious or not that performance is not being maximized, the existence of organizational slack and X-inefficiency implies that managerial effort is not solely directed towards profit maximization, which in turn implies that managers have other objectives.

A central premise of economic analysis is that individuals have well-defined **utility functions** and that they strive to maximize their utility. Many variables enter an individual's utility function, for example a concern for others, but personal gain and security are prominent, if not dominant, for all. According to Marris (1964), managers have four dominant motives: income, status, security and power. Many other motives have been suggested by other researchers, including competitiveness, game playing and a concern for non-owner stakeholders, e.g. communities in which the firm is located, but there seems widespread acceptance of the existence of the motives identified by Marris.

One way of achieving the four motives imputed by Marris to managers is by increasing the size of the firm, i.e. pursuing a strategy of growth. It is quite possible that the main reason senior managers wish to pursue a sales objective *à la* Baumol is to achieve high incomes, status, power and security. It is also possible that the same objective is being pursued because it is believed that a large market share will deliver higher profits over the longer term. Overall, the desire to increase the size of operations seems a very powerful force amongst commercial organizations. The CEO of a large public company has considerable status and power, as well as high earnings. Luxurious offices in prime locations, expense accounts, large cars and, in some cases, a company plane all boost status and the quality of life. The discretion to make investments for non-productive purposes, e.g. to fund a community or charitable event, might also be influenced by the desire for an enhanced status. These observed non-profit-maximizing behaviours by senior managers of large firms have given rise to a number of **managerial theories** of the firm.

After Baumol's **sales revenue-maximization** model, the best-known non-profit-maximizing model is Williamson's (1964) **expense preference model**. This model, which also includes a Baumol-type profit constraint, is based on the idea that managers' utility functions positively reflect their discretionary behaviour but are subject to reported profits being judged acceptable by shareholders. As a model of managerial discretionary behaviour, the Williamson model is the model that is most frequently deferred to. Essentially Williamson's model starts with the assumption that managers are utility maximizers and that their utility function (U) takes the following form:

$$U = f(S, M, I)$$ (6.1)

where S is excess expenditure on staff, M is management slack – non-pecuniary benefits such as lavish offices in excess of what is necessary for the firm's operations, and I is discretionary investment expenditure – expenditure in excess of what is actually required to maintain profits at the minimal level acceptable to shareholders. Together, these three elements comprise discretionary expenditure and to the extent that funds are devoted to these three elements the firm cannot be profit maximizing. However, in attempting to maximize their utility, managers are constrained by the need to report profits that the shareholders find acceptable. Hence, we can summarize the behaviour of senior managers thus:

$$\text{Max } U \text{ subject to } \pi_R \geq \pi_{min}$$ (6.2)

where π_R is reported profit and π_{min} the minimum acceptable level. The Williamson model is summarized in Figure 6.8. Like Baumol's model, Williamson's model reveals great difficulties when it comes to empirical verification. It is extremely difficult for external observers to identify excess staff expenditure, managerial slack and discretionary investment. With the possible exception of lavish perquisites, discretionary expenditure might be justified if the firm is attempting to increase its scale and/or its rate of growth. The funding of a sporting or charity event may add to senior managers' utility, but it might also raise the company's profile with beneficial effects for sales. Marris, as noted in the previous chapter, has argued that three factors are predominant in promoting firm growth: higher expenditure on advertising and other marketing activities; higher levels of expenditure on research and development; and diversification into new product areas. All three of these factors could be regarded as managerial discretionary expenditure, but it is far from clear that they are pursued at the cost of maximizing the firm's value; that is, maximizing profits over the longer run.

An example of senior managers exercising discretion is when a firm diversifies into new product areas. Indeed, this is an example where the firm might benefit from management discretion, as diversification

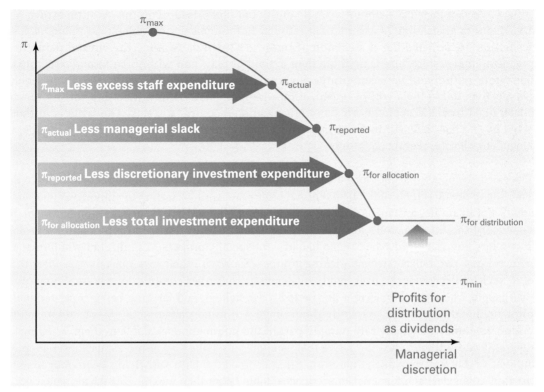

Figure 6.8: The Williamson model

into multi-products could reduce the variation in profit per production period and increase the firm's rate of growth. As demonstrated in Chapter 4, the reduction in risk will only materialize if the profit streams generated by the separate products are uncorrelated. More significantly, we observed in Chapter 5 that UK and US studies have tended to confirm that growth rates are higher for diversified firms. In itself, growth based on diversification is likely to challenge and stimulate management efficiency. Firms that are failing to grow, or even declining, are more likely to exhibit standardized procedures offering managers little scope for discretion and initiative. It would be a serious oversight to seek an explanation for diversification and firm growth rates purely in terms of the exercise of management discretion in order to raise utility. The environment within which the firm operates – in particular, the industry and related technological developments – is likely to be a major influence. We would expect firms operating in a new technology sector – e.g. mobile phones – to grow much faster than, say, a national supermarket chain. Nevertheless, a number of studies have found that in terms of profitability, owner-controlled firms outperform managerially controlled firms (see Leach and Leahy, 1991). Such studies do not confirm that managerially controlled firms seek objectives other than profit maximizing, but they are at least consistent with the Baumol-Williamson-type managerial theory of the firm.

A very different approach to the behaviour of senior managers, once ownership and management are separated, is provided by ***behavioural theories*** of the firm. Behavioural theories seek to explain the process by which a firm's senior managers decide on their objectives, which are assumed to be multiple. The father of the behavioural approach to the firm, Herbert Simon, built his theory on two pillars: the fact that firms are not a single entity but comprised of groups with their own objectives; and that it is misleading to assume that rational individuals are capable of assessing all relevant information before making a decision (Simon, 1979). For Simon, the formal structure of the organizational architecture is no more than a 'field of play' and within the formal structure, informal behaviour within and between groups governs communication and outcomes. From a behavioural perspective, individuals within organizations are motivated according to their utility functions and constrained by the accepted norms and organizational control systems. The issue is further complicated by the fact that within firms most individuals are members of one or more groups, who also have their objectives and constraints.

The existence of groups, both formal and informal, adds an additional layer of complexity to the understanding of the objectives of the firm. Formal groups are split according to authority, function, skill and so on. For example, a finance director will be a member of the senior management team, a leading member of the finance group and possibly a member of an informal group of skilled professionals. Temporary groups may also be formed to carry out specific projects. A multiplicity of formal and informal groups – particularly decision-taking groups – each with their own objectives renders the concept of a single objective for the firm highly misleading. To further complicate matters, Simon pointed out that people are neither omniscient nor perfectly far-sighted, and far from being super-rational they exhibit bounded rationality. As individuals have a limited capacity to absorb, retain and process information, they inevitably rely on only part of the information available to them when making their decisions and settle for the alternative that generates a satisfactory return rather than searching for the alternative that will maximize the return. Simon coined the term **satisficing behaviour** to explain that the firm's managers aim for satisfactory or acceptable rather than maximizing performance.

The significance of Simon's approach for senior managers in attempting to monitor and motivate behaviour within their firms is that they face a multiplicity of decision-making groups and this places limits on their ability to exercise control over their organization. The existence of separate groups with their own objectives inevitably creates the potential for conflict. This knowledge formed the basis of Cyert and March's (1963) behavioural theory of the firm. In an important milestone, Cyert and March attempted to integrate economic and organizational theory and in the process produced a theory of the firm in which bargaining between groups is continuous and **side payments** are made in order for groups to achieve their objectives. This framework applies to all groups within a firm – for example, accountants, engineers and trade union members. Here, we are primarily concerned with the senior management group and organizational goals. Note the word *goals*; Cyert and March identify areas of activity within the firm where organizational goals must be set. These specific goals are likely to include production, sales and profit goals. They then argue that the management groups responsible for these separate areas are inevitably in conflict. The desire by the production group for low-cost production makes high levels of production, ease of scheduling and investment in low-cost maintenance key objectives. But the objective of high volume production is likely to result in high stocks of finished goods inventories if sales fall below expectation. The cost of high stocks and investment are likely to conflict with the top management group's profit objectives. The goal of the marketing group is to increase sales and market share. The tendency is always to lower prices to achieve these goals, with potentially adverse consequences for profits.

The link between the behavioural approach to the firm and satisficing behaviour arises because, in resolving the conflicts between the separate groups, senior managers are forced to seek satisfactory rather than maximum levels of performance from the separate groups. Cyert and March hypothesize that satisficing behaviour gives rise to organizational slack and thus allows senior managers to concentrate, sequentially, on solving problems as they arise for separate groups. The existence of organizational slack means resources are available to investigate and improve the performance of a group that is judged to be performing inadequately in terms of its objectives. This permits performance to be improved with the minimum of impact on other groups' goals. The behavioural approach, with its emphasis on self-interest, would appear more in line with a ***governance approach*** to the firm than the ***competence approach***. The governance perspective, with its emphasis on bounded rationality and opportunistic behaviour, sits easily within the behavioural paradigm of the firm; whereas the competence approach tends to eschew opportunism in favour of the notions of trust and commitment.

Cyert and March's approach essentially takes the level of analysis below that of the organization's goals. The organization might specify maximum efficiency as a goal, but it is only when specific decisions have to be taken to meet this organizational objective that conflicts arise. For example, according to Cyert and March, human agents are myopic and reactive; hence, production managers (not to mention the workers and trade unions) would be expected to react negatively to a reduction in the numbers employed. Similarly, the reaction of research staff to less funding would be expected to be adverse. The great difficulty with the behavioural approach to the firm is that even if it were possible to identify and rank all the objectives of groups within the firm, knowledge of the objectives does not permit unambiguous predictions to be made about the firm's behaviour. Few who have observed firms at close quarters would deny the existence of goal conflicts within them. But the enormous difficulty in making predictions based on behavioural theories – and the observation that such conflicts do not seem to prevent viable and growing organizations – has resulted in little advance in economic behavioural theories.

Will a Leprechaun Bring Success?

The reasons why one company attempts to take over another are very varied. Just why Malcolm Glazer, nicknamed the leprechaun because of his ginger beard, was so keen to acquire Manchester United is less than clear and perhaps we will never know for certain. The owner of the American football team Tampa Bay Buccaneers turned his attention to Manchester United after he failed to buy the LA Dodgers baseball team. Glazer would no doubt always have received a hostile welcome from the United fans, but he did little to help his acceptance by suggesting a deal whereby Manchester

United would be pushed into debt of more than £500 million as a result of takeover.

For the fans, it is a simple choice: profits or the 'Club's heart'. They do not believe that Malcolm Glazer views the club the way they do, but they might very soon change their minds if Glazer returns United to its winning ways. Glazer's plans for the Club include generating additional income via a wider exploitation of media rights and more actively promoting the Club outside the UK. The fans may even forgive him the in-

continued

evitable hike in ticket prices that must follow the takeover if more profits bring better players and bigger wins.

Malcolm Glazer had a similar start with the Tampa Bay Buccaneers, but under his control they won the Super Bowl in 2003. Ultimately, football fans are like financiers, they dream of success and in the event do not mind who delivers it.

Principal–Agent Theory

We asked earlier how might the owners of a firm constrain senior managers from pursuing their own objectives? Ownership imparts residual decision rights and, in the case of a firm, this is the power to hire or fire the firm's executive directors. But the legal notion of ownership involves more than residual decision rights; it also involves the right of possession. Ownership of an asset means entitlement to receive and keep any returns earned by the asset. According to this notion of returns, the owner of a firm is the **residual claimant**. The owner is entitled to whatever remains after all revenues have been collected and all costs paid, and all debts discharged. That is, the owner is the residual risk bearer. If revenues are lower and costs higher than expected, then the owner may receive no return at all. In a small owner-managed firm, the residual claimant and all decision management rights are incorporated in one individual. However, in a public company where the residual risk is separated from decision rights, we find a decision-making process where decision management rights and **decision control rights** are separated (Fama and Jensen, 1983). Decision management rights are the rights to initiate and implement recommendations for resource allocations. Decision control rights are the rights to ratify initiatives and to monitor the implementation of resource commitments and in public companies these are exercised by boards of directors.

The firm is, as noted above, a nexus of contracts, both written and implicit, and the separation of ownership and control adds another dimension. Within the firm, the chief executive officer and senior managers use contracts to motivate lower-level managers in the hierarchy who, in turn, use contracts to motivate their subordinates. As we have seen, hierarchical structures inevitably provide scope for managerial discretion and hence the risk of reduced organizational coherence. A similar problem exists between the owners of the firm and its senior managers. If senior managers' and owners' goals are not aligned and the scope for discretionary managerial behaviour is not minimized, the owners' objectives stand little chance of being maximized. Our focus here is the contract between the owners and the firm's senior managers e.g. CEO. These contracts limit the risks borne by senior managers and make clear that the residual claimants bear the risk. For public companies, the residual risk is spread across many claimants whose residual claims are rights to a share of the net cash flow for the life of the firm. However, the unrestricted nature of the holders of common stock residual claims leads to an **agency cost**.

The firm's decision process is under the control of professional managers. Assuming both the residual claimants and the professional managers are utility maximizers, then there is a good reason to believe that the agent, i.e. the professional managers, will not always act in the best interests of the principal, i.e. the shareholders. Jensen and Meckling (1976) developed a theory of the principal and agent –

which is summarized in Appendix 6A – and shows how agency costs arise once ownership and control are separated. The ***principal–agent problem*** exists at all levels in a hierarchical organization, e.g. supervisor–worker. We will return to the supervisor–worker relationship in the next chapter. Our concern here is with the delegation, by the owners of a firm's capital, of the day-to-day running of the firm to a group of professional managers. The agency problem raised by the separation of ownership and control, or more correctly the separation of residual risk bearing and the decision process, is in principle addressed in public companies by the existence of boards of ***directors***; that is, the executive officers and the non-executive directors of the firm, who have the decision control rights.

The directors are fiduciaries with respect to the firm and its owners and it is the board of directors, not the shareholders, which has the right to intervene in the firm's operations. Strictly, the directors are not agents, their duties are owed to the company and they are therefore independent and in a position, if they so choose, to collude with the firm's senior managers to achieve management objectives. We can therefore still treat the relationship between the owners and the senior managers as falling within the principal–agent paradigm as an introduction to understanding how agency costs are kept to a minimum and control is exercised in a public company. At the heart of the principal–agent paradigm is the divergence of preferences between the principal and the agent. When it comes to senior managers, the problem is not so much one of incentivizing effort – most senior executives are very hard working – but rather one of ensuring they follow value-maximizing goals.

We have given many reasons in the foregoing why a senior manager would not want to exclusively pursue the profit- or value-maximizing objectives of the firm's owners. Differences in preferences are not, however, sufficient to explain why the agency problem carries costs. The agency costs arise from the reality that between the owners and the senior managers there exists asymmetric information. The owners will have information on the profit accruing to shareholders but they are unlikely to know the extent to which profits have been maximized and the effort by managers to achieve this end. And, as discussed above, this raises the possibility that the senior management team may not always act in ways that the owners, i.e. the shareholders, would view as being in their best interests. Managers have much greater knowledge of the relevant aspects of decision making and they also supply unobserved inputs such as effort. Thus, when a CEO is appointed, the owners can neither fully observe the mental and physical effort, nor accurately measure the relationship between this effort, the efforts of others and the firm's performance. This is a classic example of ***moral hazard***.

To a degree, managerial moral hazard is controlled by product and capital markets. Managers of firms in reasonably competitive product markets will be judged by their relative profit performance. The fear of unemployment and the loss of reputation associated with a poor profit performance are likely to provide senior managers with an incentive to control, but not necessarily reduce to zero, managerial slack. The ultimate weapon against managerial slack is presumed to be the threat of takeover. But again, the existence of asymmetric information suggests that managerial slack has got to be significant before an outside raider has an incentive to intervene. And if outsider raiders perceive managerial slack is sufficiently high to justify the costs of launching an attempt to take over the firm, why is it not obvious to the present owners? Presumably a rational raider has private information as to how they might improve the performance of the firm. Nevertheless, while competitive product markets and the threat of a takeover provide an incentive for managers to deliver a better profit performance, it is not possible in a world of imperfect and incomplete information to attribute precise relationships between unobservable actions and observed outcomes.

In practice, shareholders do not rely on product and capital markets to monitor and control the behaviour of the managers to whom they have delegated decision management rights. If shareholders had complete information regarding not only the actions of the firm's senior managers, but also the productive opportunities available to the firm, they could design a complete contract specifying and enforcing the precise managerial actions to be taken. Reality, of course, dictates that only incomplete contracts can be written and with such contracts come agency costs. The basic problem is to design a contract that rewards senior managers so that their self-interested behaviour approximates to the behaviour the owners want; that is, an incentive contract that achieves **goal congruence**.

If senior managers have little or no equity stake in the firm, the scope for opportunistic behaviour suggests that in maximizing utility senior managers have an incentive to appropriate the largest possible amounts of corporate resources in the form of perquisites. As it is impossible for owners to arrive at complete and enforceable contracts with senior managers, rational principals will know that whatever the threats and promises contained in a contract, if it is incomplete it cannot be relied upon to deliver a commitment that is perfectly aligned with the owners' objectives, nor avoid scope for opportunistic behaviour on the part of senior managers. If self-interested behaviour is to lead to goal congruence, then it would seem logical that senior management incentive contracts must be directly related to the profit generated. But this raises the complex issue of the sharing of risk between the principal and agent. Basing a CEO's income solely on the firm's profit leads to an imbalance in the sharing of risk. The owners of a public company, the shareholders, are likely to hold a diverse portfolio of shares in which any one company is only a small part of the risk, whereas the chief executive officer's income and prospects are more likely to be solely dependent on the compensation scheme.

Most people dislike having their incomes dependent on random factors; they are **risk averse** and would rather be entitled to a smaller income whose level is certain than a potentially larger income

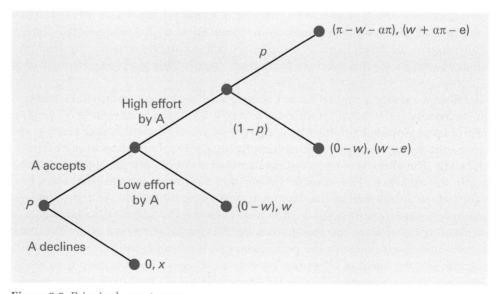

Figure 6.9: Principal–agent game

that is subject to random fluctuations (see Appendix 6B). But if senior managers are paid a fixed salary they have less incentive to put maximum effort into maximizing the value of the firm. This management of risk and incentives between principal and agent can be represented within a principal–agent game. In the game, the agent's effort is not directly observable. The outcome is observable, but this depends not only on the agent's effort, but also on random events, e.g. a downturn in the level of economic activity. The game is set out in Figure 6.9. At the start of the game, the principal (P) offers the agent (A) a salary, plus a share of the profits, α, where $0 < \alpha < 1$. The salary, w, is to be paid regardless, but the value of the profit share depends on the level of profits, π. If the agent refuses to accept the contract, the game ends with the principal obtaining zero profit and the agent earning whatever alternative opportunity is available, say x.

If the agent accepts the contract, a decision has to be made as to the level of effort expended. Low effort leads to an unsuccessful outcome, say profits are zero. The pay-offs here are $(0 - w)$ to the principal and w to the agent. If the agent puts high effort into the project, chance decides whether the outcome is successful earning profits of π, with a probability of p, where $0 < p < 1$, or unsuccessful earning profits of zero, with a probability of $(1 - p)$. In the case of an unsuccessful project, despite the higher effort the pay-off to the principal is the same $(0 - w)$ but the pay-off to the agent is $(w - e)$ as the effort involves disutility. A successful project triggers the profit share, α, and the pay-offs to the principal and agent are $(\pi - w - \alpha\pi)$ and $(w + \alpha\pi - e)$, respectively.

This game is solved by **backward induction**. In the absence of a profit share, i.e. $\alpha = 0$, the agent has no incentive to exert high effort as the utility of w is greater than the utility of w less effort, i.e. $U(w) > U(w - e)$. In the absence of a profit share, the principal must offer a contract where at a minimum $w = x$, but as we have seen this would not be rational. In order to motivate effort, the principal must offer a profit share such that:

$$pU(w + \alpha\pi - e) + (1 - p)U(w - e) > U(w) \qquad (6.3)$$

As discussed in Appendix 6B, what Equation (6.3) demonstrates is that the amount a principal has to pay to motivate high effort increases with the agent's level of risk aversion. If the agent is highly risk averse, the principal will have to put most emphasis on a fixed wage and this, as we have seen, is unlikely to motivate effort. If the agent is closer to **risk neutral**, the principal will put greater emphasis on the profit share to motivate effort.

Before leaving the issue of top management incentives, we need to say more about the fact that observable outcomes are only partly dependent on the efforts of senior managers; they are also the product of a host of factors beyond the control of the firm, e.g. the behaviour of competitors, consumers and governments. We can emphasize these issues and the implications of incentive contracts with the aid of a simple model. Profits, we will assume, are a function of the effort (E) by senior managers and also the state of the business environment (B). For example, in a time of rising demand, or reduced competitiveness, it is likely to be easier for the firm to increase profits. The business environment is not under the control of managers and we can think of its influence as being that of a random variable: in any period it will have a positive or negative influence, but the sign and strength of the influence is unpredictable. Thus for any period we can write:

$$\pi = f(E, B) \qquad (6.4)$$

where π is the firm's actual total profit and $B \approx \mu(\bar{B}, \sigma)$ i.e., the expected value of B is $\bar{B}$, and its actual value is normally distributed with a constant variance. Let us assume that the CEO is the agent and that the CEO's utility is determined by the reward received for effort (R), less the cost of the effort $c(E)$; that is, writing U_A for the agent's utility we have:

$$U_A = f(R) - c(E) \tag{6.5}$$

We must also define the owner's utility, U_O, which we can simply express as:

$$U_O = f(\pi_R - R) \tag{6.6}$$

where π_R is the firm's reported profit. The problem then becomes one of solving the joint maximization of $U_A + U_O$, i.e.

$$\text{maximize } f(\pi_R - R) + f(R) - c(E) \tag{6.7}$$

We cannot solve Equation (6.7) without knowing more about the agent's and principal's attitude towards risk — not to mention familiarity with calculus. However, we can illustrate the problem and its potential solutions. This is done in Figure 6.10, which starts with the point demonstrated above; namely, that the owners can encourage effort by including in the reward a profit element. The agent is expected to generate at least a minimum profit, π_{min}, in return for the fixed element of the reward. As profits increase above this minimum, so the reward is increased by the profit element. But note, the diagram recognizes that beyond a certain level of effort performance starts to decline: even the performance of super managers will suffer if insufficient time is devoted to rest and recuperation.

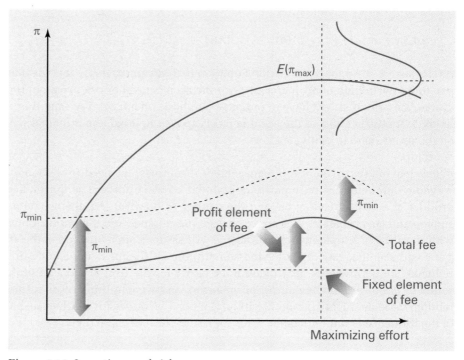

Figure 6:10: Incentives and risks

The risk posed by the business environment is represented by allowing profits to follow a normally distributed variation around the expected maximum, $E(\pi_{max})$. This is designed to show that in any period profits will be above or below the expected maximum depending on the business environment and, as illustrated, the risk is borne by the owners providing profits are comfortably in excess of the minimum.

Although highly simplified, the foregoing does provide some pointers for solving the separation of ownership and management of the firm. Firstly, it suggests that incentive contracts that include a profit element are more likely to attract managers who are risk neutral or even risk-takers than risk averse. Secondly, the risk associated with random fluctuations in the business environment can be reduced by the use of longer-term contracts that focus on performance over a number of time periods. And finally, owners could introduce penalties for performance below an acceptable level. The purpose of incentive contracts is that they help achieve goal congruence and reduce moral hazard. As a general rule for shareholders, incentive contracts are more effective than monitoring, which requires the development of alternative sources of information. As the firm's senior managers control and can therefore manipulate primary information relating to their efforts and performance, shareholders would have to rely on competition and the reported performance of rival companies. Inevitably this can only result in action after the event and in many cases is more expensive than offering explicit incentive controls.

Farmer Controlled

In 2001, the UK farming industry suffered for more than six months with a nationwide outbreak of foot and mouth disease. The industry was already reeling from five years of depressed incomes and the government set up a Policy Commission on the Future of Food and Farming. The Commission reported in 2002 and one of its main recommendations was the establishment of what is now the English Food and Farming Partnership (EFFP) to encourage farmers to collaborate via farmer-controlled businesses (FCB).

By forming a company owned by the farmer members, farmers potentially achieve the benefits of a large plc in their dealings with the food chain. As small-scale businesses producing essentially a commodity product, individual farmers have very little power, but by joining together to own a large-scale business their position is transformed. The general principle is that farmers invest in their FCBs by committing to supply only the FCB and in addition they might further invest by taking a slightly lower price for their produce.

A good example of this new type of ownership is provided by Centaur Grain Ltd. By having the assurance that it will be selling the grain of its members, not only does Centaur have some market power, but it also has the ability to enter into longer-term contracts with customers to supply particular needs. The best known is the partnership with Warburtons to supply Hereward milling wheat for their bread. Hereward is low yielding, so individually no farmer will grow it, despite its great suitability for bread. But by collaborating and selling to the company they own, farmers earn a premium on both the value of their grain and the value of their company.

Stakeholder Capitalism

Managerial and behavioural theories of the firm are, in essence, attempts to explain the ways in which the power of shareholders to control the firm they own is, in practice, shared with **stakeholders**: principally, senior managers and to varying degrees the workforce. The concept of stakeholders, however, goes further than shareholders, managers and the workforce; it also includes the firm's customers, suppliers and **complementors**. The traditional view – at least from an Anglo-American perspective – is that shareholders are the key to better performance by firms; at the very least, they provide the incentive for a better performance by allowing for the takeover of poorly performing companies. At face value, the shareholder approach is in conflict with a stakeholder approach to the firm which, according to critics, inevitably runs the risk that senior managers in exercising discretion will give too much weight to stakeholder concerns, thereby reducing efforts to maximize profits.

The stakeholder approach to the firm gained ground during the 1960s and 1970s, particularly in Europe. Starting in the 1980s, however, at least in the UK and the US, the balance of power began to swing back towards the owners of capital. As the 1990s unfolded, both global markets and global competition expanded rapidly, reinforced by the exponentially growing information and communication technology. The result was that many large, diversified firms found their corporate growth strategies of earlier decades too inflexible to respond to the rapidly changing business environment. As these conglomerates underperformed so they became vulnerable to the power of shareholders, who ruthlessly exercised their new-found powers as demonstrated by three business traits closely associated with the 1990s:

- Downsizing, which reduces the wage bill leaving more income for distribution to shareholders.
- Flexible working, which is frequently associated with lower wages and poor working conditions.
- A noticeable change in company reports emphasizing the primacy of maximizing returns to shareholders.

Senior management decisions involving any of these three traits are typically rewarded, in the short run at least, by a jump in the share price. And yet there is a distinct lack of evidence that any of the three traits outlined above have contributed to an improved longer-term performance. A survey conducted by the American Management Association of more than 500 downsizes showed that over half failed in their objective of improving operating profits; a majority had to rehire within the year; stress-related illness amongst employees jumped; and complaints from customers increased (AMA, 1996). In the UK, takeover targets, such as ICI and Pilkington, were vulnerable because they had set aside funds to provide for: employee education; buying of new equipment; improvement of quality; and development of new products. If these pay off, it is in the long term rather than the short term. But corporate raiders see the opportunity to reduce such discretionary expenditure and divert the funds to shareholders. In this way, the search for the 'quick buck' by owners threatens the creation of increased wealth over the longer term. A report published by the Royal Society for the Arts (1995) and sponsored by firms such as Cadbury Schweppes, Guinness, Midland Electricity, Unipart and NatWest, asserted that: '. . . those companies which will sustain competitive success in the future are those which focus less exclusively on shareholders and financial measures of performance – and instead include all their stakeholder relationships ... in the way they think and talk about their purpose and performance.' This observation is particularly significant as its authors were explicitly departing from the traditional Anglo-American view that a public company has one overriding goal; namely, to maximize returns to shareholders.

The report's conclusions would not have been surprising if they had been written by a group of senior Japanese or continental European managers. Companies in these regions often accept broader obligations that balance the interests of shareholders against those of other stakeholders. The proponents of stakeholder capitalism argue that wealth is created by people working together in teams in organizations – and these organizations can work only if the motivation systems recognize the basic human priorities and relationships involved. All businesses are rooted in a social context and the values that govern behaviour generally cannot be separated in business. People cannot be expected to be aggressive, selfish individuals in business but suddenly become altruists when they consider the less well-off or their own families. In short, businesses – whether a corner shop or multinational – operate through a network of co-operative working, where selfish behaviour is dysfunctional and relationships are cemented by trust and commitment.

The thrust of the stakeholder approach to the firm is the argument that companies are most successful when they build long-term relationships with everyone who has a stake in the business: employees, suppliers, customers and the community at large. This approach offers an alternative to the traditional focus on shareholders and would appear to confer the following advantages:

- Treating employees as part of a team and involving them in a firm's strategic decision making is likely to engender a co-operative environment, and give employees a stronger incentive to take the time and trouble to invest in acquiring skills that are valuable within their firm.
- Actions that foster a longer-term commitment to suppliers enable both buyer and seller to make investments that might otherwise have appeared too risky.
- A commitment to treat customers fairly and openly is likely to build closer relationships and reputation which, over the longer term, will aid the sharing of information, joint ventures and partnerships.
- The development of social responsibility has the benefit of reducing the probability of the imposition of regulations and legislation, whilst also reducing the scope for critics of private capitalism.

This last point deserves a little more attention; indeed, it has given rise to the expression **corporate social responsibility**. In a world of perfect information and complete contracts where property rights are well established and tradable, there would be little basis for complaint about a firm pursuing the interests of its shareholders (Milgrom and Roberts, 1992). In reality, decisions are made by firms, be they large or small, that affect people in ways that are not mediated by market forces. For example, in the UK the major clearing banks have in the pursuit of efficiency closed many rural branches, leaving many small towns without a bank. Such a policy is understandable as part of a profit-maximizing strategy, but it imposes significant **externalities** on rural communities – for example, a higher cost of banking and reduced development prospects for local businesses. Another example of an externality is pollution. A firm that chooses to pollute may increase its shareholders' wealth, but only at a cost to those it pollutes and hence a reduction in **social efficiency**.

The concept of corporate social responsibility has been defined as the extent to which individual firms serve social needs other than those of its owners and senior managers, even if this conflicts with the maximization of profits (Moir, 2001). The adoption of social responsibilities can in the presence of externalities be efficient for society. But it is by no means obvious. Lacking perfect information and being boundedly rational, it is unlikely that the managers of individual firms will be able to efficiently balance all the costs and benefits for society. Critics of a stakeholder approach

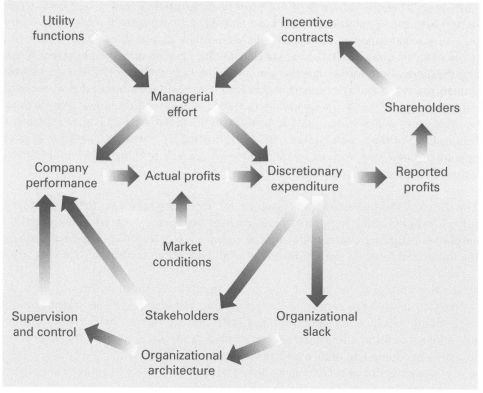

Figure 6:11: Incentives, effort and performance

argue that senior managers should not be making ethical decisions that rightly belong to society or use profits that rightly belong to their shareholders for social ends.

Critics further point out that the concept of stakeholder capitalism does not easily fit into the culture of British and American capitalism; moreover, for all their past virtues, German and Japanese companies may not be models for the future. Over recent years both German and Japanese companies have suffered low rates of growth. That future is likely to witness ever-more intense competition from global markets spurred by rapid technological advance. In such a fluid and fast-moving world, success may lie with companies who are capable of rapid changes in structure and direction and whose workforces neither expect nor desire long-term employment with one company. Support for this view is provided by the observation that most of the big new companies of the 1990s, such as Microsoft, Netscape and Oracle, have come from the entrepreneurial culture of the US, rather than from Germany or Japan.

The best companies know that serving their customers well and caring for employees is essential to their long-term health. But in a climate in which public companies suffer heavy penalties if dividends and the share price are not persistently raised, senior managers are compelled to claim that their prime objective is increasing shareholder value. At face value, this would suggest that senior managers are yoked to maximizing short-term shareholder value for owners who frequently display their lack of commitment to longer-term wealth creation. The logic is a temptation, driven by the threat of a hostile takeover, to target the investment gains from buying or selling assets rather than developing the core business. In contrast, the stakeholder approach is founded on the belief that real, sustainable wealth creation depends on co-operation, commitment and trust. Companies cannot buy and sell trust and commitment: both are 'goods' whose value actually increases the more they are 'produced' or nurtured. Good managers recognize that management confers obligations to those who invest their effort and skills on behalf of the organization and a longer-term perspective will inevitably cause managers to realize that they have a responsibility to the community within which the firm is located, from which it draws its workforce and which is vulnerable to externalities arising from their decisions. A more considered view of the many complex influences on senior managers might conclude that shareholders are likely to be viewed as *primus inter pares*. Figure 6.11 attempts to summarize the web of influences surrounding the behaviour of senior managers.

A Phoenix Snuffed Out

The experience of Rover under British ownership demonstrates a weakness of a system dominated by shareholder property rights. Britain combines an active stock market with absolute shareholder property rights; as a result there is little incentive for shareholders to commit themselves to the companies they own – they can buy and sell their shares too easily. BMW bought Rover from British Aerospace, whose short-term approach to the business was demonstrated when it bought and sold the company in five years as part of a frenzy of deal-making that nearly brought British Aerospace to its knees. BMW came with a reputation for stability, continuity and commitment of ownership that most British businesses can only envy. One of the first actions of the long-termist BMW as Rover's owner was to double investment above the level where it stood under British ownership.

But within two years, BMW had sold Land Rover to Ford and decided that only the Mini offered the prospect of a profitable future. MG Rover was sold to Phoenix Venture Holdings Group for £10 following a vociferous public campaign that effectively killed an alternative takeover from Alchemy Partners, a venture capital group. The main architect of the Phoenix takeover was John Towers, who had previously worked for Rover. So keen were BMW to be rid of Rover that in return for a £10 stake, Phoenix received £909 million, including a stock of 65,000 cars and an interest-free loan of £427 million from BMW that would not need to be repaid until 2049.

The effect of BMW's largesse in 'getting shot' of Rover was to flatten the company's 'profits'. From 2000 until the end of 2003, headline losses were £276 million, but if the non-operating goodwill benefits are stripped out, the underlying business losses climbed to £660 million. Such losses are not sustainable and in April 2005 Rover collapsed, bringing to an end the era of mass car production in Britain by a British-owned company. Many questions have been raised regarding the stewardship of Rover by Phoenix, but the sorry truth is that Britain was never prepared to invest long term in the production of cars.

Concluding Thoughts

Once we relax the highly restrictive neo-classical assumptions that firms are one-product, one-plant, profit-maximizing entities whose owner-managers are gifted with perfect information and super-rationality, we find a very complex world. We know that most firms produce more than one product and empirical studies reveal that far from minimizing costs, firms suffer X-inefficiencies and/or organizational slack. Both of these 'inefficiencies' arise from either inadequate management systems or the pursuit by managers of other objectives as well as profits. As we move away from the neo-classical paradigm of a small-scale firm producing under conditions of certainty and run by the owner, we must take account of three distinct influences – the owners, the senior managers and the workforce – on the firm's performance. This brings into focus the fact that issues of control, monitoring and incentives are at the heart of the firm. Within the firm, its organizational architecture is critical to the co-ordination and motivation of individuals and groups. The firm's organizational architecture is a nexus of relational, incomplete contracts that assign decision rights and designate residual decision rights to the firm. In addition to formal contracts, co-ordination and control is supplemented by implicit contracts.

Once decision rights have been allocated, the role of the organizational architecture is to ensure a sufficient flow of information so that performance can be monitored and rewarded. Information flows will, in part, depend on the extent to which decision making is centralized within the firm. In theory, centralizing decision making improves co-ordination, but at the cost of information asymmetries. Decentralizing all decision making incurs the risk of unco-ordinated decisions and a loss of organizational coherence. A major influence on the balance between centralized and decentralized decision making is the firm's organizational form. When it comes to large-scale, diversified firms, the M-form of organizational structure has generally replaced the U-form, though a number of firms have adopted the hybrid matrix structure. The M-form permits a much greater increase in the size of companies by pushing many decisions down to the business unit level.

In principle, organizational architecture serves to help a firm achieve high levels of efficiency, yet the persistence of X-inefficiencies and organizational slack suggest that senior managerial effort is not solely directed towards profit maximization. A central premise of economic analysis is that an individual strives to maximize their utility. This applies to senior managers who appear to obtain utility from status and power as well as earnings. These non-profit-maximizing behaviours have given rise to managerial theories of the firm, the best known of which is Williamson's expense preference model. The idea is that senior managers obtain utility from discretionary expenditure, which is pursued at the cost of maximizing the firm's value.

A very different explanation for organizational slack is provided by behavioural theories of the firm. This approach views the firm as consisting of a multiplicity of formal and informal groups, each with their own objectives, which renders the concept of a single objective for the firm highly misleading. Matters are further complicated by the belief that people are boundedly rational and hence managers engage in satisficing behaviour. The existence of many groups creates potential for conflict and an acceptance of satisfactory performance creates the scope (arising from *slack*) to resolve these conflicts.

Large firms are characterized by the separation of ownership and control. Shareholders are obviously concerned to limit the scope for managers running their companies to engage in discretionary or satisficing behaviour and to align their self-interest with their objective of profit maximization. This is a principal–agent problem, which is generally solved by incentivizing managers rather than seeking to directly control their actions. The general approach is one of setting incentives that align managers' and owners' interests, while minimizing the risk to senior manager rewards from an uncertain business environment. Typically, senior management incentive contracts link reward to the profit performance, but only to a degree. The incomes of senior managers include a fixed element so that they are not solely dependent on profit.

Finally, despite the growing power of shareholders, over the past 20 years senior managers must have regard to the interests of the firm's other stakeholders and their obligations to them. This involves the adoption of a longer-term perspective that inevitably involves the building of relationships with employees, suppliers and customers. More recently, the responsibility of firms to the wider community has attracted attention and given rise to the concept of corporate social responsibility. The conclusion drawn here is that despite the many demands for attention by stakeholder groups, shareholders remain *primus inter pares*.

Key Learning Points

- The neo-classical theory of the firm avoided issues of decision rights, monitoring and motivation by assuming owner-managers' perfect information and hyper-rationality.
- In practice ownership and control are separated in most large firms and empirical studies show that X-inefficiencies and organizational slack are widespread.
- X-inefficiencies are the result of inadequate motivation and monitoring, whereas organizational slack arises from satisficing behaviour on the part of managers.
- A firm's organizational architecture determines the allocation of decision rights, monitoring and reward systems.
- The organizational architecture is a nexus of contracts; the inability to write complete contracts being offset by a reliance on relational and implicit contracts.
- Information flows are the lifeblood of an organizational architecture and their focus and volume depend on the extent to which decisions are centralized.
- Organizational form has a direct bearing on the balance between centralized and decentralized decision making and hence the flow of information.

- Managerial theories seek to explain non-profit-maximization behaviour as the outcome of senior managers attempting to maximize their utility from the exercise of discretionary expenditure.
- Behavioural theories of the firm view non-profit-maximizing behaviour as the outcome of satisficing behaviour and as necessary in the presence of bounded rationality to resolve inevitable goal conflicts between individuals and groups within an organization.
- Rational shareholders will attempt to limit discretionary managerial or satisficing behaviour by offering incentive contracts that align managers' self interest with shareholder objectives.
- Incentive contracts combine a profit share with a fixed income so that senior managers are not unfairly exposed to the impact of the external environment and profits.
- The concept of the stakeholder firm's corporate social responsibility appears in conflict with the maximization of shareholder interests, though in practice a longer-term perspective renders shareholders *primus inter pares*.

Exercises

6.1 The existence of organizational slack and X-inefficiencies are incompatible with profit maximization. What is the difference between these two concepts and what purpose might organizational slack serve?

6.2 If a firm's organizational architecture is a nexus of contracts, why are they likely to be relational, why do they co-exist with implicit contracts and why are residual decision rights retained by the firm?

6.3 Discretionary expenditure by senior managers was seized upon by Williamson as evidence of non-profit-maximizing behaviour, but in what circumstances might such behaviour be consistent with value maximization?

6.4 The separation of residual risk and decision rights raises the principal–agent problem. Why is the emphasis in senior executive contracts placed on incentives rather than control?

6.5 In the presence of externalities, why is a profit-maximizing objective insufficient?

Problems

6.1 A firm's profits are a function of effort by its CEO, e, and the state of nature s_i. Thus $\pi = f(e, s_i)$, where there are n discrete states and the probability of each occurring is given by ρ, where $\Sigma\rho = 1$. The owner pays the CEO a fee, F, based on the outcome of π. The owner's utility is given by $U = f(\pi - F)$ and the CEO's utility is given by $U = f(F, e)$, where the disutility of effort is given by $c(e)$:

(a) Write the expression showing the CEO's expected utility.

(b) Write the expression to show the owner's expected utility.

(c) Show that the only condition under which the owner's and the CEO's expected utilities are matched is when $\Delta F/\Delta\pi = 1$.

6.2 The UK government has just announced plans to publish rankings for General Practitioners' surgeries. It is well known that the successful treatment of a patient depends only partly on the skill of the doctor and depends primarily on the severity of the illness. It is alleged that following the introduction of rankings, doctors will have an incentive to screen potential patients before accepting them:

(a) Do you think all doctors will have the same incentive to screen potential patients?

(b) Do you think the incentive to screen will be influenced by the doctor's present ranking?

(c) What other factors are likely to influence a doctor's incentive to screen potential patients?

References

Alchian, A. and Demsetz, H. (1972) 'Production information costs and economic organization', *American Economic Review*, vol. 62, pp. 777–795.

AMA (1996) *Downsizing, Job Elimination and Job Creation*, American Management Association, New York.

Chandler, A. (1966) *Strategy and Structure*, Doubleday and Company, New York.

Cyert, R. and March, J. (1963), *A Behavioral Theory of the Firm*, Prentice Hall, Englewood Cliffs, NJ.

Fama, E. and Jensen, M. (1983) 'Separation of ownership and control', *Journal of Law and Economics*, vol. 26, pp. 301–325.

Friedman, M. (1953) *Essays in Positive Economics*, University of Chicago, Chicago.

Grossman, S. and Hart, O. (1986) 'The costs and benefits of ownership: a theory of vertical and lateral integration', *Journal of Political Economy*, vol. 91, pp. 907–928.

Holmstrom, B. (1982) 'Managerial incentive problems – a dynamic perspective' in *Essays in Economics and Management in Honour of Lars Wahlbeck*, Swedish School of Economics, Helsinki.

Jensen, M. and Meckling, W. (1976) 'Theory of the firm: managerial behaviour, agency costs and ownership structure', *Journal of Financial Economics,* vol. 3–4, pp. 305–360.

Leach, D. and Leahy, J. (1991) 'Ownership, structure, control type classification and the performance of large British companies', *Economic Journal*, vol. 81, no. 3, pp. 541–562.

Leibenstein, H. (1966) 'Allocative efficiency as X-efficiency', *American Economic Review*, vol. 56, pp. 392–415.

Marris, R. (1964) *The Economic Theory of Managerial Capitalism*, Macmillan, London.

Milgrom, P. (1988) 'Employment Contracts, Influence Activities and Efficient Organizational Design', *Journal of Political Economy,* vol. 96, pp. 42–60

Milgrom, P. and Roberts, J. (1992) *Economics, Organization and Management*, Prentice Hall, Englewood Cliffs, NJ.

Moir, L. (2001) 'What do we mean by corporate social responsibility?', *Corporate Governance*, vol. 1, no. 2, pp. 16–22.

Royal Society for the Arts (1995) *Tomorrow's Company*, RSA, London.

Simon, H. (1979) 'Rational decision taking in business organizations', *American Economic Review*, vol. 69, pp. 493–513.

Williamson, O. (1964) *The Economics of Discretionary Behavior*, Prentice Hall, Englewood Cliffs, NJ,

Williamson, O. (1971) 'Managerial discretion, organizational form and the multi-division hypothesis' in *The Corporate Economy*, R. Marris and A. Wood (eds), Harvard University Press, Cambridge, MA.

Jensen and Meckling (1976) put forward the following model for analysing the agency costs of out-side equity. They start by comparing the behaviour of an owner-manager who owns 100 per cent of a firm's residual claims with the same manager's behaviour when a portion of the residual claims are sold to outsiders. The owner-manager is assumed to make operating decisions on the basis of maxi-mizing his utility and prior to selling some of the equity the situation can be represented by Figure 6A.1. Jensen and Meckling argue that the owner-manager has a choice between maximizing the value of the firm or how much non-pecuniary income – what Williamson (1964) terms discretionary spending – he will extract from the firm, e.g. lavish offices. The agency conflict between the owner-manager and outside shareholders is characterized by the manager's tendency to appropriate resources for his own consumption. The current market value of the firm is V, measured along the vertical axis and the market value of the manager's stream of expenditures on non-pecuniary bene-fits, F, is measured along the horizontal axis.

The current value of the firm is represented by $\bar{V}$ and by definition this is the maximum present value of the firm's expected net cash flows, where variable costs include a given money wage for the owner-manager; that is:

$$\bar{V} = i_0 + \sum_{t=1}^{n} \frac{pq - c(q) - w}{(1 + r)^t} \qquad (6A.1)$$

where pq is expected revenue, $c(q)$ expected materials expenditure and w wages including the owner-manager's wage. The scale of the firm depends on the initial level of investment i, hence the budget constraint $\bar{V}$ shifts to the right as the scale of the firm increases, i.e. as the level of investment rises. At point $\bar{V}$, the consumption of non-pecuniary benefits is zero. If the owner-manager's con-sumptions of non-pecuniary benefits is zero, the market value of the company is maximized at $O\bar{V}$. If the owner-manager consumes $O\bar{F}$ of non-pecuniary benefits, the market value of the firm falls to zero. Every €1 spent on non-pecuniary benefits reduces the current market value of the firm by €1; hence, the decline in the current market value of the firm as each tranche of non-pecuniary benefits is withdrawn from the firm is represented by the line $\overline{VF}$, whose slope is −1. The owner-manager's preference for wealth and non-pecuniary benefits is represented by an indifference curve map. When the owner-manager has 100 per cent of the equity, utility is maximized at point W, where the value of the firm is V^* and the consumption of non-pecuniary benefits, F^*.

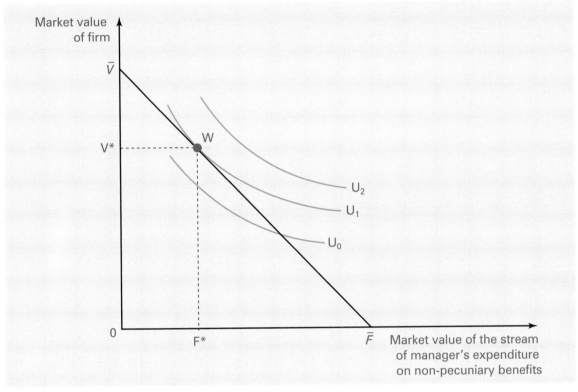

Figure 6A.1: Market value and non-pecuniary benefits

Suppose now the owner-manager sells a fraction of the firm, α, to an outsider, where $0 < \alpha < 1$, and retains $(1 - \alpha)$. If the buyer believes the owner-manager will continue to consume F^* of non-pecuniary benefits, she will be willing to pay αV^* for the share of the equity on sale as shown in Figure A6.2. However, given that an outsider now holds a claim to α of the equity, the cost to the manager of consuming an additional euro of non-pecuniary benefits now falls to $(1 - \alpha)$€1. That is, if unconstrained, the manager's choice of non-pecuniary benefits now lies on a flatter budget constraint, i.e. V_1B_1 with a slope of $-(1 - \alpha)$. If the owner-manager remains free to choose the level of non-pecuniary benefits subject only to the loss of wealth he incurs as part owner, his welfare will be maximized by increasing his consumption of such benefits. As shown, the manager will move to a point such as X on this new budget constraint, consuming F_1 of non-pecuniary benefits because only $(1 - \alpha)$€1 of wealth is given up for every €1 of non-pecuniary benefits consumed.

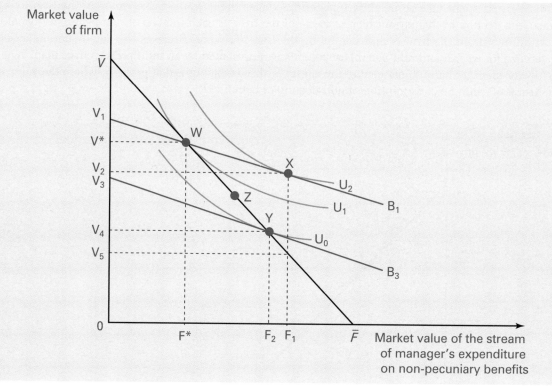

Figure 6A.2: Value to an external buyer

If the buyer is rational, she will be aware that the owner is likely to increase non-pecuniary consumption, and consequently she would be left with a share of a firm only valued at V_2. The potential owner will not therefore be prepared to pay αV^*. The market value of the firm has fallen to V_2 and the rational buyer will only pay αV_2 for a α share of the equity. This means that the decline in the value of the firm, $(V^* - V_2)$, must be entirely borne by the owner-manager. As the market value of the firm falls in response to the belief that the manager will increase consumption of non-pecuniary benefits, so the manager will have an incentive to signal a willingness to scale back on the consumption of non-pecuniary benefits associated with point X. As an equilibrium between the market value of the the firm and the manager's non-pecuniary benefits must occur on the budget constraint, $\overline{V}F$, this implies that the equilibrium will be at a point like Y, where the slope of the manager's budget constraint is tangential with an indifference curve. The budget constraint, V_3B_3, has the same slope as V_1B_1 i.e., $-(1 - \alpha)$ and is tangential to the indifference curve U_0 at Y. The rational buyer will be prepared to pay αV_4 for a α share of the equity and the owner-manager will consume F_2 of non-pecuniary benefits. In practice, a rational buyer can avoid such a loss in value by introducing formal control systems or establishing incentive systems that align the manager's interests with the outside shareholders. These monitoring costs will restrict the owner-manager's consumption of non-pecuniary benefits to an amount less than F_2. Thus, in the presence of monitoring costs we will arrive at an equilibrium value of the firm, such as Z. The agency costs associated with this outcome are the loss in value of the firm and the monitoring costs.

Pay-off uncertainty is an important consideration in contractual
relationships because most
people care about their exposure
to risk. An individual's risk preferences can be represented in
the shape of their utility function. An individual is said to be
risk averse if they prefer to get a
monetary payment for certain
rather than a random outcome
having the same expected payment. To see this, consider
Figure 6B.1.

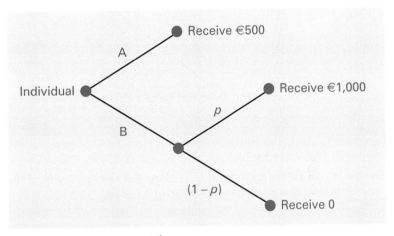

Figure 6B.1: Certainty or risk

If the probability, p, takes the
value 0.5, then the expected value of selecting option B is the same as option A in monetary terms.
But few individuals would select option B because the certainty of €500 delivers greater utility. That
is, if $U(\ )$ represents the individual's utility function then:

$$U(500) > 0.5U(0) + 0.5U(1000) \tag{6B.1}$$

This risk aversion is represented by the concave utility function shown in Figure 6B.2. If an individual prefers to get €500 for certain, this is represented as delivering a higher level of utility – point A
in Figure 6B.2 – than the expected outcome of a risk represented by point B. Given the shape of the

utility function illustrated, the individual would be indifferent between receiving the payment x with certainty and the expected value $0.5U(0) - 0.5U(1000)$, where $x <$ €500. That is:

$$U(x) = 0.5U(0) + 0.5U(1000) \qquad (6B.2)$$

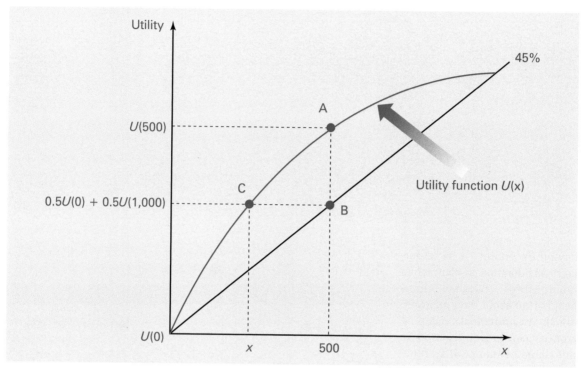

Figure 6B.2: Utility function and concavity

The more risk averse an individual, the greater the concavity of the utility function. The utility function for an individual who is **risk neutral** would lie along the 45° line.

CHAPTER 7

WAGES, INCENTIVES AND HUMAN RESOURCES

Introduction

The underlying theme of the previous chapters has been the efficiency of economic organizations. Whatever a firm's objectives, a fundamental principle is that the potential rewards to all concerned will be greater if it seeks to achieve efficiency in its use of the resources over which it has **property rights**. This economic approach may appear cold and calculating when applied to people, but in order to be efficient, the firm needs to control and co-ordinate the decisions and actions of its employees. But unlike inanimate resources, human resources must be motivated to a level of effort that will result in individuals carrying out to the full their contribution to the co-operative activity that is a firm. We have seen that central to achieving organizational efficiency is the firm's **organizational architecture**. A key aspect of an organizational architecture is its ability to attract, motivate and retain efficient employees. Much of the firm's accumulated knowledge, its particular competitive capabilities, will be embodied within its workforce, or more precisely, within its **human capital**. If the firm is to achieve high levels of **productivity** from its human capital, it will have to pay attention to the way in which it measures and rewards the performance of its workforce. Critical to achieving high levels of efficiency is the fostering of the belief on the part of the workforce that the control and incentive mechanisms are reasonable and fair.

Our focus in this chapter is the firm's workforce and in particular the relationship between the rewards system and human resource productivity. We continue to assume that people are self-interested and rational and will respond positively to pay levels and other incentives that improve their wellbeing. For its part, the firm will wish to attract individuals with the ability to undertake value-adding activities and to develop their human capital in ways that benefit the firm. Economic theories offer many valuable insights on alternative reward systems and their likely influence on the motivation and efficiency of employees. The general problem of motivating an individual to act on behalf of the firm is, as we have seen in the previous chapter, a *principal–agent* problem. As we have seen, solving this problem involves not only the design of incentive pay, but also the job design, including the allocation of decision rights and measuring of performance. When it comes to employees, the principles are precisely the same as we applied to senior management compensation; namely, providing incentives that align self-interest with the objectives of the firm. But in a world characterized by *asymmetric information* and people subject to *bounded rationality*, performance cannot be perfectly measured. Moreover, the problem of measuring performance is further complicated by the fact that firms are characterized by *team production*, rather than the output of individuals.

In addition to motivating and rewarding individuals, a firm will also wish to retain and develop productive employees. The skills, efforts, accumulated knowledge and commitment of a firm's employees are a major source of *competitive advantage* – hence, the importance of managerial skill in devising and implementing efficient human resource policies, an area of specialization that falls under the heading of *human resource management* (HRM). These policies, their structure and management, have an enormous impact on an organization's ability to create and capture value, the accumulation of knowledge and the quality of life shared by the firm's employees. Career paths are an important area of HRM, and this introduces the element of time into the issue of compensation. The reward for loyalty and commitment is virtually institutionalized in most economic organizations with career paths that increase earnings as the years of employment rise.

The relationship between employer and employee will be based on a contract, though, as previously explained, this will necessarily be a *relational contract* augmented by an *implicit contract*. The decision-making element in the employment contract grants *residual decision rights* to the firm, i.e. the employee's managers. With *imperfect information* and *incomplete contracts*, there are efficiency advantages to having the representative of the firm decide what is to be done when unforeseen contingencies arise. In introducing the subject of contracts and the relationships between employees and their managers and colleagues it serves to remind us that the firm is a social, as well as an economic, community. This is not to imply that profit-orientated firms are not first and foremost economic entities, but rather to caution that a purely economic approach can never be sufficient when dealing with such complex issues as people and their employment relationships.

People get satisfaction from their work when their efforts are appreciated and rewarded. Most people define themselves in terms of their job and many identify with their employers. A firm develops a culture based on both the formal and informal aspects of its organizational architecture. Company folklore and rituals contribute to an individual's sense of belonging. Although important, these 'softer' elements are not explicitly examined in this chapter. Our focus in this chapter is the formal aspects of human capital within the organizational architecture and in particular the use of economic analysis to help explain and understand the economic behaviour of individual employees in response to incentives designed to achieve the firm's objectives, including high levels of efficiency. By reading this chapter, you will:

- Understand why the *neo-classical approach* to employment and the determination of wage rates is a very inadequate model of reality.
- Appreciate the principal–agent problem and the wage models that it has given rise to in order to motivate employees.

- Be aware of the methods and benefits accruing to the firm from an active human resource management policy.

This chapter is divided into six sections. The first two sections provide an overview of the neo-classical approach to the supply and demand for labour. The first section outlines a model of labour supply based on rational and self-interested behaviour. The second section builds on the analysis of supply to show how, in a world characterized by **perfect information** and **hyper-rationality**, firms would determine the level of employment purely on the basis of a **'going wage' rate**. In the third section, we start to weaken the neo-classical assumptions and analyse what happens when either the firm or labour (more correctly a trade union) has the power to influence the wage rate. The section looks at both separately and closes with an analysis of the situation when a firm with market power negotiates with a trade union over the wage rate. In the fourth section, we relax the assumption of perfect information and look at the implications for employment contracts. In the fifth section, we look at the issue of motivation from a principal–agent perspective. The section sets out three wage models designed to align the self-interest of the worker with the firm. Finally, in the sixth section we turn to the issue of attracting and retaining employees and this allows us to introduce concepts such as **firm-specific human capital** and **internal labour markets**.

The Supply of Labour

An appropriate place to begin our exploration of human resources is to understand something about an individual's decision to seek employment. At its most basic, this turns out to be a choice problem between income and leisure, though for some the choice is between an income or going to school to improve their market value. We will confine ourselves to the income–leisure choice, which can be viewed as an individual's decision regarding the number of hours of work they are prepared to undertake in a particular period. For the moment, despite its deficiencies, we will adopt the neo-classical model's assumption of perfect information and assume that our individual knows for certain, without searching, what wage the market will offer someone with her skills and experience. Perfect information is also assumed on the part of employers who will know precisely the economic value of the job seeker to the firm. Finally, the neo-classical model assumes that the job seeker is a **utility** maximizer – who is both rational and self-interested – whose decision to work at the wage on offer will be determined by the utility derived from consuming the goods and services that the payment for the work will provide relative to the utility forgone; that is, the **opportunity cost** of giving up the equivalent leisure time.

As the wage on offer rises – given that inflation does not exist in microeconomic analysis – so the quantity of goods and services that can be purchased with an extra unit of work increases. In other words, in the absence of inflation, a rising money wage is equivalent to a rising **real wage**. This makes working relatively more attractive and from the perspective of economic analysis the units of work supplied, e.g. hours, will increase if the **marginal utility** derived from the last unit worked just compensates the individual for the marginal disutility of the last unit of leisure time foregone. Some individuals, based on their preferences, will choose to supply fewer labour units when higher wage rates allow them to satisfy their demands for goods and services. In these cases, the marginal utility of not working, e.g. playing golf, rises relative to the marginal utility derived from the pay for an additional unit of work. Overwhelmingly, empirical studies show that higher wages and an increasing

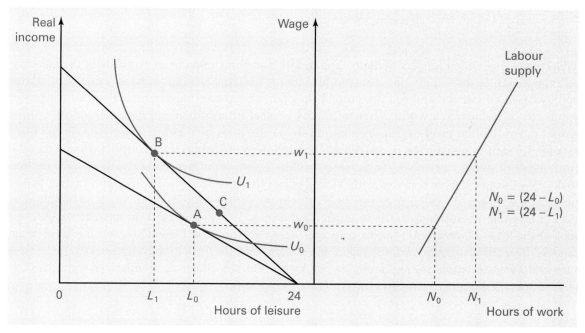

Figure 7.1: The leisure–work trade-off

supply of labour units are positively correlated, but motivating employees to supply hours in excess of their basic contract, i.e. overtime, frequently runs into the leisure–income trade-off.

Figure 7.1 is an attempt to demonstrate the relationship between the wage on offer and the supply of labour. It shows a model of individual choice between hours of leisure and the number of hours supplied to an employer per day. The analysis could alternatively be constructed for the number of hours or days per week, or per month. The left-hand graph plots the potential 24 hours of leisure (which includes sleep) on the horizontal axis and on the vertical axis the individual's real income (purchasing power) generated by the number of hours worked during the day, multiplied by the wage per hour. The **indifference curves** U_0 and U_1 represent a section of the individual's **preference map**. Point A shows the total utility (U_0) obtained by the individual if hours of leisure are L_0 and hence (24 $- L_0$) hours are devoted to work at the current wage rate, w_0. The ray running from 24 on the horizontal axis through point A to the vertical axis shows the real income obtained by working more hours at the wage, w_0. In the right-hand graph this decision to supply is recorded in the wage–labour supply space, where $N_0 = (24 - L_0)$ hours of labour supply per day. Given the individual's preference map, if the wage rate rises (e.g. to w_1), the individual is prepared to supply an increased number of hours (24 $- L_1$), because in so doing, the individual moves to point B, where a higher level of utility is obtained. Note this outcome depends on the individual's preference map. If the individual's preference map was such that curve U_1 passed through point C, then the individual would respond to the higher wage by increasing leisure time. The move from A to B involved an increase in wages and an increase in hours worked. This is translated into the right-hand graph as an upward-sloping supply curve for the individual's supply of labour.

Figure 7.1 reveals the wage rate as an incentive mechanism; a given wage rate will induce a number of individuals to supply units of work. It has been constructed in terms of hours supplied per day, but we might more realistically think of supply in terms of labour units, typically 35 hours of work per week. Nothing fundamental changes and the conclusion arrived at still holds; namely, offering a higher (real) wage will, **ceteris paribus**, attract more labour units to the firm. All but the very smallest firms need to secure a number of labour units per week. Retaining the simplifying neo-classical assumptions, we can think of workers as individuals assigned to homogeneous groups, i.e. each group having the same skills and experience, but with different income–leisure preferences. We can then think of the firm as making a wage offer to a particular 'worker' group. Conveniently, the neo-classical paradigm's assumption of **atomistic industry**

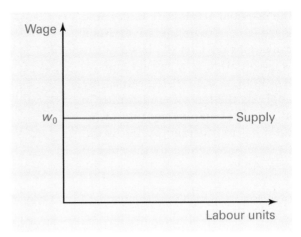

Figure 7.2: The neo-classical supply of labour to the firm

structures, placed individual firms in the position of having no direct influence over the wage on offer. The going wage for a particular worker group was determined by the market, where a wage level was generated by the coincidence of the demand generated by the large numbers of firms and the level of supply. From the viewpoint of an individual firm, which by definition is assumed small relative to the size of the market, there exists for each type of labour an abundant supply. Hence, an individual firm's demand for a particular category of labour has no noticeable influence on the available supply of labour and consequently its hiring decisions cannot affect the price of labour, i.e. the market clearing wage rate. In effect, an individual firm faces a fixed wage or 'going wage rate' for each type of labour. The situation is illustrated in Figure 7.2, which shows the neo-classical supply of labour curve facing an individual firm. The firm can hire all the labour it wants at the going wage rate, w_0.

In practice, within a town or region, a firm – even a small firm – can be a major employer of one or more categories of workers. In this situation, the firm's demand influences the wage rate and it would be more correct to represent the supply of labour units facing a firm in this situation as an upward-sloping curve, as shown in Figure 7.3. That is, the more labour units the firm wants, the higher the wage that must be offered. An upward-sloping supply curve introduces the concept of **economic rent** for labour. For an employee, a rent is the proportion of earnings in excess of the minimum amount, the so-called **reservation wage** needed to attract the individual to accept the job in question and therefore sufficient to offset the opportunity cost of accepting the job. In the neo-classical world, and in practice, it is beyond the resources of most firms hiring groups of workers to attempt to ascertain reservation wages of individuals. Hence, firms tend to offer all potential employees in each worker group the same wage rate. Facing an upward-sloping labour supply curve, the firm must raise its wage offer to a level sufficient to attract the supply of labour needed and this ensures that all but the marginal worker are earning an economic rent. This is demonstrated in Figure 7.3, where the firm is offering the wage, w_0, and at this wage the firm employs N_0 homogeneous units of labour, yielding total wage costs represented by the area ON_0Bw_0. Now, consider the marginal employee at N_1 – the last one hired when the workforce reached this level. Here, the marginal employee's reservation wage is w_1. Proving this individual ranks jobs only on the basis of the wage on offer, at w_0 a rent equivalent to $(w_0 - w_1)$ is being earned. By applying the foregoing reasoning to all levels of employment up to N_0, the total rent earned by the workforce is represented by the shaded area, ABw_0.

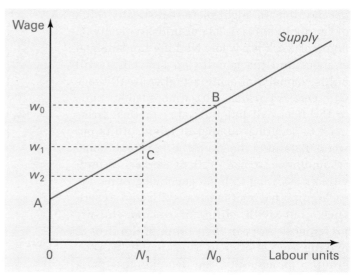

Figure 7.3: The supply of labour

If we relax the highly restrictive neo-classical assumption of perfect information, we can use Figure 7.3 to explore the concept of **quasi-rent** as it applies to employees. Whereas rents are defined in terms of decisions to enter a particular employment, quasi-rents are defined in terms of the decision to exit. A quasi-rent in this context is the proportion of earnings in excess of the minimum wage needed to prevent a worker from *quitting* his or her job. Having accepted employment and become familiar with the job – and in practice, if not in the neo-classical world, invested in skills and knowledge that are primarily of value to the current employer – quitting may involve costs associated with an uncertain period of unemployment whilst searching for a new job at a wage of at least w_1 that the individual is capable of doing. Hence a **risk averse** individual – represented once again by the marginal employee at N_1 in Figure 7.3 – may not quit until the wage on offer falls to w_2. At the going wage rate of w_0, the quasi-rent for the marginal employee at N_1 is equal to $w_0 - w_2$. This explains why, when a firm is facing the threat of closure, employees are generally prepared to take a pay cut, i.e. it may have more to do with quasi-rents than loyalty.

In the neo-classical world, the ideal of a wage rate that precisely matches the demand and supply for a particular group of workers is always achieved. This is known as the **market clearing wage** and of more interest are the implications, for firms and consumers, when a firm deviates from the market clearing wage. In principle, this cannot happen in the neo-classical paradigm, as any rise in wages above the market clearing wage will result in supply exceeding demand and hence downward pressure on the ruling wage rate. However, if we introduce a market distortion, say a powerful trade union that can control the supply of labour, then firms can be forced to offer a wage in excess of the market clearing wage. For the neo-classical school, a wage in excess of the market clearing wage is an example of **allocative inefficiency**. Consider again Figure 7.3 – the wage w_0 is the market clearing wage for our particular firm, but the creation of a powerful trade union within the firm is likely to bring about a situation where the ruling wage is pushed above the market clearing level. The result is a higher wage for those hired but not all those seeking employment will find jobs. The cost of this inefficiency is borne by the firm's shareholders, if – and as we will show below it is an if – a lower output and a higher wage rate reduce profits. As the foregoing implies, once we begin to relax the neo-classical paradigm of both firms and labour operating under conditions of **perfect competition** with perfect information and hyper-rationality, the analysis of employment and employees becomes both more complex and more interesting. Just how the situation changes once the restrictive neo-classical assumptions are relaxed will form the basis of much that follows below.

Trade Union Power

Casual workers, who on the whole tend to be low skilled, generally find themselves at the bottom of the pay ladder. In the UK, they were traditionally hired on a day-to-day basis, they had little power and in practice had little choice but to accept the wage and conditions on offer. These conditions were invariably worse than those for any permanent workers doing the same job alongside them. For example, casual workers had few employment rights, rarely received sickness pay and/or pension contributions. It was apparent from the statistics that the ranks of these low-paid, vulnerable workers were largely populated by women and ethnic minorities.

But from the start of the new Millennium, throughout the European Union, things have greatly improved for casual workers following the coming into effect of the 1999 EU Directive on Fixed Term Workers. In the UK, this resulted in the Fixed Term Employees (Prevention of Less Favourable Treatment) Regulation, which came in effect on 1 October 2002. Henceforth, casual workers must be treated equally to permanent employees in terms of pay and conditions where they are doing broadly similar work, for the same employer, in the same establishment. Under the new regulations, casual workers cannot be summarily dismissed. The new regulations do not, however, apply to agency workers who have an employment contract with a temporary work agency. It is confidently predicted that the demand for agency workers will now increase.

The Demand for Labour

We turn now to the demand for labour. The standard neo-classical approach to analysing the demand for labour is lacking in any recognition of the fact that human beings are a very different type of resource. The traditional approach treats labour in the same way as any other commodity, e.g. bananas. According to the neo-classical school, firms operating in perfectly competitive markets have no influence on the wage paid per unit of labour as the rate is determined exogenously by the coincidence of supply and demand in the labour market. We have already seen that the market supply curve for each homogeneous group of workers is upward sloping and we have explained that the point at which supply equals demand determines the market clearing wage rate. We have also explained that from the viewpoint of the individual firm, under perfect competition it faces a going wage rate and its employment decision comes down to solely determining the numbers to be hired at the ruling wage. In the neo-classical world, the going wage rate is the only remuneration paid to workers. Any firm offering a higher wage or fringe benefits would immediately find itself swamped with perfectly informed individuals seeking work and the situation would only be returned to equilibrium when the level of remuneration offered by the firm returned to the going rate.

We can represent the neo-classical model for an individual firm's hiring decision – for a particular category of worker – with the diagram shown in Figure 7.4. The individual firm is deemed to face an infinite supply of labour at the going wage rate, w, and this is represented by a horizontal line. In contrast, the individual firm's **demand curve** for labour is downward sloping, reflecting the law of **diminishing returns** and its associat-ed **marginal product of labour** (see

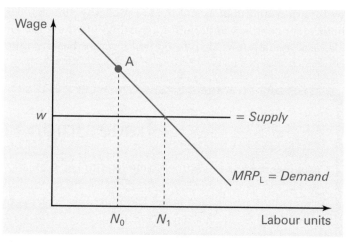

Figure 7.4: The neo-classical model

Appendix 7A). The more labour the firm hires, *ceteris paribus*, the lower will be the marginal prod-uct of labour and the lower will be the firm's **marginal revenue product** (MRP_L). The firm's demand for labour is a **derived demand**; that is, the firm's demand for labour is positively related to the demand for the firm's output. A rise in demand for the firm's output will increase the demand for labour – in terms of Figure 7.4, the demand curve for labour will move to the right.

Despite its restrictive assumptions of perfect information and hyper-rationality and (for the individual firm) an infinite supply of homogeneous labour, the neo-classical model does allow us to set down some fundamental rules for determining how much labour a profit-maximizing firm should hire. The neo-classical behavioural assumption is that the firm's managers are solely motivated by the desire to maximize profits and consequently the decision regarding employment depends solely on the answer to the question: would it be profitable to hire one more unit of labour? The answer is that it would only be profitable to increase the firm's labour resources if the additional revenue generated from the additional output is greater than – or at the margin equal to – the increase in the firm's total costs. This can be demonstrated as follows. If the firm's managers decide to hire N_0 units of labour, the MRP_L is represented by point A. As can be seen, this is greater than the wage paid, i.e. $MRP_L > w$, so the last unit of labour employed is adding more to the firm's revenue than to its total costs. A profit-maximiz-ing firm will want to hire additional units of labour as long as the $MRP_L > w$. As the number of labour units hired increases, so the MRP_L declines and when the units of labour are increased to N_1, the $MRP_L = w$. It would not be profitable for a firm to increase the number of labour units hired beyond N_1, consequently N_1 is the profit-maximizing level of employment in the current period. Thus, for a firm operating under perfect competition , we have determined its profit-maximizing level of employ-ment; namely, that level of employment where the wage just equals the value of the marginal workers' productivity, represented by the equation:

$$w = MRP_L \tag{7.1}$$

The neo-classical model outlined above is not intended to be a reflection of reality, its value rests on its ability to provide testable predictions – e.g. a rise in the wage rate will reduce employment –

while representing an 'ideal' labour market paradigm. However, as an aid to understanding behaviour within the firm, it is severely lacking. In the neo-classical firm, managers have no discretion over remuneration levels for individual workers and for their part, workers are deemed to be attracted to jobs purely on the basis of the wage on offer. In practice, many other factors will influence an employee's decision to seek new employment, though the wage is an important consideration. It follows that in such a world workers must be highly mobile. As information is both costless and instantly disseminated, employees will have perfect information regarding the going wage rate in other industries. Being hyper-rational, they will act rapidly in response to any relative change in wages. This implies that, following an increase in the demand for labour and hence the wage rate in another industry, workers will leave their jobs for the higher wage on offer. Some other characteristics would be prevalent in the neo-classical labour market: wage rates would be highly volatile; workers would have no loyalty or attachment to their existing employers; and the concept of a career would have no meaning. Thus, the neo-classical world would be one in which labour incomes fluctuate randomly in response to changes in demand. And employers, perhaps not untypical in the nineteenth century, would think of workers as commodity inputs – *'just another pair of hired hands'* to be hired or dispensed with at will.

Some labour markets do seem to come close to operating under conditions that are very close to the neo-classical model, e.g. casual farm labourers employed to pick fruit during harvest, but even in these markets there is some loyalty – workers return to the same farm year after year – and ***incomplete information*** and bounded rationality will lead to variations in pay for identical work within the same locality. In practice, even if information asymmetries are small and wage rates have largely converged, jobs vary in many dimensions, casting doubt on the validity of the going wage rate and its implication of equal remuneration. For example, the location of a job, the workplace culture and opportunities for advancement are all likely in practice to influence the relative attractiveness of employment with a particular firm. Empiricism shows that for the majority of occupations, labour markets work very differently from the form indicated by the neo-classical model. Pay and conditions vary from firm to firm within the same industry, but pay levels fluctuate much less than would be predicted by the neo-classical model. Pay cuts are very rare, and turnover and labour mobility is limited.

The Death of Orthodoxy

Following its election to power in 1997, the New Labour government set about honouring its manifesto promise to introduce a national minimum wage into the UK. Its first step was to set up the Low Pay Commission (LPC) under the redoubtable George (now Lord) Bain. One of the many issues faced by the LPC was the effect of imposing a minimum wage on the level of employment. Standard economic theory predicts job losses if minimum wages are set above market rates, but the LPC soon discovered what most government ministers already knew; namely, economists disagreed on the likely outcome. The 'new economics' of the minimum wage, as the LPC termed it, held that the existence of monopsony in the labour market meant that a moderate national minimum wage

continued

could be introduced without destroying jobs. Naturally, the LPC was interested in this viewpoint and was prepared to concede that elements of monopsony probably do exist in some parts of the UK labour market.

A particular focus was part-time, female workers, who appeared to be amongst the lowest paid. A number of economists argued that such women were being exploited by being paid below their value added, i.e. their MRP_L. In its first report, prior to the introduction of a national minimum wage in 1998, it is clear that the LPC did not quite have the confidence to side with those economists who claimed a minimum wage would not reduce employment. But four years later, the LPC was a lot more confident.

In its 2001 report, the LPC observed that using sophisticated techniques to allow for other influences on employment, e.g. the strong growth of the economy, the employment of female part-time workers had remained strong. As female part-time workers were deemed to be one of the main beneficiaries of a national minimum wage, this marked a considerable success for the policy. Indeed, the LPC felt confident enough to claim that the orthodox view that minimum wages cut employment may not be appropriate when analysing low pay and that other explanations such as imperfections in the labour market may be more relevant.

Imperfect Markets

Paradoxically, firms that do face a going wage rate are generally operating in an industry that has previously negotiated on an industry basis with a trade union. For example, in the UK, wage rates for different categories of ancillary hospital workers are negotiated with the trade union, Unison. Thus, individual hospitals are faced with a ruling wage for various categories of workers and within limits they can increase or reduce their workforces without affecting the ruling wage rate. Faced with a previously negotiated wage, $\bar{w}$, within the neo-classical paradigm, the decision rule for the firm remains unchanged; namely, set $MRP_L = \bar{w}$. Thus, to the extent that a trade union is successful in raising the wage level above the level that would be set by unfettered market forces, so it must also reduce the units of labour hired. The neo-classical model assumes that both firms and employees are price takers, i.e. neither can influence the price of what they have to sell. However, the example of trade union activity shows that market participants can influence the going wage rate. Similarly, under imperfect competition the firm will be able to influence the price at which it sells its output. In either case, the efficiency outcome of the neo-classical model will not hold.

Let us consider the outcome if the firm itself has the power to influence the price of its product – say the firm is a **monopolist**. Consider Figure 7.5, where the employer, a monopolist, recruits labour from a perfectly competitive labour market with a going wage rate, w_0. This implies that, in addition to the monopolist, many firms in other industries hire this type of labour. The figure shows that in this situation the firm will achieve a profit-maximizing position at point A by hiring N_0 units of labour. Now say the workforce of this particular firm becomes unionized and the going wage rate to the firm is raised to w_1. If the employer was operating in a perfectly competitive market, its demand for labour would be represented by $MRP_L{}^0$, the reduction in employment resulting from the rise in the wage rate would have no effect on the price of its product and a new equilibrium would be established at point B. But as a monopolist, any reduction in employment would have the effect of reducing supply and hence raising the price of its product. For a firm with market power, falling output pushes up the market price and, hence, the MRP_L for such a firm is steeper, leading to a smaller reduction in employment and a new equilibrium at point C. If this seems like a socially just outcome, remember that the losers are the consumers of the product who now have to pay a higher price for a reduced supply.

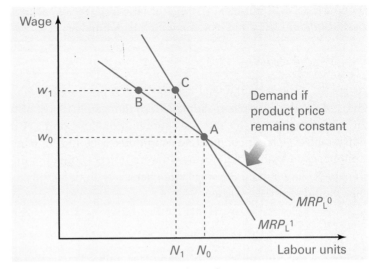

Figure 7.5: Monopoly, wages and employment

The fact that an employer has market power is not always of benefit to a workforce. Consider the example of a firm seeking to employ unskilled labour in an area with high unemployment – say, the employer is a supermarket chain opening a store in a new location. In such an area the supermarket may be the only firm hiring people and as a significant employer of labour it will have the power of a **monopsonist** in the locality. Given an upward-sloping supply curve for labour, the new supermarket will itself determine the going wage rate for the locality by the number of workers it employs. In this situation, it will be profitable for the firm to restrict the level of employment it offers so that it pays a lower gross wage to its workforce (see Appendix 7A).

This can be demonstrated with the aid of Figure 7.6, which represents a situation where the firm has monopsony power over a particular type of labour. The more units of labour the supermarket wishes to employ, the higher the wage it will have to offer, i.e. if it wishes to hire N_1 units of labour, the wage on offer will be w_1; hence, the rising wage function shown in Figure 7.6 is the firm's average cost of labour, AC_L, function. Under competitive conditions, the market clearing wage would be w_0 and at this wage, N_0 units of labour would offer themselves for work. However, a profit-maximizing

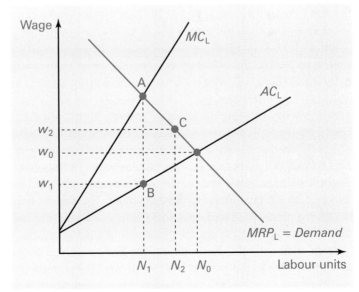

Figure 7.6: Monopsonist power

monopsonist will not hire N_0 units of labour at a wage of w_0. For a monopsonist, it is the **marginal cost of labour**, MC_L, that matters, which is defined as:

$$MC_L = \Delta TC_L / \Delta N \tag{7.2}$$

where TC_L represents the total labour costs, N the numbers employed and Δ represents change. As the AC_L rises with the numbers employed, so the marginal cost of labour curve, MC_L, which lies above the AC_L, is rising at a faster rate – as shown. Consider point A in Figure 7.6. Point A is equivalent to Equation (7.1). Under competitive conditions, each unit of labour hired costs the same as the previous unit, hence in writing $MRP_L = w$, we were in fact setting the firm's MC_L equal to its MRP_L. Now, under imperfect competition, the wage rate changes with the numbers hired, so the profit-maximizing condition should always be written:

$$MC_L = MRP_L \tag{7.3}$$

where the last unit of labour hired adds as much to revenue as to total costs, *ceteris paribus*. But in order to hirer N_1 units of labour, a monopsonist only has to pay a wage of w_1, thus point B is the profit-maximizing wage rate (i.e., w_1) and this determines the numbers hired. The result is reduced employment and a gain to the firm's shareholders at the expense of the workforce. Both the employees and those who remain unemployed suffer reductions in their welfare. To hire more than N_1 units of labour would mean paying a wage in excess of w_1 and in this situation the $MRP_L < MC_L$. The firm can 'get away' with paying less than the market clearing rate because it has no rivals bidding for labour.

An intriguing consequence of the exercise of monopsonist power is that the imposition of a minimum wage, say w_2 in Figure 7.6, would actually result in an increase in employment to N_2. This follows, because it would be illegal for the firm to hire anyone for less than the minimum wage, w_2. So now the minimum wage becomes the firm's marginal cost of labour, at least up to point C, where $w_2 = MRP_L$. Given the constraint of a minimum wage, point C is the profit-maximizing position for the firm; the outcome is a rise in income for the workforce and more people are employed. The cost is borne by the shareholders in the form of a fall in profits. The introduction of a national minimum wage in the UK in 1999, gave economists an opportunity to test this theory. One study concluded that, if anything, the effect on employment had been marginally positive for adult men and young people and there had been no effect on the employment of adult women (Stewart, 2001).

Finally, we can consider the situation where a monopoly supply of labour faces a monopsonist employer. On 1 January 1947, the post-war Labour Government nationalized the British coal industry. For the next 47 years – until the coal industry was privatized – every year the National Coal Board (renamed British Coal in 1987) engaged in wage negotiations with the National Union of Miners (NUM). The National Coal Board, with only minor exceptions, was the sole employer of coal miners. The NUM represented all coal miners; it was a monopoly supplier of labour. The annual wage negotiations were therefore a negotiation between a monopolist and a monopsonist, a situation known as **bilateral monopoly**. We can represent the wage bargaining between the monopsonist Coal Board and the monopoly NUM as a **"zero-sum game"**. To keep matters simple, let us assume the game is played only once and the negotiation concerns only the annual increase in the miners' basic wage rate. The essence of the game is set out in Figure 7.7. Both parties have got a vested interest in reaching an agreement. A strike would reduce both the Coal Board's profits and the miners' earnings for the year. Given our assumption that the pay-off is a zero sum, any increase that the NUM can secure will be matched by an identical reduction in the Coal Board's expected profits for the year. Hence, in the game shown in Figure 7.7, the maximum potential gain in profits ($\Delta\pi$) exactly matches the maximum potential gain in wages (Δw). If both sides reach an agreement, the gain is shared between them.

The pay-off from reaching a negotiated agreement is shown in the top left-hand cell. The relative pay-offs depend on the relative bargaining power of the two parties. If the Coal Board believes that the

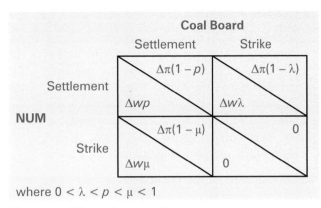

where $0 < \lambda < p < \mu < 1$

Figure 7.7: Bilateral monopoly

market for coal is going to be weak, they may be prepared to risk provoking a strike in order to achieve a low wage settlement. If the miners feel that demand for coal is rising – as was the case after the quadrupling of oil prices in 1973 – they may be prepared to risk a strike to achieve a higher wage settlement. If either side caves in, the other wins in the sense that they get the lion's share of the increase in value on offer. If, however, there is a strike, neither side wins as the loss of profits and earnings are assumed to offset the eventual settlement. What will be the outcome of a bilateral monopoly negotiation as depicted in the diagram? The answer is that it is impossible to predict the outcome of such a **bargaining situation**. No simple rule determines whether one of the parties is prepared to risk a strike and no simple rule determines how the 'cake' will be divided, that is, who will get the better part of the bargain. One party might have more time and patience, or might be able to convince the other party that it will strike (in the case of the miners) or be prepared to put up with a lengthy strike (in the case of the Coal Board). In terms of **game theory**, the root of the problem is that the game has no unique **Nash equilibrium** (a general introduction to bargaining games is set out in Appendix 7B).

Reversing Roles

In the UK, trade unions accumulated some extraordinary privileges over the course of the twentieth century. For example, they could impose a closed shop on employees, they could not be sued for damage caused by industrial action and they were immune from prosecution if they chose to picket businesses not directly involved in an industrial dispute.

Between 1982 and 1993, six successive Acts of Parliament greatly reduced these powers

for trade unions. As a result of these Acts, individuals are now free to decide whether or not to join a trade union where previously there was a closed shop, strike ballots are compulsory, trade union members have the right to inspect their union's accounts, secondary picketing is banned and legal immunities are curbed.

The result has been a dramatic improvement in industrial relations. The number of days

continued

lost, per year, due to strikes has fallen from almost 30 million in 1979 to around half a million today. Trade unions have lost millions of members over the 25 years since 1979, forcing them to consolidate and compete for members. Most trade union members now work in the public sector – the largest groupings in trade unions are now teachers, nurses and local authority workers. The outcome of the reforms of the 1980s is that unions now depend on members, but in most industries members no longer depend on trade unions. And trade unions are responding by offering members better membership services such as health and sickness insurance.

Employment Contracts

The foregoing provided an overview of the neo-classical approach to employment and it demonstrated that underlying the wage contract is productivity and relative bargaining power. The focus was the external transaction between the firm and its employees, but a major shortcoming was the complete silence on the workings of the internal relationship between worker and employer within the firm. This shortcoming of the neo-classical model is largely due to the assumption of perfect information and super-rationality. Once we allow for the reality of imperfect information and incomplete information, the neo-classical model's shortcomings become manifest. Employment is a classic example of a principal–agent relationship and it is from this perspective that we will approach the subject. The firm, in the form of managers responsible for supervising and hiring, is the principal and the employee, the agent. Employees as individuals have their own private interests and these are unlikely to be perfectly aligned with the goals of the firm. In delegating tasks and responsibilities to the agent, the principal is concerned to motivate effort; but the agent has superior information as to actual effort and the capabilities that could be brought to bear. The employee will be guided to some extent by considerations like job satisfaction, career development and relationships with fellow employees, but the disutility associated with effort suggests that there exists a conflict of interests between employer and employee.

In principle, the issue of motivation is dealt with by the employment contract, which is generally drawn up by the principal. It is the agent who decides whether or not to accept the contract, but having accepted the contract it is the agent's private information as to the level of effort likely to be applied. If it were possible to draw up a **complete contract**, then the applicant's hidden characteristics would not be an issue. The contract would specify precisely what each party has to do in all possible circumstances, that is, the contract would set out in complete detail the actions to be undertaken by both employee and employer as circumstances change. But the existence of bounded rationality means that all contingencies cannot be allowed for and when unforeseen circumstances call for the adaptation of existing contracts, the firm runs the risk of falling victim to **opportunistic behaviour**. The inability to foresee all possible circumstances and the existence of asymmetric information are not the only problems preventing complete contracting. Given the **hidden actions** of employees, it may not be possible **ex post** to tell whether the terms of the contract have been honoured.

Once we recognize that real people are neither omniscient nor perfectly far-sighted, employers are left with the problem of drawing up the best contracts they can in the circumstances. The common solution is to draw up a relational contract, which does not involve the impossible task of complete contracting. A relational contract serves to structure a relationship and a common set of expectations. It specifies in broad terms the objectives and the mechanism for decision making when unforeseen events occur. For their part, the employees agree to assign authority to the employer and to use their best efforts to undertake the tasks that the employer directs them to do. Thus, relational contracts establish the relationship between the principal and agent and set common expectations, but in all other respects the typical employment contract is imprecise and involves implicit elements.

The imprecision of contracts of employment is, at face value, surprising – given that for most people it is the major influence on their living standards and in this respect it will be amongst the most important contracts an individual will ever sign. Typically, the employer agrees to pay the employee a sum of money per period, though the full range of actions that might be required will not be spelt out. Future levels of compensation and the criteria to be used to determine promotion and career progression are also generally unspecified. It may appear – strikes and formalized grievances aside – that senior managers have all the power. But a major influence on motivation is the belief by workers that they are being treated fairly and a rational manager will be keen to build and maintain a reputation for fair dealings. In the presence of **transaction costs** – most notably, bounded rationality – contracts will always be incomplete, and they will be supported by implicit contracts that help to ensure compliance by both sides. Implicit understandings are unwritten and yet are frequently crucial to the performance of an employment contract. As observed in the previous chapter, implicit contracts by their very nature can never be enforced in a court of law, but they are self-enforcing because both sides are likely to suffer adverse consequences if the agreement is violated. They are self-enforcing because the firm believes it would suffer in some way if the worker leaves or reduces effort following a failure on the part of the firm to honour the understanding. Similarly, the worker must believe that the result of reducing effort will be a penalty, e.g. loss of bonus, that exceeds the utility gain from working less hard.

Another approach to the firm founded on its inability to sign complete contracts, and most closely associated with Cremer (1986), is the idea that the only asset a firm ultimately has is its **reputation**. According to this view, a major incentive to treat employees (and other stakeholders) fairly is the longer-term benefit to the firm of building a reputation for fairness. Reputation is like trust; the more it is used, the greater its value. The firm has a longer time horizon than an individual worker, as it expects to be in receipt of future income streams for an infinite (or at least a very extended) period. As a firm expects to be in business much longer than any individual's working life, it will do itself longer-term damage by gaining a reputation for unfairness than the short-term gain from breaking an implicit understanding. Of course, the situation changes if for some reason, e.g. the threat of bankruptcy, the firm's time horizon is shortened. The importance of reputation is not attached to individual managers; a reputation for fairness is attached to the firm itself.

It is, in practice, the firm's managers who take the actions that will either maintain or reduce the firm's reputation for fairness. As new managers enter the hierarchy, so they must become imbued with the benefits of maintaining a good reputation. This serves to raise again the issue of culture. In large organizations, a set of workable principles and routines are likely to evolve that guide managers in making decisions and also create a set of clear expectations on the part of the workforce. Culture plays two roles: it conditions and aligns managerial behaviour in accordance with a desired reputation objective; and it sends a message to all managers contracting on its behalf with employees as to what is expected of the relationship. Traditionally, companies like ICI, Marks and Spencer and Shell built a reputation for treating their employees fairly. This was not written formally into any employment contract; rather, it was a principle and an implicit promise. These firms, with their potentially unlimited lifetime, had a strong incentive to act in ways that did not damage their reputation.

Team Work

In 1994, BMW acquired the former Rover Group and when it sold out to the Phoenix Ventures in 2001, the Mini brand was the only part of the former group that it retained. BMW saw something in the Mini, or at least the Mini brand, that others had missed. BMW's new Mini was introduced in 2001 and following a successful launch production was transferred from Birmingham to Cowley in Oxford in 2002. Typical of BMW, it spent €350 million on improving production facilities at Cowley and in the ensuing years annual production has risen from 140,800 vehicles to 200,000.

What BMW has demonstrated at Cowley, as have Nissan, Toyota and Honda, is that British workers are every bit as good as their global counterparts when well managed. At Cowley, BMW introduced a change management programme, moving away from the habitual production line formula to a team-based approach. This involved more than the physical rearrangement of production facilities; it also involved a change in culture. In the Cowley plant, technology has replaced some jobs, cell production has replaced production lines and self-managed teams have replaced a command and control hierarchy.

The teams consist of between eight and 15 people, they can make production decisions and have the power to rotate jobs within the team. Plant production targets are literally in the hands of the team. BMW introduced fortnightly team talks where plans, decisions and points of view can be aired. These team talks have resulted in many productivity improvements as a result of those doing the job recognizing where inefficiencies exist. The result has been a reduction in conflict, the ending of the 'them and us' culture and much improved communication between shopfloor and managers. And a very profitable plant.

Motivating Effort

We observed above, that drawing up a contract is one thing, but ensuring that it is honoured by the worker is another. This is the hidden action problem referred to above. It may appear that the level of output is an appropriate measure of performance, but in practice the output of an individual is likely to be difficult to separately identify. Even in a work environment where a physical output is produced, say, agriculture or manufacturing, the effects of the weather or machine breakdowns, respectively, can make it difficult to identify an individual's effort. In practice, output is frequently the product of team production and, hence, an individual's contribution cannot be identified with certainty. In a service environment where the output is advice or a design, the measurement of an individual's effort may be all but impossible, as shortcomings may not be apparent, if at all, until some point in the future. In this situation of imperfect information, the informational asymmetry enables employees to engage in opportunistic behaviour. If an employee takes advantage of the existence of imperfect information in the execution of their work, it is now generally referred to as **shirking** (Alchian and Demsetz, 1972).

Hidden action problems are **moral hazard** problems. The possibility of this type of behaviour is ruled out in the neo-classical paradigm with perfect information, but it is a key issue for managers in practice. The larger and more centralized a firm, the greater the costs incurred in obtaining relevant information on team performance and individual effort. This indicates the importance of monitoring, but also the limits to the information that managers can economically gather and assess. Milgrom (1988) offers an insight into this issue with his concept of **influencing costs**. For Milgrom, influencing costs are undesired employee activities that are intended to change a superior's actions to the sole benefit of the employee. The hidden action problem may be one of reduced effort, but it may take the form of carelessness or providing inaccurate or distorted information to a supervisor. In the neo-classical model, the worst that can happen to a worker who shirks on the job is to be fired. But, since immediate alternative employment is available at the ruling market wage, this amounts to a very limited penalty for minimum effort on the part of the individual worker. In practice, a worker may not expect to easily obtain employment if fired, though this misses the point: firms have an incentive to induce workers not to shirk and indeed to work hard and use their best endeavours on behalf of the firm.

In many employment situations, monitoring actual behaviour is likely to be too expensive. Thus, firms generally resort to schemes that provide incentives for effort. A prime objective for managers is therefore to resolve moral hazard issues by devising incentive schemes that will motivate individuals, for whom they have responsibility, to high levels of effort aligned with the goals of the firm. Organizations have their goals, but so too do the individuals they employ and the purpose of motivation schemes is, as far as possible, to bring about an alignment of the employee's and firm's objectives by creating a situation where it is in the self-interest of the employee to behave as desired. Once again, it is the firm's organizational architecture, or those aspects of the architecture that reward and encourage behaviour, that must be relied on to align employee behaviour with the firm's objectives. Within the firm, individuals must be motivated to provide effort and to co-ordinate their activities with other individuals. For manual labouring jobs, effort means physical effort, but increasingly as technology and services are coming to dominate employment, effort means applying care and attention and/or high levels of intellect. In essence, it is employee behaviours and attitudes that will have a significant bearing on the success of an organization in meeting its goals – the way customers are treated, the attention to reducing waste and so on – and therefore the firm's motivation system must ensure that positive behaviours and attitudes are encouraged.

Effective motivation systems are broader than simply systems of financial incentives. Behavioural scientists will point *inter alia* to the importance of challenging jobs, cohesive teams, participation in decision making and feedback as stimulants to employee motivation. Systems in which employees feel that their efforts are appreciated, that allow them to achieve personal goals, and offer the prospect of future promotion are all likely to encourage effort. Important as these factors are for most people, the level of pay can at the very least be described as *primus inter pares* when it comes to the issue of motivation. Incentives based on pay are plentiful and varied. Piece rates, bonuses, commissions and stock options are examples of financial reward systems with the objective of motivating. To be effective, financial incentive systems must be sufficient to overcome the disutility of extra effort and the temptation to follow personal goals at the expense of the firm's goals. Unfortunately, as explained above, perfect connections between hidden activities and observed outcomes are rare in practice. Changes in output levels may be due to factors beyond the individual employee's control. Thus, managers are faced with the problem of motivating effort, while protecting the individual's income from random events that are beyond their control.

We demonstrated in the previous chapter that most people are **risk averse** and would rather have a smaller income whose magnitude is certain than an alternative expected income whose level is subject to random fluctuations. An efficient incentive contract generally means the firm accepts the risk associated with random events, but employees are responsible for their performance; that is, the employee's compensation depends to a greater or lesser extent on how much effort they put into their assigned tasks. In practice, it is never possible to avoid imposing some risk on the employees, as it is not possible for managers to obtain perfect information on employees' behaviour. We will look first at an incentive model based loosely on Holmstrom (1979), where it is possible, albeit imperfectly, to measure output before moving onto an incentive model where the desired behaviour cannot be fully observed.

Let us imagine a mushroom farm where the farm's profit depends on the effort applied by mushroom pickers. An individual mushroom picker's output, q, can be represented by a linear function of effort:

$$q = \alpha + \beta e + \varepsilon \tag{7.4}$$

where e is effort and ε is a random variable that is normally distributed with a mean of zero and a constant variance, i.e. $e = N(0, \sigma^2)$. If effort is increased, output rises, *ceteris paribus*, so β represents the individual's marginal productivity, MP_L. Now consider the mushroom farmer's profits; these will be the difference between the MRP_L and the wage paid to the individual:

$$\pi = p(\alpha + \beta e + \varepsilon) - w \tag{7.5}$$

where p is the price received per unit of mushrooms, hence $p(\alpha + \beta e + \varepsilon) = MRP_L$. There is an incentive problem with Equation (7.5). Even if the individual's manager could closely observe effort – which implies standing alongside the employee – the size and quality of the mushrooms picked will be influenced by the growing conditions; the more variable the growing conditions, the greater the value of σ^2. One way, indeed the generally adopted way, of solving the incentive problem set out in Equation (7.5) is to provide a fixed, basic wage, $\bar{w}$, plus a proportion, λ, of the value of output, i.e. the MRP_L. Thus, the mushroom picker's earnings (E) can be represented by:

$$E = \bar{w} + \lambda MRP_L \tag{7.6}$$

where $0 < \lambda < 1$. This solution is illustrated in Figure 7.8. The horizontal axis measures the picker's effort and the vertical axis measures the MRP_L and the picker's earnings. The MRP_L from the effort applied by the picker to harvesting is represented by the line, MRP_L. As drawn, the harvester receives wage $\bar{w}$ without applying effort – $\bar{w}$ might be thought of as the national minimum wage – but as the line MRP_L cuts the vertical axis above this point, it assumes that some mushrooms are picked despite limited effort.

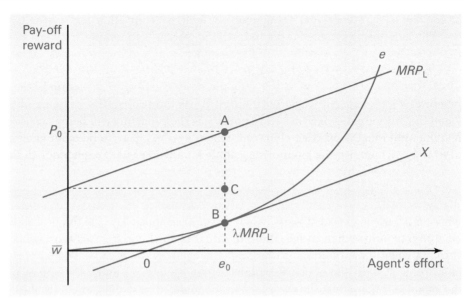

Figure 7.8: Optimal effort

The curve $\bar{w}e$ represents a constant level of utility for the harvester and points on it show the trade-off in terms of effort and reward, i.e. it is the worker's indifference curve. From the mushroom farmer's (the principal's) viewpoint, the optimal effort is e_0, because at this level of effort the vertical distance between the line, MRP_L, and the curve, $\bar{w}e$, is maximized, points AB. With a total pay-off, P_0, the farmer has to devise a scheme that will bring forth the effort, e_0. One way of doing this is **piece rates**, whereby the harvester receives a proportion of the additional value, AC, resulting from the additional effort. The farmer cannot observe the effort, but he can observe the outcome and by trial and error a piece-work scheme represented by the line $\bar{w}ox$, could be devised, whereby additional effort attracts higher rewards. Faced with the scheme represented by the line $\bar{w}ox$, a rational harvester will choose effort level e_0, where the additional piece-work payments, λMRP_L, are just equal to the vertical distance, e_0B.

Two observations follow from the foregoing. The first is that if the wage $\bar{w}$ is increased it would not increase the amount of effort and hence output. Readers can ascertain for themselves that given a normal **indifference map**, the effort level would be reduced if the fixed wage element was increased. A second observation is that the risk has to some extent, but not completely, been absorbed by the farmer. This demonstrates a very important principle of optimal incentive contracts; namely, it is more efficient for the employee to share some of the risk.

The foregoing provides an example of a particular type of incentive contract, but we can deal a little more formally with the issue of monitoring performance. We have demonstrated that to induce effort the employer must reward the individual for the opportunity cost, but ideally must also put in place a monitoring system that has a higher probability of correctly observing effort or shirking. In effect, such a compensation system presents the employee with a monitoring gamble. If the employer offers a wage with certainty, say w_0, then there is no incentive to exert effort. Hence, the employer must offer a bonus, δ_B, conditional upon being observed exerting effort and a penalty, δ_P, if observed shirking. The monitoring gamble for the industrious worker is therefore:

$$E(w^e) = p_{ee}(w_0 + \delta_B) + p_{0e}(w_0 - \delta_P) \tag{7.7}$$

where $E(w^e)$ is expected wage, with effort, p_{ee} is the probability of being observed exerting effort when the individual is exerting effort and p_{0e} is the probability of being accused of shirking when in fact the individual is exerting effort and where $p_{ee} + p_{0e} = 1$. To be a fair gamble, the expected value of $w^e > w_0$. In contrast, the monitoring gamble for a worker with a tendency to shirk is:

$$E(w^s) = P_{e0}(w_0 + \delta_B) + P_{00}(w_0 - \delta_P) \tag{7.8}$$

where $E(w^s)$ is the expected wage, when no effort is applied, p_{e0} is the probability of being judged to be applying effort when in fact the individual is shirking, P_{00} is the probability of being observed shirking when the individual is shirking and, again, $p_{e0} + P_{00} = 1$. The more reliable the employer's monitoring system, the higher the probabilities p_{ee} and p_{00} and, consequently, the more favourable the gamble for the industrious worker and the more adverse the gamble for the shirker.

The effect of a more reliable system is shown in Figure 7.9. At point A, the individual receives wage w_0 with certainty. If the system described above is now introduced, points D and C show the pay-offs to effort and shirking, respectively. This is a situation of incomplete information as neither state can be perfectly observed, and hence the expected pay-off depends on (a) whether the individual is industrious or shirks; and (b) the probability of being observed in the true state. Figure 7.9 shows the expected wage line for the two alternative hidden actions. The better the information on effort, the

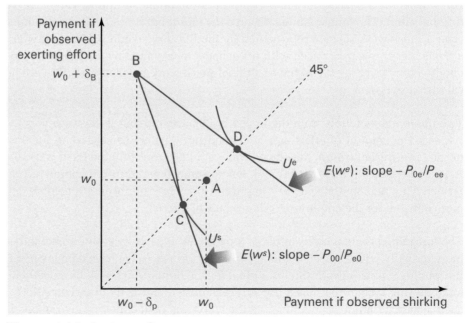

Figure 7.9: Monitoring performance

flatter the expected wage line and the better the information on shirking, the steeper the expected wage line. Hence, the best a shirker can expect (represented by the U^s indifference curve) is a point such as C; whereas by being industrious the worker is likely to achieve a point above A, such as D on a higher indifference curve (U^e).

Effective incentive systems must ensure that individuals – or groups – are held responsible for their performance. In the example set out above, the employee's earnings were at some risk from an inferior performance. Some individuals may be prepared to take the risk of their pay being reduced by an averse outcome, but as previously discussed, most individuals are risk averse. Even if the individual employee is not risk adverse, in many instances such schemes are rendered less efficient because it is not possible to measure accurately the effort, let alone the diligence and creativity, that an individual has contributed. One reason for this is that many people work as part of a team. Another reason is that the more complex and intellectual the task, the greater the difficulty in measuring effort. Where individual effort cannot be accurately measured, we need a different type of incentive system.

If it is not possible to measure individual performance, incentives must be of a more general nature and linked to general outcomes. And again, if the reward system is to be regarded as just and fair by employees, it must be designed for people who are risk averse. Another reason for an incentive system that is general rather than specific, is that where performance evaluation is subjective – as it will normally be for a team member – a manager may be tempted to engage in opportunistic behaviour, deliberately underrating the contribution of an individual team member in order to reduce costs. Finally, to be efficient – that is, an incentive system that encourages effort and minimizes moral hazard – it must be such that if caught cheating the individual has something to lose. Such an incentive system is the payment of **efficiency wages**. Figure 7.10 illustrates an example of an efficiency wage.

In Figure 7.10, let w_0 be the wage paid to a group of a firm's employees. If an individual's performance was judged to be unsatisfactory and they were forced to seek a new job, it might be that after a period of search they obtain another job paying w_0. But given a period of search, when measured over a reasonable period, say one year, the average wage received would be more likely to be w_1, after taking into account a period without employment. In other words, the vertical distance AB measures the quasi-rent

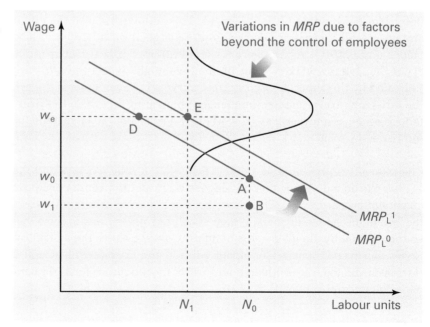

Figure 7.10: Efficiency wages

associated with current employment. The clear implication of the foregoing is that any employee who is dismissed for shirking will suffer an income penalty over the following year equivalent to the quasi-rent, AB. Set against this penalty for being caught shirking is the utility gain to the individual from shirking on the job. We can represent this dilemma facing the individual employee with the following analysis that is based broadly on Shapiro and Stiglitz (1984). Consider the equation:

$$U > p(w_0 - w_1) \tag{7.9}$$

where U is the utility gained from shirking, p the probability that the shirking will be detected and punished and $0 < p \leq 1$. Equation (7.9) must relate to a period of time, and it says that if the utility derived from shirking exceeds the expected income loss over the period, the fact that the worker is earning a quasi-rent will not be sufficient to deter shirking. Theoretically, the lowest wage that can deter shirking would be:

$$w_e = w_1 + U/p \tag{7.10}$$

The wage w_e is called an efficiency wage. It is set higher than the average wage the employee caught shirking might expect to receive over the year following dismissal in order to motivate employees to put more effort into their work. By paying a wage above what the individual might earn elsewhere, the firm is communicating to its employees the value it places on their services. But it also serves as a negative motivator in that if the worker is caught shirking and is fired, a real penalty of a significant fall in income over the period will be incurred.

The outcome of a firm paying an efficiency wage for the labour market from which it draws its employees is a reduction in the employment on offer. In Figure 7.10, the raising of wages for the group to w_e is a consequential fall in the firm's workforce. But not to point D as might be expected, but to a point like E providing N_1 employment. This follows because the efficiency wage encourages effort and as a result there is an increase in the marginal productivity of labour, pushing the demand for labour up to $MRP_L{}^1$. Again, there is the question of risk, if labour productivity is subject to random events outside the workers' control, then we might expect the MRP_L to fluctuate around point E, as indicated by the superimposed normal curve. However, even if the MRP_L does fluctuate around E, the efficiency wage remains unchanged; hence, in this case, the firm appears to bear all the risk, though again, employees may be working in teams and too large a fluctuation in MRP_L could threaten future employment.

The outcome represented by point E benefits both the workers and the employers. The workforce, N_1, has the added satisfaction of a higher wage and the firm is maximizing its profits subject to this constraint because $w_e = MRP_L$. However, if it pays one firm to raise the wages it pays above the level that would be set by the market, then it will pay other firms to raise their wages. This may appear to counter the motivational benefits of offering a wage above the market rate. But, if all firms raise their wages, the overall demand for labour will fall and unemployment will result. As unemployment has now been created, the workforce has a new incentive not to shirk; namely, the prospect of a longer period of unemployment.

In principle, incentive contracts are preferable to efficiency wages, but faced with unacceptably high costs of monitoring performance, many firms will choose efficiency wages despite having to bear the risk. However sophisticated the firm's monitoring systems, only the worker really knows how much effort is being expended. This is a situation of asymmetric information, yet it is the effort that the individual worker puts in to the job that influences the outcome for the firm. Thus, efficiency wages are more efficient when the costs of monitoring performance exceed the wage costs of discouraging shirking. The more the firm invests in monitoring performance, the greater the probability that shirking will be detected. Alternatively, the greater the difficulty of monitoring effort and performance – say, the longer-term forecasting performance of an economist – the greater the incentive to minimize monitoring costs and increase wage rates. In essence, the objective in paying efficiency wages is to increase performance without the need for a corresponding rise in monitoring costs. But there can be other justifications for paying efficiency wages; most notably, to avoid the transaction costs of replacing an efficient worker. If efficiency wages reduce turnover, the firm gains three distinct benefits: the avoidance of the disruption to the smooth running of the firm's business while a replacement is sought; the risk that it will suffer **adverse selection** in appointing a replacement; and by retaining staff over long periods the firm will increase loyalty and its employees will accumulate the knowledge benefits of learning.

In the next section, we turn to the issue of attracting and retaining employees. But before leaving the issue of incentives and monitoring, it is appropriate to say a few words about the valuation of teams. In principle, teams benefit from specialization and hence team output should be greater than the sum of the output if the individuals worked independently. For example, return to Equation (7.4) where four people working independently might produce the following output:

$$q = \sum_{i=1}^{4} (\alpha + \beta e + \varepsilon)_i \qquad (7.11)$$

but working as a team and allowing each to specialize, the output is more likely to be:

$$q = (\alpha + \beta e)^4 + \varepsilon \qquad (7.12)$$

As argued by Alchian and Demsetz (1972), teams are formed because they are more productive, but teams add a further complication to measuring performance. If teams are rewarded on the basis of team output, it creates scope for the **free-rider** problem. The larger the team, the greater the scope for free-riding and not being discovered. Supervisor or peer evaluations would appear to provide a solution, but even team members may have incomplete information on their team mates. Teams are like mini firms with respect to production. And, like a firm, effective teams develop internal architectures for allocating tasks and determining rewards and punishment. Where teams exist over a succession of production periods, punishment of identified free-riders is likely to be more effective (Radner, 1991). In a repeated context, a punishment need not involve a reduction in pay, but the contempt and ostracizing of a free-rider. Fear of this is self-enforcing, causing opportunistic individuals to behave less unselfishly and to adhere to agreements.

The foregoing indicates the complexity of the relationship between employment, incentives and pay. Of key importance to the competitive success of a firm is its ability to motivate its workforce to high levels of effort. Motivation is much more than the arm's-length market transaction between buyer and seller implied by the neo-classical labour market paradigm. Most employment actually represents a complex, long-term relationship between the employer and employee, involving personal responsibilities and the achievement of personal goals as well as the reward–goals linkages. Pay, or more generally, rewards are integral to the process of motivation but a full understanding involves behav-

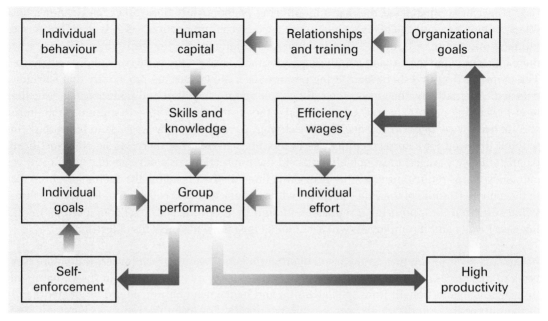

Figure 7.11: Efficiency motivation and performance

ioural as well as economic theories. Figure 7.11, which is loosely based on Vroom's (1964) expectancy theory, is an attempt to summarize some of the interrelationships. Expectancy theory predicts that an employee will exert a high level of effort if a strong relationship between effort, performance, rewards and the satisfaction of achieving personal goals is perceived. Each of these relationships, in turn, is influenced by other factors.

Attracting and Retaining Employees

The true characteristics of the potential employee, e.g. hard working, possessing the skills and experience claimed, are not known for certain by the employer; they remain the private information of the applicant. The employer will no doubt seek information on the suitability of the applicant, but information is costly. Hence, ***ex ante***, the existence of asymmetric information means that the firm may offer employment to someone who is not suitably qualified. This is the problem of adverse selection and it is not only a problem for the firm. A skilled and reliable person may not be able to convince a potential employer that their expertise has not been exaggerated. Adverse selection is a problem of pre-contractual characteristics that are hidden for the purpose of opportunism.

All firms face an ongoing need to recruit new employees. In contrast to the neo-classical model, the decision about the numbers to recruit, the skills and experience of the people to recruit and the way in which people will be recruited is a far more complex issue than merely offering a rate of pay. It will, or should, depend in part on the technology used by the firm, on its current strategy and on its forecasts about future demand. In a world of costly information, the first step in attracting applicants is to make people aware of the firm and the opportunities it offers. The information the company gives out and the image it projects will induce some self-selection; indeed, recruitment policies can be designed with the specific intention of achieving self-selection. Potential applicants hold private information as to their skills, experience and knowledge. Also relevant to a potential employer are the long-term plans of applicants. The idea is for the firm to design its recruitment policies so that they will attract only the applicants with the attributes the firm wants its employees to possess.

Offering a career with pay based on seniority is likely to deter people who are not looking for a career. A reward system based on performance is likely to attract people who are very confident of their abilities. The more a firm is seeking a long-term relationship with a suitable employee, the more care it will take to avoid hiring an inappropriate person. Managing and building the value of the relationship is the provenance of human resource management (HRM) and all managers have responsibilities in this area.

As the name implies, human resource management embraces all aspects of an employee's relationship with the firm – e.g. job design, remuneration, responsibilities and promotion opportunities – buts its underlying purpose is to build the employee's value to the organization. In the neo-classical model, an employee's value, i.e. productivity is in part a product of their innate strength and dexterity and in part the amount of physical capital they have at their disposal. The modern approach is to recognize that the level of productivity is also a product of the employee's human capital (Milgrom and Roberts, 1992). Human capital embodies the knowledge and acquired skills of the workforce. Investment in human capital has a positive impact on the productivity – in the broadest sense – and efficiency of a firm's workforce and thereby its ability to create economic value. Globalization, with its accompanying global competition, increasingly demands that firms develop the potential of their employees by helping them to enhance and utilize their skills and knowledge.

The existence of a relationship which involves investment by the firm in its employees highlights yet another deficiency of the neo-classical labour market paradigm, in that it cannot explain why firms frequently invest in training for their employees. The neo-classical labour model places productivity (MP_L) at the centre of the employment decision, but it has little to say about the nature of productivity other than to imply it is a function of the worker's innate strength. Human capital is acquired through education, training and experience and it is the factor that differentiates raw labour power from degrees of skilled expertise. Human capital and its role in helping firms become more efficient and effective must play an important role in explaining the internal workings of the firm. In short, the neo-classical model's silence on human capital greatly reduces its relevance to the actual working of labour markets in advanced economies.

Human capital can usefully be separated into two categories: firm-specific human capital and **general purpose human capital**. The former consists of specific skills and knowledge that are of most value to an individual firm, e.g. tacit knowledge of routines; whereas the latter includes more general skills and

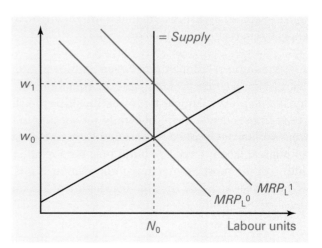

Figure 7.12: Wages, incentives and human capital

knowledge that can be utilized by a range of potential employers. Although some employers will support the acquisition of general purpose human capital by their employees, e.g. financing evening classes, in general, employers are more likely to invest in firm-specific human capital. An attempt to demonstrate the impact of such investment is set out, in Figure 7.12, by an upward shift in the MRP_L curve. Given a workforce of N_0, the impact of training to build firm-specific skills and knowledge is to push up the MRP_L^0 to MRP_L^1. But this improvement only applies to the existing workforce: workers with firm-specific skills will be of more value to the firm than new replacement workers. Hence, for the firm's existing employees with their firm-specific human capital, their supply curve becomes vertical at N_0. The figure demonstrates why firm-specific human capital justifies the payment of a rent – an increase in wage rates from w_0 to w_1. The dashed supply curve reflects the likelihood that at a wage above w_0, people outside the firm would like to be recruited but are of little or no interest to the firm as they lack the necessary human capital. The greater the firm-specific human capital embodied in the workforce, the greater the cost to the firm of resignations and hence the threat of opportunism. An employee with specific human capital who resigns is likely to inflict a greater cost on the firm than someone with only general purpose human capital. In this situation, the employee's rent-seeking behaviour is a direct challenge to the employer's property rights in the specific human capital that the firm has financed. Hence, the wage, w_1, can also be viewed as an efficiency wage, in that the firm's HRM policies have resulted in high levels of firm-specific human capital and if workers do not fulfil their contracts of employment, the alternative would be a significantly lower wage or unemployment.

What of general purpose human capital? Here, the incentive for training and education is more likely to come from employees. By developing their general human capital, they are potentially more productive and hence more valuable to a variety of potential employers. The pay-off is higher earnings over their productive lives. This explains why younger managers might study for an MBA degree and why many current employers are reluctant to help pay for such tuition. In principle, general purpose human capital could lead to behaviour similar to that indicated by the neo-classical model; namely, frequent movement from employer to employer by rent-seeking individuals. In practice, in the markets where high labour mobility is observed, human capital would appear to be limited, e.g. casual farm labourers. For most jobs – especially those requiring a high level of human capital – the labour market tends to be reasonably stable. People tend to stay with one employer for many years, so actual turnover and worker mobility is low. Both individuals and firms enter into longer-term relationships, frequently involving investment by both parties in human capital on the expectation that both will be rewarded.

A longer-term relationship between employer and employee can only be rationalized if there are longer-term pay-offs for both parties: promotion for the employee; higher efficiency and effectiveness for the employer. Longer-term relationships are the justification for internal labour markets. For many firms, outside hiring generally serves only to fill entry-level jobs and most other jobs are filled from within the firm. Pay scales and career paths are key features of internal labour markets. Using an internal labour market to build long-term relationships also builds firm-specific human capital. In addition, the prospect of a long-term relationship is likely to encourage goal congruence on the part of employees and over time the true nature of an employee's skills, attitudes and commitment will be revealed (Salop and Salop, 1976).

People who take jobs with firms who have a reputation for an internal labour market are likely, in part, to have based their employment decision on the prospect of career earnings. The expectation of a steady increase in remuneration can justify an entry-level wage that is below the employee's MRP_L. Indeed, one potential problem with systems of seniority pay is that at some point earnings rise above MRP_L and hence it is a common feature of firms with internal labour markets to encourage early retirement for those employees whose earnings have comfortably exceeded their MRP_L.

Information asymmetries and scope for opportunistic behaviour underpin the ***governance approach*** to the firm, and the idea of an internal labour market and its associated longer-term relationship would appear to be primarily designed to reduce informational asymmetries and motivate a closer alignment of employees' goals with the firm's goals. In contrast, the ***competency approach*** to the firm plays down self-interest and instead places the emphasis on the building of skills and knowledge that are unique to the firm – firm-specific human capital. Moreover, the focus is not so much at the level of the individual, but more on the collective competence of the workforce or at sub-level groups that offer bundles of skills and knowledge that the firm, through the use of HRM, seeks to develop and accumulate. The emphasis here is on longer-term relationships: continuity is more likely to allow the firm to capture the gains from specialization and co-operation. Longer-term relationships also reduce monitoring costs as managers get to know more accurately the relative productive contribution of individuals within their workforces. Thus, for the competence school, the learning inherent in longer-term relationships is an important source of competitive advantage arising from the skills, knowledge and effort contributed by individuals to the development of intangible resources such as routines and intellectual capital. Longer-term relationships are more likely to achieve not only the effort and co-ordination necessary to deliver high levels of efficiency, but also the heterogeneity necessary for competitive advantage. Learning, here, is a process of cognitive development in which business processes are adapted and changed.

Another difference between the governance and competence-based approaches is the attitude towards opportunism and trust. Whereas the governance approach views incentives as reducing the tendency for opportunistic behaviour, the competency approach focuses more on commitment and trust. For this school, the firm is a social community within which are embedded co-operative arrangements that involve not only authority, but also trust and reputation as a result of working together. Creating a culture within which knowledge is shared and innovation is encouraged is viewed as crucial to competitive advantage and the competence approach believes that co-operative discovery is more likely to be encouraged within a trusting environment.

This approach to the firm's workforce is in marked contrast to that of the neo-classical school. In spot market transactions there are no longer-term relationships and little likelihood of development and change before the contract is fulfilled. In contrast, within a trusting work environment, employees rely on each other and their managers to exercise care and discretion in their decisions so that individuals are treated fairly and with respect.

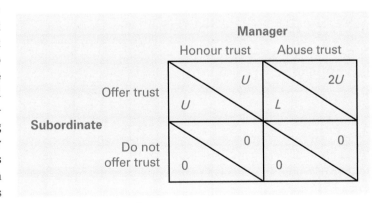

Figure 7.13: A game of trust

We can represent the interactions between a manager (the decision maker) and a subordinate with the game set out in Figure 7.13. We might think of this game as relating to the hiring of the subordinate by the manager or, within an existing working relationship, a decision relating to a new routine. The subordinate has two choices: to offer trust or not. The manager's choices relate to how to respond if trust is offered. The pay-offs are in terms of utility and if trust is offered and honoured both parties receive a valuable pay-off of U. However, for the manager there could be an opportunistic temptation not to honour the trust and in so doing receive an increased pay-off, say $2U$. In this situation, the subordinate suffers a loss of utility, L, and would have fared better if trust had not been offered.

Suppose now the game is only played once, *à la* the neo-classical approach. According to game theory, which posits that each player is rational and self-interested, the subordinate will not offer trust because of the suspicion that the manager has an incentive to abuse this trust and, therefore, the subordinate would be taking a risk in offering trust. The result is that each party receives a pay-off of zero and the opportunity to receive a valuable pay-off is missed. But now assume the game is played repeatedly. If trust is abused today, it will never again be offered and hence the manager is foregoing a repeated pay-off of U, perhaps over many years. In this situation, it would be more sensible for the manager to convince the subordinate that trust will never be abused – this might be by discussion or by the subordinate observing the manager's behaviour in other situations. The important point is that, if the subordinate is to expect trust to be honoured, the manager must be concerned to protect a

Planning for Succession

During the 1990s, companies such as Marks and Spencer and ICI that operated internal labour markets were accused of not being sufficiently responsive to the increasing speed of change in the business environment. How could a large organization plan ahead for jobs that might not exist in the future? The result was that more and more people came to be appointed to top jobs from outside the organization. The appointment of Stuart Rose to the top job at Marks and Spencer is typical; though he succeeded another 'import' who was deemed not to have performed sufficiently well.

But interest in succession planning appears to be reviving. According to the Chartered Institute of Personnel Development, the evidence is mounting that outsiders appointed to top jobs stayed for only a short time before moving on, and while in post made changes that looked superficially good, but were not to the long-term benefit of the organization. But new succession planning is in some respects very different from the old model.

The old succession planning was focused on organizational needs, whereas the 'new' takes more account of the needs of individuals and their own career objectives. Another difference concerns hierarchy. Modern organizations tend to be flatter and therefore offer fewer opportunities to gain experience by a succession of upward moves. Now succession planning is more likely to involve a sideways move equipping the individual with a wider range of generic skills that relate to the firm's desired competencies.

reputation for acting honourably and with integrity. Once trust is established between subordinate and manager, the outcome of the game is likely to be a pay-off of U to both parties and this can be repeated again and again. Note, that in a repeated game this is a Nash equilibrium, i.e. no party can gain by making a unilateral deviation in behaviour.

The simple game set-out demonstrates the importance of reputation. As played, we assumed one subordinate. But imagine the subordinate is changed for each repeated game. If the manager has established a reputation for fair and honest behaviour, a succession of subordinates, if aware of the manager's reputation, will always offer trust. Within the firm, a reputation for honourable behaviour can be the basis for competitive advantage. It is an implicit contract between subordinate and manager and it can be far more effective than detailed, costly and incomplete contracts: monitoring costs are lower and workers will be more inclined to exert effort and co-operate. In the longer term, a trusting environment is likely to encourage greater effort, the building of human capital, the development of heterogeneous skills and routines and consequently competitive advantage for the firm.

Concluding Thoughts

The neo-classical model of the labour market provides a good base from which to launch an analysis of the workings of a firm's internal labour market. Despite its highly restrictive assumptions, the neo-classical model nevertheless lays down iron laws. It explains and can empirically verify the relationship between the offer of a higher wage and the supply of labour. It shows that profit maximization occurs when workers are hired up to the point where the MRP_L is equal to the wage paid. But beyond these basic laws the neo-classical model contributes little to an understanding of the relationship between a contemporary firm and its workforce. The model's assumption of perfect information and super-rationality cannot explain the existence of incentive schemes, nor the dominance of longer-term relationships between employer and employee and expenditure on training by employers.

For most people, employment contracts determine their standard of living, yet such contracts tend to be incomplete and implicit. The problem of bounded rationality ensures that employment contracts take a relational form, whereby the framework of the employer–employee relationship is set out in broad and imprecise terms. The employment contract is, in large measure, implicit. The employer accepts an unwritten obligation to ensure, within reason, a generally risk-averse workforce against adverse fluctuations in the business environment. Implicit contracts are self-enforcing. It is to the longer-term benefit of firms to establish a reputation for fairness in their dealings with employees. For their part, if an employee is being treated fairly, abusing the trust is likely to result in the loss of such employment and possibly harsher treatment. As a member of a team, there are enormous pressures on an individual not to free ride and to adopt co-operative behaviours.

The governance approach to the firm, with its emphasis on transaction costs, provides a rationalization for a hierarchy to monitor and motivate performance, so as to minimize problems of moral hazard and opportunistic behaviour. The type of incentive scheme adopted will be influenced by the extent to which performance can be measured. Where output is observable, piece rates and bonuses might be appropriate. Where it is more difficult to measure output, efficiency wages are more appropriate as they do not require detailed measuring of outcomes and hence monitoring costs are lower. Most employees are risk averse and incentive schemes are normally structured so that the firm assumes most, if not all, of the risk of influences beyond the worker's control. With piece rates and bonuses – particularly where people are members of teams – individuals will share some of the risks, but under efficiency wage schemes, the firm assumes all the risk.

For effort to lead to good performance, an individual employee must have the requisite ability, i.e. firm-specific human capital. Human capital embodies the accumulated skills and knowledge of the workforce, some of which may be the product of a longer-term relationship with the firm and some of which may have been developed by training. The firm has a particular interest in firm-specific human capital, which is of value predominately within the context of the particular firm. In order to gain from the investment in human capital, the firm must seek to retain and motivate employees who have benefited from the investment. Not surprisingly, the firm's organizational architecture directly influences these matters. It is the firm's ability to retain and develop industrious employees through the operation of an internal labour market that builds trust and the accumulation of human capital that is so vital to both efficiency and effectiveness.

Key Learning Points

- Under the neo-classical paradigm of perfect competition, the firm faces a 'going wage rate' which it cannot influence and, in such a world, a profit-maximizing firm will seek to align productivity with unit labour costs.
- The neo-classical view of the supply of labour assumes perfectly informed and hyper-rational individuals deciding purely on the basis of the wage on offer whether or not to offer themselves for work.
- Consequently, the supply of labour function is upward sloping and this gives rise to the concept of an economic rent.
- If allowance is made for imperfections in either the demand or supply of labour, the outcome will be less employment, but the wage on offer may be higher or lower than the competitive market clearing wage depending on the balance of power.
- A monopsonist employer will limit employment and hold wages below the market clearing rate if unconstrained.

- The effect of a monopoly supplier of labour – e.g. an industry-wide trade union – is to raise wages above the market clearing level, but with the effect of reducing the amount of employment.
- Dropping the neo-classical assumptions of perfect information and hyper-rationality focuses attention within the firm where information asymmetries, bounded rationality and opportunistic behaviour abound.
- In practice, it is impossible to write complete employment contracts and firms rely on relational and implicit contracts to achieve the desired behaviours from their workforces.
- A key element of a firm's organizational architecture is to achieve the desired level of motivation and co-ordination amongst its workforce in the face of incomplete information.
- If output is measurable, then incentive schemes such as piece rates and bonuses serve

continued

to achieve these aims by aligning the individual's self-interest with that of the firm.
- Where measurement is more difficult, the introduction of an efficiency wage scheme imposes a penalty on anyone caught shirking.
- Team working is a common feature and teams develop their own architectures for dealing with free-rider problems that are more likely to achieve desired behaviour against the threat of ostracism.
- Longer-term relationships offer additional ways to motivate and develop employees by offering career paths and seniority pay.

- Efficiency wages can also be part of an internal labour market that seeks to build a long-term relationship and specific human capital with identified employees.
- Human capital refers to both innate and acquired skills and knowledge; the higher the firm's level of human capital, the more productive and therefore valuable are its employees.
- Competitive advantage depends on a firm's heterogeneity and the firm is more likely to achieve the necessary sharing of knowledge and innovation inherent in differentiation within a trusting work environment.

Exercises

7.1 Why might a reasonable and fair employer of casual harvest workers prefer a low national minimum wage?

7.2 In what sense are efficiency wages efficient?

7.3 What role does a firm's reputation play in the motivation and co-ordination of a workforce?

7.4 Career paths and seniority salaries have a number of disadvantages. What are they, and how might they be circumvented?

7.5 In contemporary, large-scale firms, employees frequently move laterally across functions. What are the benefits and costs of such practices?

Problems

7.1 The demand curve for labour in an industry is given by $L = 1200 - 10w$, where L is the labour demanded per day and w is the wage rate. The supply curve is given by $L = 20w$:

  (a) What is the equilibrium wage rate and quantity of labour hired?

  (b) If the labour force became unionized and a trade union controls the supply, what will be the quantity of labour supplied and the wage rate?

  (c) If there is only one employer of this unionized labour, draw up a normal form game and show the pay-offs.

7.2 Joe works ten hours a day and his job consists of two tasks, assembling parts and checking the quality of each assembly. He is paid a piece rate for each assembly. He works a full ten hours, so $t_2 = (10 - t_1)$, where t_1 and t_2 are the hours devoted to assembling and checking, respectively. Joe's compensation is calculated as follows:

continued

earnings = $w_1(6t_1^{1/2}) + w_2(10 - t_1)$, where w_i represents the weights the firm has placed on quantity and quality. Joe's objective is to maximize earnings:

(a) Provide an expression showing Joe's maximum earnings.

(b) If (a) is solved for t_1, show that when $w_1 = w_2$, Joe will spend nine hours assembling and one hour checking.

(c) Show this solution in the form of a graph.

References

Alchian, A. and Demsetz, H. (1972) 'Production, information costs and economic organizations', *American Economic Review*, vol. 62, pp. 777–797.

Cremer, J. (1986) 'Cooperation in ongoing organizations', *Quarterly Journal of Economics*, vol. 101, pp. 33–50.

Holmstrom, B. (1979) 'Moral hazard and observability', *Bell Journal of Economics*, vol. 10, pp. 74–91.

Milgrom, P. (1988) 'Employment contracts, influence activities and efficient organisational design', *Journal of Political Economy*, vol. 96, pp. 42–60.

Milgrom, P. and Roberts, J. (1992) *Economics, Organization and Management*, Prentice Hall, Englewood Cliffs, NJ.

Radner, R. (1991) 'Dynamic games in organizational theory', *Journal of Economic Behaviour and Organization*, vol. 16, pp. 217–226.

Salop, J. and Salop, J. (1976) 'Self-selection and turnover in the labour market', *Quarterly Journal of Economics*, vol. 90, no. 4, pp. 619–628.

Shapiro, C. and Stiglitz, J. (1984) 'Equilibrium as a worker discipline device', *American Economic Review*, vol. 74, pp. 433–444.

Stewart, M. (2001) 'Estimation of the individual level employment effects of the introduction of the national minimum wage', Interim Report to the Low Pay Commission, Warwick University.

Vroom, V. (1964) *Work and Motivation*, Wiley, New York.

When a firm employs one more unit of labour in a given period of time, its output is defined to rise by an amount equal to the marginal product of labour, MP_L. The MP_L is expressed as:

$$MP_L = \frac{\Delta Q}{\Delta N} \qquad (7A.1)$$

where ΔQ is the change in the volume of output arising from the change in labour units, ΔN. By the law of diminishing returns we know that at some point, continuing to increase the number of labour units, *ceteris paribus*, will result in diminishing marginal productivity, as shown in Figure 7A.1. Point A is an inflection point and if the firm continues to hire labour beyond N_0, the MP_L will decline, approaching zero and eventually becoming negative.

The prime motive for the firm in employing more units of labour is not the rise in output, but the revenue gain associated with higher output. The gain to the firm's total revenue from selling one more unit of output is its marginal revenue, MR. A firm operating in a perfectly competitive market has no influence on the prevailing market price and therefore the change in the firm's total revenue, i.e. its MR, is equal to the price received for the last unit produced, $p = MR$. A firm with market power, e.g. a monopolist, will, given static demand, suffer a lower price if it increases output and in this case, $MR < p$. The change in the firm's total revenue resulting from hiring one more unit of labour is defined as the marginal revenue product, MRP_L. That is:

$$MRP_L = MP_L.MR \qquad (7A.2)$$

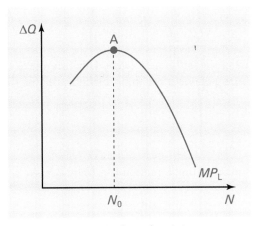

Figure 7A.1: Marginal productivity

Alternatively, the MRP_L can be presented as the change in total revenue, ΔTR, resulting from a change in the number of labour units, ΔN, which yields:

$$MRP_L = \frac{\Delta TR}{\Delta N} \tag{7A.3}$$

Turning to the supply of labour – a small firm that is one of many firms competing for a particular type of labour has no influence over the ruling market wage, w, and hence each additional unit of labour would cost the same as the one before. In this situation, the average cost of labour, AC_L remains constant no matter how much is hired. In other words, the addition to the firm's total costs from hiring another unit of labour, i.e. the firm's marginal costs of labour, MC_L, would be equal to the going wage rate:

$$MC_L = w \tag{7A.4}$$

Suppose instead that the firm is the sole buyer of a particular type of labour in a locality, i.e. the firm is a monopsonist. The more labour the firm wishes to hire, the higher will be the wage it will have to offer. For simplicity, we will assume a linear supply curve and hence the number of units of labour, N, hired is a function of the wage paid, w:

$$N = a + bw \tag{7A.5}$$

which we can conveniently rearrange to:

$$w = \alpha + \beta N \tag{7A.6}$$

where $\alpha = -a/b$ and $\beta = 1/b$. The wage rate, w, is the firm's average cost of labour, AC_L. The total cost to the firm, TC_L, of its hired labour is:

$$TC_L = w.N \tag{7A.7}$$

We are interested in the change in the firm's TC_L arising from the increase in the wage on offer. If we represent the change in the wage rate as Δw and the consequential change in the number of labour units as ΔN, the total change in labour costs, TC_L, will be:

$$\Delta TC_L = w\Delta N + \Delta w.N \tag{7A.8}$$

where w is the new wage. Our interest is the change in the firm's total labour costs arising from the hiring of one more unit of labour, that is, the firm's marginal cost of labour, MC_L, which is defined as:

$$MC_L = \frac{\Delta TC_L}{\Delta N} \tag{7A.9}$$

thus dividing Equation (7A.8) by ΔN, we get:

$$MC_L = w + \frac{\Delta w}{\Delta N}.N \tag{7A.10}$$

We have already defined w as equal to $\alpha + \beta N$ in Equation (7A.6) and therefore $\Delta w/\Delta N = \beta$. Hence, Equation (7A.10) becomes:

$$MC_L = \alpha + \beta N + \beta N = \alpha + 2\beta N \qquad (7A.11)$$

Equation (7A.11) demonstrates that the MC_L will rise at twice the rate of the increase in the wage rate when the labour supply curve is upward sloping. Finally, the firm will maximize its profits when the marginal revenue product is just equal to the MC_L, that is:

$$MRP_L = MC_L \qquad (7A.12)$$

demonstrated graphically in Figure 7A.2, which shows the MRP_L, MC_L and AC_L functions.

Say the firm hires N_1 units of labour. The wage the firm would have to offer to attract this quantity of labour is w_1. But, at this level of labour supply, the $MC_L < MRP_L$, i.e. $A < B$. The last unit of labour added more to the firm's revenue than it did to the firm's total costs. It is therefore profitable to raise the wage and it would in fact be profitable for the firm to raise the wage to w_0. At w_0, the firm attracts N_0 units of labour and at this labour supply, $MC_L = MRP_L$, point C. At point C, the last unit of labour hired added as much to the firm's revenue as it added to the firm's costs. A profit-maximizing employer will not raise the wage offer beyond w_0. If the firm were to raise the wage offer to, say, w_2, then it would attract N_2 units of labour, but now $MC_L > MRP_L$, i.e. $E > F$. The last unit of labour added more to total costs than to total revenue; it was unprofitable to go beyond w_0.

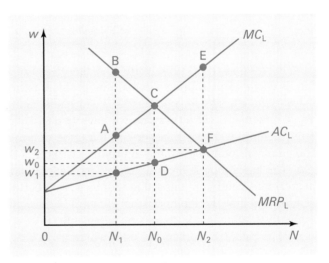

Figure 7A.2: The analytics of monopsony

Bargaining is about dividing value and the means of facilitating the division is generally money. A simple way of representing a bargaining problem is to described the alternatives available to the parties, i.e. the alternative contracts they can make, and to describe what happens if the parties fail to reach agreement. Let us assume we have two individuals, A and B. If it helps, we can think of A being an employer or a manager and B a trade union or an individual worker. Both need each other. The employer will not be able to produce without a workforce and the trade union's members need jobs. The bargaining is over the rate of pay, which essentially comes down to how much value will be created, V, and how this value will be shared between the firm and its workforce. The firm wants to introduce new working patterns, which it believes will increase the value added from V_0 to V_1. Let us finally assume that if there is no agreement, the existing arrangement continues, whereby the firm receive λV_0 and the workers $(1 - \lambda)V_0$ where $0 < \lambda < 1$.

We will call these existing pay-offs the backstop pay-offs or, in the jargon, the players' BATNAs (best alternative to a negotiated agreement). Now consider the following rule: each player is to be given their BATNA plus a share of the surplus, i.e. $(V_1 - V_0)$. We can represent the fraction A will receive from the negotiation as p, where $0 < p < 1$ and therefore B's share will be $(1 - p)$. The bargaining is therefore all about the value of p.

Writing π as the amount A will end up with and w as the amount B will end up with, we have:

$$\pi = \lambda V_0 + p(V_1 - V_0) \tag{7B.1}$$

and

$$w = (1 - \lambda)V_0 + (1 - p)(V_1 - V_0) \tag{7B.2}$$

These two expressions are known as the Nash formulas and we can represent the outcome of the bargaining as the proportions in which the surplus will be divided between the two bargainers:

$$\frac{\pi}{w} = \frac{\lambda V_0}{(1 - \lambda)V_0} + \frac{p(V_1 - V_0)}{(1 - p)(V_1 - V_0)} \tag{7B.3}$$

The first expression on the right-hand side is known as the *disagreement point* and is illustrated in Figure 7B.1 as point X. The line, $V_1 V_1$, represents the value produced if a settlement is reached and therefore we can describe this as an efficient outcome.

The outcome of the bargaining for both parties is uncertain and as we saw in Appendix 6A, the utility obtained from an expected pay-off will depend on individuals' attitudes towards risk. In this bargaining problem, reaching agreement yields the parties, in terms of utility, the joint pay-off:

$$U_A(\pi) + U_B(w) = U_A[\lambda V_0 + p(V_1 - V_0)] + U_B[(1 - \lambda)V_0 + (1 - p)(V_1 - V_0)] \tag{7B.4}$$

It is clear from Equation (7B.4) that both sides have a joint interest in maximizing the value of V_1. How this is shared out between the two sides depends on the relative bargaining power of the two players, which in turn is influenced by their attitudes towards risk – e.g. holding out for a larger share and thereby increasing the risk of a failure to agree. It also depends on the party's outside options. If the workers believe they can walk away from the deal to another one nearly as good, then they will be in a strong bargaining position. This asymmetry between the players will move the pay-off fraction for the two parties up or down the efficiency function, V_1, in Figure 7B.1.

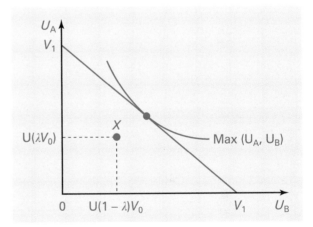

Figure 7B.1: The Nash solution

PART II
CAPTURING VALUE
FROM THE MARKET

MARKET STRUCTURE AND THE STRATEGIC ENVIRONMENT

Introduction

The study of **market structures** by the founding fathers of **neo-classical economics** was confined to the polar opposites of **perfect competition** and **pure monopoly**. Nevertheless, the neo-classical focus on these extremes of market structure served to demonstrate the link between market structure and the behaviour of firms. The neo-classical model of perfect competition remains the best demonstration of the power of competition to maximize not only consumers' welfare but also productive and allocative efficiencies. And, the neo-classical model of pure monopoly demonstrates the dangers for consumers' welfare of an absence of competition. In practice, these extremes of market structure are rarely encountered in their pure forms. Much more common in reality, and relevant for the study of strategy, are the market structures of **oligopoly** and **monopolistic competition**. It remains an article of neo-classical economics that the **strategic behaviour** of firms is to a large degree influenced by the structure of the market in which they operate. As we will demonstrate, the study of the behaviour of firms operating in oligopolistic and monopolistically competitive markets offers enormous scope for analysing the formulation and conduct of business strategy.

Market structures and the behaviour of firms are the products of economic forces. The early studies of **strategic behaviour** treated market structure as exogenously fixed and concentrated on the likely outcomes for the level of output, market prices and economic welfare. But drawing on **game theory** to analyse the strategic behaviour of firms operating under conditions of **imperfect competition**, economists came to realize that a firm's behaviour could influence not only the behaviour of rivals but also market structure. Moreover, the strategic behaviour of firms is, as we have seen, also driven by factors such as their governance structures and their core competencies. These internally generated resources determine a firm's scale and scope, its ability to lower unit costs and create superior value. Hence, a comprehensive understanding of strategic behaviour juxtaposes the individual firm's internally generated competitiveness and its external market structure. The extent to which a firm can capture the value inherent in its core competencies depends not only on its own strategic choices but also on those of its rivals. It depends on whether the outcome of these strategic interactions enables the firm to keep abreast of **exogenous** change and to add to its stock of value-creating knowledge. In short, the ability of a business unit to exploit its **competitive advantage** resides as much in the structure of the market in which it competes as in the individual firm's governance structure and core competencies.

The remaining chapters in this book are concerned with the application of economic principles to the proximate environment in which a firm operates. Our purpose is to place the formulation of business strategy and the strategic behaviour of firms within the context of market structure and other attributes of its proximate external environment, for example the behaviour of upstream suppliers and downstream customers. By strategic behaviour, we mean not just output and price levels, but also decisions regarding investments, inventories, product choice, vertical relationships and marketing. Although there is, as yet, no general theory of strategy, the economic models of oligopoly and monopolistic competition can provide deep understanding of the many dimensions of strategic rivalry and the impact of particular strategies on competition and consumers' welfare.

In this chapter, we focus on a firm's proximate environment; what might be described as the terrain upon which firms develop and play out the strategic rivalry that will be the subject of the following chapters. We approach the issue of a firm's proximate environment by first examining market structure and attempting to answer questions such as why, in a typical industry, are some firms large and others small? What factors determine the number of firms in a market? We then move on to analyse how the market structure of suppliers and customers influences the competitive environment. Finally, we ask why firms tend to cluster together in geographic concentrations and what is the contribution of governments to competitive advantage. By absorbing the information contained in this chapter, you will:

- Be able to define **seller concentration** and its relationship to market structure.
- Appreciate the extent to which **barriers to entry** can influence market structure.
- Understand how relationships with suppliers, customers and rivals contribute to the strategic behaviour of firms and their economic performance.

What follows is divided into seven sections. The first starts by widening the highly restrictive neo-classical definition of competition to embrace the strategic behaviour of firms striving to attract customers. The second moves on to outline the theoretical relationship between market structure and strategic behaviour and the third examines the ways in which market structure is measured. The fourth section brings the analysis down to the level of the **strategic group** and the fifth section investigates how strategic behaviour can influence market structure. Armed with an understanding of how strategic behaviour can itself influence market structure, we examine in the sixth section perhaps the best-known framework of strategic behaviour – Porter's **Five Forces Model** – and in the process widen the influences on strategic behaviour to include the structure of supplying industries and the nature of customers' demand. Finally, in the seventh section we study the tendency for firms to cluster together in specific locations and relax the assumption that firms are always in competition with other firms.

Competition or Rivalry?

Since the founding of economics as a discipline, the dominant view has been that competition is the force that leads to superior economic performance. However, the meaning of competition as propounded by neo-classical economists – a market condition that obliges firms to act solely as respondents to a market price set by forces beyond their control – is very different to that advanced by followers of the *strategic management* discipline. Strategic management, as a discipline, is concerned to understand how to position and manage a firm so as to generate and protect *economic rents*. Firms can only plan and act to secure this objective if they have a degree of market power; that is, the ability to influence demand for their products and the prices charged. From the neo-classical perspective, economic rents are wasteful as they imply a firm's resources are earning a profit in excess of the minimum necessary to prevent them being redeployed to alternative uses; though, as we shall discuss in subsequent chapters, this issue is not so clear cut. In contrast to the neo-classical emphasis on market structure, the strategic management approach is focused on the individual firm and competition within this paradigm essentially means succeeding at the expense of your competitors.

For the purpose of clarity, we must understand the difference between these two broad definitions of competition. As previously explained, within the neo-classical paradigm a market is said to be perfectly competitive when it consists of a very large number of small-scale firms – the phrase *atomistic industry* is frequently used to describe this structure – all selling an *homogeneous product*. In this situation, whether an individual firm increases or decreases the amount produced, it has no influence on the ruling market price and the behaviour of the individual firm is characterized as that of a *price taker*. At the other extreme is pure monopoly: a sole seller of a product or service with no close *substitutes*. For the neo-classical school, pure monopoly is the absence of competition and consequently a monopolist can engage in *opportunistic behaviour* to raise the market price and thereby extract the largest possible economic rent from the market.

In contrast, the strategic management approach to competition emphasizes the conduct of sellers in pursuit of economic rents. From a strategic management perspective, the essence of competition is viewed as the striving by the various sellers in a market for customers. This striving against other businesses for customers can be based on prices but frequently involves non-price factors, such as a superior quality, attractive design and packaging and/or an efficient distribution system and after-sales service. It can also involve behaviour designed to deny competing sellers customers. To the extent that market share is a positive reflection of superior *capabilities*, it implies that if a firm is to sustain a competitive advantage it must possess and exploit resources that are scarce, i.e. resources that other firms find it difficult to replicate.

To think of a firm striving for competitive advantage implies that the firm is operating in a market that is neither perfectly competitive nor a pure monopoly. In reality, most firms operate within such a market structure and would therefore be operating in proximate business environments that would be more accurately described as monopolistically competitive or oligopolistic. Table 8.1 is drawn from Scherer and Ross (1990) and summarizes the principle market structures identified in the economic literature. An oligopoly exists where the market is contested by only a small number of firms and it offers the ideal opportunity to investigate the link between market structure and conduct. Within the neo-classical paradigm, this is

Table 8.1: Alternative market structures

	Number of sellers (firms)		
	One	A few	Many
Homogeneous products	Pure monopoly	Homogeneous oligopoly	Perfect competition
Differentiated products	Multi-product monopoly	Differentiated oligopoly	Monopolistic competition

demonstrated by the **Cournot model** or **Bertrand model** of oligopolistic behaviour, which will be explored in more detail in the next chapter. Oligopolistic markets may be characterized by homogeneous products, e.g. oil, or **differentiated products**, e.g. cars. An example of a differentiated oligopoly – or, more correctly, a duopoly – is the washing powder market, where two giant organizations – Unilever and Proctor and Gamble – compete for market share. The washing powder market reflects all the attributes we might expect from strategic rivalry, such as the use of brands, advertising and innovation. Firms operating in an oligopolistic market will seek to anticipate and counter their rivals' strategies.

In contrast, monopolist competition describes a market structure where there are a large number of competing firms who produce differentiated products and who therefore attempt to gain competitive advantage by advertising the value inherent in their differentiated products – that is, they strive to convince potential customers that their products are in some respect unique, hence the name monopolist competition. Despite attempts at differentiation, the products produced by firms operating in monopolistically competitive – and oligopolistic – markets are functionally similar. Oligopolists seek to counter this by seeking to establish their brands as being synonymous with the market, e.g. Hoover. But as the number of competitors increases, it is not only increasingly difficult for an individual firm to establish its brand in the minds of all consumers, but also it is impossible for individual firms to anticipate and counter the strategies of competing firms.

In order to avoid confusion we will use the term **rivalry** to characterize the conduct of firms who operate in oligopolistic or monopolistically competitive markets – that is, markets where individual firms have a degree of market power, i.e. they face individual downward-sloping **demand curves** and their actions can increase or decrease their market share. We will use the term **competition** to characterize a market environment in which individual firms lack the ability to influence the market price and implicitly the behaviour of competing firms. It is for this reason that **competition policy** is well named; the competition authorities seek to achieve a situation where individual firms lack the power to control the market price. In the **European Union** (EU) it would probably be true to say that the **Treaty of Rome** viewed competition policy not as an end in itself, but as a means to promote economic integration. Today the main objective is economic efficiency (European Commission, 2000). If the power of firms operating in oligopolistic and monopolistically competitive markets to control the price is contained, the outcome, as we shall see, can be beneficial owing to low unit production costs and the incentive to search for new, improved products and procedures. This is the sought-after outcome of effective 'competition legislation'. Where appropriate, the benefits of scale without the power of individual firms to adversely influence consumers' welfare.

The fact that a firm can influence its market environment should not be interpreted as implying that rivalry necessarily yields a lesser outcome for consumers than competition, particularly when viewed over a longer time period involving the introduction of new products and processes. The fewer the number of firms contesting a market – assuming there is more than one – the greater the scope for intense rivalry. For example, the rivalry between two large companies, such as GM and Ford, is intense, each determined to prevent the other from increasing its market share. However, as we shall see, game theory suggests that the temptation to collude in such situations is also intense. In contrast, the nearer a market's structure approaches that of perfect competition, the less the intensity of the rivalry. For example, individual farmers are unlikely to be rivals in the sense that GM and Ford are: they would not increase their influence over the market by forcing their neighbour out of farming. The main difference between the competitive environments within which GM and Ford operate and that in which the typical farmer operates is, in essence, the structure of their respective markets.

EU Competition Policy

Competition policy is essential for the successful operation of the European Union's single market. The *raison d'être* of the single market is to deliver to the population of the EU the benefits that flow from the free movement of goods, services, capital and people between member states. The single market cannot operate as an efficient market if firms use their individual or collective power to frustrate effective competition. The EU's rules on competition between commercial enterprises are laid down in Articles 81 to 89 of the European Community's Treaty and EU competition policy is generally regarded as a notable success.

The 1 May 2004 will go down in history as the day eight former Communist countries acceded to membership of the EU. At a stroke, this expanded the EU's single market to embrace 454 million people and to account for 10 per cent of global GDP. But besides being an historic date for enlargement, the 1 May also has significance for EU competition policy. It marked fundamental reforms in the way Articles 81 and 82 will in future be applied. Companies will in future be trusted not to abuse their market power or enter into illegal agreements to frustrate competition. The task of policing anti-competitive behaviour and handling complaints will in future be shared between the EU and national competition authorities within a European Competition Network (ECN). This

will mean that the primary avenue for the implementation of EU competition rules will now be at the national level and the power to grant exceptions from the strict application of Article 81 is now devolved to member states. Thus, in little over ten years, the acceding Central and Eastern European countries will have moved from economies in which competition was largely absent to ones in which attempts to engage in anti-competitive behaviour are outlawed and liable to punishment. They will be helped by the ECN, whose purpose is to ensure the coherent application of competition law throughout the EU by maintaining a regular flow of information and directions.

Under the new regime, competing firms whose combined market share does not exceed 20 per cent are automatically granted a safe harbour for most agreements they enter into, though some so-called 'hard core' agreements, e.g. to fix prices, are prohibited. The idea is that after 50 years the EU authorities and business have matured, both sides have experience of the competition regime and hence a 'lighter touch' is deemed appropriate. In introducing the changes, the EU's competition commissioner, Mario Monti, claimed that they: 'will lead to a happy marriage in Europe of innovation and competition policy and further convergence between us and the United States'. Whether or not Mario Monti achieves his goal must remain a matter for conjecture.

The Structure–Conduct–Performance Paradigm

By the 1930s, many economists were becoming increasingly uneasy with the neo-classical paradigm, which although acknowledging the existence of monopoly, continued to assume that markets tended towards the 'ideal' of perfect competition. Despite the world slump, it was obvious to anyone who cared to look that the typical industry was not tending towards perfect competition. Branding and other forms of differentiation were the norm and some high-profile prosecutions in the US had demonstrated that powerful firms were prepared to collude in order to protect and enhance their economic rents. Dissatisfaction with the lack of empirical support for the neo-classical model led to a number of major developments within the subject of microeconomics. The one of interest here is the ***structure–conduct–performance*** (SCP) postulate, which can be traced back to Edward Mason (1939), who published a seminal text at the end of the 1930s. However, the SCP paradigm is now more generally associated with Joseph Bain (1959). Bain was attempting to explain the different types of competitive rivalry observed in different industries. The basic idea underpinning the SCP paradigm is that there is a causal relationship between the structure of an industry – e.g. the number and size distribution of sellers – the conduct of firms within the industry – the behavioural rules followed by sellers and buyers – and the overall economic performance of firms within the industry, e.g. profitability. Bain suggested that an industry, where a large share of output was accounted for by a small number of large firms, would exhibit collusive behaviour, tacit or otherwise, to raise prices and hence economic rents. In short, if a small number of firms work together to control the industry's supply, creating a situation of **collective dominance**, consumers will be forced to pay a high price for a restricted output. The traditional SCP approach is summarized in Figure 8.1. In this basic model, the causation runs from structure to conduct, which in turn influences performance.

At the heart of the SCP paradigm is the industry or market structure. As indicated in Figure 8.1, structure defines more than the number of competing firms and their relative sizes. These are but two of a number of intrinsic structural variables that include the extent to which competing products are differentiated, the cost structures of competing firms and organizational structures such as the extent of **vertical integration** and **diversification**. These intrinsic structural variables are to a large extent determined by the nature of the product and the available technologies for production and marketing. But a complete picture of the determinants must allow for derived influences on market structure, such as geography, accidents of history and government policies – and most importantly, as we shall see, to the strategies of the competing firms themselves.

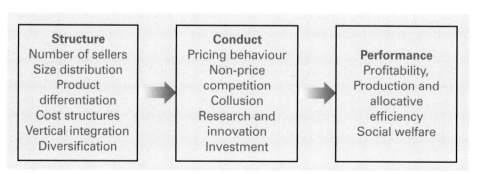

Figure 8.1: Structure, conduct and performance

If we are to measure a market's structural variables we need first to define the market's boundaries and this comes down to a definition of the product in question. The neo-classical approach avoids this complication by the assumption of market homogeneity. In practice, defining the scope of a market's boundaries is much more complex. Some products, normally described as commodities, come close to the neo-classical assumption of homogeneity, but few would seriously argue that coffee drinkers are completely indifferent as to whether the beans are arabica or robusta and to where they are grown. As Chamberlin (1933) famously pointed out *virtually all products are differentiated, at least slightly*. The issue for business strategists and empirical analysts is to know when a group of differentiated products can be defined as market competitors and when the degree of differentiation dictates that the products be placed in separate markets.

Table 8.2: A NACE industry classification

Code	Description
15	Manufacture of food products and beverages
15.5	Manufacture of dairy products
15.51	Operation of dairy and cheese making
including	Production of pasteurized, homogenized and/or heat treated milk and cream
	Production of butter
	Production of yoghurt
	Production of cheese and curd
	Production of whey, casein or lactose
15.52	Manufacture of ice cream
including	Production of ice cream and edible ice such as sorbet

Source: *EU Commission*

For practical purposes, governments need to classify individual firms by placing them within an officially defined industry. For members of the European Union, the industrial framework is provided by the NACE classification scheme. NACE is the acronym for *nomenclature générale des activités economiques dans les Communautés Européennes*. The corresponding scheme for the United States is the North American Industrial Classification System (NAICS) and both strive for compatibility with the International Standard Industrial Classification for economic activities sponsored by the UN. An illustration of the NACE classification is set out in Table 8.2. The basic code places firms in broad two-digit industry groups. For example, 15 is the manufacture of food and beverages, 45 is construction and 55 is hotels and restaurants. As can be seen in Table 8.2, the broad industry group is further subdivided into a number of three-digit sub-categories, one of which, 15.5, is the manufacture of dairy products. These sub-categories are then further sub-divided into two four-digit sub-categories. Category 15.51 includes the operations of firms known as milk processors; that is, the production of milk, butter, cheese and yoghurt, and even at this four-digit level, it is obvious that the classification incorporates a number of separate markets. In contrast, category 15.52 is confined to the manufacture of ice cream, which is more easily identified with a distinct market.

Seeking Compatibility between NACE and NAICS

A convergence of the separate industrial classifications, NACE, NAICS and the ISIC, is planned for 2007. In 2002, a joint working party involving Eurostat – the EU's statistical office – the US, Canadian and Mexican statistical bodies was set up to examine the potential for convergence between NACE and NAICS. It was realized that these discussions would have implications for the ISIC and therefore representatives from the UN and the OECD were also included on the working party. Given the number of differences, both in terms of concept and detail, between NACE and NAICS a complete convergence between the two classifications was judged impractical. Therefore the working party proposed a compromise of bringing about convergence at the two-digit level. Most of the changes will be made by NAICS.

The attempt to bring about increased comparability between the North American and European systems of industrial classification reflects in part the process of globalization and the perceived benefits of more accurately comparing industrial performance and aligning competition policies. It also reflects the desire to introduce a new two-digit information industry group. A major innovation for NACE 2007 will be a new information sector embracing books, newspapers, film, video and the internet. In principle, NACE 2007 will solve, or at least address, many of the issues e-business/commerce causes for the current system of classification. The advent of digital technology means that products can easily transfer from one classification to another. For example, the digital content of newspapers, which are currently classified in the printing sector as part of manufacturing, can easily move over to the telecommunications sector that is part of services.

Seller Concentration

As demonstrated by Table 8.2, official industry classification schemes tend to be highly aggregated and defined in terms of supply-side factors. They are, however, widely available and in practice analysts tend to settle for an officially defined four-digit *industry group* when investigating market structure. Having placed a firm within a four-digit industry group, the next stage is to assess the scope for individual firms to exercise market power. For example, a frequent reason for investigating an industry group's structure is to assess how a merger or acquisition might influence the balance of market power. Market power is assessed by measuring *seller concentration*; that is, the proportion of the total market supply that is accounted for by the production of a particular group of firms within the industry. According to the SCP paradigm, the behaviour we might expect from, say, four or five large-scale firms that account for a substantial proportion of a market's total supply will be very different from what we might expect if the same share of market output came from 500 small to medium-sized enterprises (SMEs). In the former case, we might expect rivalry to put the emphasis on advertising strategies, product research and development, even tacit inter-firm collusion. In the latter, the emphasis is likely to be much more on price competition. To complicate matters, very rarely does an industry group consist of just four or five equal-sized firms, or at the other extreme, a large number of relatively small firms. Most industry groups consist of a small number of large firms and a 'long tail' of SMEs. Typical are the data set out in Table 8.3. This shows the structure of the western European market for new cars and light vans.

Table 8.3: 2004 Western European new cars and light vans ('000s)

Firm	Sales	%	Firm	Sales	%	Firm	Sales	%
VW/Audi	2,078	13.5	Toyota	725	4.7	Volvo	237	1.5
Renault	1,752	11.3	BMW	682	4.4	Honda	206	1.3
Ford	1,434	9.3	Nissan	452	2.9	Kia	173	1.1
Peugeot	1,291	8.4	SEAT	375	2.4	Mitsubishi	155	1.0
Citroen	1,067	6.9	Hyundai	311	2.0	Alfa Romeo	148	1.0
Opel	1,043	6.8	Suzuki	252	1.6	Daewoo	135	0.9
Fiat	953	6.2	Mazda	240	1.6	Other	676	4.4
Mercedes	819	5.3	Skoda	240	1.6	**Total**	**15,452**	**100.0**

Source: *Automotive News Market Data Book*

It is obvious from Table 8.3 that merely counting the number of firms within an industry tells us nothing about the concentration of market power and rivalry. What is needed is a method of ranking firms so as to reveal the scope that exists for firms to abuse their positions of power. The most basic way of doing this is to calculate the ***concentration ratio***, which measures the cumulative market share of the largest x firms ranked in descending order of size:

$$CR_x = \sum_{i=1}^{x} s_i \qquad (8.1)$$

where CR_x = the x firm concentration ratio and s_i = the percentage market share of the ith firm where $0 < s < 100$. Equation (8.1) is used in the following manner. The analyst must first decide how many of the firms within the group are of interest; normally, attention will be confined to the largest four or five. Thus, if we are interested in the largest five firms we define the concentration ratio for five firms as CR_5. We then sum the percentage share (in descending order of size) for the five largest firms. If the resulting value is a small number say, 3 per cent, then this indicates that each firm has only a small share of the market; whereas a value approaching 100 indicates a very high level of concentration. Equation (8.2) is drawn from the data set out in Table 8.3. As can be seen the CR_5 for the western European new car and light van market amounts to about 50 per cent – a high level of concentration:

$$CR_5 = 13.5 + 11.3 + 9.3 + 8.4 + 6.9 = 49.3 \qquad (8.2)$$

The concentration ratio has the merit of being simple to calculate, but it also suffers a number of limitations as an indicator of market power and hence strategic rivalry. For example, consider two industry groups, A and B, each with 100 firms. In group A, one firm has 40 per cent of the market, four have 5 per cent each and the remaining 95 approximately half of one per cent each. In group B, five firms each have 15 per cent of the market and the remaining 95 firms approximately half of one per cent each. In both cases, the $CR_5 = 60$, but the rivalry within each group is likely to be very different. In group A, we might expect the largest firm to be a market leader and hence 'rivalry' consists of 'follow the leader' behaviour. In contrast, in industry group B there is likely to be intense rivalry between the largest five firms. A more commonly used measure of concentration is the **Herfindahl index**, which takes account of all firms in the industry group. The Herfindahl index, HI, is considered superior to the concentration ratio and is calculated by summing the squares of the individual market shares for all firms in the market:

$$HI = \sum_{i=1}^{n} s_i^2 \tag{8.3}$$

where $0 < s < 1$, s_i^2 = the square of the market share of the ith firm, and n = the number of firms in the market. As s is measured as a decimal, then HI would be close to zero when there are a large number of equal-sized firms, and equal to unity under pure monopoly. For the data set out in Table 8.3, the Herfindahl index = 0.07. The HI has the advantage that the measure of concentration can be expressed as the equivalent of a number of firms. For example, given the HI value of 0.07, taking the reciprocal shows the equivalence in the number of firms if the market were made up of equal-sized firms; in this case, the number would be close to fourteen. In the US, a variation on the Herfindahl index, the Herfindahl–Hirschman index (HHI), is used as a guide to market structure. In the HHI, s is measured in percentages, i.e. $0 < s < 100$, hence the index can take a value ranging from close to zero to 10,000. In our example, the HHI would be 719.8. As far as the US authorities are concerned, a value in excess of 2,000 merits closer investigation. The shortcoming with all these measures is that whilst they indicate a level of concentration, they tell us very little about the degree of inequality. Measuring the degree of concentration can only be a stage in the analysis, it is not conclusive. For example, consider the two industry groups set out in Table 8.4.

Table 8.4: Market shares

Market shares in group A are more unequal than for group B, yet both produce a similar Herfindahl–Hirschman

Firms (ranked by market share)	1	2	3	4	5	HHI
Group A (% share)	53	12	12	12	11	3,362
Group B (% share)	34	33	33			3,334

index. A better, or at least an augmenting, measure of inequality is the **gini-coefficient** and its associated **Lorenz curve**. An example of a Lorenz curve is shown in Figure 8.2. Using the data set out in Table 8.3, the firms are ranked by size and cumulated from smallest to largest as a percentage of the number of firms in the market and this is plotted against the cumulative percentage of output. Curve *ACB* records – starting with the smallest firm – the cumulative sales of cars and light vans as the percentage of firms in the market approaches 100 per cent. If all firms in the group had an equal share of the market, then the joint cumulation of firms and output would result in moving up the line *AB*, e.g. 50 per cent of firms would account for 50 per cent of the group's output and so on. Thus, *AB* is the line of complete equality. The greater the deviation of the curve, *ACB*, from the diagonal line, AB, the greater the inequality in the market shares of individual firms. As can be seen from Table 8.3, the market for cars and light vans in western Europe displays a high degree of inequality.

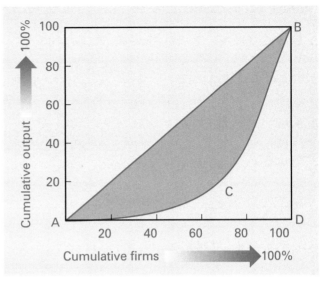

Figure 8.2: The Lorenz curve

We can give a greater measurement of precision to the degree of inequality by calculating the gini-coefficient. The gini-coefficient summarizes the deviation shown in Figure 8.2 into a single coefficient. Referring to Figure 8.2, the gini-coefficient is the product of dividing the shaded area, *ABC*, by the triangle, *ABD*.

The gini-coefficient can vary between 0, when all firms are of equal size (and hence the Lorenz curve is the same as the line of absolute equality *AB*) and 1, when a single firm produces the total market output. Thus, the closer the gini-coefficient to 1 the more unequal is the industry group:

$$\text{Gini-coefficient} = \frac{\text{ABC}}{\text{ABD}} \qquad (8.4)$$

Food Retailing

On 8 April 1999, the Director General of Fair Trading referred the supply of groceries from supermarkets to the Competition Commission. At issue was whether the larger retail outlets – defined as having a floor area in excess of 600 square metres – enjoyed a monopoly in the supply of groceries in the UK. Under UK legislation, a *scale monopoly* is taken to exist when at least one-quarter of the relevant market is supplied by one firm or when supplied by members of a group con-

trolled by one firm. The origin of the reference lay, firstly, in a public perception that the price of groceries in the UK tended to be higher than in comparable EU countries and, secondly, in an apparent disparity between farm-gate and retail prices.

The table below sets out on a national and regional basis the CR_5 and *HHI* for the share of grocery sales by UK supermarkets.

continued

%	UK	Scotland	Wales	Northern Ireland
Tesco	24.6	19.1	31.5	46.5
Sainsbury	20.7	6.3	10.1	17.4
Asda	13.4	19.3	15.7	0.0
Safeway	12.5	28.4	8.7	16.3
Somerfield	8.5	11.8	17.2	0.0
CR_5	79.7	84.9	83.2	80.2
HHI	1,506	1,795	1,788	2,935

The table shows that none of the main supermarkets supply more than one-quarter of the UK market and hence a scale monopoly does not exist for the UK as a whole. However, Tesco's share of the Welsh and Northern Ireland markets does constitute a scale monopoly. An alternative to a scale monopoly is a *complex monopoly*, which is taken to exist when at least one-quarter of a market is supplied by a group of firms who, whether voluntarily or not, and whether by agreement or not, conduct their respective affairs as in any way to restrict or prevent competition.

In order to carry out its task, the Commission had first to identify the relevant market. Their studies showed that the majority of consumers use supermarkets for the bulk of their groceries, involving a single trip to a single store once a week: so-called one-stop shopping. Having determined the behaviour of consumers, the Commission then concluded that not only were consumers generally satisfied with the service provided by supermarkets, but also a larger store – with a sales area of 1,400 square metres or more – was necessary to facilitate one-stop shopping. On this definition, 1,895 stores – out of a population of 3,927 – were identified. Although amounting to just under half of the stores with an area in excess of 600 square metres, they tend to be the larger stores and in total the 1,895 stores identified account for some 80 per cent of sales from all stores in excess of 600 square metres.

The Commission then turned to the relevant geographic market. This, they concluded, was not the national or regional market. Despite the fact that the supermarkets under investigation operated across all or most regions of the UK, in essence, for competitive purposes, the relevant market was determined by how far consumers are prepared to travel (normally in a car) to a supermarket. It concluded that the relevant geographic market for its study is essentially local, within a radius of between 10 and 15 minutes' travelling time.

The second stage of the Commission analysis was to gauge the effectiveness of competition being offered to the identified stores within the travel time catchment areas – the so-called 10- to 15-minute isochrome level. On this basis, the Commission identified *78 stores of potential concern with local 'monopoly' status and 137 stores of potential concern with local 'duopoly' status.* However, despite these findings the Commission concluded that the industry is broadly competitive and that overall excessive prices are not being charged.

Industry or Strategic Groups?

At the level of industry analysis, just as important as choosing the appropriate measure of concentration is ensuring that the market's boundaries have been properly identified. Our interest in market structure is as an aid to understanding firm rivalry and strategy, and for this businesses should ideally distinguish between structure at the level of the industry group in which they are officially classified and structure at the level of the **strategic group** in which they compete. Firms need to understand this distinction because, in practice, the definition of an industry group is an administrative convenience and it may consist of firms that are not direct rivals. Similarly firms placed in different industry groups may be direct rivals. For example, just where should the line be drawn in defining the market for a product such as beer? Is bottled beer a close substitute for keg beer? Should we go wider and include low alcohol beers and even cider? These are not easy questions to answer and ultimately can only be answered with the aid of empirical research. The situation is further complicated because a firm might produce a range of products that fall into a number of strategic groups. Within the strategic group the products of separate firms are viewed by customers as close substitutes – say, electric blankets and hot water bottles – but the fact that such products are classified into separate industry groups should not prevent a producer of electric blankets taking the output of hot water bottles into account when formulating strategy.

It is therefore the strategic group, rather than the industry group, that defines the set of products that compete directly for market share. And on the basis of the foregoing it is the extent of the boundary for a strategic group that is likely to influence the basis upon which rivalry takes place. If the market is defined too broadly, it will increase the number of firms and whether it is the competition authorities or an individual firm formulating its strategy, both are likely to obtain an exaggerated impression of the degree of competition. If the boundary is drawn too narrowly, products defined as being outside the 'group' might be disregarded but still be exerting an influence on the behaviour of firms within the 'group'. In order to make appropriate decisions regarding the degree of competition and the opportunities for firms to abuse their market power, the authorities have to be able to define a strategic group. The boundaries for a strategic group can be determined by a host of characteristics such as price, target customers, geographic location, technology and performance characteristics. One approach is to use the concept of a **product space**, which we shall return to in Chapter 13. Another approach using the example of cars is shown in Figure 8.3. The two characteristics selected for illustrative purposes are status and purpose. The figure shows four strategic groups of firms within which the products of the individual firms display similarities in respect of these characteristics. For example, cars with one-litre engines might populate strategic group A, whereas cars with

larger engines more suited to motorway driving might make up group B. Off-road vehicles are a separate group and D would be populated by top-of-the-range cars. It follows that an accurate measure of the strategic group is fundamental to business strategy, but we do not need to go as far as Alfred Chandler (1962), who in first putting forward the concept of a strategic group assumed firms within the group adopt similar strategies.

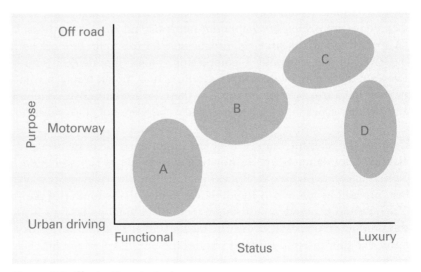

Figure 8.3: Illustrative strategic groups

The first step in defining a strategic group is to start with the official classification, e.g. NACE at the four-digit level. But this will be no more than the first step. It does not follow that four-digit industry codes are synonymous with strategic groups, e.g. hot water bottles and electric blankets. There are a number of statistical techniques that can be employed to measure the degree of interdependence between products such as **cluster analysis** and **multidimensional scaling**. These and similar techniques are beyond the scope of this book, but one measure of interdependence that we can explore is the economic concept of the **cross-price elasticity** of demand. If two products are close substitutes, changes in their relative prices will *ceteris paribus* lead to the substitution of the cheaper product for the more expensive. And it is the degree of substitution that gives us the pointer to defining a strategic group. The cross-price elasticity of demand is defined as:

$$\varepsilon_{yx} = \%\Delta Q_y / \%\Delta P_x = (\Delta Q_y / Q_y)/(\Delta P_x / P_x) \tag{8.5}$$

where y and x represent two products, Q the volume sold of product y, and P the price of product x. The symbol Δ stands for change and $\%\Delta$ for percentage change. If the two products are close substitutes, then we would expect the value of the cross-price elasticity coefficient, ε_{yx}, to be large. For example, if y is margarine and x is butter, a rise in the price of butter (P_x) – the price of margarine remaining unchanged – will result in an increase in the volume of margarine sold. The bigger the percentage change in y relative to the percentage change in the price of butter, the closer substitutes are the two products. Thus, for products within the same strategic group, we would expect $\varepsilon_{yx} > 1$. Alternatively, if the two products are completely unrelated, then the value of ε_{xy} would be zero.

A potential practical constraint with estimating the cross-price elasticity of demand is that **time series data** must be available on volumes and prices for the relevant products and in calculating the cross-price elasticity of demand care must be taken to allow for other influences such as changes in incomes or tastes. Providing data on both the volumes sold and the relative prices of a group of products are available, it should be possible to make a reliable estimate of the cross-price elasticity of demand using **regression analysis** and hence a more accurate estimate of a strategic group.

In practice, time series data may not exist for a sufficient period and consequently a number of alternative tools and techniques must be used for constructing strategic groups. Prominent amongst these techniques are **principle component analysis** and **cluster analysis**. These empirical techniques can be applied to various strategic dimensions; for example, product performance characteristics, distribution channels, customer segmentation, geographic markets and even company financial ratios. Even so, there may be no simple dividing line. When Nabisco wanted to merge with Huntley and Palmer, the European Commission, as the relevant authority, concluded that the markets for biscuits and savoury snack foods (e.g. crisps and nuts) were not close substitutes.

Defining the relevant 'market' is of key importance to competition authorities. The test that is generally used by competition authorities worldwide is the so-called **SSNIP** (Small but Significant Non-Transitory Increase in Prices) test. To find the relevant market, the EU authorities, using this test, proceed as follows. A hypothetical monopolist supplier of the product in question is assumed. The question is posed, would this hypothetical monopolist find it profitable to increase the price of the product in question above the current level in a non-transitory way, say by 5 per cent? If the answer to this question is yes, it implies the product does not face significant competition from other products, i.e. there are no close substitutes. Suppose now instead that the answer to the question is no. This implies that following the price rise, sales fall by more than 5 per cent as sales are redirected to substitute products. This is evidence that the product in question is part of a large market grouping and the test now continues by asking if a hypothetically diversified monopolist – selling all the products revealed to be substitutes – raised prices by 5 per cent, would it be profitable? By this intuitive process, the test continues until the boundaries of a separate 'market' are identified.

Going Dutch

The European Union's single market has encouraged the internationalization of European businesses. Prominent among businesses taking advantage of the single market freedoms is the Dutch agrifood sector. Dutch agrifood businesses have a long tradition of international trade, but with the single market has come a distinct shift towards the internationalization of production; namely, the acquisition of foreign companies and their production facilities. Not surprisingly, this activity has not been all one way and a number of foreign firms have gained ownership of production facilities in the Netherlands.

The internationalization strategies of Dutch companies are influenced by a number of fac-

tors, but two key influences are the number of product chains a company is involved in and the extent of vertical integration within product chains. Functionally orientated companies generally operate in a number of product group value chains, leveraging core competencies to create and capture value at one stage – e.g. processing, distribution or retail. Chain-orientated companies focus on a product group, but undertake a number of the stages in the value chain. On this basis, it is possible to place agrifood companies operating in the Netherlands into four strategic groups, as set out in the figure below.

Focused companies concentrate on just one product group, such as Heineken with beer and

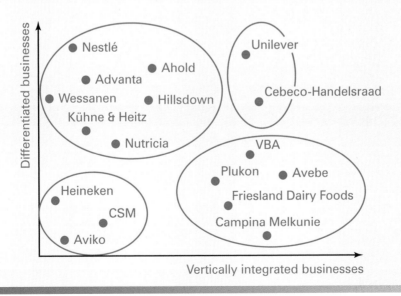

Aviko with potato products. For these companies, exporting remains the main internationalization strategy. Differentiated companies focus on one specific function but operate in three or more product groups. Companies in this strategic group, such as Nestlé and Advanta, follow a multi-domestic strategy involving the establishment of production units in individual countries to supply local or national markets. A third strategic group comprises vertically integrated companies, of which Friesland Dairy Foods, a farmer-controlled business, is typical, that primarily operate in one product group. As domestic growth opportunities for these companies are limited, these companies seek growth via foreign expansion. Finally, there are conglomerates, e.g. Unilever, that are involved in several product groups and several value chain stages. For these companies there is little synergy between the product groups and internationalization strategies are based on a diverse set of objectives.

Conduct and Performance

As we have seen, the new car and van market in western Europe displays considerable inequalities in firm size, and this observation is not untypical. Figure 8.4 shows the individual market shares – in terms of value – for the 22 firms identified by name in Table 8.3. Moving from left to right, there is an enormous difference between the share of market value accounted for by the largest four firms and the long tail of smaller enterprises. The skewed distribution displayed implies that over a period of years some firms have grown faster than others. Gibrat (1931) put forward an hypothesis which he called *the law of proportionate growth*, but which has come to be known as **Gibrat's law**. Gibrat hypothesized that over a given time period the percentage change in the size of an individual firm in an industry is independent of the firm's initial size. That is, we could start with an industry composed of a number of

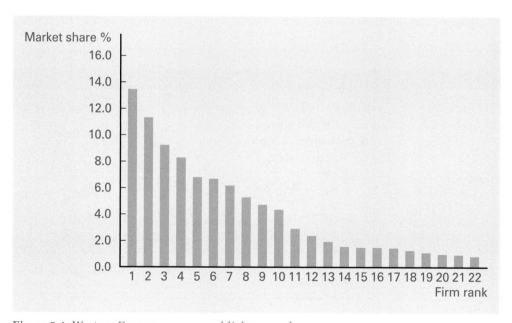

Figure 8.4: Western Europe new car and light van sales

equally sized firms, but over a period of years some firms would grow faster than others and consequently the industry group would tend towards the skewed distribution shown in Figure 8.4.

A number of explanations can be advanced to explain why the growth rate for individual firms within an industry group – and hence by association a strategic group – varies. As discussed in Chapter 6, there is considerable evidence that the most elementary 'fact' about corporate growth is that individual firm size follows a random walk (Geroski, 2000). Discrete events or 'shocks', such as the success of an innovation, have a permanent effect on the size of the firm and it means that the growth of a firm cannot be thought of as a process that is following a deterministic trend. It would not, however, be correct to view relative rates of growth as a pure stochastic process. As we examined in Chapters 5 and 6, the growth of a firm depends in large measure on its ability to develop the resources for growth, including the ability to diversify, innovate and achieve new organizational forms (Teece *et al.*, 1997). An entrepreneurial management, capable of perceiving and exploiting new productive opportunities, is a key determinant of growth; though from the outside it can appear as though growth is the product of random, discrete investments.

Closely allied to an entrepreneurial spirit in driving growth is a firm's organizational capability. We observed in earlier chapters that firms are 'social communities' and that they develop their own organizational cultures and behaviours. A firm that is not adequately enabling and motivating its workforce is likely to display a slower rate of growth and in the extreme may eventually cease to exist. Profits stemming from a successful product or process innovation provide the resources for further innovation and hence further growth, i.e. success breeds success. But success for some generates difficulties for others. A successful process innovation might reduce production costs, putting rivals under price pressure. Alternatively, an investment in an innovation that fails carries with it the possibility of reduced profits and even bankruptcy, particularly for a smaller firm. Bain (1959) argued that the risk associated with the uncertainty surrounding the success of an innovation impacts on the cost of capital and firms who have to borrow the necessary funds will pay a risk premium, i.e. a high rate of interest. The smaller a firm, the more likely that its cash flow will be insufficient to meet the capital costs of such an investment. This may discourage some firms from innovating, leading to a reduced market share or even hastening their demise.

The SCP paradigm, being firmly rooted within the neo-classical tradition, plays down the influences on industry structure arising from internal factors such as organizational and entrepreneurial capabilities in favour of more tangible or deterministic external factors. The SCP approach traditionally focused on **barriers to entry** in order to explain the skewed distribution illustrated in Figure 8.4. Strictly, a barrier to entry is defined as any factor that prevents a potential new entrant earning a sufficient profit post entry. If a barrier to entry exists, the bulk of the market will be supplied by relatively few firms and the co-existence of a long tail of small firms depends on scope provided by **niche markets**. The SCP literature views such barriers as being the product of technology and/or the behaviour of incumbent firms. Or, in the words of Bain, markets may be characterized according to whether entry barriers are structural or strategic. A **structural barrier** results when incumbent firms have a natural cost advantage – e.g. arising from the prevailing technology. A **strategic barrier** arises when incumbent firms engage in entry-deterring strategies designed to convince potential entrants that such action would not be profitable.

Technology can act as a barrier to entry if it determines that **economies of scale** are extensive and therefore the **minimum efficient scale** of production requires a high volume of output. For a single-product or highly specialized firm, such technology significantly influences unit costs at a sub-optimal scale of operation; though, as we have seen, in the presence of diversified firms and **economies of scope** scale economies may not be decisive. It is often argued that the existence of economies of scale implies large-scale expenditures on either buildings or plant and that this itself constitutes the barrier. But this would be wrong; it is not the amount of expenditure but the risk associated with the expenditure that is decisive. The more specialized the capital requirements, the more likely that entry will involve expenditures that have the nature of a **sunk cost**. For example, if the product under consideration requires high levels of **asset specificity**, the assets will have little or no value outside the industry and hence the firm will suffer high liquidation or conversion costs if it decides to exit the market. **Product differentiation** can also be a structural barrier if the nature of the market necessitates advertising, which is a prime example of a sunk cost. For example, baby foods, can involve a rapid turnover of customers, requiring high advertising expenditure to differentiate product offerings to new customers. In analysing the impact of product differentiation on market structure, Sutton (1992) highlighted the importance of sunk costs. He defined sunk costs as exogenous if they arise from a factor beyond the control of incumbents, e.g. the prevailing technology. Such structural barriers are frequently referred to as **blockaded entry**; that is, the costs of entry are such that even if the incumbent takes no action a new entrant is unlikely to take the risk of entry.

From the perspective of strategy, strategic entry barriers are arguably more interesting than structural barriers. Firms within strategic groups with low structural entry barriers may engage in strategic behaviour, i.e. conduct designed to persuade a potential entrant that entry is unlikely to be profitable; for example, incumbents may engage in excessive advertising thereby forcing a new entrant to do likewise. In Sutton's terminology in this situation, the sunk costs are endogenous; that is, they arise from the strategic behaviour of incumbents designed to discourage entry rather than meet a basic market need. The idea is that where firms can influence demand for their products, albeit by means of excessive expenditure on advertising and promotion, they will do so, thereby making it more difficult for small firms to expand and/or new firms to enter the market, with the result that the industry's concentration ratio is increased. Whether we are considering structural or strategic barriers to entry, what matters from the perspective of market structure and economic performance is not their existence *per se*, but how potential entrants view the risks post entry. We will consider entry-deterring strategies in more detail in later chapters.

As explained above, sunk costs greatly increase the risk of entry and with a reduced threat of entry, incumbents may feel able to engage in conduct that will keep prices higher and boost **economic rents**. If sunk costs are sufficient to ensure that the bulk of market output will be supplied by a small number of firms, then, as will be demonstrated in following chapters, game theory suggests that incumbents may come to the conclusion that tacit co-operation, or even **tacit collusion**, are more certain routes to economic rents than ruthless competition. Acting as a collective dominance, existing firms can raise strategic barriers, ensuring that a new entrant has to incur higher post-entry costs, e.g. entering into exclusive contracts with customers. The relationship between barriers to entry and post-entry costs has given rise to the notion of **contestability**, a concept first put forward by Baumol *et al.* (1982). More than 30 years ago, Demsetz (1968) emphasized that industries with only a few firms (or just one) could behave in a competitive manner if a threat of entry by other firms existed.

A perfectly contestable market is accessible to potential entrants, even though an apparent barrier exists. For example, the argument advanced by Bain, that a potential entrant might be deterred if the capital requirements of entry were large in absolute terms – an hypothesis that capital markets are seriously imperfect – does not now command much respect. Given reasonably efficient capital markets, a new entrant will, despite having to borrow the necessary capital, be able to serve the same market with unit costs that are similar to those of incumbent firms. And if having entered the market, profits prove disappointing they can exit the market and, subject to depreciation, recover their investment costs. That is, the costs of exit are also low, implying that not only is asset specificity low, but also emotional and legislative exit barriers are low. For example, the firm does not feel compelled to continue producing out of loyalty to employees or to avoid the image of failure. Similarly, legislation may require firms to provide generous redundancy packages in the event of ceasing production.

On this analysis, contestability is not defined in terms of the absolute costs of entering the market, but in the sense of potential entrants facing greater costs than those incurred by incumbent firms. And relative costs, post entry, are primarily influenced by the extent of sunk costs and also any proprietary cost advantages enjoyed by incumbents, e.g. monopoly rights over a prime input and/or experience arising from cumulative production. If an incumbent firm, through superior knowledge and experience, is able to produce at a low unit cost, a new entrant faces the increased risk of revenue falling below costs – the more so if incumbents react to entry by reducing prices. A contestable market is therefore a market with free entry and exit and the logic of this assumption is that it is irrelevant whether the market structure is oligopolistic or monopolistically competitive – incumbent firms will be forced towards marginal cost pricing and zero economic rents.

The concept of contestability is relevant when there are no sunk costs associated with entry. This translates to an absence of strategic behaviour since any action that can be reversed without cost does not involve a strategic commitment. In practice we need to qualify the concept of contestability. It is unlikely that a firm will contemplate entry to a market without the intention of a longer-term commitment. And it is unlikely that incumbents will be indifferent to the likelihood of entry. From the perspective of business strategy, the important point is that if a market is contestable, this, rather than the industry structure, will influence strategic behaviour. Even if the industry group is highly

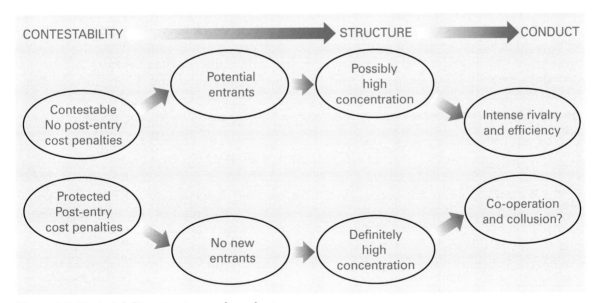

Figure 8.5: Contestability, structure and conduct

concentrated, incumbents will have to behave as if they faced competition from a large number of potential suppliers. By definition, they will not be able to sufficiently lower their unit costs or sufficiently differentiate their products so as to create a barrier that new entrants are disinclined to cross. In such a situation, incumbents must maintain high levels of supply, thereby keeping market prices low and threatening new entrants with an even lower price if they enter the market and increase supply. Moreover, in a contestable market, *X-inefficiencies* and ***organizational slack*** will be minimal as incumbents will be under pressure to minimize unit costs. The conclusion to be drawn from all this is that the conduct of firms within a strategic group is more likely to be responsive to the degree of contestability than the actual degree of seller concentration. This brief overview of concentration and contestability as major influences on the behaviour of rivals is summarized in Figure 8.5. In short, the balance between these two influences is likely to be a major determinant not only of the nature of the rivalry between incumbent firms but also the probability of more intense rivalry.

It should by now be clear that the basic SCP paradigm set out in Figure 8.1 is deficient. The diagram implies that structure is determined exogenously – that is, cannot be influenced by the behaviour and profits of incumbent firms. The SCP approach assumes a stable relation-

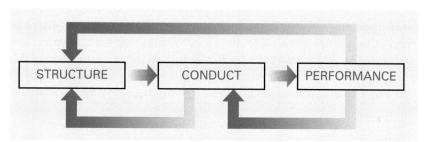

Figure 8.6: The SCP paradigm with feedback

ship that is true across industries between structural variables, e.g. seller concentration and market performance. The hypothesis is that market power is an increasing function of seller concentration. However, as we have seen, if incumbent firms have the incentive and the means to engage in building strategic barriers, their conduct with respect to entry deterrence is likely to influence the structure of the strategic group. In the light of these observations, we need to modify the original SCP diagram. Figure 8.6 modifies the earlier figure to include feedback loops that make the backward linkages explicit. For example, a performance that generates economic rents will provide funds for investment, which can be used to develop processes and/or differentiated products that serve as strategic barriers and hence maintain a highly concentrated market structure.

Structural Change

The SCP paradigm was not lost on governments anxious to improve the economic performance of their industries. In the eyes of governments, it brought to the fore tensions between: competition and competitiveness; competition and employment; competition and trade. Competition policy with an emphasis on liberalization can, in the short run, result in job losses, which are directly visible to the media and general public. In contrast, horizontal aid for industries appears to offer the benefits of longer-term competitiveness by

continued

encouraging mergers, emerging technology and suitable locations. All governments in developed and developing nations provide aid both directly and indirectly to their industries, though not on an equitable basis. So-called strategic industries, traditionally coal, steel, farming and defence, tend to be the main recipients.

A champion of such structural policies was the Netherlands. Although a competition law was passed in 1958, its prohibitions of price agreements, market sharing arrangements and collusive tendering were notoriously un-enforced. By the end of the 1980s, the Dutch government had a secret register of cartels containing some 245 agreements to divide markets, nearly 270 agreements to fix prices and some 50 exclusive dealing agreements.

Following the ratification of the Single European Act, the Dutch government began moving to correct the situation. In 1993, price fixing was officially prohibited and in 1994, market division and collusive tendering were banned. At the same time, the government decided to move towards adopting a completely new legislative basis for competition policy based on the law of the European Union. Like other EU member states, the Netherlands was finding that the old industrial policies were not compatible with the increasing interconnections between member states. But there was another force at work; namely, a growing belief that the encouragement and support for industrial 'champions' was no longer feasible in a world where speed of technological development and a capability to respond rapidly were dominant.

Porter's Five Forces Model

The SCP paradigm quickly became associated with a branch of microeconomics known as industrial economics. This school gathered momentum during the 1960s and 1970s as the growing availability of computing power allowed the empirical testing of the SCP postulates. For example, economists spent many hours with only limited success assessing, with the aid of empirical data, whether profits are higher in highly concentrated industries. Perhaps inevitably, given such a powerful new toy, industrial economists became obsessed with statistical testing and there was little attention given to the implications for business strategy. This was rectified, in a revolutionary way, by Michael Porter (1980) with the publication of his Five Forces Model, which, with some adaptation, is reproduced in Figure 8.7. Although called a model, Porter's five forces might more accurately be described as a framework: a tool for helping a systematic analysis of the forces influencing strategic behaviour and competitive advantage. The Five Forces Model views the essence of competitive strategy formulation as relating a firm to its business environment. The key aspect of the firm's business environment is the industry, or more correctly, the strategic groups in which it competes. Hence at its heart, Porter's Five Forces Model augments the industry structure approach to strategy with the market power of buyers and suppliers as an influence on the behaviour and economic performance of firms.

Porter's framework is rooted in the SCP paradigm, which by 1980 had been magisterially analysed by Scherer and Ross (1990), but places its emphasis on strategy formulation built around five competitive forces comprising a firm's proximate external environment. The Five Forces Model provides a systematic way of thinking about how competitive forces work when applied at the industry level, the strategic group level or even the individual firm. The box in the centre of Figure 8.7 reflects Porter's linking of rivalry within the strategic group to the influence of the traditional SCP factors such as the numbers and distribution of sellers, the extent of product differentiation, relative production costs and the height of exit barriers. The box labelled entry barriers represents the traditional SCP barriers to entry that influence the extent to which the market is contestable and hence open to rivalrous behaviour or, as described by Porter, *the jockeying for position* of incumbents. Porter augmented the influences of market structure on strategy with additional factors such as the relationships of business units with their parent companies, the incidence of foreign competition and the strategic importance placed on success in the market.

In Porter's model, firms within the industry, or strategic group, earn economic rents when they are in a position to impede competitive forces in either factor markets or product markets. They also earn rents if they have lower unit costs than rivals, though it is not clear in the Five Forces Model what would sustain this advantage. For Porter, industry structure matters and to a large extent in his first book (Porter, 1980), he viewed structure as being exogenously determined. Put more basically, some industries are more attractive to be in because they are not perfectly contestable and hence these structural impediments sustain competitive advantage. To this extent, the Five Forces Model was very much in line with Bain's SCP paradigm.

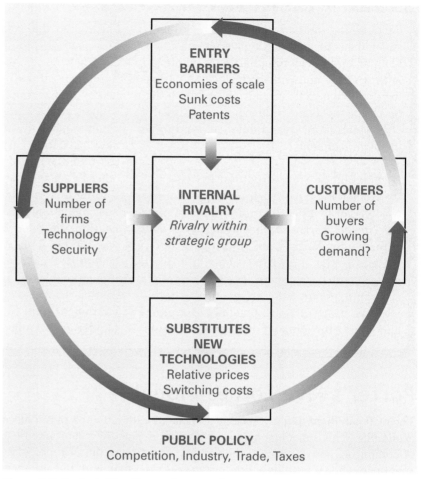

Figure 8.7: Porter's Five Forces framework

It was, however, the addition of three new external forces – represented by the other three outside boxes – that caused the Five Forces Model to become the dominant paradigm in the area of strategic analysis during the 1980s. A key influence on the demand for the products produced by firms in the strategic group are substitute products. Substitute products in Porter's Five Forces Model are not substitutes in the sense of determining the boundaries of the industry or strategic group. They are substitutes in the sense of the threat from the development of new products or processes that are likely to undermine the existing industry. Mobile telephones provide a classic example in that they circumvented existing barriers to entering the telecommunications industry – the enormous capital costs of building a terrestrial network – thereby reducing the 'monopoly' power of firms within the industry group. In order to reduce the risks posed by new substitute products, firms may engage in high levels of R&D expenditure. Alternatively, incumbents might deliberately depress prices so as to reduce the potential reward for a successful substitute product.

The two outside boxes dealing with the influence and power of suppliers and customers on behaviour within a strategic group, when taken with the centre box, and running from left to right in Figure 8.7, represent the *value chain*. The behaviour of upstream suppliers will in turn depend on factors previously discussed, such as the degree of concentration, barriers to entry and the threat of substitute products. If the strategic group's suppliers are characterized by a larger number of SMEs supplying essentially commodity products, then firms may fiercely compete, resulting in their goods and services being priced competitively. Alternatively, if suppliers provide semi-finished, niche goods or services and/or their markets are characterized by high levels of concentration, the prices of their goods and services are likely to be held above marginal cost and suppliers may engage in non-price rivalrous behaviour to secure sales, e.g. provide free advice. If suppliers are perceived to be earning economic rents, this may encourage firms in the strategic group (centre box) to engage in vertical integration or other forms of *vertical relationships* with suppliers. In addition, technological advances by upstream suppliers could impact on the success of their downstream customers in the strategic group, not only in terms of production costs, but also in areas such as quality and reliability.

Moving downstream of the strategic group, a key influence on a successful performance is the level of demand for the strategic group's output and the bargaining power of its customers. For most strategic groups, these customers will be other firms, e.g. retailers, who add value and then sell on. If the strategic group sells its output to a heavily concentrated group of buyers, then whatever the structure of the firms within the strategic group each may find that their customers have the power to reduce to zero the strategic group's ability to earn economic rents by means of persistent downward pressure on prices. For example, in the UK, food manufacturers find the power of the highly concentrated supermarket sector a major influence on performance. In many instances, the supermarkets can dictate behaviour in terms of quality, accompanying service and price. Information is also a powerful aid to negotiation by buyers. The better informed they are about production costs and the value of rivals' offerings, the greater their ability to reduce the rent-earning capacity of their suppliers. We will return to this issue when we deal with vertical relationships in Chapter 12.

Porter's Five Forces Model may be rooted in the SCP paradigm, but from a strategic perspective it is much richer. The framework is focused, as even Porter (1991) admits, on the broad principles of competitive advantage, which Porter viewed as essentially arising from the firm finding an attractive relative position within a strategic group where it could defend itself against competitive forces or influence them in its favour. For Porter, an attractive position is viewed as the outcome of one of two generic strategies: the ability to produce at a lower unit cost than rivals; and/or the ability to differentiate so as to command a premium price. In itself, this was not new, but the main contribution of Porter's framework was to add a dynamic dimension to the static SCP paradigm. The framework recognized that strategic behaviour, i.e. conduct, is formulated on a dynamic basis, responding not only to the strategic group's structure but also to a host of constantly changing conditions. Emerging technologies and changing consumer demands are but two, albeit important, dynamic influences and the strategic response of firms has to take account of the prevailing legislative environment where regulations, trade policies and tax levels will all have an influence on the behaviour and performance of firms.

Porter was not, however, the first economist to recognize the link between dynamic behaviour and competition. For one school of economists – the Austrian school – the very essence of competitive rivalry is its dynamic nature. The Austrian approach, most notably associated with Schumpeter (1942) and his emphasis on the entrepreneur, defines the key elements of competition as the development over time of product and process innovations which in turn generate product differentiation and unit cost advantage at the firm level. In Schumpeter's view it is: 'the new commodity, the new technology, the new source of supply and the new type of organization! Since it is these in the long-run that determine the survival of the firm' (1942, p. 132). For this school of thought, from an industry perspective the key issue for competitive advantage is the type of market structure that is more likely to provide scope for radical innovation. For example, Wal-Mart grew big not because of an initial market position, but because an entrepreneurial mindset had the vision to locate in small and medium-sized towns and the energy to configure its logistical system to support this vision.

Porter's framework makes explicit the dynamic influence the rate at which demand for the industry's output is growing on the intensity of rivalry within a strategic group. And this in turn depends on the maturity of the market. A very common approach to market maturity is the **_life cycle hypothesis_**, whereby most products are deemed to pass through a number of stages – introduction, growth, maturity and decline – as set out in Figure 8.8.

Firms are more likely to accommodate new entrants when the market is in its growth stage than when it reaches maturity. At the growth stage of the cycle, the impact of falling prices on revenue is offset by the rising volume of sales. When the market has matured, the rate of growth slows and if a new competitor enters the market at this stage the outcome is likely to be a reduction in the sales of existing firms. Thus, at maturity, we would expect to see conduct directed towards increasing entry barriers and greater effort to reduce production costs. Although Porter's framework amounted to a dynamic add-on to the static SCP paradigm, the Five Forces Model is not a complete explanation of the dynamic nature of rivalry.

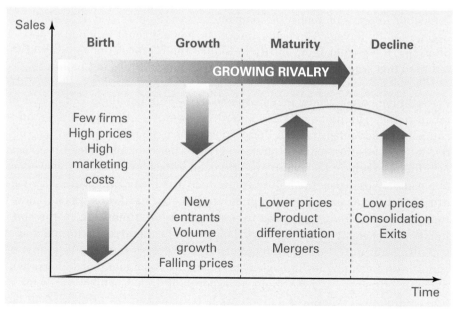

Figure 8.8: Product life cycle

A more comprehensive approach to the nature of dynamic rivalry, now more commonly referred to as the *strategic conflict* approach, was launched by Carol Shapiro's (1989) article on business strategy. The main thrust of this approach is to explore, using the tools of game theory, how strategic interactions between rivals influence market structure and economic rents. Building on the Cournot and Bertrand models of oligopoly, game-theoretic models of strategic behaviour have revealed a much richer set of interactions within a highly concentrated industry or strategic group. The strategic conflict approach argues that in such circumstances firms would soon realize their mutual interdependence and thus play more 'co-operatively' than suggested by the Cournot and Bertrand models. The strategic behaviours that game theoretic models identify range from efforts to tacitly collude to the strategic manipulation of rivals' information about market conditions. An early example of strategic interaction is provided by the tacit conclusion inherent in Sweezy's (1939) *kinked demand curve* theory of oligopoly. Above all, the strategic conflict approach teaches that only by understanding the type of competition that prevails, in an industry or strategic group, can reliable predictions of industry behaviour and performance be made.

Game theory has emerged as the predominant methodology for analysing business strategy and the capture of value inherent in competitive advantage. In many instances, game theory formalizes observed business behaviour, e.g. excessive expenditure on R&D, but crucially, equilibrium in game theoretic models of strategic behaviour depends on what one rival believes another rival will do in a particular situation. Game theory is dynamic in the sense that strategic moves can be analysed over multi-periods. That said, game theoretic models have their limitations, particularly in dynamic situations that are characterized by rapid change in technology and/or market forces. The game theoretic approach stresses the value of strategic behaviours such as commitment and reputation rather than the ability to rapidly improve and innovate. We will return to this issue in succeeding chapters.

Another major shortcoming of the Five Forces Model's rooting in the structuralist paradigm is that it misses the contribution of the individual firm's key capabilities – i.e. organizational, human and physical resources – to the nature of competition. A key empirical observation is that firms in the same industry differ from one another, often dramatically. Indeed, research has shown that differences among firms within the same industry can be much larger than differences between firms in different industries (Rumelt, 1991). Others (Levinthal, 1995) have interpreted Rumelt's finding of limited industry effects to support what has become known as the *competency approach*. This school, as we have seen, believes that heterogeneity lies at the root of competitive advantage. For the competency school, competitive advantage does not arise from the industry a firm is in, or from its strategic 'games', but from an ability to perform the required activities in ways that yield unit costs that are lower than rivals and/or create value that rivals find difficult to replicate. We have set out in earlier chapters the competency school's arguments that differences amongst firms are the product of experience and knowledge – rooted in organizational architectures and/or the cultivation of specific capabilities – that determine what resources they can muster to respond to a changing business environment. From this perspective, a firm is a bundle of resources whose activities, such as procurement, production and sales, are more valuable to the individual firm. Porter (1991) has sought to play down the distinction between his competitive forces approach and the competency school by pointing out that what gives heterogeneous resources value is their ability to create advantage in particular markets, which to Porter's mind bears a strong resemblance to industry structure.

Yet a further twist is provided by, what are regarded here, as sub-groups of the competency school; namely, the *evolutionary approach* and the *dynamic capabilities approach*. The central premise of the evolutionary approach is that competition shapes both market and organizational structures by forcing the exit of firms whose organizational form cannot deliver the capabilities necessary to align the firm with the needs of the business environment: a process of natural selection (Nelson and Winter, 1982). And closely related is the dynamic capabilities school, who interpret a dynamic capability as a firm's capacity to renew competencies so as to achieve congruence with a changing business environment (Teece *et al.*, 1997). It is perhaps inevitable that proponents of these separate approaches should seek to achieve supremacy or at least *primus inter pares*, but the issue is unlikely to be easily resolved.

What is clear is that Porter's Five Forces Model can only be a partial explanation of competitive advantage and business success. As we have explained in previous chapters, for most firms success means growth and growth means diversification – that is, operating in more than one industry. Armed with this knowledge, a focus on the structure of an industry or strategic group cannot provide a comprehensive analysis of strategic behaviour at the corporate level. A combination of the Five Forces Model and game theory provides useful guidance at the business unit level as to the nature of competition and the scope afforded to alter the nature of strategic interaction by 'game' playing. But at the business unit level, competitive success also depends on organizational capabilities. Indeed, a firm's relative position is the product of choices it has made in the past regarding the acquisition, development and use of its resources. That is, a firm's competitive advantage, at any point in time, is the product of a variety of strategic and tactical decisions ranging from actual and threatened actions to long-term investments in production facilities and intangible organizational capabilities.

The relative position of a firm is therefore largely the product of strategic commitments and by definition these must be difficult if not impossible to reverse. Earlier choices are likely to have been influenced by the firm's proximate environment and the better its managers understand and anticipate the dynamics of the firm's competitive environment, the more likely that its configuration of tangible and intangible resources is capable of creating value and thereby potentially delivering competitive advantage. But the ability to create value is not the same as capturing value, which is the measure of business success. Value is captured by strategic interaction, which involves seeking to understand and influence the behaviour of rivals; namely, engaging in game theoretic behaviour. Put another way, efficient governance, core competencies and the strategic interactions of firms are all highly relevant to the achievement of competitive advantage and this recognition is sufficient for our purpose here.

Interpreting Competition

The UK defence industry comprises less than 175 businesses; it is a knowledge-based industry whose strength rests largely on world-class technology. The importance of defence, and the need to keep abreast of technology, ensured that historically there has been very close collaboration between the industry and successive governments. In the case of defence, the government's industrial policies have had both a structural and a technology dimension. The close relationship engendered by an industrial defence policy has meant that in practice successive governments have always had to balance the twin needs of competition in the supply of defence products with the advantages of an industrial policy that delivers

continued

high-tech products at low unit costs. As a monopsonist in the purchase of defence equipment, it would appear that in practice government industrial policy has always won out over competition policy. Governments have encouraged the amalgamation of companies in order to achieve not only the benefits of scale, but also the benefits of common platforms and harmonized procedures.

The influence of the government over the structure and conduct of the defence industry was manifested in a protectionist procurement policy which underpinned its industrial policy. High levels of demand for the products of certain companies allowed these firms over time to increase market share and power. Moreover, the effect of the growing economic power of defence contractors was to create a 'pluralist corporatist' policy, whereby the industry had an increasingly powerful role in influencing government R&D expenditure.

With the collapse of the Soviet Union most developed nations took the opportunity to reduce the burden of defence expenditure and in the process some sought to give competition a higher weighting in the relationship between governments and their defence industries. In the case of European Union member states, this was reinforced by attempts to secure greater competition in government procurement following the coming into effect of the single market. Following the

end of the Cold War, in the new defence environment, UK governments have attempted to adopt a more 'neo-liberal' approach to defence procurement. This is exampled by the declared intention to source defence products from overseas suppliers if they offer greater value for money. This policy change was heralded by the cancellation of the massively over-budget Nimrod project and the purchase of AWACS from America instead. In short, the traditional sponsorship of the defence industry by the British government appeared to be giving way to a more commercial relationship between the state and its suppliers.

But, in practice, the switch in philosophy has proved more difficult than supposed. During the 1990s, doubts were expressed as to the long-term viability of a UK defence industry if it was exposed too rapidly to international competition. This led to calls for government aid to help the industry restructure and this in turn led to a new definition of 'value for money'. Previously this had been interpreted as the cheapest acquisition cost, but during the 1990s, it was redefined to include broader longer-term considerations. Another move was the development of strategic plans in relation to defence R&D and defence exports, the latter involving 'selecting winners'. The great difficulty of introducing competition into the defence industry remains not only a challenge for the UK government, but an even greater challenge for the European Union.

Clusters and Networks

The reference to game theory points up a major weakness of Porter's five forces framework in that it views all other firms, be they rivals, suppliers or buyers, as threats. This appears in conflict with the fact that firms can and do have beneficial co-operative relationships not only with their suppliers and customers, but also in many cases with their competitive rivals. Almost 100 years ago, Alfred Marshall (1920) observed that firms benefited from locating within areas of industrial *agglomeration*. These benefits arise from a host of factors such as: the existence of an *infrastructure*; the near presence of suppliers of goods and services; a pool of suitably qualified labour; and, frequently, proximity to large-scale consumer markets. During the twentieth century in developed economies, planning controls and much improved transport systems have lessened the extent of agglomerations of general industrial activity – though urban, industrial agglomerations are still an important feature of developing nations. In such countries, there is still a tendency for a large proportion of economic activity to concentrate around large cities, e.g. Bangkok.

As urban industrial agglomerations have declined in importance, so economists have started to focus on the phenomenon of **clusters**. Clusters take varying forms, but common to each is that the firms within a cluster are involved – at varying stages in the value chain – in the production of a related set of products and they are all located within a circumscribed geographic region. Clusters will generally include firms providing channels to customers, the production of complementary goods, as well as specialized inputs and supporting services. And significantly, many of these firms form vertical and horizontal relationships with each other. Clusters may also include other institutions providing a specialized infrastructure, such as training and education, research and information. By the time he published his third book, Porter (1990) had reverted to the work of earlier economists such as Marshall to extol the benefits of clusters, and in so doing ironically revived the role of *industrial policy*. Figure 8.9 shows just a few of the many industrial clusters in the UK. Similar examples could be drawn for any developed economy.

A cluster's roots can sometimes be traced to geographical or historical circumstances, e.g. the damp climate of Lancashire was ideal for cotton spinning. One of the best known clusters, Silicon Valley in Santa Clara, California, owes its existence to closely located university research expertise and an enterprising vice chancellor. Chance events may be the catalyst. Porter quotes the example of Earl Bakken, who as an electrical engineering graduate working part time at Minneapolis hospital, met and collaborated with Dr C.W. Lillehei to build the first battery-powered heart pacemaker. This breakthrough formed the basis for the creation of the Minneapolis medical devices

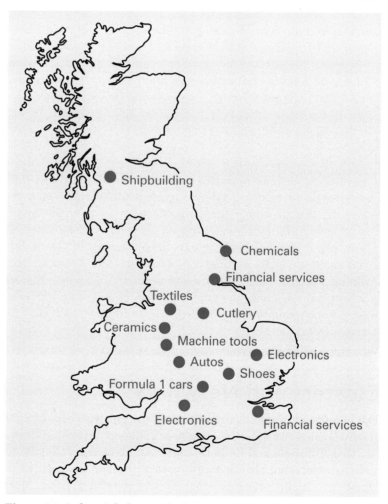

Figure 8.9: Industrial clusters in Great Britain

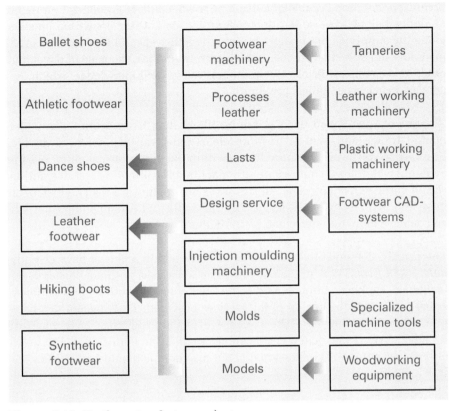

Figure 8.10: Northampton footwear cluster

cluster, which now encompasses more than 100 Minnesota companies. Clusters have grown in importance with the rise of information technology, but many clusters predate the industrial revolution. For example, Figure 8.10 shows the footwear cluster that surrounds Northampton in the heart of England, which has survived by adapting to technological change.

Our interest in clusters is their contribution to firm behaviour and performance. Firms group together in clusters to take advantage of a network of complementary strengths in neighbouring firms. Within clusters, firms heighten their competitiveness *via* a rich network of relationships, which can be separated into three groups:

- *Suppliers* – downstream firms develop close working relationships with upstream suppliers, thereby reducing the buyer's search costs and facilitating the co-operative development of inputs.
- *Labour* – firms will gain access to a pool of labour with industry-specific skills thereby reducing the need for training and the risk of skill shortages.
- *Innovation* – proximity encourages the formal and informal exchange of ideas – expressed so eloquently by Marshall (1920, quoted in Krugman, 1993, p. 37), as 'something in the air' – resulting in a faster take-up of knowledge.

It is this last point that tends to separate clusters from traditional agglomerations. By locating within a cluster and building closer relationships, the individual firm may achieve the benefits of a *spatial organizational* form capable of enhancing the benefits of specialization without the investment costs of 'doing it alone'. The co-location of suppliers and customers within clusters facilitates co-operation along the supply chain, thereby bringing together specialisms such as product design, customized materials and specialist advice. In high-tech industries, the pace of development is breathless and in order to keep abreast firms rely on the transfer of tacit knowledge, which, in turn, relies on personal contact, hence geographical proximity.

Clusters of specialized firms are more likely than firms working in isolation to quickly discern market trends and, hence, to more clearly and rapidly perceive developing consumer needs. Knowledge spillovers are more likely within clusters; consequently, participants learn early about evolving technology, component and machinery availability, service and marketing concepts. The risk of surprise technological substitutes is also reduced. Finally, clusters create a focus for government and trade lobbying. A density of firms is likely to command greater attention from government and achieve more influence than an individual firm.

The perceived competitive benefits of locating within a cluster have given rise to the concept of the **networked firm**. Think of the networks that must exist within a cluster such as the City of London – insurance, banking, shipping, and so on – where co-operation and relationships between firms offer scope to improve the quality of the services provided. This concept of a network has been taken further with the **value net**. The concept of a value net has been put forward by Nalebuff and Brandenberger (1996), and it is conceptually similar to Porter's Five Forces Model, but consists of not only rivals, suppliers and customers, but also complementors, i.e. firms producing complementary

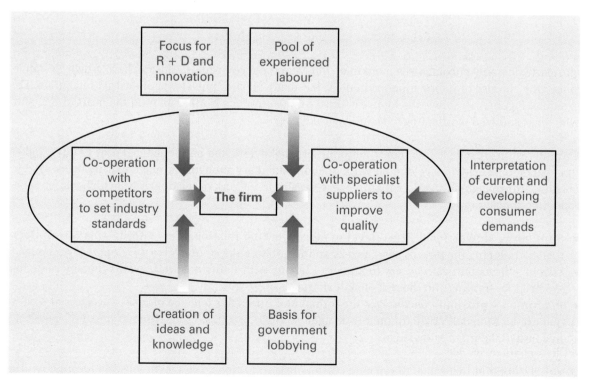

Figure 8.11: A cluster value net

goods and services. In contrast to the five forces 'competitive threat' approach, the value net analysis assesses the opportunities as well as the threats associated with each force. For example, it is not possible to comprehensively analyse the behaviour and performance of DVD manufacturers without allowing for the complementaries between manufacturers, film studios and retailers. Only by these separate elements getting together can the quality of DVDs be enhanced and, in so doing, boost demand for this form of entertainment. Complementary raises issues for strategy in terms of inter-firm relationships and joint goals. The concept of the value net and industrial clusters are inter-related and are brought together in Figure 8.11, which sums up the external benefits to competitive advantage arising for a firm of participating in a cluster.

The Community, Clusters and Competitiveness

The challenge set out by the Lisbon European Council in 2000 to make the EU, 'the world's most competitive and dynamic knowledge-based economy' has sparked interest in new approaches to economic policy. In particular, the potential of clusters is seen as critical to achieving the Lisbon strategy's ambitious goal. No consistent data exist, however, to track the prevalence and performance of clusters across the EU. The World Economic Forum's *Global Competitiveness Report 2002–2003*, provides comparative data on cluster development for 75 countries, including all European countries. On average, the EU ranks slightly lower on cluster develop-ment, but the report observes that EU economies have become more unequal since 1992 when the single market came into effect. This is consistent with the evolution of clus-ters in response to market integration. As barriers to the movement of goods, services, people and capital fall, this helps strong clus-ters to outsource low-value activities, such as manufacturing, and concentrate on high-value functions and innovation. Overall, this leads to an increasingly different composition of economic activity across regions but not necessarily to an overall increase in geograph-ic concentration.

A survey of 34 regional clusters in member states provides indicative data which show that: (1) most clusters are dominated by small or medium-sized companies; (2) most sur-veyed clusters serve global markets as well as the EU; (3) R&D and advanced services are available in many of the clusters, while stan-dard production activities are increasingly being outsourced to other locations; and (4) the surveyed clusters tend to be young, growing and at least among the national leaders in their fields. At a national level, the Netherlands and Denmark have a strong tradition of clusters, and the UK has in the last few years become very active in cluster policy and has provided significant funding for cluster development. *Ireland* has had a very conscious and success-ful competitiveness policy.

Concluding Thoughts

In this chapter, we have learnt how to define and measure the structure of an industry or strategic group. Using this knowledge, we have examined how the structure of an industry might influence the strategic behaviour of firms. We started by looking for a simple causal link between an industry's or a strategic group's structure and the behaviour and performance of its firms. Bain's contribution to the SCP paradigm was to suggest that the more concentrated the structure of production, the greater the likelihood of a restricted output, high prices and economic rents for the firms concerned. But the weight of empirical work subsequent to Bain's postulate has shown that no such simple relationship exists. Firstly, a strategic group's structure can itself be the product of the strategic behaviour of incumbents and, secondly, structure is now viewed as but one of a host of important influences on strategic behaviour.

Porter's Five Forces Model greatly enlarged the influence of a firm's proximate environment for strategy by adding the power and behaviour of suppliers and customers as well as the threat posed by the development of new substitute product groups to the SCP paradigm. Most importantly, Porter's framework recognized that strategic behaviour is formulated on a dynamic basis responding to emerging technologies, changing consumer demands and legislation. But both the SCP paradigm and Porter's framework are silent on strategic interactions and strategic influences. Game theory teaches that in highly concentrated industries, competitive outcomes are the product of strategic games involving investments, signalling and the control of information. The approach indicates that mutually interdependent firms come to realize that tacitly collusive behaviour is a rational response. The advantages of co-operative behaviour spread beyond strategic interactions with rivals to include suppliers, customers and complementors.

In contrast to these market power approaches to strategy is the competency approach and its many derivatives. This approach sees competitive advantage stemming from an individual firm's core competencies, which may be organizational and/or strategic. Success here depends on the ways in which individual firms organize their resources and develop their capabilities. Put simply, a firm's potential ability to create value can be decomposed to an industry effect and a position effect. These industry and position effects are the outcome of past strategic decisions and the capture of their inherent value depends on the skill the firm brings to bear on its strategic interactions.

The idea that behaviour and performance can be influenced by location and relationships is captured in the concepts of clusters and the value net. Within a cluster, the presence of multiple rivals not only accentuates the intensity of competition among cluster participants, but also encourages co-operation with competitors as well as suppliers to improve quality and performance. Repeated interactions and informal contacts within a cluster foster trust, open communication, and lower costs of transacting business. Paradoxically, as globalization opens up economies to foreign competition the enduring response may be the localization of production with clusters. Within the value net, competition and co-operation coexist. The existence of complementaries means that individual firms can only fully exploit their capabilities by working with firms that can add value to the products being produced.

Key Learning Points

- The neo-classical paradigm linked a firm's behaviour to market structure and this was carried forward by the SCP paradigm, which explicitly linked the conduct and performance of firms to the number and size distribution of sellers within the industry.
- In practice, firms compete within strategic groups where products are close substitutes, but the boundaries of such groups are difficult to define.
- Measures of concentration within industry or strategic groups provide only an indication of market power and should be augmented with other measures of inequality, e.g. the *gini*-coefficient.
- The SCP paradigm started from the premise that structure is the outcome of structural barriers to entry, but overlooked the existence of strategic entry barriers arising from the behaviour of incumbents.
- Researchers have drawn attention to the importance of sunk costs as the key entry barrier and this discovery underpins the concept of a contestable market.
- Porter's Five Forces Model is a framework rooted in the SCP paradigm but goes much wider by recognizing dynamic influences such as emerging technologies, life cycle development and changing consumer demands on competitive rivalry.
- Porter's model did not explicitly deal with strategic interactions. Game theory has taught that in highly concentrated industries, market outcomes are likely to be the product of strategic investments, signalling and co-operation.
- Both Porter's framework, and game theory place the emphasis on the experience of market power and both play down the importance of a firm's organizational and core competencies on competitive advantage.
- The competency approach views competitive advantage as arising not from technical or strategic barriers, but from long-term investment in learning and the accumulation of heterogeneous value-creating knowledge.
- Co-operation with suppliers, customers and complementors, particularly in geographic clusters, can contribute to competitive advantage, particularly in rapidly changing high-tech markets.

Exercises

8.1 Why can seller concentration ratios never be more than a guide to the competitive behaviour of market incumbents?

8.2 In what way does Baumol *et al.*'s (1982) contestability theory elevate the importance of sunk costs to understanding strategic behaviour?

8.3 If competitive advantage is defined as the ability to sustain an economic rent, consider whether or not Porter's five forces framework rests on the ability to impede competitive forces.

8.4 Industry structure is important but so too is an individual firm's relative position. Explain what is meant by relative position.

8.5 In what way are industrial clusters consistent with Brandenberger and Nalebuff's (1996) concept of a value net?

Problems

8.1 The following expression represents the economic rent for a firm: $\pi = pq - c(q) - (r + \delta)K$, where K is the value of the firm's capital stock, δ is the depreciation rate and r the firm's opportunity cost of capital:

(a) If rent = 0, solve the profit equation for r.

(b) Say now the firm earns r^*, that is 5 per cent above the firm's opportunity cost of capital, i.e. $r^* = r + 0.5$. Holding q constant, by how much would p have to fall to return r to its opportunity cost of capital level?

(c) Demonstrate that vertical integration by any two firms will increase profits and that integration by all three is even more beneficial.

8.2 The following equation has been estimated to test the influence of market structure on profitability. Would you be surprised if the relationship was not statistically strong?

$$\pi = 0.039 + 0.343AS + 0.0105 lnAC + 0.015GD + 0.0043CR + \varepsilon$$

where
- AS = advertising sales ratio
- AC = absolute capital requirements
- GD = growth of demand
- CR = concentration ratio

And ε is a random error term, with a mean = 0.

(a) Explain the link between a positive coefficient for the concentration ratio and industry profits. Are you surprised that the relationship is not statistically strong?

(b) Consider the other explanatory variables. Do you think it possible that these variables are correlated rather than being independent?

(c) What other variables might you reasonably expect to find in an equation that seeks to explain industry influences on profits?

References

Bain, J. (1959) *Industrial Organization*, Wiley, New York.

Baumol, W., Panzar, J. and Willig, R. (1982) *Contestable Markets and the Theory of Industrial Structure*, Harcourt Brace, New York.

Chamberlin, E. (1933) *The Theory of Monopolistic Competition*, Harvard University Press, Cambridge, MA.

Chandler, A. (1962) *Strategy and Structure: Chapters in the History of the Industrial Enterprise*, MIT Press, Cambridge, MA.

Demsetz, H. (1968) 'Why regulate utilities?', *Journal of Law and Economics*, vol. 11, pp. 55–65.

European Commission (2000) *XXIX Report on Competition Policy 1999*, Brussels.

Geroski, P. (2000) 'The growth of firms in theory and practice' in *Competence, Governance and Entrepreneurship*, N. Foss and V. Mahnke (eds), Oxford University Press, Oxford.

Gibrat, R. (1931) *Les Inégalités Économiques*, Siney, Paris.

Krugman, P. (1993) *Geography and Trade*, MIT Press, Cambridge, MA..

Levinthal, D. (1995) 'Strategic management and the exploration of diversity' in *Resource Based and Evolutionary Theories of the Firm*, C. Montgomery (ed.), Kluwer, Boston.

Marshall, A. (1920), *Principles of Economics*, Macmillan, London.

Mason, E. (1939) 'Price and production policies of large scale enterprises', *American Economic Review*, vol. 29, pp. 61–74.

Nalebutt, B. and Brandenberger, A. (1996) *Co-opetition*, Profile Books, London.

Nelson, R. and Winter, S. (1983) *An Evolutionary Theory of Economic Change*, Belknap Press and Harvard University Press, Cambridge, MA.

Porter, M. (1980) *Competitive Strategy: Techniques for Analyzing Industries and Competitors*, Free Press Macmillan, New York.

Porter, M. (1990) *The Competitive Advantage of Nations*, Macmillan, London.

Porter, M. (1991) 'Towards a dynamic theory of strategy', *Strategic Management Journal*, vol. 12, pp. 95–117.

Rumelt, R. (1991) 'How much does industry matter?', *Strategic Management Journal*, vol. 12, no. 3, pp. 167–185.

Scherer, F. and Ross, D. (1990) *Industrial Market Structure and Economic Performance*, 3rd edn, Houghton Mifflin, Boston.

Schumpeter, J. (1942) *Capitalism, Socialism and Democracy*, Harper & Row, New York.

Shapiro, C. (1989) 'The theory of business strategy', *Rand Journal of Economics*, vol. 20, no. 1, pp. 125–137.

Sutton, J. (1992) *Sunk Costs and Market Structure*, MIT, Boston.

Sweezy, P. (1939) 'Demand under conditions of oligopoly', *Journal of Political Economy*, vol. 47, pp. 568–573.

Teece, D., Pisano, G. and Shuen, A. (1997) 'Dynamic capabilities and strategic management', *Strategic Management Journal*, vol. 18, no. 7, pp. 509–533.

CHAPTER 9

IMPERFECT COMPETITION AND GOVERNMENT INTERVENTION

Introduction

An industry's structure, essentially the relative size and concentration of firms, the nature of barriers to entry and the extent of diversification and product differentiation, is a major influence on the scope and character of the strategic decisions made by industry participants. Between the neo-classical extremes of **perfect competition** and **pure monopoly**, there exists a range of market structures, generally described as states of **imperfect competition**, where the ability to think and act strategically is critical to a firm's financial success. In this chapter, we investigate the strategic behaviour of firms operating in oligopolistic industries. By definition, **oligopoly** is an industry structure in which there are a small number of active firms, each with a significant share of the total market, albeit with a tail of smaller competitors. In such an environment each firm is aware of its oligopolistic rivals and each recognizes that the actions of their rivals have a direct impact on their own performance. In order to achieve the best possible outcome for their shareholders, individual firms must choose, from a range of behaviours, how they engage with their business rivals. It is this interaction with business rivals, whether tacit or overt, that ensures that the competitive environment of an oligopolistic industry is far from passive.

Article 81 of the European Community Treaty expressly prohibits, as incompatible with the **common market**, all agreements and concerted practices between firms that have as their objective or effect the prevention, restriction or distortion of competition. Specifically outlawed is any attempt to directly fix prices, limit total supply or fix market shares; but judging by the regularity of firms being fined for contravening Article 81, there are powerful economic incentives to acting co-operatively. Both overt and **tacit collusion** is prohibited, but tacit collusion is by definition much harder to detect. In the terminology of strategy, the behaviour of firms that operate and act in their own interests is described as **non-cooperative**. This, however, is misleading as it gives the impression that such behaviour is not compatible with mutual gain. In practice, many firms come to the conclusion that they can best serve their strategic objectives by tacitly co-operating with other firms, be they competitive rivals, suppliers or customers. This poses a problem for the competition authorities, as it can be extremely difficult to distinguish between behaviour that is based on an informal agreement and behaviour that is the result of individual firms responding rationally in their own interests, i.e. acting non-cooperatively.

Although there is no general theory encompassing the entire range of strategic behaviours, models of non-cooperative oligopoly go a long way towards helping an understanding of the interdependence dimension of strategic rivalry. Theories of non-cooperative oligopolistic strategic behaviour go beyond production and pricing policies to include decisions regarding investments, inventories and product differentiation. In this chapter, we will confine our attention to explaining quantity- and price-setting behaviour and will introduce these other elements in later chapters. Modern approaches to analysing the strategic behaviour of oligopolists put great emphasis on **game theory**. **Non-cooperative game theory** is particularly suited to analysing situations in which the optimal decisions of rational players depend on their beliefs or expectations about their rivals' decisions. Since the outcome of strategic decisions taken by oligopolists depends on the reaction of rivals, the application of game theory to oligopoly is a very appropriate and insightful method of analysis. Game theoretic methodology has resulted in far-reaching changes in the way strategists think about oligopolistic behaviour and here, and in the following chapters, a concerted effort has been made to use game theory to provide greater insights into situations of interdependence. However, a small caveat: game theory assumes a high degree of rationality and for some scholars (e.g. Fisher, 1989), the subtle and complex reasoning involved does not accord with the common experience of decision makers. But a game theoretic approach does bring out the logical implications of rational oligopolists thinking hard about what each other is likely to do. These logical implications are of direct relevance to the formulation and implementation of strategy and, consequently, game theory has emerged not only as the predominant methodology for analysing oligopoly behaviour, but also many other questions of direct relevance to strategy.

Over the past 100 years, and in part due to the development of game theory, governments have come to realize that in oligopolistic markets, if left to their own devices, sellers would favour collusion over competition, with adverse consequences for the efficient allocation of resources and consumers' welfare. Viewed from the perspective of the neo-classical paradigm, there is an overwhelming case for **competition policy** to prevent firms agreeing to fix prices and/or market shares. But competition policy does not exist in a vacuum. It might correctly be viewed as a passive element of **industrial policy** and as such reflects the values and aims of society that are likely to change over time. The juxtaposition of competition policy and industrial policy can result in governments entering into agreements with industries to improve performance, whilst the competition authorities threaten sanctions on private firms seeking similar aims via private agreements. In this chapter, we will explore the incentives and outcomes of co-operative behaviour by oligopolists. Having read this chapter, you will:

- Appreciate the contribution of both static and dynamic models of oligopoly to an understanding of the concept of interdependence and its influence on strategic interaction and conflict.
- Understand why game theory is particularly well suited to analysing the dynamic strategic and tactical behaviour that underpins competitive strategy.
- Be aware of the issues and tensions involved for policy makers in applying industrial policy to improve business performance and enforcing competition law to limit co-operative outcomes in oligopolistic industries.

What follows is divided into six sections. The first, using the example of **duopoly**, demonstrates the nature of interdependence, whereby, when making strategic or tactical decisions, both firms must take into account the likely reaction of the other. The second and third sections examine, respectively, the seminal quantity-setting and price-setting non-cooperative models of oligopoly. Although valuable for the rules and insights these models generate, they are of limited value in studying business strategy because they are essentially static and do not therefore explain how firms can learn from the past behaviour of their rivals and how dynamics introduces scope for co-operative or collusive strategic behaviour. The fourth and fifth sections introduce dynamics and uncertainty and uses game theory to demonstrate the feasibility and attractiveness of collusive behaviour. The emphasis is on tacit collusion and the credibility of a punishment strategy for firms who behave opportunistically and cheat. The final section turns to the issue of overt collusion, before going on to examine the role and character of industrial policy in the European Community and the tensions between such activities and Community competition policy.

Mutual Interdependence

As outlined in the introduction, an oligopolistic market structure consists of a sufficiently small number of firms such that the output of each firm accounts for a significant share of the market, and therefore the output or price decisions by their senior managers have a direct influence on the market share or price charged by their competitors. For example, BP AMCO sales of petrol and diesel are particularly sensitive to any change in price by one or more of their competitors, e.g. Shell. But firms need not be large to operate in an oligopolistic environment. Sticking with the fuel industry, there are several thousand petrol stations in the UK and the petrol they sell – regardless of brand – is viewed by most consumers as being, in effect, homogeneous. But in an individual town there may be only four or five petrol stations serving the local market. In such a situation, it would be more correct to view the rivalry between the petrol stations serving a local market as being akin to oligopolistic rather than perfect competition.

The essence of oligopolistic competition is that the outcome of a change in tactics or strategy by a firm's decision makers, say, to alter the price of its products or to invest in increased capacity, is dependent on the reaction of rivals. This is a situation of strategic interdependence; that is, there is a tension between competitive and co-operative behaviour on the part of individual firms. Each firm is tempted to compete aggressively to increase its market share, but if all firms do so, the likely result

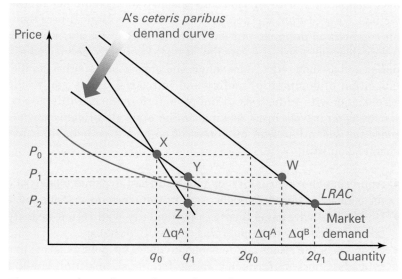

Figure 9.1: Oligopolists and mutual interdependence

would be a reduction in profits for all. A more profitable situation is likely to be achieved if they co-operate in setting prices or allocating market shares. This situation of strategic interdependence can be demonstrated using a static model of duopoly, which is just a special example of oligopoly. As its name implies, a static model cannot deal adequately with the dynamic reactions of oligopolistic rivals, e.g. the ability over time to change unit costs and differentiated products, but it does serve to bring out the key features of interdependence. Consider Figure 9.1, which shows the market demand curve for a **homogeneous product** that is only supplied by two firms, A and B. For simplicity and without any loss of generality, it is assumed that in addition to selling an identical product, both firms have a 50 per cent market share and both have identical cost functions as represented by the long-run average cost curve, $LRAC$. If each sells output q_0 – creating a market supply Q_0, equal to $2q_0$ – this generates a market price of P_0. The diagram is drawn from firm A's perspective and at point X, firm A is earning an **economic rent**, i.e. price is higher than long-run costs. An identical diagram could be drawn from B's perspective.

Now, assuming no increase in market demand, consider the impact if only firm A increases its output by Δq^A to q_1, where Δ represents a change. As firm B has not changed its output (q_0), firm A moves down its **ceteris paribus demand curve** from X to Y and the overall effect of A's decision is to increase the total market supply – represented by point W – with the effect that the market price falls to P_1 *for both firms*. The outcome for firm A is an increase in its market share and – depending on the market's **price elasticity of demand** – an increase in profits. But for firm B, who has not changed its supply, the outcome is both a loss of market share and lower profits. This is most certainly not a passive environment, it is an active and uncertain environment, where a set of actions by one firm has given rise to an unexpected and adverse consequence for another.

Firm B is unlikely to be happy with either its loss of market share or its lower profits and if it decides to respond it may act to recover its former market share, and punish firm A, by also increasing its output by Δq^B, such that, $\Delta q^B = \Delta q^A$. The effect is to increase the market supply to $2q_1$, pushing the market price even lower, to P_2. The logic of such action may not be immediately obvious, but we demonstrate below the strategic power of being able to punish a rival even if the punishment is shared by all. Of importance here is the impact of B's response on A's demand curve. When B kept its output unchanged, A's *ceteris paribus* demand curve was the relevant curve. But when B changed its output in response, the relevant curve for A was the one passing through points X to Z. The demand curve, XZ, represents the outcome when both firms lower their prices in the same proportion. As a result, market share has not changed and XZ is interpreted as the 'market share' demand curve. Both firms are now producing output, q_1; they both have a 50 per cent market share; but both firms are now making a loss, i.e. price has fallen below unit costs. This simple example demonstrates the high degree of interdependence in the behaviour of firms in an oligopolistic market. In such markets, when making either a short-run tactical decision or a longer-term strategic decision, an individual firm's decision makers must take into account the reactions of rivals to their decisions.

From the perspective of business strategy, the issue raised by the situation depicted in Figure 9.1 is that of rationality. If both players are rational, in the absence of rising demand, neither will entertain the strategy of increasing sales if their rival is in a position to rapidly respond in kind. We can demonstrate this rationality with the help of Figure 9.2. If neither firm increases its output, i.e. $\Delta q = 0$, they will continue to earn the economic rents π_A and π_B, respectively. If, however, only firm A increases its sales its profits rise to $\beta\pi_A$ and firm B's profits will fall to $\alpha\pi_B$, where $0 < \alpha < 1 < \beta$. This outcome would be reversed if only firm B increases sales, and if both firms simultaneously increase output, both make loses, $-\pi_A$ and $-\pi_B$ respectively.

The striking feature of these pay-offs is that both firms have an incentive to increase sales but only if they can be sure that their rival will not do likewise. In a world of *imperfect information*, they will lack information on their rival's sales plans, and in this situation the best tactic for each player is to choose $\Delta q = 0$. The temptation to play $\Delta q > 0$ is tempered by the knowledge that it could result in a loss, whereas the worse that could

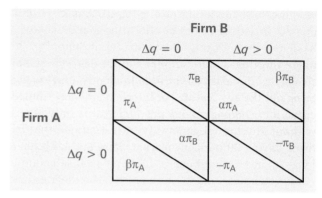

Figure 9.2: A rational game

happen by keeping output constant would be a reduced profit, i.e. $\alpha\pi$. This is a non-cooperative outcome resulting from the players thinking hard about the likely consequences of their actions – but it could equally have been the outcome of an informal agreement not to increase output.

Simultaneous Quantity Setting

Figure 9.2, in attempting to represent *rational behaviour* by oligopolistic rivals, raises a number of pertinent questions. Very conveniently, the analysis started from an '*equilibrium*', i.e. neither firm had an incentive to increase sales if their rival was likely to do the same. It is to the nature of this oligopoly equilibrium that we now turn in order to counter the model's silence as to how the firms arrived at this 'equilibrium'. The equilibrium may not represent the maximum profits that the two firms could earn if they overtly colluded to reduce output. Collusion to fix output or prices is, as noted above, prohibited under Article 81, but our interest here is to understand the process by which non-cooperating oligopolists arrive at an equilibrium output or price. For this, we need a different approach to explain how strategic interaction between oligopolists can arrive at an equilibrium. The models economists use for this purpose fall into two broad categories: quantity-setting models and price-setting models.

Quantity-setting models proceed on the basis that oligopolistic firms decide how much to produce and then let the market determine the price at which the output is sold. Such models reflect industries where production schedules are set in advance and cannot be altered without incurring a sunk cost, e.g. car assembly. Once the production line has been set up, if demand turns out lower than expected companies will, in the short run at least, put surplus cars into stock and use, say, advertising to increase demand. Price-setting models assume that firms set the price of their products and then sell whatever quantity is demanded at that price. This model is appropriate for industries that can rapidly respond if sales increase. The fast food industry provides an example. Typically, a price will be set for, say, a 'burger and chips' and outlets will then (within reason) match production to demand. In this section, we will look at quantity-setting models and in the next we will examine price-setting models.

So that we can demonstrate these models with the aid of graphs, we will continue to restrict ourselves to a duopoly market structure and for the moment we will maintain the assumption that both firms produce an identical product. The results derived from such a model can be generalized to markets with more than two firms and in which firms produce ***differentiated products***. If there are only two firms in the market, both producing an homogeneous product, there are essentially two ways in which the firms could interact: they could make their decisions regarding output simultaneously; or, alternatively, one firm may choose to be a follower by allowing the other firm to set the quantity and then to choose its own level of output. In this chapter, we will look only at simultaneous quantity setting and return to quantity leadership when considering the behaviour of a dominant firm in Chapter 10.

We can demonstrate how the assumption of rationality enables an equilibrium to be achieved with the aid of some basic equations. If you are not familiar with the analytics of profit maximization, you should first read Appendix 9A. The seminal model of simultaneous quantity setting by oligopolists was published more than 167 years ago by Augustin Cournot (1838), a French mathematician. Following Cournot, our market contains two firms, A and B. The market clearing price, P, is determined by the aggregate supply, Q, which is captured in the inverse (market) demand curve:

$$P = \alpha - \beta Q \tag{9.1}$$

where α and β are positive constants. Aggregate market supply is the sum of the outputs from both firms, i .e. $Q = q_A + q_B$; hence, as demonstrated above, the price received by an individual firm, say A, is determined by the sales of both firms. Writing Δ for change, a small increase in firm A's output (Δq_A) will lower the market price and the resulting change in its total revenue, TR_A, will be:

$$\Delta TR_A = P\Delta q_A - \Delta P q_A \tag{9.2}$$

where P is the new lower market price and ΔP the fall in price. From (Equation 9.2) we can derive firm A's ***marginal revenue*** function by dividing through by Δq_A, i.e. $MR_A = \Delta TR_A / \Delta q_A$, and recognizing from Equation (9.1) that $\Delta P / \Delta q_A = \beta$, we have:

$$MR_A = P - \frac{\Delta P}{\Delta q_A}.q_A = \alpha - 2\beta q_A - \beta q_B \tag{9.3}$$

The profit-maximizing output is determined when ***marginal cost*** equals marginal revenue; that is, when Equation (9.4) is satisfied:

$$MC_A = \alpha - 2\beta q_A - \beta q_B \tag{9.4}$$

However, to solve Equation (9.4), firm A has to have a value for q_B. As A and B must make their decisions simultaneously, neither firm knows for certain how much the other firm will supply to the market. How might the two firms choose a level of supply in this situation? The Cournot solution is that each firm's optimal output is based on what it expects the other firm to do. That is, each firm responds to the other's expected output; each has a ***reaction function***. Firm A's profit-maximizing reaction function can be derived by rearranging Equation (9.4). In order to simplify matters, without any loss of generality we will assume $MC = 0$, such that:

$$q_A = \frac{\alpha - \beta q_B}{2\beta} \tag{9.5}$$

and by similar reasoning we can determine firm B's reaction function:

$$q_B = \frac{\alpha - \beta q_A}{2\beta} \tag{9.6}$$

These two reaction functions are illustrated in Figure 9.3. They show that the optimal level of output for each firm is negatively related to the expected level of supply by the other firm. The path to equilibrium implied by the reaction function is as follows. Assume initially that only firm A is producing in this market, i.e. $q_B = 0$. As a monopolist, firm A will produce the amount where $MC_A = \alpha - 2\beta q_A$, and given the assumption that $MC_A = 0$, this fixes the profit-maximizing output at $\alpha/2\beta$: point W in Figure 9.3. If now firm B enters the market, and assumes that firm A will maintain its current level of supply, then it will produce the output represented by point X. The output X is read off the vertical axis but lies on firm B's reaction curve vertically above point W: we know from Equation (9.6) that this represents firm B's profit-maximizing output given A's existing output. The result of firm B entering the market will be a rise in total market supply and from Equation (9.1), this will result in a lower market price and therefore lower than expected profits for firm A. In the following production period, firm A must decide its response. If it expects firm B to continue to produce the output represented by X, it will reduce its output as determined by its reaction function to point Y, which is read off the horizontal axis. The output level represented by Y was determined by Equation (9.5). Given that firm B is producing at point X, firm A will earn a higher profit at Y than at W. From firm B's perspective, firm A at Y is producing less than expected and, being rational, firm B will now increase output to point Z, as determined by Equation (9.6). It can be seen that this process will continue until we reach the ***Cournot equilibrium***; but note that as each firm moves along its reaction function, total market supply is increasing and consequently economic rent for both firms is declining. In short, non-cooperative equilibrium in an oligopoly will be at a higher level of output and a lower price than would be the outcome under a monopoly.

Why having reached the Cournot equilibrium, does firm B not increase output further? The answer is, that to do so would bring forth a reaction from A that would drive them back to the Cournot equilibrium. To see this, say B increases output to point R. Firm A will respond with the output S and B will respond with T and so on. The nature of the Cournot equilibrium merits comment. The equilibrium has been arrived at by non-cooperative behaviour; that is, both oligopolists have

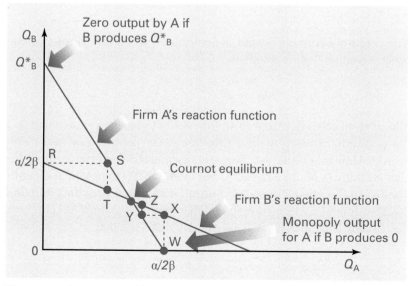

Figure 9.3: Cournot equilibrium

taken their decisions independently and they have taken them in accord with their own value systems, as represented by Equations (9.5) and (9.6). In other words, each firm's action was the best possible response to the action of its rival and at the Cournot equilibrium it is not possible for either player, acting independently, to improve its profits by deviating from the equilibrium. This concept of equilibrium is known as a **Nash equilibrium**, named after the mathematician, economist and Nobel Prize winner, John Nash (1950). Nash described the equilibrium of a non-cooperative game as the best outcome for each player given that all players are playing their equilibrium strategies. For this reason, the equilibrium shown in Figure 9.3 is now more generally known as a **Cournot–Nash equilibrium**.

Despite its restrictive assumptions, the Cournot model captures a number of important features that are common to the competitive outcome of oligopolistic rivalry. Each firm faces a downward-sloping demand curve resulting in the divergence between price and marginal revenue, i.e. $P > MR$, as demonstrated by Equation (9.3) but possesses only limited market power. The total economic rent accruing to the rival firms that have converged to a Cournot–Nash equilibrium lies between the rent that would accrue to a profit-maximizing, pure monopolist and the zero economic rent, i.e. **normal profits** earned by firms operating under a perfectly competitive equilibrium. The Cournot model also produces Equation (9.7) – see the Appendix 9B for its derivation – which captures some pertinent observations regarding market structure and profitability:

$$\frac{P - MC_A}{P} = \frac{s_A}{\varepsilon} \tag{9.7}$$

Based on Equation (9.7), we can conclude:

- Each firm possesses limited market power and can therefore charge a price in excess of marginal cost.
- This mark-up on marginal cost will be less than that of a monopolist supplying the market.
- The mark-up for each oligopolist is directly influenced by the market price elasticity of demand and the market share for its product.

Moreover, in a market consisting of n firms with varying market shares, s_i, and writing $\bar{c}$ for the average marginal cost, then the industry average mark-up is given by:

$$\frac{P - \bar{c}}{P} = \sum_{i=1}^{n} \frac{s_i^2}{\varepsilon} = \frac{H}{\varepsilon} \tag{9.8}$$

where H is the Herfindahl index (HI) of concentration. Equation (9.7) suggests a positive relationship between the HI and the industry's average mark-up, i.e. the more concentrated a market characterized by a quantity-setting oligopoly, the greater the average market power for individual sellers. Put succinctly, the more concentrated the sellers, the lower the market output and the higher the market price.

So far we have conveniently skipped over the issue of varying costs. It is just tenable that in an oligopoly producing an homogeneous product, unit costs are very similar, if not identical for each firm.

However, if oligopolists are producing differentiated products, then the assumption that marginal costs are identical for individual firms becomes untenable. From Equation (9.7) it can be seen that the lower the individual firm's marginal cost, the greater the market share. We can demonstrate the consequences of varying costs by reverting to the Cournot duopoly, shown in Figure 9.4. Say we start at the Cournot–Nash equilibrium point, X. If A discovers a new way of combining its resources so that its marginal costs of production fall, its profit-maximizing output level will rise. If you are not sure about this, return to Equation (9.4), where it is clear that if q_B remains constant, then q_A must rise if MC_A falls. The effect of firm A's new lower cost process is represented in Figure 9.4 as a shift to the right in its reaction function. Firm B's non-cooperative, profit-maximizing behaviour is to respond to this rise in firm A's output by reducing its supply; that is, the Cournot–Nash equilibrium moves from X to Y and in the process firm A's market share has risen and firm B's has fallen.

The foregoing Cournot approach to oligopoly is based on non-cooperative behaviour; each firm restricts its own output on the basis of what it *thinks* other firms will do. But this raises the question as to whether it would be possible to increase profitability if firms acted co-operatively. The effect of acting co-operatively is demonstrated in Figure 9.5, which repeats Figure 9.2 but stripped of the adjustment path to equilibrium. Superimposed on the reaction functions of firms A and B are ***isoprofit curves***, each one of which represents a fixed level of profitability. Focusing on A's reaction function, at point W firm A has no competitors and therefore the maximum pure monopoly rent is being earned at this point. Once firm B enters the market, total output rises, the market price falls and so do firm A's profits. The relevant position is now point X, and this indicates that the level of profit represented by the isoprofit curve passing through X is lower than at point W. That is, as firm A's isoprofit curves move north-west from point W, they represent successively lower levels of profitability. As can be seen, one of firm B's isoprofit lines passes through point X, representing a level of profitability that B considered sufficiently attractive to justify entry.

As previously explained, firm A will respond by moving to point Y, as this lies on an isoprofit curve that is closer to W and therefore represents a higher profit than at point X. It also lies on an isoprofit line for firm B that is nearer point R and therefore represents a higher level of profitability. Firm B will now respond with an increase in sales and this moves it to a high level of profits – and in response, firm A will further reduce its output. Eventually this process ends in a Cournot–Nash equilibrium at point E. But, say, instead of the non-cooperative equilibrium represented by point E, both firms choose to co-operate. Figure 9.5 can be used to demonstrate that the two firms could improve profitability if they were prepared to co-operate or, to give it a legal description, engage in collusion. The line EF represents a higher profit equilibrium for both firms if both firms act co-operatively. If both agree to restrict output, they can achieve a point of rest

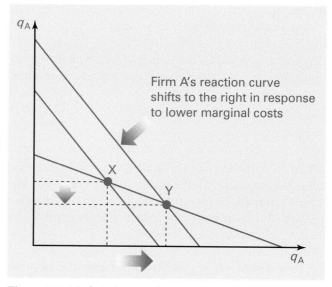

Figure 9.4: Market share and costs

somewhere between points E and F. As can be seen, points on this line lie on higher isoprofit curves for firms A and B – i.e. nearer points W and R, respectively – hence, the incentive to collude.

Armed with an understanding of a Cournot–Nash equilibrium and the scope for additional profits if firms co-operate or collude, we can return to the normal form game set out in Figure 9.2 and take it a stage further, as shown in Figure 9.6. The situation displayed in the top-left quadrant represents a non-cooperative, Cournot–Nash equilibrium and it is therefore not possible for either firm A or B to improve on their respective economic rents, π_A

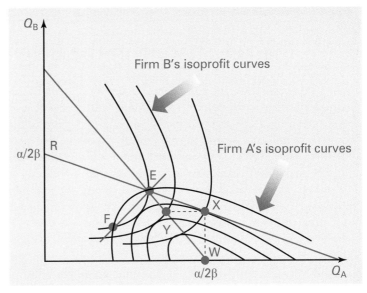

Figure 9.5: Isoprofit curves

and π_B, unless they change the rules of the game. Based on the properties of the non-cooperative Cournot–Nash equilibrium, if either firm arbitrarily attempts to increase profits by reducing sales, its rival (on the basis of its reaction function) will respond, resulting in lower than expected profits for the initiator and higher profits for the reactor, where $0 < \alpha < 1 < \beta$. However, if the two firms engage in a pre-play discussion and reach a collusive agreement or signal their intention, thereby tacitly colluding, it would be possible for them jointly to reduce sales, thereby increasing the market price and joint profits. This outcome is set out in the bottom-right quadrant of Figure 9.6, where, $\beta > \mu > 1 > \alpha$.

Figure 9.6 has the pay-off pattern of the classic **Prisoners' Dilemma:** each firm has a choice of tactics (though game theorists tend to refer to both short-term and longer-term actions as strategies); they can co-operate or they can cheat. In the absence of an 'agreement' both firms can rely on the other behaving rationally and therefore playing their dominant strategy, i.e. leave sales at their Cournot–Nash equilibrium level. Just how two (or more) independent firms might achieve the better co-operative pay-off we will return to below. The important lesson of the foregoing is that the players are in a position to change the rules of the game and in so doing increase total profitability.

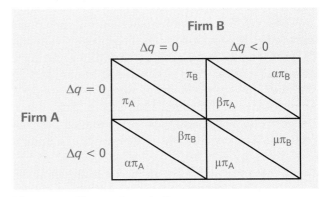

Figure 9.6: Change the rules?

Market Sharing in the Belgian Beer Market

On 5 December 2001, the European Commission fined Interbrew, Danone, Alken-Maes and Martens a total of €91 million for participating in a market-sharing agreement for the Belgian beer market between 1993 and 1998. Interbrew, the number-one brewer in Belgium, with a market share of around 55 per cent, and Alken-Maes, a subsidiary of Danone and the number-two brewer in Belgium, with a market share of 15 per cent, entered into an agreement covering a wide range of anti-competitive practices. The agreement encompassed a general non-aggression pact and more specific limitations on investment and advertising.

A striking feature of this market-sharing agreement was the close involvement of the CEOs and other top management of the companies. This included senior managers from Danone, Alken-Maes' parent company. Despite Interbrew's large market share, the driving force behind the agreement was Danone, who threatened to make life difficult for Interbrew-France if it did not transfer 5 per cent of its market share to Alken-Maes. The threat led to a 'gentlemen's agreement' between the parties, whereby they committed themselves to respect each other's market position. Throughout the period of the agreement the parties exchanged monthly information about sales values.

Price-Setting Models

In the Cournot solution to oligopolistic competition, each firm's strategic variable is the quantity supplied to the market. An objection to the Cournot model is that, in many instances, businesses choose prices rather than quantities as their strategic variables. Indeed, this was the very criticism made by Bertrand (1883), in his review of Cournot's book, and his name has since been attached to oligopolist price-setting strategies. In the **Bertrand model** of oligopolistic competition, firms are deemed to simultaneously announce the price at which they are prepared to sell their product, and then consumers determine the amount they will buy. However, an individual firm engaging in such a pricing strategy has first to forecast the prices at which its rivals will offer their products for sale. That is, its profit-maximizing price is conditional on its rivals also choosing their equilibrium profit-maximizing prices. This is a Nash equilibrium and the nature of the equilibrium that results from the Bertrand price-setting model of oligopolistic competition depends critically on whether the firms sell homogeneous or differentiated products. If, for example, the competing firms not only sell homogeneous products but also face well-behaved marginal costs, i.e. subject to the law of diminishing returns and can rapidly adjust their levels of output, there exists a unique Nash equilibrium.

Given these restrictive assumptions, it turns out that the Nash equilibrium is achieved where the competing firms all charge a price that is equal to marginal cost, i.e. they just earn normal profits. This follows because if the firms sell identical goods, then perfectly informed consumers will only buy from the firm offering the product at the lowest price. For example, imagine a market that is supplied by just two firms, A and B. Say A charges the lowest price but is still earning a rent, i.e. $P > MC$. In this situation, firm B has an incentive to slightly undercut A's price and by doing this B will capture the whole market – assuming perfectly informed consumers – whilst still earning an economic rent. Now A has an incentive to undercut B and the process would continue until the unique

Nash equilibrium is achieved; namely, the point where both firms are charging the same price and earning normal profits.

From the perspective of business strategy, this outcome is to say the least bemusing. Firms operating in oligopolistic markets are more likely than not to face increasing returns to scale. If so, marginal costs will lie below total unit costs and, consequently, $P = MC$ cannot be an equilibrium. Further, the implication of a Bertrand price-setting equilibrium for an oligopolistic market selling homogeneous products is in marked contrast to that predicted by the Cournot quantity-setting model. The Bertrand solution implies that the industry's level of concentration has no impact on market price and an individual firm's market share has apparently no influence on its market power. In a market with homogeneous products, the Bertrand price-setting model yields precisely the same outcome as a perfectly competitive market and the result – that as few as two firms will yield the competitive outcome – is referred to as the **Bertrand paradox**. It is a paradox because it seems implausible that so few firms would not find some way of colluding so as to move away from the competitive outcome in order to earn economic rents. This implausible outcome would appear to render the Bertrand price-setting model of little interest to students of business strategy. However, in practice many firms, e.g. the airlines, engage in the pricing strategy of setting a price and then selling whatever is demanded at that price. The important point is that such firms are not selling homogeneous products.

The Bertrand paradox is avoided, and price setting becomes highly relevant to business strategy, if competing oligopolist firms sell differentiated products. In a market where products are differentiated, competing firms no longer risk the all-or-nothing demand associated with the pricing of an homogeneous product. The essence of differentiated products serving the same function is that they are close but not perfect **substitutes**. For example, newspapers serve the same function but are rarely viewed as perfect substitutes. Once the assumption of product homogeneity is relaxed, individual oligopolists face downward-sloping demand curves, where a relative price cut will encourage some, but not all, consumers to switch from a rival's products. In a differentiated product market, the Bertrand equilibrium is consistent with $P > MC$, as firms retain a degree of market power by virtue of product homogeneity. We can demonstrate the essence of Bertrand price-setting competition for differentiated products with a simple example, once again involving just two firms, A and B. The demand for firm A's output depends on the relative price of its rival's product; hence firm A's demand curve is represented by:

$$q_A = a - \beta P_A + \lambda P_B \tag{9.9}$$

By manipulating Equation (9.9), for a small change in the price charged by firm A we can obtain its *reaction function* as set out below (for the derivation of Equation (9.10), see Appendix 9C):

$$P_A = \frac{a}{2\beta} + \frac{\lambda}{2\beta} P_B \tag{9.10}$$

By similar reasoning, we can also calculate firm B's reaction function. The two reaction functions represent the profit-maximizing price for each firm, given the price charged by the rival, and they are displayed in Figure 9.7.

The reaction curves for Bertrand price-setting competition are seen to be upward sloping: this follows because the profit-maximizing price depends on the rival's price; the higher B's price, the higher A can set its price. In the Bertrand model, both firms set their price simultaneously, given their beliefs about their rival's price. If we start with the assumption that A is a monopolist, in this situation it will set price W, i.e. from Equation (9.10), $P_A = \alpha/2\beta$, if $P_B = 0$. If B believes A will

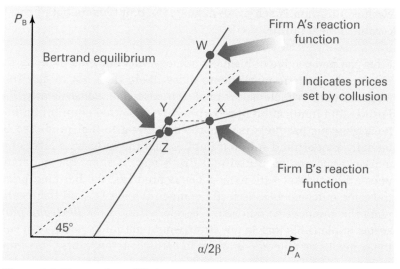

Figure 9.7: Bertrand equilibrium

set a price of W, it will plan to enter the market with a lower price, represented by point X, which is read off the vertical axis. If A believes that B, having entered the market, will set a price represented by point X, A will want to lower its price to a level represented by, say, point Y, which is read on the horizontal axis. By joining points W and Y, we construct A's reaction function, i.e. Equation (9.10). Turning to B, believing that A will set price Y, B would wish to sell for price Z and by joining points X and Z, we construct B's reaction function. Both sellers will continue to react to each other and the procedure continues until the Nash equilibrium is reached at the intersection of the reaction curves. At this point, neither firm has an incentive to change its price: both firms are doing the best they can given the price set by its rival.

The equilibrium price depends on the position of the reaction functions within the $P_A P_B$ space and this in turn depends on the extent of product differentiation. If the competing products are highly standardized, each firm will face a highly elastic demand curve for its product. In this situation, a relatively small price increase by, say, firm A will cause it to lose a large market share. Alternatively, a relatively small price cut will cause it to gain a significant market share at the expense of firm B. This would be reflected by reaction curves that intersected closer to the origin in the $P_A P_B$ space, i.e. the equilibrium price would be close to MC. At the other extreme, if the competing products are so differentiated that few consumers regard them as substitutes, a price increase by, say, firm A will result in a loss of relatively few customers to firm B. In this situation, each firm faces a low elasticity of demand and perhaps even inelastic demand and the Bertrand–Nash non-cooperative equilibrium price will, *ceteris paribus*, be considerably higher than the competitive equilibrium price. In this situation, the reaction functions will intercept much further away from the origin in the $P_A P_B$ space.

Once again, both firms could improve on their pay-offs from the non-cooperative Bertrand–Nash equilibrium if they were prepared to adopt an overtly collusive or tacitly collusive approach to setting prices. A collusive outcome is represented by the dotted line rising upwards to the right from the Bertrand–Nash equilibrium in Figure 9.7. We can illustrate this co-operative solution with, for a change, the extensive form of the Prisoners' Dilemma game set out in Figure 9.8, where the pay-offs are profits for A and B of π_A and π_B, respectively. As competition laws prohibit formal collusion to fix prices (or market shares), we will proceed on the basis of tacit collusion – which may also be declared illegal if detected by the authorities. Viewed from the perspective of firm A, it has a choice: to act non-cooperatively; or to act co-operatively by signalling a credible commitment to raise its price. The dotted line connecting both of firm B's decision nodes indicates that these two nodes are in the same information set; namely, firm B

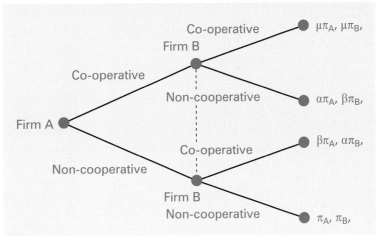

Figure 9.8: Co-operating for a behaviour

cannot tell for certain which of the two actions A has taken when it makes its decision. The co-operative outcome is achieved if firm B also chooses to act co-operatively, delivering higher profits to both players, i.e. $\mu > 1$.

If firm A signals its intention to act co-operatively, but firm B fails to correctly interpret the signal or chooses to act opportunistically by pretending to also raise its price but in the event defecting, by leaving its price unchanged, the outcome is a switch of some of firm A's customers to firm B, resulting in higher profits for B and lower profits for A, i.e. $\beta > \mu > 1 > \alpha$. Alternatively, firm A could act opportunistically by defecting from its signalled co-operative stance, placing B in a vulnerable position if it acts co-operatively, i.e. $\beta\pi_A$, $\alpha\pi_B$. The longer-term implications of cheating will be considered in more detail below. If both A and B choose to act non-cooperatively, the outcome is the Bertrand–Nash equilibrium generating profits of π_A and π_B, respectively. In the absence of a credible commitment to co-operate by both firms, this is the dominant strategy for both A and B.

Eurotunnel

In 1888, Louis Figuier, a French writer, wrote that linking France and England 'will meet one of the present-day needs of civilization'. One hundred years later, work began on building what is one of the longest tunnels in the world and, at the time it was built, the most expensive construction project ever conceived. It took €21 billion to complete the tunnel, but since its opening in 1994 passen-

ger numbers have disappointed. This may reflect a price, that in the view of potential passengers, is too high.

In September 2003, the European Commission launched an inquiry into possible price fixing by the Eurotunnel shuttle operator and three ferry companies on Channel routes. This reflected complaints from passenger groups that

continued

the prices charged by Eurotunnel and the ferries seemed high and arbitrary. In real terms, the prices charged by these Channel companies had fallen since the opening of the tunnel in 1994, though the European Commission had obviously been persuaded that there was at least a suspicion that the price of crossing the channel was being held artificially high by collusion between Eurotunnel operators and the ferry companies.

It took just three years to dig the 31-mile tunnel under the English Channel and during that period the ferry companies invested in bigger boats and better facilities. Just prior to the opening of the tunnel, the ferry companies reduced their prices – resulting in a similar response from Eurotunnel. This is the behaviour predicted by the Bertrand model. The suspicion lying behind the European Commission's inquiry is that both Eurotunnel operators and the ferry companies, having attempted to secure an increased market share by price cutting, realized that they could improve profits by adopting a co-operative rather a competitive stance when setting prices.

The economic costs of collusion are more than a welfare cost to consumers. There is an economic benefit to Britain to keep freight off its congested roads in the South East and the fact that Eurotunnel's capacity is only about half used. Despite the landmark EU directive in March 2003 requiring all member states to allow foreign operators to haul international freight across its tracks, Eurotunnel has potentially much to gain from offering a more competitive price.

Dynamics and Uncertainty

The Cournot and Bertrand models are attempts to formulate theories and predictions regarding oligopolistic competitive behaviour. Some of the assumptions underlying these models lack realism, e.g. one firm can capture all sales by simply lowering price, but their validity should ultimately rest not on their assumptions, but on a comparison of their predictions with reality. On this basis, which model is more appropriate depends on the industry being studied. Sellers in industries with high sunk cost barriers to entry are likely to pre-commit to a level of sales and such industries might therefore be better modelled using the Cournot quantity-setting approach. In contrast, competition between firms selling differentiated products without (within reason) capacity constraints, e.g. insurance, are better modelled using Bertrand's price-setting approach. But both approaches suffer a serious limitation when it comes to business strategy; namely, both are essentially static models. This may seem odd given that both employ the concept of 'reaction functions', but in both cases the focus is where the reaction functions intersect. Neither model is dynamic in the strategic sense of models of many time periods in which the business environment is changing. As demonstrated above, the static non-cooperative Nash equilibrium can be bettered if rivals co-operate and of issue here is whether this conclusion applies more generally; namely, is co-operation the optimal dynamic strategy for oligopolists?

One of the first attempts to cite tacit collusion as an explanation for the frequently observed characteristic of price rigidity over many time periods in oligopolistic markets was the ***kinked demand curve*** model, put forward by Sweezy (1939). Sweezy's approach is captured in Figure 9.9, which shows the demand curves facing two firms representing an oligopolist market. To make the example realistic, we must assume that the two firms, A and B, are producing differentiated products, i.e. consumers view the products of these two firms as close but not perfect substitutes. Starting at points Q and R, if now firm A reduces the price of its product from P_0 to P_1, the outcome, as we have seen, depends crucially on the reaction of its rival. If the rival does nothing, firm A will increase its sales to point S, which lies on its *ceteris paribus* demand curve. Part or all of firm A's increased sales will have come from consumers who have switched from firm B. The result is a noticeable fall in demand for firm B's products, represented by the shift in the demand curve facing B from point R to T.

Firm B is unlikely to be happy with its loss of market share, and if so may decide to also lower the price of its product to P_1. To avoid complications, let us assume that this decision is taken instantly as firm A lowers its price. The outcome in this situation is that firm B does not lose sales and both sellers come to rest at a new equilibrium represented by points U and V, respectively. The demand curve passing through points Q and V is firm A's 'market share' demand curve, which represents the consumption response to a price reduction by firm A *when rivals match the price change*. It should be noted that the curve passing through R and U is firm B's 'market share' demand curve and also that at the lower price of P_1, the market has expanded, i.e. both firms have increased sales.

Now consider the reaction of B to a rise in price to P_2 by A. If B also raises its price to P_2, then the outcome for both firms will be represented by points W and X, respectively. But why should firm B follow firm A's price rise? If B's price remains unchanged, then B will gain market share. That is, firm A's sales will fall to Y and demand for firm B's products will rise to Z. Unless B faces a sharply rising average cost curve, i.e. a capacity constraint, point Z is likely to be more profitable than point W. It should now be clear how Sweezy's concept of the kinked demand curve arises; it is based on the 'obvious fact that rivals react differently according to whether a price change is upward or downward' (Sweezy, 1939, p. 568). The assumption lying behind the kinked demand curve is that should firm A lower its product's price, its oligopolistic rivals will act to protect their market shares and, hence, will respond by also reducing prices to match. Thus, when considering reductions in prices, only the curve QV is relevant. However, should firm A act unilaterally in raising prices, firm B has the opportunity to increase market share if it does not follow in kind. Hence, if firm A raises its price the relevant demand curve is the *ceteris paribus* demand curve shown by curve QY. This chain of reasoning produces the kinked demand curve, YQV.

Sweezy's kinked demand curve is widely viewed as an attempt to show how dynamic tacit collusion can induce price rigidity. A fuller exposition, including production costs, is set out in Figure 9.10. We start at a point of equilibrium where the profit-maximizing oligopolist is selling quantity, q_0, at price, P_0. Given the kinked demand curve, the space below is cut by two marginal revenue curves. The curve, MR_0, equally divides the area under the curve, WX – the *ceteris paribus* portion of the demand curve – and

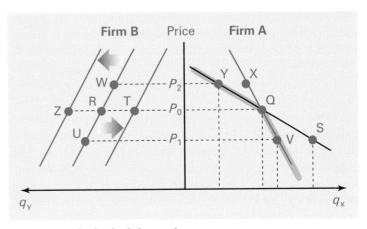

Figure 9.9: The kinked demand curve

MR_1 equally divides the area under the curve, XY – the 'market share' portion of the demand curve. Profits, it will be recalled, are maximized when marginal cost, $MC = MR$ but, as shown in Figure 9.10, when the firm is selling output, q_0, we have:

$$MR_0 > MC > MR_1 \qquad (9.11)$$

As a result, it would not benefit the oligopolist to increase output. The relevant marginal revenue curve if output is increased is MR_1, but as $MC > MR_1$, this would be unprofitable. If, alternatively, the oligopolist reduced output, the relevant marginal revenue curve is MR_0, and as falling output would coincide with a widening gap between MR_0 and MC, the loss of revenue is greater than the fall in costs. The result is that our oligopolist is better off maintaining output at q_0, as long as its rivals keep their output levels constant, and fluctuations in costs, induced by a changing business environment, within the range between X and Y will not result in either changes in output or price; implicitly, the rivals are tacitly colluding.

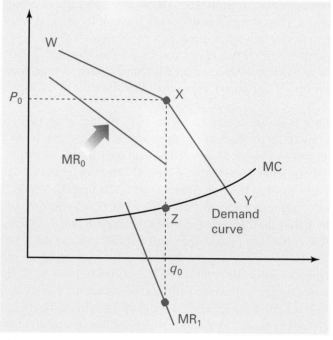

Figure 9.10: Price rigidity and the kinked demand curve

Sweezy's attempt to rationalize the observed price rigidities that characterized oligopolistic industries during the 1930s remains a popular textbook approach to dynamic tacit collusion. However, the kinked demand curve approach to oligopolistic competition remains essentially static and, as a response to demand and cost 'shocks', is flawed. Changes in demand will alter both the position of the two demand curves and also their elasticities. Thus, a fall in market demand will have the effect of shifting the kink and also increasing the elasticity of the upper branch of the demand curve and reducing elasticity in the lower branch. But the theory is silent as to the position of the new location of the kink and how the oligopolistic rivals move towards it. For example, will the new curves meet at the same or a lower price and what behaviours are likely to generate an equilibrium? In short, the model is an **ex post** rationalization rather than an **ex ante** explanation of oligopolistic competition.

From the perspective of strategic interaction, Sweezy's model is at best only a modest attempt at explaining dynamic tacit collusion; it is silent as to how rivals form views of each others' responses. In this respect, Sweezy's model suffers the same criticism as the Cournot and Bertrand models of oligopoly; namely, it is essentially static and firms know for certain how their rivals will respond. Some years before Sweezy introduced the concept of a kinked demand curve, a mathematician, Arthur Bowley, suggested the concept of **conjectural variations** (Bowley, 1924). Conjectural variations are an attempt to explain how, in a world of **imperfect information**, expectations are formed by a firm's decision makers about the reaction of rivals to changes in the firm's tactics or strategy, e.g. an increase in output. The Cournot quantity-setting model was based on the assumption that each oligopolist, in deciding its profit-maximizing output, believed that its rivals would collectively hold their output constant. This static solution can be converted into a simple model of dynamic interactions, incorporating uncertainty, by including conjectural variations in the analysis. The ith oligopolist's conjectural variation can be represented with the following elasticity coefficient:

$$v_i = (\%\Delta Q_{-i})/(\%\Delta q_i) \tag{9.12}$$

where Q_{-i} is the output of all firms in the industry except the ith firm. Thus, the conjectural variation coefficient v_i should be interpreted as measuring the firm's decision makers' collective belief regarding the output response of rivals to a change in its own output (Δq_i). If the ith firm expects its rivals to exactly match its change in output, then $v_i = 1$. For example, a 1 per cent rise in q_i leads to the expectation of a 1 per cent rise in Q_{-i}. If $v_i = 0$, this means that the ith firm believes its rivals will not alter output in response to its output decisions, i.e. the basic Cournot assumption regarding behaviour. Another possibility is $v_i = -1$. This says that if the ith firm increases its output, its rivals will reduce their output to exactly offset the rise in output. In fact, v_i can take a wide range of values reflecting the many factors that enter into a strategic response. Conjectural variations can be incorporated in the ith firm's profit-maximizing price mark-up equation if its market share, s_i, is replaced with the formula $v_i + (1 - v_i)s_i$. Thus, for the ith firm, Equation (9.7) becomes:

$$\frac{P - c_i}{P} = \frac{v_i + (1 - v_i)s_i}{\varepsilon} \tag{9.13}$$

where c_i is its marginal costs. If the ith firm expects an aggressive one-for-one matching of its output decisions $v_i = 1$, the right-hand side of Equation (9.13) reduces to that of a monopolist. $1/\varepsilon$, i.e. if all firms move in unison, then they are in fact acting like one firm, a multi-plant monopolist. If the ith firm expects a passive response to an output decision $v_i = 0$, this reduces Equation (9.13) to the basic Cournot–Nash equilibrium, s_i/ε. As noted above, v_i can take a wide range of values and it is logical to assume that its value is influenced by the size of the firm. If the ith firm only has a small market share, say, $s_i = 0.05$ and $v_i = -0.1$, then the numerator on the right-hand side of Equation (9.13) is negative, i.e. -0.045, which implies (after being divided by the elasticity coefficient) that the firm cannot hold price above marginal costs. The higher the value of the conjectural variation parameter v_i, the greater the incentive for the firm's decision makers to behave co-operatively.

Conjectural variations are a convenient way of parameterizing the uncertainty of rivals' reactions to dynamic strategic changes, but they are silent as to how a firm's decision makers form their views of the likely reaction of rivals to changes in output or price and they are incapable of allowing these views to be modified on the basis of experience. In a world of imperfect information, a firm may not easily observe the response of its rivals to change in its output, but to the extent that over time it may be able to assess how rivals react, this should influence its conjectural variations. It is now widely accepted by economists that a fuller understanding of the strategic behaviour of oligopolists demands more realistic dynamic models. To be of value, dynamic models must have two major advantages: firstly, they must reflect the ability of decision makers to learn about the reactions of their rivals by observing their behaviour over a number of time periods; and, secondly, they must show how tacit or overt collusion in the current period can be compelled by the credible threat of punishment in the future for opportunistic behaviour by a rival in the current period. Paradoxically, aggressive competitive behaviour can be reserved as a threat to a rival who undermines tacit collusion. From the perspective of business strategy, dynamic models need to show how firms might adjust their tactical or strategic behaviour in response to changes in the business environment that is of interest.

Testing Market Power

Competition authorities and academics are constantly seeking new ways of measuring or identifying the existence of oligopoly power. One way in which empirical researchers have attempted to obtain evidence is by making use of conjectural variations. This approach is built on the expectation that a limited market response to a change in an individual firm's output reflects a market that is competitive, while a measurable market response is suggestive of the existence of oligopoly market power. In principle, a conjectural variation approach to measuring market power is based on the specification of an econometric model that allows the empirical data to provide estimates of the size of the conjectural variation's elasticity coefficient.

Although this represents an attractive and practical basis for empirical research, the methodology is open to criticism. It relies crucially on accurate estimates of the underlying market and technological conditions, but above all, on accurate firm-level data. In practice, such data are frequently not available and consequently researchers, more often than not, have to resort to industry-level data, yielding a measure of industry- rather than firm-level market power. The conclusion is that the results derived from a conjectural variation approach to the econometric measurement of oligopolistic market power are greatly weakened by the lack of firm-level data.

A Game Theoretic Approach

In the preceding sections, we have demonstrated how game theory can be used to analyse situations of interdependence. We now take a step further by using game theory to analyse dynamic strategic behaviour. Dynamic behaviour incorporates the ability to learn from experience and also to react to the observed behaviour of rivals. This can be modelled by means of **repeated games**. A repeated or ongoing relationship between players introduces the possibility that resort to opportunistic behaviour (i.e. cheating) by any player is likely to lead to the collapse of co-operation in the future. If the value of longer-term co-operation exceeds the short-term value of opportunistic behaviour, then the desire for an ongoing relationship is likely to encourage rivals to engage in at least tacit collusion. At its simplest, a repeated game is played over two successive time periods, allowing each player to respond in the second period to its rival's actions in the first.

We can demonstrate a two-period game with the simple example set out in Figure 9.11. Once again, the analyses is confined to two firms, A and B, engaged in a quantity-setting strategy. Each firm's strategy consists of two parts: its first period output; and its second period output, which is conditional on its rival's first period output. If both firms choose a non-cooperative stance the Cournot–Nash equilibrium prevails, yielding the pay-offs for both A and B of profits π_{At}, π_{At+1} and π_{Bt}, π_{Bt+1}, respectively, where the subscripts t and t + 1 refer to the two time periods. A co-operative outcome results in both firms constraining output below the Cournot–Nash equilibrium level and consequently profits rise to $\alpha\pi$, where $\alpha > 1$ for both firms for both time periods. If, however, either firm switches to non-cooperative behaviour, having indicated otherwise (i.e. cheats), it will reap the benefits of its rival's reduced output in the form of higher profits, $\beta\pi$, and its rival will suffer reduced profits $\mu\pi$, where $\beta > \alpha > 1 > \mu$.

How will this two-period game be played? In the first period, if either firm cheats, i.e. adopts a non-cooperative stance, it will ensure a non-cooperative solution for the second

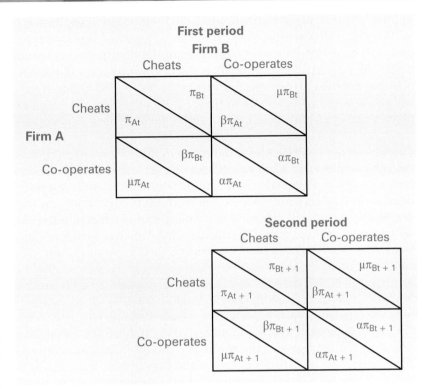

Figure 9.11: A two-period game

period. It might also appear that both firms have an incentive to co-operate in the first period, as failure to do so ensures that non-cooperation will follow in the second period – but this does not automatically follow. To see this, consider Equation (9.14), which shows the present value of the theoretical pay-offs to firm A from co-operating in both periods (where δ represents the discount factor, i.e. $\delta = 1/(1 + r)$ where r is an appropriate rate of interest):

$$PV_A = \alpha\delta\pi_{At} + \alpha\delta^2\pi_{At+1} \qquad (9.14)$$

This pay-off is not as large as the theoretical pay-off shown in Equation (9.15) from adopting a non-cooperative stance in the second period:

$$PV_A = \alpha\delta\pi_{At} + \beta\delta^2\pi_{At+1} \qquad (9.15)$$

Thus, both firms have an incentive to cheat in the second period and, being rational, decision makers will choose a non-cooperative stance in the second period. But if they are likely to choose a non-cooperative stance in the second period, there is no risk of being punished for cheating in the first period. Consequently, there is reason to doubt a signalled intention to co-operate in the first period and rational decision makers are likely to also choose non-cooperation in the first period. Thus, by the process of **backward induction**, also sometimes described as 'rollback', it can be demonstrated that unless the pay-off from co-operating in both periods exceeds that for cheating in either period, the likely outcome of the game is non-cooperation.

In principle, this result could be applied to three-, four-, five-, indeed any finite-period game. As long as the relationship between two players in a Prisoners' Dilemma-type game lasts a fixed and known period of time, the dominant behaviour in the final period is non-cooperation, i.e. to cheat. And backward induction logically predicts that if cheating is the dominant behaviour for the final period, it is also dominant behaviour for the next-to-last period and also for the next-to-next-to-last period, and so on. Working backwards in time, period by period, the conclusion would appear to be that the players cannot credibly threaten to do other than act non-cooperatively.

The logic of applying backward induction to finitely repeated Prisoners' Dilemma-type games is that the **sub-game perfect Nash equilibrium** for the entire game is non-cooperation, which implies that tacit collusion is an unlikely outcome. This general result is known as the *paradox of backward induction*. It is a paradox because the irrefutable logic does not accord with reality; empiricism demonstrates that tacit collusion is a widespread practice in oligopolistic markets. In practice, there are two approaches to countering the paradox. One way is to introduce imperfect and **incomplete information** as well as **bounded rationality**. Firstly, players' information may be imperfect as to the number of times the game will be repeated. Secondly, players may have incomplete information on their rivals, i.e. they do not know their rivals' pay-offs for different strategies. And finally, in reality a firm's decision makers are unlikely to be able to anticipate all possible outcomes. Lack of information as to the number of time periods over which the game will be played increases the present value of the cost of a decision to cheat in an early time period. Say a game is expected to last at least n periods, where n is large and the profit per period from co-operating is $\alpha\pi$, where $\alpha > 1$, and from non-cooperation, π. If firm i cheats in the first period, then unless the pay-off for cheating in that period is very large, it will incur the cost of non-cooperation for an indeterminate number of time periods, which can be represented as:

$$PV_i = \sum_{t=1}^{n} \pi_i (\alpha - 1)\delta^t \qquad (9.16)$$

where δ is the discount factor. Unless α is close to unity and δ significantly less than unity, co-operation is likely to deliver a higher present value. It follows that if the players perceive an infinitely-repeated game, i.e. expect it to continue indefinitely, then co-operation is always the preferred option as retaliation for cheating would also prove more costly.

Infinitely repeated games or **supergames** are well suited for the exploration of the dynamics of tacit collusion. They allow a greater focus on the conditions that would discourage cheating; namely, the credibility of punishment strategies. For example, if $\alpha\pi_t$, where $\alpha > 1$ is the annual flow of profits earned by co-operating, $\beta\pi_t$, where $\beta > \alpha$ is the profit earned by cheating and, $\mu\pi_t$, where $\mu < 1$ is the annual flow of profits if rivals adopt punishment strategies, we have for a single instance of cheating in the first period the following outcome for the ith firm:

$$\beta\pi_{it}\delta + \sum_{t=2}^{\infty} \mu\pi_{it}\delta^t < \sum_{t=1}^{\infty} \alpha\pi_{it}\delta^t \qquad (9.17)$$

providing $\alpha\pi > \mu\pi$, any short-run gains from cheating will be outweighed by the collapse of tacit collusions. Indeed, the inequality Equation (9.17) suggests that only mild punishments (i.e. $\mu < \alpha$) and bounded profits from cheating (i.e. only available for a limited number of periods) are necessary for the inequality in Equation (9.17) to hold if δ is close to unity. But Equation (9.18) also assumes that a firm cheating can be identified and punished. If, in a world of imperfect information, the actions of rivals are not perfectly observed, then tacit collusion may not prevent cheating. Conversely, short detection lags and realistic values for δ make tacit collusion highly feasible.

So far we have tended to focus on quantity-setting supergames, but the foregoing also applies to price-setting games. The general conclusion that tacit collusion is the likely outcome in a supergame is equally applicable to price-setting supergames. Pricing strategy will be explored in more detail in the following chapters, so the issue will not be pursued here. But whether the focus is a quantity-setting or a price-setting strategy game, the general propensity towards a co-operative outcome needs some qualification. The assumption that firms have sufficient, if not perfect, information regarding their rivals, i.e. they can reasonably accurately observe their behaviour, is crucial; whereas a time lag before responding is less critical in supergames. In practice, imperfect information is the norm and it can be very difficult for a firm to interpret market signals. For example, a firm can accurately observe a weakening market price but not the production levels of rivals. This places decision makers within an oligopoly having to distinguish between a downturn in demand and expansion (i.e. cheating) by a rival.

Given a world of imperfect information, efforts by firms to facilitate the exchange of output and pricing information via trade associations, trade magazines and conferences might reasonably be viewed as an attempt to counter the lack of accurate information on the behaviour of their rivals. Firms also have to cope with incomplete information on rivals. A high-cost rival will seek to keep such information private and will therefore opportunistically signal an ability to respond swiftly and effectively to any cheating by rivals. In a world of imperfect and incomplete information, supergames demonstrate the importance of patience, the importance of learning from experiences and the importance of building a **reputation** for responding aggressively to cheating.

The foregoing only scratches the surface of dynamic models of strategic interaction for oligopolists operating in conditions of uncertainty over multiple time periods. For those wishing to go further, we can but indicate some of the areas of interest; not only are we approaching the frontiers of economics, but also the subject is highly mathematical (Shapiro, 1998). If change arises from the strategic manoeuvring of rivals, then we can describe dynamic change as being **endogenous**. Factors here will include the types of strategies discussed in the earlier chapters on firm-level behaviour, such as investment in new capacity and the accumulation of heterogeneous capabilities, as well as the building of horizontal and **vertical relationships**. Such strategies will be driven in large measure by the beliefs and expectations held by senior managers as to the strategic manoeuvring of rival firms. In a dynamic world where future periods are part of the decision-making process, prices and quantities can take on an additional role to that of maximizing rents; namely, that of signalling to rivals and manipulating information.

In practice, the strategic variables available to firms are wider than just output levels and prices. Investment takes on the significance of commitment. An investment in excess capacity sends signals to rivals and potential new entrants regarding future potential behaviour. For example, the combination of holding prices above marginal costs in the presence of excess capacity sends a strong signal to rivals that any attempt, in future periods, to take advantage is likely to be punished by increased output and a lower market price. But physical capacity is not the only type of strategic investment. As dynamic problems inevitably invoke uncertainty about the future, information is also a strategic variable. Investment in acquiring information regarding, say, future demand and costs will allow the individual firm to adjust its own behaviour and also to attempt to influence that of its rivals – e.g. by attempting to convince them that its costs are low.

Strategy can also be driven by external forces and the resulting dynamic change is described as **exogenous**. One obvious external source of change is technological progress, which may act on costs, products or both. Another major influence is **globalization**, where falling trade barriers expose industries to low-cost competition. Yet another example would be a declining industry where demand is falling over time. Factors such as these are bound to be influential when oligopolistic rivals are formulating strategy. Firms whose strategy is to always be the first to adopt a new technology can, if the technology is successful, influence their market share. Though first movers in the area of technology have to bear the risks of unanticipated problems, there are many examples, e.g. the VHS video system, where a follower has eventually gained market advantage from a new product or process.

In terms of studying and analysing the link between the tactical and strategic choices made by a firm's decision makers and the nature of its industry, its market position and its configuration of activities, game theory is an invaluable tool. As explained above, supergames provide a framework for analysing the logical, dynamic consequences of strategic behaviour. Above all, such models highlight the importance of information and beliefs about the reactions of rivals and the conditions required if firms are to engage in tacit collusion. But game theory is not, and cannot be, a general dynamic theory of business strategy and the building of competitive advantage. It is but one of a number of complementary approaches to understanding strategy and competitive advantage that includes Porter's Five Forces Model, the building of firm-level efficiencies through governance structures and firm-level capabilities.

Vitamins and Healthy Competition

The EU market for pharmaceutical vitamins was worth around €800 million at the end of the 1990s. In May 1999, following a number of complaints, the European Commission opened an investigation into a number of companies producing vitamin supplements for the food, animal feed and cosmetic industries. In November 2001, the Commission announced the result of its investigation and fined several companies, including Hoffmann-La Roche and BASF AG, a total of €855 million. The bulk of the fine, €758 million, was levied on these two companies, who were deemed to have played a major role in setting up eight (separate vitamins) secret market colluding agreements. The size of the fine reflected the Commission's concern at the sheer scale of the collusive agreement and the fact that the substances concerned were judged vital elements for nutrition and a healthy life.

The participants in each of these illegal market-fixing arrangements agreed to fix prices and adhere to sales quotas, as well as exchange sales and prices data and participate in regular meetings to monitor their collusive arrangements. The prime mover and main beneficiary of these schemes was Hoffmann-La Roche, the largest vitamin producer in the world, with some 50 per cent of the overall market. The involvement of some of its most senior executives confirmed, according to the Commission, that the 'market agreements' were part of a strategic plan conceived at the highest levels to control the world market in vitamins by illegal means.

Cartels and Industrial Policies

The previous section examined the factors that open rational decision makers to the potential advantages of tacit collusion – in effect, to co-operate in price- or quantity-setting without resort to explicit or formal collusion. Collusion, be it formal or tacit, is prohibited under Article 81 of EU competition policy. Formal collusion involves establishing and maintaining a **cartel**, whereas tacit collusion can achieve the same outcome, but arises solely from the recognition by decision makers that robust competition is not in their best interest. Below we will examine how the authorities attempt to place legal obstacles in the way of collusion, but first we will examine why oligopolists, given a choice, might prefer to form a cartel rather than engage in tacit collusion.

Whether firms collude tacitly or overtly, they face a number of problems in ensuring that co-operating firms do not cheat. In a world of imperfect information, it may take a considerable time lag before a cheating firm is identified and this may encourage a firm to boost market share or give secret price discounts. Another problem arises if firms' costs or demands differ markedly. To see this, consider Figure 9.12, which illustrates the issue with the aid of a duopoly: firms A and B. To simplify matters, we assume that both firms have equal market shares. This means that both firms (given the output of the other) face the residual demand curve, D_R, that coincides with the market demand curve's marginal revenue curve, i.e. $MR = D_R$. In this situation, each firm's MR curve is not the MR associated with market demand, but the MR associated with D_R, i.e. MR_R. The MCs for A and B are represented by MC_A and MC_B, respectively, and the industry's supply curve is given by the horizontal summation of the two marginal cost curves, MC_{A+B}. The problem is revealed by inspection. The profit-maximizing price for A is P_A and for B is P_B. Neither of these prices maximize industry profits, which requires an industry output of Q_M. In order to achieve Q_M firm A has to reduce its profit-maximizing output from W to Y and firm B should increase its output from X to Z.

Both of these problems can be solved by the formation of a cartel. The pooling of information within a cartel makes it much easier to overcome imperfect information on individual firm's costs. Members of the cartel are more likely to accept the existence of varying costs if confirmed by the cartel and, most importantly, a cartel can, in principle, facilitate the side-payments that would be necessary to compensate those firms whose profits would fall as a result of joining the cartel. But even with cartels, firms are unlikely to have complete information on other members of the cartel and in industries with rapid

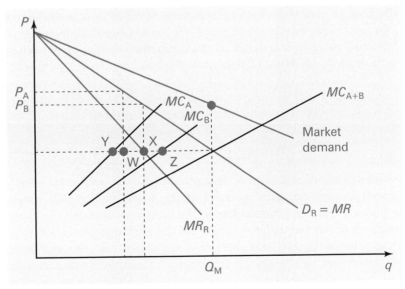

Figure 9.12: Colluding when costs differ

technological change are likely to find it particularly difficult to reach collusive agreements. Reaching an agreement is only the start of the process. Having reached a collusive agreement to raise prices, the more successful the cartel in raising prices, the greater the incentive for individual firms to *chisel*. Also, the more successful a cartel, the more attractive it will be to firms operating in the industry; but the larger the number of sellers in the cartel, the more difficult it will be to detect a secret price cutter. Although important, a heightened ability to detect cheating is not sufficient; the cartel must be able to deter such behaviour – that is, the cartel must be able to punish the offender.

As discussed in Chapter 4, horizontal relationships, a form of collusion – whether tacit or overt – can serve to achieve multiple goals including learning, the utilization of under-exploited capabilities and the reduction of risk. Here, we are concerned with prices and output, but in all cases there needs to be a credible threat to the firm that is tempted to act opportunistically. In the case of the horizontal relationships discussed in Chapter 4, this discipline was provided by the loss of reputation and the longer-term cost of being excluded from knowledge-enhancing collaborative ventures. In the case of horizontal collusion to secure market share or a higher price, the credible threat must involve the certainty of a longer-term output or price penalty if caught cheating. Pre-commitment is a way of making a threat credible. For example, if the cartel members pre-commit to match a lower price – via a 'most favoured customer contract clause' – their hands are tied and any firm tempted to cheat will rationalize that any gain will be short lived.

Given the interdependence of the strategic decisions of oligopolistic firms and the positive benefits of co-operation, the behaviour and outcome of 'competition' in oligopolistic markets is in practice 'planned'. Largely as a result of the developments in game theory set out above, most countries accept the need for some form of competition policy. Behind this acceptance is the belief that competitive markets are socially optimal and that therefore oligopolistic industries must be 'encouraged' to behave competitively by means of competition policy. In the case of natural monopolies where competition is not an option, competitive outcomes should be mimicked by resorting to **nationalization** or **regulation**. Competition policy, nationalization and regulatory policies are all elements in the set of industrial policies; that is, policies designed to influence industrial change and performance by affecting, or overriding, market incentives. What follows is a brief overview of industrial and competition policy in relation to oligopolistic markets and the focus is more on competition policy than industrial policy. More detail on the competition policy issues raised can be found in texts devoted to the subject, e.g. Furse (2002).

Competition policy does not exist in a vacuum; it, along with industry policy, is an expression of society's values and aims. The founding fathers of the European Community gave a high priority to competition policy. The **Treaty of Rome** contained provisions to outlaw both private and publicly owned companies engaging in uncompetitive behaviour and the **European Commission** was given the responsibility for ensuring that competitive market forces would be the basis upon which internal Community trade would grow. This presumption in favour of market forces was in some respects challenged by the industrial policies of the founding member states and, indeed, the widespread application of interventionist **Keynesian** macroeconomic policies at the time. The rather cosy view of a world in which industrial structure and development can be left to competitive market forces is confronted by issues such as economies of scale, tacit collusion and labour market rigidities that increase the social costs of adjustment. Thus, from the start there was a tension, if not a fundamental contradiction, between the economic (and political) integration of member states – which implies the removal of trade barriers and greater influence for the forces of competition – and attempts by the governments of member states to enhance the competitive performance of their national industries, if not to support and protect them.

The founding fathers gave the Commission overall control of competition policy and extensive powers to investigate and punish prohibited behaviour. Nevertheless, political realities ruled out a frontal assault by the Commission on national industrial policies deemed to be

Table 9.1: A nomenclature of industrial policies

Policies	Description
1. Passive and negative	Competition policy and regulation to prevent the abuse of market power
2. Passive and positive	Creation of a favourable economic climate via macroeconomic and supply-side policies
3. Active and positive	Co-ordination of economic policies, including direct and indirect support for potential 'winners'
4. Active but negative	Sectoral policies, with barriers to restrict competition
5. Direct involvement and control	The state enterprises and partnerships

in conflict with the aims of competition policy. The Commission had to accept reality and find a way to allow competition policies and protective industrial policies to co-exist. Industrial policy can generally and conveniently be placed under five headings, as set out in Table 9.1. The policies shown are not mutually exclusive and most member states use all five of the policies shown. A minimalist approach to industrial policy would be represented by policies 1 and 2. Under policy 1, the abuse of market power by a dominant firm or oligopoly acting in concert is condemned. Competition policy is geared towards preventing behaviour likely to frustrate the 'proper functioning' of the market and thereby to ensure that the allocation of productive resources is determined by the free choices of consumers rather than the exercise of market power by suppliers. Policy 2 seeks to use fiscal and monetary policies to create a business environment conducive to competition and an improved industrial economic performance. The achievement of price stability, limited government borrowing and the orderly conduct of labour relations would be the key objectives of government economic policy. Increasingly **supply-side** policy is focused on particular issues, e.g. productivity and market incentives.

Policy 3 represents what is commonly understood to be industrial policy; that is, governments engage in proactive policies to directly influence the restructuring of a failing industry or the development of new industrial capacity and skills. Since the 1970s, and the rise of Japan and the Asian Tigers, positive industrial policy has been given a new urgency within Western Europe. National governments selected certain industries, e.g. computers, as of strategic importance and therefore their development justified state support in the form of funding, credit, information and education. But, given limited resources, the state is also forced to 'pick winners' who benefit from active supply-side policies. Policy 4 best captures the approach of most Community members to industrial policy in the 1960s and 1970s – in essence, a defensive policy, driven largely by political consideration to help 'traditional' or 'declining' industries. This type of industrial policy usually includes **voluntary restraint agreements** (VRA) and other non-tariff barriers to restrict competition and is ultimately a negative policy, because rather than foster change it is aimed at maintaining the *status quo* by restricting competition. Policy 5 ranges from the nationalization of industries to public–private arrangements where firms nominally in the private sector are partly or wholly owned by the government. Such firms may pursue a number of goals, ranging from the production of military products to the social purpose of reducing regional employment.

Despite the prevailing climate of intervention in the 1950s, the Treaty of Rome did not mention industrial policy – nor was it mentioned in the 1986 **Single European Act** (SEA) – and the industrial economic history of the Community could be characterized as the slow but steady ascendancy of competition policy to dominate industrial policy. Since the founding of the European Community, industrial policy has been the province of national governments. In the 1960s, it was mainly driven by the desire on the part of member states to catch up with the technologically more advanced US and the increasingly threatening Japan. During the 1970s, the emphasis switched to defending more traditional industries, e.g. steel, as growing global competition threatened the economic viability of labour-intensive primary industries in high-wage, developed nations. It was also the decade that witnessed the demise of Keynesianism and the rise of 'new classical economics', which sought to convince governments of the merits of deregulation and reduced intervention. To varying degrees, these views started to gain influence from the start of the 1980s and industrial policies in all member states began to change, ushering in greater market liberalization. Consequently, member state industrial policies have been converging towards a greater emphasis on competition policies; a process that has been greatly helped by the advent of the single market. In many respects France, with its traditional use of intervention and state planning, is the most reluctant; but attitudes are changing, demonstrated in particular by the wave of privatization at the end of the 1980s and in the early 1990s.

Thus, the 1990s witnessed a shift in industrial policies by member states placing less emphasis on policies 4 and 5 in Table 9.1 and more on policies 1 to 3 e.g. the **Lisbon strategy**. Nevertheless, the continued existence of state-owned enterprises remains particularly awkward for the Commission. With state-owned enterprises, it is impossible to distinguish between legitimate investment in the business and subsidies designed to provide a competitive advantage. Even if it were possible to calculate the level of investment that might be made by a similar enterprise if it was in private ownership, the authorities still face a difficult problem. Namely, what is the purpose of taking a firm into public ownership if private sector rules are to apply? With the current trend towards privatization, this is a problem that is past its peak and will probably be largely solved within a decade.

One consequence of these changing attitudes is that fears that the single market would encourage greater emphasis on policies 4 and 5 – the so-called Fortress Europe – have proved unfounded. Article 130 of the 1992 Treaty on European Union (Maastricht Treaty) explicitly excludes the Community from action that could lead to the distortion of competition, e.g. picking winners. Community measures are allowed only in support of action taken by member states. To the extent that the Community has an industrial policy, the emphasis is comprehensively focused on horizontal measures – that is, initiatives aimed at influencing the overall competitive framework in which firms operate, i.e. policy 2 in Table 9.1. Such policies are to be directed towards education and science and include support for generic technologies such as ICT. In practice, this constrains the Commission to use its limited funds to provide some indirect aid. For example, the *European Strategic Programme for Research and Development* (ESPRIT) in information technology is representative of the EU's approach to industrial policy.

The EU, unlike member states, lacks both the funds and the legal status to provide direct aids to industries. Without a fundamental change in attitudes and a substantial increase in the funds available to the Commission, Community industrial policy will remain a matter largely for member states and hence unplanned at the European level. Despite changing attitudes at the member state level, governments continue to provide a vast range of subsidies and aids to their industries. A task force was set up and in 1989 produced the first survey of state aids in the Community, showing that these amounted to just over €100 billion per annum and within the (then) 12 member states they accounted for between 10 and 20 per cent of public expenditure and between 3 and 5 per cent of GDP. Subsequent surveys suggest that state aids have fallen, but only slightly – the last published estimate is for 2003, which shows national aids totalling €90 billion for a Community of 15. These figures suggest that despite the efforts of the Commission the granting of state aids remains a major instrument of industrial policy at the level of the nation state. There is no evidence that member states are prepared to hand over such powers to the Commission. In any event, there appears little consensus amongst Community governments as to industrial policy – other than convergence to the broad areas represented by policies 1–3 in Table 9.1. The French government is the strongest advocate of an industrial policy to foster Euro-champions in place of the former approach of national champions, but such an active policy does not find favour with the British or the Germans. Even if there was a consensus for a Community-wide industrial policy, the instruments available at a European level for such a policy are very limited and the Commission appears to have reconciled itself to the global realities, i.e. competition policy with its emphasis on liberalization rather than industrial policy.

The unique position of the Commission and the Community's competition policy means that both the policy and Commission officials have had to address the behaviour and actions of both private companies and member state governments. As set out in Chapter 1, policy towards private companies is covered in Articles 81 and 82 of the Treaty of Rome and of particular relevance here is Article 81, which outlaws agreements, either vertical or horizontal, between companies that are designed to restrict or distort, 'competition within the common market'. The actions of governments, as they affect competition, are limited under Article 37, which deals with state monopolies, Article 86, which deals with companies to whom their governments have granted special or exclusive rights, and Articles 87–89, which deal with state aids. Article 81(1) sets out the behaviours that are prohibited and is deliberately worded so as to include all agreements between rivals and applies equally to formal and tacit collusion. It is this aspect in particular that makes the application of Article 81 so fraught with problems. Apart from the difficulty of detecting tacit collusion, the authorities must also be able to separate conduct which is the result of each firm responding non-cooperatively to the actions of rivals.

During the Community's formative years competition policy developed uncontroversially, partly because the founding member states were enjoying rapid economic growth and partly because the Commission was conscious of the need to avoid conflict with **The Council**; from its earliest days, the Commission took a pragmatic approach to competition issues. In 1962, when it called for firms to provide information on collusive agreements that might fall within the provisions of Article 81, it was swamped with more than 35,000 applications for clearance. Using its discretion, most of these were dealt with by **block exemptions**. The small number of cases pursued to a formal decision reflected reality and were selected on the basis of establishing policy precedents. Traditionally, the Commission alone has the power to select cases and it is then responsible for the investigation, prosecution and decision, which includes the power to impose fines where breaches of the law have occurred. The use of the Commission's powers to levy fines is overseen by the Court of First Instance, with the possibility of an appeal to the European Court of Justice. But the use of the Commission as effectively police officer, prosecutor and judge, coupled with a lack of transparency in its formal procedures, has remained a matter of concern.

The Commission's pragmatic approach was very much in evidence as economic conditions worsened in the 1970s. In the harsh conditions of the 1970s, the Commission was forced to take an almost perverse approach to competition. As European industries attempted to come to terms with a quad-rupling in oil prices and rising inflation, so member states sought to protect their industrial bases by aiding and encouraging restructuring. Member states redoubled their efforts to build national cham-pions, i.e. dominant firms, capable of challenging the power of US and Japanese multinationals. The intention was to improve international competitiveness by providing state aids and facilitating merg-ers. Such behaviour constitutes an aggressive, active industrial policy and as such is in direct conflict with the aims of competition policy. Under Article 81(3), the Commission had the sole power to exercise discretion with respect to Article 81(1) and in the late 1970s, as observed above, it made full use of these powers. Indeed, on occasion it did more than exercise discretion – it actively supported the creation of crisis cartels. For example, the Commission required 11 dominant Community synthetic fibres firms to sign an agreement to co-operate in reducing capacity and market sharing. This was an example of a Community-wide industrial policy and, as such, in direct conflict with the EC's competition rules.

The swing back to the dominance of competition policy came with the preparations for the single market programme and with it – or because of it – the revival of the Community's dynamism. Peter Sutherland, the Commissioner responsible for competition at the time, took full advantage of the single market programme to enforce the Community's competition rules with increased vigour. For example, in 1986 15 oil companies were found guilty under Article 81 of price fixing and market sharing and were fined €57 million. Under Peter Sutherland, the Commission also began to take a tougher line on state aids. Since the coming into effect of the single market in 1993, the Community has continued to give a high priority to competition. But conscious of the need to balance the pursuit of competitive markets with the advantages of agreements amongst firms to share information, under-take joint ventures and build alliances, it has also striven to adopt an appropriate and, where possible, informal approach.

A collusive agreement between two or more firms will not be caught within Article 81(1) if it does not prevent, restrict or distort competition and, traditionally, the Commission confirmed such a posi-tion by granting negative clearance. But the time and cost of notifying the Commission and the competition officials' increasing workload steadily built up a case for reform. The Commission took the opportunity of the enlargement of the European Union to embrace Central and Eastern European countries to publish significant reforms to the conduct of competition policy. One of these reforms has the effect of no longer requiring firms entering into an agreement to notify the Commission pro-viding they have taken steps to ensure the agreement is not caught within Article 81(1). In addition, a certified *de minimis* rule has been increased so that agreements between competing firms accounting for less than 15 per cent of the relevant market are deemed to escape the prohibition of Article 81(1). The Commission's power under Article 81(3) to grant exemption is similar to, but not the same as, the application of the 'rule of reason' in American antitrust law. Under the rule of reason, a plaintiff must show that the collusion is likely to damage competition. If this is established, it is then up to the defendant to demonstrate that clear benefits flow from the agreement and that the agreement is necessary for these benefits to be realized, e.g. an agreement to share transport costs.

Under Article 81(3) the procedure is less formal, leaving the Commission maximum flexibility in dealing with essentially illegal agreements that offer wider benefits. Under the reforms announced to coincide with the enlargement of the Community on 1 May 2004, the Commission effectively re-moved its monopoly on the application of Article 81(3). In future, the Commission will act on complaints on its own initiative, but it will do so alongside member states' competition authorities and costs. The intention is to speed up procedures, cut the cost of compliance and reduce regulatory uncertainty. The new decentralized framework is to be underpinned by a European Competition Network to encourage co-operation and congruence in the application of Community competition rules. In effect, the Commission is empowering national competition authorities and national courts to apply Article 81(3).

Airbus Industries

Back in the 1960s, when government intervention represented the main instrument of industrial policy, three European aircraft manufacturers – Hawker Siddeley Aviation (UK), Sud-Aviation (France) and Deutsche Airbus Gmbh (Germany) – decided to jointly design a wide-bodied aircraft. In September 1967, a meeting between ministers from these countries agreed to invest €1 billion (at today's prices) in the development of what was to become the A300. The vision was an aircraft capable of carrying up to 300 passengers for a distance of 3,000 km at an economic cost. The aircraft design was very advanced for its time, in fact so advanced that the British government decided not to fund the construction of a plane that its 'experts' said would not be viable. Presumably these same 'experts' considered Concorde to be viable. Hawker Siddeley Aviation was the only manufacturer from Britain to join the consortium that by 1970 included Fokker-VFM (the Netherlands) and CASA (Spain).

The consortium made good progress, confounding their detractors and in 1970 Airbus Industries was officially created. Britain now became a full member along with Belgium, France, German, the Netherlands and Spain. Airbus Industries set about constructing a 250-seat aircraft called the A300B. Initially, the aircraft was to be powered by two Rolls-Royce RB207 engines, but Rolls-Royce decided to stop the development of the RB207 and concentrate instead on the development of RB211 for the Lockheed Tristar – a decision that actually resulted in Rolls-Royce going bankrupt. The first prototype A300B made its maiden flight in October 1972. The first commercial flight between Paris and London took place in May 1974 under Air France's colours. Despite the fact that the A300B was a very advanced plane, the airlines remained sceptical and Airbus decided to build a new version of the A300B capable of flying 270 passengers 4,800 km and later 5,800 km. Now the airlines started to take an interest and in the years since, Airbus Industries has developed bigger and more efficient versions of the A300 and in the process has overtaken Boeing as the world's number-one producer of wide-bodied aircraft.

Airbus Industries' A300 was in part the result of an industrial policy that placed a high emphasis on developing in Europe the ability to build aircraft capable of competing with Boeing. The coming together of Europe's leading aircraft manufacturers to counter the world dominance of Boeing – in effect to create a duopoly in the production of wide-bodied aircraft – would not have been possible without the financial support of European governments.

Concluding Thoughts

The study of oligopoly is central to an understanding of business strategy. Unlike the polar extremes of pure monopoly and perfect competition, these market structures are more in accordance with the experience of most firms. In practice, most firms face only a limited number of rivals – through location or specialization – and seek competitive advantage by differentiating their products. In such a world, concepts such as interdependence, reactive behaviour and product positioning are the very essence of competitive rivalry and strategic manoeuvrings.

In this chapter, we have identified and critically examined the behaviour predicted by the seminal models of non-cooperative oligopoly and more recent game-theoretic models. We have demonstrated using the Cournot and Bertrand models that, under oligopoly, the likely outcome is that market output will be higher, and prices and profit mark-ups lower than would be the case under pure monopoly. We have also shown that this mark-up will vary according to the individual oligopolist's market share and (assuming differentiated products) the price elasticity of demand for the firm's output. We have also demonstrated, using game theory, that the non-cooperative Cournot and Bertrand equilibrium can be bettered if firms are prepared to engage in collusive behaviour. Game theory's ability to analyse dynamic interactions makes it particularly appropriate for analysing the strategic manoeuvrings of firms under imperfect competition, which is a dynamic process not a static event. Competition is dynamic in that the behaviour of rivals in the next and subsequent periods will be influenced by behaviour in the current period. This aspect of imperfect competition greatly increases the importance of information and signalling as well as collusion, whether tacit or overt. One of the great advantages of a game theoretic approach is that by extending the interaction between rivals over an infinite number of time periods, the incentive to collude and the credibility of punishment for cheating are revealed.

Overt collusion to fix prices or market shares, i.e. a cartel, is outlawed under European Community competition policy, but tacit collusion to achieve the same ends is difficult to detect. In principle, a cartel has some benefits in policing an agreement and where firms would lose by joining, it can facilitate side payments. Not all collusion is prohibited by the European competition authorities. By applying a **rule of reason** approach, where collusion results in lower costs, e.g. by sharing distribution, or the more rapid development of a new technology, the authorities are likely to judge that on balance the collusion is in the public interest. Moreover, the industrial policies of member states frequently involve collusion between the government and industries in an attempt to achieve competitive advantage. Nevertheless, imperfectly competitive market structures do offer scope for behaviour that results in a loss of consumers' welfare from paying higher prices than would be the case under perfect competition. Moreover, by engaging in collusive behaviour firms may have a lower incentive to invest in new technologies, products and processes. We will return to these issues in later chapters, but in the firm belief that competitive market structures benefit both current and future consumers' welfare, the European Community has at its core an extensive and powerful competitive policy.

Key Learning Points

- Many industries, particularly when separated into strategic groups or geographical locations, are characterized by imperfect competition, where only a small number of firms compete for market share.

- Such markets are described as oligopolistic and represent situations of strategic interdependence. Oligopolists have a degree of power, but in making decisions regarding output or selling prices the outcome depends critically on the actions of rivals in response.

- The seminal models of oligopolistic behaviour were developed by Cournot and Bertrand. In both cases, firms act non-cooperatively to maximize their profits by assuming the output or prices set by their rivals will remain unchanged.

- The problem with the Cournot and Bertrand models is that they are essentially static. In practice, strategic interaction is dynamic, whereby competitors learn from the past behaviour of their rivals and adjust to changes in the business environment.

- By employing game theory to analyse dynamic interactions, it can be shown that both the Cournot and Bertrand non-cooperative outcomes can be bettered if rivals are prepared to collude, either overtly or tacitly.

- Sweezy's model of the 'kinked' demand curve is an early attempt to cite tacit collusion as an explanation for the frequently observed characteristic of price rigidity in oligopolistic markets, but it lacks the explanatory powers of game theory.

- The great advantage of the game theoretic approach to analysing oligopolistic competition is that repeated games can incorporate learning and strategic responses.

- Infinitely repeated games, or supergames, are well suited to analysing the incentives and efficacy of collusive behaviour. They demonstrate the credibility of a threat to punish a rival for cheating and hence explain why collusion is a likely outcome of strategic interaction.

- Tacit collusion to achieve price- or quantity-setting outcomes is illegal but more difficult to detect than the formation of a cartel. A cartel has a number of advantages in ensuring compliance and is likely to be exempt from legal proceeding if judged to be serving an overall economic benefit, e.g. lower transport costs.

- Industrial policy is a generic description of government policies aimed at creating efficient industries and some industrial policies amount to overt collusion between government and businesses to achieve specific goals.

- Competition policy is correctly viewed as a passive but important element of industrial policy. Community competition policy – essentially Articles 81 and 82 of the European Treaty – dominates for firms operating within the European Community.

- Article 81(1), in principle, prohibits all collusive agreements, but owing to Article 81(3), the authorities have been in a position to apply a 'rule of reason' and more recently they have extended this power to national authorities.

Exercises

9.1 Explain what is meant by the statement: 'Cournot and Bertrand strategies are just special cases, indeed polar opposites, of assumptions regarding the elasticity of an oligopolist's supply curves.'

9.2 Bowley's concept of conjectural variations provides a convenient way of parameterizing oligopolistic behaviour. How would you expect the conjectural variations coefficient to be influenced by:

- Sunk cost barriers to entry?

- Publicity emanating from the fining of the members of a cartel?

- The arrival of a new low-cost technology?

9.3 In what way do repeated games represent an advance on Sweezy's kinked demand curve model as a means of explaining the strategic behaviour of oligopolists?

9.4 The Commission by its actions under Article 81(3) has already adopted an approach to collusive agreements that in effect is similar to the rule of reason. What might be the advantages of its sharing of its powers under Article 81(3) with national competition authorities and countries?

Problems

9.1 Consider a market for apples in a remote rural town. Demand is given by $Q = 1,000 - 1,000p$. The market is supplied by two growers, hence $Q = q_1 + q_2$:

(a) Define the residual demand curve for grower 1 selling q_1.

(b) If grower 1 believes that grower 2 will sell 300 apples, calculate grower 1's profit-maximizing output.

9.2 Two firms compete with differentiated variants of the same product. Each has a constant marginal cost of c per unit and each faces the demand curve $q_i = a - p_i - $

$\lambda(p_i - p_A)$, where p_A is the average price, i.e. $p_A = 0.5(p_1 + p_2)$. The function λ means the degree of product differentiation – if $\lambda = 0$ there is no substitution:

(a) Rewrite the conditions for profit maximization as $(p_i - c)(\Delta q_i / \Delta p_i) - q_i = 0$ and use it to obtain both firms' reaction functions.

(b) Obtain the equilibrium price by solving the equations for both reaction functions.

(c) Graph the reaction functions. Show how they shift as λ changes from 0 to 2.

References

Bertrand, J. (1883), 'Review of *Théorie Mathematique de la Richesse Sociale*', *Journal des Savants*, pp. 449–508.

Bowley, A. (1924) *Mathematical Foundations of Economics*, Oxford University Press, New York.

Cournot, A. (1838) *Recherches sur les Principles Mathématiques de la Théorie des Richesses* [Transl. 1987, *Researches into the Mathematical Principles of the Theory of Wealth*] Macmillan, New York.

Fisher, F. (1989) 'Games economists play: a non co-operative view', *Rand Journal of Economics*, vol. 20, pp. 113–124.

Furse, M. (2002) *Competition Law of the UK and the EC*, 4th edn, Oxford University Press, Oxford.

Nash, J. (1950), 'Non co-operative games', *Annals of Mathematics*, vol. 54, pp. 286–295.

Shapiro, C. (1998) 'Theories of oligopoly behaviour' in *Handbook of Industrial Organisation*, R. Schmalensee and R. Willig (eds), North-Holland, Netherlands.

Sweezy, P.A. (1939), 'Demand under conditions of oligopoly', *Journal of Political Economy*, vol. 47, pp. 568–573.

APPENDIX 9A
THE ANALYTICS OF
MONOPOLY

A single supplier of a product faces the downward-sloping inverse demand curve:

$$P = \alpha - \beta Q \qquad\qquad (9A.1)$$

where P is the market price, Q the quantity supplied and α and β are positive constants. Writing Δ for a small change in the firm's output, ΔQ, the effect as shown in Figure 9A.1 will be an inverse change, ΔP, in the market price.

The changes shown in Figure 9A.1 will alter the firm's total revenue, ΔTR, in the following manner:

$$\Delta TR = P.\Delta Q + \Delta P.Q \qquad\qquad (9A.2)$$

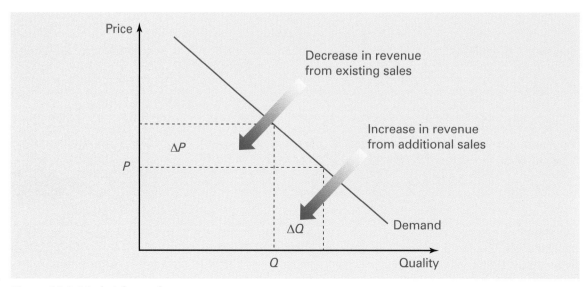

Figure 9A.1: Market demand

where P is the new market price. What we are interested in is the firm's marginal revenue, MR, which is the change in revenue resulting from a marginal change in output, thus:

$$MR = \frac{\Delta TR}{\Delta Q} = P + \frac{\Delta P}{\Delta Q}.Q \qquad (9A.3)$$

where $\Delta P/\Delta Q$ is the decline in price necessary to sell the additional unit of output. We can now rewrite Equation (9A.3) to get:

$$MR = P\left[1 + \frac{\Delta P}{\Delta Q}.\frac{Q}{P}\right] \qquad (9A.4)$$

but the second term in the squared parenthesis is the inverse of the price elasticity of demand. Writing ε for the elasticity of demand, it is defined as:

$$\varepsilon = \frac{\%\Delta Q}{\%\Delta P} = \frac{\Delta Q}{\Delta P}.\frac{P}{Q} \qquad (9A.5)$$

where $\%\Delta$ means percentage change. Given the inverse relationship between price and quantity, the elasticity coefficient is always negative, but inserting its absolute value in Equation (9A.4), we can write:

$$MR = P\left[1 - \frac{1}{\varepsilon}\right] \qquad (9A.6)$$

All firm's maximize profits when the addition to revenue from selling one more unit of output just equals the extra cost of producing the last unit of output, which under the law of diminishing returns will be rising. The cost of producing the last unit of output is the firm's marginal cost, MC, of production. Hence, the profit-maximizing condition is given by:

$$MR = MC \qquad (9A.7)$$

and from Equation (9A.6), the firm's profit-maximizing condition is:

$$MC = P\left[1 - \frac{1}{\varepsilon}\right] \qquad (9A.8)$$

By rearranging Equation (9A.8) and dividing through by P, we get the profit-maximizing price–cost mark-up more generally referred to as the ***Lerner index*** of market power:

$$\frac{P - MC}{P} = \frac{1}{\varepsilon} \qquad (9A.9)$$

Equation (9A.9) shows that the monopolist's profit-maximizing price should be close to MC when demand is very price elastic. When demand is relatively price inelastic, the mark-up may be substantial.

APPENDIX 9B
SOME ANALYTICS OF OLIGOPOLY

The market clearing price, P, is determined by the aggregate supply, Q, where $Q = \sum_{i=1}^{n} q_i$, giving the inverse (market) demand curve:

$$P = \alpha - \beta Q \tag{9B.1}$$

where α and β are positive constants. Writing Δ for a small change in the ith firm's output, (Δq_i), will alter the market price and the change in its revenue will be:

$$\Delta TR_i = P\Delta q_i - \Delta P q_i \tag{9B.2}$$

where P is the new market price and ΔP the change in price. From Equation (9B.2), we can derive the ith firm's marginal revenue function by dividing through by Δq_i, i.e. $MR_i = \Delta TR_i / \Delta q_i$:

$$MR_i = P - \frac{\Delta P}{\Delta Q} \cdot q_i \tag{9B.3}$$

multiplying and dividing the right-hand side by q_i/Q, we get:

$$MR_i = P - \frac{\Delta P}{\Delta Q} \cdot q_i \cdot \frac{Q}{q_i} \cdot \frac{q_i}{Q} \tag{9B.4}$$

and recognizing that q_i/Q is the ith firm's market share, i.e. s_i Equation (9B.4) reduces to:

$$MR_i = P[1 - \frac{1}{\varepsilon_i}]s_i \tag{9B.5}$$

where $\varepsilon > 0$ is the market price elasticity of demand. The profit-maximizing condition for the ith firm is then given by:

$$\frac{P - c_i}{P} = \frac{s_i}{\varepsilon} \tag{9B.6}$$

where c_i is the ith firm's marginal cost. If all the firms in the oligopoly have an identical market share, then (9B.6) reduces to:

$$\frac{P - c_i}{P} = \frac{1}{n\varepsilon} \tag{9B.7}$$

where n is the number of firms. Equation (9B.7) captures the notion that firms of relatively equal size are more likely to price competitively and as the number of firms grows, so the mark-up on marginal costs reduces towards zero.

APPENDIX 9C
BERTRAND
PRICE-SETTING
MODEL

Focusing on the ith firm, if P represents the average price charged by the ith firm's competitors, firm i's demand curve is given by:

$$q_i = \alpha - \beta P_i + \lambda P \tag{9C.1}$$

where P_i is the price charged by the ith firm for its differentiated product. As $P_i q_i$ equals the ith firm's total revenue (TR_i), multiplying Equation (9C.1) by P_i generates:

$$TR_i = \alpha P_i - \beta P_i^2 + \lambda P_i P \tag{9C.2}$$

For a small change in price (ΔP), Equation (9C.2) becomes:

$$\Delta TR_i = \alpha \Delta P_i - \beta[(P_i + \Delta P)(P_i + \Delta P) - P^2] + \lambda \Delta P_i P \tag{9C.3}$$

For a very small change in price, the second expression on the right reduces to $-\beta 2\Delta P.P_i + \Delta P^2$. As ΔP is very small, ΔP^2 will approach zero and thus Equation (9C.3) becomes:

$$\Delta TR_i = \alpha \Delta P_i - \beta 2\Delta P.P_i + \lambda \Delta P_i P \tag{9C.4}$$

and from Equation (9C.4) we can derive the ith firm's marginal revenue function with respect to a change in price. As $MR_i = \Delta TR/\Delta P_i$, by dividing Equation (9C.4) by ΔP_i, we obtain:

$$MR_i = \alpha - 2\beta P_i + \lambda P \tag{9C.5}$$

and setting marginal cost (MC) equal to marginal revenue in order to maximize profits, we have:

$$MC_i = \alpha - 2\beta P_i + \lambda P \tag{9C.6}$$

In order to simplify matters, we can assume that $MC = 0$ without any loss of generality and by rearranging Equation (9C.6) we obtain the ith firm's *reaction function*:

$$P_i = \frac{\alpha}{2\beta} + \frac{\lambda}{2\beta} P \tag{9C.7}$$

CHAPTER 10

THE DOMINANT FIRM AND PREDATION

Introduction

The previous chapter presented a number of models designed to aid an understanding of the strategic behaviour of oligopolists. Implicitly, these models characterized rivalry between firms of a similar size and market power. This chapter is concerned with the strategic behaviour of a firm that has a large share of an industry's sales. There are many examples of such industry structures persisting for many years, where one large firm accounts for a substantial share of an industry's output and a tail of significantly smaller rivals supplies the remainder. For example, Eastman-Kodak, IBM and Boeing each accounted for more than 60 per cent of the sales in their respective industries over many years. Such industries are described as containing a **dominant firm** and a tail of **fringe competitors**. A dominant firm is not a **monopolist**, but such firms have enormous power to act independently, and in so doing are capable of influencing the performance and strategic behaviour of their smaller rivals.

Dominance is a legal as well as an economic concept. European competition law defines dominance as the economic power that enables a firm – or a group of firms acting collusively – to hinder efficient competition for a specific product. There is no presumption in the European Community's competition policy that the possession of a dominant position is unacceptable in itself. What is unacceptable is the abuse of a dominant position. A dominant firm faces a downward-sloping **demand curve** and from a legal perspective much depends on the reasons for the price or quantities offered by the dominant firm. A dominant firm is by definition in a position to act in ways that are harmful to its actual and potential competitors and if it does so efficient **competition** is frustrated to the detriment of customers. In other words, a dominant firm, in formulating its strategy, has not only to consider the impact on its smaller rivals in the competitive fringe and potential entrants, but also the reaction of the competition authorities and the consequences if it is judged to be abusing its powerful market position.

In this chapter, we will examine the key strategies that can be employed by a dominant, incumbent firm. We will largely ignore **collective dominance**, or as it is more generally known a **cartel**, as we have already discussed in the previous chapter some of the issues raised by such a grouping. Dominant firms, in setting their strategies, can choose to be co-operative or ***non-cooperative*** and, according to what they choose, will either have the objective of maximizing short-run profits or protecting market share against competitive attacks by smaller-scale incumbents and potential entrants. Depending on which of these strategic objectives is pursued, the outcome will be very different not only for the dominant firm, but also for its smaller-scale rivals and customers. Strategies designed to maximize short-run profits are likely to have longer-term consequences that invoke increased competition, a declining market share for the dominant firm and greater choice for consumers. Strategies designed to protect a dominant firm's market share have the characteristic of limiting the expected level of profits for the competitive fringe and also, at least in the short term, the profits of the dominant firm. In this respect, the strategic behaviour of a dominant firm differs from the strategic behaviour of oligopolists, who generally would benefit from co-operative arrangements.

In pursuing the goal of short-run profit maximization a dominant firm's decision makers are likely to adopt ***quantity fixing*** or ***price leadership*** strategies; that is, using its market power to control market supply or raise market prices. Such behaviour results in allocative inefficiency. With quantity fixing, the dominant firm chooses how much to supply, leaving smaller rivals to share a relatively small proportion of the market and, hence, to forgo additional scope for economies of scale arising from increased output. Price leadership involves controlling and holding the market price above where it would otherwise be. With price leadership, smaller rivals can sell for a higher price, with the effect that customers pay a higher price than would be generated by competition. A strategy of price leadership should not be confused with the notion of ***barometric price leadership***, where the price leader acts only as a barometer of market conditions, i.e. setting prices that would emerge under competition.

If the dominant firm's senior managers choose instead to follow a ***deterrence strategy***, they will develop and deploy strategies designed to disadvantage existing rivals and deter potential entrants, thereby reducing, over the longer term, the number of, and power of, competitors. In the extreme, these deterrence strategies can amount to hostile and exclusionary behaviour designed to cause the exit of existing rivals. The deliberate attempt to drive a rival from the market so that the dominant firm can exercise greater control over prices or the quantity sold is described as a strategy of ***predation*** and is considered to be an abuse of the dominant firm's dominant position. In the European Community, competition law outlaws predatory behaviour by a dominant firm or a collective dominance. In this chapter, we will explore in some detail these alternative strategies and use economic theories to shed light on the likely outcomes; not only for the dominant firm, but also for the nature of competition, market structure and consumer welfare. At the end of this chapter, you will:

- Understand the difference between a strategy of quantity leadership and price leadership, as well as the longer-term consequences of price leadership for market structure.
- Appreciate the limitations of a deterrence strategy, and in particular a strategy of limit pricing.
- Know why a strategy of predation, and in particular ***predatory pricing***, is both difficult to detect and an unlikely strategy in practice.

What follows is divided into six sections. In the first section we examine the concept of dominance as defined by the competition authorities. Dominance implies the existence of entry barriers and the first section takes further the analysis set out in Chapter 8 to examine the barriers facing a potential entrant to a market dominated by one firm. The second section introduces von Stackelberg's model of quantity leadership and demonstrates why even for a dominant firm there is still an incentive to co-operate with smaller rivals. The third section outlines the theory of price leadership and demonstrates both the short-run and the longer-term consequences of pursuing such a policy. The fourth section turns to deterrence strategies. The main focus is how prices can be used to limit rival's opportunities, but it also deals briefly with non-price deterrence. The fifth section analyses extreme deterrence in the form of predation. Again, the emphasis is on the use of price, but non-price predation will also be analysed. Finally, the sixth section considers the issues that confront the competition authorities in attempting to prevent a dominant firm abusing its dominant position.

Dominance and Entry Barriers

The first issue we must address is the meaning of dominance and why it is, or could be, a matter of concern. From an economic perspective, dominance is more akin to the market power of a monopolist than an **oligopolist**. We demonstrated in the previous chapter that an oligopolist has the power to influence price, but in doing so it is not independent of the reactions of its rivals. In contrast, a dominant firm has sufficient market power to enable it to raise price or act in some other way independently of its rivals, though such actions may bring forth a longer-term reaction. As noted in the introduction, in principle, under European Community (EC) law there is no automatic presumption that a dominant position *per se* produces an adverse outcome; indeed, as we shall demonstrate, dominance can in principle be beneficial. Only if the dominant firm abuses its power and engages in opportunistic behaviour is it likely to fall foul of the competition authorities. Nevertheless, the European Commission sought, and was granted, in the 1980s the power to prevent **mergers** that it considered would not be conducive to encouraging competition. Since it was granted the power to vet potential mergers, the Commission has blocked 18 notified mergers to prevent the emergence of dominant positions.

In the UK, a firm is deemed to have a scale monopoly, in essence a dominant position, if its sales account for more than 25 per cent of a specified market. In contrast, under Article 82 of the European Community Treaty, there is no threshold and the existence of a dominant position must be demonstrated. Under EC law, a dominant position is more easily conceptualized than demonstrated. A dominant position must be established in relation to a specific market, which must be analysed from three perspectives: the product market; the geographical market; and the temporal market. Although there is no formal test, European Court of Justice (ECJ) rulings have made it clear that product substitutability is key to defining the relevant product market. For example, products are likely to be competing for the same market, i.e. be close substitutes, if it can be demonstrated that they have a high **cross-price elasticity of demand**. Market share cannot be calculated in the absence of a geographic boundary to the market. But defining the geographic boundary is complicated and in this day and age is unlikely to be based on national boundaries and may instead be based on the cost of transport or, in the case of airlines, routes. Finally, market share may reflect transient temporal factors such as the effect of seasonal supply or the weather on market share. For example, both the supply and the cross-price elasticities of demand for some products, e.g. bananas, may fluctuate depending on the supply of alternative fruits.

Having identified the relevant product, geographic and temporal markets, the next stage for the EC competition authorities is to decide what constitutes dominance. The assessment of market power is a complicated task and when applying Article 82 it does not rest on market share alone. In this respect, Article 82 is in accord with more modern approaches to market power. Factors such as *contestability* and superior *capabilities* are relevant to the behaviour and performance of a dominant firm. The focus in the years following the pioneering work of Bain (1951) was to predict (where possible) likely behaviour and (more commonly) performance from a range of structural characteristics. High profits associated with high *concentration ratios* were suggestive of the abuse of market power. The modern approach does not automatically take high profits as indicating the abuse of market power – it might, for example, reflect superior capabilities.

Whatever path brings a firm to a position of dominance, it would be paradoxical if it was not earning an economic rent. The neo-classical paradigm views the earning of *economic rents* by incumbent firms as providing the incentive for new suppliers to enter the market and the persistence of economic rent as evidence of market failure. In the neo-classical world of *perfect information*, new entrants and incumbents are deemed to be equally efficient and super-rational. Each firm can imitate the products and services of rivals and all market entry and exit expenditures are potentially recoverable. Such a market, as explained in Chapter 8, is described as a *contestable market* and new entrants will be attracted to the market as long as they believe that post-entry they will earn an economic rent. Baumol *et al.*'s (1982) theory of contestable markets assumes that entry does not involve *sunk costs*, cumulative production generates little or no learning advantages and there is no *product differentiation*. Significantly, a new entrant faces the same *long-run average cost curve* as the dominant firm and customers view market output from whatever source as homogeneous. Thus, in a contestable market, in the long run the force of competition, actual or potential, prevents the emergence of a dominant firm and consequently the prevailing market price is reduced to a level that offers an efficient entrant zero economic rent.

But the contestability assumptions are a long way from reality, as evidenced by the persistence of a dominant position in many industries. There are, in practice, a number of ways in which a firm can achieve a dominant position. Dominance may be the outcome of a long period of competition, where a combination of a well-planned strategy and adverse stochastic shocks has reduced the number of rivals. A dominant firm may have achieved its position by means of a significant cost advantage. This may be the outcome of a technological advance that is protected by a *patent*, a super-efficient organizational architecture, a heterogeneous capability, e.g. product design, a favourable location or the control of a key input. Alternatively, there are strategies that a firm can employ to reach a dominant position through internal growth. Such strategies have the advantage of raising rivals' costs, either directly or indirectly, by forcing them to invest in technology, human resources and/or marketing. Once the dominant firm achieves a scale advantage over its smaller rivals, any cost advantage is likely to be reinforced by *economies of scale* and in a multi-product firm, *economies of scope*. In principle, a low-cost firm could achieve dominance via a strategy of low prices, providing rivals find it impossible to match the developing dominant firm's unit production costs. Alternatively, dominance might have been achieved by aggressive merger and acquisition activity, though over the past 20 years adopting this route to dominance would have involved satisfying the relevant competition authorities that it posed no threat to competition.

To remain dominant, a firm must be able to prevent the growth of small rivals and new entrants. Given that smaller incumbents and potential entrants are likely to suffer cost disadvantages relative to the dominant firm, it is possible, as discussed in Chapter 8, for the larger firm to engage in strategic behaviour to exploit the barriers facing the growth of smaller rivals or new entrants. Sunk costs and economies of scale allow a dominant incumbent to commit to a level of output that increases the risk associated with investment in additional capacity by smaller rivals. The more specific is a productive asset to a particular industry, the more likely it is that the investment will be a sunk cost, e.g. an electric arc furnace. Investments by the dominant firm in intangible assets – such as **brands**, advertising and research – are classic examples of sunk costs. Sunk costs can also influence the cost of capital. When a firm borrows funds, the loan is secured by the promise that if the debt cannot be paid, lenders will be able to sell off the firm's assets in order to recover (at least a portion of) their capital. The more a firm's assets are sunk, the lower their *ex post* value relative to their purchase price and the greater the likelihood of a risk premium charged by lenders.

Obstacles to growth and/or entry are created by **exit barriers**. A high level of **asset specificity**, where in the extreme **opportunity costs** are zero, will prevent a firm moving its assets into alternative industries. Such assets may be human or intangible. It is hard to sell a **reputation** for anything like the cost of creating it, especially if business is so bad that the seller is leaving the industry. The company may have technological skills, marketing experience or a reputation for service that are of little value in an alternative industry. Managerial specificity may be another impediment to exiting an industry if the performance of physical assets is specific to the executive style of a particular management team. Legal and regulatory commitments can also act as exit barriers, such as an undertaking to the workforce for severance pay or, in a regulated market, the prohibition on a firm abandoning a market without assurances on future supply.

In addition to the foregoing, once we move away from the restrictive assumption of the **neo-classical paradigm**, a smaller-scale incumbent or a potential entrant, contemplating an investment that will increase the industry's productive capacity, faces the risk arising from incomplete and **imperfect information**. For example, smaller firms, whether within or without the industry are likely to have **incomplete information** regarding the influence of an incumbent dominant firm's experience and scale of operation on its unit costs. This is private information and to reduce the risks associated with an investment, the **transaction costs** of gathering and evaluating information on the dominant incumbent must be incurred. Such expenditures create an asset – information – but the firm will only be able to recover what it has invested if the information suggests that the larger firm is unlikely to enjoy a significant cost advantage. Having obtained sufficient information on the dominant firm's unit costs, the smaller firm will also suffer the disadvantage of being only imperfectly able to assess the likely behaviour of the dominant firm post-investment in additional capacity.

In a world of imperfect information, there exists scope for dominant firms to create strategic barriers for smaller incumbents and potential entrants by signalling misleading information that may cause a smaller firm to doubt its ability to compete at a larger scale. A fringe firm, or potential entrant, will have to base its decision, in part, on its interpretation of the signals it receives from the dominant incumbent. This situation is represented in the game theoretic literature by a dynamic game in which the potential entrant will, in principle, apply **Bayes' rule** to update beliefs regarding the incumbent's competitive strength. Before taking the decision to invest in additional productive capacity, a smaller-scale firm's decision makers must form a view as to the likely response of a dominant incumbent. Fear that the dominant firm's response may be aggressive resulting, for example, in a price war may be sufficient to deter investment and hence the opportunity for greater competition.

Figure 10.1 illustrates Bayes' rule using the example of a small-scale fringe firm who is contemplating investing in additional capacity, but who has incomplete information regarding the dominant firm's unit costs. The fringe firm can, however, observe the prices charged by the dominant firm and might use these as a guide to its unit costs. To keep matters simple, we will assume there are only two states of nature concerning the dominant firm: low unit costs and high unit costs. The probability that

Figure 10.1: An illustration of Bayes' rule

		Observed price	
		Low	High
Dominant firm's unit costs	Low	$p\alpha$	$p(1-\alpha)$
	High	$(1-p)(1-\beta)$	$(1-p)\beta$
	Sum	$p\alpha + (1-p)(1-\beta)$	$p(1-\alpha) + (1-p)\beta$

unit costs are low is p, where $0 < p < 1$, so the probability of high costs is $(1-p)$. The probability that observing a low price reflects low unit costs is α, where $0 < \alpha < 1$, and hence the probability of observing a high price when unit costs are low is $(1-\alpha)$. The probability of observing a high price when unit costs are high is β, where $0 < \beta < 1$, and therefore the probability of low price when unit costs are high is $(1-\beta)$. Each cell in the first two rows of the matrix shows the overall probability of the combination of an observed price and the true state of nature. The last row shows the sum of the first two rows in each column.

Writing *LC* for low cost and *HP* for high price, the probability that the dominant firm has low unit costs given the observation of a high price is:

$$\text{Prob}(LC \cap HP) = \text{Prob}(LC) * \text{Prob}(LC \text{ conditional on } HP) \tag{10.1}$$

and inserting the probability from Figure 10.1, this gives:

$$p(1-\alpha) = [p\alpha + (1-p)(1-\beta)] * \text{Prob}(LC \text{ conditional on } HP) \tag{10.2}$$

which, by rearranging, becomes:

$$(\text{Prob}(LC \text{ conditional on } HP) = \frac{p(1-\alpha)}{p\alpha + (1-p)(1-\beta)} \tag{10.3}$$

The foregoing serves to explain the barriers facing smaller firms within the competitive fringe or potential entrants who might contemplate investing in additional capacity so as to increase scale and compete on more equal terms with a dominant firm. As we shall see, the long-run outcome cannot be determined solely by an analysis of economic barriers. Much depends on strategic purpose and intent, most importantly by a dominant firm. If a dominant firm adopts aggressive and exclusionary behaviour, the outcome is likely to be very different than would be the case if the dominant firm adopted a more accommodating strategy.

Competing for Market

By any yardstick, Microsoft is the dominant firm in the markets for personal computer operating systems and internet browsers. By the end of the 1990s, Microsoft's share of Intel-based personal computer operating systems was estimated to be of the order of 90 per cent. Given the scale of Microsoft's domination a competitor would be hard-pressed to achieve a foothold in the market, let alone directly challenge Microsoft. It was widely reported that IBM – itself a dominant player in the manufacture of computers – spent more than $1 billion developing, testing and marketing its OSA/2 operating system as an alternative to Microsoft's Windows. But, IBM's alternative operating system was a commercial failure in part because IBM could not overcome the chicken-and-egg problem of network effects. That is, the demand for a specific personal computer operating system increases with the number of other uses of the product and/or with the number of complementary goods or services. The desire on the part of consumers for a variety of applications ensures that the cost of switching to a new operating system is unacceptably high until the new operating system is widely used and has a large set of available applications.

Microsoft argues, in defence of its market dominance, that the very fact that its dominant position depends on the network effect of computer operating systems makes it extremely vulnerable to technological progress and, hence, what it describes as catastrophic entry. That is where a new operating system is sufficiently superior that it creates a network bandwagon that rapidly replaces the existing system. According to this view, rivalry in personal computer operating systems and internet browsers takes the form of competition to become the dominant firm; that is, competition for the market rather than competition within the market.

Quantity Leadership

We turn now to the strategic behaviour of a dominant firm. We will start with the not-unreasonable assumption that its senior managers are motivated by the goal of maximizing long-run profits. In order to achieve this goal, the dominant firm's senior managers must essentially choose between deterrence and accommodating strategies. We will examine first strategies of deterrence and in this and the next section strategies designed to disadvantage smaller fringe competitors and/or potential entrants. In this section, we analyse the behaviour of a dominant firm operating in a commodity market, i.e. rivals' products are not differentiated.

We can analyse the situation with the aid of Figure 10.2, where, to keep matters simple and without any loss of generality, we will assume only two firms: a dominant firm – firm A – and a smaller-scale firm considering entering the market – firm B. To reduce the number of lines in the figure and allow a focus on the key elements, we will assume – without displaying its marginal revenue and marginal cost curves – the dominant incumbent is maximizing profits at output q_0 and for both firms we will ignore fixed capital costs. We will further assume that market demand is static and for the moment that firm B believes that the output of firm A will remain unchanged. What we need to ascertain is how much firm B, as a profit maximizer, will wish to produce, given firm A's output.

As the dominant firm is fully meeting demand at price p_0 and is expected to maintain output at q_0, the only market demand available to the potential entrant, B, is the additional sales represented by all points on the market demand curve to the right of point X. Hence, the demand curve facing firm B is obtained by subtracting A's output from the market demand curve at all feasible prices below point X. The demand curve obtained by subtracting the dominant incumbent's output from market demand at all prices is known as the ***residual demand curve***. In Figure 10.2, the residual

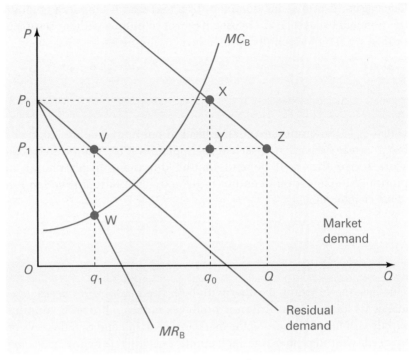

Figure 10.2: A new entrant's residual demand curve

demand curve facing firm B has been shifted back to the vertical axis, where starting from point p_0, its slope is identical to the market demand curve. As the market price falls below p_0, so the 'residual' demand for firm B's additional output is represented by the horizontal distance between the vertical axis and the residual demand curve. As is always the case for a downward-sloping demand curve, firm B's residual demand curve has an associated marginal revenue curve, MR_B. As a profit maximizer, we can assume that firm B will set its marginal revenue equal to its marginal cost, i.e. $MR_B = MC_B$, shown as point W in Figure 10.2. This gives firm B a profit-maximizing output of q_1 and determines the total market supply of Q where $Q = q_0 + q_1$, which in turn yields a lower market price of p_1. The horizontal distance $p_1 V$ represents firm B's output at price p_1 and the distance $p_1 Y$ represents firm A's (unchanged) output. It follows that the horizontal distance $p_1 V = YZ$.

The model set out above demonstrates that the strategy for a fringe firm contemplating expansion, or a new entrant, involves determining the most profitable level of output given an assumption about the dominant firm's output *ex post*. One way of capturing the asymmetric rivalry involving a dominant firm and a smaller rival is to employ von Stackelberg's (1934) leader–follower model. Stackelberg's model, now more often called a model of ***first-mover advantage***, demonstrates the value of being in a dominant position. Stackelberg's model is based on non-cooperative behaviour and is very similar to the Cournot approach to oligopolist equilibrium set out in the previous chapter, which, it will be recalled, relied on each firm choosing its desired level of output in response to its rival's output. Stackelberg's leadership model assumes a dominant firm is able to precommit itself to a particular level of supply and we can demonstrate some of the model's subtleties if we use the approach shown in Figure 10.3, which is similar to the Cournot model.

Once again, firm A is the dominant firm and firm B the representative of the competitive fringe. As the dominant player, if A chooses its level of output without regard to B and seeks to maximize its profits, we can represent its optimal level of output as:

$$q_0 = \frac{\alpha}{2\beta} \tag{10.4}$$

where q_0 is the profit-maximizing level of output. Equation (10.4) should look reasonably familiar, but a formal derivation is set out in Appendix A10. The profit-maximizing choice for the smaller-scale fringe firm will depend on the dominant firm's choice of output; therefore firm B's profit-maximizing level of output is given by the Cournot **reaction function** as explained in the previous chapter, namely:

$$q_1 = \frac{\alpha - \beta q_0}{2\beta} \tag{10.5}$$

This reaction function, together with both firms' **isoprofit curves**, are shown in Figure 10.3. Firm A makes its largest profit if firm B produces nothing. If firm B supplies the quantity q_1, total market supply will increase, causing the market price to fall and as it does A's profit level declines, represented by north-west movements in its isoprofit curves. The figure makes explicit B's choice. If firm A has chosen to produce q_0 then, subject to this constraint, B will maximize its profits by choosing output q_1, which lies on its reaction function. Visually in Figure 10.3, B's profit-maximizing level of output is determined where its reaction function is tangential to A's isoprofit curve that is nearest the Q_A axis.

This solution is the **Stackelberg equilibrium**. Despite producing the same output that a monopolist would produce, the dominant firm does not earn such a large economic rent. This, as we have seen, is because the follower's positive level of output drives down the market price. The existence of a first-mover advantage carries over to Stackelberg's pricing game with differentiated products, of which more in later chapters. The Stackelberg game is at the very least a two-period game. The dominant firm moves first and makes a commitment to a level of output. This is observed by its smaller-scale rival before making a decision: thus, in this respect, the Stackelberg model is a non-cooperative game of perfect information. Despite the

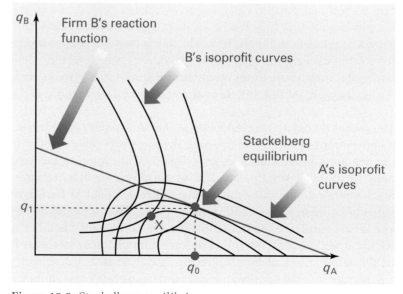

Figure 10.3: Stackelberg equilibrium

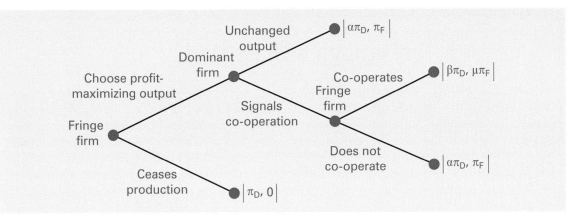

Figure 10.4: A dynamic Stackelberg game

leaders precommitment to a level of output of its choosing, as previously demonstrated for oligopolistic rivalry, there are potential gains if the two firms are prepared to adopt a co-operative stance.

The two firms can increase their profitability if they are prepared to jointly reduce output, i.e. co-operate. Point X in Figure 10.3 shows the co-operative solution involving lower output from both A and B. At point X, the two firms' isoprofit curves are tangential at a higher level of profits for both firms than provided by the Stackelberg equilibrium. The incentive to reach a co-operative outcome is more clearly presented with the aid of a Stackelberg first-mover extensive game, as set out in Figure 10.4. The Stackelberg game is inherently dynamic, which raises the possibility of actions being threatened or promised and possibly being acted upon. In practice, we are only concerned with promises and threats that are credible. To rule out incredible threats – e.g. a threat by the dominant firm to vastly increase output lowering its economic rent to zero – we require that the predicted outcome of the game be sub-game perfect. To find the **sub-game perfect Nash equilibrium** we apply the principle of **backward induction**. The game starts with the smaller rival responding to its observation of the leader's level of output. The fact that the fringe firm can observe the dominant firm's output before choosing its response alters the predicted behaviour of the two firms.

In Figure 10.4, π represents profits and the subscripts $_D$ and $_F$ relate to the dominant firm and the fringe rival, respectively, and the coefficients α, β and μ have the following values: $0 < \alpha < \beta < 1 < \mu$. In order to determine the optimal strategy for either firm using backward induction, we start by evaluating the pay-offs from the information set at the penultimate nodes, i.e. the nodes that immediately precede the terminal nodes. When the optimal decision at each of these nodes has been determined we move back down the tree to the immediately preceding node, choose the optimal decision at this point and continue the process until we arrive at the initial node. In Figure 10.4, there are two nodes at which the fringe rival has to make a decision and one that requires the dominant firm to make a decision.

At the fringe firm's penultimate node a decision has to be made as to whether to remain non-cooperative or to signal a co-operative stance. On reaching this node, the only rational decision for the smaller-scale rival is to co-operate – assuming no legal impediment – as $\mu\pi > \pi$. The dominant firm, being rational, can anticipate this outcome and in making a decision at the previous node will rationally choose to signal co-operation as $\beta\pi > \alpha\pi$. Finally, at the initial node where the follower has a choice between producing or leaving the market, it will anticipate a rational decision by the dominant

Through a Glass Darkly

In 1861, Ernest Solvay, a man with a passionate interest in science, research and innovation, developed a revolutionary ammonia-soda process, the Leblanc process, for producing sodium carbonate. Sodium carbonate is used in a wide range of manufactured products including glass, paper and soaps. Solvay patented every stage of his process and founded a company in 1863 to exploit its potential. Licenses to the Leblanc process were sold around the world and licensees were required to share their technical improvements with Solvay. In the ensuing years, Solvay's company has grown into a transnational pharmaceutical and chemical company, the Solvay Group, specializing in three sectors: pharmaceuticals, chemicals and plastics. And by the 1980s, it had achieved a dominant position in the production of soda ash.

During the 1980s, Solvay, together with ICI, was accused by the European Commission of abusing their dominant positions in the European soda ash market. In the course of the 1980s, they had established a system of rebates designed to avoid any danger of real competition in their respective territories, that is to say, western continental Europe in the case of Solvay and the United Kingdom and Ireland in the case of ICI. Conduct of this kind is contrary to Article 82 of the EC Treaty.

Solvay and ICI each set up a system of what were called 'top-slice' rebates aimed at keeping competitors out of the market. Most glass manufacturers, the major users of soda ash, have one main supplier for their core requirements, but like to have a second supplier, too, so as not to be completely dependent on the first. To minimize the competitive impact of second suppliers of this kind, Solvay and ICI developed a two-tier pricing system. The core tonnage was sold at the normal price, but the additional quantities that the customer might otherwise have bought from another supplier – the 'top slice' – were offered at a substantial (and secret) discount. In some cases, this meant that the marginal tonnage was being offered by Solvay or ICI at virtually half price. It was made clear to customers that the special price for the top slice depended on their agreeing to take most, if not all, of their requirements from the dominant producer.

The effect was to prevent other producers from entering into genuine competition with Solvay and ICI. In order to compete, they would have had to offer very large discounts on their entire sales volume, whereas Solvay and ICI were doing this only on the top slice. The Commission took the view that these were very serious infringements of Article 82, and on 19 December 1990 it adopted decisions imposing fines of €20 million on Solvay and €10 million on ICI. These were considered heavy fines at the time, but it took another ten years of legal wrangling before the fines were paid.

firm at the second node and will therefore choose to produce. The fringe firm's action is optimal as it is likely to yield a pay-off of $\mu\pi$, which is greater than the pay-off of 0 for leaving the market. The strategy profile just discussed is called a sub-game perfect Nash equilibrium, as it specifies a Nash equilibrium at every sub-game in the decision tree.

Price Leadership

The Stackelberg game described above showed the dominant firm's asymmetric advantage in a quantity-setting model. The presence of a dominant firm's asymmetric advantage carries over to pricing models. Logically, pricing models are more suited to dealing with markets in which products are differentiated. However, we can demonstrate the essence of a strategy of price leadership by a dominant firm – and most importantly its longer-term consequences – by assuming homogeneous products in order to simplify the analysis.

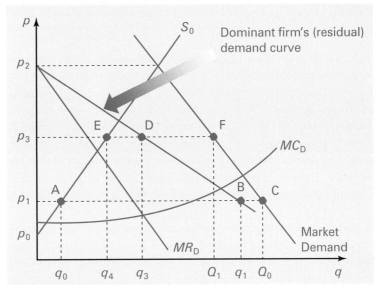

Figure 10.5: Price leadership

We can demonstrate the economics of this strategy with the help of Figure 10.5, where for ease of exposition we will ignore the dominant firm's fixed capital costs. The market demand is represented by the market demand curve and we now seek to ascertain the dominant firm's output under price leadership. As the dominant firm sets the price, of relevance here is how incumbent smaller-scale fringe rivals or new entrants react to the price set.

Under a strategy of price leadership by the dominant firm, the competitive fringe is composed of price takers. This follows because as profit maximizes, smaller-scale firms in the competitive fringe will set their output at the level determined by the equality of their marginal costs with the leader's price. Given the law of diminishing returns, each of the price-taking firm's marginal costs will be rising at the profit-maximizing level of production and therefore we can represent the collective supply of the competitive fringe at different market prices with the upward-sloping short-run **supply curve**, S_0, in Figure 10.5. As drawn, the supply curve for the smaller rivals suggests that some of them have lower marginal costs than the dominant firm – a not-unreasonable assumption if the dominant firm's powerful position has resulted in its tolerance of **X-inefficiencies**. If the market price falls below p_0, no firm will find it profitable to supply the market.

At a market price p_1, the competitive fringe would supply the quantity, q_0 to the market – represented by the horizontal distance from the vertical axis to point A – leaving the dominant firm to supply q_1 – represented by the horizontal distance from the vertical axis to point B. Note, at output q_1 and price p_1, the dominant firm's $MC_D > p_1$. This is therefore not a level of output that the dominant firm would choose, but here we are only demonstrating the consequences if the dominant firm as price leader wanted to achieve a market price of p_1. When the dominant firm's output q_1 is added to the output produced by the competitive fringe, q_0, the total market supply is Q_0, where $Q_0 = q_1 + q_0$, is sufficient to meet market demand at p_1, represented by point C. Now consider the situation if the market price were p_2. At this price it would be so profitable for the smaller firms to produce that they would supply the whole of market demand: represented by the intersection of S_0 with the market demand curve. Thus, at a price of p_2, the dominant firm would in principle supply nothing to the market. Armed with these two points of reference, we can now construct the dominant firm's residual demand curve.

At a market price of p_2, the dominant firm's residual demand curve cuts the vertical axis and at a price of p_1, it supplies the quantity represented by the horizontal distance from the vertical axis to point B. Joining these two points with a straight line (assuming for simplicity that the demand curve is linear) yields the dominant firm's residual demand curve. Associated with this residual demand curve is a marginal revenue curve – shown as MR_D. As a profit maximizer, the dominant firm will set its marginal revenue equal to marginal cost, yielding a profit-maximizing output of q_3, at a market price of p_3, represented by point D. At this price the competitive fringe will collectively choose to supply q_4, represented by point E, which is equivalent (by construction) to the horizontal distance, DF. At this short-run equilibrium, total market supply is Q_1, where $Q_1 = q_3 + q_4$ equivalent to the horizontal distance, p_3F.

In the example set out above the dominant firm is not abusing its dominant position. This would only apply if it sought to prevent one or more of the firms comprising the competitive fringe from offering a lower price. Indeed, it is worth noting that the existence of a low-cost dominant firm can improve market performance in the short run. In the absence of the dominant firm, the market price would be p_2 at the intersection of supply and demand. Consumers would be worse off because they would not have access to the low-cost production of the dominant firm. Over the longer term, as we shall see, consumers' welfare benefits from a growing supply from the competitive fringe, however in the absence of a price leadership strategy by the dominant firm, competition would have forced prices to lower levels. The long-term effects of a strategy of price leadership can be demonstrated by reference to Figure 10.6, which shows how Figure 10.5 is likely to alter over a period of years.

The high market price implied by a price leadership strategy will earn economic rents not only for the dominant firm, but also for the smaller-scale followers. This will encourage investment in additional capacity by the existing competitive fringe and/or new entrants. The effect of this – over a period of years – is to push the collective supply curve for the smaller-scale firms that comprise the competitive fringe, S_0, to the right – S_1 – so that the competitive fringe can now fully supply market demand at price p_4. At price p_1, the smaller firms have increased their combined output from point A to point B. The effect of this is to force the dominant firm's residual demand curve to the left, running from p_4 on the vertical axis to point C – where distance $CD = p_1B$. To avoid overcrowding, the dominant firm's MR curve is not shown, but setting its new $MR_D = MC_D$ yields the dominant firm a low price and a profit-maximizing output that is lower than previously. Thus, the

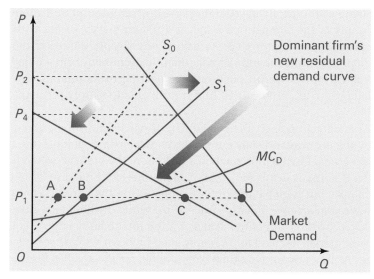

Figure 10.6: Dynamic outcome of price leadership

paradoxical outcome of a strategy of price leadership leads over the short run to a procyclical market share for the dominant firm, i.e. market share rises in booms and declines in recessions, and over the longer term to a declining market share. In this attempt to represent the dynamic consequences of price leadership, demand has been held constant so the leader suffers not only a fall in market share, but also an absolute fall in output. If market demand is growing, then the consequence of price leadership is a falling market share, but the absolute volume sold may still be rising.

A dominant firm is in a strong position to punish a smaller rival who seeks to grow market share more rapidly by reducing its selling price. Price leadership is **tacit collusion** and its enforcement can be modelled within a game theoretic framework. On the assumption that the dominant firm enjoys lower unit costs than its smaller rivals – say, as a result of economies of scale – it has the scope to reduce the market price to a level that would be unprofitable for a smaller rival. The game can be viewed as infinitely repeated and sequential. In a repeated game there is a different information set for each period and a history of play; thus, strategy for each player is conditional on what has taken place in the past. A dominant firm pursuing a price leadership strategy must seek to build a reputation for rapid and effective punishment of any defection by a smaller rival. To capture the idea of reputation in this game we can introduce the concept of a **trigger strategy**. In a trigger strategy game a player, in this case the dominant firm, has two courses of action: price leadership and ruthless price competition. The game, for three sequential periods is set out in Figure 10.7 and the subscripts $_D$ and $_F$ refer to the pay-offs to the dominant firm and a representative member of the competitive fringe, respectively.

The dominant firm sets the price and the smaller scale rival now has to choose whether or not to co-operate. If the follower co-operates, the dominant firm makes a profit of €100m and the smaller-scale follower a profit of €2m; moreover, this pay-off is repeated for the next two periods. If, however, the fringe player defects it gains market share and an increase in profits to €4m, whereas the leader's profit falls to €90m. At the start of the next period, having observed that the follower has not co-operated, the leader's trigger strategy comes into play. During this period, the follower has no choice but to suffer the ruthless price competition, the result of which is shown as a €2m loss. At the start of the next period the dominant firm again sets the price, leaving the fringe firm to make its choice. The **present value** of the fringe player's pay-off for a strategy of defecting every other period is:

$$PV_F = 4 - 2\delta + 4\delta^2 - 2\delta^3 + 4\delta^4 - 2\delta^5 + 4\delta^6 - 2\delta^7 + \ldots \qquad (10.6)$$

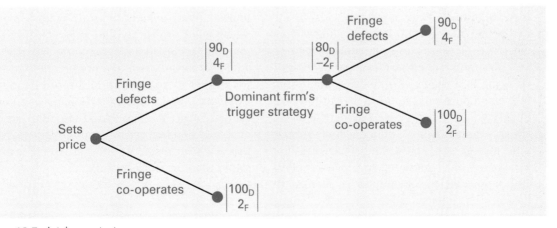

Figure 10.7: A trigger strategy

where δ is the discount factor, i.e. $\delta = 1/(1 + r)$ and r is the opportunity cost of capital. Equation (10.6) can be expressed as:

$$PV_F = 4[1 + \delta^2 + \delta^4 + \ldots] - 2\delta[1 + \delta_2 + \delta^4 + \ldots] \tag{10.7}$$

And if treated as an infinitely repeated game, can be reduced to:

$$PV_F = \frac{4}{(1 - \delta^2)} + \frac{4 - 2\delta}{(1 - \delta^2)} = \frac{4 - 2\delta}{(1 - \delta)(1 + \delta)} \tag{10.8}$$

Alternatively, if the fringe competitor chooses to co-operate the pay-off from an infinitely repeated game will be equivalent to the first expression on the right-hand side of Equation (10.8). This will always be greater than a strategy of defection involving a trigger response from the price leader:

$$PV_F = \frac{4}{(1 - \delta)} > \frac{4 - 2\delta}{(1 - \delta)(1 + \delta)} \tag{10.9}$$

Taking the Lead

By its very nature, price leadership is difficult to detect. In practice, the observation of *parallel pricing*, the tendency for sellers' prices to move in the same direction, may be due to three types of price leadership: the ability of a dominant firm to ensure smaller rivals follow its lead; collusive behaviour by oligopolists; or barometric leadership, where one firm does no more than act as a barometer of market conditions, i.e. the price change reflects a general increase in costs. Parallel pricing is also likely to be the outcome of intense competition where products are close substitutes. Over the years competition authorities have investigated firms in a range of industries, including telecommunications, motor fuels and tobacco, for price leadership. Some 30 years ago, the UK government commissioned a study of parallel pricing in the UK. The report was not exhaustive but concluded that price leadership appeared to have been a feature of industries as diverse as bread, electric lamps, petrol and tyres.

More recently, the Competition Commission investigated the issue of price leadership in the UK supermarket sector. Supermarkets typically sell in excess of 20,000 products, but researchers had deduced that in terms of price competition a much smaller range of so-called *known value items* materially influenced consumers' perceptions of the store's overall price level. In order to examine the extent of price leadership, the leading supermarkets were asked to supply weekly price data for 18 products. The analysts then attempted, using statistical techniques, to link a change in the price of a product by one supermarket to coincident and rapid changes by rivals. The Competition Commission concluded that it was satisfied that some common pricing occurs, though it believed this was the result of competitive pressure rather than price leadership.

Strategic Deterrence

The quantity and price leadership models analysed above provide an overview of two alternative strategies for a dominant firm. But they do not represent the only strategies that might feasibly be pursued by a dominant firm. Indeed, retaining the assumption that a firm's decision makers are primarily motivated by the goal of long-run profit maximization, price leadership may not be the most effective pricing strategy for a dominant firm. In the long run, the present value of a dominant firm's profits might be maximized if it adopts behaviour designed to deter the competitive fringe from investing in additional capacity or potential entrants. Such strategies are known as **deterrence strategies** and are designed to convince an existing rival or potential entrant that the creation of additional productive capacity is unlikely to be profitable. Our focus here is pricing strategy, but a deterrence strategy need not be confined to pricing behaviour and we will return to non-pricing deterrence strategies in this and later chapters. We will focus in this section on behaviour designed to deter potential entrants; in the next section we will explore behaviour whose purpose is to cause the exit of an existing rival or rivals.

In essence, a deterrence strategy is designed to deter a specific action by an existing or potential rival by convincing its senior managers that their firm's profits will not be sufficient to justify the cost. Such a strategy can only be effective if the senior managers of the target firm not only believe that post the specific action an adverse cost asymmetry will exist with the dominant firm, but also that it will continue to exist under all future market conditions. As observed previously, lack of scale and learning by doing are likely to place a smaller rival at a cost disadvantage compared to the dominant firm, and this situation will be exacerbated if the investment under consideration will *ex post* be a sunk cost. A deterrence strategy must have, therefore, the objective of convincing a firm that poses a potential threat that even if it is prepared to forego short-term profits it cannot expect over the longer term that the situation will improve and allow the firm to earn an economic rent. The classic strategic deterrence strategy is the **limit pricing model** of behaviour by a dominant firm. Such a strategy is more likely to be successful, i.e. protect longer-term profits for the dominant firm, if the existing production technology exhibits economies of scale that can only be realized at a large scale of output.

One of the first economists to examine the manner in which economies of scale can be used to secure competitive advantage was Sylos-Labini (1962), whose work gave rise to the concept of a limit price. We can again greatly simplify the analysis of this concept – without any loss of generality – if we view the industry's current level of output as being solely supplied by a dominant firm

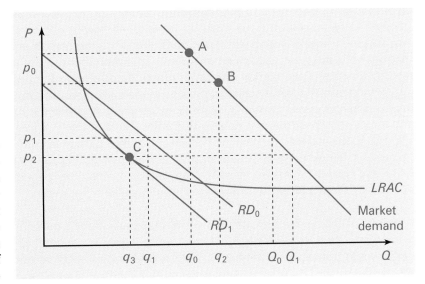

Figure 10.8: Limit pricing

who is facing a competitive threat from one smaller-scale rival. We will assume that both the dominant firm and its smaller rival have access to the same production technology and the scope for additional learning from cumulative production is limited. This assumption implies that both firms face the same long-run average cost curve ($LRAC$). We can further simplify matters by assuming for the moment only one time period and, most importantly, consumer indifference between the two firms' output, i.e. both produce an homogeneous product. In order to analyse this situation we need behavioural assumptions for the dominant firm and the smaller-scale rival. One assumption is the **Sylos postulate**, which owes much to the Stackelberg leader model. The postulate holds that the dominant firm commits to an output level and the smaller follower believes that the dominant firm's output level will be maintained in future periods regardless of the action of the smaller firm. Given the Sylos postulate, the situation faced by the smaller rival is illustrated in Figure 10.8.

A major influence on whether or not the smaller firm chooses to invest in additional capacity depends, as previously noted, on whether it expects to earn an economic rent and hence the target for the dominant firm is to make it difficult for a smaller rival to earn a rent. This can be demonstrated in Figure 10.8, which makes use of the previously introduced concept of the residual demand curve In this case, we are concerned with the smaller firm's residual demand curve which, as explained above, is obtained by subtracting from the market demand curve the dominant firm's output at every price. As the dominant firm has pre-fixed its output at q_0, this would generate a market price of p_0, in the absence of the smaller rival. The potential sales for the smaller firm are represented by the residual demand curve, RD_0, which has moved point A on the market demand curve to the point where it intercepts the vertical axis at price p_0. Whether or not a firm earns an economic rent depends on the price it receives and its unit costs; or in terms of cost curves it is its average, not marginal, production costs that are relevant for calculating rent. As can be seen in Figure 10.8, if the dominant firm produces output q_0 – which we can assume represents its profit-maximizing output, ignoring its smaller rival – the smaller rival can earn an economic rent if it produces output q_1. At this level of output, market supply is $Q_0 = q_0 + q_1$ and the market price is p_1.

The dominant firm can, however, remove the scope for the smaller firm to earn a rent by increasing its output to q_2. The effect of this is to shift the smaller firm's residual demand curve from RD_0 to RD_1, which is tangential to its $LRAC$ at point C. At output q_3, the smaller firm now only earns a normal profit. Market supply increases to $Q_1 = q_2 + q_3$ and market price falls to price, p_2. It follows that the limit price, or perhaps more correctly the deterrent level of output, is determined by three factors: the size of the market, the **price elasticity of demand** and the smaller firm's average cost curve. In Figure 10.8, an increase in the size of the market would show up as a rightward shift in the market demand curve. Similarly, the higher the elasticity of demand, the flatter the demand curve, and the greater the additional volume that will be sold at lower prices. An increase in demand or an increase in the elasticity of demand – caused, say, by a change in consumers' tastes – would mean an increase in the output a dominant firm would have to pre-fix to deter a smaller rival. On the other hand, the greater the extent to which the smaller firm's unit costs exceed those of the incumbent dominant firm, the lower the volume of output needed to limit entry.

A dominant firm pursuing a deterrence strategy must also be concerned to deter potential entrants. What Figure 10.8 illustrates is **blockaded entry**, where a potential entrant observing market supply of Q_1 would not expect to earn even normal profits post-entry, as entry implies a market output of $> Q_1$ and a price $< p_2$. Whether or not the output level Q_1 amounts to what Bain (1956) referred to as an *effective impediment*, depends on the dominant firm's profitability. We know by assumption that the dominant firm has chosen not to maximize short-term profits by choosing a level of output where $q_2 > q_0$. A rational firm will only choose this option if it believes that in the long run this level of output will maximize the present value of its profits. Given the assumption of rational decision makers, a dominant firm will pursue the strategy that yields it the largest, expected present value of profits and, therefore, the fact that a dominant firm *can* control and limit the options for smaller incumbents and potential entrants does not mean that it will choose to do so.

We can demonstrate how a dominant firm will choose whether or not to pursue a deterrent strategy by relaxing the restraint of a single time period. Viewed from a multi-period perspective, if the expected present value of the dominant firm's long-run profits is greater by choosing to supply at a higher price rather than limit pricing, it should rationally choose this option. Central to this strategic choice is the fact that rational decision makers will have a positive **rate of time preference**, thereby attaching much greater weight to profits expected to be earned in the near term than at more distant dates. In principle, the dominant firm can choose between strategic alternatives by constructing a discounted value formula, as set out in Equation (10.10), to obtain the present value of future profits (PV_π):

$$PV_\pi = \sum_{i=1}^{n} \frac{\pi_{t+i}}{(1+r)^{t+i}} = \frac{\pi_{t+1}}{(1+r)^{t+1}} + \frac{\pi_{t+2}}{(1+r)^{t+2}} + \dots + \frac{\pi_{t+n}}{(1+r)^{t+n}} \tag{10.10}$$

where π represents the expected profits accumulated over each year, r is the firm's opportunity cost of capital and t represents the number of years under consideration and takes the value $t = 0$ in the first year. As can be seen, as the timing of the expected profit recedes further into the future the value of the denominator increases, causing its present value to decline. Of course, as implied by the phrase expected profits, the firm's senior managers cannot know for certain the level of future profits and this increases the risk element of the firm's opportunity cost of capital. The idea lying behind limit pricing is that by taking a lower profit today, the firm can maintain this level of profitability into the future because existing smaller-scale competitors will be dissuaded from investing in additional capacity and potential entrants will not mount a threat. However, the longer the period under consideration, the greater the uncertainty attached to a forecast of profits. On this basis, it may be perfectly rational to prefer a large profit in the short run, albeit at the cost of a declining market share and a lower profit in future years.

The Sylos-Labini model of limit pricing is based on the hypothesis that a dominant firm or a cartel – a collective dominance – will continue to produce the pre-entry level of output regardless of whether or not a smaller rival expands or entry occurs. Such an assumption is, at best, questionable. A smaller fringe competitor is also concerned with the present value of future profits and if it is efficient it may wish to expand its production base. Whether it chooses to or not will depend on its decision makers' conjectures regarding the behaviour of the dominant firm post the coming on stream of its additional capacity. The dominant firm's limit price and associated output will not be regarded as a deterrent by the smaller firm's senior managers if the dominant firm's refusal to alter its level of output is believed not to be credible following an increase in output by the competitive fringe. Returning to Bain's classification, the dominant firm's deterrence strategy will be an *ineffective impediment* if the smaller firm's decision makers believe that it would be more profitable for the dominant firm to be accommodating. For example, following the smaller firm's investment the dominant firm may adopt a non-cooperative Cournot strategy – all firms adjust to new market shares in order to maximize profits – or it may seek a co-operative solution, i.e. tacit collusion. The important point is that if **ex ante** conjectures such as these are plausibly held by the competitive fringe or potential entrants, then there is no rational basis for limit pricing in the first place. Put in the language of game theory, *ex post*, the dominant firm and the smaller rival are in a two-person game, whose structure and form are entirely independent of the *ex ante* strategy of the dominant firm. It is the *ex post* game that matters and *ex ante* behaviour matters only to the extent that it influences a small rival's conjectures about *ex post* behaviour.

We can demonstrate something of the greater complexity attached to the behaviours of a dominant firm and the competitive fringe with the game theoretic model illustrated in Figure 10.9. The game reflects the choices open to a dominant firm and a smaller-scale rival considering investing in additional capacity. The pay-offs are in terms of rankings of the present value of future profits; the dominant firm's are placed first and 7 represents the highest pay-off. The game starts with a decision by the dominant firm whether to adopt a limit price or a price leadership strategy. We now move to the smaller rival's decision, represented by the first oval. We assume that the smaller rival can observe perfectly the incumbent's price and output and on this basis the smaller rival has to make a decision whether to invest in additional capacity or leave output unchanged. If the dominant firm adopts a price leadership strategy, but the smaller rival chooses not to invest in additional capacity, the pay-offs are 7 and 0, respectively. Note, the pay-offs to the small rival reflect only the change in profits if the investment is undertaken. If, alternatively, the dominant firm adopts a deterrent limit price strategy and the smaller rival decides not to invest, the pay-offs are 5 and 0, respectively. If, however, the smaller firm invests, the dominant firm then has to make a decision as to its response.

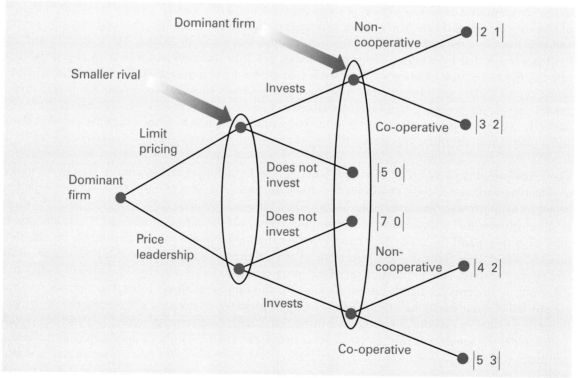

Figure 10.9: A game theoretic approach

Let us assume that it has two choices: a non-cooperative strategy; or the seeking of a co-operative strategy. If the dominant incumbent had been pursuing a strategy of limit pricing it might adopt a non-cooperative Stackelberg stance assumed by the Sylos postulate. Alternatively, it may judge that its *ex ante* strategy had failed and seek instead to accommodate the new situation by signalling a willingness to co-operate. If it adopts the Stackelberg stance the market price falls, but it could even rise if both firms tacitly collude. If the dominant firm had been pursuing a policy of price leadership it will logically seek a co-operative outcome with the new entrant. Note, the pay-off to the dominant firm, 5, is ranked higher here because implicitly the dominant firm has been maximizing profits. If the smaller rival chooses a non-cooperative stance, the dominant firm has to decide whether to adopt a Cournot strategy – implicitly illustrated in the figure – or adopt a punishment strategy involving action to drive down the market price.

Employing backward induction to the example set out in Figure 10.9, the dominant strategy for the dominant firm is to adopt a price leadership strategy followed by co-operation *ex post*. Different pay-offs are likely to yield different behaviours from both the dominant firm and its smaller rival, but the important lesson is that future profits are interdependent and it is their expected present value that drives behaviour. For example, the dominant firm cannot achieve a co-operative pay-off if the smaller rival adopts a non-cooperative stance. In practice, the critical variables underlying the relative size of the pay-offs to alternative strategies are market size and the extent of sunk costs. If the market is large and sunk entry costs are small, a strategy of limit pricing implies that a dominant firm will have to produce significantly more than the profit-maximizing level of output, resulting in a much lower price and substantially lower profits. In large markets with easy entry, a dominant firm will earn a greater rent by adopting a price leadership strategy and sharing the market with a competitive fringe of small firms than it will by setting a low price to deter expansion by existing rivals or potential entrants.

If we allow for the dynamic nature of the game set out in Figure 10.9, the choice between price leadership and limit pricing may not be so stark. Over a number of production periods it might be possible for a dominant firm to follow both strategies sequentially. The extensive game model shown in Figure 10.9 ignores the fact that investment in additional capacity is a process that takes time. It might take several years to bring new capacity to the market and during this period a dominant firm may choose to maximize its profits by limiting its output. Once the output from the investment comes on stream, the dominant firm can continue to maximize its profits – albeit at a lower level – if it adopts a Cournot or Bertrand non-cooperative strategy. The dominant firm will, as a result, lose market share to the competitive fringe, but in practice this may occur gradually over many years. The classic case is United States Steel (USS), whose policy of price leadership continued over more than 50 years. At its inception in 1906, USS had a 60 per cent market share, which by 1960 had fallen to 22 per cent. At some point a dominant firm may have to choose between continuing to lose market share and eventually the loss of its dominant position, or switch to a limit pricing strategy. Rationally, the decision will depend on the present value of the expected profit streams associated with the alternative strategies at that future date.

Once we take a dynamic perspective we have also to consider the influence of technological progress and knowledge acquisition on the relative position of the dominant firm and its smaller rivals. In many cases, the maximum rate at which smaller firms can increase their output will depend on technological factors. If technology enables smaller rivals to rapidly increase their output and more rapidly take market share away from the dominant firm, the dominant firm will gain little by setting a high price: both short-run rents and market share will evaporate quickly. The three factors just discussed – the extent to which investment costs are sunk, the rate at which technology allows smaller firms to expand and the present value of alternative profit streams – will determine how rapidly a dominant firm will bring the price down to the limit level.

So far we have said little about how smaller-scale rivals form their conjectures about the dominant firm's **ex post** behaviour. The senior managers of a firm within the competitive fringe, in addition to observing the market price and profit reported by the dominant firm, should also consider the growth of demand for the industry's output, the prospects for rivalry or co-operation, the share of the market it expects to capture and associated projected production costs. In judging these determinants, the dominant firm's *ex ante* price and profits need play no direct role. For the smaller rival strategic considerations are the anticipated *ex post* price and its expected market share. In assessing these factors, paramount should be an appraisal of the sort of rivalry, including price policies, likely to be encountered.

The traditional, naïve, limit price model employed the Sylos postulate because it facilitated a definite solution to the problem of the long-run equilibrium price and output under limit pricing. Once one abandons the assumption that a smaller rival uses the incumbent's *ex ante* behaviour as determining its *ex post* behaviour, the success of a deterrence strategy hinges on the extent to which the dominant firm can influence the formation of conjectures about its likely *ex post* behaviour. Figure 10.10 shows a limit pricing game under conditions of incomplete information, where the dominant firm seeks to deter a smaller rival from investing in additional capacity The pay-offs are shown as the present value of future profits, in millions of euro: in each column the dominant firm's and the

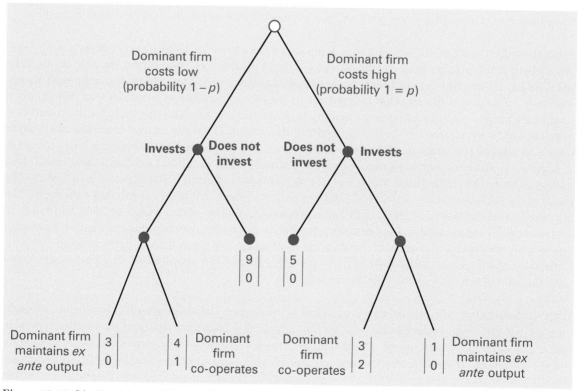

Figure 10.10: Limit pricing and incomplete information

smaller rival's pay-offs are shown first and second, respectively. The dominant firm's unit costs of production are private information; the firm may be highly efficient, in which case unit costs are low or it may suffer X-inefficiencies or organizational slack, in which case unit costs are higher. Game theorists describe such situations as *states of nature*, in the sense that nature determines whether or not the incumbent is low cost. For the smaller rival, its senior managers have incomplete information as to whether the price charged by the dominant firm reflects high costs or the exploitation of the dominant firm's rent-generating abilities. Only the dominant firm knows its unit costs and hence the sustainability of a price war *ex post*. The game starts with a **chance node** – depicted by an open circle – where nature determines whether the dominant incumbent is high or low cost. The smaller rival can proceed by attaching probabilities to these states of nature; thus, the dominant firm is high cost (with probability p) or low cost (with probability $1 - p$).

As can be seen from Figure 10.10, if the smaller rival invests, the dominant firm earns a greater pay-off by adopting a co-operative stance, i.e. sharing the market, than by producing the limit price output. Let us assume that the smaller firm's senior managers believe this to be the case, but are not satisfied with a profit stream the present value of which is €1m. The smaller firm's senior managers will, therefore, only proceed with the investment if they believe the dominant firm's costs are high: this is therefore the critical decision factor for entry. From the dominant firm's point of view, a decision on limit pricing may in this situation be predicated on an assessment of the way the smaller rival's senior managers form their beliefs about their larger rival's costs. Unlike its smaller competitor, the dominant firm will potentially play the game shown in Figure 10.10 over and over again with a succession of would-be entrants. It may then make sense for a weak, i.e. high-cost, dominant firm to produce the limit output, if by so doing it creates or maintains a reputation for having low unit costs, which discourages smaller rivals from expansion.

The foregoing has focused on using price as the strategic variable, but in practice a dominant firm might employ a non-price strategic variable to place smaller rivals at a competitive disadvantage. Such a strategy can include all behaviours that are credible and signal the ability to place a rival or new entrant under asymmetric pressure. Analysis of this strategic approach was initiated by Salop and Scheffman (1983). A strategy of deterrence to secure and defend a dominant position by increasing smaller rivals' production and selling costs is potentially superior to lowering price. For example, a dominant firm might seek to raise smaller rivals' unit costs by limiting access to essential resources or, in a differentiated market, spending lavishly on advertising. These are just two of a number of ways in which a dominant firm with deep pockets can put additional pressure on smaller rivals. Given the likelihood that the dominant firm will have lower unit costs than its smaller rivals, it may be rational for the larger firm to engage in action that while raising its own costs also raises those of its smaller rivals. Raising rivals' costs places the burden on smaller rivals or potential entrants. By accepting higher costs, the dominant firm can actually protect itself from competition and thereby strengthen a position that will allow it to exercise greater control over the market price to recoup higher costs. For example, in a highly unionized industry, acceding to a generous pay demand or granting its employees improved benefits is a way of placing smaller rivals under pressure to offer similar deals. More generally, a dominant firm may bid up the price of an essential input, acquire control of low-cost suppliers or generate internal organizational resources that create some advantage, e.g. lower costs of serving the market. Other examples include **vertical integration** or an **alliance** with a supplier to control a key input. Actions to impair the growth of demand for smaller rival's products also ultimately come down to raising costs. If the dominant firm uses its size and funds to induce customers to sign longer-term contracts or to offer a wider product range it will force additional promotional costs on smaller rivals.

The dominant firm can also indirectly raise rival's costs by investing heavily in new products and distribution networks. But in terms of deterrence, investment in spare capacity sends a clear signal to smaller rivals and potential entrants that the dominant firm is willing and able to defend its market share. For such a signal to be convincing, the capacity must be sunk: an investment that can be liquidated with relatively small capital losses does not demonstrate the same commitment. If excess capacity is sunk, then it can permit a dominant firm to maintain its position without suffering the reduction in profit or of market share predicted by limit price models. A dominant firm may invest in excess capacity for reasons other than attempting to limit competition. Excess capacity may be dictated by the prevailing technology. For example, if short-run average costs increase markedly with increased output and market demand is volatile, the only efficient way to increase output is for the dominant firm to maintain some excess capacity. Where distributors' services are essential to commercial success and a dominant firm has not integrated forward into distribution, it will have to convince distributors to support its product. Investment in excess capacity can demonstrate a commitment to distributors that the firm is in the market to stay.

Upstream vertical integration to control the production of a key input may have as a prime purpose the security of supplies and this consideration may outweigh a consequential rise in the firm's production costs. Alternatively, a decision to integrate upstream, even if it raises costs, could be designed to influence the entry decisions of potential rivals. A decision by a would-be dominant firm to integrate vertically to secure access to a vital resource could place an entrant at a cost disadvantage. If a dominant firm manufactures consumer goods, it may integrate forward into wholesale and retail distribution. By integrating forward, the dominant firm can guarantee itself secure access to the final consumer, control efforts to differentiate its product, and possibly impede the access of rivals to the final consumer. For example, if the entrant comes in at the manufacturing level only, it will have to distribute its product through independent wholesalers and retailers. It will have to pay for their support, either directly or by offering the product to retailers at a discount. If it tries to avoid these costs by cultivating a powerful brand image these costs will also be sunk; and, if unsuccessful, the entrant could hardly expect to sell its goodwill and recover its investment.

In Chapter 13, we will examine the strategic relationships between product differentiation and advertising in some detail. Both can be employed as a strategy for market dominance. Funds may be invested in developing distinctive product varieties. Advertising and other sales efforts can be used to cultivate a favourable brand image among final consumers and distributors. The resulting product and/or brand loyalty can create a dominant position because it raises entry costs for potential rivals who would have to persuade the incumbent's loyal consumers to switch. Forward vertical integration into retail distribution can facilitate product differentiation, as it promotes the flow of information from consumers to producers. A firm that controls access to final consumers is in a strong position with respect to rivals, especially if that access cannot be duplicated without some sunk investment and some passage of time.

Having established a dominant position a firm can employ various tactics – other than lowering price – to make it harder for new firms to obtain a foothold in the market. For example, by offering a variety of brands (as in the breakfast cereal industry), a dominant firm can pre-empt opportunities for a new firm to come in on a small scale and serve a narrowly focused segment of the market. This is a particular problem if learning by doing is important. In such an industry, small-scale entry may be the only practical way a firm can enter a market. Finally, as we will discus in some detail in the next chapter, a firm could employ *vertical restraints* as part of a dominance strategy. Vertical restraints are applied to the sales of *intermediate products* between buyers and sellers in the *supply chain*. There can be many motives for a firm engaging in such restraints, but one can be to raise entry barriers and frustrate competition. We will return to these strategies in subsequent chapters; at this stage the point to note is that deterrent strategies encompass a wide range of actions, some of which are likely to be judged an abuse of a dominant position by the competition authorities.

Locking-In

Having invested heavily in telecommunications networks, operators have enormous incentive to lock in subscribers through agreements that make it difficult for them to move to another operator. Examples include long-term contracts and discounts for exclusive dealing. Most such arrangements are perfectly legal, but the practice becomes more questionable when a dominant firm locks in subscribers before the market is being contested by a number of players.

The arrival of mobile phones presented the European Commission with a particular issue. All mobile phones have a Subscriber Identification Module – or SIM – card that is uniquely associated with a particular handset. Operating companies placed a 'lock' on the SIM as, in principle, it acted as a theft deterrent, but it also effectively locked the handset and subscriber to a particular mobile

phone operator. Locking the SIM card and preventing its replacement in the handset prevented subscribers from switching provider. The SIM could be unlocked, but service providers tended to impose significant charges for overriding the SIM 'lock-in'.

In 1996, the Commission Directorate responsible for competition policy wrote to all EU network providers notifying them that it considered the practice had anti-competitive effects. After a period of consultation the operators agreed to modify their handsets so that subscribers could unlock the SIM lock feature. But the Commission demanded more. In the future, operators were to provide customers with full information as to how they could unlock their handsets and where handset were subsidized, the amount of subsidy and terms for recovery had also to be disclosed.

Predatory Pricing

So far we have considered the strategies that a dominant firm might adopt to protect its market share and deter entry. There are, however, a wide range of hostile and aggressive strategies that can be employed by dominant firms that are designed to force existing competitors out of the industry and as explained earlier these are known as predation strategies. Predation falls under the ambit of Article 82 of the European Community Treaty as it amounts to an attempt to harm the competitive process. The result of predation might paradoxically be intense competition for a short while, but its longer-term purpose is the removal of competitors. Article 82 prohibits actions designed to harm the competitive process: if undertaken by a dominant firm it is an 'abuse of a dominant position' that sooner or later will be adverse for consumers. Predation can involve both price and non-price strategies and the suspicion of such behaviour is likely to be carefully scrutinized by the competition authorities. We will focus here mainly on predatory pricing as non-price predation amounts to the more extreme pursuit of the non-price deterrence strategies just outlined above.

The prevalence, indeed even the existence, of predatory pricing has been the subject of much debate. The best-known example of predatory pricing is the Standard Oil Company, which under the leadership of the 'church going' John D. Rockefeller ruthlessly attained a 90 per cent market share of the US oil refining industry between 1870 and 1899. Standard Oil attained this dominant market share, in part, by using predatory pricing to drive its rivals out of the industry (Scherer and Ross, 1990). Other well-documented examples of predatory pricing include the activities of shipowners' 'conferences' (i.e. cartels) who resorted to 'fighting ships' with very low freight rates to undercut any new entrant attempting to compete for business. The theoretical literature on predatory pricing defines two distinct models: one based on the concept of a '***deep pocket***' and one based on reputation signalling. The idea underpinning the 'deep pocket' model is that access to financial resources is asymmetric and the firm with greater financial resources can outlast its rival in a 'fight to the death'. Reputation models are based on the idea that in driving a rival out of the industry, the firm is focused not so much on the current situation, but the signal such behaviour sends to firms in the competitive fringe or potential entrants.

Predatory pricing can be illustrated by working through a stylized version of the Standard Oil story. There are two questions to keep in mind. First, what kind of market structure is required for predatory pricing to be feasible? Second, in what circumstances is predatory pricing likely to be profitable? The stylized story is this: a dominant firm operates in a number of geographically separate markets. In some of those markets, it enjoys market power, in others, it does not. In one market where its actions are constrained by competitors, it sets a price below unit cost. By so doing, it loses money in that market but is sustained by its operations in other markets. Small firms, whose unit costs are likely to be higher than the dominant firm, are now faced with a market price too low to cover their costs of production. Consequently they suffer losses and, lacking a 'deep pocket', will sooner or later exit the industry. With the departure of the smaller rivals, the dominant firm becomes a monopoly in the targeted geographic market. It then restricts output, pushing up price, and maximizes its economic rent in the target market. The economic rent is presumed to (more than) compensate for its profit sacrifice during its period of predatory pricing. Note that we have not said that the large firm raises price in other markets when it cuts price in the target market. This argument is sometimes called the ***recoupment fallacy***. If the dominant firm is already maximizing its profits in these other markets, price increases would reduce its overall profits. Although this story concerns spatial markets, the logic would be much the same for a dominant firm producing multi-brands of a differentiated product, competing with many rivals that each produced a single competing brand.

A strategy of predatory pricing is an investment in market power and, like all investments, it is inherently dynamic. We can attempt to capture something of the dynamics with the aid of Figure 10.11, which illustrates the three stages of the process of predatory pricing assuming homogeneous products. To keep things simple, let us assume that the predator has constant marginal costs, MC_p, and this allows us to minimize the number of lines in the diagram as implicitly unit costs equal marginal costs, i.e. $SRAC = MC$. The assumption of constant MC may not be such an unrealistic assumption if, for example, the predator can produce in other markets to supply the target market, and if transportation costs are small relative to price. The victim, which by assumption is smaller scale and operates in only the target market, has a conventional U-shaped, short-run total, average total cost curve ($SRAC$) and rising marginal cost curve, MC, as shown in Figure 10.11.

In the first stage the dominant firm and its small
rival co-exist with a
market price of p_0, where
total market output, Q_0, is
split between the smaller
rival, q_0, and the dominant firm, q_M, where $q_M =$
$(Q_0 - q_0)$. We can view
this 'equilibrium' as non-
cooperative Cournot. In
the second stage the dom-
inant firm adopts a
predatory stance and in-
creases its output, causing
the market supply to in-
crease to Q_1. The effect of
this is to push the market
price below unit produc-
tion cost for both firms,

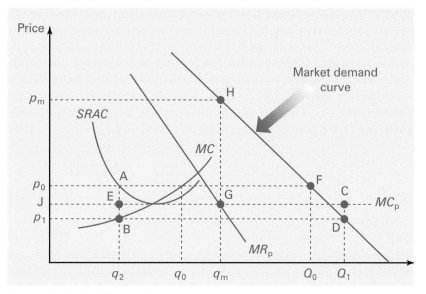

Figure 10.11: Predatory pricing

i.e. p_1. In response the victim can minimize its losses by reducing output from q_0 to q_2 – its point of
minimum loss at price p_1. The victim is now losing money on every unit sold and its total losses are
given by the area, p_0ABp_1. Since Figure 10.11 is a representation of the market's operations for a
single period, the victim will lose this much, per period, as long as predation continues to operate.
Lacking deep pockets the smaller firm is now threatened with bankruptcy. If the predator succeeds in
forcing its smaller rival out of the industry, we move to the third stage. Once the rival has exited the
industry, the dominant firm uses its newly gained **monopoly** power to earn an economic rent that
compensates for its first-stage losses.

Now consider the position of the predator. To maintain a market price of p_1, the quantity supplied
must be maintained at Q_1. At the same time, the quantity supplied by the victim has fallen to q_2, so
the predator must greatly increase its own supply to $Q_1 - q_2$ in order to maintain the low predatory
price. As long as the victim remains in the market the predator is failing to cover its variable costs by
a margin of $MC_P - p_1$ on every unit sold – let alone making a contribution to fixed costs. The predator's total losses on variable costs per period are given by the area, $CEBD$. By comparing these losses
($CEBD$) for the predator with the victim's losses (p_0ABp_1), it is evident that the predator loses substantially more, per period, than the victim. The economic losses suffered by both firms are offset by
the consumers' gain, i.e. there is an increase in consumers' surplus. In this simple example, it would
appear that the sum of the firms' losses is less than the gain in consumers' surplus, suggesting there
is the net welfare gain from predation – at least in the first stage.

Let us now consider in more detail the third stage of the predation process. The victim has left the
market and the dominant firm now remains as **a monopolist** in this particular geographic market. As
a profit-maximizing monopolist, the predator will now reduce output to the level that equates its
marginal revenue to its marginal cost, q_m in Figure 10.11, yielding a market price p_m. Economic rent
– ignoring fixed costs – is given by the area, p_mHGJ. This is the rent earned in a single period but for

a predatory strategy to be 'profitable' the present discounted value of the profit stream expected by the predator must exceed the expected present value of profits from its *ex ante* policy of accommodation. The expected profits for the predator are set out in Equation (10.11). During the predation period the dominant firm will suffer losses ($-\pi$) but once the victim has left the market it can then use its market power to raise its price and earn a positive rent of π per period. Much depends on how many periods the victim might hold on for, but for illustrative purposes this is set at two periods in Equation (10.11). Taking r to represent the risk-adjusted opportunity **cost of capital**, the **present value** (π_{PDV}) of the dominant firm's income stream is:

$$\pi_{PDV} = \frac{-\pi_t}{(1+r)^1} + \frac{-\pi_{t+1}}{(1+r)^2} + \frac{\pi_{t+2}}{(1+r)^3} + \frac{\pi_{t+3}}{(1+r)^4} + \dots \tag{10.11}$$

A rational dominant firm will consider predatory pricing as a strategy toward rivals only if π_{PDV} is both positive and more profitable than any other strategy at the dominant firm's disposal. For example, merger might be a preferred alternative to predation, but subject to approval by the competition authorities. It follows that whether or not Equation (10.11) satisfies these conditions will depend in part on the available alternative strategies and also on three issues arising from predation: the predator's losses in the predation stage; the pay-off in the succeeding periods; and the value of r.

The key influence on losses in the predation stage is the predatory price chosen by the dominant firm. The choice here is the trade-off between losses per period during the predation stage and the number of periods it takes to drive the victim from the market. The lower the predatory price the greater are the losses per period during the predation period. However, the lower the price set by the predator, the more rapidly the victim is likely to depart. And, the shorter the first stage, the more rapidly will the predator recoup its losses by exercising its monopoly profits. If the discount rate is very high, a predator will give greater weight to the short-run losses entailed by a campaign of predatory pricing and less weight to the monopoly rent expected after the victim has been driven from the market. On the other hand, if the discount rate is very low, the present value of long-term monopoly rents will be higher. The lower the discount rate, *ceteris paribus*, the more likely is predation to occur. A major influence on the length of the predation period is the extent to which the victim's capital investment is a sunk cost. If the assets employed are sunk, the victim may be earning a **quasi rent** and the price war upon which successful predation depends will tend to be of longer duration. Sunk costs thus stretch out the period of predation, reducing the likelihood for recoupment after the victim has departed. It is possible that if the target firm decides to sell out, the predator firm would be interested in purchasing its assets. This raises a possible additional motive for predatory pricing: to drive down the purchase price of the assets of the target firm before acquisition by the predator.

Finally, the pay-off from predation depends on how great the monopoly profits are once the victim is driven from the scene. A rational firm will not precipitate a period of substantial losses without the expectation of being able to raise the market price at the end of that period to (more than) recoup its losses. But here we find ourselves in a situation of circular reasoning. The longer it takes to drive a victim from the market, the more uncertain are future monopoly profits. A protracted price war might attract greater scrutiny from the competition authorities or cause the predator to lose ground in areas such as R&D. If the market is contestable – i.e. there are no sunk entry costs – the victim might rapidly exit the market, but once the predator is earning an economic rent, new firms can enter with the effect that monopoly profits will be short lived. Moreover, if economic rents are likely to be available in the future it would be more profitable for the target firm to stay put: the more so, if there are sunk costs. If it is profitable for the target firm to stay put it should be able to obtain the financial resources – loans or equity – needed to sustain it through the price war. If the target firm can obtain such financial assistance, it cannot be driven from the market. A rational dominant firm, in recognizing the logic of this argument will, it is argued by some economists, conclude that predatory pricing is doomed to fail and will therefore never embark on such a strategy.

Unfortunately, the argument that funding from the capital market will prevent successful predation depends critically on efficient financial markets; namely, capital markets that can accurately assess return and risk. The flaw in this 'predatory pricing is illogical' approach is that even if financial markets are efficient, there are sound reasons to think that real-world capital markets will systematically refuse to fund target firms, or at least that such firms will be able to acquire funds only at differentially high interest rates. The very act of predation is likely to lower the victim's net asset value and suppliers of financial capital would have incomplete information about the target firm's ability to survive a period of predatory pricing. There would be uncertainty about the predator's resources and the determination of its management to pursue a predatory strategy to the bitter end. As pointed out by Fudenberg and Tirole (1986), the factors that make the smaller firm vulnerable to predation may also foreclose it from access to the financial markets. Given incomplete information on the target firm, coupled with the opportunism of the predator, financial markets are unlikely to provide capital to a target firm, except at a risk premium that pushes the costs of the target firm above those of the predator.

We noted above, that the theoretical literature on predatory pricing also defines a second model based on reputation signalling. A dominant firm is unlikely to face only a single rival. The competitive fringe is likely to contain a number of firms and there is also the issue of potential entrants. For example, a dominant firm operating in a number of separate geographic markets will rationally take into consideration the effects of a strategy of predation in one market on the conjectures and behaviour of existing and potential rivals in other markets. Say, for example, a dominant firm is operating in two geographically separated markets. It would seem logical for the dominant firm, in considering a strategy of predatory pricing in one of the markets, to take into consideration the impact on rivals in the second market. That is, by building a reputation for 'aggressive competition', the dominant firm might cower smaller rivals in the second market and in the extreme cause some to exit the market.

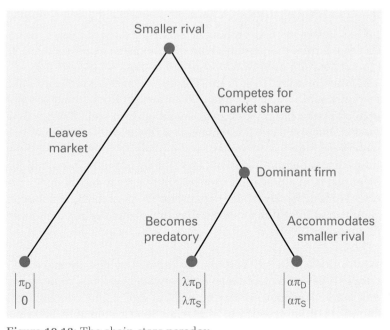

Figure 10.12: The chain store paradox

This logic is, however, flawed as can be demonstrated by the *chain store paradox* game, which was set out some 25 years ago by Reinhard Selten (1978). The game can be demonstrated as follows. Suppose that a single dominant firm operates a chain of stores in 20 separate geographic markets. In each of the 20 markets the dominant firm confronts *sequentially* an existing smaller-scale rival; that is, in the first time period it faces a rival in one market, in the next time period it faces a rival in another market, and so on. A game tree for one of the 20 geographic markets is shown in Figure 10.12. The smaller rival's pay-off, measured in millions of euro, π_S, relates only to the single game set out in Figure 10.12. The dominant firm's pay-off is also in millions of euro, π_D, and for the dominant firm this profit is potentially available for capture in the other 19 markets in which it operates. The smaller player has two choices: either to compete for market share or to leave the market.

If the smaller firm exits the market, it earns a zero profit and the dominant firm earns a monopoly rent, π. If the smaller firm chooses to compete for market share, the game moves to its second stage. The dominant firm must now decide whether to co-operate with its smaller rival or engage in predation. The pay-offs to the dominant firm are $\lambda\pi$ and $\alpha\pi$, where $\lambda < 0 < \alpha < 1$ for a strategy of predation and accommodation, respectively. Now the dominant firm has an incentive to engage in predation in the first market in the first time period if:

$$\delta\lambda\pi_D + \sum_{i=2}^{n} \delta^i\pi_D > \sum_{i=1}^{n} \delta^i\alpha\pi_D \qquad (10.12)$$

where δ is the discount factor, i.e. $\delta = 1/(1 + r)$. But even if the inequality shown in Equation (10.12) does not hold, might the dominant firm not have an incentive to engage in predation in order to cower smaller rivals in the other 19 markets? It might appear that having ruthlessly dispatched one rival in the first market, the other rivals will choose not to fight, leaving the dominant firm to capture π_D in all of the other 19 markets. The answer is, however, no, providing we assume rational behaviour. Consider the twentieth market, which the dominant firm would turn to in the twentieth time period. In this market, a rational smaller player will expect the dominant firm to behave in a manner that maximizes the present value of its expected profit stream. If the inequality shown in Equation (10.12) does not hold in the twentieth market, then regardless of what happened in the first 19 markets, the dominant firm is unlikely to engage in predatory behaviour. Predation in the twentieth market would cost the dominant firm lost profits without any possibility of later gains in other geographic markets; thus, a rational dominant firm would adopt an accommodation strategy in the final market. But if the small incumbent in the next-to-last period is clever enough, it will realize that a pay-off-maximizing dominant firm is likely to co-operate in the twentieth market; then again, if the inequality shown in Equation (10.12) does not hold, the dominant firm would have nothing to gain by engaging in a predation strategy in the next-to-last period. This is an example of backward induction. Working backward in time, period by period, the conclusion is reached that the dominant firm cannot credibly influence the behaviour of smaller firms in markets 2 to 20 by its behaviour in the first market.

Why is this a paradox? Because the irrefutable logic of backward induction fails to destroy the plausibility of behaviour in one market influencing rivals in other markets. The belief that behaviour in one market influences the conjectures and behaviour of rivals in other markets is widespread (Scherer and Ross, 1990). In fact, it can be shown that by relaxing one or another of the assumptions of Selten's model, it is possible to build a model within which predatory behaviour could emerge as

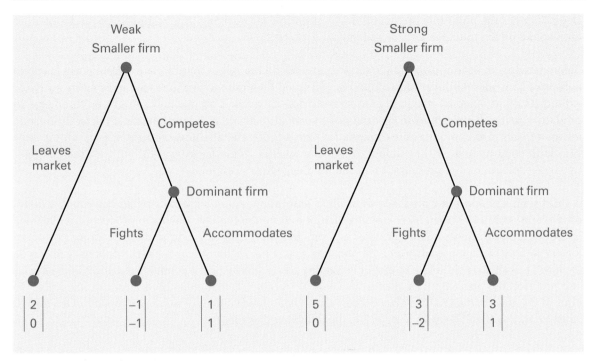

Figure 10.13: Imperfect information

the optimal strategy. One such relaxation concerns information. If the smaller firms have incomplete information it can be shown that predation may emerge as the best strategy if smaller rivals are uncertain about the dominant firm's pay-offs. Figure 10.13 shows a possible game tree for a single market in the chain store game with incomplete information. As before, the smaller competitor's pay-offs are the second figure in the columns. With uncertainty, the smaller player does not know the dominant firm's pay-offs. It may be that the dominant firm is weak, in the sense that it earns more by accommodating than by fighting. If the dominant firm is weak, its pay-offs are shown on the left-hand side of Figure 10.13. The smaller firm earns a pay-off equal to zero by leaving the market. If the smaller firm competes, the dominant firm makes a profit of €1m if it accommodates its smaller rival. If, however, the dominant firm is weak and it decides to fight, it makes a loss of –€1m in the current period. It would appear that if the dominant firm is weak, and smaller rivals believe this to be the case, then by backward induction the dominant firm will accommodate in every geographic market and time period.

Alternatively, the dominant firm may be strong, in the sense that it if it fights it will win. Pay-offs for the strong incumbent are shown on the right-hand side of Figure 10.13. If the incumbent is strong, it will fight. But, in fact a weak incumbent also has an incentive to fight, at least in early periods, because by fighting it can establish a reputation for being strong. Such a reputation is a valuable asset, and therefore worth investing in, because it discourages future entrants from coming into the market. The foregoing is an important observation. It suggests that predation can emerge as strategic behaviour because information is incomplete. This would appear to accord with reality: in the real world, information is both incomplete and imperfect, and it makes sense for smaller rivals in the separate geographic market to consider whether or not a dominant firm has fought aggressively in other markets when it tries to anticipate the behaviour of the dominant firm if it competes for market share. It also reinforces the point that the overall level of profitability arising from a strategy of predation does not depend on the outcome for a single period or market.

Before moving on, it is appropriate to once again remind ourselves that predation frequently involves non-price strategies. Ordover *et al.* (1983) have argued that a dominant firm may have an incentive to extend its dominance by vertically integrating downstream. The incentive might be to engage in predatory **price discrimination** or predatory vertical restraints. Advertising is a perfectly normal means of informing potential customers of a firm's products, attitudes and intentions. But a large firm with deep pockets will be able to out-spend smaller rivals, making it difficult for the competitive fringe to counter the presentation of the dominant firm's products.

A third source of non-price predation is product innovation. All other factors remaining equal, a dominant firm is more likely than its competitive fringe to have the funds to devote to product improvement. Introducing a new higher-quality product in a differentiated market would normally capture those customers who value higher quality and are prepared to pay the higher price. But if the dominant firm sells the new product at a price close to that of its smaller rivals' products, the competitive fringe finds its sales and profits under pressure. If smaller rivals cease to remain viable the dominant firm can then raise the price of the new product to earn an economic rent. These three sources of non-price predation are not exhaustive, but each will be dealt with within the following chapters.

The Practice of Dominance

A large company like the Coca-Cola Company, together with its bottlers, has enormous power in the European carbonated soft drinks sector. After a complaint by a competitor, the European Commission reached agreement with Coca-Cola whereby it would cease to include in its commercial agreements a number of practices judged by the Commission to be potentially anti-competitive.

One such practice was the offering of rebates or other advantages to customers purchasing all, or a specified minimum, of their carbonated soft drinks from Coca-Cola and its bottlers. In addition, the Commission required that the practice of conditioning rebates or other payments on a customer reaching an individually set purchase threshold or requiring customers to purchase other Coca-Cola brands must

cease. The purchasing of shelf-space from retailers and the advance of funds for facilities to customers were to be limited.

A significant commitment regarded beverage coolers and the common practice by Coca-Cola and its bottlers of placing coolers with customers free of charge, providing the customer had no other installed chilled beverage capacity. In future, customers must be able to use 20 per cent of the free beverage cooler's capacity for non Coca-Cola products. Finally, the Coca-Cola Company had to give an undertaking that it would publish the details of the settlement and the countries to which it applied on its website and each year it must provide the Commission with a written report detailing the steps taken to comply with the undertaking.

Competition Law and Predation

We have demonstrated above, that when a dominant firm adopts a strategy of predation, its tactics are designed to impair the competitive process and for customers the longer-term consequences are likely to be adverse. We have also pointed out that such behaviour is outlawed under Article 82 of the EC's competition policy. However, in practice detecting, let alone successfully prosecuting, predatory pricing raises a host of problems. The main problem for the competition authorities is that there are many reasons why prices might fall, and mostly they are beneficial – reflecting increased competition or technological advance rather than predation. It is perhaps understandable that fringe competitors who find themselves under price pressure will have a tendency to complain to the competition authorities that they are the subject of predation. In response, the competition authorities need a test that serves to differentiate between competitive and anti-competitive behaviour on the part of a dominant firm. Such a test – a cost-based test – owes much to Phillip Areeda and Donald Turner (1975), whose seminal article recognized the difficulty of specifying a standard that would detect predatory pricing without making it too easy for a rival, under the pressure of competition, claiming predation for the purpose of frustrating competition.

Areeda and Turner suggested the use of neo-classical profit-maximization rules to identify predatory situations. Their argument is based on the fact that if a firm is engaged in predatory pricing, it must be making a profit sacrifice in the short run in the expectation of an offsetting future profit. A firm operating under **perfect competition** maximizes its profits by picking the level of output that equates marginal cost to price (i.e. $p = MC$). Under imperfect competition, in order to maximize profits a firm with market power will choose a level of output that equates its marginal cost to its marginal revenue and consequently profit maximizing occurs where price exceeds marginal cost (i.e. $p > MC$). Areeda and Turner argued that it would therefore require some explaining if a firm with market power deliberately set a price less than its marginal cost. In their view, if a firm with market power deliberately sets a price at less than its reasonably anticipated short-run marginal cost, such behaviour should be held to be predatory and therefore unlawful.

This rules out limit pricing as predatory. In Areeda and Turner's view, a limit price is acceptable as long as the price is above the firm's short-run marginal cost. In essence, they treat a price above marginal cost as reflecting a competitive environment and for that reason they would not condemn a strategy of limit pricing. This, however, focuses attention on whether the marginal cost is the appropriate floor price. An efficient dominant firm might reasonably be expected to have much lower unit costs than a smaller rival and might be able to place the rival under extreme financial pressure without resort to lowering its price below its marginal cost. More to the point, as discussed above, predatory pricing might be employed to signal a reputation. As such, it is a tool in a game of dynamic strategic interactions and in this situation the dominant firm's prices need only convey to a smaller rival the signal that it would not be profitable to expand, or in the extreme remain in the market. This might be achieved by occasional, temporary price reductions (e.g. promotions) or the installation of sufficient additional capacity to significantly increase output if a smaller rival appeared to be contemplating an expansion or a potential entrant had emerged.

As a smaller rival or a potential entrant considering expansion must invest in facilities, personnel training, distribution development and product promotion, both may be deterred if they interpret temporary price reductions by the dominant firm as indicating a lower price will be adopted in response. In such circumstances, dominance may be maintained without resort to a predatory price war. A number of theorists have put forward alternatives to the Areeda–Turner test. One approach put forward by Ordover and Willig (1981), defines predation as 'a response to a rival that sacrifices part of the profit that could be earned under competitive circumstances' (p. 372). This is a much broader definition and requires demonstration that the dominant firm had available to it a less harmful reaction to expansion by a smaller rival or a potential entrant. Yet another approach is that of Krattenmaher and Salop (1986). These authors stated that a dominant firm should be deemed to be engaged in anti-competitive behaviour if its strategy is designed to raise smaller rivals' costs, forcing them to reduce output or leave the market. The dominant firm can then increase its own output or raise its price.

The problem with all of these tests of predation is that they present investigators with formidable problems. The simplest, and most explicit, test is that proposed by Areeda and Turner. A firm's marginal costs would appear to provide a definite floor price, yet in practice calculating a firm's MC is likely to be difficult. Recognizing this, Areeda and Turner propose that the firm's short-run average variable cost ($SRAVC$) be used as a proxy for MC. A price below $SRAVC$ can be presumed to be anti-competitive, as the firm is not covering **avoidable costs**. A further problem posed by predatory pricing is that it usually has to be dealt with in what is alleged to be the predation stage before the victim has been driven from the market. What the authorities and, possibly ultimately, the courts have to decide is whether they are dealing with a justified temporary reduction in price, e.g. resulting from competitive conditions, or whether a dominant firm is engaging in predation. If the competition authorities are satisfied it is the latter, they can take action – such as fining the predator and even forcing its break-up. From the perspective of the victim it would be better if predation had been prevented. One course of action, proposed by Baumol (1979), is for the authorities to prohibit the predator from reversing a price cut once a rival has exited the market. But Baumol's suggested approach, even if enforceable, would not prevent non-price strategies of predation. Areeda and Turner provide three good reasons why such a policy would be difficult to operate in practice and why therefore the authorities are constrained to only acting after predation has started. The three reasons are that, if the authorities:

- Were simply to forbid dominant firms to maximize their economic rents, then they would be transforming themselves into regulatory agencies, necessitating continual monitoring of the prices and costs of industries and firms under their jurisdiction.
- Held it illegal for a dominant firm to lower price in response to expansion or entry by a rival, they would in effect provide a protective umbrella over entrants that might prevent a dominant firm from competing on its merits; the authorities would also have to decide when technology or a new organizational design justified a lower price.
- Allowed price reductions but insisted that having reduced price in the face of entry a dominant firm cannot reverse the price cut, the courts would have to find a way to allow exceptions for changes in costs or demand, placing detailed administrative work on the authorities.

In practice, it is extremely difficult to prove intent and to balance the longer-term benefits for society. The pursuance of a pricing strategy by a dominant firm that creates difficulties for smaller rivals could be the result of superior skills and acumen, in which case attempts to restrain or penalize such behaviour serve only to discourage competition and its undoubted benefits for society. A further problem for the authorities is that weak competitors may have the incentive to claim predatory pricing by their rivals when they find it difficult to compete. Thus at an initial stage the authorities have to be convinced that the alleged predator has the necessary market power and that the market is not contestable.

Newspaper Price Wars

In September 1993, Rupert Murdoch reduced the cover price of *The Times* from 45p to 30p. In so doing, Murdoch lit a fuse. It appeared to his rivals that he was trying to provoke a price war and *The Independent* went further, complaining to the Office of Fair Trading that Murdoch was engaged in predatory pricing. Within weeks, Sir Bryan Carlsberg, the OFT's director, announced that the action was 'a calculated commercial decision by News International, which I would not be justified in treating as predatory'.

So what was Rupert Murdoch up to? One consideration was circulation; the higher a paper's circulation, the greater the leverage for negotiation with advertisers. Given the high fixed costs associated with the production of broadsheet newspapers, a higher circulation would have the twin benefits of lowering unit costs and increasing advertising revenue. From this perspective, the price cut might just have paid off, but it is unlikely to have been Murdoch's true motive.

For this we must look to the tabloid market and the considerable circulations of papers like the *Daily Mail* and the *Daily Express*: together these two titles had sales in excess of the total broadsheet market. By lowering the price of *The Times* to a level that put the paper in direct price competition with the tabloids, Murdoch might reasonably have expected to attract many more readers from this market than from rival broadsheets, where issues of politics and values ensured a highly differentiated market. Certainly *The Times* attracted readers from the *Daily Mail* and particularly the *Daily Express*. And in 2005, *The Times* was re-launched as a tabloid.

Concluding Thoughts

A dominant firm has more than the power to influence its market price, it has the power to operate independently of its rivals. Although such power can only pertain in the long run if there is some impediment to the operation of normal competitive forces, it does not automatically follow that a dominant firm will abuse its power by engaging in opportunistic behaviour. A dominant firm can be a price leader, generating not only higher profits for smaller rivals in the short run, but over the longer term providing them with the means to compete on more equal terms. Nevertheless, having achieved dominance a firm does have the option of engaging in strategies to disadvantage smaller rivals and potential entrants so as to reduce competition and thereby to protect its dominant position.

There are, in essence, two types of deterrent strategy: limiting rivals' options; and predation. The best-known model of limited deterrence is limit pricing, but strategies designed to raise rivals' costs or restrict access to key inputs can be just as effective. The hoped-for pay-off from limit pricing and other limited deterrent strategies is the longer-term absence of aggressive competition from an enlarging competitive fringe or the emergence of larger-scale rivals. Predation is an extremely aggressive strategy of deterrence. The idea is to force a rival out of the market and therefore to establish a market structure whereby the dominant firm can more-or-less act like a monopoly and extract a substantial economic rent. The best-known and most researched strategy of predation is predatory pricing.

In the European Union predation is viewed as an abuse of a dominant position and outlawed. The less aggressive limit pricing is not outlawed and in principle delivers to consumers over the longer term lower-priced products. Both strategies require a dynamic perspective for a full understanding. To be effective, the smaller rival or potential entrant must be convinced that the dominant firm's behaviour would not be accommodating following an expansion of production by the competitive fringe. Yet, a rational dominant firm will only be prepared to suffer the inevitable reduction in profits by aggressively resisting in the short run if losses can be offset by expected future profits. Once a dynamic perspective is adopted, factors such as sunk costs, technology and the opportunity cost of capital inform the strategic decision.

If a dominant firm chooses a strategy of accommodation rather than deterrence, it may adopt a Cournot or Bertrand non-cooperative stance or the co-operative stance implied by price leadership. From a dynamic perspective, over the longer term the effect of a price leadership strategy is to create scope for rivals to steal market share. The overriding rule is to adopt that policy which, subject to uncertainty, is likely to deliver the greatest present value from a discounted profit stream. Nevertheless, given the uncertainties associated with the long-term policy of limiting a rival's options – uncertainties that are greatly increased in industries where technology and/or consumer tastes are subject to continual change – the best course of action might be to maximize short-run profits and use the funds generated to strengthen brands and/or develop new products and processes.

Key Learning Points

- Dominance describes a situation where a firm with a large market share has the ability to use its market power to place smaller rivals at a competitive disadvantage.
- A dominant firm has the option of choosing a strategy of price leadership. This maximizes profits in the short run, but encourages expansion by smaller rivals and/or new entrants with the result that in the longer term the dominant firm loses market share.
- A dominant firm can engage in deterrence strategies. These may be pricing strategies such as limit or predatory pricing or non-price strategies to increase smaller rivals' costs.
- Economies of scale are not sufficient for a strategy of limit pricing; the dominant firm's unit cost advantage must be reinforced by accumulated learning and/or the presence of sunk costs. In short, if the market is contestable limit pricing is infeasible.
- Any strategy of deterrence is inherently dynamic. Whether or not it is rational depends on the conjectures of smaller rivals as to the dominant firm's behaviour following investment in additional capacity. If smaller rivals believe that it would be less profitable for a dominant firm to persist with a strategy of deterrence, then such a strategy will be ineffective.
- Predation is the most extreme strategy of deterrence. Its purpose is to physically drive a rival from the industry so that the dominant firm can raise output or price to increase its economic rent.
- Predatory pricing involves lowering the market price below unit production costs so that all firms in the market are incurring losses. The predator must therefore be able to sustain losses in the short run and must believe that the present, discounted value of the longer-term profit streams will more than offset the short-run loss.
- Non-price forms of predation include vertical integration to control a key input or a downstream market; advertising and innovation can be just as effective and may involve a smaller profit sacrifice on the part of the predator.

continued

- In principle, deterrent strategies are anti-competitive, but in practice it is extremely difficult for the competition authorities to determine when a dominant firm's intent is deterrence and when it is competitive. Predation is in principle easier to detect and will incur the wrath of the competition authorities if discovered.

Exercises

10.1 What is the essential difference in terms of a quantity solution when comparing a Stackelberg and Cournot equilibrium?

10.2 Is the Sylos postulate a realistic assumption for a potential entrant? Explain when it might and might not be.

10.3 What strategies other than reducing price might a dominant firm adopt to maintain dominance?

10.4 By setting a price far above the limit price, a dominant firm invites expansion by the competitive fringe and/or new entry. In what situation might price leadership not be challenged by the growth of the competitive fringe or new entrants?

10.5 In what way does, or should, the rate of time preference influence preferences for strategies of deterrence?

Problems

10.1 Consider a duopoly consisting of a dominant firm and a 'fringe' competitor. Given the market demand curve $p = 1,000 - 0.05(Q + q)$, where Q is the output of the dominant firm and q the output of the fringe, and the cost functions Q and $80 + q$, respectively, for the dominant firm and the fringe:

(a) How much output will the dominant firm have to produce to remove the fringe firm from the market?

(b) If the fringe firm observes the dominant firm producing $Q = 400$ and expects this to be maintained, construct the residual demand curve for the fringe firm.

(c) Using the answer to (b) what is the fringe firm's profit-maximizing level of output?

10.2 Consider a Stackelberg game between two firms. Firm 1 is the leader, market demand is given by $p = 1,000 - 4Q$ and each firm has a constant unit cost of €20:

(a) Determine the profit-maximizing output for the leader.

(b) Solve the Nash equilibrium for the follower, firm 2.

(c) How far below €20 would the follower's unit costs have to fall so that it achieved the same market share as the leader?

References

Areeda, P. and Turner, D. (1975) 'Predatory prices and related practices under Section 2 of the Sherman Act', *Harvard Law Review*, vol. 88, pp. 697–733.

Bain, J. (1951) 'Relation of profit rate to industry concentration: American concentration', *Quarterly Journal of Economics*, vol. 65, pp. 293–329.

Bain, J. (1956) *Barriers to New Competition: Their Character and Consequences in Manufacturing Industries*, Harvard University Press, Cambridge, MA.

Baumol, W. (1979) 'Quasi-permanence of price reductions: a policy for prevention of predatory pricing', *Yale Law Journal*, vol. 89, pp. 1–26.

Baumol, W., Panzar, J. and Willig, R. (1982) *Contestable Markets and the Theory of Industry Structure*, Harcourt Brace Jovanovitch, New York.

Fudenberg, D. and Tirole, J. (1986) 'A "signal-jamming" theory of predation', *Rand Journal of Economics*, vol. 17, pp. 366–376.

Krattenmaher, T. and Salop, S. (1986) 'Anticompetitive exclusion: raising rivals' costs to achieve power over price', *Yale Law Journal*, vol. 96, pp. 209–295.

Ordover, J. and Willig, R. (1981) 'An economic definition of predation: pricing and product innovation', *Yale Law Journal*, vol. 91, pp. 8–53.

Ordover, J., Sykes, A. and Willig, R. (1983) 'Unfair international trade practices', *New York University Journal of International Law and Politics*, vol. 15, pp. 323–337.

Salop, S. and Scheffman, D. (1983) 'Raising rivals' costs', *American Economic Review*, vol. 73, pp. 267–271.

Scherer, F. and Ross, D. (1990) *Industrial Market Structure and Economic Performance*, Houghton Mifflin, New York.

Selten, R. (1978) 'The chain store paradox', *Theory Decision*, vol. 9, pp. 127–159.

Sylos-Labini, P. (1962) *Oligopoly and Technical Progress*, Harvard University Press, Cambridge, MA.

von Stackelberg, H. (1934) *Marktform und Gleichgewicht*, Vienna, Springer [translation, 1952, Peacock, A. *Theory of the Market Economy*, William Hodge, London].

As the leader, firm A does not have a reaction function, but when making its output decision it will recognize the influence that it will exert on the follower. Both firms face the following inverse demand curve:

$$p = a - \beta(q_A + q_B) \qquad\qquad (10A.1)$$

Firm B, as the follower, has the reaction function (10A.2) as derived in the previous chapter:

$$q_B = \frac{a - \beta q_A}{2\beta} \qquad\qquad (10A.2)$$

A's total revenue function is obtained by multiplying Equation (10A.1) by q_A and as A knows that B will set its output in response to A's output, we can substitute Equation (10A.2) for q_B, to obtain:

$$TR_A = a q_A - \beta q_A{}^2 - \beta q_A \left[\frac{a - \beta q_A}{2\beta} \right] \qquad\qquad (10A.3)$$

which can be simplified to:

$$TR_A = \frac{a}{2} q_A - \frac{\beta}{2} q^2{}_A \qquad\qquad (10A.4)$$

If firm A makes a small change to its level of output, Δq_A, the change in total revenue, ΔTR, is given by the following:

$$\Delta TR = \frac{\alpha}{2}\Delta q_A - \frac{\beta}{2}[(q_A + \Delta q_A)(q_A + \Delta q_A) - q^2_A] \tag{10A.5}$$

Note the second term on the right-hand side of Equation (10A.5) in squared parentheses reduces to $2\Delta q_A + \Delta q^2_A$ and for small changes in q_A, $\Delta q_A{}^2$ approaches zero, giving:

$$\Delta TR = \frac{\alpha}{2}\Delta q_A - \beta\Delta q_A q_A \tag{10A.6}$$

Marginal revenue is defined as $\Delta TR/\Delta q$, so dividing through by Δq_A, we obtain:

$$MR_A = \frac{\alpha}{2} - \beta q_A \tag{10A.7}$$

Setting Equation (10A.7) equal to marginal cost (which as before we can assume to be zero without any loss of generality) determines the profit-maximizing level of output and rearranging to get q_A on the left-hand side yields:

$$q_A = \frac{\alpha}{2\beta} \tag{10A.8}$$

CHAPTER 11

PRICE DISCRIMINATION AND BUNDLING

Introduction

Arguably, **_price discrimination_** is one of the most widely practised forms of pricing. At its most basic, price discrimination is present whenever the same product is sold to different customers or consumers at different prices. As we shall see, this simple definition needs some qualification; for example, the product must be identical in all respects, including the transport costs of delivery. The examples of price discrimination are numerous, ranging from airfares to discount coupons on groceries. There can be little doubt that firms, or rather their senior managers, believe there are real benefits in taking advantage of variations in customers' price sensitivities. Our interest in this chapter is to understand what these benefits are in order to explain why firms engage in strategies of price discrimination. We also investigate what forms price discrimination might take and the consequences for competition and social welfare.

For a firm to engage in price discrimination, three conditions are necessary. Firstly, the firm must have sufficient market power to be able to exercise some control over the price at which it sells its product. Secondly, it must be possible to separate customers or consumers into separate groups according to their price sensitivity. Finally, the firm must be able to prevent those customers or consumers who are sold the product at a lower price, reselling to customers and consumers who are being charged a higher price. Despite its prevalence, price discrimination can be illegal if it is judged to deter competition. We dealt with deterrence strategies in the last chapter, and while it would be possible for a dominant firm to engage in price discrimination in order to disadvantage rivals, it would be incorrect to assume that deterrence is the prime motive for firms with market power to price discriminate.

Price discrimination is an important strategy in pursuit of maximizing profits. The essence of price discrimination is to charge customers or consumers the price they are willing to pay. Whenever a product is sold where $p > MC$, there is an incentive to engage in price discrimination, because there are buyers who are willing to pay more than it costs to produce the product. Charging a uniform price means lowering the price to those customers or consumers who are prepared to pay a higher price and, hence, the firm is foregoing a higher revenue without any change in unit costs. Price discrimination is a practice widely promoted by the marketing literature. It exists in many forms, but has recently been taken to new levels of sophistication by low-cost airlines. As a passenger on, say, an EasyJet flight, the one thing of which you can be certain is that the passenger in the seat next to you paid a different price for the journey.

By definition, a firm can only be maximizing its profits when the difference between total revenue and total costs is maximized. A **monopolist** or **oligopolist** that sells its output at a uniform price and sets $MR = MC$ is only maximizing profits given the constraint that all customers are charged the same price. As will be demonstrated below, profits can be increased if those customers that are less price sensitive are charged a higher price and those that are more price sensitive are charged a lower price. The charging of non-uniform prices does not, however, always reflect price discrimination. There are many other explanations for charging customers varying prices. Quantity discounts are an example, where price varies with the quantity purchased: the larger the quantity purchased, the lower the unit price. In this case, the price variation is more likely to reflect the lower per unit cost of administering and delivering a larger order.

It is tempting to think of price discrimination as existing when the cost of supplying each customer is identical but different customers are charged different prices. Unfortunately this is not a sufficiently precise definition, as price discrimination could exist when all customers are charged the same price, but the costs of supplying each customer vary. We will study these variations in more detail below. Our starting point, as ever, is the assumption that the pursuit of maximum profits underpins business strategy and as price discrimination does not influence unit costs, then business interest in price discrimination implies a positive effect on revenue and hence profits. Price discrimination is therefore a key business strategy and by reading this chapter, you will:

- Understand how price discrimination works to increase revenue and profits for a firm with market power.
- Appreciate the many ways in which firms may apply a strategy of price discrimination in practice.
- Be familiar with the legal aspects of price discrimination.

This chapter is divided into seven sections. In the first, we will look first at the economics of charging different customers a different price for essentially the same product. This practice is known as price discrimination and it remains the most prevalent form of pricing strategy. We will also examine the conditions that must be present if a firm is to be able to engage in such discrimination and briefly define three types of price discrimination. The following three sections are each devoted to a detailed analysis of the three types of price discrimination using the traditional approach of assuming a **monopoly** supplying an homogeneous product. In the fifth section we relax these two assumptions and consider in broad terms the form and output of price discrimination in markets where there is more than one supplier and product heterogeneity is the norm. We then extend the concept of heterogeneity to explore how spatial geographic markets can be used as a means of price discrimination. In the sixth section we will turn our attention to a closely related pricing practice; namely, **bundling**, which refers to the practice of selling two or more goods in a package. The final section is devoted to a brief overview of the EU's competition authorities' attitude towards price discrimination.

Price Discrimination

We have defined price discrimination as the act by an individual firm of selling essentially the same product at different prices to different buyers. This, however, is not sufficiently precise. There are a large number of reasons why apparently homogeneous products are in fact heterogeneous. Price variations for essentially the same product could reflect real or imagined differences in the accompanying service, credit policies or transport costs if the product is sold in different locations. And perversely, price discrimination would exist if all consumers, regardless of their location, were charged the same delivered price. A comprehensive survey of price-discriminating practices is provided by Phlips (1983), where such practices are categorized under four headings: quality, income, time and geography. If a firm offers consumers essentially the same product at a choice of different qualities at the same price or at prices that do not fully reflect the cost of the quality differential, it is engaging in price discrimination. Consumers with different incomes are likely to have different demands for a particular product and an aware seller can exploit this fact to charge lower prices to those with the greater demands and in the process increase revenue. Time can be a source of price discrimination: a fairly common feature of booking a flight, train journey or theatre seat is to be charged a higher price the nearer the booking to consumption. A firm serving customers in a number of separate geographic markets may have the scope to spatially discriminate, usually by forcing customers in one or more markets to cross-subsidize customers in another.

Our prime focus here is to understand the economics of price-discriminating strategies and we need to start with an unambiguous definition of price discrimination. A more precise definition of price discrimination is provided by Stigler (1966), who argues that price discrimination exists when 'the sale of two or more similar goods are sold at prices which are in different ratios to marginal cost' (p. 209). Hence price differences for products having essentially the same purpose may not constitute price discrimination, unless the sales are made under identical cost conditions. Sales by a firm to wholesale distributors and final retail outlets provide an example. If a manufacturer sells to both wholesalers and retailers under competitive conditions, the wholesaler will typically pay a lower price. It costs a manufacturer less to supply a wholesaler than a retailer, because the wholesaler performs the storage and distribution functions that the manufacturer must perform for direct sales to retailers. For the manufacturer, the reduced cost of supplying wholesalers will result in a lower marginal cost and this must, to some degree, be passed on in terms of lower prices if the wholesaler is to earn a profit by supplying to retail outlets. Such price differences are not price discrimination because units of the product, although physically identical, are different goods in an economic sense. However, this distinction becomes blurred as the marginal costs of supply narrow. The **marginal cost** to an airline of carrying a business class passenger across the Atlantic may be modestly higher than the cost of carrying an economy class passenger, but the actual difference for the two categories will not justify the variation in prices normally charged. It is for this reason that Stigler's definition is superior to the conventional definition.

Bearing in mind theses subtleties, it is conceptually easier to demonstrate the advantages of price discrimination if we assume the marginal costs of supplying the separate markets are identical. Price discrimination is a widespread feature of imperfectly competitive markets and a characteristic of such markets is that sellers face downward-sloping demand curves. If a firm facing a downward-sloping demand curve charges each customer the same uniform price, in order to sell an additional unit, as demonstrated in Chapter 9, it must lower its price, not only to the customer buying the additional unit, but also to all of its customers who were previously prepared to pay a higher price. If the firm is operating where $MC = MR$, the result of lowering its price would be to reduce its profits. Consequently, the firm is unlikely to choose to supply potential customers who would be prepared to buy at a lower price. The result is a loss of welfare for potential consumers and allocative inefficiency. For the firm, if it was prepared to adopt a non-uniform pricing strategy and charge a lower price only to those customers who would enter the market at a lower price, it would increase its economic rent and reduce allocative inefficiency.

We can demonstrate, without any loss of generality, the benefits of price discrimination by analysing the behaviour of a monopolist. In order to price discriminate, a monopolist must be able to separate its customers into separate groups with different **reservation prices**. For products where customers are likely to purchase only one unit of the product per period, e.g. a refrigerator or transatlantic flight, a downward-sloping demand curve is an explicit ordering of customers by their reservation prices. Those at the top of the demand curve are prepared to pay a higher price than those lower down. For many products customers can be induced to buy more than one unit of a product per time period, e.g. glasses of wine, DVDs and fairground rides. In the case of such products, a lower price will encourage each individual customer to purchase more than one unit. In this situation, the translation of the demand curve is more complicated. We will return to this complication below; but for the moment we will assume that each customer buys only one unit per time period.

In order to price discriminate, the monopolist must have sufficient knowledge to know how groups of, if not individual, customers differ in their demands for its output. Lacking **perfect information**, the firm must garner information on its customers. There are a number of ways in which the firm can proceed. It may place restrictions on buyers; for example, offering a lower price above a certain age or coupons for specific groups, e.g. students. Alternatively, prices can be structured so that buyers 'self-select' into an appropriate category, e.g. a transatlantic fare class. Another way in which customers might be separated is by their costs of search. Search activities represent a price paid by consumers that is not captured by the firm. If consumers differ in their costs of search, price discrimination may be an effective means of sorting consumers and dividing the market. For example, the opportunity costs for a high-paid executive of searching for a bargain transatlantic fare may be prohibitively high.

Having separated consumers into market segments, according to price sensitivity, there must be no opportunities for individuals to engage in **arbitrage**, otherwise a customer who is charged a low price could profit by resale to a customer who has been offered a higher price by the supplier. Where the nature of a product is such that it could be resold, e.g. an airline seat or a car, firms will attempt to prevent or frustrate resale, respectively, by linking the seat to a specific individual and voiding warranties if the car is resold. By increasing the **transaction costs** associated with resale, a price discriminator is likely to curtail profitable resale. Successful price discrimination also depends on being able to prevent (too many) existing customers trading down. The effect of price discrimination will be that some customers find themselves facing a higher price than previously and inevitably some customers will seek to switch their demand to the lower-price segment. To minimize the transfer of demand, the seller must attempt to design the options so that individual consumers who are willing and able to pay a higher price do not transfer demand to a lower-price category. Some products, e.g. medical, legal and educational services, are not transferrable and in many cases transport costs will outweigh the price difference, e.g. the same book sold at different prices on either side of the Atlantic. Again, a price discriminator must seek to raise the transaction costs associated with transferring demand to a lower-price segment by, for example, increasing the search costs of identifying bargains. But, customers who attempt to resell or switch their demands are not the only concern for a price discriminator. The competition authorities may seek to frustrate attempts at price discrimination. Within the European Community the overriding objective in creating a single market was to ensure greater competition, particularly between firms in different member states. A crude form of price discrimination would be to sell essentially the same product at different prices in member states that have no relationship to transport costs. For example, pharmaceutical companies find it increasingly difficult to charge different prices for the same products in different countries as a result of legislation enabling parallel imports.

Price discrimination comes in a number of forms and the traditional classification of the forms of price discrimination is due to Pigou (1920). He distinguished three types of price discrimination, the economics of which are dealt with in the following sections:

- *First-degree price discrimination* – where a supplier with sufficient market power sells each unit of output at a different price to individual customers equivalent to each individual's reservation price.
- *Second-degree price discrimination* – where a supplier with sufficient market power divides output into successive tranches and charges customers successively lower prices for each tranche consumed.
- *Third-degree price discrimination* – where a supplier with sufficient market power divides customers into distinct groups and charges each group a different profit-maximizing price.

Parallel Imports

Since the early 1980s, consumer organizations, competition agencies and academic researchers have produced a large number of studies showing considerable price differentials across European countries. For example, between 1981–1993, BEUC, a consortium of European consumer organizations, conducted a series of studies that consistently found that pre-tax car prices were lowest in Denmark, followed by Greece and the Benelux countries. Car prices in France, Germany and Portugal were found to be about 30–40 per cent above the level in Denmark and in Italy, Spain and Sweden they were found to be in the range of 30–50 per cent above Denmark. In Ireland, the gap was estimated at between 40 and 60 per cent, but the UK demonstrated the highest differential, in the range of 50–80 per cent above the level in Denmark.

The BEUC studies initiated a lot of public attention and in 1992 the European Commission published its first report on car price differentials within the European Community. The study found that price differentials across member states for individual car models frequently exceeded the levels that might be justified for different specifications and the Commission decided to publish bi-annual reports on specification-adjusted car prices so as to better monitor price differentials across the European Community.

In January 1993, the single market was launched and with it the expectation that car price differentials across the Community would narrow in the following years. Yet, study after study continued to find large differences in the general car price level

continued

between countries. Neither the public nor the car companies were happy with this state of affairs. The former suspected discrimination in favour of the car producers and the latter felt that insufficient attention was being given to the factors that might justify significant price differentials across member states.

In an attempt to clarify matters, the Commission commissioned a study from the London-based Centre for Economic Policy Research (CEPR), which was published in November 2000. The CEPR first calculated the pre-tax prices in a common currency and these are set out in column (1) of the table below. If taxes paid on new cars are included, the data in column (1) would have to be adjusted by the data in column (2), and once taxes are included, Denmark is no longer the cheapest country to buy a car. Column (3) adjusts for exchange-rate fluctuations. In principle, the effect of this is to reduce the year-to-year volatility, but most of the countries shown had become members

of the Economic and Monetary Union (EMU) at the start of 1999 and were therefore in the last stages of preparing to adopt the euro for cash transactions. The UK shows the biggest variation, reflecting its decision not to adopt the euro.

Column (4) shows the price differentials after adjusting for taxes and exchange rates. In principle, CEPR should have further adjusted the data for dealer discounts and margins and also for any right-hand drive surcharge, but the authors concluded that insufficient information was available to construct reliable price adjustments. Nevertheless, the effect of these adjustments is to reduce the range of price differentials and although the UK remains the most expensive country, the differential is smaller. Whether or not it is appropriate to adjust for taxes and the exchange rate is a matter for debate. What is clear is that the single market does seem to have caused post-tax car prices to converge.

Systematic price differentials, 1999–2000

	Pre-tax price index* (1)	Tax adjustments (2)	Exchange rate adjustments (3)	Adjustment price index (4)
Austria	103.7	1.0	0.2	104.9
Belgium	101.4	−0.2	0.1	101.3
Denmark	81.6	24.7	−0.4	105.8
Finland	94.5	9.1	−1.0	102.6
France	101.1	−0.4	−0.4	100.3
Germany	107.5	−0.8	0.2	106.9
Greece	92.7	3.7	3.2	99.6
Ireland	99.3	4.9	−0.4	103.8
Italy	100.7	−0.1	−0.6	100.0
Luxembourg	101.7	−0.8	0.2	101.1
Netherlands	96.8	3.8	0.5	101.1
Portugal	99.5	5.1	0.8	105.4
Spain	96.1	0.3	1.2	97.7
Sweden	103.5	0.3	−1.3	102.5
UK	119.8	−0.7	−8.2	110.9

continued

In its latest report on car prices, based on November 2004 data, the European Commission claims that car prices are converging across the European Union. Nevertheless, differences remain. In the euro-zone, prices are lowest in Finland and highest in Germany. Looking at the EU as a whole, cars are less expensive in the new member states, with Estonia being the cheapest market. The UK, however, remains the most expensive on average.

First-Degree Price Discrimination

First-degree price discrimination is also known as perfect price discrimination. In the extreme, it transfers to the firm all available **consumers' surplus** in the form of higher profits. In the absence of price discrimination the effect of charging a single, high price to the market transfers only some of the total consumers' surplus to the firm and then only from those customers with high reservation prices. Potential customers with reservation prices below the market price transfer their demand to other products, thus the firm forgoes the opportunity to increase profits. In principle, a monopolist can increase its profits – and in the process remove the **deadweight loss** – if each customer is charged a price that they are willing to pay, i.e. their reservation price. Charging each customer a separate price according to their individual reservation prices calls for a great deal of information on individual customers and the ability to be able to sell an additional unit without lowering the prices to existing customers. Returning to our simplifying assumptions of a monopolist and customers that buy only one product unit per period Figure 11.1 demonstrates the concept of first-degree price discrimination.

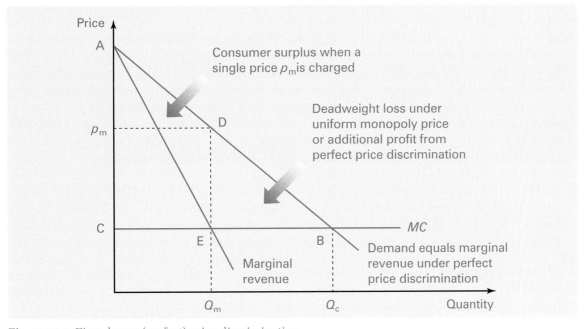

Figure 11.1: First-degree (perfect) price discrimination

To simplify matters, without losing the general point, we will assume constant marginal costs for the supplier. If the market was perfectly competitive, $p = MC$, the total quantity supplied would equal Q_c and consumers' surplus would amount to ABC. As a profit maximizer, our monopolist, selling at a uniform price, would maximize **economic rent** by selling output Q_m, where $MC = MR$. As can be seen from Figure 11.1, limiting output to Q_m yields a uniform price, p_m, and earns the monopolist an economic rent of $p_m DEC$ – strictly net revenue before deducting fixed costs. Consumers' surplus is reduced from ABC to ADP_m and potential consumers suffer a deadweight welfare loss equivalent to DEB.

Now, what happens if the firm can charge each customer their individual reservation price? In a market where customers buy just one product per period, the demand curve represents all potential customers' reservation prices ranged from the highest to the lowest as we move down the curve. Since each customer is charged exactly what he or she is willing to pay, the conventional marginal revenue curve is no longer relevant to the firm's output decision. Instead, the incremental revenue earned from each additional unit sold is the price paid for that unit. As the demand curve determines the price paid for each addition unit sold, under perfect price discrimination the demand curve becomes the firm's **marginal revenue** (MR) curve. Since, by assumption, price discrimination does not affect the firm's cost structure, the profit from producing and selling each incremental unit – ignoring unit fixed costs – is now the vertical difference between the demand and marginal cost curves. As long as $p > MC$, the firm can increase its profit by expanding production until it produces total output, Q_c. At Q_c, the price charged for the last unit sold had fallen to $p = MC$. At this point, first-degree price discrimination profits are maximized, given by the area ABC. It is obvious from Figure 11.1, that total profit is now much larger. The economic rent earned by first-degree price discrimination is ABC, which is greater than the uniform price monopoly rent of $p_m DEC$.

An interesting side effect of first-degree price discrimination is that it eliminates the deadweight welfare loss associated with uniform-price monopoly. Recall that deadweight welfare loss is the consumers' surplus lost on output that is not produced when a profit-maximizing monopolist sells at a uniform price. In Figure 11.1, if the product was sold under competitive conditions, i.e. $p = MC$, output would be Q_c. In restricting output in order to drive the price back up the demand curve, a deadweight welfare loss equivalent to BDE is incurred. Under first-degree price discrimination, however, there is no output restriction. The monopolist charges each consumer the maximum price that the individual consumer is prepared to pay for each unit of output, and the monopolist is prepared to sell to anyone willing to pay at least the marginal cost of production. Since there is no restriction of output under first-degree price discrimination, there is no deadweight welfare loss.

In practice, perfect price discrimination or attempts to apply first-degree price discrimination are not as rare as might be imagined. Suppliers of personalized services who charge on the basis of 'what the customer will pay' are attempting and, presumably in many cases succeeding, in applying first-degree price discrimination. This happens frequently when professionals, such as doctors, lawyers, accountants or architects, who know their clients reasonably well, are the 'firms'. Then the client's willingness to pay can be assessed, and fees set accordingly. For example, a doctor may offer a reduced fee to a low-income patient whose willingness to pay or insurance coverage is low, but charge higher fees to upper-income or better-insured patients. And an accountant, having just completed a client's tax return, is in an excellent position to estimate how much the client might be willing and able to pay for the service. Sellers who engage in haggling – be they selling aircraft or concert tickets – are also attempting to sell to each individual customer at their reservation price. However, for mass markets, e.g. washing powder, it is impractical to charge each and every customer their reservation price. Even in markets where the number of customers is relatively small it is most unlikely that a firm knows the reservation price of each customer and asking each customer what they would be willing to pay is confounded by the rational customers' interest to claim that they would pay very little. Any firm attempting perfect price discrimination will incur the transaction costs associated with determining the reservation prices of different customers. Thus, strictly in terms of Figure 11.1, in order for the monopolist to engage in perfect price discrimination the transaction costs must be taken into account and a rational monopolist will only proceed if $(ABC - p_{m}DEC) > T$, where T is the transaction costs of implementing perfect price discrimination.

So far, we have assumed that each customer buys only one unit per period, no matter how low the price. In markets where the quantity purchased by individual customers depends on the price charged, e.g. glasses of wine, a monopolist could also engage in first-degree price discrimination. In this situation, the demand curve shown in Figure 11.1 should be viewed as representing the demand of one individual. A perfectly discriminating monopolist charges a lower price for each additional unit purchased by an individual customer. In this way, the monopolist again appropriates all the consumers' surplus. An alternative and equivalent method of perfect price discrimination would be to charge an optimal ***two-part tariff*** to extract consumers' surplus. A two-part tariff is a pricing scheme where each customer pays a lump-sum fee for the right to purchase plus a per unit price for each unit consumed regardless of how many units are purchased.

The rationale for a two-part tariff is easily discerned in Figure 11.1. If the owner of the amusement park charged a price per ride equal to marginal cost, i.e. $p = MC$ and then set an admission fee, A, so that $A > P_{m}DEC$, the economic rent would be nearer to the rent generated by perfect price discrimination than the rent arising from charging a uniform price. A classic example of a two-part tariff is an amusement park where one price – an entrance fee, A – must be paid to enter the park and additional prices are charged for individual rides. Total revenue is then given by $TR = A + \Sigma p_i q_i$, where subscript i's refer to individual rides. If the marginal cost of each ride is the same, then total revenue is given by $TR = A + pQ$, where $Q = \Sigma q_i$. If, as would generally be the case, individuals differ in their demands, each individual would be charged a different entrance fee – that varied positively with each individual's demand – in order to extract all the available consumers' surplus. Hence for the jth consumer, we would have $TR_j = A_j + pQ_j$ and total revenue would then be given by $TR = \Sigma TR_j$. In practice, most firms would not have a detailed knowledge of individual demands and in such cases the transaction costs associated with measuring individual's demands are likely to be prohibitive. There are exceptions. A firm that rents out equipment, e.g. a photocopier, might be able to monitor usage and adjust the rental accordingly, i.e. the greater the usage, the higher the demand. But realistically, in markets where customers purchase more than one unit per period and where individual demands vary, sellers will be constrained to charging a single entrance fee.

If a monopoly supplier does not know the individual demands of its customers it faces an additional complication in optimizing its two-part tariff. Consider the owner of an amusement park whose profit function is given by the equation:

$$\pi = A.N + pQ - c(Q) - \delta K \tag{11.1}$$

where implicitly the price charged for each ride, p, is the same, A is the entrance fee and δK, as described previously, is the annual capital deprecation. N is the number of customers, where N is a function of the price of the rides and the entrance fee, i.e. $N = N(p, A)$. The number of rides sold, Q, is also a function of the price charged and the entrance fee, i.e. $Q = Q(p, A)$. The owner of the amusement park faces a dilemma. If A is set too high, a lower number of people will pay the entrance charge, but in setting a lower entrance fee, a high price per ride will need to be charged, reducing the number of rides. The mathematical solution to this problem is beyond the scope of this book (but interested readers should consult Varian, 1984), in essence it depends on how many rides the marginal customer, i.e. the customer who is indifferent between buying and not buying, will demand. Generally, the marginal customer is likely to buy less than the average customer and in this case the price per ride should be set above marginal cost, i.e. $p > MC$. If, however, the marginal customer does not value the amusement park very highly but having paid the entrance fee wants to consume a large number of rides, an optimal solution could be to set a low price per ride, even less than marginal costs, i.e. $p < MC$ and make up the lost revenue through a higher entrance fee (Schmalensee, 1981). In the extreme, the amusement park owner could use **_block pricing_** to achieve the same result. With this type of system the entrance fee includes a number of free rides. The mathematics aside, charging a single entrance fee will be too high for some potential customers, but in principle a tariff plus marginal cost pricing is likely to increase overall profitability.

We have already observed that first-degree price discrimination eliminates the deadweight welfare loss associated with uniform, monopoly pricing. Faced with a product that can be consumed more than once in a given period and consumers with varying demands, the welfare effect of a two-part tariff is more complicated. If the outcome is a price set so $p > MC$, then from society's perspective welfare would be increased by lowering the price. Thus, in summary, we may conclude that the use of a two-part tariff as a means to achieve the benefits of first-degree price discrimination reduces, but may not eliminate, the deadweight welfare loss associated with a uniform price monopoly.

Road Sense

In a speech to the Social Market Foundation, in June 2005, Alistair Darling, the UK Secretary of State for Transport, raised the possibility of a radical change in policy; namely, road pricing, whereby people would be charged according to the amount of congestion on the road. The main economic argument for road pricing is efficiency. As roads become congested, so road space becomes scarce and this imposes costs not only on travellers, but also on the infrastructure and more generally in terms of pollution.

As set out by Alistair Darling by way of provoking a debate on the issue, the amount charged per mile could rise sharply depending upon the level of congestion. He suggested that on this basis the highest charges would be levied on, say, London's orbital motorway, the M25, during the rush hour. During the early hours of the morning the charge per mile on the M25 would be a lot lower. Many roads would attract little by way of changes as, despite rising congestion and environmental costs, it remains a fact that only a small fraction of the road network rated capacity is used. According to the Secretary of State, road pricing will improve conditions because only motorists who attach the highest value to travelling in the rush

continued

hour will do so and others will stagger their travel times according to their perception of the value received for the price paid.

The principle of road pricing has much merit, but in practice it will be important to set the prices for varying levels of congestion, so that efficient outcomes are achieved. Too high a price will result in under-utilization – and excessive pressure on other transport systems – and too low a price will not achieve the desired outcome. It would seem that the government has at last got the message. Charging efficient prices via fuel taxation and excise duty is impossible. Road pricing at least offers the prospect that future congestion will reflect the fact that those involved value the benefits of the travel greater than the cost.

Second-Degree Price Discrimination

In the discussion of first-degree price discrimination when more than one unit can be consumed per period and customers have varying demands, it fell to the seller to attempt to identify the characteristics of individual customers and their demands. A seller of personal services, who gets to know individual customers, may accumulate sufficient information on individual customers to engage in first-degree price discrimination, but the larger the market, the more difficult it is for a seller to identify different customers. However, it is in principle possible for a monopolist to devise a pricing silence that will induce customers to reveal their demands. Such a pricing scheme is known as second-degree price discrimination. Second-degree price discrimination is also known as **non-linear pricing**, as the average price paid varies inversely with the quantity purchased. It is a form of price discrimination whereby a firm with monopoly power separates sales into volume bands or tranches. Customers purchase one or more tranches and are charged successively lower prices for each tranche purchased. Examples of second-degree price discrimination are widespread – e.g. railway tariffs specify charges based on weight, volume and distances of each shipment; electricity tariffs are based on total kilowatt hours used in a given period; and airlines will allow 'frequent fliers' credits towards

free tickets. In all these situations, the supplier finds it profitable to price discriminate according to the quantity consumed by charging successively lower prices to consumers who purchase larger volumes of output. The effect of this, is that the more that is purchased, the lower the average price, hence non-linear pricing.

The general approach to analysing second-degree price discrimination owes much to Oi (1971). Recall our monopolist has no way of knowing an individual's demand, so the pricing scheme must result in individual customers revealing their demands. We will, to simplify matters, assume that there are

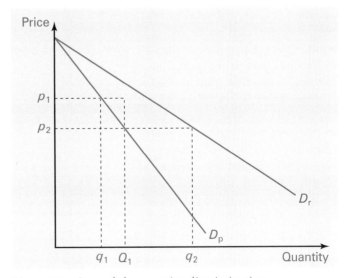

Figure 11.2 Second-degree price discrimination

just two types of customer: a poor customer and a rich customer. The two types are distinguished by their **reservation outlay** – richer consumers are prepared to spend more on the particular product. Figure 11.2 shows the demand curves for a poor consumer, D_p, and a rich consumer, D_r. For the first tranche of consumption all customers are charged a price of p_1. For this, they can consume up to Q_1 units, and consumption beyond Q_1 is charged at a lower unit price of p_2. Given our poor consumer's demand curve, a quantity of q_1 units will be purchased, resulting in an outlay of p_1q_1. The outlay for our rich consumer is $p_1Q_1 + p_2(q_2 - Q_1)$. This, it will be observed, largely removes most of our poor customer's consumers' surplus, but leaves our rich customer with a larger share of consumers' surplus.

Monopolists whose production technology is subject to large-scale capital investment, e.g. an electricity generating plant, have an additional incentive to engage in second-degree price discrimination. The more units that are sold, the lower unit production costs. The option of achieving a high volume of sales by offering a low uniform price is not a profit-maximizing strategy.

Figure 11.3 illustrates the advantage of second-degree price discrimination for a profit-maximizing monopolist whose fixed capital costs are so high that short-run average production costs, $SRAC$, steadily decline with rising output. Note, in this situation because $SRAC$ is declining, marginal costs must lie below $SRAC$. If a single uniform price were charged, it would be, say, p_0, where $MR = MC$ (neither curve is drawn to reduce the complexity), yielding the uniform price, profit-maximizing quantity of output, Q_0. This, as can be seen, will result in the installed capital – e.g. the electricity generating plant – being under-utilized and consumers paying a high price for all they buy. In this situation, it makes more sense to charge different prices according to the volume that individual consumers purchase.

Figure 11.3, for the purpose of illustration, shows three different prices: the first block of sales is priced at p_1, the second at p_2 and the third at p_3. Customers attach a high reservation price to the first tranche as it would be used for necessities, e.g. lighting and electrical appliances. All customers have to pay p_1 and, given the market demand, total sales for the first tranche are given by Q_0, where $Q_0 = p_1\Sigma q_{1j}$ and q_{1j} is the jth individual customers' purchases of units in the first tranche. Only customers whose purchases of q_1 exceed the threshold can purchase from the second tranche at a lower price, p_2. At this lower price consumers with higher demands as a result of owning additional electrical products – e.g. electric heaters, lawn mowers – will purchase additional units of electricity, increasing total sales of electricity by $Q_2 - Q_1$. For the third tranche, a price equal to the

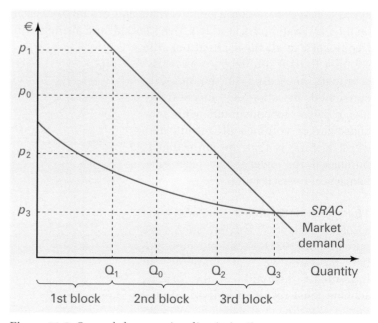

Figure 11.3: Second-degree price discrimination

SRAC of production is charged, p_3. At this price consumers who have the highest demand for electricity, possibly arising from an installed electric central heating system, more than fulfil the second tranche, pushing total sales to Q_3. The monopolist is not earning an economic rent on the third tranche but, as can be seen, selling tranches one and two at prices p_1 and p_2, respectively, has generated more economic rent than would have been the case if a uniform selling price of p_0 had been offered. And, most importantly, by increasing output to Q_3, the first two tranches have benefited from the lower unit production costs, thereby further increasing rent.

Utilities frequently combine second-degree price discrimination with a two-part tariff. This enables the firm to capture an even larger proportion of consumers' surplus and/or offer lower prices for successive tranches. There is a conceptual similarity between second- and first-degree price discrimination. If the tranches of output that are priced at successively lower prices under second-degree price discrimination were made smaller and smaller, until each tranche contains only one unit, this would reduce second-degree to first-degree price discrimination. First-degree price discrimination is therefore a limiting or extreme version of second-degree price discrimination.

As noted above, the essential difference between first- and second-degree price discrimination is that the supplier does not know individual customer's demands. But, let us assume the seller knows there are two types of customer: type 1, who will only purchase a limited quantity; and type 2, who will purchase a much larger quantity. The seller can offer two different two-part tariff schedules. For customers only likely to purchase a limited quantity a low tariff is charged, but customers pay a higher price per unit consumed. For customers likely to consume a large volume, a high tariff is set accompanied by a low price. This two-part tariff is illustrated in Figure 11.4. The intercepts on the vertical axis represent the tariffs paid by each type. The low demanders are charged the lower tariff, T_1, but because they pay a high price per unit, their expenditure schedule rises steeply. High-demanding customers are charged a higher tariff, T_2, but a lower price.

The two-part tariff scheme set out in Figure 11.4 allows customers to self-select. Why do all customers not choose the lower tariff? Because despite choosing the higher tariff, the area under a big demander's demand curve is increased further by a low price and hence despite the tariff, big deman-

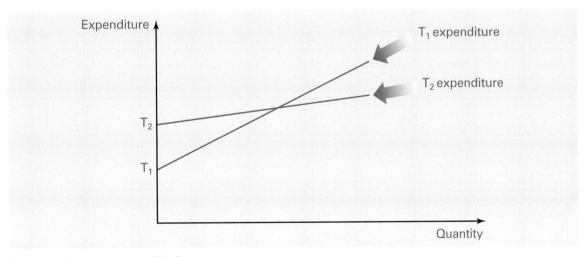

Figure 11.4: A two-part tariff scheme

ders gain a larger consumers' surplus. Telephone services frequently involve a different service charge according to the number of calls likely to be made. A high service charge and a low price per call benefits customers who make frequent calls, and a relatively low service charge and a higher price per call benefits customers who make few calls. Importantly, customers self-select the service charge–unit price combination that suits their demands. Similarly, health clubs frequently charge an annual membership fee and an entrance price each time the facilities are used. These payments vary inversely, by setting a higher membership fee coupled with a lower entrance fee, high demanders will use the club's facilities regularly. Restaurants that seek to attract families frequently use two-part tariffs as part of a strategy of second-degree price discrimination. For example, customers are offered the choice of an 'all you can eat' fixed price buffets, i.e. the tariff is high and $p = 0$, and also an *à la carte* menu where there is no tariff but a high price, i.e. charged per dish – $T = 0$ and $p > MC$. Finally, Disneyland charges one (high) price for admission, but then the attractions inside are free. In these cases, the logic would appear to be that the marginal cost of the rides is less than the transaction costs of collecting a separate payment for them.

Turning the Screw

It is a common complaint by food processors that when supplying supermarkets, particularly in the UK, the balance of power is generally firmly tilted in favour of the buyer. Many suppliers are small relative to the supermarkets and they are also heavily reliant on them. In reality there is little they can do against practices that involve unilaterally reducing the price agreed. Supermarkets are in a position to use their negotiating strength to achieve a range of discounts as volumes increase. If a particular level of sales is achieved, supermarkets often insist on a discount and when a particular level of sales is not achieved, some supermarkets then insist on receiving the discount. They might also seek annual or quarterly payments for agreeing to promotion plans and demand contributions towards the opening or refurbishment of stores. Suppliers also are required to offer concessions to secure shelf-space for a wider range of products and/or the stock of a new product line – so-called listing fees.

An alternative to discounts are margin support payments, sometimes requested by the multiples to protect the buyers' margins when retail prices are reduced and/or when the volume of sales is declining. If suppliers make errors, say in bar-coding, or make a late or incorrect delivery, then they are frequently required to pay compensation. If suppliers seek a display area, such as a 'gondola end', to promote products then they will be expected to negotiate a lower price for the privilege. Some suppliers even claim that they are subject to *ad hoc* demands for payments on what they regard as spurious goods. Credit terms are another feature of the way the multiples use their power, with periods ranging from 7 to 60 days. Suppliers are expected to offer rebates for prompt payments and for compliance with certain logistics such as use of pallets and EDI.

Third-Degree Price Discrimination

Returning to markets where customers are likely to purchase only one unit per period, if these are mass markets suppliers are unlikely to have sufficient information to enable them to identify individual customer's demands and hence willingness to pay. They may, however, have enough information to imperfectly price discriminate providing they can separate customers into distinct groups according to their price sensitivities and willingness to pay. If a firm knows the aggregate demand curve for each group and can prevent resale between the groups, then it is in a position to engage in third-degree price discrimination. This form of price discrimination – the charging of different prices to different groups of customers – is, in practice, the most frequently encountered form of price discrimination and is often referred to as linear pricing. Groups or, more correctly, market segments may be determined by age, income, education and so on. Each segment is charged a different price, but within each segment individual consumers face a constant price for all units purchased. In order to exploit third-degree price discrimination a firm must possess sufficient market power to be able to charge different prices for its product to each of the separate market segments and it must be able to enforce the division between the segments in order to prevent **arbitrage** from customers charged a low price reselling to those facing a higher price.

As implied, examples of third-degree price discrimination abound. Discounts for senior citizens, students and young children are very common forms of discrimination. Such groups are likely to have lower incomes and hence display greater price sensitivity. Another example is the use of discount coupons to buy groceries. People on low incomes are not only generally more responsive to lower prices, but also they are likely to have the inclination to make the effort to cut out coupons. Offering end-of-season clothes at a lower price is yet another form of third-degree price discrimination, based on time of purchase, as is charging an audience a higher price to see a newly released film than the price to view a repeat. A widely practised form of discrimination is whether the customer has been a previous customer. For example, the price of a software program may depend on whether the customer purchased an earlier version. Airlines in particular, and travel companies in general, are adept at applying third-degree price discrimination. A common feature of this type of price discrimination is that it is implemented by placing restrictions on the characteristics of the ticket – a lower price may be available to passengers who purchase tickets a long period in advance of travelling, who are prepared to stay over on a Saturday, who are frequent fliers and so on.

If third-degree price discrimination is feasible, how should the firm decide what price to charge each market segment? We can answer this question by focusing on the marginal revenue associated with each segment's demand. If profit is to be maximized, total output should be divided between the market segments, so that the *marginal revenues for each segment are equal*. If the marginal revenues for each segment were not equal the firm could increase its revenue by switching output between the segments. For example, given two segments, if marginal revenue for the first segment, MR_1, is lower than the marginal revenue for the second segment, MR_2, the firm could increase its total revenue by shifting output from the first segment to the second. It would do this by increasing the price to customers in the first segment, and lowering the price to customers in the second segment. So whatever the prices charged to the two segments, they must be such that the marginal revenues for the two segments are equal.

Maximizing revenue is not the same as maximizing profit and given that the purpose of third-degree price discrimination is to maximize economic rent, splitting sales between the two (or more) segments, so that $MR_1 = MR_2$, will only equate with profit maximization if supply to each segment is such that marginal revenue is equal to the marginal cost. If this is not the case, the firm can increase its profit by raising or lowering total output. For example, suppose the marginal revenues were the same for each group of consumers, but marginal revenue exceeded the marginal cost of production. Assuming a rising or constant marginal cost curve, the firm will increase its overall profits by increasing its total output. To achieve this, it would lower its prices in all market segments, so that the marginal revenues for each group fell (but remained equal to each other) until they reached the level of marginal cost.

This solution can be demonstrated with the following equations. To simplify matters, we will assume just two market segments. Let p_1 and q_1 be the price charged and quantity supplied, respectively, to the first market segment; while p_2 and q_2 are the price charged and quantity supplied, respectively, to the second segment. The expression $c(Q_0)$ represents the total cost of producing output Q_0, where $Q_0 = q_1 + q_2$, and hence total profit, before capital costs, is given by:

$$\pi = p_1 q_1 + p_2 q_2 - c(Q_0) \tag{11.2}$$

For convenience, and without any loss of generality, we will ignore fixed capital and organizational costs and assume $c(Q_0)$ displays constant average cost, i.e. c = marginal cost. In order to maximize profits, the firm must set marginal revenue equal to marginal cost for all market segments. As demonstrated in Chapter 9, for a monopolist setting $MR = MC$ can be expressed as:

$$p_1 + \frac{\Delta p_1}{\Delta p_1} q_1 = c = p_1 \left[1 + \frac{1}{\varepsilon_1} \right] \tag{11.3}$$

$$p_2 + \frac{\Delta p_2}{\Delta q_2} q_2 = c = p_2 \left[1 - \frac{1}{\varepsilon_2} \right] \tag{11.4}$$

where ε_1 and ε_2 are the absolute value of the elasticity of demand coefficient. Given that marginal costs are the same in both segments, the third-degree price discrimination profit-maximizing condition is satisfied when:

$$p_1 \left[1 - \frac{1}{\varepsilon_1} \right] = p_2 \left[1 - \frac{1}{\varepsilon_2} \right] = c \tag{11.5}$$

From Equation (11.5) it can be seen that if $\varepsilon_1 < \varepsilon_2$, then $p_1 > p_2$. Hence the market with the more elastic demand – the market that is more price sensitive – is charged the lower price. This can be easily demonstrated with the following simple example; if the price elasticity of demand in the two segments is 2 and 4, respectively, we will have $p_1/p_2 = (1 - 1/4)/(1 - 1/2) = (3/4)/(1/2) = 1.5$. In other words, the price charged to the first market segment should be 1.5 times the price charged to the second segment. Figure 11.5 illustrates the condition set out in Equation (11.5), where a monopolist has segmented its market into two enforceable segments with no prospect of arbitrage. The important point, as just demonstrated, is that the two sub-markets must display different price elasticities of demand. It is logical that consumers with a higher need, or high search cost, will have lower price elasticities of demand and that consumers with a lower need, or low search cost (and hence are better informed about prices), will have a higher price elasticity of demand. In such a case, a profit-

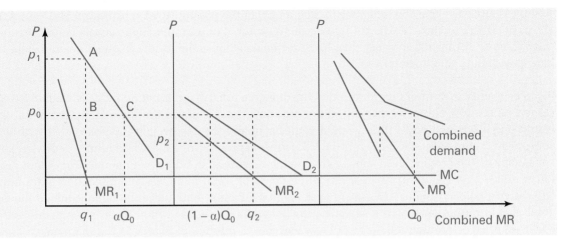

Figure 11.5: Third-degree price discrimination

maximizing firm will reduce sales in the low-elasticity market by raising the price in this segment and expand sales in the high-elasticity market by reducing the price to this segment.

In the absence of price discrimination, the relevant demand and marginal revenue curves are the combined curves shown in the right-hand graph of Figure 11.5. Given the MC function, the profit-maximizing output for the monopolist is Q_0, yielding a uniform price in both markets of p_0 and earning the firm an economic rent. At price p_0, the proportion of Q_0 sold in the D_1 market is αQ_0, where $0 < \alpha \le 1$ and $(1 - \alpha)Q_0$ in the D_2 market. Note that the demand curve D_1 for the first market segment is less elastic than the demand curve for the second market segment, D_2, and both demand curves have an associated MR curve: MR_1 and MR_2, respectively. By equating MR_1 and MR_2 with MC, the price rises to p_1 in the low-elasticity market and falls to p_2 in the more price-sensitive market. Sales in the less price-elastic market fall from αQ_0 to q_1 and sales in the market with more elastic demand rise from $(1 - \alpha)Q_0$ to q_2. Providing the demand curves are linear, total output is unchanged by the move from a uniform price to price discrimination. But the effect of price discrimination is to increase the firm's revenue and as total output and marginal costs remain unchanged, this must result in an increase in economic rent. This can more readily be seen by rewriting Equations (11.3) and (11.4) as:

$$\frac{p_1 - c}{p_1} = \frac{1}{\varepsilon_1} \tag{11.6}$$

$$\frac{p_2 - c}{p_2} = \frac{1}{\varepsilon_2} \tag{11.7}$$

where, as before, ε_1 and ε_2 are the absolute value of the elasticity coefficient. Equations (11.6) and (11.7) show that the mark-up for each segment's price over its marginal cost is inversely proportional to its elasticity of demand. The higher the segment's elasticity of demand, the lower the mark-up. In practice, a monopoly seller may not be able to separate the two segments clearly. The lower price charged in one segment will reduce demand in the higher-priced segment, for example some business travellers will switch to an economy ticket. This follows because the products being offered in the two segments are substitutes and hence there will be a ***cross-price elasticity of demand***. This serves to emphasize that the seller has to be mindful of the possibility of substitution and, hence, the efforts by sellers to make it difficult for people to switch. For example, high-income consumers typically value their time more highly than low-income consumers, hence the frequent need to engage in lengthy search to find lower prices.

It can be readily seen from Figure 11.5 that third-degree price discrimination reduces welfare for consumers in the low-elasticity market. There are some consumers in the low-elasticity market who would purchase the product if they could get it for p_0 and the deadweight loss associated with these consumers is shown as ABC in Figure 11.5. It is this aspect of price discrimination – depriving some consumers of the product even though they value it more than others who are able to obtain it at a lower price – that ensures price discrimination does not result in an efficient allocation of resources. Allocative efficiency among consumers requires that all consumers place the same value on the marginal unit of output and price discrimination prevents this equal valuation. However, the welfare effects of price discrimination may not be as extreme as implied in Figure 11.5 if the demand curves are non-linear. If demand is non-linear, total output could increase under price discrimination and this would mitigate the overall effect of price discrimination on welfare. Indeed, in the presence of non-linear demand curves, it is possible that price discrimination could increase welfare if it allowed markets to be served that would not be served under single-price monopoly.

Low-Cost Airlines

In Europe, the rise of the low-cost airlines at the expense of established flag carriers catches the headlines and the attention of analysts in equal measure. In May 2002, EasyJet became the leading European low-cost carrier with its acquisition of GO. The new leader's combined passengers will exceed 1.2 million per year, up more than 50 per cent over the 12 months to May 2002. The takeover has left the national carriers in no doubt of the challenge they are facing. Both EasyJet and Ryanair have the potential to pass the biggest national carriers – including British Airways, Air France and Lufthansa – and become Europe's biggest short-haul operators by 2010.

What is the secret of EasyJet's – and for that matter, Ryanair's – success? Both, drawing inspiration from Southwest Airlines in the US, use highly variable pricing that reflects demand for individual flights and both strive to keep the marginal cost of every passenger journey as low as possible. Both airlines are labelled as low-cost, but it would be more correct to describe EasyJet as an airline whose prices are lower than those of the national carriers. Although its youthful chairperson, Stelios Haji-Ioannou, launched EasyJet by offering flights to Edinburgh at the same price as a pair of jeans – in essence, treating a short flight as an impulse purchase – it is the care and sophistication that EasyJet put into pricing that is a major cause of its phenomenal success.

Aircraft are extremely expensive – to purchase and maintain – thus low fares are only feasible if aircraft utilization is high. To achieve this, EasyJet's aircraft have a greater number of seats than the national carriers, they fly to and from uncongested airports and avoid food and drink on board. By not providing food and drink, less crew are required, and clearing and load-

continued

ing times are reduced. Moreover, by not providing passengers with a seat number EasyJet ensures that passengers reach the departure gate in good time to find a preferred seat. The effect of this strategy is to significantly reduce the turnaround time at airports and hence increase the time the aircraft are in the air: EasyJet's utilization rate averages 10.7 hours per day, compared to BA's 7.1 hours a day.

In order to achieve maximum load factors, EasyJet uses price discrimination. Their model approximates third-degree price discrimination, but passengers self-select into price categories on the basis of time-dependency. The idea is this. Airline travel is a service: production and consumption cannot be separated. As far as passengers are concerned, the value they attach to a flight is not only dependent on its consumption, but also when it is consumed. Amongst passengers, the costs of arriving late at a destination are asymmetric. For example, if the flight is being made to attend a meeting, arriving late – due to a too-late reservation – will be costly in terms of wasted time and the need to reschedule. In contrast, students, the unemployed and retired people will be more flexible as the costs of a late reservation are small.

Since passenger characteristics with respect to time of travel and willingness to pay vary widely, the objective of EasyJet's price discrimination model is to charge passengers a price that varies inversely with flexibility and positively with willingness to pay. The result is that on an EasyJet flight there is wide price dispersion.

Interestingly, this is despite the fact that a large proportion of reservations are made via the internet – a medium that is supposed to reduce search costs and hence price dispersion.

It would be going too far to say that the low-cost airlines are turning short-haul flights into a commodity. Even low-cost flights are horizontally differentiated, i.e. in the attributes they offer, as passenger ranking is likely to be based on the convenience of the flight's time and the destination. This suggests a relationship between the price paid and the time between booking and the flight that follows an inverted U-shape. Passengers booking one month or more in advance tend to pay the lowest prices because they tend to be flexible regarding the time of flight and have a low willingness to pay. However, tickets purchased two weeks prior to travelling, sell at a higher price. This reflects passengers who place a higher value on securing a seat on a particular flight and are booking sufficiently far in advance to ensure they get their desired flight. Finally, in the days just prior to the flight, if there remains capacity, yield management considerations result in seats being offered at very low prices. Thus EasyJet have succeeded by understanding and responding to uncertainty on the part of passengers. Those who want to minimize uncertainty book two weeks in advance and pay a relatively high price – compared to other passengers – and those who are less concerned about their time of flight will either book well in advance or at the last minute in response to the offer of a very low price.

Differentiation and Discrimination

For heuristic purposes we have analysed price discrimination in terms of pure monopoly, though, in practice, most examples of price discrimination occur in markets with free entry. For example, magazine subscriptions and cinema seats are frequently sold to students at a discount, pensioners can travel more cheaply and airlines sell trips of different durations at different prices. These products – and many more

– could not be thought of as being provided by a monopolist. It would be more correct to describe the markets supplying them as being characterized by rivalry and significant product differentiation, i.e. differentiated oligopolistic or monopolistically competitive markets. In the foregoing examples, the demand curve facing the monopolist was exogenously given. Under **oligopoly** or **monopolistic competition**, the demand curve facing an individual firm depends on the behaviour of other firms. Only if we assume **Cournot–Nash** equilibrium, whereby each firm takes the quantities supplied by other firms as given, is the foregoing discussion on monopoly an adequate representation of oligopolistic and monopolistic competition providing we are concerned only with the behaviour of an individual firm.

Once we allow for multiple, product-differentiated firms, a number of new issues need to be considered. Not least is to examine what form of price discrimination is the most effective in markets characterized by product differentiation. Other pertinent questions might be whether price discrimination influences the number of products on offer and indeed the number of firms competing for market share. These are complex issues and research in this area is relatively thin. A study by Katz (1987) approached the issue of price discrimination for heterogeneous products from the perspective of information. The study hypothesized two types of consumer: the informed and the uninformed. The informed consumers know the relative prices being charged by alternative suppliers and the uninformed know none of the prices. If suppliers engage in price discrimination then, Katz concluded, the price paid by informed consumers would be lower than the price paid by uninformed consumers. Interestingly, the study also suggested that price discrimination would support a larger number of firms than the alternative of a uniform price. He also observed that if the uninformed account for only a small proportion of the market, then in terms of consumers' surplus uniform pricing is better, but if the uninformed account for the majority of consumers, the result is reversed.

An alternative approach to price discrimination under product heterogeneity is provided by Borenstein (1985). He assumes consumers have not only varying reservation prices, but also brand preferences. Differences in reservation prices reflect differences in taste, whereas a willingness to travel to purchase a particular brand indicates brand preference. In his study, Borenstein finds that the effectiveness of price discrimination based on reservation prices or brand preference depends on market structure. If the monopolistically competitive market is highly competitive, reflecting a large number of competitors, then discriminating on the basis of brand preference is more effective than discriminating by reservation price. If, alternatively, the monopolistically competitive market is more 'monopoly' than 'competitive', then discriminating on the basis of reservation price is more effective.

If it is difficult to make much progress on the relationship between price discrimination and the structure of differentiated oligopolistic and monopolistically competitive markets, there is more that can be said about product differentiation. We have defined price discrimination as existing whenever a firm sells an identical product to different buyers at prices that are in varying ratios to their marginal costs. In practice, what we normally observe are differentiated products where variations of the basic product sell for different prices. Ski resort hotels are more expensive in the winter than in the summer, restaurant meals are more expensive in the evening than at lunch time and business class air travel is more expensive than economy. In these and many more examples, we observe that the differentiating elements involve material differences – the weather, greater choice and more space, respectively. But closer inspection of these and many other examples suggests that the deviation in the prices charged for product variation greatly exceeds any differences in the cost of supplying the variation. One explanation for this observation is that rather than offering a wider choice to all consumers, the variations in the basic product are aimed at distinctly different market segments.

It has long been recognized that firms may use quality differences to discriminate among consumers. Phlips (1983), following Stigler (1966), argues that price discrimination should be defined as existing when two varieties of a product are sold by the same seller to different buyers at different net prices, i.e. the net pricing being the price paid by the buyer after correction for any costs associated with the differentiation. Using this definition it would not be discriminating to charge a transatlantic business class passenger the extra cost of the additional space, improved seating, entertainment and service. But with the business class fare costing up to four times the economy fare, it seems unlikely that the difference in price accurately reflects the difference in cost. In other words, the difference between the business class and economy version of a transatlantic flight amounts to price discrimination.

The foregoing throws a new light on price discrimination. Quite simply, it suggests that by offering different varieties of the same product, a firm with market power enhances its ability to price discriminate. It will be recalled that in order to engage in price discrimination a seller must overcome two difficulties: individual or group demands must be capable of identification before they can be separated into different segments; and arbitrage between customers being charged different prices must be preventable. By offering different versions of its product, a seller may be able to overcome these problems. Different consumer types may buy different versions of a product, and by so doing reveal the nature of their demands. Quality enthusiasts are prepared to pay a higher price for a higher-quality level, while other consumers are content to purchase quality levels below the highest available. An example is provided by improvements in the speed of computers. Not all consumers buy the best, because the best generally carries a higher price, suggesting that given the choice some consumers do not judge that the price of the higher quality matches the benefits. Selling different versions of a product has another advantage for a price discriminator. As different customers are purchasing different varieties of the product, the problem of resale is significantly reduced.

For airlines, the issue of arbitrage is easily solved. In order to travel business class, a business class ticket is required. But in charging the business class passenger a higher price, the airline has to try to ensure that the price differential will not cause too many business passengers to choose to fly economy. This problem is minimized by making conditions for an economy passenger, if not intolerable, then uncomfortable, e.g. little leg room and, if supplied at all, small DVD screens. In contrast, business class passengers are given plenty of leg room, a surfeit of seat positions and lavish services. It is not that the airline wishes to be mean to economy class passengers, but rather the airline is attempting to prevent passengers who value higher quality and can afford to pay the business class fare switching to economy seats.

The essence of the problem facing a supplier who wishes to price discriminate on the basis of quality rather than quantity is the fundamental constraint of devising a pricing scheme that induces consumers of each quality level to prefer their quality to any other quality. Formally, as pointed out by Pepall et al. (2005), price discrimination based on product quality variations can be modelled using the techniques outlined earlier. In principle, consumers are placed in type categories, not according to the quantity of the product they are willing to consume at different prices, but according to the quality of the product. Consumers self-select according to their demand for particular levels of quality and the seller seeks to reinforce their commitment to a particular quality class by exaggerating the quality choice, hence the lavish services provided to business class airline passengers and the superfluous comforts provided to first-class passengers.

The marginal cost of supplying the separate quality markets will not be identical; we would logically expect a positive relationship between higher quality and marginal cost (we will explore this issue in

Chapter 12). Allowing for this qualification, profit maximization is achieved by identifying the quantity sold to each market segment that equates marginal revenue with marginal cost. As observed above, quality choices are exaggerated in order to ensure self-selection, but passengers willing and able to pay more for higher quality can be reinforced in that decision if costs are imposed by switching to a low-quality segment. For example, airline passengers who want the lowest-priced seats are generally required to stay over a weekend. This is unlikely to be viewed as a cost for someone who is flying to a holiday, but for a business traveller it represents a cost most – or rather their firms – are willing to pay to avoid.

The technique of offering different quality levels of the same product has been taken to new heights by suppliers of information technology products and this form of discrimination to discriminate between consumers with different willingness to pay has been described as **versioning**. This technique was christened and analysed by Shapiro and Varian (1999), and it describes a situation where a firm offers a range of slightly different versions of the same broad product at different prices, leaving the consumer to self-select the product (or quality of products) they wish to buy. Versioning can extract consumers' surplus provided the menu of choices offered to consumers creates incentives for higher valuation consumers to opt for high-price versions, whilst lower valuation consumers retain the opportunity to purchase the cheaper products. The arbitrage problem is circumvented as the strategy involves offering the same options to all customers, but priced in a way that consumers with different levels of willingness to pay self-select according to the production version. As observed above, versioning is particularly suited to information products and a menu of versions drawn from Shapiro and Varian is set out in Table 11.1.

Table 11.1: Versioning and consumer characterization

Product differentiation	Consumers
Delay	Patient/impatient users
User interface	Casual/experienced users
Convenience	Business/home users
Image resolution	Newsletter/glossy users
Speed of operation	Student/professional users
Format	On-screen/printed users
Capability	General/specific users
Features	Occasional/frequent users
Support	Casual/intensive users

The foregoing has focused on price discrimination in consumer markets, but the practice is also found in **intermediate markets**. We will return in more detail to pricing behaviour in intermediate markets in the next chapter. In many respects the analysis of price discrimination in intermediate markets remains unchanged but, as pointed out by Katz (1987), there are two important differences. Firstly, a buyer's demand for an intermediate product is dependent on the prices paid by its competitors for the same product. Secondly, search costs for buyers in intermediate markets are likely to be small relative to their overall costs and in some cases they may have the possibility of vertically integrating upstream to produce the intermediate product themselves. The first point means that the welfare analysis must take into account the indirect change in the intensity of competition engendered by price discrimination, e.g. charging a high price for an intermediate good will lower the supply of the final product and lower competition. The second point means that it would be hard to maintain discrimination based solely on high search costs – the calculation of the impact on welfare must compare the impact on production costs (and hence welfare) of vertical integration as opposed to price discrimination.

We noted above that Phlips defined space as a basis for price discrimination. In geographically spatial markets, delivery of a product involves transport costs and this cost must be added to the selling price. Phlips examined practices employed by sellers that depart from the charging of a uniform price for an homogeneous product in geographically spatial markets. Assuming that unit transport costs, t, are constant and per unit of distance is d, the delivered price, p_d, at a specific spatial location is given by:

$$p_d = p + td \tag{11.8}$$

where p is the uniform product price. If consumers are charged the transport costs in full, then, all other factors remaining equal, consumers will go to the firm for which td is lowest. This implies that individual firms in separate locations will have spatially distinct markets. If, however, a firm only supplies the product at a price inclusive of transport costs, it has a basis for price discrimination. By absorbing all or part of the transport costs associated with more distant markets and charging 'phantom freight' rates, i.e. rates in excess of the true costs of transport, to customers in closer markets the firm discriminates in favour of more distant customers.

The advantage of this form of price discrimination for a profit-maximizing firm can be demonstrated with some simple theory. In an oligopolistic market supplying an homogeneous product, the market price, p, is determined by the total quantity supplied, that is:

$$p = \alpha - \beta Q \tag{11.9}$$

where $Q = \Sigma q_i$ and q_i are the quantities supplied by each firm. If we assume each firm has an equal market share, then $q_i = Q/n$. As each firm supplies spatially located customers, its marginal cost of supply consists of two elements: the marginal cost of production, c_i, and also the transport costs, td. Setting marginal costs, $c_i + td$, equal to marginal revenue, it can be shown (see Appendix 11A) that the optimal delivered price is given by:

$$p = \frac{c_i n + \alpha}{n + 1} + \frac{n}{n + 1} td \tag{11.10}$$

This delivered pricing schedule is illustrated in Figure 11.6. The first term on the right-hand side of Equation (11.10) is the phantom freight addition to marginal production costs and the second term is the proportion of transport costs passed on to the buyer. If there are only two producers (i.e. a **duopoly** where $n = 2$), then only two-thirds of the transport cost is passed on to the buyer. As the value of n increases, so the pricing schedule converges to the competitive outcome shown in Equation (11.8).

A second discrimination practice is that of **basing point pricing**. This is a co-operative pricing system whereby industry rivals agree that delivered prices will be based on published product prices at specific locations, plus the costs of transport from these locations to the point of delivery. The basing point system is suited to commodities where per-unit product value is relatively low and transportation is a relatively large proportion of the delivered price – cement, wood and steel are examples of products that have been subject to basing point pricing. Under a single basing point system, one location within a geographic market is the basing point and for delivery anywhere in the market the delivered price is the basing point product price plus the cost of transport from the basing point regardless of the location of the plant where the product was made relative to the point of delivery.

In practice, basing point systems have a number of price points. Under a multiple basing point system, the delivered price to any location is the basing point that offers the lowest delivered price regardless of the location of the plant at which the product was made. Figure 11.7 is based on Phlips (1983) and shows a simplified market with two firms, i.e. a duopoly, and hence two basing points: 1 and 2. Plant 1 has marginal costs, MC_1, and plant 2 has MC_2. The lower curves rising from locations 1 and 2 show the rising cost of delivery from locations 1 and 2. The higher curves rising from locations 1 and 2 show the delivered price to the con-

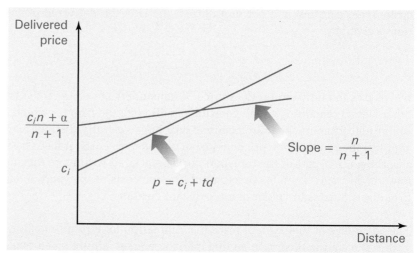

Figure 11.6: Freight absorption

sumer, where $p_1 > MC_1$ and $p_2 > MC_2$. Over the interval from 1 to A, the lowest delivered price is from location 1. Between A and B, the delivered price from location 1 is lower than the delivered price from location 2. Between B and C, the delivered price from location 2 is cheaper, but beyond D only location 1 would find it profitable to sell to consumers located in this region.

Basing point pricing creates the appearance of rivalry in the sense that there are some regions, A to E and F to D, where customers have a choice of more than one supplier. In fact, the basing point system acts as an efficient method of reducing a co-operating firm's incentive to cheat. Consider the shaded areas in Figure 11.7. Location 1 could supply customers located between points B and E at the same price as location 2, providing it was prepared to reduce its price; at E, the delivered price would be equal to the marginal cost of production, plus the cost of delivery. Similarly, by reducing its price–cost margin, location 2 could undercut location 1 between G and A. But the incentive to cheat is greatly reduced because the cost to a rival of punishing cheating – i.e. lowering its price – is much lower under a basing point system. Normally, a punishment strategy requires the enforcer to reduce the price of all it produces, im-

posing a considerable reduction in profits on both the enforcer as well as the victim. But with basing point pricing a retaliatory price cut can be made by shading the delivered price to just the areas where the cheating firm violated the agreement, i.e. the shaded areas in Figure 11.7. As a result, the retaliation can be more precise and, more importantly, less costly. This considerably enhances the credibility of retaliation, which in turn discourages cheating in the first place.

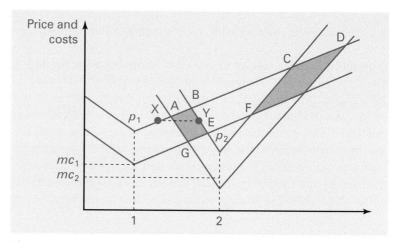

Figure 11.7: Multiple basing point pricing

Under a basing point pricing system all firms should offer the same price for delivery to the same location, but firms discriminate between customers in terms of net price – delivered prices less marginal cost. In Figure 11.7, for example, the marginal profit to the firm at location 1 at point X is $p_1 - MC_1$, while its marginal profit from supplying a customer located at Y is somewhat less. Sales at X and Y are both profitable for the firm at location 1, but a greater profit is made on sales to customers at X than to customers at Y. When firms have different costs of supplying different locations, identical delivered prices mean discriminating net prices.

Lessening the Noise

Some commentators are of the view that the internet will reduce the scope for price discrimination and push the 'new economy' towards the neo-classical ideal of perfect competition. In many markets consumers are faced with a bewildering array of similar products and services at different prices, which is evidence of suppliers attempting to leverage the benefits of price discrimination. Such price variation is described as 'noisy', as prices seem to vary from supplier to supplier in a random and unsystematic way. Thus, consumers with low opportunity costs to their time can search out the best bargain, but those with higher opportunity costs are unlikely to search and expect to pay over the odds. Marketers have more recently coined the term 'confusion marketing' to describe the practice of segmenting markets in this way.

In principle, the internet makes it much easier and less time-consuming to monitor a bewildering arrays of prices. There are now many websites that continually monitor prices of durable products so that potential buyers have a good idea of what is being offered. The effect of rapid and timely information is one of the main ingredients for perfect competition and therefore, over time, according to this view we should witness less 'noisy' price discrimination and greater convergence of prices to low levels.

It is important to distinguish between 'noisy' and systematic price discrimination. If people know that a particular product variety delivers greater value, they will still choose it despite a higher price. But where high prices relied on the positive costs of searching, such discrimination will in the future be more difficult to sustain. There is finally also the power of the internet itself. The same technology that allows people to search more efficiently can also help sellers to devise ever-more complex and personalized pricing schemes. The more information a seller gathers on customers, through repeat purchases, the easier it gets to devise customer-specific tariffs that approach first-degree price discrimination.

Bundling

Another price discriminating practice identified by Phlips is that of bundling. This practice was analysed in a seminal article by Adams and Yellen (1976). Their contention was that bundling enables a firm to discriminate between customers with the purpose of capturing a larger share of consumers' surplus and hence generating a greater economic rent. Bundling is a widely used marketing practice, where two or more products are sold together in a package. At first sight it may appear to have little resemblance to other price discrimination schemes, but its objectives are the same. Bundling comes in two forms. ***Pure bundling*** refers to a situation where two or more products can only be purchased together in a package, for example fixed priced menus and mandatory service contracts. ***Mixed bundling*** is a pricing system that allows individual products to be sold separately or as a bundle. An example of mixed bundling would be a travel agent offering a roundtrip airfare to a distant location and a package that includes an inclusive holiday. Formally, bundling is a form of second-degree price discrimination, i.e. non-linear pricing arising from purchasing one product and getting another at a lower price. It will only be feasible where a firm, or more than one firm in some form of alliance, produces at least two products for which their customers have heterogeneous demands such that there is a negative correlation among buyers' reservation prices for the two products – that is, their valuations differ so that some prefer one product more than the other and *vice versa*.

It is important to stress that we are not referring here to complementary goods. For example, a left shoe is always bundled with a right shoe, car bodies are generally bundled with engines, wheels and seats. In the case of such complementary goods there are many production and transaction cost benefits in selling the separate parts as a bundle. In many cases, bundling is undertaken to take advantage of ***economies of scope*** in distribution. Potential examples include the different sections of newspapers sold as a single product, or the bundling of cable television and cable telephones. Our interest here is in bundling that does not involve goods that are complementary or only weakly so, or that necessarily deliver economies of scope. Our focus here is the motive of exploiting the willingness of heterogeneous consumers to pay different prices. In the next chapter, we shall return to another possible motive; namely, entry deterrence. Figure 11.8 is highly simplified, but it demonstrates how bundling increases revenue. The figure represents a diversified firm who is in a position to benefit from bundling, i.e. customers for the two products have heterogeneous demands. As a pricing tactic, bundling does not increase the firm's unit production costs for either of the bundled products – though it could lower unit costs if it results in higher output – and therefore to the extent that it increases the total revenue, it must increase profits. The figure is interpreted as follows. The dots *A* to *J* represent a group of individuals' reservation prices for the firm's two products: Product 1 and Product 2. Tastes are such that consumers only purchase one unit of each product in a given period and the products are not complementary. This last assumption allows us to set the reservation price for the bundle as being the sum of the reservation prices for the two products. For example, point *A* represents an individual who has a

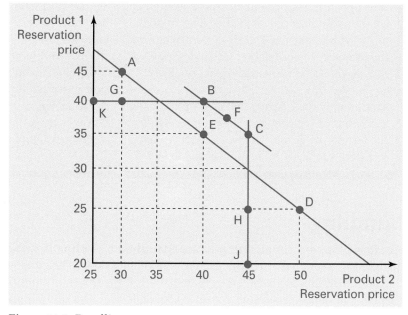

Figure 11.8: Bundling

reservation price of €45 for Product 1 and a reservation price of €30 for Product 2; individual B has reservation prices of €40 for both products and so on. Say our firm sets market prices of €40 and €45, respectively, for Products 1 and 2, then only consumers with reservation prices equal to, or above, these prices will buy the products. Thus, individuals A, B, G and K will buy Product 1 but not Product 2. Consumers C, D, H and J will buy Product 2 but not Product 1. Consumers E and F will buy neither.

In this situation, we can improve the firm's cash flow markedly with bundling. In the absence of bundling – in this highly simplified example – the firm will generate €160 from Product 1 and €180 from Product 2, yielding a total revenue of €340, as shown in Table 11.2. If the firm sells the two products separately it is over-looking the fact that each consumer logically has a maximum bundled price (p_B) they will pay for the bundled products, i.e. if sold jointly. This is generated by the following equation:

Table 11.2: Cash flow and bundling

	Product 1	Product 2	Bundle	Cash flow
No bundling	160	180		340
Pure bundling			450	450
Mixed bundling	120	135	240	495

$$p_B = R_1 + R_2 \qquad (11.11)$$

where R_{1i} and R_{2i} are the individual's reservation prices for the two products. We can see from Figure 11.8, that individuals A, E, D have the same p_B, namely €75, which is represented by the line passing through points A and D. Individuals B, F and C have a higher p_B equal to €80, i.e. for these consumers, $p_B < R_{1i} + R_{2i}$. Consumers G, H, J and K have reservation prices < €75, so for these consumers, $p_B > R_{1i} + R_{2i}$. If a pure bundled price of €75 is offered, then consumers A, B, C, D, E and F will all buy the two products, generating a total revenue flow of €450; see row 2 of Table 11.1. An alternative approach is to adopt a mixed bundling strategy. One example would be as follows: a bundled price of €80 is offered and at the same time the individual price for Products 1 and 2 are set at €40 and €45, respectively. In this example, the consequence is that A, G and K only purchase Product 1 and consumers D, H and J only purchase Product 2. Consumers B, F and C purchase the bundled product and E does not participate. In total, in this specific very simple example of mixed bundling, the strategy raises a total revenue flow of €495. Generally, mixed bundling will prove the most profitable option, though a perceptive student will have realized that given the distribution of buyers set out in Figure 11.8, a pure bundled price of €65 would generate the highest revenue.

Adams and Yellen argued that mixed bundling always dominates pure bundling and McAfee *et al.* (1987) derived a condition whereby if the buyers' reservation prices are independently distributed, then this guarantees that mixed bundling will dominate unbundled sales. Given the expectation that mixed bundling always dominates, we will examine a strategy of mixed bundling in a little more detail. Consider Figure 11.9, where consumers have been partitioned into four groups – W, X, Y, Z – as indicated by the solid lines. The bundled price is given by p_B and the prices at which Products 1 and 2 are sold individually are p_1 and p_2, respectively. Consumers in area X will purchase the bundled products and those in area Y will purchase nothing. Now let us consider consumers in areas W and Z.

Focusing on W in the area, p_1Ap_B, consumers are not willing to purchase the bundle since the sum of their reservation prices is less than p_B. These consumers purchase Product 1 on its own. However, consumers in the triangular area, W, could purchase the bundle but are likely to purchase only Product 1 because they derive more consumer surplus from it ($R_1 - p_1$) than from the bundle ($R_1 + R_2 - p_B$). If consumers in area W are likely to purchase only Product 1, then by similar reasoning consumers in area Z are likely to purchase only Product 2. This follows, because only consumers with low reservation prices for the two products buy the bundle, while higher prices for the two products extract the surplus of those with higher reservation prices.

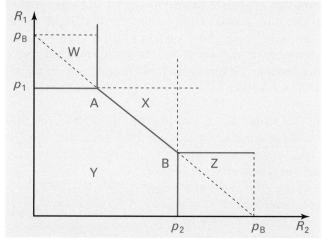

Figure 11.9: Strategy of mixed bundling

An example of mixed bundling is provided by broadband services where for varying monthly fees subscribers can access different bundles of film, sports and music content, in the process forcing competing suppliers of single services to 'play the game' against bundles. A pertinent question is whether bundled content represents a separate market from unbundled services. It may be far cheaper to buy the bundled content than individually, in which case individual services would not exert a competitive threat. Alternatively, consumers may attach a premium to buying a bundle, in which case a separate higher-priced market for the bundle may be justified as a 'one-stop' supply. As will be made clear in the next section, unless it can be demonstrated that discrimination exists between consumers in a specific market, the authorities cannot begin to even investigate whether the practice is to consumers' benefit or amounts to anti-competitive behaviour.

Bundling is inherently a pricing tactic that exploits differences in both tastes and a willingness to pay across consumers. It works providing the distribution of consumers' reservation prices for the two products are independently distributed. Given this, it follows that the **standard deviation** of consumers' valuation of the bundle will always be less than the sum of the standard deviations of the reservation prices for the individual products. By reducing the dispersion of consumers' valuation the monopolist is better able to capture consumers' surplus, though whether the practice enhances consumers' welfare is far less certain. Indeed, price discrimination and bundling are only two of many marketing devices employed to capture consumers' surplus. Other devices include discount coupons, matching offers, price promotions and discount brands. To what extent these devices improve welfare and industry performance remains a moot point.

Micro Bundling

In March 2004, the European Commission found Microsoft guilty of abusing its dominant position in the software market and ordered them to 'unbundle' the Windows Media Player from Windows software. It also fined Microsoft €497m. As is its right,

continued

Microsoft appealed against the decision and further argued that while the appeal was taking place they should not need to start the 'unbundling' process. On 22 December 2004, the European Court of the First Instance disagreed. The court argued that justice delayed would be justice denied.

As a result of the ruling, Microsoft is required to provide European Economic Area (EEA) countries with a stripped-down version of its Windows operating system, without its media player. The issue at the centre of this case is not bundling *per se*, but rather the use of bundling to protect and reinforce a dominant position. Microsoft's Windows operating system is *de facto* the industry standard and by bundling new software with Windows, Microsoft was making it more difficult for rival producers of media software to gain entry to the market. The European Commission is charged with encouraging competition with the EEA and in addition to ordering Microsoft to unbundle its media player, it also ordered Microsoft to license technical information to rivals so that their products can interface with Windows as efficiently as Microsoft's own media player.

Microsoft appears to be taking its time in fully complying with the court ruling. In February 2003, the European Commission threatened to fine Microsoft 5 per cent of its global revenue for failing to comply with the landmark court ruling. But Microsoft is no doubt looking beyond its Media Player to the longer-term threat to its strategy of dominating markets by bundling software. As it fights Google and Yahoo in the field of search technology, the court ruling makes it more likely that Microsoft will have to fight on a more level playing field, one on which merit is likely to be the victor.

Competition Policy and Price Discrimination

Price discrimination has long been regarded as a dubious practice by competition authorities both in the EU and the US. From a legal perspective, there may be objective reasons for a firm charging different prices to different customers, such as different transport costs – **price differentiation** – whereas price discrimination is viewed as a situation where differences in prices cannot be justified by differences in costs. As far as the competition authorities are concerned, price discrimination raises two potential competition issues: it may be anti-competitive in that it excludes competitors from a market; or it may allow a firm (or group of firms) to exploit market power and charge excessively high prices to certain customers.

There are two ways in which price discrimination could act as a **barrier to entry**. First, if it involved **predatory pricing** in one segment of the market; and second, if there were effects in downstream markets. We will deal with **vertical relationships** and downstream effects in the next chapter; here, we will confine attention to the direct impact of price discrimination and those aspects that might be judged unlawful. We should also recall, as observed in the previous chapter, that it is extremely difficult for the competition authorities to demonstrate predatory pricing, and consequently it would be difficult to demonstrate that price discrimination is anti-competitive and in the long run damaging to consumers.

Demonstrating an adverse effect for social welfare is far from easy. As observed in earlier sections, price discrimination involves some individuals or groups paying a higher price – but price discrimination can still be beneficial for such groups. A relevant example is peak and off-peak rail travel.

Charging leisure travellers (who have a lower willingness to pay than commuters) a lower price may allow the rail company to recover a bigger proportion of the fixed capital and overhead costs. The result of price discrimination could be to increase the overall level of output, as charging both peak and off-peak travellers the same price is likely to result in off-peak travellers switching to another mode of transport. High output lowers the unit cost of capital and overheads to the benefit of all customers. In general, the competition authorities will not view price discrimination as an abuse if it can be demonstrated that it leads to a higher level of output in the relevant market(s) than could be achieved if all customers were charged the same price. Similarly, charging the same price when costs are different may also be more efficient in some cases.

There is therefore no presumption by the EU competition authorities that price discrimination by a dominant firm is necessarily an abuse of its dominant position. This has not always been the case. In the US in the 1930s, the spread of chain stores, particularly grocery stores, brought great pressure to bear for strengthening the law against price discrimination and in 1936, Congress passed the Robinson–Pateman Act. An interesting observation on the Robinson–Pateman Act was that in seeking to protect small, independent stores from the larger-scale chain stores, the Act focused on powerful buyers who used their power to negotiate more favourable terms than their smaller competitors. The Robinson–Pateman Act has been described by one leading economist as 'the misshapen progeny of intolerable draftmanship coupled to wholly mistaken economic theory' (Bork, 1993, p. 310). Bork aside, what the Robinson–Pateman Act throws into sharp focus is the gulf between lawyers seeking to prevent unfair competition and the concern of economists to encourage efficient pricing.

Turning specifically to the attitude of the EU's competition authorities, two points should be emphasized at the outset when considering price discrimination. Firstly, EU competition law is directly applicable in all member states – indeed, it applies throughout the **European Economic Area** – and this necessitates legal certainty as to what constitutes competition and what is likely to be judged unlawful price discrimination. Secondly, the EU authorities are above all concerned to achieve single market integration and the maintenance of price differentials from one member state to another is likely to attract attention. As noted above, price differentiation might be justified by transport costs, but inter-member state price discrimination, indeed any attempt to isolate national markets from one another, is likely to be severely punished. There is no doubt that **horizontal agreements** to discriminate would infringe Article 81; indeed, Article 81(1)(d) specifically refers to agreements which, 'apply dissimilar conditions to equivalent transactions with other trading parties, thereby placing them at a competitive advantage' (European Commission, 2002, p. 64). Also, horizontal agreements that attempt to discriminate against importers and so protect domestic markets are likely to fall foul of the law, as are discriminating loyalty rebates.

Price discrimination may be condemned under Article 82 where it is carried out by a dominant firm. In several cases, price discrimination has been condemned because of the harm it might cause to a discriminator's rivals. **Primary line injury** may result from predatory pricing, discounting practices and delivered pricing. By definition, predatory pricing is designed to harm a competitor and the **European Commission** has been particularly penal where a company has sold a product at a loss in a member state – the 1992 *Tetra Pack II* is an example. The Commission and the European Court of

Justice (ECJ) have also been strict on loyalty retailers, declaring as long ago as 1979 in the case of Hoffmann La Roche & Co, that loyalty rebates conditional on a customer obtaining all or most of its requirements from a firm in a dominant position were unlawful. The ECJ did, however, accept that not all discounts can be treated as abusive. For example, the Court pointed out that quantity discounts exclusively linked to the volume of purchases and fixed objectivity would be permissible. In 1988, the European Commission held that British Sugar's delivered pricing systems constituted an abuse of a dominant position, although it did not impose a fine in respect of this offence as it was the first decision on this phenomenon. Until 1986, British Sugar had refused to allow customers to collect sugar at ex-factory price. In the Commission's view, uniform delivered pricing was to be viewed with scepticism. The brief overview of primary line injury reflects the EC and ECJ's view of the circumstances in which price discrimination harms a rival producer.

The foregoing does, however, raise the concern that even if it is possible to distinguish prices, discounts and delivered prices that reflect efficiency rather than discrimination, there is a danger that Article 82 might actually discourage price competition for fear that offering customers favourable terms might be unlawful. Getting the balance right is rarely easy. In the opinion of many economists, the EC is more likely to arrive at economically sound decisions if it focuses on the output effects of discriminatory pricing practices. If the size of the market increases under price discrimination there is scope for a net increase in consumers' plus producers' surplus.

Concluding Thoughts

Price discrimination is a pricing strategy that can either lower welfare by taking advantage of imperfect information and high search costs or increase welfare by more accurately targeting prices at consumers' demands and lowering the costs of search. The fact that price discrimination results in a firm appropriating a larger share of consumers' surplus and economic rent is not of itself sufficient grounds for condemning the practice. For firms that face declining average costs, price discrimination and/or a two-part tariff are efficient ways of utilizing installed capital. Price discrimination can take a number of forms, but they share in common a need to identify – either by research, experience or self-selection – individual or group demands. Providing these individuals or groups have varying reservation prices and/or price sensitivities, price discrimination will yield higher revenues without additional costs for the firm.

In order to engage in price discrimination, the firm must have sufficient market power; that is, it must face a downward-sloping demand curve; and it must be able to prevent arbitrage if consumers sold the product at a lower price can resell it to consumers who would otherwise pay a higher price.

In practice, firms that engage in price discrimination are likely to produce differentiated products and hence the marginal costs of production for each separate price category are likely to vary. In such markets, firms are likely to reinforce the choice of a high-priced product by exaggerating the quality difference. A two-part tariff becomes an efficient instrument of price discrimination when consumers are likely to purchase more than one unit of the product in any given period. Yet another method of discriminating is bundling where firm's seek to exploit variations in consumers' valuations of products offered jointly for a fixed price.

Key Learning Points

- Only firms with market power can engage in strategies of price discrimination.
- The essence of price discrimination is to separate consumers of a particular product into segments – according to the valuation the individuals place on the product – and then attempt to capture as much of this value as possible.
- First-degree price discrimination appropriates all the market's consumers' surplus by selling units of output separately to individuals according to their reservation price.
- A more practical method of applying first-degree price discrimination is to employ a two-part tariff.
- Second-degree price discrimination – sometimes known as non-linear pricing –

arises where a firm with monopoly power separates output into tranches and charges successively lower prices as successive tranches are consumed.
- Third-degree price discrimination separates a market into two or more segments and charges prices to the segments inversely proportionate to their price elasticity of demand.
- Price discrimination can only be effective – in terms of increasing a firm's revenue and profits – if consumers can be prevented from retrading.
- An alternative approach to capturing consumers' surplus is bundling, where consumers' valuations of two or more products are uncorrelated and offering the two (or more) products at a bundled price increases the number of joint consumers.

Exercises

11.1 In what way do the low-cost airlines approach the ideal of perfect, or first-degree, price discrimination?

11.2 The EU competition authorities take a negative view of price discrimination between countries, but is there an economic justification for parallel imports?

11.3 What is the link between third-degree price discrimination and information asymmetries?

11.4 Why does a firm with market power enhance its ability to price discriminate by offering different varieties of the same product?

11.5 In what way can bundling be described as price discrimination?

Problems

11.1 Given a monopolist's demand curve, $p = 1,000 - 0.1Q$, and unit costs $= 100Q$:

    (a) If the monopolist can engage in first-degree price discrimination, how much will be produced?

    (b) Suppose the monopolist can divide ouput into tranches of 3,000 units and charges €700 per unit in the first tranche, €400 per unit in the second tranche and €100 per unit in the third.

continued

Calculate consumers' surplus.

(c) If the market can be divided into two groups, with demand curves, $p = 1,000 - 0.5Q$ and $p = 1,000 - 0.05Q$, respectively, how much is sold to each group and at what price?

11.2 A bar has both students and adult customers. The demand for beer by students is given by the demand curve, $q = 18 - 3p$, and for adults by the demand curve, $q = 10 - 2p$. There are equal numbers of students and adults and the marginal cost of beer is constant at €2:

(a) What price should the bar owner set if students cannot be separately identified from adults?

(b) If the owner can discriminate and adopts third-degree price discrimination, what price would be charged to members of each group?

(c) The owner turns the bar into a private club and issues membership cards that distinguish students from adults. If members are charged a cover price and given drink tokens, what should be the cover price for each group and how many tokens should be issued to each group?

References

Adams, W. and Yellen, J. (1976) 'Commodity bundling and the burden of monopoly', *Quarterly Journal of Economics*, vol. 90, pp. 475–498.

Borenstein, S. (1985) 'Price discrimination in free entry markets', *Rand Journal of Economics*, vol. 16, pp. 380–397.

Bork, R. (1993) *The Antitrust Paradox*, 2nd edn, Free Press, New York.

European Commission (2002) 'Consolidated Version of the Treaty Establishing the European Community', *Official Journal of the European Communities*, C 325, p. 64.

Katz, M. (1987) 'The welfare effects of third-degree price discrimination in intermediate market goods', *American Economic Review*, vol. 77, pp. 154–167.

McAfee, R., McMillan, J. and Whinston, M. (1987) 'Multi-product monopoly, commodity bundling and correlation of values', Working Paper 1296, Harvard University.

Oi, W. (1971) 'A Disneyland dilemma: two-part tariffs for a Mickey Mouse monopoly', *Quarterly Journal of Economics*, vol. 85, pp. 77–96.

Pepall, L., Richards, D. and Norman, G. (2005) *Industrial Organization: Contemporary Theory and Practice*, 3rd edn, Thomson-South Western, Ohio.

Phlips, L. (1983) *The Economics of Price Discrimination*, Cambridge University Press, Cambridge.

Pigou, A.C. (1920) *The Economics of Welfare*, Macmillan, London.

Schmalensee, R. (1981) 'Monopolistic two-part pricing arrangements', *Bell Journal of Economics*, vol. 12, pp. 445–466.

Shapiro, C. and Varian, H. (1998) 'Versioning: the smart way to sell information', *Harvard Business Review*, November–December, pp. 106–114.

Stigler, G.J. (1966) *The Theory of Price*, 3rd edn, Macmillan, London.

Varian, H. (1984) *Microeconomic Analysis*, 2nd edn, Norton, New York.

Suppose an industry consists of n identical oligopolists producing an homogeneous product. All the suppliers are concentrated in one location, but the market they serve is geographically dispersed. The inverse market demand curve is given by:

$$p = a - \beta Q \qquad (11A.1)$$

where $Q = \Sigma q_i$ and q_i are the supplies of each firm. For each firm, the marginal cost of production is represented by c_i and common transport costs can be represented by td, where t is the transport cost per unit of distance and d the unit distance. The marginal cost of supply is therefore, $c_i + td$. If an individual firm changes its supply, Δq_i, the change in its total revenue, TR_i, is given by:

$$\Delta TR_i = p\Delta q_i + \Delta p.q_i \qquad (11A.2)$$

The change in price, Δp, is determined by the change in total supply:

$$\Delta p = \beta \Delta Q \qquad (11A.3)$$

Marginal revenue is defined as $\Delta TR_i / \Delta q_i$ dividing Equation (11A.2) by Δq_i and replacing Δp with Equation (11A.3), we get:

$$MR = p + \beta \frac{\Delta Q}{\Delta q_i}.q_i \qquad (11A.4)$$

Assuming a Cournot conjecture of $\Delta Q/\Delta q_i = 1$, recalling that $q_i = Q/n$ and substituting from Equation (11A.1) for Q we get $(a - p)/n$, Equation (11A.4) becomes

$$MR = p\left[\frac{n+1}{n}\right] - \frac{a}{n} \tag{11A.5}$$

Setting $MC = MR$, where $MC = c_i + td$, the profit-maximizing price is given by:

$$p = \frac{c_i n + a}{n+1} + \frac{n}{n+1} td \tag{11A.6}$$

CHAPTER 12

REPUTATION AND VERTICAL RESTRAINTS

Introduction

Throughout this book we have made much of the disparity between the neo-classical paradigm's assumptions of **perfect information** and **hyper-rationality** and what is observed in a world characterized by **asymmetric information** and **bounded rationality**. The reality is a **business environment** characterized by **imperfect information** and positive costs of obtaining information, which creates an imbalance of power between buyers and sellers. If buyers lack perfect information there can be no expectation that they will hold identical views as to the value and price of goods and services. Markets will be populated by a distribution of consumers ranging from the uninformed to the well informed in terms of the value and prices offered by sellers. If obtaining information is costly, a single firm may find that modestly raising the price of one of its products will not induce much search amongst its customers and therefore its sales volume may decline very little or not at all. Alternatively, it may choose not to lower its price when cost conditions are favourable if it believes that its (non-)action is unlikely to induce its customers to search out lower prices. In short, even in an industry with large numbers of firms, the existence of search costs may well be sufficient to allow prices to remain above marginal costs.

In this chapter, we extend our analysis of the relationship between price and sales to include imperfect information, and in so doing, we move further away from the **neo-classical paradigm** whereby it is assumed that firms within an industry sell at a uniform price – sellers treating all customers on an equal basis. As demonstrated in the last chapter, this assumption is some way from reality. It is quite common for an **homogeneous product** to be sold at different prices to different groups of buyers. For example, the price of electricity is likely to be lower the larger the volume purchased and passengers on low-cost airlines pay different prices for their seats. These practices, known as **price discrimination**, along with **bundling**, remain the most prevalent form of pricing strategy. Here, we focus again on different consumers paying different prices and the role of, or rather the lack of, information in bringing about a distribution of prices within a market. In practice, a distribution of prices may reflect a number of factors, including differences in quality and location, but with imperfect information some of the distribution is likely to reflect pure price variance.

Imperfect information also has consequences for the distribution of varieties and qualities of products produced. Aligning consumers' preferences to particular varieties or qualities of product is more of a challenge when consumers have only imperfect information. A strategy to invest in varieties and/or higher-quality products is only rational if the firm can capture the value it has created and we will explore the strategies firms adopt to achieve this objective. But capturing value is not the only issue thrown up by imperfect information. In a world characterized by imperfect information, positive search costs and **opportunistic behaviour**, there is scope for firms to cheat their customers into paying for a higher quality than they receive. The existence of imperfect information gives rise to a demand for information and in the next chapter we will consider at some length the use of advertising as a medium for supplying information. In this chapter, we focus on the behaviour of buyers and sellers, operating with imperfect information and in the absence of advertising. We will look first at the influence of imperfect information on price distribution before moving on to examine the behaviour of firms seeking to capture the value embedded in their products.

With the exception of Chapter 3, we have implicitly assumed throughout this book that a firm's output is sold to final consumers. However, in a modern economy only a small proportion of producers sell their products to final consumers. If the output is a raw material, a semi-finished product or a component, the customer will almost certainly be another firm. And even for firms who produce finished consumer products, they are likely to reach final consumers through intermediaries such as wholesalers and retailers. Thus, it would be more correct to think of most products produced by firms as being **intermediate products** and this raises a whole new set of issues regarding buyer–seller relationships. For most firms, their customers or suppliers are one stage removed in a vertical chain of production. The exchange of products between them is rarely based on **spot market** transactions, but on contractual agreements designed to reduce transaction costs, including the better co-ordination of the actions of buyers and sellers and greater security of quality and supply. The contractual relationships are referred to as **vertical restraints** and in the second half of this chapter we will examine their nature and purpose.

There is, perhaps inevitably, a tendency to view vertical restraints as falling between the two extremes of spot market exchange and **vertical integration**. Another perspective views vertical restraints as a special case of the **principal–agent problem**. Neither viewpoint is satisfactory, though both add important insights. As the word 'restraint' implies, one party to the transaction is attempting to influence, if not control, the behaviour of another party at a different stage in the vertical supply chain. This raises a key issue in the field of **competition policy**; namely, is it possible for a firm at one stage in the **supply chain** to use anti-competitive practices in its dealings with a firm at another stage in the chain to protect or enhance its market power. From its earliest days, the **European Commission** demonstrated a suspicion of **vertical agreements**, with the effect that since most types of vertical restraints were regarded as falling under the general prohibitions of Article 81, a large demand for exemptions emerged. The Commission has now adopted a more tolerant approach, where the positive efficiency effects of such restraints can be set against any potential anti-competitive effects. A positive approach to vertical restraints would view them as an attempt to counter imperfect information and bounded rationality. From this perspective, vertical restraints are viewed as a means of capturing the value of the extra effort that has been applied, to achieve a higher-quality product. As such, they are the means by which customers and consumers are offered wider choice and higher quality. After reading this chapter, you will:

- Understand how imperfect and asymmetric information impact on the prices charged by firms with or without variations in the quality on offer.
- Be aware of the many types of vertical restraint and their positive role in a world characterized by imperfect information and bounded rationality.
- Appreciate why the European Commission now essentially takes a *rule of reason* approach to vertical restraints.

What follows is divided into five sections. The first section examines the impact of imperfect information on pricing and in particular the scope for a price distribution to exist in markets selling homogeneous products. In the second section, we explore how strategic pricing can capture the higher value embedded in higher-quality products and the issues that are raised when quality cannot easily be assessed at the time of purchase. In the third section, we focus on vertical exchange relationships between buyers and sellers in the supply chain. In part this is to illustrate some of the issues that arise in selling intermediate products to other firms rather than selling to final consumers and also to show, using *game theory*, why co-operative vertical relationships are attractive. The examination of vertical exchange relationships also provides a platform for the fourth section, which builds on the previous section to analyse the nature of vertical restraints and how they can serve to improve efficiency by delivering higher quality to final consumers. Vertical restraints can also have anti-competitive effects and in the final section, we consider how vertical restraints might be used in such a manner and the response of the EU competition authorities in attempting to balance the efficiency-enhancing effects of vertical restraints with the potential for anti-competitive outcomes.

Pricing with Imperfect Information

Once we dispense with the neo-classical assumption of *perfect competition*, we enter a very different world when it comes to analysing the behaviour of both suppliers and consumers. In this section, we will consider how different sellers can charge different prices for the same product when customers have imperfect information as to the average level and distribution of prices charged by sellers in the market. According to the neo-classical paradigm, the *Law of One Price* applies to product categories and differences in offer prices are due only to differences in transport costs or quality. But in a world of imperfect information and positive search costs, it is not only possible for prices to have a distribution around the mean, but also it is possible for market prices to be above marginal cost (Stiglitz, 1998). Consider Figure 12.1. This shows the neo-classical convention of an infinitely elastic *demand curve* facing a firm producing a single homogeneous product. This curve assumes consumers have perfect information and any attempt by the firm to raise its price will result in sales falling to zero. Alternatively, the act of lowering its price would reduce profits and the firm would be unable to meet the rise in demand for its output. But if consumers have only imperfect information as to the prices charged by different firms – who might conveniently be thought of here as retailers – when a firm raises its price it may lose some customers but not all, because those with high search costs will assume that the price everywhere has been raised. Similarly, if it lowers its price, it may gain some new customers, but it does not attract the whole market because most people in the market will be unaware of the reduction in price.

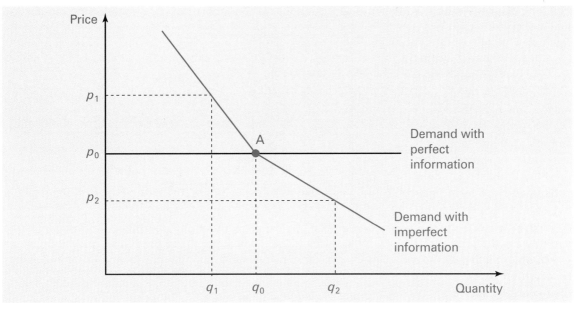

Figure 12.1: Demand and imperfect information

In Figure 12.1, we start at point A, with the firm facing a market price of p_0 and selling quantity q_0. With imperfect information, raising the price to p_1 results in sales falling to q_1 and reducing the price to p_2 results in the quantity of sales rising to q_2. As illustrated, the demand curve facing the firm under imperfect information is kinked. There is no significance in the shape of the kinked curve. It implies that the price elasticity of demand is higher when the price is reduced than when it is raised, but explanations could be advanced to reverse these elasticities. The important point is that in markets characterized by imperfect information on the part of customers, the firm does not face an infinitely elastic demand curve.

The analysis set out above applies to the short run and over time, **ceteris paribus**, as search activity and word-of-mouth increase the acquisition of information by consumers, so the **elasticities** on the kinked demand curve increase, straightening out the demand curve and moving it towards the horizontal. The time lag, however, may be considerable, particularly if the product in question is only purchased infrequently. Advertising does not necessarily resolve the problem outlined above. Firstly, only the firm that has lowered its price has the incentive to advertise and this would add to selling costs. Secondly, the more homogeneous a market, the more likely that advertising will be deployed at a generic level. Thirdly, advertising is not always designed to better inform a potential consumer. We will deal with advertising in the next chapter; here we will explore how a price distribution arises under imperfect information. We can start our analysis with an individual firm's profit function – assuming a single product, q – which can be represented by:

$$\pi = pq - c(q) - (r + \delta)K \tag{12.1}$$

where p is the product's price, $c(q)$ is variable production costs, K is capital expenditure and $(r + \delta)$ the cost of capital and the rate of depreciation, respectively, where $0 < r, \delta < 1$. Now imagine a market in which a number of firms, n, produce an homogeneous product and further imagine that there are two types of seller: a higher-price seller q_H; and a low-price seller q_L. If all consumers – represented by N – are well informed, then only low-price sellers will have customers. However, if only a proportion of consumers, a, where $a < 0 < 1$ are well informed, then there will exist $(1 - a)N$ consumers who have positive search costs and having arrived at a firm are prepared to pay the price asked – assuming it is below their ***reservation price*** – rather than continue searching. In this situation, it is tempting for a firm to increase its price above the minimum level. The firm will not attract any well-informed customers, but it will attract a share of the uninformed.

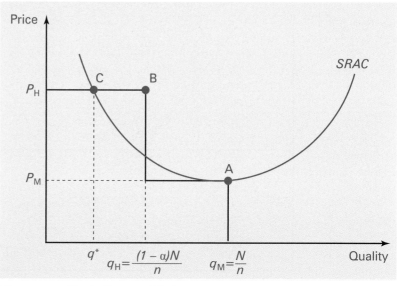

Figure 12.2: Single-firm equilibrium

Whether or not it is profitable for the individual firm to raise its price depends on the number of customers it is likely to retain and this, in turn, depends on the numbers of consumers and the proportion that are uninformed. The demand curve facing the individual firm that raises its price is shown in Figure 12.2. Given the ***law of diminishing returns***, we know that total, short-run average costs for the ith firm, $SRAC = [c(q_i) + (r + \delta)K]/q_i$, will follow a U-shape, as shown. If it charges the minimum price, p_M it attracts its proportional share of the market, i.e. N/n, but earns a zero rent: point A. Charging a price above the minimum, e.g. p_H, it sells fewer products but earns an **economic rent**: point B (see Appendix 12A for an explanation). The limiting factor is the proportion of uninformed consumers. If sales fall below q^*, then it will not be profitable for the firm to raise its price to p_H.

We can extend in broad, if not rigorous, terms, the thinking behind Figure 12.2 to indicate a multi-price equilibrium. Again,

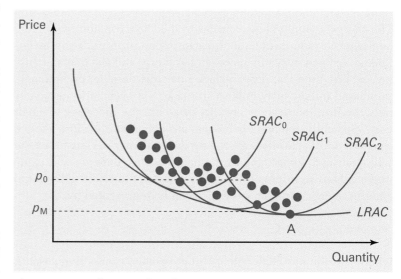

Figure 12.3: Multi-price distribution

to simplify matters we will assume all firms face the same short-run ($SRAC$) and long-run ($LRAC$) costs depending on their scale of operation. We will further assume that consumers purchase only one unit per period and both consumers and firms have positive search costs and, therefore, imperfect information as to the distribution of prices. Each firm offers a quantity for sale at $p > SRAC$ and if satisfied with sales takes no further action. The prices charged by the firms therefore lie on a continuum ranging from the highest to the lowest, but sales are distributed randomly as represented by the dots shown in Figure 12.3. As search costs are positive for all consumers, it does not automatically follow that a firm reducing its price will attract more customers. However, even with positive search costs over time – as implied by the $LRAC$ curve – some consumers will acquire some information on firms selling at a lower price. Note the caveat here: if a customer of a firm charging a relatively high price acquires information regarding a firm selling at a lower price, the low-price firm is likely to be charging prices above the minimum in the market. Thus, with limited search it does not follow that customers will immediately move to the lowest-priced firm represented by point A, the point of **minimum efficient scale** (MES) in Figure 12.3.

At a particular point in time, the average weighted market price might be p_0. The short-run equilibrium represented by price, p_0, in Figure 12.3 amounts to price discrimination amongst individuals partly according to their costs of search, and partly due to chance, i.e. the price charged by the first firm approached may not have been high enough to induce search. The average, p_0, can only be a short-term equilibrium because in successive time periods it is reasonable to assume that consumers' acquisition of information improves and as it does, so consumers will start to switch from higher-priced sellers to the lower-priced sellers. The effect of this, is a fall in demand for firms with high prices and a rise in demand for firms with low prices. This process lowers the weighted average market price, a process reinforced by high-price firms choosing to lower price rather than exit the market. Given sufficient time, the market will arrive at the equilibrium price, p_M, which is where individual firms will produce output A, but earn a zero rent. How fast the market moves to A depends on the costs of search.

Another factor is the market's **contestability**. If the market is **contestable** over successive time periods, higher-priced firms will find themselves challenged by lower-priced entrants, who have the effect of lowering demand for existing firms and at the same time increasing the price elasticity of demand. It is not, however, automatic that increasing the number of firms will rapidly reduce the market price. As search costs are positive, there is a limit to the number of firms a consumer will include in a search. Indeed, if entry is limited, with fewer firms in the market, information might be expected to spread at a faster rate regarding relative prices as there are fewer firms to visit. This suggests the paradox of a lower mean price and a tighter price distribution with fewer firms.

So far, we have only considered firms producing homogeneous products, but the addition of product varieties adds a new dimension. If, in the minds of consumers with heterogeneous tastes, different varieties of a particular product – say colours – are imperfect substitutes, then this raises the likelihood that, subject to search costs, consumers will seek varieties of a particular product that are matched to their preferences. Introducing product heterogeneity increases both choice and the search costs of satisfying this choice. With imperfect information, consumers will not know how prices for different varieties vary, but now they have to search across two dimensions, e.g. colour and price. As we have seen, the higher the costs of acquiring information, the lower, *ceteris paribus*, the price elasticities of demand and the greater the scope for price dispersion. In such conditions many consumers will purchase a variety of a product that is not well matched to their preferences, thereby revealing that the ill-matched product's price represented its **reservation price** and hence indifference to continuing to search.

Once we introduce product heterogeneity, the appropriate model is that of **monopolistic competition**, which we briefly referred to in Chapter 8. Chamberlin's (1933) model of monopolistic competition is summarized in Figure 12.4. In contrast to an **oligopoly**, under monopolistic competition the market is assumed to be perfectly contestable and its structure is characterized by a large number of sellers. Sticking with our example of colour variety, each firm produces and sells only one colour product, but we can assume there are large numbers of firms each selling the same colour. For the moment, we will further assume that all firms have identical production costs and an individual firm is represented by the short-run and long-run average cost curves – SRAC and LRAC, respectively – set out in Figure 12.4. The curve, D_M, is the **market response demand curve**, i.e. the relevant demand curve when all sellers change their prices in the same direction. The curve, d_i, running through point A, is the **ceteris paribus demand curve** facing an individual seller. This is assumed to be more elastic than the market response curve, as an individual firm, in lowering its price, is assumed to have no appreciable impact on rivals' sales and therefore rivals do not react in kind; formally, firms hold zero **conjectural variations** regarding rivals' behaviour. For convenience, this is drawn as a straight line, but it could in principle be kinked at A to represent different price elasticities of demand, depending on whether the price is raised or reduced.

Starting at point A, the ith firm's price, p_0 is above its SRAC and therefore it is earning an economic rent. As the market is contestable, new entrants will be attracted by the prospect of earning a rent, with the effect that over time the market share for incumbents will decline – represented by the shift from point A to B. New entry ceases when rents are reduced to zero, i.e. point B, where d_i^1 is tangential to the LRAC curve. The figure shows the situation for an individual firm, but because there are a large number of firms and each holds zero conjectural variations, the repercussions for other firms are ignored when a firm lowers its selling price. Each is assumed to act as though facing the d_i curve, but as all firms are lowering their prices in response to falling market share, they are in fact all moving down the market response curve, D_M.

The long-run equilibrium, represented by point B, gives rise to Chamberlin's *excess capacity* prediction of monopolistic competition. But the model's equilibrium is seriously compromised by the assumption of product heterogeneity. Heterogeneous products will not necessarily have the same production costs – we might reasonably expect a positive relationship between quality and production costs – and, as we shall explore in the next

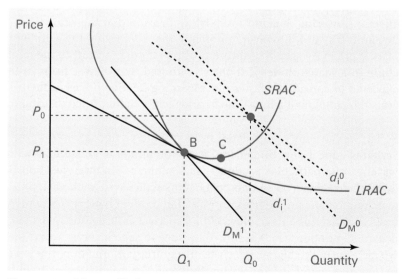

Figure 12.4: Monopolistic competition

chapter, they may also have very different selling costs. There is, in short, a logical inconsistency of combining downward-sloping demand curves, derived from product heterogeneity, with identical cost curves. Another problem, indicated in Figure 12.4, is that new entrants will increase the range of substitutes available, thereby increasing the price elasticity of demand for each firm's products, i.e. flattening the curve, d_i. But with potentially no limit to the number of firms, it is not possible to rule out infinite demand elasticity for each firm and with zero conjectural variations, this is the outcome that would be generated by perfect competition.

Chamberlin's model was constructed within the neo-classical paradigm, which assumes perfect information on the part of consumers and sellers. However, the existence of imperfect information and positive search costs does provide a plausible basis for individual firms continuing to face downward-sloping demand curves. With product heterogeneity and imperfect information, a firm reducing its price might be expected to capture additional sales, but the increase would be restricted by the fact that products of different varieties are not perfect substitutes and only some consumers would find it beneficial to engage in search. Similarly, a firm raising its price might be expected to suffer a loss of sales, but, again, many consumers would remain customers because the limited information available to them shows that the offerings of the firms they are aware of are not perfect substitutes and they are not prepared to incur the costs of a wider search. In such circumstances, the effect of an individual firm reducing its price might be to cause so few consumers to switch that the impact for the individual firm is no different than if the average market price was reduced.

Vanishing Variety

A common trend across OECD countries is the increasing concentration of retail markets, particularly in Europe. Within the European Union, the consolidation process increasingly involves cross-country mergers, so that within the EU the largest ten supermarket chains now account for more than 30 per cent of sales of food and daily products. Amongst retailers that are now active in more than one country of the EU are Germany's Rewe and Metro, the UK's Tesco and France's Intermarché. Also, the US Wal-Mart is operating in several European countries following a string of acquisitions including that of Asda in the UK and Wertkauf in Germany.

One of the concerns raised by the concentration of retailers' buying power is that it may have negative consequences for upstream product in-novation and variety. There are two reasons for this concern. Firstly, following a merger the consolidated retailer is likely to delist some suppliers, thereby reducing variety and a better fit to individual preferences. Secondly, larger supermarkets have developed their own brands so as to differentiate themselves from their rivals selling similar products.

The loss of variety due to retail merger and subsequent sourcing from just one or two suppliers is further aggravated by suppliers, in anticipation of further consolidation among their buyers, repositioning their produce to be more widely acceptable and thereby further reducing product variety. The increased buying power of consolidated retailers puts downward pressure on supplier prices, with the effect that the profits of suppliers are reduced,

continued

which in turn leads to a reduction in R&D and marketing expenditures.

The selling of own-label products by retailers is an important form of differentiation for retailers, reinforcing the store's image and building customer loyalty. As the retailers own-label products become a source of variety, so the upstream suppliers find their power to differentiate weakened. In response, upstream suppliers become more concentrated in the hope of creating a countervailing power, but in the process further reduce product variety.

Pricing Quality

In the previous chapter, we explained that although in practice price discrimination frequently involves variations in quality – e.g. business and economy class airline seats – as a strategy it does not depend on differences in quality. In the last chapter, we also discussed how quality itself is a variable that firms can use to discriminate among consumers. Given heterogeneous consumers, whose taste for quality and willingness to pay for it will by definition vary, firms can in principle discriminate by choosing a pricing scheme that induces consumers facing varying levels of quality to purchase the quality that best meets their demand. But there is a more fundamental question surrounding quality; namely, in a world of imperfect information and positive search costs, how can a supplier of a single product, who invests effort in producing to a higher quality, capture the additional value of the quality? When it comes to quality, consumers are faced not only with imperfect information regarding the distribution of prices, but also with imperfect information concerning the quality of products at the time of purchase. The existence of quality heterogeneity forces consumers to balance seller claims of value with limited information and positive search costs.

The problem of capturing value in the presence of imperfect and asymmetric information was neatly captured by Akerlof (1970), in his famous model of the market for slightly-used cars. Akerlof used the example of a low-quality car, known in America as a 'lemon'. When purchasing a new car consumers, generally, trust to the producer's system of quality control in the expectation that there is only a small probability that the car will turn out to be a lemon. Once the car is bought, some buyers may find that they have, in fact, purchased a lemon and such buyers are more likely than other buyers to try and quickly resell their cars. This means that the market for slightly-used cars has a much higher percentage of lemons than the market for brand new cars. But buyers suspect this and in consequence adjust their offer prices downwards, resulting in sellers of 'non-lemons' facing market prices that are below the true value of the cars they are offering for sale. The result is that sellers with non-lemon, slightly-used cars withdraw from the market, thereby increasing the proportion of lemons and further depressing market prices. This is a problem of ***adverse selection*** – a product version of Gresham's law; namely, bad quality drives out good quality.

We can start our analysis of this issue by separating products into three categories with respect to quality. Nelson (1970) defined two categories: ***search goods*** and ***experience goods***; and a third category, ***credence goods***, was introduced by Darby and Karni (1973). Only in the case of search goods, where search costs are low and quality can be evaluated effectively before purchase, are consumers likely to approach a situation of being fully informed with respect to quality – though not to the distribution of prices for that quality. For example, the quality of a jacket or a dress can be fairly accurately assessed by pre-purchase inspection. With experience goods, search costs are high and quality can only be evaluated effectively after consumption. For products that are frequently purchased, e.g. pre-prepared meals, consumers will quickly become informed as to relative quality, but in the case of infrequently purchased experience goods, e.g. a car, quality may only be revealed after a lengthy period of time and buyers have to take most of the suppliers' quality claims on trust. In the case of credence goods, consumers may never be able fully to evaluate quality, even after purchase and consumption, as quality has to be taken on trust, e.g. the advice of a solicitor. Darby and Karni (1973) focused on a unique feature of service industries; namely, the joint provision of diagnoses and service such as repairing a car. In such situations, buyers can never be sure that they needed the service. But physical goods can also have credence characteristics such as the claim that fruit or vegetables have been grown organically. In this respect, credence goods and experience goods, where quality takes time to be revealed, amount to purchasing a *pig-in-a-poke* – not in the sense of unscrupulous sellers ruthlessly exploiting the asymmetry of information and the trust of consumers, but rather in the sense that sellers offer their products for sale as fair samples of their production systems and associated quality control systems (Andersen, 1994). The more committed a firm to quality, the more likely that its quality control system will ensure that there is only a small probability that a product will turn out to be of low quality. For example, some cars will break down shortly after purchase, but overall quality is maintained if the proportion is very small.

Zeithaml (1981) placed these three types of goods on a continuum, ranging from easy-to-evaluate products to pure services that can never be fully evaluated, as set out in Figure 12.5. Goods, she proposed, generally have more search characteristics, while services exhibit more experience and credence characteristics. Search qualities, Zeithaml concluded, include attributes such as colour, style and touch, while experience qualities include taste, durability and satisfaction. As service become more difficult to evaluate, so uncertainty increases and hence the incentive on the part of consumers to bear the transaction costs of seeking more information.

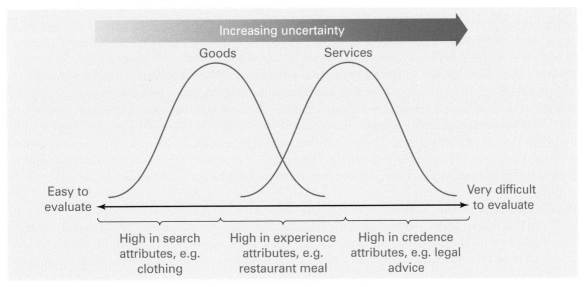

Figure 12.5: Evaluation continuum

The difficulty for consumers of distinguishing between good and bad quality is an important example of how uncertainty enters the calculus of pricing products. Producers of higher-quality products have a vested interest in helping potential customers to detect quality. But the detection of quality is not unambiguous. Buyers seek to detect quality by attempting to discern between intrinsic indicators (e.g. colour, texture), extrinsic indicators (e.g. brands, trademarks) and external authorities (e.g. in the case of food safety, the Food Standards Agency in the UK and the Food and Drug Administration in the US). Food safety is a credence good, rarely can it be judged before purchase or after unless it causes illness. More generally, when faced with credence goods or infrequently purchased experience goods, buyers use surrogate extrinsic indicators. **Reputation**, which is frequently manifested in brands, is a common extrinsic indictor of quality. We will look in more detail at **brands** in the next chapter. Here, we will focus on reputation.

Reputation only makes sense in a world characterized by imperfect information, e.g. when quality is not perfectly observable prior to purchase. In such a world, a firm that has a good reputation owns a valuable asset. But developing a reputation for producing high-quality products takes time and the expenditure of resources. It follows that a seller who chooses to enter a high-quality segment of the market must invest in reputation and this involves two distinct types of investment. Firstly, the firm must acquire **property rights** over the resources capable of producing higher quality, and, second, the seller must invest in informing potential customers of the quality being offered for sale. Here we are concerned with how price can be used to signal and eventually capture the value embodied in a firm's products. Price is the only vehicle for capturing the value of quality produced, but in the absence of an advertising campaign during the 'investment' period, the firm must sell at less than cost or settle for a low volume of sales. A price associated with high quality is unlikely to be achieved until reputation is established. The necessity of investing in reputation implies that in equilibrium, high-quality items must sell for a premium above their costs of production, i.e. they must earn a rent which represents the return on the initial investment.

This raises an interesting question. Why do firms earning a rent from a reputation for quality not take advantage of imperfect information and reduce quality, thereby reducing production costs and earning an even larger rent by continuing to sell at the premium-quality price? We do not need to resort to notions such as 'morality' or 'social pressures' to answer this question – there are good economic reasons why a firm that has built up a reputation would do itself greater harm in the long run if it attempted to cheat its customers. And this knowledge leads to an important observation. The price charged by a firm with a reputation for quality and fair dealing must exceed marginal production costs. In the absence of such a margin, firms would have little incentive not to cheat. Hence, firms that have built a reputation for quality own a self-enforcing mechanism for continuing to treat their customers fairly and honestly. In this respect, firms with a reputation for quality differ fundamentally from the neo-classical paradigm; namely, free entry will not reduce this rent to zero.

We can demonstrate the persistence of a quality rent with a dynamic model put forward by Carl Shapiro (1983). The model must be dynamic because reputation is fundamentally a dynamic concept. We can start by representing the cost of producing different levels of quality, α, with the function $c(\alpha)$ that is increasing in α, i.e. the higher the quality, the higher the costs of production. By definition, our seller operates within a monopolistically competitive market where the price achieved at a particular time, t, reflects the seller's reputation, R, at that date, and to a lesser extent the quantity sold. Monopolistically competitive markets are characterized by many sellers with varying reputations and all products will be subject to some minimum quality, α_0, below which it is illegal to offer products for sale. If we think of quality in this example as being an experience product we can define reputation as the quality expected by consumers and the simplest adjustment mechanism is:

$$R_t = \alpha_{t-1} \tag{12.2}$$

namely, the reputation held by the firm in the current period depends on the quality it delivered in the previous period, which in turn depends on the resources devoted to producing quality. Equation (12.2) implies that through experience, information on reputation is accurately held by all consumers who purchased and consumed the firm's products in the previous period. Turning to the demand side, this consists of heterogeneous consumers who differ in their willingness to pay and their taste for quality. Once again, for simplicity we will assume consumers are only willing to purchase one unit per period. A consumer will only purchase one unit if the expected utility from the quality exceeds, or at the margin equals, the disutility of the price paid. Expectations are formed as set out in Equation (12.2). Finally, we can denote the price associated with quality, α, as $p(\alpha)$, the higher the perceived quality, the higher the price that can be charged.

Given these parameters, we are now in a position to demonstrate why a firm with a reputation will not wish to risk its reputation – unless it intends to exit the market. Given a reputation for producing the quality, α, and therefore selling at the associated price, $p(\alpha)$, milking its reputation would yield a rent of $p(\alpha) - c(\alpha 0)$, where $c(\alpha_0)$ is the unit cost of producing minimum quality. That is, the firm would charge prices consistent with the higher quality, α, while only incurring the lower costs of supplying the minimum legal quality over a short period, i.e. $c(\alpha_0) < c(\alpha)$. The alternative strategy of maintaining quality yields a constant flow (say, for convenience, forever) of rent given by $p(\alpha) - c(\alpha)$, which has a present value of $[p(\alpha) - c(\alpha)](1 + r)/r$ when r is the **cost of capital**. Only if $[p(\alpha) - c(\alpha)](1 + r)/r > p(\alpha) - c(\alpha_0)$, will the firm have the incentive to avoid milking its reputation. With some manipulating, we can rewrite this condition as:

$$p(\alpha) \geq c(\alpha) + r[c(\alpha) - c(\alpha_0)] \tag{12.3}$$

Shapiro describes Equation (12.3) as the *no-milking* condition. It puts a floor under the price at which items of a given quality can be sold and the normal monopolistic competition assumption of free entry places a ceiling on the price at which a product of a particular quality, α, can be sold. In between the floor and ceiling prices, there will be a continuum of prices determined by the balance of supply and demand for products

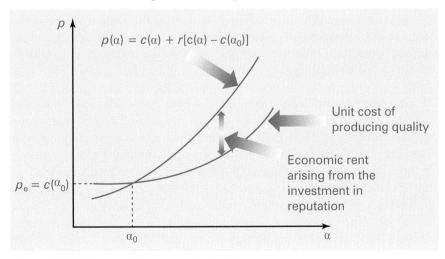

Figure 12.6: Price–quality and cost schedules

of varying quality. Free entry requires that the potential longer-term economic rent for a new entrant into the quality, α, market segment is positive, but in the short run rent it will be negative. It takes time for a new entrant to establish a reputation for quality; hence, in the absence of a successful and presumably expensive advertising campaign, they will have to settle for a lower entry price, say $p_e = c(\alpha_0)$. We might think of p_e as an introductory discount, a response to free entry which demands that $p_e \leq c(\alpha_0)$ as $p_e > c(\alpha_0)$ implies that a new entrant could earn a rent selling products of minimum quality. Thus, initially, for a new entrant producing a higher-quality product, profits will be negative, i.e. $p_e - c(\alpha)$, but rising (given Equation (12.2)) to $p(\alpha) - c(\alpha)$ in subsequent periods.

The entrance price reflects consumers' willingness to pay for 'unknown' products. Consumers expect products to be at least of minimal quality, hence they are prepared to pay $p_e = c(\alpha_0)$. On these assumptions, the price–quality schedule set out in Equation (12.3) is shown in Figure 12.6. It demonstrates that products with qualities in excess of the minimum earn a rent equivalent to $r[c(\alpha) - c(\alpha_0)]$, i.e. the higher the quality, the higher the rent. There is a simple interpretation of Equation (12.3). The cost of providing items of quality, α, is the production cost, $c(\alpha)$, plus a return on the investment in establishing and signalling a reputation for quality, i.e. $c(\alpha) - c(\alpha_0)$. The seller incurs this cost in the initial period and the premium price reflects the return on this investment in the form of ownership of an asset of reputation.

We observed above that reputation is a dynamic concept. It is an ongoing relationship between a firm and its customers and its strategic value depends on expectations formed on the basis of how the firm has behaved in the past. The relationship between past behaviour and expectations about future behaviour is captured in a repeated game where *players* condition their decisions on the history of their relationship. Firms that nurture a good reputation can expect over the longer term to be trusted and rewarded, whereas firms with a bad reputation are more likely to be punished. In order to examine the relationship between pricing and reputation using a game theoretic perspective, we start by hypothesizing a game played over an infinite succession of discrete time periods; that is, T time periods and in each period, the players – buyers and sellers – simultaneously and independently make decisions regarding their actions. These actions lead to pay-offs. Furthermore, we assume that in each time period, t, the players have observed the history of play from the first period through to $t - 1$. The pay-off from the entire game is defined as the sum of the pay-offs from each period's game from periods 1 through to T. We can capture the essence of this game with Figure 12.7, which shows a pricing game that is repeated, i.e. played over two periods, $T = 2$, where the product being offered for sale is an experience good.

The pay-offs are in the form of an economic rent, π to a seller with a reputation for quality and in the form of **utility**, U, to buyers. We will further simplify matters by assuming the buyer is only likely to buy one unit per period. In the first period, the buyer has to decide whether or not to buy and if this is the first period, as there is no history to guide the buyer's action, much will depend on the trust the buyer has in the seller's claims of quality. One way to gain a buyer's trust, as previously observed, is to offer a discount as a good experience is likely to lead to repeat purchase in the next period. The combination of the extra cost of producing higher quality and the introductory discount reduces profits below the maximum, i.e. $\alpha\pi < \pi$, where $0 < \alpha < 1$. But once the supplier has established a reputation for quality, a repeat purchase can be sold without a discount yielding a rent of π. If the firm can convince a buyer of its quality claims but then cheats by not delivering the quality expected, it gains the additional profits from its lower production costs in the first period of $\beta\pi$, where $\beta > 1$, but does not sell any products in the second period. Letting r represent the cost of capital, the firm has an incentive to be honest if:

$$\left[\frac{\alpha\pi}{(1+r)}+\frac{\pi}{(1+r)^2}\right]>\frac{\beta\pi}{(1+r)} \tag{12.4}$$

The outcome here might appear finely poised, but if the game is played over a large number of time periods, say for simplicity an infinite succession of periods, the outcome clearly favours being honest:

$$\left[\frac{\alpha\pi}{(1+r)}+\frac{\pi(1+r)}{r}\right]>\frac{\beta\pi}{(1+r)} \tag{12.5}$$

What Equations (12.4) and (12.5) show is that a seller who sells an experience or a credence product to one-time consumers and who cannot be sued for sub-standard quality has a strong incentive to cut quality – on the assumption that producing quality is costly – to the lowest possible level. This is a **moral hazard** problem, which explains why so often items purchased for tourist markets turn out to be of low quality.

If we drop the simplifying assumption that reputation takes only one period to establish, then the higher the quality produced, the larger the initial losses on the investment (in reputation) and, *ceteris paribus*, the higher subsequent rent. A longer lag between market entry and the establishment of a reputation for quality leads to a larger value of r and hence the price–quality schedule steepens, this effect is set out in Figure 12.8(a). Another insight revealed by Equation (12.3) is that any move by the authorities to alter the minimum quality will influence the rent associated with higher quality. An increase in α_0 to, say, α'_0, arising from, say, a new minimum standard, raises the price at which entry will take place, but it also *reduces* the profits that a firm can earn by milking its reputation and hence reduces the rent necessary to induce the maintenance of quality merchandise. This may seem odd at first, but the rent is the return to building up a reputation, which to some extent the authorities have done by raising minimum standards. This effect is set out in Figure 12.8(b).

Pricing is only one way in which information about

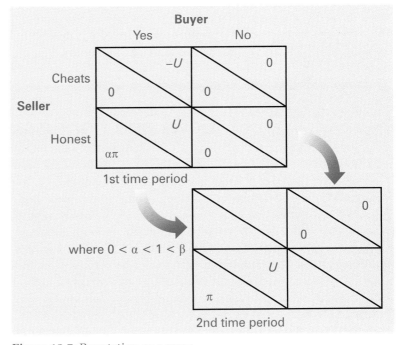

Figure 12.7: Reputation as a game

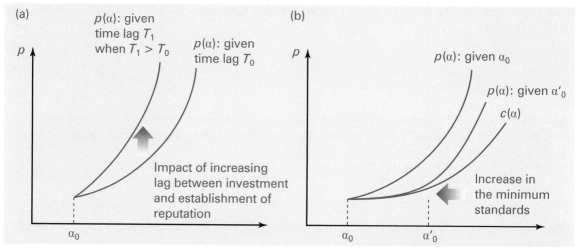

Figure 12.8: The influence of time and minimum standards

quality can be conveyed. If the interaction between a buyer and seller is likely to be repeated over many time periods, then it is a foolish firm that raises its price so as to imply a higher-quality product if in fact it is merely attempting to fool consumers into paying a higher price than other firms are charging for a product of similar quality. We have demonstrated that the use of a discount in the first time period is one way of conveying information about quality in the presence of imperfect and asymmetric information. Other mechanisms include warranties or guarantees, third-party endorsement and, for consumers with low search costs, disclosure of relevant technical details. As observed by Tirole (1993), in reality these mechanisms are compromised by the fact that very often quality, say for example durability, depends on the way the product is consumed. This, again, is a moral hazard problem, as the buyer has no incentive to take care of the product if they are to be fully reimbursed. Thus, the way to proceed for a product whose quality is durability is to make the consumer internalize some of the cost by, say, giving less than a full warranty.

Cows and Confusion

In March 1996, a hapless Stephen Dorrell, Secretary of State for Health, announced to a hushed House of Commons that ten young people had contracted a new variety of the harrowing and inevitably fatal Creutzfeldt-Jakob disease. Stephen Dorrell went on to say that scientists had concluded that the new variant disease, which quickly became known as vCJD, had probably been caught from eating beef from cattle suffering from Bovine Spongiform Encephalopathy (BSE). The Secretary of State's announcement was a bombshell, coming as it did after ten years of vigorous denial by the government that BSE could cross the species barrier and infect human beings. Consumers who had literally trusted government and scientists with their lives were now being told that those they trusted had got it wrong. The government's announcement marked a turning point in British and European food safety. It had a devastating impact on UK beef farms, the

continued

meat export industry, public finances and Britain's reputation abroad. Most importantly, public confidence in the claims of governments and scientists regarding food safety was seriously undermined.

A major conflict from the outset was created by the twin objectives of the Ministry of Agriculture, Fisheries and Food in being expected to simultaneously promote the economic interests of beef farmers while protecting the public from food-borne health hazards. Many observers believe that this conflict resulted in the government playing down the risks and although the feeding of bone meal – the suspected cause of BSE – was banned, many in the industry took their lead from the government and behaved as though there was little or no risk. Following the government's announcement in March 1996, the government's claims for food safety lacked

credibility. In the short term, consumers turned to the supermarkets as being influential and having a reputation for safety and quality. The New Labour government acknowledged the loss of public confidence in the statements of ministers and established an independent Food Standards Agency (FSA) in April 2000 to take over responsibility for the health and protection aspects of food policy.

Fortunately, since 1996 the number of BSE cases has declined steadily – following much tougher government action to remove bone meal from the food chain – and the number of vCJD cases, although now well over 100, does not appear to be rising as once feared. Nevertheless, the World Health Organization has warned that more than 100 countries that had imported meat or feed containing bone meal from Western Europe during the 1980s and 1990s were at risk from BSE.

Vertical Exchange Relationships

Although throughout this book we have referred frequently to firms and their customers, with the exception of Chapter 3, we have implied by omission that firms sell to final consumers. In fact, most firms sell to other firms in a vertical supply chain. Most firms do not produce final consumer goods, but intermediate goods that become inputs to downstream firms. Whether a firm sells to another firm or to final consumers, it faces the problem of capturing the value of what it produces; but arguably for sellers of intermediate products the situation is complicated by the nature of vertical exchange relationships with buyers in the supply chain. In a world of imperfect and asymmetric information, intermediate goods markets differ fundamentally from final or consumer markets. Firstly, intermediate goods markets generally involve large-scale transactions made by sophisticated buyers who typically will have more information than the average consumer. Secondly, the products being sold may possess attributes the value of which can be lessened by the behaviour of downstream buyers, raising the problem of moral hazard. Thirdly, the intermediate buyers' demands are derived from consumer demands, the level of which will be influenced by the nature of competition between the buyer or buyers and the rivals who purchase from other intermediate suppliers. Finally, the seller of the intermediate good is naturally keen to maximize profits, but in so doing the seller increases the probability that a buyer will engage in backward vertical integration.

We explore below the alternative contractual arrangements between an upstream producer and a downstream buyer. All rational upstream suppliers want their products to be used by downstream customers in ways that benefit the supplier, but it is impossible for the supplier and buyer to write a

complete contract. Some of the complexity of vertical exchange relationships can be demonstrated by considering the relationship between a producer of consumer goods and a retailer who will actually sell the supplier's products to final consumers. Here, the producer (the principal) contracts with the retailer (the agent) to sell its product. The producer cannot perfectly observe the effort the retailer puts into selling the product and therefore the seller is vulnerable to moral hazard and opportunistic behaviour. Common to principal–agent problems is the desire to reduce ***transaction costs*** on the part of the principal; but when it comes to vertical relationships, the problem is complicated by the existence of multiple agents, i.e. the buyers. Significantly, the positing of an offer price, so typical of consumer markets, is only one of a number of exchange mechanisms that exist between buyers and sellers of intermediate products. Frequently, buyers and sellers in a vertical chain sign contracts of various types in order to reduce transaction costs, guarantee stability of supply and better co-ordinate actions. These vertical contractual provisions are commonly referred to as vertical restraints. Vertical restraints are contractual relationships between buyers and sellers that fall between the polar extremes of spot markets and vertical integration.

Before looking specifically at a number of vertical restraints, we will briefly outline the economics of vertical relationships. Firms are involved in a vertical relationship if they operate at different, but complementary, levels in the supply chain, or as it is now frequently known, the ***value chain***. As the supply of goods or services proceeds through successive vertical stages of the supply chain, the complementary nature of the vertical linkages means that co-ordination between them takes on considerable importance. As a starting point for analysing the relationship between an upstream seller and a downstream buyer, we will for the sake of simplicity and clarity assume both are monopolies. In order to further simplify the analysis, we will assume that the product produced by the upstream firm is the key input to the downstream firm's production function and the downstream firm is the sole buyer of the upstream firm's output; that is, the buyer is a ***monopsonist***.

Figure 12.9 shows the inverse demand curve, D_q, facing the monopsonist. If we make the simplifying assumptions that there is a one-to-one relationship between the intermediate product, x, and the downstream firm's output, q, such that one unit of q requires one unit of x, i.e. $x = q$ and also that x is the downstream firm's only variable production cost then the price of x represents the buyers ***marginal costs*** of production. The monopsonist's ***marginal revenue*** curve, MR_q, is also the demand curve facing the upstream monopolist: see Appendix 12B for a more detailed analysis. Under these assumptions, the profit-maximizing output for the monopsonist would be q_0 the price of input, x, is equal to its marginal costs of production, i.e. MC_x. But the upstream monopoly supplier maximizes profits when the

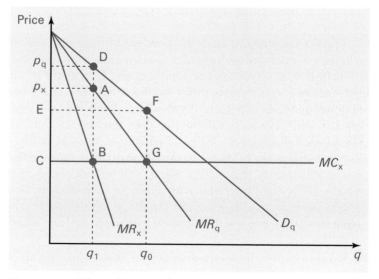

Figure 12.9: Bilateral monopoly

monopsonist's output is q_1: ignoring fixed costs, this level of output yields the upstream monopolist a rent equal to $p_x ABC$. At this level of output, the monopsonist is forced to pay p_x for x and it will then add its monopoly mark-up to this cost, resulting in the market price, p_q, for q; and again, ignoring fixed costs, the buyer earns a rent equal to $p_q DAp_x$. This situation is known as the double mark-up or **double marginalization** problem first identified by Spengler (1950). A number of researchers (see, for example, Shepard, 1993; Slade, 1998) discuss the effect of double marginalization on consumer prices and, as can be seen in Figure 12.9, from the customer's perspective it results in a loss of welfare.

Whether or not the outcome of the vertical exchange relationship between the two monopolists is a supply of q_1, depends on the relative bargaining power of the buyer and seller. Total profit is maximized with output q_0 and a market price equivalent to E. In principle, both firms have an incentive to increase output to this level providing they can agree on a basis for sharing the additional profits. The upstream monopolist would ideally like the downstream monopsonist to agree to all the economic rent ($CEFG$) accruing upstream. The downstream monopsonist might have an incentive to agree to such a contract if the alternative was to go out of business, but otherwise there is little incentive for the downstream buyer to put in the effort to ensure sales of q_0. This poses a problem for the upstream seller, who must incur the transaction costs associated with attempting to monitor the contract to ensure that the buyer is putting effort into achieving the sales target. Moreover, the presence of **bounded rationality** ensures that it would be impossible to draw up, let alone administer, a contract that would anticipate all possible contingencies. The essence of the problem is one we encountered when dealing with oligopoly; namely, the action of one party affects the profits of both. In this example, the problem takes the form of buyer moral hazard. One solution, if the upstream manufacture had the power to implement it, would be a **two-part tariff**, which is frequently also known as a **franchise fee**. We introduced this concept in Chapter 11 and will therefore only deal briefly with it here. The upstream monopolist would charge the downstream buyer a fixed fee and then sell the buyer all the intermediate product it wants at the marginal cost of producing it. This contract would encourage the downstream buyer to sell the maximum quantity, as this would reduce unit costs yielding an economic rent.

It is unlikely that a monopoly supplier facing a monopsonist buyer would have the power to impose a profit-maximizing two-part tariff and in such a situation the outcome of a vertical exchange relationship would reflect the willingness of the two parties to co-operate and their relative bargaining power. Both need each other and both have a vested interest in achieving the maximum economic rent. The issue is, therefore, how the increased rents from co-operation would be shared and this, as noted above, comes down to relative bargaining power. We can represent the situation as a game whereby the seller has to decide whether to exercise its monopoly power (i.e. sell at a high price) or sell at a low price in return for a share of the increased rent that the buyer would earn. A normal form game is set out in Figure 12.10, and we can illustrate the pay-offs to the players by referring back to Figure 12.9. If the buyer and seller agree to co-operate, the best strategy would be a variant of the two-part tariff. The seller would sell at marginal cost, $p_x = MC_x$. The buyer should set $MR_q = p_x$, generating the economic rent equivalent to the area, $CEFG$. This would then be shared between seller and buyer, respectively, on the basis of $\alpha\pi_q$ and $(1 - \alpha)\pi_q$, where $0 < \alpha < 1$, providing that $\pi_q \alpha > p_x ABC$.

If both firms adopt a non-cooperative stance, a profit-maximizing seller would restrict output; in terms of Figure 12.9, downstream output would be restricted to q_1. In this situation, we return to the double marginalization problem with the result that the consumer price is p_q and the seller and buyer earn the non-cooperative rents of $p_x ABC$ and $p_q DAp_x$, respectively. These two pay-offs sum to the monopoly rent π_m of $p_q DBC$, and the buyer's and seller's shares can be conveniently expressed as $\lambda \pi_m$ and $(1 - \lambda)\pi_m$, where $0 < \lambda < 1$ in Figure 12.10. What would be the outcome if one or both players refused to co-operate? Say the buyer adopts a co-operative stance and agrees to sell at marginal cost, i.e. $p_q = p_x$, believing that the seller will also honour a commitment to sell at marginal costs, i.e. MC_x. In this situation, the downstream buyer's demand curve is also the upstream supplier's demand curve and, hence, $MR_q = MR_x$. However, if the downstream buyer has only incomplete information on the upstream supplier's costs, and knowing this the upstream monopolist chooses to act opportunistically, i .e. cheats by setting $MC_x = MR_x$ so that $p_x > MC_x$, then the seller earns a rent, π_x, which in terms of Figure 12.9 is equal to $CEFG$, and the downstream buyer earns a zero economic rent. Alternatively, the seller might agree to co-operate for a fixed share of the downstream buyer's economic rent. Accordingly, the seller sets $p_x = MC_x$, but the buyer cheats by failing to put in the agreed selling effort. In this situation, the upstream supplier will find that total sales are lower than expected and consequently profit share could be less than the non-cooperative profit, e.g. $\pi_s < \lambda \pi_m$, whereas, by reducing selling costs, the downstream buyer could end up with a profit greater than the non-cooperative profit, e.g. $\pi_B > (1 - \lambda)\pi_m$. The various outcomes are set out in the normal form game shown in Figure 12.10.

In the absence of co-operation, this game has a **Nash equilibrium**; the seller charges a monopoly price and the buyer adds a profit-maximizing mark-up. However, if the game is repeated, then buyer and seller could agree to co-operate, because if either party cheats, the other will have the opportunity to punish the cheat in the next period. In order to attract the seller's co-operation the buyer must be prepared to hand over a profit share, such that $\alpha \pi_q > \lambda \pi_m$. Thus, for a repeated game, a stable outcome is likely to be a co-operative solution – whereby the seller will charge a low price, preferably equal to marginal production costs – and the economic rent will be shared, such that $\alpha \pi_q > \lambda \pi_m$. A co-operative solution may not involve the price of x being set at MC_x. The upstream firm may have motives other than greed for charging a price above marginal production costs. The upstream seller may believe that final consumers equate a high price for the intermediate product with high quality and in this situation it may charge a high price in order to protect a reputation for quality. For example, the manufacturer of an amplifier that will be combined downstream with a tuner and CD player is likely, in the minds of consumers, to have a decisive influence on the quality of the stereo system. Alternatively, the upstream seller may provide promotional support for the downstream product, thereby justifying an intermediate price in excess of marginal production costs.

In practice, the upstream seller, and possibly the downstream buyer, may not know the level or growth of market demand for the final product. Without knowledge of market demand it is not possible to set the franchise fee so as to maximize the seller's economic rent. Moreover, the seller will find it impossible to accurately compute the influence of the buyer's behaviour on the level of demand. In this situation of imperfect information, there is a need for both parties to share the risk of sales, and hence returns, falling below an expected

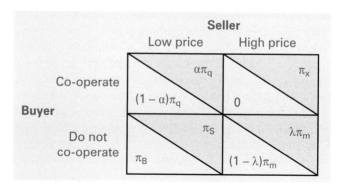

Figure 12.10: A game theoretic approach to vertical exchange

level. The franchise fee must be set so that neither the downstream buyer nor the upstream seller bear all the risk. Generally, we might expect the upstream seller and the downstream buyer to be asymmetrically informed, with the downstream buyer having better knowledge of market conditions. The seller, in drawing up a contract, must seek to elicit this private information. If there is more than one potential buyer, then the seller could, by offering potential buyers exclusive dealing, start with a high franchise fee and reduce it by small amounts in successive rounds of bargaining until one party accepts. If there is only one potential buyer, then the buyer's private information might be elicited by allowing the buyer to choose the volume of purchases, i.e. x. A buyer who is prepared to put in more effort is likely to choose a higher value for x. The greater the contracted volume of sales, the closer the seller's price can be to marginal production costs and the greater the franchise fee. Finally, we have assumed up till now that the seller faces the problem of buyer moral hazard. But the reverse could also be the case, with a seller, having agreed a contract with a buyer, then not applying sufficient effort to ensure that the intermediate product is of the quality contracted for. In this situation, it is the seller who must be incentivized and in this case it may be appropriate to set price above marginal cost and lower the franchise fee accordingly.

We have used the extreme of a vertical exchange relationship between two monopolies to demonstrate the issues raised. We can now extend the model to incorporate less extreme vertical relationships – e.g. the outcome if the upstream supplier is a monopolist, but the downstream market is competitive. Figure 12.11 redraws the earlier figure, but we now change the assumptions accordingly. In this situation, the aggregate demand curve for the downstream firm is, given our simplified assumption that $x = y$, also the demand curve for the intermediate product. As the downstream market is perfectly competitive, the price of the downstream product will be set equal to marginal cost, i.e. $p_q = p_x$, and as demonstrated above, on this basis the upstream supplier will fix output at q_0 and collect the monopoly rent by charging buyers p_x. This is a situation in which the upstream monopolist would do better to impose a two-part tariff, whereby buyers pay a fixed franchise fee plus a constant per-unit price for the intermediate product, where $p_x = MC_x$. An alternative polar example of a vertical exchange relationship has an upstream competitive sector selling to a downstream monopsonist. Again, we have implicitly covered this in the analysis of the buyer–seller game set out above. In essence, the price charged by upstream firms will be equal to their marginal costs, MC_x, and the downstream monopsonist sets its marginal revenue, $MR_q = MC_x = p_x$, yielding the profit-maximizing output, q_0. This determines the volume of x demanded and the market price of p_q.

We can further extend the model to deal with oligopolist sellers, oligopsonist buyers or monopolistic competition at one or both stages. It should be recalled that under a **Cournot–Nash**

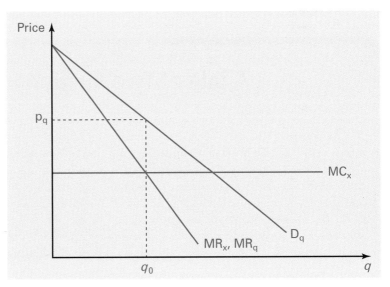

Figure 12.11: Polar extremes

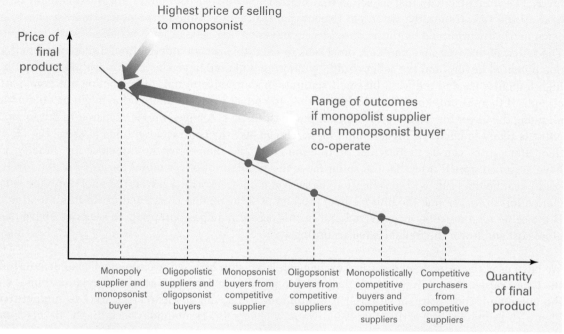

Figure 12.12: Pricing and vertical exchange relations

equilibrium, market output for an oligopoly is higher than for pure monopoly and hence the market price is lower and total economic rent smaller. As market structures move along a continuum towards perfect competition, the principles demonstrated above continue to hold, but equilibrium progressively involves a higher volume of sales and a lower price. Figure 12.12 summarizes the outcome of vertical exchange relationships under different market structures. In essence, as sellers and buyers move towards competitive structures there is an unambiguous increase in consumers' welfare as the price of the final product falls.

A Tale of Two Auction Houses

Christie's and Sotheby's are two names that are synonymous with the auction of fine and decorative artworks. These two London fine art auction houses consider themselves to be distinct from smaller auctioneers and dealers operating on a national or local scale, in part because they operate on an international scale and also because the auctioneering of high-value items calls for a particular expertise. Like all auctioneers, Christie's and Sotheby's compete to auction the property of fine art sellers largely by the level of vendor commission they charge; but other elements are also important, such as a guarantee of a minimum sale price, advances paid to sellers and insurance. A further parameter of competition is the payment of introductory commissions to third parties (a finder's fee) for bringing in new customers.

continued

Even though vendor commission is the main source of revenue, these two fine art auction houses sometimes reduce the charge to 0 per cent in order to obtain a high-profile sale. This is especially the case for high-value items where the auction house would in any event secure considerable income from the buyer's premium and many new customers from the widespread publicity. If competition for customers is intense, the same cannot be said for buyers. Indeed, there is no direct competition for buyers. Apart from attracting high-value items for sale and publicizing the details in a manner and medium that is likely to be noticed by wealthy, would-be purchasers, there is relatively little that the auction houses can do. The buyer's premium is a fixed amount on which no negotiation is possible.

At the start of the 1990s, the international art market was in recession and both Christie's and Sotheby's were not achieving the desired levels of revenue. Some time during 1993, the two companies entered into an agreement to end various incentives to sellers, to limit the payment of introductory commissions and to fix a scale of vendor commission that both auction houses would adhere to. The effect of the secret agreement was that Christie's and Sotheby's, nominally a duopoly, were to behave vis-à-vis vendors as though they were one auctioneer. Acting as a monopoly fine art auctioneer, Christie's and Sotheby's could force the sellers of high-value works of art to absorb much higher selling costs. Between 1995 and 2000, both Christie's and Sotheby's enjoyed a significant increase in revenues and profit. In October 1995, the *Rapaport Diamond*, a trade paper, reported that selling at auction had been, 'as close to a free ride as a businessman gets. As at the beginning of September 1995 the free ride came to a halt. Both Christie's and Sotheby's instituted new commission structures effective as of this season that pass some of the marketing costs onto sellers making the entire process more expensive from the trader's viewpoint and far more remunerative for the auctioneers.'

Vertical Restraints

A two-part tariff or a franchise fee is a form of vertical restraint. Any departure from spot market transactions, whereby sellers and buyers of intermediate products enter into contractual arrangements in order to reduce the transaction costs of exchange, are called vertical restraints. The analysis presented below is simplified by focusing on products for resale where upstream suppliers produce brands that are sold to retailers or dealers for sale to final consumers. Despite the simplification, it should be apparent that the general arguments set out below carry over to intermediate production in general. As noted in the introduction, traditionally competition authorities in both the EU and the US tended to view vertical restraints with suspicion. The traditional view of vertical restraints, particularly between a producer and retailer, saw them as an interference with the distribution mechanism for the benefit of suppliers. However, as we have demonstrated above, the outcome of a vertical restraint agreed between a seller and buyer can also be beneficial for consumers, for example by removing a double marginalization, and thereby lowering the price and increasing supply. More generally, the economics of many industries have changed, with increased demand for high-quality, reliable service in both foremarkets and aftermarkets, and both economists and competition authorities are now more cautious in their condemnation. Vertical restraints arise in many different circumstances and have a variety of effects on economic efficiency and competition. We will examine the anti-competitive effects of vertical restraints in the next section; here, we focus on the ways in which vertical restraints might benefit economic efficiency. Specifically, we examine how they might beneficially influence the quality of the services provided by retailers and the value received by consumers.

In a world of imperfect and asymmetric information, vertical restraints can play an important role in reducing transaction costs. For example, consider an upstream producer who puts effort into producing a high-quality intermediate product that takes the form of an infrequently purchased experience or credence good. In such a situation, the supplier's reputation is likely to determine how much of the value of the intermediate product will be captured and in a vertical exchange relationship this raises the issue of a **reputational externality**. A reputational externality exists where consumers' perceptions of quality and hence the upstream supplier's reputation are dependent on the behaviour of the downstream buyer, say a retailer. A retailer's actions, by influencing consumers' perceptions of quality, not only impact on current demand, but also on future demand in the form of repeat purchases. Reputational externalities are particularly prevalent in the case of a franchise where retailers present themselves under the upstream supplier's trade name. In this situation, the supplier will be concerned to protect a hard-won reputation but the transaction cost of minimizing reputational externalities – specifically, reducing the moral hazard involved in relying on the buyer to put appropriate time and effort into selling – could be prohibitive. At the very least it would involve monitoring costs, and in the extreme, vertical integration.

A sensible response to reputational externalities is for the upstream seller to enter into a contractual relationship with the downstream buyer that will provide the buyer with an incentive to protect the upstream firm's reputation. The services provided by a retailer will vary according to the nature of the product. An upstream producer who supplies a chain of franchised fast-food outlets will be concerned that the quality of the service in one outlet will be taken by imperfectly informed consumers as a guide to quality in the supplier's other franchised outlets. For more expensive, complex products such as stereo systems, the upstream supplier will expect the retailer to provide not only information, but also demonstration facilities and possibly after-sales service. If these services are provided in a manner that potential consumers find helpful and valuable they have the additional benefit of lowering search costs for consumers and thereby helping them make more informed choices, as well as protecting the reputation of the upstream supplier. However, the more resources that are absorbed by the services provided by retailers, the higher the selling costs, many of which may be **sunk costs**, e.g. learning about the supplier's product. In the absence of a vertical restraint that rewards a retailer for providing potential customers with accurate information and better service, and generally more effort put into selling, there is a real possibility that quality will decline and consumers forced to make less well-informed choices.

All vertical restraints involve some degree of vertical control within a principal–agent relationship. Under the assumption of perfect competition, transactions between independent firms at different stages in a supply chain would be conducted on an arm's-length basis: once a firm has sold an intermediate product it need take no further interest in its fate. Only when a seller has a degree of market power and a situation of imperfect and asymmetric information exists between seller and buyer, is there scope for a principal–agent relationship and an incentive to employ a vertical restraint. In this framework, vertical restraints should be viewed as a mechanism by which the principal – the seller – seeks to minimize any actions by the buyer designed to maximize their own profits, but which act against the seller. For example, retailers might be tempted to reduce the level of service and/or reduce its quality. Alternatively, a retailer may engage in competitive practices, e.g. cut-price promotions that lower consumers' perceptions of value and thereby impact adversely on the supplier's profits.

Formally, a vertical restraint involves the placing of a contractual limitation on downstream customers. They most often arise in retail settings, with the upstream supplier or manufacturer typically restricting or controlling, to some degree, the way in which the retailer sells the upstream supplier's products. Subject to competition law – of which more in the next section – this may involve placing limits on the selling price, the volume or range of products sold, the market they sell in or the level of service support. Vertical restraints take a variety of forms, but generally will be one of the following:

- *Resale price maintenance* – where the seller specifies a minimum (or maximum) price below (above) which the buyer (normally a retailer) may not sell the product.
- *Exclusive dealing* – where a downstream buyer is required to purchase the type of product only from the seller and not to stock rival brands.
- *Territorial restrictions* – in the extreme assigning to each downstream buyer exclusive rights within a geographical location.
- *Quantity forcing* – where buyers are required to purchase minimum quantities from the supplier.
- *Full-line forcing* – which constrains the buyer to carry the full line of the supplier's product.
- *Tying* – where the sale of a product is conditional on the buyer taking one or more complementary products.
- *Service provision* – whereby the buyer is contracted to supply a specified supporting service or promotion effort.

As shown by the restraints listed above, a vertical restraint may take the form of a price or non-price restraint. We will look first at resale price restraint, or as it is more generally known, resale price maintenance (*RPM*), which is the strongest form of vertical control (short of vertical integration). In most countries the treatment of vertical price restraints is much more harsh than non-price restraints. In the EU, resale price maintenance is *per se* illegal, this is despite the fact that from a strategic perspective, price and non-price restraints are often substitute methods of achieving the same objective. Despite the competition authorities' attitude, *RPM* can deliver improved efficiency. Our interest in *RPM* is to explore how, in principle, it could benefit both sellers and consumers in a world characterized by imperfect information and intra-brand competition at the retail level. *RPM* directly affects the price at which the buyer, normally a retailer, can resell the product. In principle, the restraint can set either a minimum or a maximum retail price, but in practice a minimum resale price is much more common. Under the European Community's competition laws, a manufacturer can no longer fix a retail price, but they can 'suggest' retail prices, so an analysis of resale price maintenance is still relevant where the 'suggested' price applies.

We have demonstrated above (see also Appendix 12B) that the elimination of double marginalization results in both a higher overall profit and lower retail prices. If the upstream supplier can set a maximum retail price, say $\bar{p}$, then by setting the supplier's $MC = \bar{p}$, the retailer is forced to act like a competitive firm in seeking to sell the maximum number of units. The downstream retailer should be prepared to accept such a restriction if the upstream supplier offers, in return, a share of the profits, i.e. the standard two-part tariff solution. Thus, in the presence of double marginalization, a *RPM* agreement acts to the benefit of both the supplier and consumers. But double marginalization cannot be the sole justification for *RPM*; indeed, generally the purpose of *RPM* is to raise rather than lower the consumer price.

One reason why an upstream supplier might wish to impose a minimum retail price is to counter a retailer who is in a position to engage in price discrimination. For example, suppose a retailer serves two markets – in one the retailer is a monopolist and the other is contestable – and the retailer faces the threat of an entrant who will set the retail price equal to marginal cost. Still retaining the simplifying assumptions used above, this would mean setting $p_q = p_x$. In the first market, the incumbent retailer will set $MR_q = p_x$ and earn an economic rent; in the second, the retailer will set $p_q = p_x$. Assuming the upstream supplier can only sign one contract determining the price of the intermediate product – the wholesale price – and a franchise fee, no single contract will allow the seller to maximize profits. To maximize profits the wholesale price should be set equal to marginal cost, i.e. $p_x = MC_x$, and the largest possible franchise fee charged. But it is not possible to charge a franchise fee in the competitive market. The only way for the upstream supplier to earn an economic rent is to sell at marginal cost but impose a *RPM* agreement on the retailer, fixing the minimum retail price above the marginal cost. This now creates scope for the upstream seller to extract some or all of the downstream rents by means of a franchise fee.

From the perspective of consumer welfare and the encouragement of quality, there is arguably a more important and certainly more justified reason for an upstream seller imposing a *RPM* agreement fixing a minimum retail price. Quality involves higher production costs and the upstream manufacturer's reputation – particularly where consumers are unable to observe the product's full quality prior to purchase – is vulnerable to the behaviour of the retailer. If we relax the assumption of a monopsonist retailer, an upstream seller has a vested interest in retailers not only stocking and selling its products, but also in taking care to protect and enhance their qualities by the addition of services and/or promotional support. We can demonstrate this with the aid of Figure 12.13. Once again, let us label sales of the downstream product as q and sales of the intermediate product as x – the retailer at the very least will have added some service to the intermediate product before sale. The (inverse) demand curve, D_q, is the market demand for q. The manufacturer sells to the retailers at the wholesale price, w, which includes a mark-up on its marginal costs, but only on the condition that the retailers do not sell the final product below the price, p_q. The seller agrees to hold the wholesale price constant and fixes the minimum retail price at p_q. This raising of the retail price will enable the retailer to earn an increased profit on every unit sold, but it is not obvious how the manufacturer directly benefits from the *RPM* agreement. Indeed, it would appear that the manufacturer is made worse off. As can be seen, the effect is to reduce total sales from q_0 to q_1, which begs the question as to the manufacturer's motive.

When retail outlets increase the quality of their service, indeed develop their own reputation for quality, it contributes not only to enhancing the value of the products they sell in the eyes of consumers, but also to enhancing the reputation of intermediate suppliers. As noted above, this can be of benefit to an upstream supplier where the quality has to be taken on trust, e.g. a credence good. The contribution to quality enhancement on the part of the retailer is not easily observed or measured, yet the interests of the seller of the intermediate

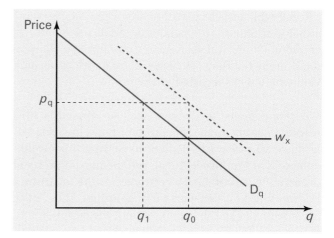

Figure 12.13: Resale price maintenance

product are undoubtedly better served if the retailer puts maximum effort into explaining the product's inherent qualities to potential consumers. By supporting high retail margins, *RPM* can increase the retailer's incentive to provide a high-quality service, which benefits consumers by providing them with more information so as to make an informed choice. Moreover, if the positive impact of the additional point-of-sale information more than offsets the detrimental impact of the higher retail price, *RPM* will be profitable for both the retailer and the manufacturer. The effect of greater effort on the part of retailers could be to increase demand, as indicated by the dotted line in Figure 12.13.

The foregoing provides an efficiency justification for vertical restraints as an upstream supplier's response to informational imperfections in the retail market. A prerequisite for this market failure argument is that demand for the manufacturer's product is dependent to a significant degree on services provided by the retailer. These services must be specific to the manufacturer's product, and there must be something about them that prevents the retailer from charging for them separately. The most common example of an integral service is presale effort in explaining and demonstrating a product's quality. This may involve additional investment by retailers in demonstration facilities and higher-quality staff. For example, a consumer electronics shop may employ experts who can assist customers in choosing a digital camera that best meets their requirements and to demonstrate its compatibility with computer software and peripherals. In some cases, the manufacturer may invest in providing retailers with demonstration facilities and training their staff. But both the retailer and the upstream manufacturer have to guard against opportunistic behaviour, i.e. ***free-riding***.

For the manufacturer there is a risk that both retailers and consumers will free-ride. A manufacturer who invests in improved facilities for a retailer or who engages in heavy advertising that attracts consumers to the retailer will need to charge the buyer a higher price to cover the cost. But the manufacturer runs the risk that retailers might behave opportunistically and encourage people who visit their outlet to purchase a competing brand that has a higher retail margin. If an upstream supplier attempts to counter such behaviour by offering discounts to selective retailers selling a wide range of competing brands, the retailer has an incentive to peddle news of the discount in the hope of eliciting matching price cuts from other suppliers. For the manufacturer, the transaction costs associated with attempting to monitor the performance of retailers are likely to be prohibitive. Alternatively, entering into a profit-share arrangement might prove effective in incentivizing retailers and hence reduce the risk that expenditure on retail facilities or advertising will not be recovered. But incentivizing retailers to apply effort on behalf of the manufacturer may not be sufficient if consumers can free-ride by visiting retailers who provide a high-quality pre-sale service and then purchase the product from a retailer whose prices are lower because no pre-sale service is provided. By engaging in *RPM* and imposing a minimum price on all retail buyers, the manufacturer could in principle prevent the adverse selection inherent in consumer free-riding, which could eventually result in no pre-sale services being offered.

Consumers will place differing values on the pre-sale services supported by vertical restraints. Some, perhaps most, consumers might prefer to have the product at a lower price without the services. Under *RPM*, these consumers suffer a welfare loss because they have to pay more for the special services (via a price increase for the final product) than they feel the services are worth. If there are large numbers of consumers who are unwilling to pay for pre-sale services, an upstream seller may find it impossible to make a suggested minimum price stick. On the assumption that consumers' expectations of quality are raised when they observe a product being sold in a store with a reputation for high-quality goods, upstream sellers could as an alternative strategy – and subject to competition laws – price discriminate. The upstream supplier could counter adverse selection by introducing a two-part tariff and reducing the tariff for retailers with a reputation for high-quality service. This would provide compensation for free-riding consumers with low search costs, while the upstream supplier enjoys a positive reputational externality.

If the justification for *RPM* is that consumer demand for the final product depends upon product information provided at the retail level, then, as we have seen, the manufacturer has a concern to prevent free-riding by retailers. If the provision of information and demonstration cannot be perfectly appropriated by the retailer supplying these services, i.e. there are spillovers that benefit rival retailers carrying the same product, then these services take on the nature of a ***public good***. This creates an horizontal externality on which rival retailers will free-ride. Resort to a *RPM* would prevent discount stores free-riding on information provided by other retailers by cutting the price to attract customers with low search costs. The idea that *RPM*, by preventing one retailer from undercutting another, enhances efficiency by protecting value-adding retailer services was first advanced by Telser (1960). It is, however, far from clear whether *RPM* can be advanced to justify all retailer services or just pre-sale services. Moreover, it would appear that for many goods and services, pre-sale information and demonstration facilities play a limited role. Post-sale services are frequently used to justify vertical restraints and are now an important feature for many markets, e.g. warranties, finance and servicing, but they do not at face value justify *RPM per se*, as such services can be charged for separately and are likely to be better supplied under conditions of competition.

RPM can also play a role in launching a new product for which demand is uncertain. If demand is weaker than expected, retailers operating under competition conditions will discount heavily to unload stock and in the process drive down the market price. Either fearing such an outcome or observing it, retailers may be reluctant to stock the new product and in this situation a *RPM* agreement that establishes a minimum price could overcome the risk inherent in a new product that takes time to establish itself. Another frequently argued justification for *RPM* concerns the number of retail outlets. If demand for a product depends not only on price and quality, but also on the number of outlets choosing to stock the product, then *RPM* enables small retailers (and indeed wholesalers) to counter the power of large multiples to under-price them. According to this viewpoint, *RPM* can actually increase the number of retail outlets offering consumers greater variety in pre-sales service and lower travelling costs. Until the demise of the Net Book Agreement on 1 October 1995, this argument justified *RPM* for UK booksellers. Another argument for *RPM* is the 'loss-leader' argument, where price cutting is likely to reduce the reputation of the product and by implication the manufacturer. Finally, in a world of imperfect information and positive search costs *RPM*, by providing uniform pricing, could reduce the hidden cost to consumers of searching for lower prices.

We noted above that price and non-price vertical restraints are, from a strategic perspective, frequently substitute methods of achieving the same objective. An alternative vertical restraint that solves the moral hazard problem of dealer opportunism is an exclusive dealership that binds a downstream buyer, e.g. a retailer, to a specific supplier. Typically under such contracts, a retailer must pay a penalty if it breaks such a contract and switches suppliers. Exclusive dealerships can also be justified as promoting product-specific information and/or investments. Manufacturers of consumer products often expend considerable resources promoting their products, but the ability to provide information on the benefits of a particular product will be lessened if retailers are in a position to offer customers an alternative, unadvertised and therefore cheaper product, that delivers the same or similar benefits. Advertising the benefits of a new product can be viewed as a specific investment and as such it is a sunk cost. More generally, as noted above, specific investments by either the manufacturer or retailer will lose most of their value outside the seller–buyer relationship and therefore an exclusive agreement can reduce the risks and encourage longer-term relationships with knock-on benefits for learning and developing specific capabilities.

Behind the protection of exclusive dealerships, upstream manufacturers could be more certain of selling to consumers attracted by their advertisements. They could also offer secret price cuts to dealers in order to allow them to engage in non-price competition (advertising, other sales efforts), thereby increasing sales for the upstream manufacturer's product. A further incentive for entering into exclusive contracts with a limited number of spatially differentiated retailers is that it constitutes a barrier to entry at the upstream manufacturing stage. If a sufficient number of retailers have exclusive contracts with a manufacturer, a new entrant at the upstream manufacturing stage is then faced with the problem of attracting customers who have signed exclusive dealing contracts with incumbents. The entrant must offer the retailer a cost saving great enough to make up for the penalty of breaking the contract, but as this reduces the entrant's expected profitability it makes it less likely that entry will occur. This kind of exclusive dealership contract therefore acts as a barrier to entry.

It may appear, at first sight, that there is great similarity in exclusive dealerships and exclusive territorial contracts. But there is a subtle difference. Exclusive dealerships are aimed at limiting inter-brand competition between manufacturers, whereas exclusive territorial contracts are aimed at restricting intra-brand competition between downstream retailers. We demonstrated above that competition between retailers provided a solution to the problem of double marginalization, but we also showed that intra-brand competition at the retail stage gave rise to opportunistic behaviour in the form of free-riding. When the upstream supplier is selling to a competitive or more likely a monopolistically competitive retailer sector, inter-brand competition is more likely than double marginalization to be the issue of concern. The closer competing retailers are located to each other, the more likely that information provided by one will become a public good for other retailers. Moreover, if one retailer lowers its price to attract customers its rivals will be forced to follow and this will impact adversely on the manufacturer.

Since the issues raised by inter-brand competition at the retail level arise from the presence of competing buyers, an obvious way for the seller to restore control is to credibly restrict itself to supplying only one buyer in each, distinct geographic market. By entering into a contract to supply only one buyer within a specified area, the manufacturer solves the problem of horizontal externalities. For example, Bang & Olufsen have chosen to sell their high-quality, distinctive home entertainment products mainly through a network of exclusive dealers located in exclusive territories. Owning a Bang & Olufsen franchise is not cheap, on average around €300,000, but for those selected, Bang & Olufsen provides a five-week intensive training programme and help with locating an exclusive territory.

Bang & Olufsen's exclusive dealerships and territorial agreements remedy the horizontal externality problem. By limiting the number of competitors – selling Bang & Olufsen's products – retailers reap the benefits of any price and service decisions. Hence exclusivity can serve to raise both the price and service level. High prices and an excellent service are the hallmarks of a Bang & Olufsen dealership. The result is higher profits for the manufacturer and dealer jointly. The higher the returns, the greater the ***opportunity cost*** for a dealer who allows the level of service to fall below that expected by the manufacturer and hence the termination of the agreement. The combination of exclusive selling and territorial restrictions results in the creation of a local monopoly for the dealer. This takes us back to the earlier analysis of double marginalization and scope to make use of a two-part tariff.

Quantity forcing, full-line forcing and tying are vertical restraints that have in common the intention of leveraging additional sales from a vertical exchange relationship. In the case of quantity forcing, the buyer is required to purchase a minimum quantity; in the case of full-line forcing, the buyer is required to stock all the upstream firm's product lines; and in the case of tying, the sale of an intermediate product is conditional on the buyer agreeing to buy another product exclusively from the same supplier. Tying might seem very similar to **bundling** discussed in Chapter 11, but there are two crucial differences. Firstly, the tie does not prescribe how much of the individual products must be bought and, secondly, tied products are typically **complementary goods**, whereas bundled goods are not. Tying also introduces the notion of applying vertical restraints to **aftermarkets**, whereby dealers or retailers are contracted to stock only spare parts and ancillary products that are manufactured by the producer. The central issue here is whether a firm that does not have monopoly power in the foremarket can effectively exercise it in the aftermarket. In a world of imperfect information and bounded rationality, it is unlikely that many customers will be able to adequately take into account the future costs of service when making a purchase, and, secondly, there is no credible way for a firm to commit itself into an unforeseeable future to low prices in aftermarkets.

An economic justification for a manufacturer making supply conditional on a quantity-forcing contract is to benefit from **economies of scale** and in the case of full-line forcing or tying to benefit from **economies of scope**. If the upstream supplier benefits from either economies of scale and/or economies of scope, then the result could be lower prices for the range of intermediate products. Another positive justification for full-line forcing and tying is that such practices maintain the quality of complementary inputs and thereby protect the reputation of the firm that is imposing the restraint. Parent firms of a franchise operation, for example, often argue that they must require franchisees to purchase supplies from them. A bad reputation based on the use of substandard inputs at one franchise will, it is argued, harm the whole operation long after the delinquent firm is gone. Although in principle the franchiser could specify acceptable inputs, allowing the franchisee to purchase from any supplier that meets the specifications, the transaction costs might be prohibitive. Tying will be the preferred method of quality control when it is less expensive for the parent firm than the transaction costs of monitoring and evaluating the quality of inputs purchased from other suppliers.

So far we have adopted a principal–agent approach to vertical restraints, whereby the upstream supplier (the principle) uses a position of market power to adjust the agent's behaviour (the retailer) so as to correct market inefficiencies. From this perspective, retailers are denied by assumption real market power and their role is confined to providing a sales service when selling the upstream supplier's products. In principle, there is no reason why powerful retailers should not instigate vertical restraints, though the existence of market power by upstream manufacturers raises a problem for retailer sponsorship of vertical restraints. It is precisely the manufacturers with the highest reputation and best-known brands that will be in the strongest position to resist any attempt to reverse the principal–agent model. However, multiples now possess considerable market power and studies suggest (see Sharp, 1985; Shaffer, 1991) that in the past, retailer-sponsored resale price maintenance has occurred in the pharmaceutical, cosmetics and alcohol industries. These are all industries that have active trade organizations.

In these cases, the retailers' motivation seemed to involve not only higher prices, but also protection from mass-marketing, discounting retail outlets and new entrants. In principle, the benefit of *RPM* to an oligopolist retail sector is that it can use an upstream supplier to impose and police minimum retail prices as a way of furthering collusive behaviour by the retailers. A suggested retail price eliminates, or at least reduces, the pressure on suppliers from retailers to provide a discount. Recall the game of **Prisoners' Dilemma** as applied to oligopolists. The key problem that besets oligopolists seeking to collude is adherence. If oligopolists are to exercise control over price, they must secure agreement on a common pattern of behaviour and once such agreement is obtained, the oligopolists must be able to enforce adherence, overcoming the incentive of each firm to defect, i.e. to reduce price and increase its own profits. A generally accepted pricing rule, e.g. a suggested retail price, can greatly facilitate tacit collusion and make successful collusion (tacit or overt) at the retail level easier. However, unless the upstream supplier is a monopolist, or oligopolist manufacturers act as a multi-plant monopolist, a suggested retail price could not be enforced as consumers would simply switch to a cheaper brand at a lower price.

RPM has also been justified for some products as providing the incentive for retailer investment in highly specific assets that better display or protect suppliers' specialist products. Pharmacists, for example, may need to invest in refrigerated storage space with elaborate temperature controls to maintain the quality of certain medications. If such equipment is of little use for retailing other products, its purchase amounts to a sunk cost. Whatever the incentive in the past, retailer-sponsored vertical restraints are now regarded as remote, not only because *RPM* is now outlawed, but also because of the growing number of rivals in retail markets, e.g. the supermarkets now sell medicines. As UK food manufacturers have discovered to their cost, as the number of channels to market increases, an oligopolistic retail sector has turned to open price wars and demanded lower prices from manufacturers.

The foregoing has tended to focus on intra-brand competition and has had little to say about the influence of vertical restraints on inter-brand competition. However, a number of economists have analysed the strategic rationale for vertical restraints under **imperfect competition** (see, for example, Bonanno and Vickers, 1988; Rey and Stiglitz, 1988). The idea that has attracted the interest of economists is that the competition that exists between rival manufacturers operating under imperfect competition is better viewed as competition between vertical supply chains. The strategic rationale is to soften the competition at the retailer end of the chain, so as to achieve higher final prices and higher profitability. One type of vertical restraint that can be used strategically is a two-part tariff. By choosing a higher wholesale price, a manufacturer will force the retailer to charge a higher price and this, in turn, will make rival retailers more willing to raise prices. Another vertical restraint that can relax inter-brand competition is exclusive territories. By removing intra-brand competition and giving retailers the power to act like local monopolies higher retail prices are likely to be set. By being visible and not easily renegotiated, exclusive territories aid tacit co-operation. Finally, it should be noted that the strategic use of vertical restraints delegates price decisions to the retailers. For this reason, *RPM* cannot be used in the strategic manner outlined above as the pricing decision is made by the upstream manufacturer.

A Chip Off the Old Block

When it comes to motor vehicles, the link between sales and service is an important aspect of the system by which vehicles are sold. Vehicle manufacturers are very dependent not only on the selling skills of their dealership networks, but also on the quality of the servicing and repairs undertaken by individual dealerships. A dealership will generally consist of three distinct services and sometimes a fourth if forecourt services (e.g. fuel, carwash) are offered. The three main services are: new car sales, used car sales and workshop facilities.

New car sales require investment in showroom facilities and signage and used car sales require the maintenance of a stock of used vehicles. The most heavily invested part of the business is the workshop and associated stock of parts. In terms of profit, gross margins on new car sales are very low and this aspect of the business is in effect run by the vehicle manufacturer via the mechanism of *ex post facto* bonus payments and the provision of incentives such as no-cost finance and free insurance. The gross margins on used cars are even lower, frequently negative, in part because there is considerable competition in this area. The most profitable element, indeed the financial heart of most dealerships, is the service–repair workshop. Building a reputation for high-quality servicing and repairs builds relationships with consumers and loyalty to the dealership.

The idea that motor vehicles are potentially dangerous if subject to inferior maintenance and repair is cited by the European Commission to justify its decision to allow vehicle manufacturers and dealerships to enter into vertical agreements to create selective and exclusive distribution systems, a so-called block exemption. In July 2002, after a long investigation, the Commission, with some significant adjustments, allowed the block exemption system to continue. One adjustment was the requirement that vehicle manufacturers must only use qualitative criteria for selecting authorized repairers and any repair shop that meets the criteria must be allowed to become an authorized repairer.

Within months, the Commission announced that it had reached agreement with Audi AG on an exclusive distribution network. In order to ensure the provision of repair and maintenance services that meet its quality criteria, Audi had established a network of authorized dealers who both sell cars and provide after-sales services. In addition, Audi had entered into vertical agreements with repairers in order to authorize repairs and after-sales service for Audi cars. Following the coming into force of the new block exemption, Audi confirmed to the Commission that it would extend to any repair shop that met its quality criteria the status of an authorized Audi repairer. By this requirement the Commission hoped to increase competition for the provision of after-sales repair and maintenance service. The hoped for outcome would be an increased number of repairers, including many small repair shops within the Audi authorized network. From Audi's perspective, the concern was to ensure that new additions to the authorized network would quickly build a reputation for high-quality servicing and repairs. By building such a relationship with customers not only do the repair shops build loyalty for their business, but also for Audi vehicles.

Vertical Restraints and Competition Policy

The economic effects of vertical restraints can be grouped into two broad categories: the effects on vertical co-ordination; and the effects on competition. As observed above, vertical restraints have traditionally been viewed with suspicion by competition authorities, in effect playing down the problems that might arise in supply and distribution and focusing primarily on the potential anti-competitive effects. The main worry for the competition authorities in both the EU and the US when it comes to vertical restraints is the possibility that their use will facilitate collusive behaviour by retailers and/or foreclose entry at some stage in the vertical supply chain. The concern is that vertical restraints raise barriers to entry and hence impact on a market's horizontal structure and/or reduce the effectiveness of competition to lower prices. For example, the imposition of a minimum price under *RPM*, by helping retailers to enforce a high price, prevents opportunities for lower prices to materialize. Similarly, an exclusive territory agreement removes intra-brand competition and makes it easier for inter-brand rivals to seek co-operative market outcomes.

Exclusive dealing contracts can also serve the purpose of raising rivals' costs and typically a firm's profits are an increasing function of rivals' costs. For example, if there are economies of scale and/or scope in distribution, a firm with a large market share will have a unit distribution cost advantage in supplying its larger network of exclusive dealers. By reducing unit distribution costs for a large firm, exclusive dealing contracts place smaller firms with smaller networks at a cost disadvantage. The situation is exacerbated if firms with large market shares, by demanding exclusive dealing arrangements, tie up dealers with locational advantages or who offer the greatest economies of scope. In this way, tying contracts can serve to raise potential rivals' costs. Typically, a new entrant could be expected to have a smaller market share and hence will suffer the higher distribution costs if confronted by exclusive dealing arrangements. But if incumbents have established tying contracts with retailers, potential rivals will have to enter more than one market simultaneously, i.e. the main product plus the tied products.

An example of the effects of exclusive dealing and tying contracts is provided by the EU ice cream market. In 1991, the Mars group lodged a complaint with the European Commission claiming that exclusive agreements linking retailers with two leading firms, Langnese-Iglo and Schöller, limited its penetration of the German ice cream market. Entry into the ice cream market involves persuading retailers who are not tied to an incumbent producer to install an additional ice cream cabinet and the new entrant has to incur the sunk costs of establishing a distribution system and building brand reputation. The Commission decided that the exclusive dealing and tying arrangements had infringed Article 81 and this was ultimately upheld by the European Court of Justice. But if a large international firm like Mars, already established in Germany with a range of products other than ice cream, finds itself facing barriers to entry, the difficulties for smaller firms would appear considerable.

Vertical contracts involving quantity forcing, full-line forcing and tying can also be anti-competitive. Firstly, they may serve strategically to deter or impede entry by raising entry costs. If potential entrants at the retail level must purchase a large volume, the costs and risk of entry are increased. If an upstream entrant must enter two (or more) markets in order to compete effectively, they must make a greater capital investment than would otherwise be necessary. This not only increases the new entrant's unit production costs – when allowance is made for fixed costs – but also by entering two markets simultaneously the risk that entry will be unsuccessful is increased.

Secondly, they may allow the upstream firm with market power to increase profit, by price discrimination (see, for example, Burstein, 1960). Subject to appropriate competition laws an upstream supplier engaged in quantity forcing could adjust the minimum quantities to favour certain outlets. In the case of full-line forcing or tying, an upstream profit-maximizing monopolist who also produces complementary products has an incentive to lower the price of its main product, say a computer, and price discriminate, i.e. increase the price of a tied complementary product where the price elasticity of demand is likely to be much lower. By lowering the price of the main product a greater volume will be sold and the tied product will be used more intensively in the process, paying the supplier a higher revenue for the bundled package. Full-line forcing allows a firm with market power over a range of complementary products to price discriminate across the full range for maximum profits.

The foregoing provides examples as to how vertical restraints might adversely influence an industry's structure; nevertheless, the impact of vertical restraints on the horizontal structure of an industry is ambiguous. In the case of *RPM*, by protecting retailer margins they may make it easier for a new firm to enter the market. Exclusive dealing and tying may also benefit the selling of new products by making it more attractive for an incumbent to market a new product and attract dealers willing to do missionary work. If a product is new, *all* consumers are marginal and benefit from pre-sale service. In such circumstances, vertical restraints may improve welfare. These arguments, however, do not justify permanent restraints. As consumers acquire information about the product, the net effect of restraints might become negative if the majority of consumers come to place less value on special services. Economists favour the price system as a method of resource allocation, partly because they believe the price system induces firms to seek efficient (least cost) means of production. The existence of vertical restraints can therefore only be justified from the perspective of social welfare when there is market failure, e.g. the information-transmitting properties of markets are frustrated by imperfect information and high transaction costs, which is efficiently countered by a vertical exchange contract (Mathewson and Winter, 1986).

When Levi Strauss famously was forced to abandon *RPM*, which it justified as preventing intra-brand competition between two types of outlets – department stores and discounters – retail prices fell, but Levi prospered. Once Levi abandoned *RPM*, chains of jeans stores were free to experiment with lower prices. They discovered that demand for jeans was very price elastic and that increased sales more than compensated for the lower price. If the jeans stores had been wrong, they would have been able to raise price. This kind of experimentation generates information about market demand. Resale price maintenance (and, to a lesser extent, other vertical restraints) prevents dealers from developing this kind of information.

In recent years, the competition policy of the EU concerning vertical restraints has undergone considerable development. In principle, vertical restraints will fall foul of Article 81(1) if they lead to a restriction of competition between member states, but Article 81(3) states that the prohibition may be declared inapplicable if the agreement contributes to improving the production or distribution of goods or to promoting technical or economic progress. In consequence, considerable demand for exemptions under Article 81(3) emerged and the Commission began issuing **block exemptions** where the pro-competition benefits were considered to outweigh their anti-competitive effects. By the end of the 1980s, the Commission's list of block exemptions was very large and contained exhaustive lists of the restrictive agreements that were exempted (white list) and restrictive agreements that were disqualified (black list).

In the mid-1990s, the Commission started an in-depth review of EU competition policy concerning vertical restraints. In its Green Paper on Vertical Restraints (1996), the Commission acknowledged that block exceptions suffered from a legalistic, inflexible approach and that in future a more economics-based approach was required. The in-depth review ended in 1999 and from it emerged a renewed framework for assessing vertical restraints and block exemptions. New block exemption provisions came into force for all vertical restraints with the exception of the motor vehicle sector, which was viewed as a special case. The reforms were taken a stage further as of 1 May 2004, whereby the system of clearance for individual agreements under Article 81(3) was abolished and in future providing agreements satisfy the conditions of Article 81(3) they are not prohibited.

The Commission's new economic approach to vertical restraints focuses on the assessed effects of an agreement on the efficient allocation of resources and consumer welfare. As we have seen, vertical restraints have a number of efficiency features and in some circumstances potential anti-competitive effects. A *per se* prohibition rule is therefore inappropriate and the Commission's new approach is recognition of this fact. Because the effect of a vertical restraint depends heavily on the particular circumstances, which may vary over time, it is not possible to recommend a *priori* that a given vertical restraint should be considered illegal, or legal, in all situations. Indeed, the Commission's new approach might be considered to be more of a **rule-of-reason** approach in which the negative effects on competition have to be balanced against the efficiency effects. Only a small number of vertical restraints, such as *RPM* involving a minimum price, are viewed as nearly always having anti-competition effects – so-called hardcore restrictions – and are therefore subject to a *per se* prohibition.

A rule of reason approach to vertical restraints implies that all vertical restraints should be examined by the competition authorities. This however, would be impossible and with the abolition of the system of clearances the onus has now been placed on parties to agreements to ensure they are within the law. However, there remains a *safe harbour* for firms. The block exemption regulations remain in force and providing agreements remain within their scope they are permissible, enforceable and immune from prosecution.

The Commission identifies four types of anti-competitive effects that may arise from vertical restraints: foreclosure by raising barriers to entry; a reduction in inter-brand competition facilitating both explicit and tacit collusion; the removal of intra-brand competition; and the creation of obstacles to integration within the single market. In the Commission's view, these effects can only emerge if the firms involved hold a degree of market power. Thus the Commission has set market share thresholds of 10 per cent for agreements between competitors and 15 per cent for agreements between firms that are not direct competitors. In effect, the Commission will not apply Article 81(1) to agreements amongst SMEs since they are rarely capable of affecting competition and trade within the EU. The favourable treatment accorded to SMEs finds its rationale in the *de minimis* rule. The idea that there is little point in wasting investigative resources on firms that can have little impact on competition and welfare is now reinforced by the **Lisbon strategy**. This strategy has elevated the contribution of SMEs in terms of job creation, innovation and economic development. In general, the Commission takes a favourable view of SMEs and sees vertical agreements involving SMEs as balancing the disadvantages of their smaller scale.

No sooner had the Commission put in place its new framework for the assessment of vertical restraints that allowed the motor vehicle sector to carry on as before than it announced a critical review of vertical restraints in the motor vehicle sector. The review showed that every car manufacturer in the EU employed a qualitative selection distribution system – whereby dealers are selected for exclusive dealing on the basis of specific criteria – involving exclusive territories, with the effect that innovation at the retail level was practically non-existent. This brought forth, in 2002, a new Regulation for the motor vehicle sector, the intention of which was to stimulate innovation in the motor vehicle retail and aftermarkets (Vezzoso, 2004). The result is that some of the vertical restraints previously allowed under the block exemption for the motor vehicle sector are no long exempt; in particular, in future dealers cannot be obliged to provide aftermarket services, e.g. repair facilities, and the manufacturers must choose between selective distribution and exclusive territories.

Central to the European Commission's new approach to vertical restraints is the importance of innovation at both the product and retail stages in the supply chain. The roots of this emphasis can be traced back to the work of Schumpeter (1934) and more recently the evolutionary approach to the firm exemplified by Nelson and Winter (1982). We have incorporated this approach within the **competency approach** to the firm discussed at some length in earlier chapters. This approach emphasizes the importance of knowledge accumulation and the development of specific capabilities to the achievement of efficiency in production, technical progress and growth. From this perspective, building co-operation and trust between firms in order to create and share knowledge is beneficial and more likely to be achieved within some form of vertical contractual arrangement (Håkansson, 1989). This thinking is exemplified by the European Commission's new block exemption for the motor vehicle industry, where the emphasis is firmly on innovation, though in the case of motor vehicles the judgement has been made that more rather than less competition at the dealer state would be beneficial.

In emphasizing the contribution of the competency approach to the firm to a new perspective on vertical restraints, we should not underestimate the contribution of the **governance approach**. By focusing on problems such as specific investments, bounded rationality and opportunism, the governance approach provides further insights into the efficiency arguments for vertical restraints. According to this approach, the reduction in transaction costs associated with vertical restraints compensates for the associated reduction in flexibility and freedom.

Concluding Thoughts

The underlying theme of this chapter has been the encouragement of higher-quality goods and services in a world characterized by imperfect and asymmetric information. Chamberlain's model of monopolistic competition sought to explain behaviour in markets characterized by heterogeneous products, but the combination of imperfect information, heterogeneous consumers and production costs that are positively related to quality, seriously compromised his model. In a world of product heterogeneity firms face downward-sloping demand curves, but we established that the existence of imperfect information and positive search costs could result in a price distribution that was unrelated to variations in quality.

We went on to demonstrate that when quality can only be assessed by experience or only rarely, as in the case of credence goods, reputation plays an important role in the delivery of quality. The problem with capturing the value inherent in higher-quality experience or credence goods given the asymmetry of information between seller and buyer has given rise to a number of extrinsic indicators of quality such as trademarks and external authorities. In this chapter, we focused on reputation. Rational firms should be prepared to invest in building a reputation because once established it provides a basis for the earning of an economic rent on an ongoing basis. Thus once established, reputation, by signalling quality, rewards firms for the extra effort involved in devising and delivering higher quality.

The supply of most products proceeds through successive stages of a vertical supply chain and for most firms customers are not final consumers, but complementary firms at the next stage in the chain. Consequently, most firms are the suppliers of intermediate products. The analysis of such vertical exchange relationships gives rise to two categories of issue: the advantages of vertical co-operation; and the potentially anti-competitive effects of such relationships. The former is concerned with the benefits which may result from solving problems that might otherwise arise between an upstream supplier and a downstream buyer and detract from aggregate profits, e.g. double marginalization. The latter category refers to the effects co-operative vertical relationships might have on horizontal market structure and the softening of inter-brand competition. When firms operating at complementary levels in the supply chain enter into vertical contractual relationships the agreement is known as a vertical restraint.

At first sight such restraints appear to only raise retail prices and reduce welfare, but in a world where information on quality is asymmetric and costly to obtain, they can actually contribute to both greater satisfaction on the part of consumers and enable intermediate producers to capture the value inherent in the quality they produce. Vertical restraints make sense in the context of imperfect information and transaction costs and are a means of restructuring incentives so that downstream buyers put effort into protecting the upstream supplier's reputation. Vertical restraints also raise concerns for the competition authorities as they can be employed strategically to restrict competition and lower consumers' welfare. By raising the costs of competing they can create a barrier to entry, resulting in foreclosure, collusion and reduced competition. If these actions translate into higher prices per unit of utility gained they will lower consumers' surplus.

Recognition by the competition authorities that vertical restraints can, depending on the circumstances, either enhance efficiency or result in anti-competitive behaviour has resulted in a move away from a *per se* prohibition to essentially a rule of reason approach for all but the most extreme practices, e.g. minimum *RPM*. Vertical restraints can be justified as a counter to market failure; namely, that a manufacturer who relies on a high level of pre-sale service is vulnerable to horizontal externalities such as free-riding. More generally, the economics of many industries have changed, with greater emphasis now on the demand for high-quality service in foremarkets and aftermarkets, e.g. computers. Recent reforms of EU legislation on vertical restraints have taken cognisance of these changes and placed the emphasis on the role of vertical contractual arrangements in encouraging greater efficiencies and innovation.

Key Learning Points

- Once we dispense with the neo-classical assumption of perfect information, we enter a world in which variations in prices may not reflect variations in quality.

- Imperfect information on the part of consumers means that individual firms face downward-sloping demand curves. As search costs are positive a firm lowering its price may capture more sales, but in the short run the volume will be restricted.

- The problems caused by imperfect information are compounded once product differentiation is allowed for. Consumers now have to search in two dimensions – price and quality – in order to meet their heterogeneous demands.

- Imperfect information is a plausible basis for individual firms facing downward-sloping demand curves, but the existence of product heterogeneity seriously compromises the assumption of identical production costs in Chamberlain's model of monopolistic competition.

- The existence of asymmetric information and positive search costs poses a major problem for producers of quality products in capturing the value produced; particularly, for infrequently purchased experience goods and credence goods.

- Producers of high-quality products have a vested interest in helping potential customers to detect quality. The detection of quality is not unambiguous and consumers use extrinsic indicators, one of which is reputation.

- Investment in the building of a reputation only makes sense in a world characterized by imperfect information. And reputation is a dynamic concept. By nurturing a reputation for quality, a firm builds an ongoing relationship with its customers and can expect to be trusted and rewarded over the longer term.

- Most firms do not sell to final consumers but to complementary firms within a vertical supply chain. As a seller of an intermediate product, a firm faces the additional problem that the value of what they produce can be lessened by the behaviour of downstream buyers.

- Upstream suppliers selling to buyers operating in imperfectly competitive markets face the problem of double marginalization. This results in a high price to consumers and consequently lower sales for the upstream producer.

- If both buyers and sellers in a vertical exchange relationship are operating under conditions of imperfect competition they can improve not only profitability, but also consumers' welfare by engaging in co-operative behaviour.

- A vertical restraint defines a contractual relationship between a buyer and seller at successive vertical levels that lies between the extremes of spot market exchange and vertical integration.

- Vertical restraints can be grouped into two general categories: those designed to improve vertical co-ordination; and those designed to restrict or soften competition.

- By placing contractual limitations on downstream buyers with the intention of controlling the price, the mix of products, or the geographic area for retailers, vertical restraints are a means of protecting upstream sellers from reputational externalities.

- Vertical restraints can be used to counter transaction costs by motivating a retailer to provide advice and support that will enhance the seller's reputation, and in so doing, to limit the scope for buyers and/or consumers to free-ride.

- Anti-competitive outcomes will result if vertical restraints are used strategically to raise rivals' costs and create a barrier to entry. This can lead to foreclosure, collusion and reduced competition.

- Vertical restraints have traditionally been viewed by competition authorities as being

continued

anti-competitive, but contemporary thinking recognizes that they can improve efficiency by better informing consumers and enabling firms to capture the value of quality.

- Recognition of the potential benefits of vertical restraints has resulted in the European Commission switching from a *per se* prohibition to essentially a *rule of reason* approach to vertical restraints.

- Most, but not all, types of vertical restraint are now subject to block exemptions in line with the contemporary view that the encouragement of efficiency and innovation offers a longer-term benefit than a determination to prevent any form of anti-competitive behaviour.

Exercises

12.1 In what way does imperfect information and positive search costs on the part of consumers add plausibility to Chamberlin's model of monopolistic competition?

12.2 In principle, a two-part tariff where the upstream producer sells at marginal cost, generates the largest joint profits. Why in practice might the vertical contract involve setting the upstream price above marginal costs.

12.3 Bang & Olufsen's strategy of giving dealerships exclusive territories and restricting them to exclusive dealings results in their products selling at much higher prices than competing brands. The benefits for Bang & Olufsen and the dealerships are clear. What are the claimed benefits for the customers?

12.4 What is the different between 'bundling' and 'tying'?

12.5 Vertical exchange relationships raise issues for intra-brand and inter-brand competition. Why might the competition authorities fear that a reduction in the former will also result in a reduction in the latter?

Problems

12.1 Ace Cars is a dealership with a local monopoly for the sale of Morgan cars. Ace pay Morgan w for each car it sells and charges each customer, p. The demand curve facing Ace is $Q = 30 - p$, where p is in €'000 and it costs €5,000 to make a Morgan:

(a) What is the profit-maximizing price and quantity for Ace Cars if Morgan sell with a 20 per cent mark-up?

(b) Calculate the demand curve facing Morgan and how many cars it would sell if customers were charged the profit-maximizing w price?

(c) What price p would Ace set if it was charged the profit-maximising w by Morgan?

12.2 Consider the situation where a retailer sells in two markets: one is a monopoly and the other is competitive. Demand in each market is given by $p = \alpha - \beta Q$. Manufacturing cost is c per unit and there are no additional retail costs:

(a) Derive the formulae for the retailer's profit-maximizing quantity, price and profit in the monopoly market.

(b) Derive the formulae for the retailer's profit-maximizing quantity and profit in the competitive market?

(c) Calculate the formula for the manufacturer's optimal wholesale price w and franchise fee.

References

Akerlof, G. (1970) 'The market for "lemons": quality uncertainty and the market mechanism', *Quarterly Journal of Economics*, vol. 84, no. 3, pp. 488–500.

Andersen, E. (1994) *The Evolution of Credence Goods: a Transaction Approach to Product Specification and Quality Control*, MAPP Working Paper, 21.

Bonanno, G. and Vickers, J. (1988) 'Vertical separation' *Journal of Industrial Economics*, vol. 36, pp. 257–265.

Burstein, M. (1960) 'The economies of tie in sales', *Review of Economics and Statistics*, vol. 42, pp. 68–73.

Chamberlin, E. (1933) *The Theory of Monopolistic Competition*, Harvard University Press, Cambridge, MA.

Darby, M. and Karni, E. (1973) 'Free competition and the optimal amount of fraud', *Journal of Law and Economics*, vol. 16, pp. 67–68.

European Commission (1996) *Green Paper on Vertical Restraints in Community Competition Policy*, Com (96) 721, Brussels.

Håkansson, H. (1989) *Corporate Technological Behaviour: Cooperation and Networks*, Routledge, London.

Mathewson, G. and Winter, R. (1986) 'The economics of vertical restraints in distribution' in *New Developments in the Analysis of Market Studies*, J. Stiglitz and G. Mathewson (eds), MIT Press, Cambridge MA

Nelson, P. (1970) 'Information and consumer behaviour', *Journal of Political Economy*, vol. 78, pp. 311–329.

Nelson, R. and Winter, S. (1982) *An Evolutionary Theory of Economic Change*, Harvard University Press, Cambridge MA.

Rey, P. and Stiglitz, J. (1988) 'Vertical restraints and producer competition', *European Economic Review*, vol. 32, pp. 561–568.

Schumpeter, J. (1934) *The Theory of Economic Development*, Harvard University Press, Cambridge, MA.

Shaffer, G. (1991) 'Slotting allowances and resale price maintenance: a comparison of facilitating practices', *Rand Journal of Economics*, vol. 22, pp. 120–135.

Shapiro, C. (1983) 'Premium for high quality products as returns for reputation', *Quarterly Journal of Economics*, vol. 98, pp. 659–679.

Sharp, B. (1985) 'Comments on Marvel: how fair is fair trade', *Contemporary Policy Issues*, vol. 11, no. 3, pp. 37–42.

Shepard, A. (1993) 'Contractual form, retail price and asset characteristics', *Rand Journal of Economics*, vol. 24, pp. 58–77.

Slade, M. (1998) 'Beer and the time: did divestiture of brewer-owned public houses lead to higher beer prices?' *Economic Journal*, vol. 108, pp. 1–38.

Spengler, J. (1950) 'Vertical integration and anti-trust policy', *Journal of Political Economy*, vol. 58, pp. 347–352.

Stiglitz, J. (1998) 'Imperfect information in the product market' in R. Schmalensee and R. Willing (eds) Handbook in *Industrial Organisation*, North Holland, Amsterdam.

Telser, L. (1960) 'Why should manufacturers want free trade?', *Journal of Law and Economics*, vol. 3, pp. 86–105.

Tirole, J. (1993) *The Theory of Industrial Organization*, MIT Press, Cambridge, MA.

Vezzoso, S. (2004) 'On the anti-trust remedies to promote retail innovation in the EU car sector', *European Competition Law Review*, vol. 4, pp. 170–181.

Zeithaml, V. (1981) 'How consumer evaluation processes differ between goods and services' in *The Marketing of Services*, J.Donnelly, and W. George (eds), America Marketing Association, Chicago.

APPENDIX 12A

Imagine a market with two groups of consumers: one group is well informed on available prices, i.e. they have zero search costs; the other comprises individuals who have only limited information, i.e. they have positive search costs. There are n equal-sized firms (e.g. retail outlets) supplying this market and all are assumed to have identical production costs. Of the N consumers in the market, aN, where $0 < a < 1$, are well informed and therefore $(1 - a)N$ are uninformed. Each consumer buys one unit per period providing the price is no higher than p_R, which is the common reservation price. Uninformed consumers are distributed equally amongst firms regardless of whether they are high- or low-price firms. Finally, of the n firms, λn, where $0 < \lambda < 1$, charge a high price, p_H, and $(1 - \lambda)n$ charge a low price p_L.

The high-price firms sell only to the uninformed, but only to that proportion of the uninformed who by chance have come to a high-price firm. By definition, the uninformed have high search costs and therefore they will not search for a firm offering a lower price. Thus, we can express the total quantity sold by high-price firms, Q_H, as:

$$Q_H = (1 - a)N\lambda \tag{12A.1}$$

whereas the total quantity sold by low-price firms will reflect not only their share of the uninformed, but also all of the well informed:

$$Q_L = aN + (1 - a)N(1 - \lambda) \tag{12A.2}$$

and so each high-price firm will sell:

$$q_{Hi} = \frac{(1 - a)N}{n} \tag{12A.3}$$

where $Q_H = \Sigma q_{Hi}$ and each low-price firm will sell:

$$q_{Li} = \frac{\alpha N + (1 - \alpha)N(1 - \lambda)}{n(1 - \lambda)} \qquad (12A.4)$$

where $Q_L = = \Sigma q_{Li}$. If all firms sell at the same low price, which implies that not only are they selling at the point where p = minimum average costs, but also that $\alpha = 1$ and $\lambda = 0$, Equation (12A.4) reduces to:

$$q_{Li} = \frac{N}{n} \qquad (12A.5)$$

The outcome for the distribution of market prices depends on the proportion of well-informed consumers. The smaller the proportion of well-informed consumers, the greater the scope for an individual firm to raise its price providing it does not raise its price above p_R. As shown in Figure 12A.1, if all individual firms sell at the same price, the equilibrium for each firm will be a price of p_L and $q_L = N/n$. If now a firm raises its price to p_H, then what matters is that the quantity sold is greater than q^* ie, $q_H > q^*$. At q^*, the price received is equal to the unit cost of production, i.e. $p_H = SRAC$, and a smaller volume of sales would result in a loss. As illustrated, there are sufficiently few well-informed consumers to allow the firm to produce an output in excess of q^* and hence we have a short-run equilibrium for a firm charging p_H, represented by point A, whereas low-price firms, charging a price of p_L, have an equilibrium at B.

As can be seen from Figure 12A.1, a firm charging a high price, p_H, earns an economic rent providing there are relatively few well-informed consumers. There cannot be an equilibrium for all firms at A because if one firm lowers its price below p_H it would capture all the well-informed consumers and hence the rise in its sales would increase its profits.

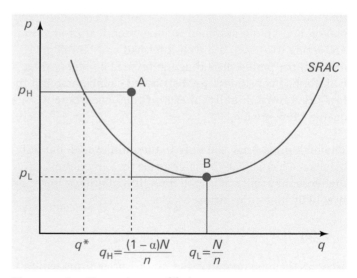

Figure 12A.1: Two-price equilibrium

We will examine the alternative outcomes for quantity and price of vertical exchange relationships between an upstream monopoly supplier of an intermediate good and a downstream buyer who is also a monopolist. Let us represent the volume of the intermediate product sold by the upstream firm as x, and the volume of the product produced by the downstream firm as q. We will further simplify matters by assuming a one-for-one relationship between a unit of x and a unit of q, i.e. $q = x$, and the downstream firm has no other variable production costs. The price the downstream firm receives for q is determined by the inverse demand curve:

$$p_q = \alpha - \beta q \qquad\qquad (12B.1)$$

Armed with this simple model we can attempt to answer some interesting questions, such as what price should the upstream monopolist charge and can the monopsonist influence the price charged for the intermediate product? The monopsonist's profit function, ignoring fixed capital and administration costs, is:

$$\pi_q = p_q q - p_x x \qquad\qquad (12B.2)$$

where p_x is the price of the input x. As $x = q$, the monopsonist's marginal cost is p_x. The downstream buyer's marginal revenue, MRq, is defined as the change in total revenue divided by the change in output, Δq, which yields:

$$MR_q = p_q + \frac{\Delta p}{\Delta q} q \qquad\qquad (12B.3)$$

Setting marginal revenue equal to marginal cost and recalling from the inverse demand curve that $-\beta = \Delta p_q / \Delta q$, we have:

$$p_q - \beta q = p_x \tag{12B.4}$$

and replacing p_q with $\alpha - \beta q$, we have:

$$\alpha - 2\beta q = p_x \tag{12B.5}$$

from which we can see that the monopsonist's profit-maximizing output is influenced by the price of the inputs, x; the higher the price of x, the lower the profit-maximizing value of q:

$$q = \frac{\alpha - p_x}{2\beta} \tag{12B.6}$$

Since the monopsonist demands one unit of x for each unit of q, Equation (12B.5) also determines the downstream firm's demand for x:

$$x = \frac{\alpha - p_x}{2\beta} \tag{12B.7}$$

Now consider the position of the upstream firm. It also wants to maximize profits. From Equation (12B.7) we have the demand curve facing the seller, which, by rearranging to the inverse demand curve, is revealed as the monopsonist's marginal revenue curve, i.e. Equation (12B.5):

$$p_x = \alpha - 2\beta x \tag{12B.8}$$

recalling that total revenue is $p_x x$, that $\Delta p_x < 0$ and $\Delta p_x / \Delta_x = 2\beta$, we can calculate the supplier's marginal revenue:

$$MR_x = p_x + \frac{\Delta p_x}{\Delta x} x = p_x - 2\beta x \tag{12B.9}$$

and replacing p_x with Equation (12B.8) and letting MC_x be the seller's (constant) marginal cost, we can set marginal revenue equal to marginal cost:

$$\alpha - 4\beta x = MC_x \tag{12B.10}$$

which gives us the profit-maximizing amount of x produced:

$$x = \frac{\alpha - MC_x}{4\beta} \tag{12B.11}$$

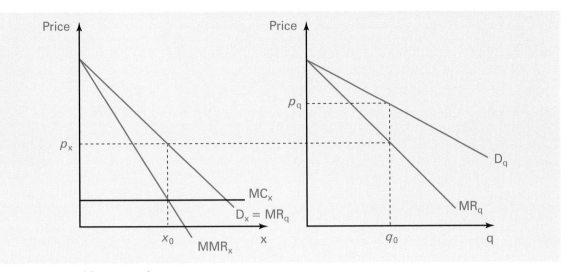

Figure 12B.1 Double marginalization

By comparing Equations (12B.11) and (12B.7), it is clear that the monopoly supplier wishes to supply a smaller quantity than the monopsonist buyer wishes to purchase. This outcome is illustrated in Figure 12B.1. The monopsonist faces the inverse demand curve (D_q), Equation (12B.1), and its associated marginal revenue curve is MR_q, Equation (12B.5). This in turn is the demand curve facing the upstream monopolist, D_x, Equation (12B.9) and the marginal revenue curve associated with the upstream firm's demand curve is shown as MMR_x. The seller sets output at x_0, where $MMR_x = MC_x$, which generates a price of p_x. The downstream buyer purchases x at a unit price of p_x and setting this marginal cost equal to MR_q sells output q_0, where $q_0 = x_0$ at a market price of p_q.

CHAPTER 13

PRODUCT DIFFERENTIATION AND ADVERTISING

Introduction

In the last two chapters we have modified the neo-classical tenets of markets characterized by **homogeneous products** and consumers with **perfect information**. In studying the strategic interactions of firms we have, however, largely retained the notion that the way in which firms compete is either by quantity or price. In practice, most industries are characterized by **product differentiation** and typically individual firms within the industry will produce a range of differentiated products. In such a world, in order to generate a profit, firms must do more than just produce, they must also market their products to their customers and consumers. Consumers, in turn, perceive the differences amongst products to be real and are therefore confronted with the need to choose between the many different products that might satisfy their needs. As we have seen, constrained by **incomplete** and **asymmetric information** as well as **bounded rationality**, consumers tend to choose from only a subset of the products that are offered for sale by any one industry. Although this may in part reflect heterogeneous tastes and consequently disinterest in many of the products offered for sale, it also reflects the cost, financial or otherwise, of seeking information on the full range of products.

Recognition of these realities raises the issue of marketing and its role in the strategic behaviour of firms. Marketing might conveniently be defined to include all aspects of selling a product once it has been produced, though modern marketing theories, e.g. **consumer relationship marketing** (CRM) view the process of marketing as being integral to the complete production process (Christopher *et al.*, 1991). For example, differences in a product's design, packaging, location and post-sales service are some of the characteristics that differentiate a product and all are considered to be legitimate aspects of marketing, but CRM would reach further back to influence other differentiating characteristics such as durability and features. It follows that marketing has the purpose of helping individual firms to adjust the nature of their products so as to capture the greatest possible value from the market. The aspect of marketing that is the subject of this chapter is advertising. Advertising has only a limited role in markets characterized by homogeneity, e.g. milk, but a key role in markets characterized by product differentiation. Advertising can be an aid to price competition, but more generally it is the principle form of non-price competition.

In order to make headway in appreciating the strategic implications of advertising we need to understand more clearly the relationship between advertising and the formation, development and alteration of consumers' preferences for differentiated products. That advertising and product differentiation are dominant features of modern business life is beyond dispute; yet the precise role played by advertising is less clear. We do not know exactly how advertising affects a consumer's choice of product variety and a decision to buy. Our goal in this chapter is to understand how advertising might influence consumers' choice and the implications for strategic interaction and consumer welfare. By definition, a differentiated product is not – in the eyes of a purchaser – a perfect substitute for a competing product. But if consumers are to find a product that is closely aligned with their preferences there must be a mechanism for disseminating relevant information. The fact that different consumers will prefer different product varieties reflects consumer heterogeneity and implied differences in consumer profiles and preferences. A major influence on a consumer's profile is income, but the behaviour of consumers in purchasing different product varieties cannot be accounted for by differences in income alone. Purchasing patterns will be influenced by whether a consumer is a parent, a teenage or a pensioner, but underpinning a consumer's profile is the individual's preferences emanating from culture, upbringing, experiences, tastes and values. In a world of **imperfect information**, firms can never be certain of the behaviour of consumers, but the greater the effort that has been made to align a product with individual consumers' preferences, the more likely it is to meet expectations of satisfaction and result in a purchase decision. Incomplete information implies positive search costs, which in turn suggests that in valuing competing products consumers are likely to be influenced by the level of trust they have in the credibility of the claims made by a seller.

In imperfectly competitive markets characterized by large numbers of sellers and differentiated products, i.e. **monopolistic competition**, advertising serves primarily as the means of disseminating information and thereby supports the operation and effectiveness of competitive forces. But in imperfectly competitive markets characterized by small numbers of sellers, i.e. **oligopoly**, advertising can take on the role of a strategic tool, with a purpose other than disseminating information such as creating a **barrier to entry** by increasing pre- and post-entry **sunk costs**. The effectiveness of advertising as a barrier to entry is a matter of some dispute; but beyond dispute is the very high levels of advertising expenditure typical of oligopolistic markets. Having read this chapter, you will:

- Understand how allowing for the preferences of heterogeneous consumers brings a new dimension to Chamberlin's model of monopolistic competition.
- Appreciate the need for advertising as a source of information and how it may be used and abused in a world characterized by boundedly rational people who suffer incomplete and asymmetric information.
- Be aware of the use of advertising as a strategic weapon when deployed to create a barrier to entry.

What follows is separated into five sections. In the first, we will look at ways of defining product differentiation and in particular at models that seek to explain two key issues left unresolved by the standard model of monopolistic competition. They are, what determines the sub-set of products that individual consumers choose from and why under free entry is the range of differentiated products produced much less than the number of possible products that could be produced? Product heterogeneity raises the issue of marketing and, in particular, the costs of selling and in the second section we introduce advertising expenditure as a major instrument of marketing. The section examines the concept of optimal advertising and the factors that should determine the level of advertising expenditure. In the third section, we turn to the economic rationale for advertising. The combination of differentiated products and positive search costs provides a justification for advertising as the means of informing consumers of the existence, nature and price of competing products. Advertising that provides objective information to potential customers enhances and makes more efficient market competitiveness and thereby raises social welfare. In the fourth section, we explore an alternative motive for advertising; namely, to change consumers' preferences. Many advertisements contain no useful information but seek instead to create an image. The section examines the purpose of such advertising and critically analyses the claim that such advertising is wasteful. In the last section we focus on the relationship between advertising and market structure. In the process we seek to ascertain the strength of the argument that advertising serves the function of a strategic barrier to entry.

Product Differentiation and Consumers' Preferences

Understanding the economics and strategy of product differentiation involves both a ***demand*** side and a ***supply side*** analysis of the issues. We know from casual empiricism that the bundles of goods and services purchased by individual consumers comprise a very wide range of differentiated products. A moment's thought confirms the truth of this observation. Consider the different ways that people with similar incomes furnish their homes, dress and entertain themselves. The variety of goods and services purchased by individual households reveals a spectrum of preferences amongst consumers which cannot be accounted for by variations in income, culture or family status alone. Given a spectrum of consumers' preferences, it is not surprising that in most industries firms produce a spectrum of products. Typically, the number of differentiated products produced by an industry will greatly exceed the number of firms, which implies that individual firms find it profitable to offer a range of differentiated products. Yet the range of products produced is limited; always much less than the number of possible products that might be produced to meet the full range of consumer preferences. This reflects the costs of developing and producing large numbers of product variations. While technology has enabled much greater product variety, ***economies of scale*** and ***set-up costs*** are still influential. This implies that attempting to satisfy the spectrum of consumers' preferences is constrained by the positive costs associated with an increasing range of differentiated products.

The foregoing raises some pertinent strategic questions; in particular; how many product variations should an industry produce, and what are the implications for market prices? There are no easy answers to these questions. We touched briefly on these issues when considering Chamberlin's (1933) model of monopolistic competition in the previous chapter. Chamberlin's model lies within the ***neoclassical paradigm*** and therefore assumes that consumers benefit from ***perfect information*** and ***hyper-rationality***, the effect of which is that their preference for differentiated products are defined over the set of all products. The model is based on a representative consumer who views product variations as equally good substitutes and firms compete equally for all consumers. A example that approximates to this model would be a city's restaurant market, in which the individual restaurants produce differentiated experiences but compete for the same customers who, in a given period, will buy from more than one restaurant. There have been a number of serious attempts to provide rigour to Chamberlin's model – the best known is by Dixit and Stiglitz (1977) – but the assumption that all individuals' preferences are defined over the set of all products is not in accord with the fact that most consumers purchase only a sub-set of available varieties of a product and consumers do not generally view all product varieties as good substitutes – e.g. listen to any discussion by students as to the merits of alternative beers.

A number of researchers have attempted to provide a more robust micro foundation for Chamberlin's model by allowing individual consumers to exhibit differences in preferences (see, for example, Perloff and Salop, 1985) and this is advanced to explain the observation that most individuals purchase different bundles of differentiated products. But, even with the assumption of consumer heterogeneity, Chamberlin's model still finds it impossible to escape the criticisms levelled at it. The model does not address the issue as to the optimal number of product variations in a monopolistically competitive market, nor the implication for costs. And without some criterion for limiting the substitutability between the products produced by the industry, the ***cross-price elasticity*** will be very high. This is in conflict with the negligible cross-price elasticities implied by the assumption of zero ***conjectural variations*** (a concept we introduced in Chapter 9), whereby each firm sets its price on the assumption that others will not respond.

A model of product differentiation therefore requires something that limits substitutability thereby allowing individual firms to face downward-sloping demand curves. One approach discussed in the previous chapter is incomplete information. With positive search costs, consumers will limit their choices to a sub-set of the available product varieties. But even the reality of incomplete information does not ensure a downward-sloping demand curve if within the sub-set there are very close substitutes so that a change in the price of a product would have significant effects for close substitutes. Unhappiness with the failure of the various restatements of Chamberlin's monopolistic competition model to resolve the boundaries of a product's ***strategic group*** has given rise to a very different approach. We start with the recognition that no two goods are ever perfect substitutes. Goods are almost always differentiated by some characteristic, e.g. quality, location or even time. This new approach does not seek to describe all the many characteristics that make up a product, rather it focuses on two broad characteristics by invoking the concept of a ***product space*** (Tirole, 1993). The product space assumes a diversity of consumer preference such that individual consumers are defined to have preferred *addresses* within the product space. Within the product space, consumer demand, *D*, can be represented by:

$$D = f(p, \theta) \tag{13.1}$$

where *p* is a product's price and θ is its address within the product space. We can illustrate this concept if we confine attention to a two-dimension space, as shown in Figure 13.1. The two axes show the characteristics or ***attributes*** associated with a set of differentiated products. The vertical axis reflects differences in attributes that determine quality such as durability, performance, features and service support. Moving up the axis reflects products embodying an increasing quantity of quality attributes. For example, if the product set shown was passenger cars, then a basic Renault 4CV would be near the bottom and a Mercedes S type nearer the top. Products differentiated in this way – by the quantity of resources that are used in their production – are known as ***vertically differentiated***. Moving along the horizontal axis reflects variety. For example, the Renault 4CV comes in a variety of

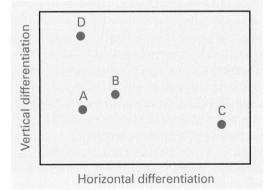

Figure 13.1: An illustrative product space

colours. Products that are differentiated in this way require the same quantity of resources for their manufacture, but are different in respect of their design or packaging. This type of differentiation is known as **horizontal differentiation**.

In Figure 13.1, individual products occupy an *address* in the product space; thus we can in principle describe a differentiated product sold by an individual firm by its individual address in the product space. This is a convenient simplification. We know in practice that the vast majority of firms occupy multiple addresses. In most industries, firms produce a range of differentiated products; indeed the typical pattern in consumer goods markets is for a large number of differentiated products to be produced by a smaller number of firms. Similarly, an individual consumer, with a given profile and set of preferences, will occupy a specific area within the product space according to taste and willingness to pay. What is of interest to firms is consumers' willingness to pay; hence, firms are implicitly only concerned with those areas in the product space where there is a high density of consumers, which implies a high probability of purchase and hence the capture of value. A key aspect of the product space approach is that it allows for the diversity of consumers' tastes – heterogeneous consumers – while allowing for some products to be closer substitutes than others. For example, in Figure 13.1 products A and B might be described as **near neighbour** products. Intuition suggests that the cross-price elasticity between near neighbour products such as *A* and *B* will be higher than, say, between *A* and *C*. Hence, if the price of *A* rises relative to both *B* and *C*, consumers of *A* are more likely to switch to *B* rather than both *B* and *C*.

In Figure 13.1, product *D* is vertically differentiated from product *A* and therefore its price will normally be higher than *A*'s reflecting the greater volume of resources used in producing its higher quality. Vertically differentiated products might be homogeneous in most respects but only differentiated by supporting service. For example, fresh milk delivered to individual houses is more expensive than fresh milk sold in a supermarket. In this example, the product is differentiated by the accompanying service; namely, delivery to a specific location. It does not follow, however, that consumers will purchase *D* in preference to *A*. An individual may appreciate the value of having fresh milk delivered every day, but given their preferences, income constraint and the higher price of delivered milk, may choose to purchase milk from a supermarket at a lower price. The concept of a product space is analogous to the concept of strategic groups discussed in Chapter 8; we can think of groups of near neighbour products forming strategic groups.

Horizontal differentiation we have observed reflects differences in the variety of products yielding similar levels of quality. A particular case of horizontal differentiation is **spatial differentiation**, which we analysed in Chapter 11 as a means of **price discrimination** for an homogeneous product. Our interest in spatial differentiation here is the insight it provides into the competitive behaviour of firms competing on the basis of differentiated products. Consider Figure 13.2, which is loosely based on Salop's (1979) circle model, and represents two vendors selling ice cream on a particular beach. Matters are simplified by the assumption that customers are uniformly located around the circle and further simplified by the restriction that each consumer buys only one ice cream and that the price charged by

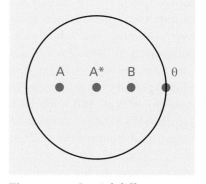

Figure 13.2: Spatial differentiation

each vendor is identical. Finally, let us assume that one vendor, *A*, sells only vanilla ice cream and the other, *B*, sells only chocolate ice cream. The utility an individual consumer located at θ gets from consuming their favourite ice cream can then be represented by:

$$U(p, \theta) = U(p) - c(\theta_B + \theta_A) \tag{13.2}$$

where *U* is the utility from consuming the preferred flavour of ice cream, say vanilla, from vendor *A*, at price *p* and *c*( ) is the cost to the individual in terms of utility of having to walk to the location of vendor *B* or *A*. Assuming our consumer wishes to maximize utility – and given that each vendor is charging the same price – whether or not vanilla or chocolate ice cream is purchased depends on the cost of the further walk to vendor *A*.

But the location of vendors *A* and *B* does not represent a stable equilibrium. This follows because neither vendor has an incentive to stay in their location. For example, if vendor *A* was to move to a new address represented by point *A**, then *A* would steal some of vendor *B*'s customers. However, vendor *B* can also reason this, so *B* will also attempt to move to the centre. This simple model provides a wider insight into differentiated products. It demonstrates the temptation for producers of differentiated products to focus them so that they appeal to the largest potential number of customers. That is, there is an incentive for rival firms to reduce the degree of differentiation between competing products, thereby increasing the degree of substitutability between products. This has the apparent advantage of making individual products attractive to a larger proportion of consumers in the product space, but it also has the effect of increasing the cross-price elasticity of demand. The outcome is to reduce the firm's market power and in failing to cater for consumers with more diverse tastes there is an increased likelihood of new entrants to meet the demands of consumers with atypical tastes.

Arguably the best-known model that attempts to reconcile heterogeneous consumers and near neighbour effects was put forward by Kelvin Lancaster (1966), who proposed a framework for analysing consumers' behaviour in differentiated markets. His framework starts from the premise that what consumers desire are not goods themselves but the attributes, i.e. the quality characteristics embodied in those goods. The location approach to the address-specificity of differentiated products implicitly assumes consumers purchase only one good, i.e. they do not get additional satisfaction from consuming a variety of differentiated products. In contrast, Lancaster's attribute approach, by focusing on the consumption of attributes rather than the product itself, allows in principle for the consumption of more than one differentiated product by individual consumers. If a bundle of attributes can best be achieved by consuming a mix of products, then this will be the preferred

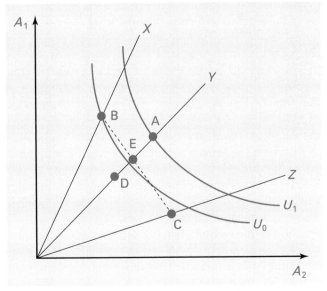

Figure 13.3: Product attributes and demand

consumption pattern. In keeping with mainstream theory of the rational consumer, Lancaster's approach is founded on the belief that consumers prefer more attributes to less, but that the ***marginal utility*** associated with an increasing consumption of a particular attribute increases at a diminishing rate. This leads to the framework set out in Figure 13.3, where the ***marginal rate of substitution*** is diminishing along an ***indifference curve*** in the attributes space.

Each ray, *OX*, *OY* and *OZ*, represents the proportion of the attributes, A_1 and A_2, supplied by the three competing differentiated products, *X*, *Y* and *Z*. The points *A*, *B* and *C* represent the amounts of these attributes that can be obtained for a given unit of expenditure, say €5. By superimposing an individual's preference map on the rays, it is clear that utility will be maximized at point *A*, so this individual will, for the expenditure of €5, purchase product *Y*. If now the price of good *Y* is raised, the consumer (for the expenditure of €5) will only be able to consume a smaller amount of product *Y*, represented by, say, point *D*. Given the preference map, our consumer will wish to switch to point *B* in this situation. The rise in the price of *Y* will therefore result in a sudden fall in the consumption of *Y* as consumers with similar preferences switch to product *X*. However, if the attributes are separable – that is, the desired combination of attributes can be obtained by purchasing bundles of both *X* and *Z* – then point *E*, which reflects combinations of products *X* and *Z* that give the attributes of product *Y*, is obtainable and is preferred to point *B*. In practice, the separability of attributes is more the exception than the rule. In the case of fresh fruit and vegetables, if the attributes sought are vitamins and nutrition, then a desired mix of these attributes can probably be obtained by purchasing a variety of fruit and/or vegetables. But more generally, it is not possible to consume attributes in the desired proportion by purchasing combinations of products, a criticism that Lancaster (1979) accepted. This brings us back to the importance of near neighbour effects rather than generalized competition between products in monopolistically competitive markets.

How can we relate Figure 13.3 to Chamberlin's model of monopolistic competition? As the price of *Y* rises, this is in principle equivalent to moving up the individual firm's ***ceteris paribus demand curve*** in Chamberlin's model. Adopting Lancaster's approach, the switch away from *Y* by consumers may initially be minimal – implying a very small cross-price elasticity of demand – but as the price gap widens there will come a point where larger numbers of consumers will switch away. The redirected expenditure is not, however, spread evenly over a large number of competing firms, but is concentrated to the benefit of a small number of near neighbour products. If the price increase is sufficiently large to invoke the substitution of near neighbour products, zero conjectural variations with respect to a price change is an unrealistic assumption. This explanation of behaviour suggests that if the price of *Y* rises sufficiently to cause demand to switch to near neighbours, the market segment supplied by product *Y* will shrink, and in the extreme could cease to be viable. In other words, raising the price would, at some point, shift the *ceteris paribus* demand curve to the left. The key feature of Lancaster's approach is that the seller of a differentiated product has limited autonomy in setting price, the extent being determined by near neighbour products. The implication for pricing strategy is that, in practice in differentiated markets, near neighbour effects are likely to be more important when setting prices than generalized competition between products implied by monopolistic competition. In terms of Chamberlin's model, if the effects of a price change are not spread across all other products in the market, then the *ceteris paribus* demand curve is not relevant to the analysis.

If, contrary to Chamberlin's assumption, firms expect near neighbours to react with a similar price change, i.e. its senior managers hold positive conjectural variations, the outcome is likely to be less price competition and hence higher equilibrium prices. We can demonstrate this with a

Bertrand–Nash analysis. Consider Figure 13.4, which shows on each axis the prices charged by the two firms in a differentiated duopoly: firms *A* and *B*. Starting at point *X*, this represents the price of firm *A*'s differentiated product in the absence of a rival. If firm *B* now enters the market and *à la* Chamberlain holds zero conjectural variations regarding firm *A*, it sets the price for its differentiated product at *Y*, which is read on the vertical axis. Point *Y* lies on firm *B*'s **reaction function**, R_B, which shows the price firm *B* would set having observed price *X* set by firm *A*. By similar reasoning, firm *A* observing firm *B*'s price *Y* and holding zero conjectural variations, now reduces its price to *Z*, which lies on firm *A*'s reaction function, R_A. This process of reaction will continue until, as indicated in Figure 13.4, a Bertrand–Nash equilibrium is reached at point *E*. If, however, firm *B* views firm *A* as a near neighbour and holds positive conjectural variations with respect to firm *A*, i.e. it expects a similar (even aggressive?) reaction from firm *A* if it reduces its price, it is likely to be more cautious in its response. It will not seek to significantly undercut firm *A* and this is represented by the reaction function, R'_B. By similar reasoning, if firm *A* holds positive conjectural variations it will have a more muted reaction function, represented by R'_A. On this analysis the outcome of near neighbour effects is a higher market price, as indicated by the non-cooperative equilibrium at point *E'*.

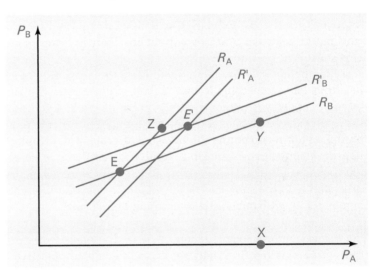

Figure 13.4 Positive conjectural variations

Figure 13.4 cannot be the end of the matter. If firms in this industry are earning **economic rents**, then this will attract new entrants or encourage incumbents to widen the range of products supplied. And, as previously discussed, entry into a differentiated product market raises additional complications. In markets with differentiated products, buyers can be expected to prefer the familiar products of established firms over the unfamiliar products of a new entrant. In terms of the foregoing analysis, the new product has to find an address within the product space and this implies that the new entrant's costs will depend on where it chooses to locate within the product space. If we write θ_i for the *i*th product's specific address within the product space, then total production costs (*TC*), including a normal return on capital, *r*, will be:

$$TC = c(q_i, \theta_i) + (r + \delta)K_\theta \tag{13.3}$$

where *q* is the volume produced, K_θ is the capital costs associated with θ_i, and δ, which takes a value $0 < \delta < 1$, is the depreciation rate. The term $c(q_i, \theta_i)$ is a positive function of higher quality, reflecting at the very least the greater effort in terms of care and control at the production stage that higher quality necessitates. Most importantly, a proportion of the capital costs associated with producing the *i*th product for a specific product space address, θ_i, is likely to be a sunk cost. Product development is a sunk cost and the physical capital required to meet the attributes associated with θ_i might be highly specific. In order to enter θ_i with the expectation of a profitable future, the new entrant must be able to attract sufficient customers from near neighbour products. In these circumstances, a new entrant's strategy is likely to involve choosing a mix of attributes that appeal to consumers whose specific needs lie between the addresses occupied by a group of near neighbour products. The intention must be to achieve a cash flow with a positive **net present value** after allowing for the likelihood that, in a world of imperfect information, it may take a number of time periods to establish a **reputation**.

It is reasonable to assume that the greater the horizontal space between the addresses of a group of near neighbour products, the greater the likelihood of attracting customers. If the number of heterogeneous consumers is increasing, there may be opportunities for new entrants, but in principle the more firms that enter the market (or increase their product range), the more crowded becomes the product space, thereby reducing the likelihood of post-entry economic rent. Moreover, the incumbent firms most threatened by a new entrant are likely to lower prices in response. This follows because it is reasonable to presume that the incumbent firms have incurred sunk costs in establishing address-specific differentiated products, opening up the possibility of earning a **quasi-rent**. Sunk costs imply that firms have something to lose if their expectations of post-entry profits prove optimistic. If the only form of entry is to increase the number of product addresses, then in the presence of sunk costs there will exist barriers to entry. As the number of firms in a market increases potential entrants run the risk of not recuperating the investment costs of developing a new product and, for incumbents, their development costs are sunk, implying that fierce price competition is more likely than relocation to a new address. Hence, the need to produce for a specific product space address and the risks associated with the sunk cost of developing a specific differentiated product create barriers to entry, thereby limiting Chamberlin's assumption of free entry.

The discussion on barriers to entry essentially focused on horizontal differentiation, but a new entrant, or an existing firm, may seek to achieve a competitive advantage by improving quality, i.e. vertical differentiation. As observed by Sutton (1986), if a firm improves the quality of its product, it gains not only a vertical differential advantage by virtue of an improved price–quality combination, but also a horizontal advantage as some consumers may switch from near neighbour horizontally differentiated products. Entry via vertical differentiation offers a greater likelihood of success providing the costs of delivering the higher quality are such that a rent can reasonably be expected. This follows because high-quality production tends to drive out lower-quality products, whereas entry at the same quality relies heavily on increasing numbers of consumers to outweigh the price depression effects of increasing numbers of firms competing in a horizontally differentiated space. Just where a firm positions its product, or products, within the produce space is therefore of key strategic importance. If the firm's resources have the capability to deliver a higher-quality product, it still faces the issue of persuading consumers to search for, experience or place their trust in the producer's quality claims for the new product. This raises the issue of marketing, and specifically, advertising; but before turning to these issues there is for some consumers an intriguing aspect of their preferences that attracts them to the address of an extremely vertically differentiated product within the product space.

By definition, the more vertically differentiated a product, the greater the cost of the resources absorbed in its production and therefore the more expensive the product to buy. A **Veblen good** is an expensive vertically differentiated product, the demand for which is not based solely on its attributes, but in part on the notion that the utility associated with the act of consumption is enhanced by the consumer's belief that in the eyes of others, consumption confers considerable affluence and it is this by-product of consumption that is highly valued by the consumer. It was Thorstein Veblen

(1934) who gave rise to the phrase ***conspicuous consumption***, reflecting extreme vertical differentiation and the idea that ostentatious expenditure by the rich was a way of flaunting their wealth: 'the only practical means of impressing one's pecuniary ability … in an unremitting demonstration of ability to pay' (p. 87). The notion of a Veblen good is that the more people that can afford to consume a particular good or service, the less attractive it is to those who value the product for flaunting their affluence. One of the theoretical outcomes of Veblen goods is set out in Figure 13.5(a). Over at least part of its price range, the Veblen effect will result in an upward-sloping demand curve; that is, the effect of an increase in supply – from S_0 to S_1 – lowers the price, thereby encouraging 'Veblen consumers' to purchase less. A Veblen good is an extreme form of snob effect; less extreme 'snob effects' may result in a downward-sloping but highly inelastic demand curve.

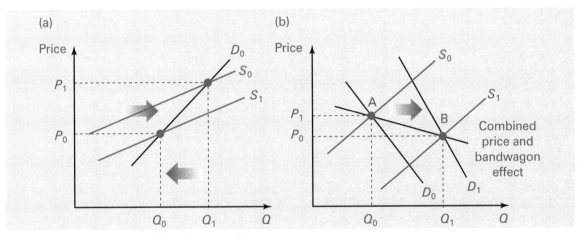

Figure 13.5: Veblen good and bandwagon effects

Snob goods and Veblen goods represent products whose demand depends on the behaviour of other people. That is, their consumption is influenced by a ***network externality***. In the case of a snob or Veblen good, the externality is negative. A negative network externality exists if the utility gained by an individual consumer declines in response to an overall growth of consumption of the product. In terms of the product space, a combination of growing affluence on the part of consumers and increased competition would force suppliers of Veblen goods to seek ever-higher levels of vertical differentiation. More generally, firms seek to secure an address within the product space with a positive network externality. The extreme example of a positive externality is a ***bandwagon effect***. The frequently observed phenomenon in the run-up to Christmas of a child's toy – e.g. the latest Playstation – that is in great demand is an example of bandwagon effect. Building a bandwagon effect is a key objective of many marketing campaigns, for example the manufacturers of fashion clothing, and the effect is illustrated in Figure 13.5(b). Starting at point *A*, when a new fashion product is launched, only a relatively small number of people will have purchased the new item of fashion clothing. However, should potential consumers now come to believe that in order to 'be in fashion' they must be seen in the new clothing, demand will increase dramatically, represented by the move from D_0 to D_1. As illustrated, the supply has increased to keep pace with demand, allowing a small reduction in price at point *B*. It would, however, be conceivable that if demand outstrips the growth of supply, the price would rise and the curve representing the combined price and bandwagon effect would be upward sloping.

Conspicuous Consumption

When it comes to wine, France believes that its cuvées of vintage wines remain the best in the world. For many wine experts, wines from the Panillac region of France embody the quintessential characteristics of a fine Bordeaux wine. Indeed, three of the top Premier Cru Classé, Lafite, Mouton-Rothschild and Latour are from Panillac.

These wines are amongst the most expensive in the world. Outstanding vintages from what are regarded by many as the best vineyards in the world can sell for many thousands of euro per bottle. Red wines, because of their greater shelf life, tend to be the most expensive. Such wines are normally at their best a decade or more after being bottled. Part of the expense associated with rare, vintage wines comes from the risk that after ten years the quality will not have stood the test of time, or even worse, the wine may have turned to vinegar. Purchasers of such wines, be they wealthy individuals or expensive restaurants, must be prepared to discard a vintage wine if upon opening the bottle the wine has not matured as expected. A restaurant can cover this risk by charging a high price for a vintage wine, but an individual purchaser of vintage wines is demonstrating sufficient wealth to absorb the risk.

There is in fact a great deal of snobbery attached to wine, particularly the super premium wines and there is no better way to demonstrate affluence and success than to grandly order a bottle, or two, of Chateau Mouton-Rothschild 1986 in a crowded restaurant. The bill will run into thousands of euro, but there is a fair chance – at least in the mind of the host – that dinner guests and near neighbours will believe they are in the presence of a very wealthy individual and possibly even a wine expert.

Optimal Advertising

We defined marketing, in the introduction, as including all aspects of selling a differentiated product, including not only its price but also its design, packaging, location, durability, features and post-sales service. Indeed, this broader view of marketing would encompass product innovation and new product development. We deal with the economic aspects of product innovation and development in the next chapter; here, we focus on the traditional role of marketing which, through a number of dimensions, has the purpose of favourably differentiating an existing product in the minds of consumers. Distinctive packaging, selective sales outlets and superior after-sales service are all elements of the ***marketing mix***. Another element is pricing, including tactics such as coupons, buy-one-get-one-free and free samples, which are all forms of price discrimination that we analysed in Chapter 11. The element in the marketing mix that is of interest here is advertising. We can define advertising as the non-personal presentation of a product to existing or potential consumers. Advertising has many purposes, but for commercial firms it is essentially an instrument for promoting and positioning their product offerings within the product space. Advertising may be conveyed via a variety of media – TV, billboards, newspapers – and in a modern economy it is a ubiquitous presence. The emergence of large-scale advertising and its association with mass consumerism over the latter half of the twentieth century certainly suggests that many firms view it as a necessary activity. And a consistent finding in consumer product markets is that there is a positive correlation between advertising and profitability. The pioneering work in this regard is that of Comanor and Wilson (1967). Their basic finding that profits are associated with a higher advertising-to-sales ratio has been replicated many times (see, for example, Schmalensee, 1989). We may not know precisely how advertising affects consumers' decisions as to what **brand** to buy, but we do know that if consumers are to approach efficiently exercising their choice they must be aware of the attributes and prices of all near neighbour products if not the complete set of competing products.

The economic function of advertising has long been an issue of interest to economists. In the neo-classical world of perfect competition, advertising, indeed marketing *per se*, has no purpose. However, once the reality of product differentiation, bounded rationality and asymmetric information is acknowledged, advertising can serve a vital role. Even in markets characterized by homogeneous products, the existence of incomplete information creates a role for advertising, albeit limited to generic advertising, e.g. informing consumers about the natural properties of milk. In the 1950s, economists tended to view advertising as a socially wasteful way for firms to compete (see, for example, Kaldor 1950). This early view focused on advertising's potential to create anti-competitive outcomes, whereby the building of brand loyalty resulted in a softening of both intra- and inter-brand price competition, as well as the deterrence of new brands. In short, economists focused on the potential inherent in advertising to confer monopoly power and thereby to weaken price as a vehicle for bringing about efficient allocations of resources. The idea that advertising fosters monopoly powers was soon to be challenged by Telser (1964), and in the ensuing years economists have come to realize that the effects of advertising are more subtle and complex. For example, causation may be reversed, with market power driving advertising rather than advertising causing market power. It may be that advertising reflects vigorous inter-brand competition, particularly in consumer markets. What is beyond dispute is the fact that advertising is a widely used instrument for firms operating in markets where a large number of functionally similar but differentiated products are offered for sale. It is these markets that we are primarily concerned with in this chapter.

Advertising may appear to be a ubiquitous presence, but in **advertising intensity** – the ratio of advertising expenditure to sales – there are substantial variations between product groups. In industrialized countries, measured advertising expenditure generally accounts for between 1 and 2 per cent of GDP, but at the industry or product group level it can be much higher. For example, in the UK, over-the-counter medicines frequently display advertising intensities of 20 per cent or more. At the other extreme, advertising intensities for cars, beer and wine are typically 2, 1 and 0.5 per cent, respectively. It should also be noted that much promotional activity is not measured, e.g. coupons, so advertising intensity is not a complete measure of either promotional effort or expenditure. There are a number of explanations for the observed variations in advertising intensity between industries and product groups. One significant influence is whether the products are being sold to industrial or consumer markets. Industrial markets consist of both **intermediate products** and finished products, e.g. machines. In the case of intermediate products, the volumes involved are generally large and the transactions made by sophisticated buyers. Given the volumes involved and/or the sophisticated nature of industrial goods, buyers will not be concerned only to identify a lower-priced source, as expected scale economies have to be balanced against the loss of profits arising from an error of judgement. Intermediate products and almost certainly finished industrial products are likely to possess complex bundles of attributes and, consequently, buyers require more information than can be communicated effectively via an advertisement. Industrial advertising may be efficient where product characteristics change rapidly. In such markets, there will be a need to advertise regularly to help ensure potential customers are aware of product developments, e.g. computer software.

In the case of consumer products another significant influence on advertising intensity is whether the product in question is durable or non-durable. Durable goods such as refrigerators and washing machines generally have lower levels of advertising intensity than non-durable consumer goods such as beer and confectionary. Durable goods tend to be expensive in terms of consumers' incomes and consequently the loss of utility from an unsuitable purchase is likely to be significant. Rational consumers will therefore be more willing to incur the costs of searching out information on the competing merits of the alternatives on offer. Moreover, when it comes to purchasing an expensive item such as a car, a DVD system or a Caribbean holiday, people are more likely to consult specialist magazines or seek the advice of experts in order to obtain accurate information. In contrast, relatively cheap, non-durable products do not justify a great deal of search effort by people with positive search costs. The opportunity cost of a mistake is likely to be small and most will be available in local convenience outlets. For such products consumers must be constantly reminded of their existence and hence the intensity of advertising will be relatively high. Other influences on the intensity of advertising are customer turnover and geography. Where there is a rapid turnover of customers (as in the baby food market), relatively high levels of advertising will be necessary to inform new consumers. If a market is large and geographically scattered, a mass communication form of advertising such as television is required, and this will tend to increase the measured intensity of advertising.

Despite the widespread use and apparent benefits for firms of advertising, consumers are generally disparaging. A frequent complaint about commercial television is the frequency of advertising and a fear increasingly voiced by firms is that technology such as Sky+, which enables viewers to fast-forward advertisements, is reducing the effectiveness of advertising and confirming the parochial attitude of consumers towards the medium. If, as appears to be the case, most people given the option avoid watching or listening to advertisements, and skip the majority of advertisements in newspapers and magazines, this implies that from the viewpoint of consumers there is an excess of advertising. This is not altogether surprising because consumers do not directly pay for it and from their perspective the marginal cost is zero. But what of firms? From their perspective, how much advertising is optimal?

Advertising differs in one important respect from most resources purchased or created by firms; *ceteris paribus*, resources devoted to advertising expenditure have the purpose of maintaining or increasing demand for a firm's output. Other resources absorbed by firms may also have the effect of increasing demand, e.g. high-quality materials, but their effect on demand is generally indirect via higher quality or lower costs. Advertising is a costly activity and rational managers will engage in advertising only to the extent that it is profitable to do so. A firm that faces a downward-sloping demand curve may be able to influence demand – that is, the position of the demand curve in the price–quantity space – by advertising. For most firms, achieving a higher volume of sales by advertising is preferable to selling more by lowering price. This choice is illustrated in Figure 13.6. Assuming for simplicity that the firm is a monopolist who faces market demand of D_0 and who is maximizing profits by selling output, Q_0, at price, p_0. Lowering the price from p_0 to p_1 will reduce profits, even though sales increase from Q_0 to Q_1. If, however, the firm spends a fixed sum each period on advertising, A, this has the effect of increasing long-run average costs, from $LRAC$ to $LRAC + A$, and also increasing demand represented by the shift in the demand curve from D_0 to D_1. The outcome can be either a rise in sales, or a rise in price or, both. In Figure 13.6, the outcome is shown as a rise in sales to Q_2, which implies that the increase in sales revenue exceeds the advertising costs. As illustrated, advertising has done more than increase demand, it has also reduced the **price elasticity of demand**. We will return to the issue of price elasticity later; but first we will explore how much a profit-maximizing firm should spend on advertising.

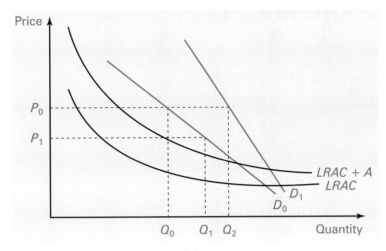

Figure 13.6: Price cuts or advertising?

As shown in Figure 13.6, if price remains unchanged at p_0 and there is a rise in demand, the results will be an increase in **gross revenue**. Efficient firms will want to balance any increase in **net revenue** – the rise in gross revenue less any rise in variable production costs – against the costs incurred by advertising. It is therefore natural to ask whether there is some rule linking advertising expenditure to profits. The answer was provided by Dorfman and Steiner (1954), and it has become known as the **Dorfman–Steiner condition** for optimal advertising intensity. We can demonstrate the Dorfman–Steiner condition, as presented by Schmalensee (1972), with the aid of two simplifying assumptions: a profit-maximizing **monopolist**; and advertising expenditure consisting only of a fixed sum per period on a national television campaign, which ensures that sales are not influenced by where a unit of advertising expenditure is spent. We can then express the **demand function** as the outcome of the relative price and the level of advertising, such that:

$$Q = f(p, A) \tag{13.4}$$

where A is advertising expenditure per period. The profit function is then:

$$\pi = pQ - c(Q) - (r + \delta)K - A \tag{13.5}$$

where r is the firm's cost of capital, δ is the depreciation rate and $0 < r, \delta < 1$. To further simplify matters, without any loss of generality, we will assume that variable costs $c(Q)$ per unit of output are constant, represented by c. We know that for a profit-maximizing firm $MR = MC$, and for a small increase in advertising expenditure, (ΔA), the profit-maximizing condition becomes:

$$p\Delta Q = c\Delta Q + \Delta A \tag{13.6}$$

where $(p\Delta Q)$ is the marginal revenue, c is the marginal cost of producing ΔQ and ΔA is the marginal change in advertising expenditure. Dividing through by ΔQ, taking c over to the left-hand side and multiplying and dividing the right-hand side by A/Q, Equation (13.6) becomes:

$$p - c = \frac{A}{Q} \cdot \frac{\Delta A}{\Delta Q} \cdot \frac{Q}{A} \tag{13.7}$$

now the trick is to realize that:

$$\frac{\Delta A}{\Delta Q} \cdot \frac{Q}{A} = \frac{1}{\varepsilon_{QA}} \tag{13.8}$$

where ε_{QA} is the elasticity of demand with respect to advertising. Substituting Equation (13.8) into Equation (13.7) and multiplying and dividing both sides by ε_{QA}, and p, respectively, we get:

$$\frac{A}{pQ} = \frac{p-c}{p} \cdot \varepsilon_{QA} \tag{13.9}$$

Equation (9) is the Dorfman–Steiner condition. The left-hand side shows the ratio of advertising expenditure to total sales revenue; the intensity of advertising. The right-hand side consists of the product of the price–cost margin and the elasticity of demand with respect to advertising. The equation says a profit-maximizing firm will advertise more, the larger its price–cost margin and the more sensitive sales are to advertising. Recalling that the price–cost margin is equal to the inverse of the price elasticity of demand, ε_{QP} (Appendix 9A, Chapter 9), we can express Equation (13.9) as:

$$\frac{A}{PQ} = \frac{\varepsilon_{QA}}{\varepsilon_{QP}} \tag{13.10}$$

Say a firm's sales are €100m per year, the price elasticity of demand (ε_{QP}) is 2 and the elasticity of demand with respect to advertising (ε_{QA}) is 0.4, i.e. a 10 per cent rise in advertising expenditure leads to a 4 per cent rise in sales. The optimal expenditure on advertising is then given by solving Equation (13.10), which produces a value of £20m. The Dorfman–Steiner condition is, however, a little too simplistic. We have assumed that only current advertising influences demand, whereas the building of a brand and/or a reputation via an accumulation of advertising is likely to indirectly boost demand. For example, the Coca-Cola brand has been built over many years of advertising and in the unlikely event that Coca-Cola suddenly stopped advertising the influence of past advertising would take many years before its influence was nullified. The idea that advertising contributes to a stock of goodwill was first suggested by Nerlove and Arrow (1962). This requires that Equation (13.10) be modified to include past levels of advertising. The effects of past levels of advertising expenditure on demand will decay over time and the Nerlove–Arrow contribution allows for the lagged effects of advertising, in essence by substituting the long-run elasticity of demand with respect to advertising for the short run ε_{QA} in Equation (13.10).

The simplifying assumption of a monopolist overlooks another important aspect of advertising; namely, the reaction of rivals to a firm's advertising expenditure. Firms advertise to increase demand for their products; sometimes the increase in demand will be achieved at the expense of rivals' sales; sometimes it may increase consumers' general interest in the product line and boost demand for all producers, giving rise to a free-rider benefit for other producers. One way to model strategic interactions when advertising impacts on demand for other firms' products is with a **Cournot duopoly model**, as shown in Figure 13.7. There are two players, firms A and B, and firm A selects a level of advertising expenditure, α_0, before firm B enters the market. In Figure 13.7, firm A's level of advertising expenditure is measured along the horizontal axis, labelled α_A. Observing α_0, firm B now enters the market and chooses the level of advertising expenditure represented by α_1 – which is read on the vertical axis. Firm A, observing this level of advertising, now increases its own advertising expenditure to α_2, which lies on its reaction function, RF_A.

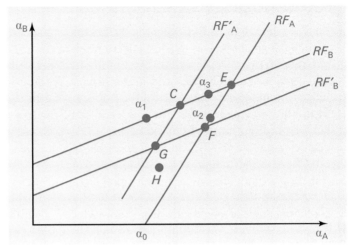

Firm B, observing α_2, increases its own advertising expenditure to α_3, which lies on its reaction function, RF_B, and this process continues until the non-cooperative **Cournot–Nash equilibrium** is reached, at point E. As profit is decreasing as we move up the reaction functions, both firms could increase profits by taking ac-

Figure 13.7: Advertising and strategic interactions

count of the expected strategic response of their rivals to their actions. The classic way of incorporating the expected strategic response of rivals is to introduce the concept of conjectural variations. If firm B's managers hold positive conjectural variations they will realize that increasing the level of advertising expenditure will bring forth an increase in firm A's level of advertising expenditure, the effect of which will be to constrain the increase in demand for firm B's products that might otherwise have occurred. Hence, being rational, firm B's managers will modify their response to A's advertising expenditure. If firm B holds positive conjectural variations, its reaction function shifts down to, say, RF'_B, yielding a new non-cooperative equilibrium at point F. Point F could be viewed as the **Stackelberg equilibrium**, where firm A has first-mover advantage and it should be noted that point F gives both firms higher profits than at point E. If now firm A also holds positive conjectural variations, then its reaction function shifts to the left – to RF'_A – yielding a new, high-profit equilibrium at point G. This point could be interpreted as one of **tacit collusion**. However, both firms could do better if they were prepared to engage in **explicit collusion**; a collusive solution would lie somewhere in the area represented by point H.

Fatal Attraction

Internet marketing has become a phenomenon of the last decade. More than any other form of marketing, speed is the hallmark of an internet site. It has the potential to deliver more information, to more customers, more quickly, more continuously and more interactively than any other form of marketing.

Potential internet customers are less reactive to what is offered and more proactive in defining what they want. The potential customer has not only chosen the method of communication but also is likely to be better informed and more active in seeking solutions than earlier generations.

continued

The internet, by providing potential customers with much greater access to comparative product details, prices and availability, results in much reduced search costs and less information incompleteness. Yet many of the dot.com firms that emerged in the 1990s and relied heavily on the internet to market their products have not survived. Extensive research by McKinsey and Company has pointed to a salient fact that contributed to the collapse of the dot.com boom. McKinsey termed it 'the fatal attraction', whereby sites were successful in luring visitors, but not at getting them to buy. However, a small number of players have been successful. These websites convert more than 12 per cent of visitors into customers, compared to less than 2 per cent for average sites, and achieve repeat purchase rates in excess of 60 per cent.

What differentiates these sites? The most successful sites focus on the entire customer experience rather than the economic transaction. They have a high degree of functionality by being easy to use and reliable, they are intimate by being customized and consistent and their ability to provide information inspires trust. A successful website is a living brand visually changing and developing in response to customers' demands.

Successful websites reflect the importance of information, but they are also mindful that even the internet cannot provide the potential customer with perfect information. There is still a need to gain the visitor's trust and to build a strong, favourable impression of the firm and its products. A website is a direct link between the customer and the supplier and it is in effect the sum of all the elements that contribute to customer experience brought together in front of the potential customer. In the digitized world of internet marketing, the customer experience really is king.

Advertising as a Source of Information

Advertising (and promotional activity in general) is impossible to explain within the context of the neo-classical model, which assumes a hyper-rational calculating individual in possession of all pertinent information and armed with the ability to use it. In such an environment it would be irrational for a firm to incur the costs of promotion as consumers would already be aware of the existence, quality, price and service surrounding its product. In practice, markets are characterized by consumers who are not only boundedly rational but also suffer from incomplete and asymmetric information. In such an environment there is value to be gained by incurring the costs of providing information. Typically, markets are characterized by firms that possess more knowledge about their products' attributes than potential consumers and in the presence of this asymmetry of information advertising can play an important role.

In the world described, the provision of timely, accurate and succinct information to boundedly rational consumers will help them make better choices and in the process support the efficient operation of the market. As a source of information, advertising serves three purposes. Firstly, it provides information on the existence of individual sellers. Secondly, it can provide information on the nature and characteristics of the attributes embodied in the differentiated products offered for sale. Thirdly, it helps potential consumers to evaluate relative quality and price. Without such information it is not possible for consumers to make informed choices. In essence, the purpose of informational advertising is to help potential customers identify the *address* of a product within the product space; but the provision of information can also extend beyond a product's price or attributes, to how the product might be used, e.g. a food ingredient.

By broadening potential consumers' understanding of how a product might be used, a firm is seeking to extend the reach of its brand and thereby attract new customers. As the costs of search are positive, it does not follow that in the absence of information consumers will search out the relevant information. The optimal level of search for information in differentiated product markets will be higher, the greater the distribution of prices, the higher the level of expenditure on the product, the less frequently the product is purchased and the greater the complexity of the product's attributes. These **transaction costs** of acquiring information are positive – though it should be noted that technology, e.g. the internet, is reducing these costs – and individuals being boundedly rational are limited in the amount of information they can consider at any one point in time. It follows that most individuals will make purchase decisions based on incomplete information and where advertisements contain truthful, objective information on a product's attributes and price, so they reduce the information incompleteness and help match consumers to products that closely meet their demands.

To investigate the role and impact of advertising as a source of consumer information we need first to understand that the firm is the prime source of information on its products. As time goes on the experience of consumers who have purchased the product will also become a major source of information, thereby reducing the asymmetry between the firm and consumers on a product's attributes and value. There is therefore a relationship between the amount of advertising that a firm does in a particular period and the proportion of the market whose purchasing decision is reliant on the advertising. Following Stigler (1961), expenditure A on advertising the same message will inform α of the market where $0 < \alpha < 1$, such that $\alpha = f(A)$. In addition, a certain proportion of the market β, where $0 < \beta < 1$, will turn over each period, implying that the value of β will vary with the nature of the product: the less frequently a product is purchased, e.g. a house, the closer β will be to unity. If, to simplify matters, we assume that the number of potential customers, N, remains constant in each successive period, then, in the first period of advertising, αN will be informed by the advertisement. In the second period, $\alpha N(1 - \beta)$ of the first period's potential customers will remain informed and $\alpha\beta N$ new potential customers will be informed. In addition, $\alpha N(1 - \alpha)(1 - \beta)$ potential customers from the first period will be informed for the first time. In total, in the second period the number of informed potential customers will be:

$$\lambda N = \alpha N[1 + (1 - \alpha)(1 - \beta)] \tag{13.11}$$

This generalizes for k periods, to:

$$\lambda N = \alpha N[1 + (1 - \alpha)(1 - \beta) + \ldots + (1 - \alpha)^{k-1}(1 - \beta)^{k-1}] \tag{13.12}$$

And if k is large, this approaches:

$$\frac{\alpha N}{[1 - (1 - \alpha)(1 - \beta)]} = \lambda N \tag{13.13}$$

That is, the proportion, λ, of potential customers informed by the advertising depends on the value of α and β and the number of time periods. We can now incorporate Equation (13.13) into the long-run elasticity of demand with respect to advertising. Recalling that $\varepsilon_{QA} = (A/Q)(\Delta Q/\Delta A)$ this can now be expanded to:

$$\varepsilon_{QA} = \frac{A}{Q} \cdot \frac{\Delta Q}{\Delta \lambda N} \frac{\Delta \lambda N}{\Delta a N} \frac{\Delta a N}{\Delta A} \tag{13.14}$$

where $\Delta Q/\Delta \lambda N$ measures the response of demand to the proportion of informed customers. Over time, the value of $\Delta Q/\Delta \lambda N$ is increasing because, as demonstrated above, the ratio $\Delta \lambda N/\Delta a N$ is increasing. Finally the response will increase further if A is increased as $\Delta a/\Delta A$ – the effectiveness of an additional unit of advertising expenditure on the proportion of the market that is informed – is likely to be positive but displaying **diminishing returns**. All of this suggests that information advertising is likely to be most effective, and therefore at its highest level of intensity, when the product is new. As the product matures, so the optimal advertising intensity declines, reflecting the fact that an increasing proportion of the market is informed with time, but as consumers are boundedly rational they will not retain all the information they have previously been given so there will continue to be a need for some level of advertising. In addition to the effectiveness of the advertising to inform potential customers, the optimal level will be influenced by the rate of turnover of people in the market. As the rate of turnover of potential customers rises, so the optimal level of advertising increases – at least up to a point. At some point, a rapid turnover in the market destroys the cumulative effect of information advertising. At a high level of turnover there will be little retention, so less advertising is optimal. Stigler's theory has been confirmed by Doyle (1968), who showed that the frequency of purchase was negatively correlated with advertising intensity.

We observed above, that the purpose of informational advertising is to help potential customers identify a product's *address* within the product space. Grossman and Shapiro (1984) provide some valuable insights into the issues raised when individual consumers have a preferred product specification. In the absence of information, Grossman and Shapiro assume that consumers buy at random. Firms engage in advertising in order to reduce this randomness by providing information on the address of their products; however, as they cannot identify consumers with a preference for their products' specifications, they are forced to advertise to the whole market. As just discussed, the proportion of the market reached by an individual firm is a function of the intensity of advertising expenditure, but for Grossman and Shapiro, advertising in the situation described has both favourable and unfavourable consequences. It helps potential customers whose preferences are close to the attributes of the firm's product to identify it as the product they wish to buy. But it also dissuades other potential consumers, who might otherwise have bought at random, who now realize that the product does not match their preferences.

Grossman and Shapiro go on to show, with some simplifying assumptions, that the intensity of advertising expenditures will be higher, the smaller the number of firms contesting the market and the more strongly held are consumers' preferences. The first insight is based on the fact that with fewer firms consumers will have to compromise in attempting to precisely match their preferences to a particular product. In accepting a less than perfect match, less advertising will be 'wasted' telling potential customers about a particular product's attributes. The second insight rests on the knowledge that the more strongly held are the preferences of consumers, the less elastic are the demand curves facing individual firms and hence the greater the potential profit margin.

We explained above, when introducing the concept of a product space, that moving up the vertical differentiated axis implied increasing quality. Thus, one of the concerns firms have when engaging in informational advertising is to convey information about quality. When dealing, in the last chapter with the issue of conveying information about a product's quality to potential consumers, under conditions of incomplete and asymmetric information, we made use of Nelson's (1974) concepts of **search goods** and **experience goods**, as well as Darby and Karni's (1973) concept of a **credence good**. Nelson, it will be recalled, defined a search good as a product such as an item of clothing, the quality of which could be ascertained at the time of purchase. Thus, buyers can shop around until they find the appropriate quality by inspection. In contrast, for experience goods, consumers can only learn of the inherent quality after purchasing and experiencing the product. In the case of a credence good, quality may never be accurately assessed, even after purchase, e.g. the advice of a doctor.

As the quality of a search good, as defined by Nelson, can be ascertained before purchase, the role of informational advertising is to guide potential consumers to a particular product. To influence sales of search goods advertising must provide detailed, descriptive information; they are, for example, likely to include photographs or detailed specifications. This favours newspapers and magazines as the medium rather than television, as the potential consumer can reread and compare the information in the advertisement. In the case of experience goods, detailed advertisements are of little value. The qualities of an experience good cannot be ascertained by looking at a photography, but only by consumption; so informational advertising for experience goods should be directed at encouraging people to try the product. Providing the information is accurate, a secondary purpose is to encourage repeat purchases. As consumers cannot perceive the quality of an experience product prior to purchase, advertising expenditure will need to be high to attract customers from substitute products. Nelson concluded that the intensity of advertising is likely to be positively correlated with quality. High-quality goods are more likely to generate repeat purchases from satisfied customers, so over the longer term, the elasticity of demand with respect to advertising, i.e. ε_{QA}, will be higher and hence more advertising will be undertaken.

Nelson's conclusions have been explored by a number of economists. Schmalensee (1976) shows that although higher quality gives rise to more repeat purchases and therefore higher returns to advertising, higher quality is also more costly to produce and this – depending on market conditions – could reduce profit margins and hence the incentive to advertise. For Nelson's conclusions to hold, the firm's **marginal costs** of production must not increase too greatly with quality and the repeat purchase mechanism must be strong. Another perspective on the notion that there is a positive relationship between quality and advertising intensity has been explored by Milgrom and Roberts (1986). The issue they focus on is that a firm producing a low-quality product might seek to convey the impression of quality by mimicking the high pricing of high quality products. By combining the signals of a high price and a high intensity of advertising, a firm is signalling its belief that purchase will lead to repeat purchases, though in the case of a low-quality product the firm would expect to make its profits on the basis of first-time buyers.

Thus, advertising that provides factual information on attributes and prices makes more effective the competitive process and thereby raises social welfare. Informational advertising can increase competition by allowing new entrants to make themselves known to potential customers. It enables incumbents to communicate their products' mix of attributes and it can inform on relative prices. In this way, informational advertising (and other forms of informational activity) help consumers to identify, within the product space, the address of a product that is likely to match more precisely their preferences. Where consumers hold strong preferences and, in terms of attributes, products are clearly differentiated, information advertising is likely to lower price elasticities and cross-price elasticities of demand for an individual firm's products. However, where there are near neighbour products and preferences are not strongly held, advertising to inform can increase price elasticities and cross-price elasticities of demand. In such markets, advertising to inform will lower the profit-maximizing price and firms will be under more pressure to offer attractive prices.

Frightfully British

The BBC corporate brand is synonymous with everything that is British. The BBC has viewers and listeners in every part of the world. Despite the onslaught of cable and satellite television the BBC brand reigns supreme. It does so because more than any other organization, the BBC product is the BBC brand: every aspect of the Corporation reflects its brand values. And audiences are able to readily identify with the strategic identity of the BBC. Regardless of where one is in the world, sight or sound of the BBC brand evokes a clear sense of what it stands for: fair play, objectivity and quality.

The primary cause of the BBC's success is its consistency. Whatever the programme, viewers and listeners can experience Britishness. The BBC offers a unique and differentiated identity that evokes all that is good about Britain. The BBC has established a loyal relationship with its audience through the provision of trusted news, reliable information, high-quality entertainment and educational opportunities. The brand is differentiated for different nationalities, but it always remains high quality and very British. For example, in India the news is presented by an Indian but it is read in English and presented in the same way as it is presented in London. In terms of adopting its brand for different nations, the BBC has its strongest affinity with those nations that were former colonies. In all cases the adaptation is limited to a greater emphasis on regional representation. The BBC brand is well established, but regional adaptations only serve to enhance its identity. Being easy to understand and interpret, secures for the BBC audience loyalty – a loyalty that is passed on from generation to generation.

But being frightfully British has not prevented the BBC embracing change and innovation. The BBC website is amongst the best in the world and its long association with the Open University makes its educational role unique. The BBC can undertake these innovations with confidence because it has a very strong understanding of its own values as well as those of its audiences.

Persuasion or Signalling?

The idea that advertising serves customers by providing information on alternative choices would be questioned by many economists. Most advertising is not informative. The long-running Marlborough advertisement featuring a cowboy smoking a cigarette conveys no useful information concerning the attributes of the product being sold. Firms spend money on such advertisements because they believe they can persuade people to buy by creating or stimulating images that the consumer wishes to be associated with. If an advertising message that is devoid of any true information can persuade consumers to favour a particular brand, then this amounts to saying advertising can change consumers' preferences. This view of advertising as a means of persuasion implicitly assumes that advertising has the ability to distort consumers' preferences, causing them to select advertised products in preference to unadvertised products. By altering consumers' preferences to favour the advertised product, demand for the product becomes less sensitive to price changes (i.e. less elastic) and cross-price elasticities of demand between the advertised product and close substitutes are also reduced. The intention, according to this viewpoint, is to make consumers less responsive to relative price changes and so to confer a degree of monopoly power on the firm.

At face value such advertising is socially wasteful to the extent that, if successful, persuasive advertising not only enhances a firm's profits at the expense of consumers' welfare, but also it uses resources which could have been used productively elsewhere, e.g. developing new products. The notion that persuasive advertising is wasteful was widely shared by economists of the **structure–conduct–performance** school. The fear was that established firms would build, through accumulated advertising, a market identity for their products that a new entrant would find difficult to overcome. A focus on the persuasive role of advertising demands an excursion into consumer behaviour. Figure 13.8 illustrates a consumer's **preference map** between two goods, A and B. Initially we will assume that neither good is advertised and the pre-advertising indifference curve is labelled U_0. With the **budget line**, XX, the consumer is in equilibrium at point E, purchasing the bundle A_1 of good A and B_1 of good B. If now the producer of good A decides to advertise and by creating a positive image successfully persuades the consumer that A is superior to B, the consumption of a unit of A will now generate more **utility** than previously. This is represented by a rotation in the consumer's preference map, resulting in the indifference curve, U_0, swivelling through point E to give a new indifference curve, U_1. As illustrated, the relative price of products A and B remains unchanged so with an unchanged income both the position and slope of the budget line XX remain unchanged. These assumptions isolate the effect of image advertising, which has the effect of increasing the amount of utility delivered by a unit of the advertised product. A new equilibrium is now established at point F on a higher indifference curve, U_2, with the consumer buying more of A and less of B.

The ability of advertising – that may in the extreme be devoid of any true information – to change individual preferences may not *per se* be either harmful or inefficient. Consumers' tastes change over time and in a real sense these changes in preferences are always developed in response to some form of persuasion. Developing a taste

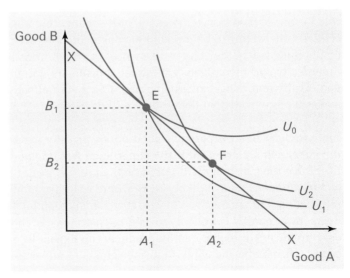

Figure 13.8: Changing preferences

for fine wine, foreign food or opera are all likely to be the outcome of persuasive effort, though generally by partners, parents or colleagues. Indeed, children have to be persuaded of the value of education and adults the value of a healthy diet. Far from disapproving, society generally welcomes such forces of persuasion that start by awakening interest or curiosity in a particular experience, activity or taste. In short, it is far from clear as to whether changing a consumer's preferences is socially harmful. As there is no fixed basis for comparing welfare before and after advertising, this is not something we are going to resolve here. People are the best judges of their own welfare and it is difficult to draw strong conclusions relating to advertising. Nevertheless, an attempt to calculate the welfare effects of advertising is set out in Appendix 13A.

If the foregoing serves to caution criticism of persuasive advertising it can be reinforced by the observation that in a world of asymmetric information, persuasive or image advertising may be more informative than appears at first sight. One of the enduring problems for firms that put effort into producing higher-quality products is how to capture higher value in a world in which consumers are imperfectly informed – that is, cannot observe the behaviour of firms – suffer positive search costs and are boundedly rational. Advertising to convey product quality may call for more than an attempt to convey factual information. Product quality has multiple dimensions not only attributes such as taste, appearance and enjoyability, but also for many products, effectiveness – how well does the product do its job – durability – how long will it do its job – and safety – whether the use of the product involves risk of injury. It will be apparent that the assessment of quality is hampered where products are experience goods or credence goods. The role of advertising for such products is to persuade consumers to try the experience. As quality and production costs are positively related, higher-quality products must attract a higher price. Given that consumers are heterogeneous in both their attitudes towards quality and their willingness to pay for quality, the problem becomes one of matching consumers to the standards of quality that they seek and are prepared to pay for.

By separating products into search, experience and credence goods, we focus attention on the nature of advertising. As observed above, advertising for search goods must provide detailed, descriptive information, whereas for experience goods advertising has the purpose of getting people to try the experience. It was for experience goods – to which we can add credence goods – that Nelson saw a role for image-based advertising. Advertisements that are devoted to building a brand image are essentially attempting to help potential consumers identify the quality or other relevant characteristics of a product before they buy it. In a world in which firms know the quality of what they produce, but imperfectly and incompletely informed consumers do not, the producers need to signal the embedded quality and image advertising might be a very effective signally device. Building a brand name makes it more likely that the product will be tried.

The producer of an experience good hopes that the experience of a purchase will result in gaining the consumer's patronage. If the experience was as good, or better, than expected, then it is very likely that the consumer will purchase the product again. However, if the experience proved unsatisfactory the consumer is likely to continue searching for a substitute product that delivers greater satisfaction. Put another way, a firm that signals high quality through image advertising but then delivers lower quality is unlikely to gain the patronage of those who sampled the product. Accordingly, only producers of higher-quality products can expect to profit from image advertising. This will encourage firms offering good quality products to advertise more heavily because of the prospect of earning larger returns on their advertising outlays. And the process will be reinforced if consumers interpret high advertising as evidence of product quality.

Where a product has the characteristics of a credence good, then advertising alone cannot provide sufficient information. Credence goods reflect an asymmetry between buyer and seller with respect to knowledge. In essence, buyers have to decide whether they find the sellers' quality claims credible. These may relate to the production process, e.g. organic food, or the existence of a large set of minimum standards that a buyer would find impossible to test, e.g. a car. When quality is a matter of credence, the role of advertising is not so much to impart detailed information, but rather to establish the seller's reputation for quality and fairness. Nelson pointed out that as advertising expenditure is incurred before any sales are made and is also a sunk cost, it can only be justified if the net present value of the additional revenue stream generated by advertising exceeds the expenditure. The more the advertised product has the nature of an experience or credence good, the more important that it delivers the expected quality and therefore the expected utility. Consumer products that deliver the quality expected can be interpreted as having a low price per unit of utility and consequently a higher probability of repeat purchases and hence the greater the expected net present value. The positive relationship between the delivery of expected utility and repeat purchases implies that firms whose products have a low price per unit of utility have a greater incentive to advertise, *ceteris paribus*.

This notion of advertising as a signal of quality has been the subject of much research. Schmalensee (1978) makes the point that Nelson's argument that a firm that believes its products yield better value for money has a greater incentive to advertise than a firm who knows its products are of lower quality. But the perception that a product that is heavily advertised indicates that it is likely to have a low price per unit of utility opens up the possibility of opportunistic behaviour. Producers of cheap, inferior goods may have an incentive to advertise, even if no repeat purchases are expected providing sales to first-time buyers generate a profit after allowing for production costs and advertising expenditure. Consumers will be unable to distinguish plausible from implausible advertising claims before purchase and hence all advertising claims will be discounted to some extent.

Another important study of the notion that image advertising signals quality was undertaken by Kihlstrom and Riordan (1984), who demonstrated a strong incentive for high-quality producers to lure repeat buyers by advertising heavily in the early stages of a product's life cycle. Kihlstrom and Riordan argue that repeat purchases are driven, not by advertising, but by the quality of the product which is fully revealed in use. In this situation, advertising serves as a signal of high quality as firms can only justify the high price necessary to offset advertising costs because customers are satisfied with the quality and make repeat purchases. We can demonstrate the model with the following game theoretic example. The model is based on the assumption that:

$$c_H(q) > c_L(q) \tag{13.15}$$

where $c(q)$ is the unit cost of production and the subscripts $_H$ and $_L$ refer to high- and low-quality production. Consumers can costlessly observe expenditure on advertising, A, and draw the inference that the higher A, the higher the quality. Writing p_1 for the post-advertising price and p_0 for the pre-advertising price, then by assumption a high-quality firm will be able to sustain $p_1 > p_0$, but for a low-quality firm the price will revert to $p_1 = p_0$. Writing A/q as the unit cost of advertising, it follows that it will only be profitable to advertise if

$$p_1 - \frac{A}{q} \geq p_0 \tag{13.16}$$

But in the absence of advertising, a firm producing a high-quality product will be severely constrained in its ability to charge a higher price to capture the higher quality. We can now demonstrate with the game theoretic pay-off matrix shown in Figure 13.9, that a Nash equilibrium will be achieved when the high-quality firm uses advertising to signal its quality and the low-quality firm does not. By assumption, unit production costs are higher for the higher-quality firm, but the higher quality will result in repeat purchases. A low-quality product will not be able to sustain the higher post-advertising price. The importance of the Kihlstrom and Riordan study is that it demonstrates a strong incentive for high-quality producers to capture repeat buyers by advertising heavily in the first period. Having established a reputation for quality, image advertising still has a role in reinforcing the brand image and encouraging repeat purchases.

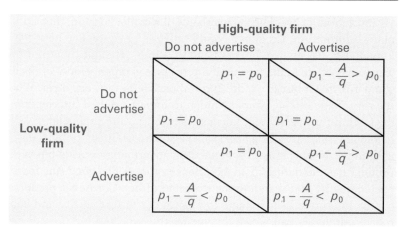

Figure 13.9: Advertising as a game

When it comes to empirical studies designed to test Nelson's contention that advertising serves as a signal of quality, the results might best be described as mixed (Pepall *et al.*, 2005). In the first place, the idea that consumers link advertising intensity to quality presupposes that they are aware of the value of total sales and advertising expenditure. Further, the analysis applies specifically to experience goods, but this presupposes that in practice it is easy to distinguish between a search good and an experience good. Finally, the signalling approach to advertising is only relevant to a new product or potential consumers of an existing product. Once the product has been purchased and information on the experience gained, the underlying logic of the signalling approach is that the role of advertising is reduced. Yet we know from causal empiricism that the producers of major consumer brands, be they cosmetics, food products or beer, apparently find it profitable to repeatedly advertise their products. We will investigate in the next section one possible reason why firms with established products continue to advertise.

Before leaving the issue of advertising to persuade, we will return briefly to the notion of changing preferences. A different view of the persuasive role of advertising is taken by Becker and Murphy (1993). They acknowledge that image advertisements do stimulate demand, but not necessarily by changing consumers' preferences. The idea they advance is that image advertising rather than changing preferences can actually be a complement to the product being purchased. That is, consumers value the product more, the more it is advertised; the fact that an item of clothing is widely advertised serves to enhance its value in the eyes of consumers. In a similar manner to price enhancing the value of a Veblen good, so some consumers gain utility from consuming a product that is widely advertised. In a sense, this view of advertising involves an element of persuasion, but here consumers are not required to change their preferences. This perspective reinforces the idea that advertising is a means of building brand value. The greater the expenditure on advertising, the more popular the product and the greater the willingness of consumers to pay.

Monopolizing Merchandising

Sport merchandising has grown to become a billion-euro global businesses. In 2001, Manchester United made some €30m from its merchandising activities alone. The revenue generated from merchandising has allowed top football teams to buy expensive players and to fund high salaries for players. It is therefore not surprising that there is a strong interest in maximizing income from merchandising and preventing competition from 'unofficial' sources.

In April 2001, Arsenal FC brought proceedings against a Mr Reed under the 1994 European Trade Marks Directive, alleging trade mark infringement and passing-off. Mr Reed had for over 30 years been selling, on Arsenal's premises during matches, football memorabilia and souvenirs such as badges, hats and scarves bearing the names 'Arsenal' and 'Gunners', together with the team's cannon logo. But, in the high court, Arsenal FC was unsuccessful. The judge took the view that the memorabilia and souvenirs served as evidence of allegiance and did not carry any message regarding the essential function of the club or establish a trade connection between the goods and the club.

The matter was, however, then referred to the European Court of Justice (ECJ) for clarification, who concluded that the function of a trademark is to guarantee the identity of the origin of goods. To facilitate this, the ECJ opined that all goods bearing the marks must offer the guarantee that they have been manifested and supplied under the quality control of a single entity. For the ECJ, whether or not the name Arsenal was perceived as a badge of support, loyalty or affiliation was immaterial. What mattered was that the use of the name Arsenal created the impression of a connection between Mr Reed's goods and Arsenal FC and as Arsenal FC did not control the production or supply of Mr Reed's goods, the essential function of a trademark was in jeopardy.

The matter then returned to the English court, where it eventually ended in the Court of Appeal. The Court of Appeal agreed with the ECJ's view that the unchecked use of a trademark by a third party was likely to threaten the guarantee of origin. The outcome creates a wider monopoly for Arsenal FC in the area of merchandising, but it has implications beyond football for other areas of merchandising, most notably in the entertainment business involving pop stars, film stars and video game characters.

Advertising and Market Structure

Yet another approach to explaining variations in advertising intensity between markets, which also has implications for the 'persuasion v information' debate, links advertising intensity to differences in market structure. We have already noted that under the neo-classical model of perfect competition – with its assumptions of perfect information, homogeneous products and an atomistic industry structure – an individual firm cannot benefit from advertising. And to a large extent minimal advertising remains a feature of markets whose products and structures approach the neo-classical model, such as farming. At the other extreme, it would appear that a monopolist producing a single product has little incentive to advertise unless there are potential consumers who are unaware of the product.

This suggests that we might expect to see high levels of advertising intensity in markets characterized by small numbers of rivals and this is reinforced once we relax the assumption of homogeneity and include differentiated products. As monopolistically competitive markets are characterized by large numbers of competing firms, it might appear logical to expect that the intensity of advertising would be at its highest in such markets and then decline as the number of sellers declines. But researchers have found that the intensity of advertising, and other forms of promotional activity, are highest in oligopolist markets (Sutton, 1991). Empirical studies reveal, *ceteris paribus*, that an industry's advertising intensity varies with its **concentration ratio**, but the relationship is not linear. Advertising intensity rises to a peak at intermediate concentration levels – say a CR_5 in excess of around 60 per cent – and then declines at higher levels of market concentration. This finding is often referred to as the *inverted-U hypothesis*, which is shown schematically in Figure 13.10.

Figure 13.10 shows that monopolists tend to have a lower level of advertising intensity than oligopolists. We saw in Equation (13.9) that the optimal advertising intensity is given by the product of the price–cost margin and the elasticity of demand with respect to advertising. We have also discussed the factors that are likely to influence the advertising elasticity over the longer term. One of the factors deemed to influence the long-run advertising elasticity was conjectural variations. Conjectural variations are only applicable in highly concentrated markets where the degree of interdependence amongst firms is high. We have already demonstrated in Figure 13.7 how, in principle, if firms operating in oligopolistic markets hold positive conjectural variations then they are aware of the self-defeating nature of attempting to outspend rivals in the area of advertising. This would imply that the more concentrated a market, the more certain that advertising initiatives would be matched and hence the rational oligopolist would desist from a self-defeating escalation of advertising expenditure, even seeking a co-operative solution.

However, if such logic is impeccable when it comes to pricing, it may not be so clear cut when it comes to advertising. For oligopolists, a strategy of competitive advertising has two advantages over a strategy of competitive pricing. Firstly, a price reduction is likely to be immediately countered by rivals, whereas an increase in advertising expenditure may not result in a rapid reaction. Indeed it

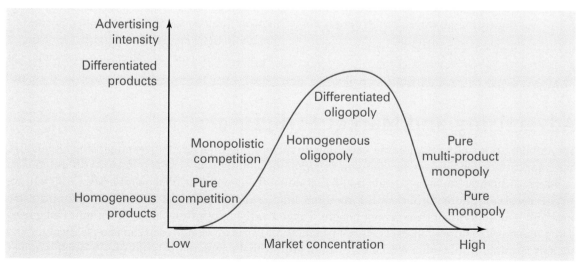

Figure 13.10: Advertising intensity and market concentration

takes time to mount an advertising campaign and strategic advertising has the further advantage over a price reduction in that it can more easily be reversed. Secondly, while the response of a rival will almost certainly be to match a price cut, in the case of an advertising campaign a firm might believe that an original campaign will not be easily matched by rivals or its effects nullified. All of this casts doubt on how we might expect conjectural variations regarding advertising to vary with market structure. The smaller the number of rival firms in a market, the greater the incentive for an individual firm to pursue a strategy that will take sales from its rivals. In oligopolist markets there is therefore both an incentive to compete and an incentive to collude, preferably tacitly. The incentive to advertise is to gain market share, while the disincentive is the cost of advertising campaigns and the uncertainty of the outcome, both in terms of market share and the response of rivals. We can demonstrate this interdependence with the aid of the game theoretic, normal form matrix shown in Figure 13.11.

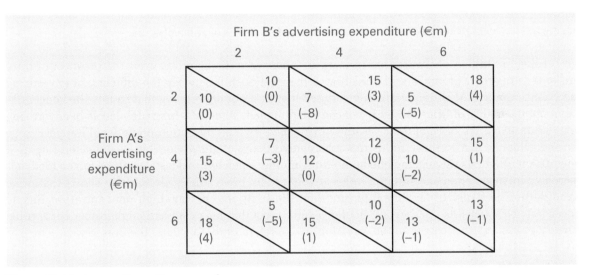

Figure 13.11: A game theoretic approach

The pay-offs shown in Figure 13.11 need some explaining. They show the gains in gross revenue from increases in advertising expenditure and also (in parentheses) the net revenue gain after allowing for the *increased* cost of advertising. Thus, starting in the top left-hand cell, both firms are spending €2m on advertising, per period, and this is generating for both firms a sales revenue of €10. This is our reference cell. If now firm A increases its advertising expenditure to €4m, it achieves a gross revenue of €15m and a net revenue gain of €3m (shown in parenthesis). If, however, firm B also increases advertising expenditure to €4m, then for both firms gross revenue rises to €12m, but after deducting the €2m rise in advertising expenditure, the gain in net revenue is zero. If both firms simultaneously increase their advertising expenditure by a further €2m to €6m, market shares are unaffected, but due to the higher advertising costs the net revenue gain is now negative at –€1m. However, both firms have the incentive to increase advertising if they believe their rival will not respond or if they suspect their rival might increase expenditure. Whether this game is played once or repeatedly, both firms have the incentive to spend more on advertising. If either firm adopted a **minimax** strategy, they would choose to increase advertising expenditure by €4m to €6m. By doing this the worst that could happen to them is a reduction of €1m in net revenue, but there is also the opportunity to increase net revenue by €4m.

Thus, the Nash equilibrium for the game shown in Figure 13.11, the **saddle point**, is for both firms to increase advertising expenditure to €6m, even though it is not profitable to do so.

The game set out in Figure 13.11 is consistent with the *inverted-U* hypothesis set out in Figure 13.10, but it is not a sufficient explanation. In differentiated markets the free-rider problem is reduced and most firms appropriate the benefits of their advertising. However, in monopolistically competitive markets it is hard to stand out from the crowd, whereas in oligopolistic markets, there is a greater likelihood that by advertising a firm can stand out. Or in the words of Comanor and Wilson (1974), 'when there is a noise in the market one must shout louder to be heard'. The suggestion that the intensity of advertising is higher the more concentrated an industry, is reinforced by the work of John Sutton (1991). He focuses on the fact that there is a positive correlation between the extent of sunk costs and an industry's equilibrium concentration ratio. Advertising is a sunk cost. Once an advertising campaign is mounted, the associated costs can never be recovered. Hence, argues Sutton, in industries where product differentiation enables firms to appropriate the gains from advertising, such industries will be characterized by both considerable sunk costs and a high degree of concentration.

According to Sutton's analysis, only in markets where advertising offers firms the prospect of truly differentiating their products will one observe the relationship between the intensity of advertising and concentration. Most importantly, he argued that it is not advertising that causes the concentration, but the ability of firms in highly concentrated markets to benefit from high levels of advertising expenditure. On the basis of the case study evidence provided by Sutton, there would appear to be strong evidence that in those industries where advertising might reasonably be expected to play a significant role in distinguishing one brand from another, such as breakfast cereals or frozen food, advertising intensity and concentration ratios are both high. Interestingly, Sutton also shows that price competition is likely to be very intense when the high advertising–high concentration link is strongest. This suggests that beyond the large sunk costs that heavy advertising creates, fierce price rivalry places a further barrier in the way of firms hoping to profitably enter the industry.

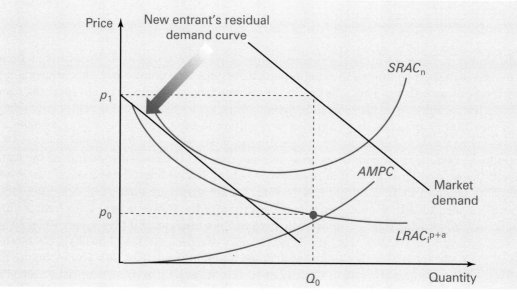

Figure 13.12: Market penetration costs

By definition, a highly concentrated industry will have **barriers to entry** and it has frequently been argued by economists that advertising can serve as a **strategic barrier to entry**. One approach to this issue is to recall Equation (13.9), which showed, *ceteris paribus*, a positive relationship between higher price–cost margins and advertising. The greater a firm's market power, the higher will be its price–cost margin. Thus, larger firms with higher profit margins will be able to profitably maintain higher advertising to sales ratios than smaller rivals and this may be sufficient to deter potential entrants. An alternative approach is to reverse the causation. Advertising can build up a stock of brand loyalty that makes it harder for a new entrant to attract customers. In this situation, a new entrant will need to advertise extensively to overcome the brand loyalty created by the incumbent firm's accumulated advertising. In contrast, the incumbents, having established their brands in the minds of consumers, can spend less on recurring advertising to protect their brands' identities. We can demonstrate this with the aid of Figure 13.12.

To simplify matters, let us assume that the market represented in Figure 13.12 is supplied by a monopolist. When unit advertising costs are added to the incumbent's long-run total unit production costs the outcome is represented by the curve, $LRAC_i^{p+a}$. For an incumbent firm, the cumulative effect of advertising in previous periods is the creation of a stock of brand loyalty, which implies that there will be fewer people switching between brands, and hence likely to try a new product. Thus, to counter brand loyalty, a new entrant has to overcome this attachment and must either advertise more heavily, bearing in mind that advertising is a sunk cost, or offer directly or indirectly, e.g. coupons, significant price discounts. In either case, a new entrant will require substantial additional funds in order to penetrate the market and consequently the entrant's profitability will be adversely affected in the short run and the risks associated with entry increased. In Figure 13.12, these additional market penetration costs are shown on a unit basis by the curve, $AMPC$, which is illustrated as a rising function of the scale of entry. These market penetration costs are added to the potential entrant's production and normal advertising costs and included in the short-run cost curve, $SRAC_n$. This curve shows unit production and advertising costs falling at first, but then starting to rise, as $AMPC$ is included as the scale of entry is increased. Turning now to the incumbent, if its output is Q_0, then the market of p_1 generates an economic rent. Indeed, the price p_1 is the **limit price** and the incumbent has the margin, $p_1 - p_0$, to conduct a more extreme deterrence strategy if necessary. Providing the market price is kept below p_1, it will not be profitable for a potential entrant to enter, even on a small scale.

The importance of advertising as a barrier to entry depends on how long lasting the effects of advertising are. And in this respect, the empirical support for advertising as a barrier to entry is mixed. A number of studies lend support to the entry barrier hypothesis; for example, Rizzo and Zeckhauser (1990) showed that US manufacturing industries with high advertising intensities have significantly lower entry rates. But a more complex picture of advertising and entry is painted by Geroski and Murfin (1991), whose study suggests that advertising initially fosters competition by easing entry to the market; however continued advertising makes it harder for later entrants. Yet other studies have shown that a high advertising intensity either reduces or has no impact on barriers to entry. In their study of generic pharmaceuticals between 1984 and 1988, Grabowski and Vernon (1992) found that high ratios of advertising to sales did not act as an effective barrier to entry and Kessides (1991) provides evidence that advertising can facilitate entry. Kessides views his results as a rejection of the *advertising as persuasion* view and support for the *advertising as information* view. If advertising is advantageous to existing firms by informing potential customers about details of their products, then

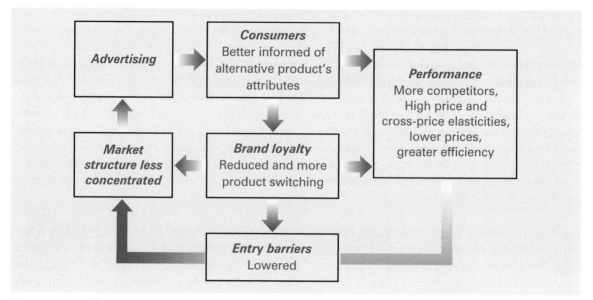

Figure 13.13: Advertising and market entry

the same advantages will accrue to a new entrant. Behaviour in the market for optician services in the UK since advertising was permitted in 1985 is also consistent with the latter view. Many new opticians have set up, for example Lenscrafters and Vision Express. Advertising intensity has been greater amongst the new entrants, for whom advertising is a way of facilitating entry. Figure 13.13 summarizes the view that, in a world of asymmetric information and bounded rationality, advertising can actually facilitate entry.

It might appear that one way to resolve the *persuasion v information* debate is by investigating the relationship between advertising and market prices. If empirical studies suggested an inverse relationship between advertising expenditure and prices, this would be consistent with the *advertising as information* hypothesis. Alternatively, if a positive relationship was discovered, this would lend weight to the *advertising as persuasion* hypothesis. Yet again the empirical results prove to be contradictory. Heavily advertised brands do appear to command a price premium over rivals with lower advertising intensities, but studies of the effect of advertising on market prices face the difficulty of finding relevant comparisons and allowing for the many factors that contribute to a higher price, e.g. vertical differentiation. Rizzo and Zeckhauser's examinations cited above caused them to conclude that advertising actually leads to higher prices and higher-quality services.

Concluding Thoughts

The publication in the 1930s by Chamberlin of his theory of monopolistic competition was a response to the difficulty of reconciling the neo-classical theory of the firm with the general observation that individual firms seek to differentiate their products – frequently with the aid of a unique brand name. Chamberlin's model remains an important milestone in the development of economic thought, but the model's failure to supply a criterion for limiting substitutability undermines its central tenet of a downward- sloping demand curve. This challenge was taken up by other economists. One approach was the concept of a product space within which differentiated products have unique addresses, limiting the degree of substitutability. But within the product space, products can have near neighbours, allowing for high levels of substitutability. Lancaster's attributes model has done much to foster research into near neighbour products, but has itself been criticized because the sudden switches in demand implied by near neighbour effects are not generally observed in the real world.

The lack of a widely accepted model of product differentiation is all the more frustrating given the ubiquitous presence of differentiated products and advertising. In a world where consumers are challenged by incomplete and asymmetric information as well as positive search costs, most will be forced to make their purchase decisions based on extrinsic indicators. As firms have more complete information on the true value of their products, this raises the question as to whether advertising can serve a useful purpose in supporting and enhancing the efficiency of markets. Advertising to inform would appear to be necessary if consumers are to make more informed choices, which in turn, makes the competitive process more responsive to consumers and thereby increases consumers' welfare. But not all advertising sets out to provide objective information. Much advertising is focused on creating an image that is designed to persuade consumers to change their preferences in favour of a particular product.

Just what purpose and medium advertising should adopt depends on the frequency and complexity of the item being purchased and also on whether it is a search, experience or credence good. A search good requires detailed information, whereas for experience and credence goods the purpose is to encourage consumers to try the product and to reinforce a seller's reputation. The notion that image advertising is a quality-signalling device has gained support with the acceptance that producers of higher-quality experience goods have a greater incentive to advertise than lower-quality producers. But doubts as to the efficiency of advertising remain, with the knowledge that the intensity of advertising reaches a peak in highly concentrated differentiated markets. This suggests that advertising might take the form of a strategic barrier to entry. In addition to protecting market share, strategic advertising has the purpose of increasing the costs and hence risk for a potential new entrant. In this way, advertising can influence market structure and soften competition. However, the empirical evidence on this and the other hypotheses concerning the purpose of advertising remains ambiguous.

Key Learning Points

- The neo-classical theory of the firm cannot explain the persistence of industries characterized by firms producing ranges of differentiated products, usually under a brand name.
- Chamberlin's model of monopolistic competition sought to deal with product differentiation, but its central tenet of a downward-sloping demand curve was compromised by an inability to explain how substitution was limited.

- Close substitutes implies high cross-price elasticities of demand and hence a demand curve approaching the horizontal.
- One attempt to impose limited substitutability is provided by the concept of a product space, where individual products have a unique address depending on the degree of vertical and horizontal differentiation.
- This concept takes explicit account of the fact that consumers, characterized by heterogeneity in their preferences and willingness to pay for

continued

higher quality, have their preferred addresses within the product space.

- However, products close to a specific product's address are described as near neighbours and to the extent that these products are close substitutes, so the cross-price elasticities will be high, comprising a downward-sloping demand curve.
- Another influential attempt to link consumers' heterogeneity to limited substitutability for differentiated products is Lancaster's attributes model, where consumers' consumption choices are not based on products *per se*, but on the varying attributes embodied in differentiated products.
- In making their consumption decisions, consumers are handicapped by incomplete and asymmetric information regarding the distribution of prices and product attributes. Lack of information on the choices available limits substitutability and can result in a downward-sloping demand curve.
- Product differentiation increases the amount of information a consumer must possess to purchase efficiently. However, as the search for information involves positive costs, individuals are constrained to make their market choices with incomplete information.
- An extreme form of product differentiation is a Veblen good, which offers rich consumers the opportunity to flaunt their wealth and can result in an upward-sloping demand curve.
- Incomplete information and bounded

rationality on the part of consumers implies an important role for advertising in markets characterized by product differentiation. By providing information on the alternative choices, advertising reduces search costs and makes the competitive process more efficient.

- Most advertising is not informative, but designed to persuade by creating an image and thereby to change consumers' preferences with the intention of building brand loyalty.
- Economists traditionally question the efficiency of image advertising which confers quasi-monopoly power on individual firms, thereby resulting in reduced competition, lower price elasticities and a loss of social welfare.
- More recent studies are less condemning of image advertising, viewing it as a means of conveying product quality, particularly for experience goods and credence goods.
- Studies show that, within industries, advertising intensity varies with the concentration ratio. This has given rise to the suggestion that advertising may have a strategic role in raising entry barriers and hence encouraging high levels of seller concentration.
- The belief that advertising raises prices is not unambiguously confirmed by empirical analysis. Some studies have demonstrated that advertising facilitates market entry because it offers an effective means for new firms to make potential customers aware of their existence and of the attributes of their products.

Exercises

13.1 Why is the issue of the degree of a product's substitutability so important to Chamberlin's model of monopolistic competition?

13.2 Both Chamberlin's and Lancaster's models assume decision makers hold zero conjectural variations. Is this realistic and

what are the consequences if senior managers hold positive conjectural variations?

13.3 In what way should the Dorman–Steiner optimal advertising intensity relationship be adjusted to take account of longer-term influences?

13.4 Why is it likely that the producer of a low-quality experience good would not find it profitable to spend heavily on advertising?

13.5 In markets with small numbers of producers, game theory suggests co-operative behaviour is optimal for pricing strategies. Why might this conclusion not hold for advertising?

Problems

13.1 A firm's marketing department has estimated that the demand for a recently launched product is $Q = 15{,}000 - 60*P + 6*A^{1/2}$, where Q is annual output, P is the price charged by the firm and A is the level of advertising expenditure, which is paid as a lump sum at the start of the year. If the firm's marginal production costs are $MC = 0.0015Q + 9$:

(a) Calculate the firm's profit-maximizing output, price and profit if the firm's annual advertising budget is zero and ignoring fixed costs.

(b) If the firm spends €50,000 per year on advertising, provide an estimate of the marginal revenue from spending an additional €1 on advertising.

(c) Estimate the firm's optimal intensity of advertising.

(d) Show the firm's output, price and profits ignoring all fixed costs except advertising.

13.2 A specialist firm advertises its product in a market by means of newspaper advertisements. The effectiveness of these advertisements in informing potential customers is given by the function $a = 5*(A^{1/3})/100$, where A is annual expenditure on advertising. Customers may buy more than one of the firm's products per year but turnover in the market, which we can represent with β, is 10 per cent a year. The size of the potential market remains constant, at N customers per year, as does A, but the foregoing implies that the number of potential customers informed each year, λN where $0 < \lambda < 1$, is increasing at a rate determined by the value of α and β. Demand is given by the function $Q = 2.5*\lambda N$. If $N = 10{,}000$ and the firm spends a constant €1,000 per year on advertising:

(a) How many potential customers will be informed in year two?

(b) Calculate the level of demand in the first year and year five.

(c) If the elasticity of demand with respect to advertising in the first year is 0.2, what is its long-run value in year five?

References

Becker, G. and Murphy, K. (1993) 'A simple theory of advertising as a good or bad', *Quarterly Journal of Economics*, vol. 108, pp. 941–964.

Chamberlin, E. (1933) *The Theory of Monopolistic Competition*, Harvard University Press, Cambridge, MA.

Christopher, M., Payne, A. and Ballantyne, D. (1991) *Relationship Marketing: Bringing Quality, Customer Service and Marketing Together*, Butterworth Heinemann, London.

Comanor, W. and Wilson, T. (1967) 'Advertising, market structure and performance', *Review of Economics and Statistics*, vol. 49, pp. 423–440.

Comanor, W. and Wilson, T. (1974) *Advertising and Market Power*, Harvard University Press, Cambridge MA.

Darby, M. and Karni, E. (1973) 'Free competition and the optimal amount of fraud', *Journal of Law and Economics*, vol. 16, pp. 67–68.

Dixit, A. and Stiglitz, J. (1977) 'Monopolistic competition and optimum product diversity', *American Economic Review*, vol. 67, pp. 293–308.

Dorfman, R. and Steiner, P. (1954) 'Optimal advertising and optimal quality', *American Economic Review*, vol. 44, pp. 826–836.

Doyle, P. (1968) 'Advertising expenditure and consumer demand', *Oxford Economic Papers*, vol. 20, pp. 395–417.

Geroski, P.A. and Murfin, A. (1991) 'Entry and industry evolution: the UK car industry 1958–83', *Applied Economics*, vol. 23, pp. 799–810.

Grabowski, H. and Vernon, J. (1992) 'Brand loyalty, entry and price competition in pharmaceuticals after 1984 Drug Act', *Journal of Law and Economics*, vol. 35, pp. 331–50.

Grossman, G. and Shapiro, C. (1984) 'Informative advertising with differentiated products', *Review of Economic Studies*, vol. 51, pp. 63–81.

Kaldor, N. (1950) 'The economic aspects of advertising,' *Review of Economic Studies*, vol. 18, pp. 1–27.

Kessides, N. (1991) 'Entry and market contestability: the evidence from the United States', *Entry and Market Contestability*, P. Geroski and J. Schwalbach (eds), Basil Blackwell, Oxford.

Kihlstrom, R. and Riordan, M. (1984) 'Advertising as a signal', *Journal of Political Economy*, vol. 92, pp. 427–450.

Lancaster, K.J. (1966) 'A new approach to demand theory', *Journal of Political Economy*, vol. 74, pp. 132–57.

Lancaster, K.J. (1979) *Variety, Equity and Efficiency*, Columbia University Press, New York.

Milgrom, P. and Roberts, J. (1986) 'Price and advertising signals of product quality', *Journal of Political Economy*, vol. 94, pp. 796–821.

Nelson, P. (1974) 'Advertising as information', *Journal of Political Economy*, vol. 82, pp. 729–754.

Nerlove, M. and Arrow, K. (1962) 'Optimal advertising policy under dynamic conditions', *Economica*, vol. 29, pp. 129–142.

Pepall, L., Richards, D. and Norman, G. (2005) *Industrial Organization: Contemporary Theory and Practice,* 3rd edn, Thomson-South Western, Ohio.

Perloff, J. and Salop, S. (1985) 'Equilibrium with product differentiation', *Review of Economic Studies*, vol. 52, pp. 107–120.

Rizzo, J. and Zeckhauser, R. (1990) 'Advertising and entry: the case of physician services', *Journal of Political Economy*, vol. 98, pp. 476–50.

Salop, S. (1979) 'Monopolistic competition with outside goods', *Bell Journal of Economics*, vol. 10, pp. 141–156.

Schmalensee, R. (1972) *The Economics of Advertising*, North Holland, Netherlands.

Schmalensee, R. (1976) 'Advertising and probability: further implications of the null hypothesis', *Journal of Industrial Economics*, vol. 25, pp. 45–54.

Schmalensee, R. (1989) 'Inter-industry studies of structure and performance' in *Handbook of Industrial Organizations*, vol. 2, in R. Schmalensee and R. Willig (eds), North Holland, Amsterdam.

Stigler, G. (1961) 'The economics of information', *Journal of Political Economy*, vol. 69, pp. 213–225.

Sutton, J. (1986) 'Vertical product differentiation: some basic themes', *American Economic Review*, vol. 72, pp. 393–399.

Sutton, J. (1991) *Sunk Costs and Market Structure*, MIT Press, Cambridge, MA.

Telser, L. (1964) 'Advertising and competition', *Journal of Political Economy*, vol. 72, pp. 537–562.

Tirole, J. (1993) *The Theory of Industrial Organization*, 6th edn, MIT Press, Cambridge, MA.

Veblen, T. (1934) *The Theory of the Leisure Class* (p. 87), The Modern Library, New York.

What are the relative gains for producers and consumers of advertising? The answer depends, very largely, on what happens to the price of the product. Consider Figure 13A.1, which represents a profit-maximizing monopolist.

Letting c represent (constant) marginal production costs, in the absence of advertising, the firm maximize profit at output Q_0, yielding price, p_0. To reduce congestion, the firm's marginal revenue curve is not shown, but at output Q_0, the firm earns a maximum rent equal to p_0JCB – ignoring fixed capital costs per period. Consumer welfare is measured by consumer surplus, which is equivalent to the area, p_0JZ. If now the firm spends A on advertising, unit costs increase to $c + a$, where $a = A/Q$, and demand shifts from D_0 to D_1, increasing the profit-maximizing output from Q_0 to Q_1. As the firm has

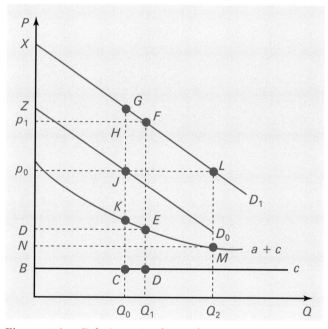

Figure 13A.1: Relative gains from advertising

spent a lump sum, A, on advertising, marginal costs remain constant at c and, again, marginal revenue is not shown. At output Q_1, price rises to p_1, generating a new rent of p_1FED, ignoring fixed capital costs. For the firm's owners any rise in profits is a welfare gain, which is equal to the increase in profit ($\Delta\pi$):

$$\Delta\pi = \Delta pQ_0 + p_1\Delta Q - c\Delta Q - A \tag{13A.1}$$

where $\Delta p = p_1 - p_0$ and $\Delta Q = Q_1 - Q_0$. What are the welfare effects for consumers? This is equivalent to the increase in consumers' surplus. The welfare for existing consumers is now equivalent to the area p_0JGX, less the area p_0JHp_1 (ie, $\Delta p Q_0$), which is transferred to the firm's owners. For new consumers, the gain in welfare is the area, FGH. Thus, after deducting the transfer to the firm's owners, the consumers' surplus amounts to the area, p_1FX, which may or may not be greater than the area, p_0JZ. Recalling that $\Delta p / \Delta Q$ is the slope of the inverse demand curve and the distance $p_1F = Q_0 + \Delta Q$, the gain in welfare ($\Delta\omega$) is given as:

$$\Delta\omega = \frac{1}{2}\frac{\Delta p}{\Delta Q}[Q_0 + \Delta Q]\,[Q_0 + \Delta Q] \tag{13A.2}$$

The total gain in welfare is then given by the sum of Equations (13A.1) and (13A.2). Recalling that $\Delta p = p_1 - p_0$ and dividing through by $[Q_0 + \Delta Q]$, we get:

$$\frac{\Delta\pi + \Delta\omega}{[Q_0 + \Delta Q]} = p_1 - \frac{p_0Q_0}{[Q_0 + \Delta Q]} - \frac{c\Delta Q}{[Q_0 + \Delta Q]} + \frac{1}{2}\frac{\Delta p}{\Delta Q}[Q_0 + \Delta Q] - \frac{A}{[Q_0 + \Delta Q]} \tag{13A.3}$$

The left-hand expression can be interpreted as an overall gain in welfare per unit of sales, if:

$$p_1 - \frac{p_0Q_0}{[Q_0 + \Delta Q]} - \frac{c\Delta Q}{[Q_0 + \Delta Q]} > \frac{A}{[Q_0 + \Delta Q]} - \frac{1}{2}\frac{\Delta p}{\Delta Q}[Q_0 + \Delta Q] \tag{13A.4}$$

As the second element on the right-hand side of this inequality will always be positive, an overall gain in welfare requires that the enhanced unit profit be greater than the unit cost of advertising less the gain in consumers' surplus. This result is based on some strong, simplifying assumption, not least that our firm is a profit-maximizing monopolist. If now we relax this assumption, the existence of rivals makes a price rise much less likely. Under oligopoly the likelihood of retaliation – in the absence of collusion – discourages price rises. In such markets, the purpose of advertising may be to protect market share by neutralizing the advertising by rivals. However, if market share does rise following an advertising campaign – or the market grows in size – this is represented by point L in Figure 13A.1, generating a total profit of p_0LMN for the firm and an increase in consumers' surplus for existing and new customers ($\Delta\omega$) equivalent to:

$$\Delta\omega = 1/2\,\frac{\Delta p}{\Delta Q}\left[Q_2 - Q_0\right]^2 \tag{13A.5}$$

CHAPTER 14

COMPETITIVE ADVANTAGE, INVENTION AND INNOVATION

Introduction

The underlying theme throughout this book has been efficiency. We have demonstrated the importance of **productive** and **allocative efficiency** and the importance of competition to the achievement of these goals. We have also shown the importance of profits and how the attempt to maximize **economic rents** is the driving force behind strategies designed to reduce costs, improve quality and deliver **competitive advantage**. But there is an alternative, or more correctly, a complementary view that firms engage in strategies to develop and maintain their resource capabilities over successive time periods in a search for new sources of economic rent. From this perspective strategies are focused on achieving **dynamic efficiency**. A key consideration for all firms when it comes to dynamic efficiency is the extent to which they can successfully introduce new products or processes or, to use the language of Chapter 5, new knowledge and **capabilities**. New products and more efficient ways of producing products represent **technical progress** and improving **living standards**.

In Chapter 5 more than any other chapter, we focused on the growth of the firm and the importance to this end, of enabling and encouraging new knowledge. We argued that for any organization to improve its position, indeed to remain viable, it needed an **organizational architecture** that encouraged entrepreneurial activity and the capabilities to persistently seek new sources of competitive advantage. Although Michael Porter is recognized as a major proponent of an alternative perspective on firm strategy – see Chapter 8 – he very forcibly makes the point (Porter, 1990) that competition is, '... dynamic and evolving ... constantly changing [the] landscape in which new products, new ways of marketing and new production processes and whole new market segments emerge' (p. 29). Porter's approach to competitive advantage owed much to Joseph Schumpeter, who more than 50 years earlier wrote that it was not price competition but, 'competition from the new commodity, the new technology, the new source of supply, the new type of organization ... competition that commands a decisive cost or quality advantage' (Schumpeter, 1942, p. 82).

For Schumpeter, competition was the ability of a firm to exploit opportunities for profit that other firms either ignored or were unable to exploit. Schumpeter was concerned to explain how and why firms developed new ways of doing things that generated new sources of value-adding activities. He represented this as an inherently disruptive process, whereby markets are characterized as switching between periods of calm, during which firms might be earning rents, and periods of turbulence when fundamental 'shocks' or 'discontinuities' destroy existing sources of competitive advantage and replace them with new ones. The **entrepreneurs** who perceive and have the ability to exploit the new opportunities these shocks create go on to generate economic rents in the ensuing period of calm. Schumpeter described this process as one of **creative destruction** and it had two important consequences: it revealed the superiority of dynamic efficiency over static efficiency – i.e. the achievement of long-term **growth** rather than the optimal allocation for society's resources at any one point in time – and also the importance of competition based on new products, new technologies or new organizations rather than the traditional focus on price competition.

As is made clear in the quote above, Schumpeter's concept of creative destruction applies equally to organizational architectures. An example of such a Schumpeterian creative destruction would be a lessening of the dominance of hierarchical governance structures in some sectors of a modern market economy and their replacement with flatter management structures. Command and control has in many firms given way to increased empowerment and autonomy for individuals and teams – particularly in industries dedicated to creative design and intellectual products. Intra-firm relationships have also changed. **Partnership alliances** and **joint ventures** are but two modern forms of intra-organizational relationships that have emerged to provide their participants with a source of competitive advantage. These internal and external organizational innovations have in common governance relationships that *ex post* create productive and transactional efficiencies capable of capturing additional market value.

This chapter focuses on the innovating firm within its strategic environment. It builds on the internal incentives to build knowledge and capabilities set out in some detail in Chapter 5 by concentrating on **investment** in new products and processes and the motivating forces of profits and competitive advantage. Here, the purpose is to understand how market structures, market shares and **patents** influence and motivate firms to devote resources to these activities. We seek to shed light on what constitutes success in the areas of new products and processes and how investment in such activities differs from investment in **fixed** and **human capital**. We further explore how the existence of more than one firm seeking competitive advantage from a new product or process influences the level of resources devoted to the activity by rivalrous firms and why greater co-operation in such activities is likely to improve dynamic efficiency. Most new products and processes – essentially new knowledge – have a social value that exceeds the private value. Sooner or later the new knowledge will be disseminated widely to the benefit of industry in general and society as a whole. Indeed, without diffusion, new knowledge would have little economic or social impact. A key issue is therefore the ability of firms that invest in new products or processes to appropriate the rewards of their endeavours. We will examine how effectively patents and licences balance the conflicting needs of innovating firms with the wider benefits of rapid diffusion. By reading this chapter, you will:

- Understand the contribution of new products and processes to economic progress, living standards and the competitive process.
- Appreciate how market structures augment internal forces to motivate investment in new knowledge and also influence the level of such investment.

- Be aware of the advantages and limitations of patents in the encouragement and diffusion of new knowledge.

This chapter is divided into five sections. In the first, we will examine the concept of competitive advantage from a Schumpeterian perspective; that is, the advantages inherent in new products or processes. For Schumpeter, the creation of competitive advantage was the outcome of a path-dependent stock of knowledge and capabilities built up in the search for new knowledge. In the second section, we focus on market structure and its influence on the incentive to invest in **research and development** (R&D) effort. This section introduces some basic economic models in order to demonstrate some key influences. The third section turns to strategic innovation behaviour in **oligopolistic** markets. It builds on the previous section and introduces a game theoretic approach to the issue of incentives under conditions of uncertainty and bounded rationality. In the fourth section, we consider the issue of patents and the diffusion of new knowledge. The main concern is the trade-off between the life and breadth of a patent and the social benefits of rapid diffusion. The last section returns to the issue of organizational architecture and its influence on technical progress. The section brings out the increasing importance of inter-firm collaborations in the area of R&D.

Competitive Advantage

Before analysing the relationship between innovation and competitive advantage it is critical to distinguish three steps or stages in the process by which new or superior knowledge permeates the marketplace. Schumpeter is credited with defining the classic trilogy that has informed and conditioned many of the debates on technological development: **Invention** – constitutes the first development of a new product or process; **Innovation** – describes the transformation of these new products or processes into marketable products or practical processes; and **Diffusion** – is concerned with the spread of the new knowledge to the economy, in general and beyond. The cumulative economic impact of all three stages is generally referred to as the process of **technological change**. The first two stages – invention and innovation – are typically carried out in private firms through a process that is normally described as R&D. A successful innovation is one that delivers not only a unique product or process to a firm, but also offers the prospect of the firm gaining profits and an advantage over its rivals. Moreover, the longer the period of diffusion is drawn out, the longer is likely to be the period over which the firm will enjoy the benefits of its advantage.

In a general sense, economists have always recognized the central importance of technological change. In the first chapter of his book, *The Wealth of Nations*, Adam Smith (1776) plunges immediately into a discussion of machinery improvements and how the **division of labour** promotes specialized inventions. Alfred Marshall (1890) had no hesitation in describing knowledge as the chief engine of progress. Yet, until the latter part of the twentieth century, technical progress had been an area of relative neglect for economists, due in part to the restrictive assumption of **neo-classical economics** that tended to view new knowledge as an **exogenous** variable. The neo-classical school focused on the short term, which by definition takes the technological environment as a given. There were exceptions, the best known of which was the Austrian school, and in this respect the most influential proponent is Joseph Schumpeter, who gave technical and organizational change a central place. Schumpeter, as we have seen in Chapter 5, always stressed the role of the entrepreneur in the invention–innovation process, but it was only in his later work that he recognized the internalization of much R&D activity within the firm.

If we refashion the Schumpeterian theory of profits and growth through innovation into contemporary language, then he contended that innovation relies on the creation of a technological capability through learning and problem solving. As discussed in Chapter 5, the development of new products and processes is a path-dependent outcome that builds upon established capabilities. Hence, for Schumpeter, innovation must be understood as a continuous learning process and not as a discrete event which gives rise to a flash of entrepreneurial insight. This approach to innovation is very much in accord with Penrose's (1959) theory and growth of the firm, as well as Nelson and Winter's (1982) *evolutionary theory* of economic change. For Schumpeter, a successful innovation might confer a quasi-*monopoly* position on firms enjoying *first-mover advantage*, but the incentive to engage in R&D comes from competition or rivalry in the classic sense; namely, the recognition by firms that survivability depends on a better ability than rivals to assimilate new learning and take advantage of a new market opportunity. The fact that, for Schumpeter, path dependency implies that the sources of innovation were increasingly concentrated in large firms – an hypothesis we will qualify below – does not mean that only firms with market power are the drivers of technological progress and it should be set alongside Schumpeter's belief that successful innovation rendered existing monopoly power ineffective.

The Schumpeterian idea that competitive advantage is an evolutionary process has also been advanced by Michael Porter (1985). His thesis is that firms gain competitive advantage by altering the basis of competition and that technological change is a key influence on the nature of competition. Porter points out that technology is embodied not only in the production of the firm's products but also in its support activities as captured by his concept of the *value chain* and, like Schumpeter, is manifested in the firm's relative *production* costs or the extent of *product differentiation*. Porter's observation that technological change by altering the degree of substitution can alter the boundaries of an industry and reduce entry barriers is as Schumpeterian as one can get. Thus, both Schumpeter and Porter view technological change and competitive advantage not as a permanent state, but rather as dynamic processes where winners and losers constantly emerge. Both believe that in this environment competitive advantage may be sustained for a longer period if firms invest in improved or new sources of advantage, but that sooner or later this position will be threatened by technological change. From this perspective, competitive advantage does not lie in the ability to charge the lowest price for a good or service, but rather arises from an ability to do something that rivals find impossible – at least for a time – to imitate.

There are therefore two approaches to understanding the relationship between innovation and competitive advantage. The view here is that the two approaches are largely complementary but reflect subtle differences in emphasis. One is grounded in the neo-classical tradition, whereby the effect of a successful innovation is analysed in terms of price, quantities and economic rents. Economic rents derive from positions of market power since in perfectly competitive markets economic rents are driven to zero. Thus, in the traditional setting of prices and quantities, a successful innovation, by conferring quasi-monopoly power, also confers opportunity to maximize economic rents. This approach allows innovation to be analysed within the paradigm of productive and allocative efficiency and comparative equilibrium states. The alternative approach is based on the Schumpeter concept of creative destruction. From this perspective, economic rents derive not from a position of market power *per se*, but from the value added inherent in the creation of new fields of economic activity. This approach focused on the way in which firms organize and manage the process of innovation inside the firm. It is concerned to understand how they identify new opportunities and organize effectively and efficiently to create and capture the inherent value.

This approach to firms as, *in primis*, structures to accumulate competencies, as discussed in Chapter 5, is very much at the heart of the **competency approach** to the firm. The competency approach can be traced back to Penrose (1959), who viewed firms as placing the primary emphasis on the internal accumulation of knowledge and skills. In contrast, the **governance approach** places the emphasis on efficient co-ordination through hierarchies to deal with **principal–agent problems**. In this respect, the governance perspective is aligned with the Schumpeter–Penrose perspective; new organizational forms are part of the creative process. Where they differ is in the latter's emphasis on firms as being engaged in a continual process of seeking new rent-earning activities, an incessant process that leads sooner or later to change. It is this notion of a firm, whose organizational architecture supports not only productive activity but also the capabilities or competencies to persistently seek and adapt to new sources of value, that has been described by Teece *et al.* (1997) as **dynamic capabilities**. Teece *et al.* argue that over the longer term successful firms are those that can demonstrate timely responsiveness and rapid flexible product innovation coupled with the management capability to effectively co-ordinate and redeploy internal and external competencies. Teece *et al.* view these dynamic capabilities as new forms of competitive advantage. The term dynamic refers to the capacity to renew competencies, including the ability to innovate in response to a changing business environment.

The creation of capabilities to anticipate and meet the challenge of change is the hallmark of the dynamic capabilities school, which is taken here as a sub-group of the competency approach to the firm. It may be that an innovating firm has a degree of market power, but from a competency perspective this is not the source of the new value, but rather the coincidental by-product. This approach to understanding technological change is very much what Nelson and Winter (1982) had in mind when they described the process of innovation as a search for economic rents, not within the standard neoclassical framework, but within the context of experimentation. We need to be clear not to interpret the foregoing as implying that all firms are constantly innovating; indeed, many firms do not appear to innovate at all. Where firms do have a history of innovation, very few do so persistently (Geroski, 1990). Rather, the process of seeking and accumulating new knowledge should be separated from the decision by a firm to exploit the new knowledge with an innovation. When we discuss patents below, we will also consider why firms may delay or speed up an innovation. What we do know, as observed in Chapter 5, is that the growth of firms follows a **random walk** and this is consistent with an erratic pattern of innovative activity.

The neo-classical paradigm with its assumption of **perfect competition**, including **perfect information**, cannot explain inventions. This is because in a world of perfect information there would be no return on the invention of a new process or product. All agents in the market would immediately adopt the new process or product and hence all economic rents would be rapidly competed away. As perfectly competitive markets, in which imitation of a new product or process is assumed to be instantaneous and widespread, do not exist in practice, we must confine our attention to imperfectly competitive markets if we are to understand the factors that motivate R&D expenditure. Induced invention – as opposed to spontaneous invention arising out of human inquisitiveness – is, as discussed above, promoted by the prospect of financial reward. A more realistic approach to investment in R&D is therefore to recognize that in a world of **bounded rationality** and **incomplete information**, it is possible for a firm to gain advantage from a new process or product. In the case of the former, this might be achieved by keeping the details secret. Where secrecy is not possible – say in the case of a new product – the inventor of an original product or process can be granted a patent. The patent system operates by assigning to the inventor a **property right** on the new knowledge for a limited number of years. We will return to the issue of patents below.

Whereas the neo-classical assumption of profit-maximization assumes agents are **hyper-rational** in the sense that they can foresee the outcomes of their actions, those engaged in innovative search for new sources of rents are necessarily subject to bounded rationality. Since knowledge is open-ended it can never become a routine process. Innovation will always involve search, the outcome of which can never be fully anticipated or factored into prices and quantities. In this respect, innovation, and the growth it begets to the firm are distinct from the issues addressed by neo-classical theory. Innovation is a process of rent-seeking rather than rent-maximizing behaviour. Maximum profits better describes the profits that arise from the efficient allocation and use of a firm's existing resources at a point in time and with a given technology. But over the longer term, profits from innovation are more important (Cantwell, 2002). As observed above, whether or not these profits occur to firms with market power is not the issue, but there is an analogy with the cycles of innovation within large, successful firms in which knowledge becomes codified and as it does so it creates the basis for a new round of evolution and learning (Nelson and Winter, 1982).

The defining characteristic of a modern, market economy is change. Technological and organizational innovations are the drivers of change and the pay-off for society is rising living standards and thereby hopefully increasing welfare. Over time, expenditure on R&D, by bringing both new and better products to the market, or existing products at lower **real prices**, is a necessary condition if a country's population is to enjoy a rising standard of living. It is a necessary, but not sufficient condition because this simplified materialistic view of living standards ignores the costs of natural resource depletion and pollution. The fact that throughout the developed and developing world living standards – including the quality of life – are steadily rising is due ultimately to R&D in both the private and public sectors. Although universities and governments spend large sums on R&D, the contribution of profit-orientated firms to the development of new technologies and organizational innovations should not be underestimated. Figure 14.1 summarizes the process by which research and development is transferred to rising living standards.

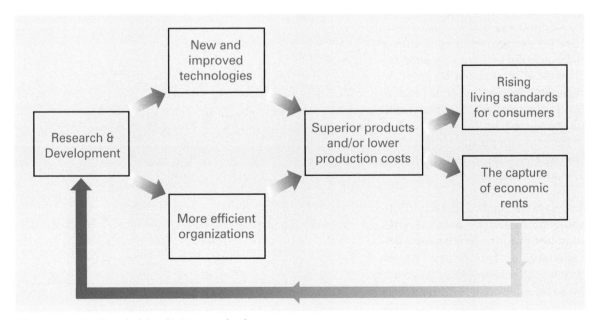

Figure 14.1: R&D and rising living standards

Our focus here is the **supply side** and the motivating forces that lie behind R&D. As implied by Figure 14.1, the pay-off will be in the form of economic rents and strategic advantage. Whether these rents arise from the emergence of a new product or a more efficient process, if we think of the firm as operating in isolation the profit incentive can, in the words of Katz and Shapiro (1987), be regarded as the *stand-alone* incentive. The second incentive, as discussed above, is relevant when, as is generally the case, the firm has to compete with rivals for market share. In this environment firms engage in R&D to deepen and broaden their capabilities and thereby to give themselves a strategic or competitive advantage.

We can demonstrate the impact of advances in knowledge for the firm with the aid of an **isoquant** diagram. Once we have entered Schumpeter's *period of calm*, we can think of an industry as using the new technology. The older technology will have been superseded by the new, technically more efficient technology, whereby the industry's products, assumed here to be homogeneous, can now be produced using a smaller or lower-cost bundle of resources. In practice, some firms will continue to use the older, technically less efficient process – in the sense that they utilize more factors of production than the new technology – but in a competitive market such inefficiency must be compensated for by low wages and/or low profits. Figure 14.2 represents the technological position of an industry with the isoquant Q_0, which shows the technically efficient frontier of all possible techniques – represented by the inputs, x and y – that could be employed by individual firms to produce Q_0 using the prevailing technology. The points lying above the isoquant represent bundles of resources that would produce the output Q_0 but are defined to be inefficient. This may result from the continued use of the older technology or the inefficient use of the current technology, i.e. the outcome of organizational routines that result in the under-utilization of the firm's resources. In the neo-classical paradigm, these inefficiencies will not be tolerated as the assumption of perfect information and super-rationality will result in a rapid convergence to the point of efficiency. That is, firms will adopt the techniques and supporting organizational structures that not only place them on the isoquant, but also they will be concentrated at the point of highest efficiency. As briefly discussed in Chapter 2, given the relative prices of the factor inputs, x and y – providing they are determined in competitive markets – the point of economic efficiency is represented by point A, where the **isocost line** C_0 is tangential to the isoquant, Q_0. In a world characterized by incomplete and asymmetric information, the period over which firms converge to point A could be lengthy.

In a dynamic context, the equilibrium represented by point A will only last until the next technological change in the industry. Sooner or later the current technology will be superseded with the emergence of a new, or variant, technology. The dynamic process of technological

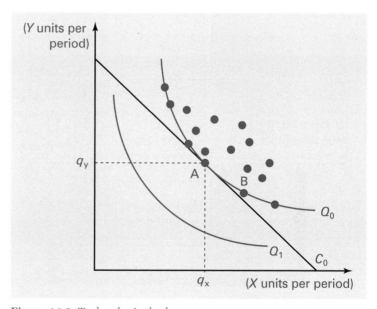

Figure 14.2: Technological advance

advance is represented, in Figure 14.2, as shifting the isoquant towards the origin as represented by the isoquant, Q_1. However, in this instance the level of output represented by Q_1 is identical to the previous level of output, i.e. $Q_1 = Q_0$. In this example, the pay-off to the innovation is the same volume of output for a reduced volume of inputs, i.e. a rise in **total factor productivity**. An alternative perspective on technological change is to view it as resulting in a change in the relative prices of x and y. Say x becomes cheaper owing to a new technology. The effect would be, *ceteris paribus*, to shift the **short-run equilibrium** from point A to point B. Not so easily shown in diagrammatic form is the alternative outcome of an innovation; namely, a higher-quality product. Either way, if an individual firm can secure one of these improvements in advance of its rivals it can choose how it will exercise its competitive advantage by adjusting prices or levels of output. When Schumpeter spoke of the superiority of dynamic efficiency, it was the productivity performance (i.e. output per unit of input) represented by the move from Q_0 to Q_1 that he had in mind. The profitability of such movements depends on firms being willing to invest in ever-more efficient ways of producing goods and services.

Recording a Competitive Advantage

An excellent example of the link between competitive advantage and research and development was the development and successful exploitation of the video cassette recorder (VCR) by the Victor Corporation of Japan (JVC). The attempt to develop a commercially successful VCR goes back to the early 1960s, when the American-based Ampex Corporation invented video tape. Over the next 25 years many firms attempted to exploit this new technology and, although American and European firms at first led the way, in the latter stages they were forced to give way to JVC's Video Home System (VHS) and the rest, as they say, is history. JVC's success no doubt owed something to luck but it also reflected a longer-term belief in the VCR and a commitment to making it commercially viable. The Japanese success was not based on imitation, but involved a whole series of product and process innovations. JVC achieved competitive advantage when Philips was forced to give way, and licenced the VHS technology in 1985.

The VHS system was said to be technically inferior to another Japanese standard – Sony's BETAMAX system – but JVC's system won out because of its superior sales and distribution system and the alliances JVC had forged with European and American companies. By securing a large share of the market, the VHS system created a lock-in just as had the much earlier technology involving the less than optimal QWERTY system of typewriters. The success of the VHS system therefore serves to remind us that not only is it necessary to anticipate an unmet consumer need by investing in the development of technologies to meet that need; but also the new product must be carefully marketed and its market position secured by the exploitation of an extensive network of outlets, by economies of scale and eventually by the learning inherent in producing large volumes. Despite all this, it should not be overlooked that the success of the VHS system also depended upon very complex, precision engineering and even when production of VCRs was transferred to cheaper locations in the 1980s and the 1990s the precision machinery was still supplied from Japan.

Market Structure and Pay-off

In the previous section, we categorized the competency school's approach to the process of innovation as a search for economic rents, that is only coincidentally related to the innovating firm's degree of market power. In this section, we will explore this issue more formally. It may not be strictly correct to ascribe to Schumpeter the view that large firms with market power better serve society in the long run because they have both the means and the incentive to invest in R&D, but what is of interest is whether firms with monopoly power have a greater incentive to engage in innovative activity than a firm operating in a competitive market. If a **monopolist** has a much greater incentive to invest in innovation, then it is possible that in a dynamic analysis monopoly improves overall welfare. We can test the hypothesis that a monopolist has a greater incentive to engage in innovation by resort to Kenneth Arrow's (1962) classic paper that sought to establish the reverse proposition; namely, that more competitive environments give a greater incentive to innovate.

We can start our analysis with the simplifying assumption that the technology employed in the industry delivers constant returns to scale. Say this industry is served by a monopolist who faces the inverse demand curve shown in Figure 14.3 and whose unit costs are represented by $LRAC_0$. The profit-maximizing monopolist would set output equal to Q_0 (where $LRAC_0 = LRMC_0 = MR$) and economic rent would be equal to the area, p_0ABp_2. Following the spirit of Schumpeter's *creative destruction*, we will assume the monopolist discovers new knowledge that leads to a **drastic innovation** in the production process. Process innovation can be conceptually separated into non-drastic or minor innovation and into drastic or major innovations. In broad terms a drastic process innovation is one that reduces the firm's unit costs to such an extent that even if it charges the profit-maximizing monopoly price associated with the new marginal cost of production, it will under-price the competitive price that would have been charged under competition. Hence, a drastic process innovation

creates a monopolist who is unconstrained by any fear of entry – at least in the short run. The effect of this drastic innovation is to reduce long-run average costs from $LRAC_0$ to $LRAC_1$. Following the drastic process innovation, the monopolist's output rises to Q_1 and despite the lower market price of p_1, economic rent rises to p_1CDE.

For a monopolist, the **opportunity cost** of gaining the economic rent represented by the area p1CDE is the economic rent represented by the area, p_0ABp_2. If we let R represent the research cost of inventing the new process – and again to simplify matters we will assume that R was spent in one go at the start

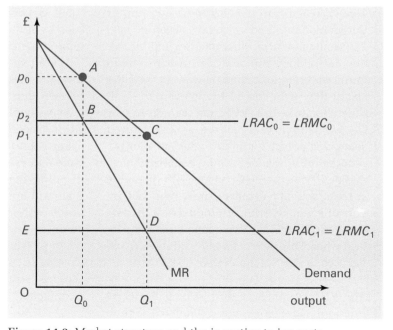

Figure 14.3: Market structure and the incentive to innovate

of the current period, t, and that there is only one further period of pay-off, then the incentive for the monopolist to innovate is given by the present value of the net cash flow for the following two-period model:

$$PV = \left[\frac{p1CDE_{t+1}}{(1+r)} - \frac{p0ABp_{2t+1}}{(1+r)} - R_t \right] \tag{14.1}$$

Providing PV is positive, the monopolist has an incentive to innovate. In practice, the monopolist might reasonably expect to earn rents from the process innovation over a number of future periods, particularly if the invention is protected by a patent, hence equation (14.1) should be rewritten as:

$$PV = -R_t + \sum_{i=1}^{n} [p_1CDE_{t+1} - p_0ABp_{2t+1}]/(1+r)^i \tag{14.2}$$

Now consider the situation if the market is competitive; that is, its structure consists of many firms but the neo-classical assumption of perfect information is lacking. As $LRAC_0$ for all firms is equal and economic rents are competed to zero, the price charged by all firms will be p_2. Arrow argued that if one firm in the industry now invents a new process that amounts to a drastic innovation, it can patent the invention and licence it to all the other firms in the industry. If the inventing firm exploits its invention to the full, it can gain p_1CDE in licence fees. That is, $LRAC$ for competitive firms, incorporating the licence fee, falls to p_1 – where p_1CDE is the licence fee. Note that the patent holder must adopt a **two-part tariff** and charge a lump sum rather than a royalty per unit of output. As $p_1CDE >$ $[p_1CDE - p_0ABp_2]$, Arrow concludes that competitive markets provide a greater incentive to innovate. Another perspective on this conclusion, is that the smaller firm (or new entrant) can replace the monopolist, but the monopolist can only replace itself: consequently, Arrow's insight is often called the **replacement effect**.

Once we depart from the assumption of a monopoly, or what Katz and Shapiro (1987) refer to as the *stand-alone* incentive for innovation, we can focus on what we described above as the alternative incentive. Where a firm competes with rivals for market share they are likely to engage in R&D activity as part of the process of strategic interaction. This perspective on R&D activity is closer to the Schumpeter–Penrose spirit, whereby firms seek new knowledge and capabilities as an explicit part of their strategy. If a firm knows, or believes, that a rival is engaging in R&D activity, then its own competitive position is under threat and the fear of losing out to a rival is likely to be a significant influence on its behaviour. This competitive threat, generally referred to as the replacement effect, is measured in an oligopolistic market as the difference between the pay-off for a successful innovation and the pay-off (i.e. loss) if the firm loses out to a rival. The cost of losing out to a rival is likely to be large – in the extreme it could mean being 'replaced' by a victorious rival.

We can begin our analysis of the strategic interaction between oligopolists in the area of R&D with a relatively simple, static, i.e. one-period, model where rivals make simultaneous decisions about the level of R&D expenditure. The following model is based on Dasgupta and Stiglitz (1980), which despite its simplicity provides some key insights. Decisions within the model are based on a **Nash–Cournot** approach, which we discussed in Chapter 9, and by reducing the complexity we can better focus on R&D expenditure as a strategic weapon. Dasgupta and Stiglitz assume an industry comprised of n identical firms, producing an homogeneous output. In each period, the rival firms must make a decision regarding the level of R&D expenditure. We demonstrated in Chapter 9 that the profit-maximizing equilibrium for an oligopolist occurs where the profit margin equals the inverse of the market's price elasticity of demand multiplied by the individual firm's market share. If each firm has an identical market share, we can represent the profit-maximizing outcome as:

$$\frac{p-c}{p} = \frac{1}{n\varepsilon_{pQ}} \tag{14.3}$$

where ε_{pQ} is the market demand **price elasticity of demand**. Equation (14.3) does not tell us how much R&D expenditure each firm will find optimal. To determine this, we must find a way of incorporating the situation when individual firms engage in R&D expenditure. To simplify matters we will assume all firms have the same constant unit variable costs, and with the exception of R&D expenditure we will ignore fixed costs (including normal profits). The profit equation for the individual firm is then given by:

$$\pi_i = [p(Q) - c]q_i - R_i \tag{14.4}$$

where π_i is the economic rent, for the ith firm, p is the market price, which is determined by total supply Q, c is the unit variable cost, q_i is the quantity produced and R_i is the R&D expenditure. In practice the firm's variable costs, $c(q_i)$, are likely to be inversely related to the amount spent on R&D, i.e. $c(q_i R_i)$. For the individual firm, given the assumption of constant unit costs, we can rewrite Equation (14.4) so that:

$$\pi_I = [p(Q) - c(R_i)]q_i - R_i \tag{14.5}$$

Returning to our assumption of common, constant unit costs, summing for all firms in the industry and assuming that free entry will drive economic rents to zero we have:

$$0 = [p - c]Q - nR \tag{14.6}$$

where $Q = \Sigma q_i$ and n the number of firms in the industry. By rearranging Equation (14.6) and dividing through by pQ, we arrive at:

$$\frac{p-c}{p} = \frac{nR}{pQ} \tag{14.7}$$

We can interpret the right-hand side of Equation (14.7) as the intensity of R&D expenditure. Combining Equation (14.3) with Equation (14.7) gives:

$$\frac{nR}{pQ} = \frac{1}{n\varepsilon_{pQ}} \tag{14.8}$$

which tells us that the industry's profit-maximizing optimum expenditure on R&D is inversely related to the market's price elasticity of demand multiplied by the number of firms. From Equation (14.8) we can draw an important conclusion; namely, if the number of firms rises, the R&D expenditure per firm must fall to satisfy Equation (14.8) and so the unit cost of production will be higher. A second insight, going back to Equation (14.3), is that with more firms the price–cost margin will be lower. We know from the **Cournot model** that an increase in the number of firms increases the industry's total output, but reduces the profit-maximizing output for each firm. The net effect for society is higher output and lower prices, which raises a question about the contribution of R&D to social welfare. It should further be noted from Equation (14.8) that as individual firms reduce R&D expenditure in response to rising numbers, it does not follow that total industry expenditure, nR, will fall. Dasgupta and Stiglitz show that aggregate spending on R&D might actually rise if the price elasticity of market demand is sufficiently large. This follows because a large elasticity of demand implies that an increase in industry output will not depress the price too much or, more formally, the reduction in marginal revenue will not be too large.

In practice, given a linear demand curve, we know that price elasticity will decline as output increases. This implies that total R&D spending is more likely to decline as the number of firms increases. At this level of simplicity, we can take the Dasgupta and Stiglitz model as tending to support the popular interpretation of the Schumpeterian–Penrosian hypothesis that industry concentration fosters innovation. As ever, we must guard against the possibility that the simplifying assumptions have biased the outcome. There are at least three questions that are raised by the assumptions set out above. The first is the assumption that R&D expenditure is only indirectly rivalrous. We might expect in oligopolistic markets that a rival's expenditure on R&D will enter into the decision variables when considering the amount to spend on R&D – that is, the ith firm's expenditure will to some extent be a function of the jth firm's expenditure, i.e. $R_i = f(R_j)$. Secondly, the assumption that free entry drives economic rents to zero implies a long-run, not a one-period, model. Once we allow for a dynamic perspective, we turn to the longer-term benefits of investment in knowledge and the advantages this is likely to confer in situations of strategic interaction. A third consideration is the assumption that R&D expenditure equates to success, i.e. true innovations. In practice, this may not be the case.

We can measure innovative effort by calculating the ratio of R&D spending to total sales, but this is not the same as measuring the efficiency of such expenditure. In a one-period analysis we would expect the effectiveness of R&D expenditure to be subject to **diminishing returns** and in practice the value of any innovation will depend partly on how efficiently the firm is organized to create and capture the benefits and partly on luck, i.e. there will be a stochastic element. Finally, the Dasgupta–Stiglitz model assumed demand remained constant, but this implies that R&D expenditure has no impact on demand. As we demonstrated when considering Dorfmann and Steiner's (1954) model in the previous chapter, expenditure on advertising is designed to increase demand and it is a reasonable assumption that expenditure to improve product quality will also increase demand and, like advertising, at a diminishing rate. On this reasoning, the quantity sold by the ith firm holding price constant will be a positive function of the level of expenditure, R, devoted to product innovation, i.e. $q_i = f(p_i, R_i)$.

The foregoing suggests that the Dasgupta–Stiglitz theoretical conclusions are not sufficient to resolve the question as to whether there is an inverse relationship between the number of firms in an industry and the level of R&D intensity. Unfortunately, empirical studies are less than convincing. At best it appears that R&D intensity increases with industry concentration, but only up to a modest level before levelling off. This was the conclusion of one of the first studies exploring the link between industry structure and R&D intensity that was undertaken by Scherer (1965) and subsequent studies have tended to confirm his findings (see, for example, Geroski, 1990; Blundell *et al.*, 1995), though we will return to this issue below. Scherer focused on the output of patented innovations, but it is possible that some process innovations are kept secret by the inventing firm for reasons we will explore below.

Innovation or Imitation?

Perhaps inevitably given its dominant position, public opinion appears divided on the fining of Microsoft by the European Commission. One view sees Microsoft as guilty of improving its products so successfully that rivals find it very difficult to compete. But improving products is the very essence of economic progress and rising living standards.

The alternative view claims that Microsoft is an imitator rather than an innovator. Excel, the Microsoft spreadsheet, is an imitation of Lotus 123, which in turn was an imitation of VisiCalc. Microsoft's Word was introduced into the market long after several other popular word processing products and Microsoft's PowerPoint imitated programs such as Harvard Graphics and Freeland. And, having achieved a position of dominance, Microsoft used its wealth to buy itself into the relational database market, where it was a late entrant.

Today Microsoft so completely dominates these software programs that few would consider funding R&D programmes in an effort to dislodge Microsoft. What is beyond doubt is that Microsoft is a very successful company whether or not it owes its position to imitation or innovation.

Strategic Innovation Behaviour

The Dasgupta–Stiglitz model outlined in the previous section was an attempt to get closer to the Schumpeterian–Penrosian paradigm by making R&D expenditure an explicit part of a firm's strategy. But the model lacked a very important feature of strategic rivalry; namely, under ***imperfect competition***, particularly in oligopolistic markets, innovation has both winners and losers. From this perspective, innovation might be thought of as a race, a race that has the added complication of uncertainty. For an individual firm operating under imperfect competition, there are three complications that must enter the calculation when considering investment in R&D as opposed to investment in, say, fixed capital. Firstly, investment in R&D must be set against the expected stream of returns in the years ahead. These returns will have a much higher degree of uncertainty than would normally be the case for investment in additions to existing plant, buildings and machines. Secondly, achieving a successful invention is not certain; despite expenditure on R&D there will be a probability of failure. Thirdly, a number of firms are likely simultaneously to be investing in a search for the same invention, giving rise to the added risk that another firm will be first and consequently the pay-off to the firms coming second will be less than expected and may even be negative.

Faced with these uncertainties, one strategy is to spend more on R&D in the expectation that the higher the expenditure in the current period, the greater the probability of not only obtaining the invention but also being first. This raises the question of the source of funds and suggests that firms with '***deep pockets***' would have greater access to funds for such high-risk strategies and by spending more would improve their chances of winning the race to invent first. But even if a firm has the resources to commit large sums to R&D, the date of the invention – one, two, three or more years into the future – will be stochastic, making present value calculations extremely difficult. Moreover, the existence of venture capitalists can offset much of the disadvantage inherent in small scale when funding areas of new technology.

We can represent the foregoing as a game. Let us assume that the firms are 'racing' to develop a new product. The gain to the firm that is first with the invention can be represented as the present value of the stream of profits generated by the new product over its life. For the winner, the present value of the profit stream will be the present value of the net cash flow over the product's life, less the expenditure on R&D. We will make the not-unreasonable assumption that the probability of a successful innovation is proportional to the level of expenditure on R&D, i.e. as set out above, the firm improves its probability of winning if it spends more on R&D. Much now depends on the behaviour of rivals. Rivals will also increase their probability of success if they increase their expenditure on R&D. We can demonstrate the essence of this situation by defining just two strategies for an individual firm: a high expenditure strategy; and a low expenditure strategy. To simplify matters, let us assume that the industry is a **duopoly**: firm A and firm B. The expected pay-off of a high expenditure strategy to firm A would then be:

$$E(PV)_A = (1 - \lambda)[\rho(\frac{CF_A}{r} - R_A)] + \lambda[(1 - \rho)(-R_A)] \tag{14.9}$$

where $E(PV)$ is the present value of the expected profits, CF_A/r is the present value of an infinite annual net cash flow at the date of discovery, R_A is firm A's expenditure on R&D – assumed to be a one-off payment at the start of the process – and ρ is the probability of achieving the invention, where $0 < \rho \le 1$. In addition to the probability of achieving the invention there is also the probability of winning the race. Whether or not firm A wins the race depends on the level of expenditure by firm B. Firm B increases its probability of winning the race λ, where $0 < \lambda \le 1$, by also spending more on R&D and therefore firm A faces the additional probability, λ, of receiving a negative return, i.e. $-R_A$. By similar reasoning, the alternative low-expenditure strategy can be represented as:

$$E(PV)_A = (1 - \lambda)[\rho(\frac{CF_A}{r} - \alpha R_A)] - \lambda[(1 - \rho)(-\alpha R_A)] \tag{14.10}$$

We have represented the low-expenditure strategy as αR_A, where $0 < \alpha < 1$. By assumption, there is a positive relationship between ρ and α and if spending less on R&D delays the date of discovery, then the net present value of $CF_A - \alpha R_A$ will be proportionally reduced. The outcome of the foregoing can be demonstrated in the normal form game shown in Figure 14.4.

Figure 14.4 presents only the pay-offs to firm A – i.e. the game is assumed to be a **zero-sum game** – in order to reduce complexity. The pay-offs arising from the probabilities set out in Equations (14.9) and (14.10) are obviously only illustrative but consistent. The top row of the matrix reflects Equation (14.9) above and the second row Equation (14.10). As can be seen, a non-cooperative Nash equilibrium solution will result in both firms devoting high levels of spending to R&D and as implied in the matrix, spending for both is too high relative to the likely pay-off. If both firms were prepared to cooperate and spend less on R&D, the expected pay-off is shown as lower than both spending highly, i.e. $E(\beta\pi) < E(\pi)$, but this largely reflects an expected longer period before the innovation comes to the market and the longer the payback period, the closer β will be to unity. In essence, what the game set out in Figure 14.4 implies is that if the firms were prepared to invest co-operatively in R&D, the solution would be to both spend less on R&D.

The foregoing makes clear the strategic element of timing in the face of technological uncertainty. The situation described is normally referred to as a **tournament model** because the game has a winner and loser and carries the implication that the innovation can be effectively protected. The model differs

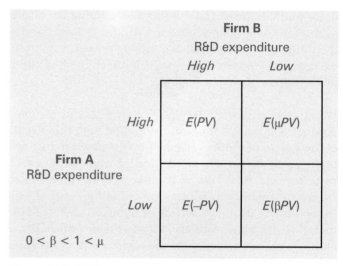

Figure 14.4: R&D as a game

from the Dasgupta–Stiglitz model in that it allows for asymmetry between the players – both in terms of the pay-off to the winning firm and the probability of success – and the relationship between R&D expenditure and success is stochastic. Before examining these asymmetries in a little more detail, we will demonstrate the efficiency advantages of co-operation. To simplify matters, we treat expenditure on R&D as an up-front payment. More realistically, expenditure on R&D is likely to be a flow per period and the probability that the firm successfully innovates first is a positive function of the flow rate of R&D expenditure. This conditional probability is called the **hazard rate** in the innovation literature. As discussed in the first section of this chapter, one reason for asymmetries is accumulated knowledge and capabilities that are path dependent. For the moment we will put this complication to one side, i.e. we will assume there is no accumulated knowledge and therefore each firm's accumulation of knowledge depends on the flow rate of R&D expenditure chosen. By treating R&D expenditure as a flow, it allows for game theoretic interactions, whereby firms increase or reduce their R&D expenditure depending on their **conjectural variations** regarding their rivals' expenditure and likelihood of success. Equation (14.9) therefore becomes:

$$E(PV)_A = (1 - \lambda)[\rho(\frac{CF_A}{r} - \frac{[1 + (1 + v)]R_A}{r})] + \lambda(1 - \rho)\frac{-[1 + 1 + v)]R_A}{r} \tag{14.11}$$

where ρ is a positive function of R_A, i.e. $\rho = f(R_A)$, and firm B's probability of success is a function of its expenditure on R&D, i.e. $\lambda = f(R_B)$ and v is the conjectural variation, i.e. $v = (R_A/R_B)(\Delta R_B/\Delta R_A)$.

We can interpret Equation (14.11) as firm A's **reaction function**, which is illustrated in Figure 14.5. As a monopolist, firm A spends R_0 on R&D and as there are no rivals this delivers the highest expected pay-off. When firm B enters the market, it observes A's expenditure of R_0 and on this basis B reacts by spending R_1 on R&D. A, observing B's expenditure of R_1, now increases its own expenditure to R_2 and B, observing A's behaviour, increases its level of expenditure to R_3 and so on until the **non-cooperative equilibrium** is arrived at at point E. Point E in Figure 14.5 equates to the high-expenditure non-cooperative **Nash equilibrium** as previously described. It will be recalled that the expected value of the pay-off is decreasing as we move out along the reaction functions and the expected pay-off is represented by the *isoprofit curves*. As can be seen for both firms a co-operative outcome is shown at point *F*, which lies on higher isoprofit curves for both firms. Thus, again, we have established that in the absence of co-operation firms have a tendency to spend too much on R&D.

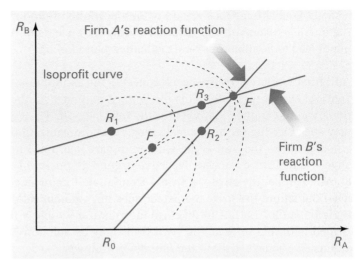

Figure 14.5: R&D expenditure reaction functions

In order to simplify matters we have so far dealt with only two firms. As the number of firms increases so does the likelihood of an early invention by one of the firms. In terms of the foregoing analysis, the probability of being first declines and with this lower probability the expected pay-offs. Consequently, in calculating the lower expected pay-off, firms are likely to modify their R&D expenditure as indicated by the Dasgupta–Stiglitz model. On the basis of the foregoing, we can identify four significant factors that combine to determine which firm has a strategic advantage. First, firms will differ in their valuation of the innovation. Second, they may have different rates of discount. Third, the efficiency by which they perform the research will vary and, finally, firms will differ in their accumulated knowledge.

What does all this have to say for the influence of market structure and firm size on the incentive to invest in R&D? The profit incentive and the competitive threat will depend on a firm's current market position. A firm's current market position, *ceteris paribus*, influences its current profit flow and even if it is the market leader, if it loses the innovation race it could find itself dislodged. All this suggests, *à la* Schumpeter, that the larger the firm, the greater the incentive to innovate; but this may not necessarily be the case. Beath *et al.* (1989) show that the incentive depends on whether imitation is easy or difficult. The reaction functions shown in Figure 14.5 imply that imitation is difficult and hence the competitive threat outweighs the profit threat. However, if imitation is easy it could, in the extreme, result in negatively shaped reaction functions. Another perspective on the current market leader's incentive to invest in R&D is provided by Scherer and Ross (1990), who observe that there is abundant evidence to support the view that actual and potential new entrants play a crucial role in stimulating technical progress, both as direct sources of innovation and as a spur to existing industry members. Scherer and Ross go on to point out that new entrants contribute a disproportionately high share of all really revolutionary new industrial products and processes.

Before leaving the issue of strategic R&D expenditure, we should draw a distinction between process and product innovation. In the case of a process innovation, we might expect success to be determined by the most cost-efficient technology, but when it comes to product innovation matters are more complicated. If we return to the concept of **vertically differentiated** goods introduced in the previous chapter, we can envisage a sequence whereby a firm builds up successively higher quality goods so that it can better target the *addresses* of different consumer groups within the product space. This complicates matters because we now have to deal with a portfolio of products rather than a single innovation. Once we allow for a portfolio of products, then it is possible, indeed likely, that there will be **economies of scope** favouring the successful firm and if technical progress is slow, this might lead to dominance over an extended period of time.

And finally, another reality check concerns the assumption that the firm only wins if it makes the invention, i.e. the innovator wins the 'lottery' and receives the pay-off. However, in practice patents do not always guarantee the inventor the total pay-off. The very act of engaging in an innovation race may speed up the process of technological and organizational progress. The act of investing in R&D, whether or not the firm is the winner, imparts learning and adds to the firm's accumulated knowledge – and future success we have argued is positively related to the degree of accumulated knowledge, i.e. the greater a firm's accumulated knowledge the greater the probability of winning. Even the failure to secure the patent does not automatically result in a negative pay-off. When seeking a patent a firm has to disclose information which is then made generally available to others. Armed with this information rival firms may be able to reverse engineer a new product or process and receive some benefit as the *imitator* or follower.

Racing for a Prize

A study by Cockburn and Henderson (1994) researched the R&D expenditure by ten major pharmaceutical companies. On a confidential basis, the authors collected data from the firms on not only the level of R&D investment, but also the outcomes at the level of individual R&D programmes over a period of more than 17 years. The pharmaceutical companies provided an ideal context to study innovation rates, as being first to market with a new drug drives competition within the industry rather than price or quantity.

Cockburn and Henderson were particularly interested in the hypothesis that with free entry innovation rates resulted in excessive expenditure on R&D. The authors focused on research for cardiovascular drugs and a particular product group whose existence could be traced back to the original discovery in 1977. Their measures of output included patents, new drug approvals, new drug introduction, sales and market share.

Interestingly, Cockburn and Henderson showed that in the period since the original discovery there were lengthy periods of apparently unproductive effort and an extensive exchange of knowledge between competing firms and the public sector. They observed that it was only in the last stage of the R&D effort that the competitive dynamics took on the characteristics of a race. Moreover, the evidence suggested that far from firms dropping out when it looked as though one firm was succeeding, this tended to encourage rivals. By 1992, some 12 patents based on the original discovery had been awarded, showing that a patent race may award several prizes.

Patents and Diffusion

Patents, *copyrights* and *trademarks* are needed to create the incentive for innovation and creative effort. An invention or an original idea is new knowledge and new knowledge is a *public good*. But, if the new knowledge is freely available, imitators will drive the price down, reducing economic rents to zero. R&D expenditure is a *sunk cost* and to warrant such investment the inventor must expect, in a commercial environment, to earn a return that exceeds the cost and this can only be done if once commercialization occurs price is held above marginal cost. Patents are designed to create the incentive to invest by conferring an exclusive property right on the owner of a patent. In this section we will focus on patents. Copyrights can be analysed in a similar manner to patents, whereas trademarks are primarily designed to protect a firm's reputation and convey information to consumers regarding quality. One important distinction between patents and copyrights is that the latter protects an idea, whereas the former protects the tangible embodiment of an idea.

Within the EU a patent confers exclusive property rights for a period of 20 years. Rather surprisingly, the EU does not have its own patent system – though after many years of negotiation an outline agreement on a new Community-wide patent system was agreed in March 2003. It was agreed in principle that there would by 2010 be a centralized Community Court to deal with infringements, but to date member states have been unable to agree on the text of the proposal and there is now a real possibility that the proposed system will be abandoned. At present, individuals or firms who wish to obtain patents valid in a number of European countries must either make a separate application in each country or make a single application via the European Patent Office. This is not an EU institution and was created by intergovernmental agreement in 1973; though all 25 EU member states, plus six other nations, are members.

Patents do more than confer exclusive property rights for new inventions. In addition to providing the incentive to invent and innovate, they also result in the disclosure of new knowledge and facilitate orderly diffusion. By conferring exclusive property rights a patent empowers inventors to restrict unauthorized use of their invention, and in effect the award of a patent creates a monopoly that the inventor is free to fully exploit with the support of the authorities. This raises something of a paradox for Arrow's (1962) conclusion that competitive markets provide a greater incentive to innovate. The 'benefits' for an inventor operating in a competitive market can only be realized if the invention can be patented and the patent successfully protected. That is, the benefits can only be secured by creating a monopoly and in so doing this gives rise to the welfare costs of allocative inefficiency and, possibly, productive inefficiency. In practice, a process innovation may not need a patent if the firm can keep it secret, but the benefit to a firm would only arise if as a result it developed market power. Although Arrow's observation is pertinent, it is not conclusive. In practice, R&D is rarely a one-off event, but rather a dynamic process, and this process will tend to favour firms who are existing patent holders and have a structure and culture that encourages invention (Geroski *et al.*, 1996).

It is therefore possible that the patent system actually reinforced monopoly power over the longer term. The basic argument is that of Gilbert and Newberg (1982). Whenever the award of a patent to a monopolist makes entry into the market more difficult, the monopolist has a strategic incentive to invest in the necessary R&D. This *pre-emption* effect arises from the desire to prevent the dissipation of industry profits that would follow new entry. In contrast, a potential entrant's R&D must either result in a drastic innovation that allows the entrant to replace the monopolist or, more likely, will result in creating a duopoly. For the new entrant a duopoly rent might be very attractive, but on the reasonable assumption that the total rent earned by two non-cooperative duopolists is less than the rent earned by a monopolist, the monopolist has the greater incentive to innovate.

The pre-emptive effect is consistent with Scherer's observation that potential entrants act as a spur to incumbents and the effect can also encourage incumbents to engage in complementary innovations. One reason for complementary innovations is to exploit to the full market demand by patenting vertically differentiated versions of a new product. Another reason, which is more directly connected with market structure, is to accumulate **sleeping patents**. Large firms typically hold hundreds, if not thousands, of patents and in most cases each product or process will have a significant number of patents. Many of these patents are not used; these are the sleeping patents and they serve as a strategic device to pre-empt the economic rents generated by the truly valuable patent. For example, a sleeping patent may relate to a technology that is not superior to the technology used by the patent holder, but the patent serves to prevent an entrant from competing.

As explained above, a patent confers an exclusive property right for a finite period of years, but the exclusive rights are also limited in their breadth. In fixing the length of the patent and its breadth, the authorities are attempting to optimally solve the trade-off between the necessity of granting firms, institutions and individuals appropriability of their inventions, whilst balancing the desire that the benefits of new knowledge should be spread widely throughout the economy as soon as possible. There is a large literature on the optimal length and breadth of patents (see Tirole, 1993, for a good summary), which seeks to identify and analyse the key issues. In essence, the problem is that if the authorities give too lengthy and broad protection, innovation by rivals will be discouraged. However, if the protection is short lived and/or too narrow, the incentive to innovate will be reduced.

The appropriate theory of patent life is due to Nordhaus (1969) and is based on the following principles. During the life of the patent the holder can behave as a monopolist and earn the maximum economic rent. When the patent protection expires, market forces will in principle drive the economic rent to zero. The social cost of the patent is therefore the **deadweight loss** associated with monopoly, which will be transferred to consumers as **consumers' surplus** when the patent expires. The authorities have therefore to choose the length of the patent, T, such that invention is induced, which in turn creates the potential for consumers' surplus. The higher the value of T, the greater the potential consumers' surplus, but T will always be finite. This follows, firstly, because there will be diminishing returns to R&D expenditure and, secondly, the present value of the future gain in consumers' surplus – the removal of the deadweight loss – will be small if T is spread over a long period.

Turning to the breadth of patent protection, this can be defined in two dimensions: horizontal breadth and vertical breadth. Klemperer's (1990) analysis of patent breadth showed that conceptually breadth poses a similar problem to patent life. The greater the breadth, the more difficult it is for other firms to *invent around* the patent, and consequently the greater the economic rent accruing to the patent holder. However, as there is no universally accepted measure of breadth in practice, this issue is more problematic than defining the patent life. The idea is to set a minimum amount – both horizontally and vertically – by which the innovation differs from an existing process or product. The UK Patent Office's approach is to require all applicants for a patent to specify all related patents and how the patent being applied for is …*novel, and inventive over all matter published before the filing date of the patent application.*

Matters are further complicated by the fact that there is, in principle, a trade-off between a patent's life and its breadth. Economists are not very helpful on this matter. Klemperer (1990) argues that patent breadth is related to product differentiation and there is a case for controlling the number of patents that would otherwise be sought for every minor differentiation. In contrast, Gilbert and Shapiro (1990) suggest that patent breadth is more directly related to the flow of economic returns. By not unreasonably assuming an inverse relationship between social welfare and economic rents, they favour a longer life and a narrower breadth. The problem with a longer life, according to Gallini (2002), is it increases the likelihood that a rival will *invent around* the patent and this may actually reduce the incentive to invent.

In practice, empirical studies show that imitators can *invent around* a patent to bring out similar, if not identical, products in a shorter period and at a lower cost. Scherer (1981) observes that in a ten-month period in 1974, 16 companies, including IBM and Kodak, obtained 390 patents in the field of xerography. In short, even with patents, innovators face the problem of knowledge spillovers. Other firms quickly learn of new developments and the leakage of information from one firm to another reduces the cost of inventing around a patent. One consequence of such leakages might be to discourage small firms and would-be new entrants from investing in R&D activity. Another is that where possible, say a process or organizational innovation, the firm attempts to keep the development secret and therefore does not apply for a patent.

Social efficiency demands that new knowledge should be made widely available at the earliest possible date, consistent with providing an incentive for its discovery. In principle, a patent is a device to prevent diffusion of new knowledge, but this is not necessarily the case. Firstly, the award of a patent is accompanied by the details of the patent. Secondly, a patent can assist the orderly dissemination of new knowledge to a limited population before the patent expires by means of a **patent licence**. There are a number of reasons why a patent holder might choose to enter into a licensing agreement with other firms. The first is the situation outlined by Arrow, where the inventor is a small firm lacking the size and supporting knowledge to make full use of the invention. Another situation in which a patent-holding firm may choose to license the patent is where the new knowledge applies to a market in which the licensor does not operate or wishes to **diversify** into. The justification might also apply to operations in a foreign country. Faced with the choice of setting up a foreign subsidiary, the patent-holding firm may choose to license the new technology.

There are also a number of reasons why a patent holder may choose not to license the invention. The licensor may fear that the licensee – by acquiring the new knowledge – may improve its chances of developing the next generation of the new technology. A firm operating under **Bertrand competition** in a differentiated product market who discovers a way to better differentiate its products would have little incentive to license the new knowledge. Again, a firm operating in a Cournot oligopoly who discovers a drastic process innovation would not want to license its discovery.

The fruits of technological advance are only fully realized for society when the new products, processes or organizational capabilities are spread throughout industries. In practice, the adoption of an invention by rival firms may take many years. An important empirical observation regarding the commercialization of an invention is that adoption is typically delayed; and firms do not adopt the innovation simultaneously. Instead, innovations diffuse into use over time (Reinganum, 1998). Diffusion may be thought of as a *rate of learning*. If the new knowledge has been licensed it may be diffused to a degree by the time the patent expires. If the new knowledge has not been licensed, the process of diffusing starts with the first firm adopting the new process or producing the new product and it proceeds as more firms adopt the new invention. Overall, diffusion measures the aggregate usage of the new technology as a proportion of all firms within the industry. Attempting to understand the forces that determine the speed of diffusion also raises another question; namely, why do some firm's adopt earlier than others, leading to a diffusion process that typically follows the S-shaped pattern illustrated in Figure 14.6.

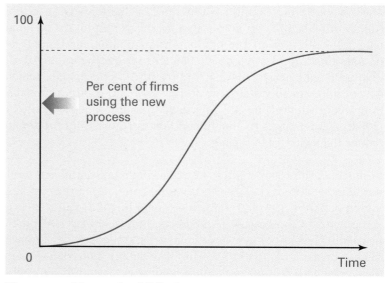

Figure 14.6: Time path of diffusion

One explanation, based on incomplete information as to the profitability of the innovation and varying attitudes towards risk, has been put forward by Jensen (1982). The idea is that information incompleteness will be reduced over time as information regarding the innovation accumulates. Thus, some firms will choose to wait before adopting the innovation. The more favourable the firm's initial assessment, the sooner the firm is likely to adopt. The more costly the costs of gathering the relevant information, the slower the rate of diffusion. Reinganum (1998) argues that an S-shaped diffusion curve will result even in situations of perfect information if an innovation, particularly a process innovation, involves installation costs and is time consuming. The larger the disruption to current operations, and the faster the speed of adoption, the higher the cost to the adopting firm. Thus, setting an adoption date further into the future – the date at which the adoption will be completed – will reduce installation costs. As different firms will face different installation costs, the result is an S-shaped curve as shown in Figure 14.6.

Another explanation for the S-shaped diffusion curve is that all firms likely to adopt the innovation are aware of the innovation but differences in the vintage of each firm's capital stock lead to differences in the optimal time to adopt. Yet another explanation likens the diffusion process to the spread of epidemics, e.g. flu. The epidemic gains momentum as the number of people with flu increases, because this increases the rate of infection but only up to some point; beyond this the number of people left to catch the disease is declining and hence the rate at which it spreads slows down. Finally, as noted above, diffusion is likely to be faster if the innovation has been licensed. Indeed, as we have seen, in sectors such as chemicals and pharmaceuticals, which are highly dependent on innovation for competitive advantage, firms are actually more willing to exchange information by granting licences reciprocally. Empirical studies suggest that larger firms tend to adopt a more liberal attitude towards the granting of licences. One reason may be that refusal to grant a licence seldom has a serious impact on competitors. Usually firms are able to find a substitute technology or in the case of a process innovation, be prepared to purchase the key component from the patent holder.

Delayed Diffusion

Commercially grown, genetically modified (GM) crops are concentrated in a few countries, mainly the US and Argentina. The two crops where GM is most widely diffused are soyabeans and maize, though cotton, rapeseed, tobacco and potatoes also have some GM varieties. Almost all GM crops are herbicide tolerant as a result of the inserting of a herbicide-tolerate gene into the plant. Two-thirds of GM corn is insect resistant as a result of inserting genetic material from the *Bacillus thuringiensis* (Bt) into seeds. The degree to which farmers can realize the potential gains – higher yields or lower production costs – differs across countries. New technologies are always developed in a given technological, economic, social and cultural context. If circumstances in the adopting country differ widely from those in the inviting country, the potential gains are likely to be smaller.

In its report on the economic impact of GM on the EU farm sector, the European Commission observed that larger farms and better educated farmers – often the two go together – are more likely to be earlier adopters. A higher degree of education appears to be aligned with the ability and/or willingness to undertake the necessary changes in management practices or it might reflect a greater ability to visualize the longer-term benefits. Another influence on the diffusion of GM crops is consumer resistance. In the EU, following the lowering in esteem of scientists following the BSE debacle, consumers have been very wary and both food retailers and food processors have been very reluctant to introduce new products that are developed with the aid of modern biotechnology. The EU demonstrates that social acceptance can play an important role in the diffusion of new knowledge. Consumer attitudes are not the only constraining influence. Also relevant is the Common Agricultural Policy (CAP). Despite recent reforms, farmers are still protected to a significant degree from external competition. Put another way, the need to adopt higher-yielding or lower-cost crops is that much less pressing.

Organizing for Innovation

In this final section, we return again to the firm's organizational architecture. Our focus is its influence on the creation of new knowledge and the ability to successfully innovate and capture competitive advantage. We have considered at length the relationship between market structure and the incentive to invest in R&D activity and, by implication, firms that account for a significant market share are likely to be large scale. But scale also enters in its own right as an influence on the incentive to innovate. The first obvious point is that large firms are more likely to benefit from any economies of scale inherent in R&D activity. For larger firms indivisibilities and specialist staff mean that the cost of R&D activity can be spread across a wider range of projects, thereby lowering unit costs. When it comes to product innovation, large firms usually have well-established marketing channels and may realize scale economies in advertising and promotional activities. But large firms also suffer a number of disadvantages associated with R&D activity. Associated with invention and innovation are the agency costs of organizing and motivating activity that is congruent with the organization's goals. As observed by Cyert and March (1992), in their **behavioural** approach to the firm managers may spend their time defending their projects and engaging in bureaucratic activities rather than creative endeavour. As discussed in Chapter 5, in large organizations there is a greater danger that entrepreneurial flair will be stifled as decisions to go ahead with a R&D project might need to filter through a large chain of command.

Set against these disadvantages small firms have some distinct advantages. Smaller firms may be more adept at risk taking. On the issue of scale and funds for investment, despite the growth of venture capitalists seeking to invest in small, high-tech enterprises, there is evidence that size still confers advantage in the provision of financial resources. There is empirical evidence to show that very small firms rarely engage in R&D activity. One of the EU leaders' justifications for focusing on SMEs, in what is now known as the **Lisbon Strategy**, is that it is generally more difficult for these smaller firms to acquire the necessary resources and knowledge for innovation. A European Commission (2001) staff working paper identified the costs of collecting and interpreting information, the lack and/or failings of the advice services on offer to SMEs and capacity constraints arising from the small scale of operation, task-structured organizations and limited access to financial markets.

The balance of empirical evidence regarding firm size and R&D intensity has shifted over the past 50 years. Studies in the 1960s suggested that the hypothesis that R&D intensity increased more than proportionally with size was only weakly supported and then only up to a threshold whereupon the relationship ceased to exist or became weakly negative. During the 1980s, more sophisticated techniques identified the size of the business unit rather than the overall firm size as influential, but in most studies firm size was found to be a relatively minor influence. As observed by Cohen and Levin (1992), the most notable feature of the considerable body of empirical research on the relationship between firm size and innovation is its inconclusiveness.

The attempts to test for a positive relationship between firm size and R&D intensity derive their exegesis from the hypothesis wrongly or rightly attributed to Schumpeter (1942). But this hypothesis has to be set against the fact that most large firms, as discussed in earlier chapters, are diversified and consequently operate business units in a number of industries. But again, attempts to find a significant relationship between diversification and R&D expenditure have met with failure. None of this would come as a surprise to those who take as their starting point the Schumpeterian–Penrosian approach that links innovation to complex relationships within and between firms. What firms do, and how they do it, owes more to fundamental uncertainty and differences in perceptions, as well as variations in feasible paths based on accumulated knowledge. Viewed from this perspective, size is not necessarily dominant in this necessarily dynamic process.

What can be said with some confidence is that the institutional conditions for innovation in larger firms have changed over the past 50 years. Innovative profits, as opposed to the profits associated with market power, are now more significant with the contemporary emphasis on technology and the reduced protection afforded by border tariffs and other trade barriers. Back in the 1950s technological development was centred on mass production, with its economies of scale. Since then the emphasis has shifted towards economies of scope and the achievement of plant flexibility and intra-firm networks all drawing heavily on information and communication technologies. Freeman (1987) has termed this new environment, a techno–economic paradigm, whereby firms must now rely on more complex combinations of related technologies to serve ever-more narrowly defined product markets.

Firm size also raises the issue of organizational architecture. We might reasonably expect that as a firm's organizational architecture is a major influence on the way its members interact, co-operate and learn, it is also likely to be a major influence on the area, pace and exploitation of R&D activity. Consideration of a firm's organizational structure brings us inevitably to the governance approach to the firm and its contribution to understanding technological change. We have devoted considerable space in this chapter to the importance of accumulated knowledge, capabilities and path dependencies in the process of acquiring new knowledge. All these influences tend to be primarily associated with the competency approach to the firm. In fact, despite Schumpeter's observation that new products and processes might require different organizational structures, i.e. governance structures, the governance approach appears largely to have ignored the issue of technological change.

The essence of the governance approach is that when **asset specificity** is high, hierarchical governance is more efficient than market exchange. Williamson (1985), as described in Chapter 3, compares the incentive impairing effects of **transaction costs** on a cost-reducing process innovation at the supply stage in the presence of high asset specificity and concludes that new organizational forms – e.g. **vertical integration** or alliances – are constructed because they economize on transaction costs and at the same time provide innovation incentives. But he does not go on to discuss in any detail the relationship between different organizational forms and innovation. Today, large firms frequently take minority stakes in small innovative firms in order to potentially profit from their technological competencies without destroying the entrepreneurial culture of the smaller firm. This knowledge serves to warn that as firms grow in size, so they not only increase in complexity, but also, to the extent that for many firms diversification is the route to faster growth, they tend to operate in an increasing number of distinct technological areas. Consequently, they will begin to develop a capability in these diverse technological areas and in turn the existence of a diversified portfolio of products offers a greater probability that an invention can be successfully applied. As firms grow and diversify they become more knowledgeable and in the process this exerts an upward pressure on R&D budgets and makes greater demands on the firm's organizational capabilities as it struggles to benefit from its increasingly diverse, intangible resources.

Within large-scale **M-form** firms, the divisional structure itself can act as a disincentive to innovate. If the division has to bear the costs (including the risks) of the innovation project, but headquarters can then redistribute the benefits to other divisions, the incentive to innovate is likely to be lower. Moreover, in the absence of freely flowing information within the firm, there is a danger of duplication if more than one division is devoting resources to solving the same problem. The key issue, in terms of innovation, is to ensure that the firm's organizational architecture encourages new learning and minimizes the transaction costs of transferring the new knowledge to other divisions.

The Schumpeterian–Penrosian approach to the firm as a place of learning and knowledge accumulation has provided the platform upon which much of the more recent competency approach to the firm is built. Yet it is precisely in the area of Schumpeterian invention and innovation that the competency and governance approaches overlap. A central purpose of the competency approach to the firm is to explain why firms differ. According to this school, the heterogeneous characteristics of the firm – its resources and organizational architecture – give rise to idiosyncratic patterns of development upon which competitive advantage is built. But if a firm's internally generated resources create heterogeneous capabilities in the area of invention and innovation, the realization of their potential is dependent on the way in which the firm organizes its activities – in short, the firm's governing hierarchy determines how its individual resources are organized to deliver specific capabilities. Organizational and human intellectual capital is invested in invention and innovation within the firm's existing organizational structures, which will balance authority and control with patterns of trust.

Accumulated capabilities within the firm gives rise to increasing returns on their application, i.e. the return on the firm's invention and innovation activities increases with the scale of its activities in these areas. Thus, an organizational perspective not only informs as to why invention and innovation activities vary between firms, but also why the outcomes are varied and unpredictable. Viewed as additions to the firm's stock of knowledge, inventions and innovation necessarily rest in the minds of individuals, are shared within teams and expressed in new products or processes. Many of these interactions are less than transparent to the external observer and even the firm's management. In short, the link between invention, innovation and competitive advantage is not readily decipherable and consequently, the process of generating knowledge has been described as one of causal ambiguity. Typically for a firm that invests consistently in research and development, it is likely to find itself continually faced with emerging opportunities that are both the product of existing capabilities and also the genesis of new capabilities.

Nelson and Winter (1982) have argued that firms can best be understood in terms of a hierarchy of practised organizational routines which define not only how the firm's resources are co-ordinated, but also to what endeavours they will be put. In an environment of Schumpeterian competition, some of the firm's resources must be devoted to R&D routines which must be practised if the firm is to build the capability to innovate successfully again and again as the external environment changes. Within this evolutionary framework it is inevitable that firms will choose somewhat different strategies and this will lead to firms having different organizational structures and different capabilities, including R&D.

The foregoing views organizational change not as a separate influence on economic progress, but as being central to technological advance. New organizational architectures are not devised; when the business environment changes they, like technologies, evolve according to the perceptions of their decision makers and their accumulated knowledge and capabilities. One way in which organizational structures are changing is the development of inter-firm collaborations that are increasingly motivated by the need for joint development of new technologies. It is increasingly the case that technological innovation can rarely be accomplished by individual firms acting independently. It is more and more common for firms to engage in horizontal or vertical collaborations in the search for new rent-generating opportunities. To talk of firm attributes and innovation is no longer sufficient as many firms, particularly in the more technologically orientated industries, are embedded in various knowledge-developing interactions with other firms.

Inter-firm co-operation in R&D offers efficiency improvements. As explained above, in a non-cooperative invention race only one firm is likely to be the winner and therefore the duplication of R&D expenditure by other firms is, at least in part, wasteful. To this we can add technological diversity (Coombs and Metcalf, 2000), whereby innovations increasingly draw on an ever-widening range of technologies and knowledge. Technological diversity implies that individual firms are unlikely to have accumulated all the necessary knowledge and this limits the firm's capability to deliver technological advances. In contrast to the Penrose argument that firms grow by discovering a profitable use for an under-utilized capability, the view advanced above implies the problem in the area of technological advance is one of missing capabilities that can be rectified by entering into horizontal or vertical co-operative arrangements with other firms. Put succinctly, the creativity and capabilities necessary for technological change can be constrained within single firms (Cohen and Klepper, 1992).

Article 81(1) of the Treaty of Rome (as renumbered in 1999) prohibits **horizontal agreements** and **vertical agreements** between firms that may affect trade between member states. But Article 81(3) states that the prohibition does not apply to any agreement, decision or concerted practice which contributes to improving the production or distribution of goods or to promoting technical or economic progress. What the founding fathers had in mind in allowing co-operation in the discovery and development of new technologies was the advantage of common standards. Official sanctioning of co-operation on R&D – subject to allowing consumers a fair share of the resulting benefits – reflects two potential efficiency gains. Firstly, as noted above, if there can be only one winner of the race to innovate then it is potentially wasteful for other firms to duplicate each other's efforts in a non-cooperative race. Secondly, modern technology is so complicated and frequently draws on a wide range of expertise and experience that it is unlikely that one firm will possess all the necessary knowledge.

The recognition that intra-firm co-operation is for many firms an indispensable tool in the successful conduct of R&D activity has resulted in a phenomenal increase in the number of collaborative ventures. Researchers tracking the trend have observed that the overwhelming majority of collaborations being formed today occur in rapidly changing industries and involve complex linkages in technology, R&D and other knowledge-intensive activities and are characterized by reciprocal knowledge flows of a tacit nature (Mowery *et al.*, 1997). Such inter-firm relationships can take many forms and range along a spectrum from the purchase of licences for specific technologies, to the purchase of firms in order to obtain specific knowledge. The broad organizational forms of inter-firm collaborations are set out in Figure 14.7.

The diagram is viewed from the perspective of an individual firm and shows some alternative inter-organizational R&D relationships within its two dimensions. The horizontal axis indicates the degree

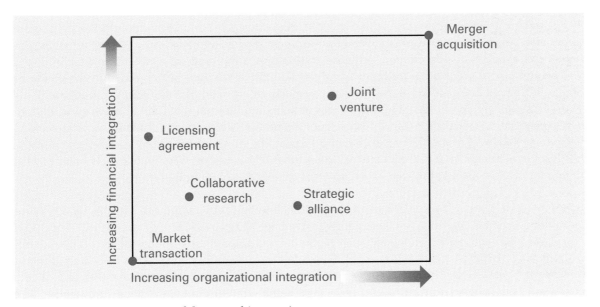

Figure 14.7: Inter-organizational forms and innovation

to which the collaboration involves the firm sharing accumulated knowledge and the vertical axis indicates the potential commitment of R&D expenditure. At the bottom left-hand corner of the diagram the firm judges that it can acquire the specific knowledge from its own resources. The other points – in the somewhat simplified diagram – represent longer-term relationships that involve the firm working with one or more collaborators to produce new knowledge. A licensing agreement is a relationship that involves the transfer of knowledge, but the knowledge flow is one way and there may be no expectation of developing the relationship. Technology-focused collaborative research, e.g. 'research clubs' – frequently involving universities – would be an example where organizations share staff and capital and where the outcome is generic and therefore unlikely to take the form of a viable process or product without further innovative activity. The same outcome arises from a strategic alliance where the commercial benefits and/or the potential longer-term opportunities arising from the collaboration are not capable of being codified and require a continuing alliance to fully exploit their potential. Joint ventures are more application-orientated, the output being a marketable product or process. They also provide an alternative to licensing new knowledge. Finally, the firm can merge with or purchase a firm with the purpose of acquiring the firm's otherwise ***tacit knowledge*** in the area of invention and innovation.

Inter-organizational relationships have a number of advantages. Firstly, the costs of the development and its risks are shared. Secondly, the parties do not need to be of equal size, hence collaboration offers small firms access to the benefits of large-scale research and larger firms access to creative, innovative cultures. Thirdly, where new products or processes offer opportunities for complementary activities, these are likely to be more quickly exploited with collaboration. Finally, the collaborations will bring a wider range of knowledge and perspectives to bear on specific developments as a result of the varying knowledge and skills of the participants. Consequently, jointly discovered new knowledge is likely to be diffused more rapidly, thereby providing a more rapid benefit to society.

Concluding Thoughts

The Schumpeterian theory of profits and growth brings invention and innovation to the very centre of understanding a firm's performance and development. For Schumpeter, the dynamic efficiency inherent in the process he described as *creative destruction* is the basis upon which new technologies and organizational forms bring forth new products and processes upon which rising living standards are based. The Schumpeterian hypothesis is popularly interpreted as linking innovation positively with market power, but in fact Schumpeter was at pains to point out that Capitalism is an evolutionary process and over time profits derive from a process that is best described as rent-seeking behaviour that seeks to profitably develop and employ the firm's accumulated knowledge and capabilities. For Schumpeter, it did not matter if the sources of innovation were increasingly concentrated in large firms, the effect of innovation was to overturn existing monopoly power.

Schumpeter also provided the characterization of technological development with his trilogy of invention, innovation and diffusion. Competitive advantage arises from the first two stages – invention and innovation – but for a firm, securing an economic rent from the investment in R&D is always uncertain. Not only are the returns from a yet to be invented new product or process extremely difficult to estimate, there is a probability that the invention or innovation will not work and that even if successful, a rival might appropriate the gains by being first to patent the new knowledge. The uncertainties and a misreading of Schumpeter led to the view that monopolists are more likely to innovate than firms operating in a competitive environment.

The monopolist, it is argued, has both the incentive – as a barrier to entry – to invest in invention and innovation and also the means – resulting from a monopolist's ability to earn economic rents. However, if the monopolist is successful, the pay-off will be the economic rent from the new development less the economic rent previously earned. On this reasoning, a firm in a competitive market has a greater incentive to invest in R&D as the pay-off for a 'success' would be the total economic rent which a competitive firm could capture via the patent system and licensing. In practice, matters are not so clear cut; in part because the patent system is at best only an imperfect guarantee of a firm's ability to appropriate all the value it has created. Other firms quickly learn the new developments and the leakage of information can enable competitors to rapidly produce substitute products. In practice, most firms operate under conditions of imperfect competition and the existence of rivals whose R&D efforts could result in the loss of a firm's market raises wider issues. One response to this situation is to adopt a high-spending strategy for R&D on the grounds that this will increase the chance of success. However, in a non-cooperative environment rivals will also adopt a similar strategy, resulting in the industry spending too much of its resources on invention and innovation activity. As the number of firms in an industry rises, so each individual firm's probability of being the 'winner' declines and hence the expected pay-off will decline. The larger the number of competing firms, the lower the proportion of resources individual firms will devote to R&D activity.

Another concern is whether firm size influences the incentive to invest in new technologies. One argument is that large firms are almost certainly diversified and hence will be operating in a number of markets with a range of technologies. Such firms have not only gained a considerable amount of knowledge and experience in building up their scale of production, but also they have a greater probability of a pay-off from one of their diversified sectors. However, large firms do not necessarily have all the advantages. They are more likely to suffer from managerial inefficiencies, e.g. managers engaged in bureaucratic activities rather than creative endeavour. Moreover, the existence of venture capitalists can provide small-scale firms with the means to exploit promising innovative ideas.

Society can only fully gain from R&D activity when its fruits are fully diffused. Paradoxically, in order to encourage investment in invention and innovation the patent system is designed to slow down the diffusion of knowledge by granting the originator a monopoly. During the life time of the patent diffusion depends in part on the security of the patent and whether the new product or process is licensed. With or without a patent, over time the knowledge inherent in all new products and processes spreads throughout an industry, but its progress tends to be S-shaped. Differences in capital, experience and information lead some firms to adopt earlier than others.

Finally, as noted above, non-cooperative behaviour leads to wasteful expenditure on R&D. Co-operation is more efficient and this creates interest in the forms of inter-organizational relationships that might give rise to successful joint investment in R&D. Such relationships can take a number of forms ranging from the purchase of a licence or consultancy service to merger and acquisition. Inter-organizational relationships have a number of advantages. The development costs and risks are shared, the collaborators do not need to be of the same size and the bringing together of groups with varying knowledge and skills offers a broader capability and hence chance of success.

Key Learning Points

- Schumpeter characterized technological development with the trilogy of invention, innovation and diffusion.
- Invention and innovation are manifested in new products, new processes and new organizational forms and are the essence of competitive advantage.
- The pay-off to investment in R&D activity is more uncertain than to conventional investment as there is a risk that the yet to be invented product or process will not work and/or rivals may invent first.
- The incentive, inherent in coming first, is the likelihood of earning economic rents.
- These may be secured by keeping a new process secret or, as in the case of a new product, gaining the protection of a patent.
- A patent may not guarantee the originator full appropriability as rivals may be able to produce substitutes within a short period.
- As the returns to R&D activity depend in part on coming first, one strategy is to increase the funding on such activity.
- The result of such a strategy is that the industry tends to devote too many resource to R&D activity.
- A monopolist would appear to have an incentive to invest in invention and innovation as success might serve as a barrier to entry and hence a protection for economic rents.
- However, the opportunity cost to the monopolist is the economic rent previously being earned. On this basis a firm in a competitive market has a greater incentive to invest in R&D activity.
- Large-scale firms are deemed to have an advantage in the area of R&D as they are almost certainly diversified and therefore possess both a wider range of knowledge and opportunities to exploit a successful invention.
- The existence of venture capitalists offers some offset to smaller firms and smaller firms can also engage in collaborative ventures.
- Inter-organizational collaboration in R&D has a number of advantages, including the sharing of costs and risk and the enhanced capabilities inherent in the knowledge and skills of the collaborators.

Exercises

14.1 Justify the observation that Schumpeter provides a good analytical starting point for the development of a theory of innovation as an evolutionary process.

14.2 Why is a focus on market structure and firm size insufficient when attempting to explain the incentive to invest in R&D activity?

14.3 If Arrow's replacement effect is unchallengeable from a theoretical perspective, why in practice is a small firm likely to be at a disadvantage in appropriating the value of their invention?

14.4 List the four significant factors that combine to determine which oligopolist has a strategic advantage in R&D activity.

14.5 In what ways might a joint venture to fund R&D be superior to a firm working alone?

Problems

14.1 Assume that demand for an homogeneous good is $p = 100 - Q$, and a process innovation reduces the costs of production from €75 to €60 per unit:

(a) Confirm that this is a non-drastic innovation. How much would marginal costs need to be reduced for the innovation to be classed as drastic?

(b) If the market was served by two Cournot duopolists who have identical marginal costs of €75 per unit, calculate the pre-innovation price and profits for the firms?

(c) If now one of the firms is awarded a patent for the innovation, confirm that the market price will fall.

(d) Assuming a cost of capital of $r = 0.8$, show that the duopolist is prepared to

pay more for the innovation than the monopolist.

14.2 A firm faces the demand curve $p = 6 - 5Q$. The marginal and average cost of production is 1, the firm's opportunity cost of capital is r and if two firms make a discovery simultaneously they split the patent rights:

(a) Under a patent, a firm obtains exclusive rights to act like a monopolist. Calculate the present value of the annual profits if the firm is awarded a patent.

(b) How much is this patent worth if the patent lasts for five years?

(c) How much is the expected value of a patent if it lasts for five years but there are two firms with an equal probability of making the discovery?

References

Arrow, K. (1962) 'Economic welfare and the allocation of resources for invention' in *The Rate and Direction of Inventive Activity*, NBER, Princeton, NJ.

Beath, J., Katsoulacos, Y. and Ulph, D. (1989) 'Strategic R&D Policy', *Economic Journal*, vol. 99, pp. 74–83.

Blundell, R., Griffith, R. and Van Reene, J. (1995) 'Dynamic count data models of technological innovation', *Economic Journal*, vol. 105, pp. 333–344.

Cantwell, J. (2002) 'Innovation, profits and growth' in *The Growth of the Firm*, C. Pitelis (ed.), Oxford University Press, Oxford.

Cockburn, I. and Henderson, R. (1994) 'Racing to invest: the dynamics of competition in ethical drug discovery', *Journal of Economics and Management Strategy*, vol. 3, pp. 481–519.

Cohen, W. and Klepper, S. (1992) 'The trade-off between firm size and diversity in the pursuit of technical progress', *Small Business Economics*, vol. 4, pp. 1–14.

Cohen, W. and Levin, R. (1992) 'Empirical studies of innovation and market structure' in *Handbook of Industrial Organization*, 3rd edn, R. Schmalensee and R. Willig (eds), North Holland, Amsterdam.

Coombs, R. and Metcalfe, J. (2000) 'Organising for innovation: coordinating distributed innovation capabilities' in *Competence, Governance and Entrepreneurship*, N. Foss and V. Mahnke (eds), Oxford University Press, Oxford.

Cyert, R. and March, J. (1992) *A Behavioral Theory of the Firm*, 2nd edn, Blackwell, Cambridge, MA.

Dasgupta, P. and Stiglitz, J. (1980) 'Industrial structure and the nature of innovative activity', *Economic Journal*, vol. 90, pp. 266–293.

Dorfmann, R. and Steiner, P. (1954) 'Optimal advertising and optimal quality', *American Economic Review*, vol. 44, pp. 826–836.

European Commission (2001) 'Creating top-class business support services', Staff Working Paper, SEC, 1937, Brussels.

Freeman, C. (1987) *Technology Policy and Economic Performance: Lessons from Japan*, Frances Pinter, London.

Gallini, N. (2002) 'The economics of patents: lessons from recent us patent reform', *Journal of Economic Perspectives*, vol. 16, pp. 131–154.

Geroski, P. (1990) 'Innovation, technological opportunity and market structure', *Oxford Economic Papers*, vol. 42, pp. 586–602.

Geroski, P., Hossein, S. and Van Reenen, J. (1966) 'How persistently do firms innovate?', CEPR Discussion Paper, 1433, London.

Gilbert, R. and Newberg, D. (1982) 'Pre-emptive patenting and the persistence of monopoly', *American Economic Review*, vol. 72, pp. 514–527.

Gilbert, R. and Shapiro, C. (1990) 'Optimal patent length and breadth', *Rand Journal of Economics*, vol. 21, pp. 106–112.

Jensen, R. (1982) 'Adoption and diffusion of an innovation of uncertain profitability', *Journal of Economic Theory*, vol. 27, pp. 182–193.

Katz, M. and Shapiro, C. (1987) 'R&D, rivalry with licensing or imitation', *American Economic Review*, vol. 77, pp. 402–420.

Klemperer, P. (1990) 'How broad should the scope of patent protection be?', *Rand Journal of Economics*, vol. 21, pp. 113–130.

Marshall, A. (1890) *Principles of Economics*, Macmillan, London.

Mowery, D., Oxley, J. and Silverman, B. (1997) 'Strategic alliances and interfirm knowledge transfer', *Strategic Management Journal*, vol. 17, pp. 77–92.

Nelson, R. and Winter, S. (1982) *An Evolutionary Theory of Economic Change*, Harvard University Press, Cambridge, MA.

Nordhaus, W. (1969) *Invention, Growth and Welfare*, MIT Press, Cambridge, MA.

Penrose, E. (1959) *The Theory and Growth of the Firm*, Blackwell, Oxford.

Porter, M. (1985) *Competitive Advantage: Creating and Sustaining Competitive Performance*, Free Press, New York.

Porter, M. (1990) *The Competitive Advantage of Nations*, Free Press, New York.

Reinganum, J. (1998) 'The timing of innovations: research, development and diffusion' in *Handbook of Industrial Organization*, 3rd edn, R. Schmalensee and R. Willig (eds), North Holland, Amsterdam.

Scherer, F. (1965) 'Firm size, market structure, opportunity and the output of patented innovations', *American Economic Review*, vol. 55, pp. 1097–1125.

Scherer, R. (1981) 'Comments on patents, sleeping patents and entry deterrence' in *Strategy, Predation and Antitrust Analysis*, S. Salop (ed.), Federal Trade Commission, Washington DC.

Scherer, F. and Ross, D. (1990) *Industrial Market Structure and Economic Performance*, 3rd edn, Houghton Mifflin, Boston.

Schumpeter, J. (1942) *Capitalism, Socialism and Democracy*, Harper, New York.

Smith, A. (1776) *An Enquiry into the Nature and Causes of the Wealth of Nations*, 1976 Bicentary Edition, Clarendon Press, Oxford.

Teece, D., Pisano, G. and Shuen, A. (1997) 'Dynamic capabilities and strategic management', *Strategic Management Journal*, vol. 18, no. 7, pp. 509–533.

Tirole, J. (1993) *The Theory of Industrial Organization*, 6th edn, MIT Press, Cambridge, MA.

Williamson, O. (1985) *Economic Institutions of Capitalism*, Free Press, New York.

GLOSSARY

Adverse selection arises when there is *asymmetric information* between buyers and sellers with the effect that eventually only consumers with the least desirable characteristics buy the firm's products. Customers lacking sufficient information to make an informed choice do not enter a market leaving only those prepared to pay a low price as customers. Suppliers, of say, health insurance will attempt to select only those customers whom they judge to be healthy, forcing the less healthy to rely on the public sector.

Advertising intensity the ratio of advertising expenditure to revenue. The ratio can be measured at the firm or industry level. See also the *Dorfman–Steiner condition*.

Aftermarkets exist where a good or service once sold will need an additional service from time to time, e.g. maintenance. If buyers impose the condition that the service is purchased from them, then it might be judged to be a *vertical restraint*.

Agency theory see *principal–agent theory*.

Agency costs are the costs that arise when agents (e.g. employees) engage in behaviours that are not fully aligned with those of the principal who hires them. The principal must either bear the cost of monitoring and motivating the agent or accept the costs of *hidden actions* on the part of agents and accompanying loss of efficiency.

Agglomeration refers to the gathering together in a region or locality of many firms. By gathering together firms hope that their production costs will benefit owing to the increased supply of key inputs, e.g. labour attracted to the area and the infrastructure typically found in industrial areas.

Alliances agreements between firms, usually motivated by the benefits accruing to the partners as a result of sharing capabilities.

Allocative efficiency in the case of a firm, it describes a situation where its resources cannot be reallocated so as to increase the firm's profits. More generally, it applies to any allocation of resources where it is not possible to make one person better off without making someone else worse off. See also *Pareto efficiency*.

Arbitrage riskless trading activity based on buying where a product is cheap and selling where it has a higher price.

Asset specificity refers to the extent to which a particular asset is specialized. A very high degree of asset specificity implies that the asset has only one specialist use.

Asymmetric information describes a situation in which one party to a transaction is in possession of relevant information that is not held by the other party, who consequently is vulnerable to opportunistic behaviour. The two most common examples are (1) in markets, where sellers have more detailed information on the quality of the goods and services they are selling than their potential customers, and (2) in labour markets where potential employees (sellers) do not reveal *hidden information* on their abilities.

Atomistic industry consists of a large number of small-scale sellers. See also *perfect competition*.

Attributes separate tangible and intangible elements that comprise a good or service and determine its value to consumers. In a famous attempt to explain behaviour in *differentiated product* markets, Kelvin Lancaster argued that people consume attributes not products, e.g. the value of a house depends on attributes such as its physical size, its location and so on.

Average fixed costs total *fixed costs* divided by the units produced per production period.

Average product this is calculated by dividing a firm's total output by one or more of its inputs. For example, the average product of labour is calculated by dividing total output by the number of people employed. The resulting average product is more generally referred to as labour productivity. When output is divided by a weighting of all inputs used, e.g. capital, labour and materials, the result is known as total factor productivity. See also *productivity*.

Average total costs the sum of *average variable costs* and *average fixed costs*.

Average variable costs total *variable production costs* divided by the number of units produced in a given period.

Avoidable costs costs that are positively linked to a rise in the level of production. Although generally viewed as equivalent to *variable production costs*, they also apply to *fixed costs* at the planning stage, i.e. all costs are avoidable *ex ante*.

Backward induction an intermediate process for solving non-cooperative extensive form games with finite horizons. First, the optimal strategy for the player who makes the last move is determined, then, taking this move as given, the optimal strategy for the player who makes the next to last move is determined and so on. This process continues back to the start of the game, thereby determining the optimal strategy for each player. Effectively, *Nash equilibrium* is determined for each sub-game.

Backward integration describes the situation when a firm vertically integrates *upstream*. See *vertical integration*.

Bandwagon effect arises when demand for a product rises sharply as a large section of the population believe the product in question generates additional utility by virtue of the fact that it is popular, e.g. a new style of cloth.

Bargaining situation refers to an economic exchange where the outcome in terms of the price or wage paid and/or the quantity sold or labour hours supplied depends on the relative bargaining power of the parties.

Barometric price leadership emerges where one firm, possibly a *dominant firm*, is first to gather information on cost and demand conditions, which it then uses to set its price. In this respect, the firm will be first to set a price that cost and demand conditions will cause others to follow. See also *price leadership*.

Barriers to entry anything that prevents a firm from entering an industry and being able to earn at least a *normal profit*. See also *learning by doing, strategic barriers to entry, structural barriers* and *sunk costs*.

Barter the trading of goods directly for other goods.

Basing point pricing a pricing system whereby industry rivals designate certain geographic points as pricing points and customers are charged the product price at this point plus the cost of delivery, i.e. the further the point of delivery, the higher the delivered price.

Battle of the sexes a game in which there is no solution unless one of the parties capitulates. The game is representative of many negotiation situations.

Bayes' rule a formula by which prior probabilities of various states of nature can be revised as a result of an experiment. Bayesian techniques provide a way in which subjective impressions may be included in quantitative analysis.

Behavioural *theories* an approach to understanding the firm whereby behaviour is the outcome of a continuous process of bargaining between individuals and groups, e.g. the marketing group, the research group and so on.

Bertrand competition see *Bertrand model*.

Bertrand model a model of oligopolistic behaviour that implicitly refers to markets with *differentiated products* where firms simultaneously and non-cooperatively adjust their prices on the basis of conjectures regarding the prices they expect their rivals to charge.

Bertrand–Nash see *Bertrand model*.

Bertrand paradox the demonstration that if an oligopolistic firm selling an undifferentiated good follows pricing strategies their profits will be the same as would have been generated under perfect competition. It is a paradox because a small number of firms should be able to use their market power to do better.

Bilateral monopoly describes the bargaining situation between a *monopoly* seller and a *monopsonist* buyer. Both firms (or groups) have conflicting interests as regards the price charged and both parties have the power to influence the price. The outcome, as demonstrated by *game theory*, will be determined by the two firms' relative bargaining abilities.

Black market a market in which goods are sold illegally at prices that violate the legal restrictions on prices.

Block exemptions as the name implies, firms are given exemption from EU *competition policy* restrictions on agreements between firms where the Commission judges that on balance such agreements are in the public interest.

Block pricing see *second-degree price discrimination*.

Blockaded entry if a market is small and unit costs are very sensitive to *economies of scale* and/or *learning by doing*, it may not be possible for a new entrant to achieve sufficiently low unit costs to make entry profitable. Consequently, the market is served by either a monopoly or an oligopoly.

Bounded rationality a counter to the neo-classical assumption that individuals are *hyper-rational*. Herbert Simon is credited with coining the term to describe the reality whereby the limitations on human mental abilities mean that individuals cannot possibly absorb, store and retrieve all the information that will enable them to always select the course of action that will maximize their benefits.

Brands trade names given to differentiated goods and services with the purpose of establishing a reputation for quality and the ability to charge a price premium.

Break-even price the price at which a firm is just able to cover all of its costs, including the opportunity cost of capital.

Budget constraint a household's (or firm's) income per period that places an upper boundary on the goods and services that can be purchased. In principle, the budget includes any borrowed funds.

Budget line a graphical representation of a consumers' or households' *budget constraint*. Points on the line represent the largest consumption bundles that could be purchased with a given money income at the ruling set of prices. Points lying below the line represent feasible but inefficient consumption bundles, i.e. part of income is being wasted.

Bundling exists where a seller combines two or more products and sells the 'bundle' for a fixed price. If the products that are bundled were unlikely to have been bought in such quantities if sold separately, the benefit is to increase *revenue* and possibly reduce *unit cost*.

Business environment the combined influence of the many factors external to the firm that influence its level of profitability. At its broadest, the business environment embraces global forces and government policies. More narrowly, it reflects the behaviour of existing and potential rivals. See also *Five Forces Model*.

Business strategy refers to decisions concerning the deployment of a specialist firm's or *business unit's* resources so as to achieve the goals of the business.

Business unit a division of a *corporation* that has adopted an *M-form*.

Capability an activity that a firm is particularly good at. More frequently referred to as a *core competency*.

Capital generally refers to all man-made goods that are used in the process of making other goods and services rather than consumed for their own sake, such as tools, machinery and factories. It also refers to the funds available for investment in these capital goods. See also *fixed investment*; *investment and stocks*.

Capital deepening increasing the ratio of capital to labour, in a particular production process.

Capital goods products whose function is to produce goods and/or services, e.g. machinery. In practice, it is any product purchased by a firm that provides a flow of services over more than one production period.

Capital stock the total quantity or value of capital available to a firm or industry.

Capital widening increasing the quantity of capital without changing the proportions in which the factors of production are used.

Capitalist system a broad description of an economic system in which productive resources are privately owned and allocated primarily on the basis of market forces. In such a system, *property rights* must be clearly defined and capable of being enforced. See also *free market economy*.

Cartel a group of firms that agree to act as if they were a single unit.

Ceteris paribus 'other things being equal', as when attempting to isolate and analyse the impact of one variable, say a change in price on the quantity consumed, all other factors that might influence the outcome are held constant.

Ceteris paribus **demand curve** the demand curve facing an individual seller when all other sellers in the market leave their prices unchanged. See also *market response demand curve*.

Chance node with reference to *game theory*, it is a point in the *game tree* when chance determines the outcome.

Change in demand *a shift* in the whole demand curve, i.e. a change in the amount that will be bought at *each* price.

Choices the consequence of *scarcity*. The fact that resources are scarce means that any individual or firm has only a limited quantity of resources available to them and therefore choices must be made between competing uses for these resources.

Classical economics strictly refers to the body of thought on economics that had built up between 1776 when Adam Smith published the *Wealth of Nations* and the birth of neo-classical economics around 1850. More generally, often used to describe the period before the 1930s and *Keynesian economics*.

Cluster analysis a statistical technique for solving classification problems by sorting variables (people, products and so on) into groups, or clusters, so that the degree of association is strong between members of the same cluster and weak between members of different clusters. Each cluster thus describes, in terms of the data collected, the group to which its members belong.

Clusters see *industrial clusters*.

Collective dominance a situation in which a group of firms either tacitly or secretly agree to act as one and have the power to ensure all participants co-operate. See also *dominant firm*.

Collusion a situation where firms work together to achieve an agreed goal, though normally used where the agreement is secret. See also *tacit collusion* and *explicit collusion*.

Commodities in the world of commerce, a term that usually refers to primary or basic goods, such as wheat and iron ore, that are produced by the primary sector of the economy. Sometimes also used by economists to refer to all goods and services. See also *products*.

Common market the popular name for the EU *single market*.

Comparative statics short for 'comparative-static equilibrium analysis', it refers to studying the effect of an economic change, say a rise in the price of a product, by comparing the positions (e.g. level of sales) of static equilibrium before and after the change is introduced.

Competence approach the modern description of the resource-based approach to the firm, whereby firms are viewed as collections of resources, some of which are purchased in the market and some of which are created and developed internally, e.g. knowledge. Internally created resources include organizational and productive systems that are largely based on the skills, experience and co-operative routines that individuals and teams have accumulated during their working lives. Such resources are described as the firm's competencies and amount to tacit knowledge and cannot be fully codified and therefore be easily copied. According to this view of the firm, such competencies provide a basis for heterogeneity amongst firms and therefore a source of competitive advantage.

Competency see *capability*.

Competition describes the behaviour of firms within a market where each is attempting to maximize their profits by delivering equal or better value than their rivals. Normally used to describe a market in which no player has any influence over the market price.

Competition policy a range of policies designed to enable markets to operate under the forces of competition. In essence, these policies prohibit and seek to discourage a *dominant firm* abusing its power and groups of firms entering into a secret *restrictive agreement*. See also *industrial policies*.

Competitive advantage describes a situation in which a firm has a commercial advantage over rivals in supplying a particular market. This advantage may take the form of lower production costs, a superior quality product or an innovative design. Whatever the form of the advantage, it must result in a higher *profit* for the firm.

Complementary goods two goods for which the quantity demanded of one is positively related to the price of the other.

Complementors see *networker firms*.

Complete contract a hypothetical contract that describes what action is to be taken and payments made in every possible contingency.

Concentration ratio the fraction of total market sales (or some other measure of market power, e.g. fraction of industry's capital) controlled by a specific number of an industry's largest firms. For example, the four-firm concentration ratio measures the combined percentage of total sales accounted for by the largest four firms measured in descending order.

Conglomerate describes a firm that has diversified into unrelated markets. See also *diversification*.

Conglomerate merger when firms selling unrelated products merge. Also called a *lateral* or *horizontal merger*.

Conjectural variations an attempt to explain the dynamic behaviour of oligopolists, whereby a firm's decision regarding a change in its level of output or its price is based on conjectures regarding the responses of rivals.

Conspicuous consumption consumption of expensive goods that are desired because they imbue the consumer with the knowledge that others recognize their wealth. See also *Veblen good*.

Constant prices when applied to economic data, is a means of indirectly estimating volume growth by recalculating sales at points in time using one period's prices. Particularly useful when the firm produces a range of products.

Constant returns to scale situation that occurs in the long run when a firm's output increases exactly in proportion to the rate of increase in inputs, i.e. if inputs double, output doubles. It is represented by a horizontal long-run average cost curve.

Constrained optimization describes behaviour of an individual or firm, whereby the achievement of a goal is subject to a constraining influence, e.g. costs. For example, higher levels of production within the current period are constrained by rising unit costs. Alternatively, the pursuit of the satisfaction incurred by consumption is constrained by the costs of purchasing consumer goods.

Consumer relationship marketing no one definition but essentially a marketing system that seeks to identify individual customers and build a lasting relationship that will attract repeat business in the future.

Consumers' surplus the difference between the total value consumers place on all units consumed of a product and the payment they must make to purchase the units consumed.

Contestable market see *contestability*.

Contestability a theory which states that a market is perfectly contestable if there are no *sunk costs* associated with entry or exit. The effect is that potential entrants are not disadvantaged by incurring higher capital costs than incumbents. Consequently, incumbents have to limit the extent to which they abuse their market power, i.e. earn *economic rents* if they wish to discourage new entrants.

Control loss from a business perspective, the difficulties of receiving accurate and timely information as the size of an organization grows. See also *influencing costs*.

Co-operation refers to the practice of individuals or firms working together to achieve a commonly agreed goal. See also *collusion*.

Co-operative game theory see *game theory*.

Co-operatives where a number of independent enterprises pool all or part of their businesses for the purpose of achieving some cost or profit benefit.

Co-opetition a word introduced by Barry Nalebuff and Anthony Brandenberger to capture situations where the best strategy is to co-operate with other firms so as to be more competitive.

Copyrights are unregistered rights associated with the arts that come into effect the moment something that can be protected is created, e.g. a book.

Core competency an activity or function that the individual firm can undertake more efficiently and effectively than rivals. For example, a software company may have a core competency in designing particular operating systems.

Corporate social responsibility a business ethics concept based on the idea that companies have a social responsibility to their *stakeholders*. From this perspective, companies should be aware of, and attempt to minimize, harmful *externalities* arising from the conduct of their business.

Corporate strategy in a large-scale organization, particularly if *diversified*, it is the pattern of decisions that determine how its resources will be marshalled to achieve its goals. See also *business strategy*.

Corporation a large-scale, *diversified*, firm.

Correlation coefficient takes a value between zero and unity and provides a numerical summary measure of the degree of correlation between two variables. A coefficient equal to one means perfect correlation.

Cost–benefit analysis (CBA) a procedure for making long-run investment decisions, whereby benefits exceed costs over some succession of future time periods. Generally, only explicitly applied to large-scale public projects, e.g. a new airport.

Cost of capital is more than the cost of borrowed funds, as it embraces the opportunity cost to the firm of using its internally generated financial resources for *investment*.

Cost minimization the corollary of profit maximization; a level of output cannot be profit maximizing if the unit costs of producing the specific output are not the lowest attainable.

Cournot equilibrium see *Nash equilibrium*

Cournot model a simplified quantity-adjusting model of oligopoly that demonstrates how rivals providing an homogeneous product, non-cooperatively simultaneously adjust the quantities sold to achieve a *Nash equilibrium*.

Cournot–Nash equilibrium the *Nash equilibrium* associated with the *Cournot model*.

Covariance measures the co-movement between two variables.

Creative destruction a theory put forward by Joseph Schumpeter that the potential *economic rents* arising from the discovery of new knowledge regarding a product or process, spurs entrepreneurs to invest in such activities. As they succeed, so they 'destroy' existing products and processes and replace them with the preferred replacements, thereby raising living standards.

Credence goods goods and services whose true quality can rarely be accurately assessed even after consumption, e.g. the services of a solicitor. See also *search goods* and *experience goods*.

Cross-price elasticity of demand the responsiveness of demand for one product to changes in the price of another, defined as the percentage change in quantity demanded of product A divided by the percentage change in the price of product B.

Deadweight loss a measure of the loss of *allocative efficiency* associated with the exercise of monopoly power resulting in a less than optimal level of production, a high price and a reduction in *consumers' surplus*.

Decision control rights are the powers to ratify and monitor the implementation of resource commitments by senior managers.

Decision management rights are the powers to initiate and implement recommendations concerning the allocation of resources within a firm.

Decision tree see *game tree*.

Decreasing returns to scale see *diseconomies of scale*.

Deep pockets refers to the ability of a cash-rich firm to fund a large-scale investment in an uncertain project or fund anti-competitive behaviour, such as predatory pricing, that involves a period of losses.

Demand summarizes the many factors that determine the quantity of a product that will be purchased at all feasible prices. For example, the level of consumers' incomes, their tastes or preferences, and the prices of competing products.

Demand curve a graphical representation of *demand* showing the quantity of a product that would be purchased at different prices assuming the other elements of demand are held constant, i.e. *ceteris paribus*.

Demand function the formal representation of the factors that influence the *demand* for a specific product.

Derived demand refers to secondary demand created in response to an initial demand, e.g. demand for labour is the result of people demanding goods and services.

Deterrence strategies a class of strategies employed by incumbent firms designed to prevent firms entering the market or *fringe firms* expanding.

Differentiated product a product that is sold in a competitive market but is sufficiently different in design, quality or brand packaging to distinguish it. Products that are differentiated according to their mix of *attributes* are known as *horizontally differentiated* and products that are differentiated by having a larger or smaller quality of the attribute are known as *vertically differentiated*. Another form is *spatial differentiation*, that is, two identical products may be differentiated by the place of sale, e.g. retail outlet or home delivery.

Diffusion the speed, pattern and methods by which an *invention* or *innovation* is spread throughout the economy.

Diminishing marginal utility refers to the experience of obtaining successive smaller additions to utility as more of a product is consumed.

Diminishing rate of technical substitution refers to a movement along an isoquant whereby successively larger amounts of the increasing output must be available to compensate for the input being substituted.

Diminishing returns strictly this is short for diminishing marginal returns. The concept, popularly known as the *law of diminishing returns*, states that for any production function, as the volume of one or more inputs is steadily increased, and at least one input remains fixed, there will come a point where the addition to output resulting from the last (or marginal) unit of the variable input(s) employed will start to decline. The effect of diminishing returns is to cause the firm's output to increase at a diminishing rate and eventually to actually decline.

Directors are elected by the shareholders to manage or direct the affairs of publicly owned companies. Directors have a fiduciary duty to the owners. It is a relationship of trust and, typically, the directors make only minor business decisions, their main function being to monitor the activities of the firm and its managers. See also *principal–agent problem*.

Discounted cash flow (DCF) calculation of the present value of cash flows generated over future periods of varying length.

Diseconomies of scale a situation that occurs in the long run when a firm's output increases less than proportionately to inputs as the scale of production increases. This results in the firm's long-run average cost curve rising as output increases; a situation that is frequently referred to as decreasing returns to scale.

Disequilibrium a state of imbalance between opposing forces so that there are forces leading to change.

Disposable income the after-tax income that consumers have to spend or to save.

Diversification refers to the horizontal expansion of a firm into another product line. Diversification may be related or unrelated: the former occurs when a firm expands into a similar product line; and the latter occurs when the diversification involves the production of products that are very different, e.g. food and footwear. Diversification is usually undertaken to exploit *economies of scope* and is the normal means by which a firm grows in size.

Diversified firm see *diversification*.

Diversified growth see *diversification*.

Diversify see *diversification*.

Division of labour the breaking-up of a production process into a series of repetitive tasks, each done by a different worker.

Dominant firm is defined to have sufficient market power to be able, to an appreciable extent, to behave independently of its competitors, customers and ultimately its consumers.

Dominant strategy in a 'game', a dominant strategy describes a situation where a particular strategy always generates a higher return than any other strategy, regardless of the behaviour of rivals.

Dorfman–Steiner condition a formula for determining the optimal *advertising intensity*.

Double marginalization the potential outcome of a vertical exchange relationship involving two firms with market power at adjacent stages in the supply chain. The seller charges a price above *marginal cost* and this price then increases the downstream buyer's marginal cost, who also charges a price in excess of marginal cost.

Downstream refers to a movement along the *supply chain* towards final consumers.

Drastic innovation a production process *innovation* that reduces the innovator's unit cost of production to such an extent that it can under-price all of its industry rivals.

Duopoly an industry containing only two firms and therefore a special case of *oligopoly*.

Dynamic capabilities an approach to the firm rooted in the *competency approach*, whereby a firm's unique capability is the ability to react rapidly and efficiently to rapidly changing market conditions. See also *core competencies*.

Dynamic efficiency in relation to firms, the organization and development of their resources over successive time periods so as to maintain their capabilities.

Dynamic games games that take place over a number of time periods allowing participants to react to previous actions of rivals as well as conjectures about future actions of rivals.

Economic liberalization refers to the relaxation or removal of government restrictions and direct involvement in the conduct of economic activity. In the extreme, all prices and resource allocations are determined solely by market forces.

Economic models a term used in several related ways sometimes as a synonym for theory, sometimes for a specific quantification of a general theory, sometimes for the application of a general theory to a specific context, and sometimes for an abstraction designed to illustrate some point but not meant as a full theory on its own.

Economic profits or losses the difference between the revenues received from the sale of output and the opportunity cost of the inputs used to make the output. Negative economic profits are economic losses. Also called pure profits or pure losses, or simply profits or losses.

Economic rent the excess that a factor of production is paid above what is needed to keep it in its present use. Frequently used to describe a situation where a firm with market power, e.g. a monopoly, charges a price that is in excess of marginal costs, resulting in profits that are in excess of normal profits, i.e. those necessary to encourage investment in the industry. In this situation, economic rent is often referred to as super-normal profit. The expectation of earning an economic rent is presumed a sufficient incentive for a firm to enter a market and in this situation economic rent is an *ex ante* influence.

Economies of massed reserves the reduction in production costs arising from the reduction in risk associated with large numbers. For example, a firm with 100 machines is less vulnerable to breakdown than a firm with one machine.

Economies of scale are reductions in unit production costs that are potentially available as the scale of production increases. They are defined to exist when a firm's output increases more than proportionately to the cost of production; these are also known as *increasing returns*. A key driver of such economies if the prevailing technology, but scale itself increases the firm's ability to negotiate more favourable terms with suppliers. Economies of scale can only be achieved in the *long run* and are represented by a declining *long-run average curve*.

Economies of scope potentially arise from multi-product production, where jointly producing two or more products enables unit costs to be lower than if each was produced separately. Some of these cost savings are identical to those that arise from scale, e.g. large-scale distribution, advertising and purchasing, but they can also arise from the exploitation of a firm's *core competencies*, e.g. good management.

Efficient capital market a financial market in which there is *perfect information*. New information is available to all agents and is very quickly reflected in asset prices. If such a market existed in practice, no investment would be better than a coin toss.

Efficiency wages a system that sets wage rates above *market clearing* levels with the intention of attracting and retaining the best workers – thereby reducing the *transaction costs* of hiring new employees – as well as providing the employees with an incentive to improve their performance. The payment of an efficiency wage means that if the employee is caught *shirking* and dismissed, there will be a significant reduction in pay. Efficiency wages help to explain why wage rates do not adjust to clear labour markets.

Elastic describes the situation where the percentage change in quantity is greater than the percentage change in price (elasticity greater than 1).

Elasticity formally, the ratio of the incremental percentage change in one variable with respect to an incremental percentage change in another. For example, by what percentage does the quantity sold change when price is changed by a given percentage?

Elasticity of demand see *price elasticity of demand*.

Elasticity of supply see *price elasticity of supply*.

Endogenous literally, from within the model. For example, consumers' expenditure is a function of their disposable income; a rise in income will therefore increase consumption.

Entrepreneur the classical interpretation is someone who innovates and is prepared to take the risk of investing their own capital in the production of new products and/or new ways of making existing products. In more modern parlance, it is someone who seeks new knowledge and having acquired this knowledge uses it to their own, or their firm's, profitable advantage by having the vision as well as the energy and drive to bring about the necessary reallocation of resources.

Entry barrier see *barriers to entry*.

Equilibrium a state of balance between opposing forces so that there is no tendency to change.

European Commission is the executive of the European Union. Its primary roles are to propose and enact legislation, and to act as guardian of the treaties which provide the legal basis for the EU. The Commission also regulates *competition policy* for the EU.

European Economic Area is an economic area encompassing all the members of the *European Union* and three members of the European Free Trade Association – Iceland, Liechtenstein and Norway – who agree to be bound by the rules of the single market.

European Union is an inter-governmental, supranational organization made up of 25 European countries. Established by the Treaty on European Union in 1992 many aspects of the EU can be traced back to the Treaty of Rome that established the European Economic Community in 1957.

Evolutionary approach see *evolutionary theory*.

Evolutionary firm see *evolutionary theory*.

Evolutionary theory as applied to the firm, is associated with Richard Nelson and Sidney Winter. In essence, it is a theory whereby survival or growth is part of an evolutionary process in part influenced by random events, but also influenced by the way the firm accumulates and acts upon its own knowledge.

Ex ante refers to the situation before the event. A practical example is the planning stage for an investment. In this period the firm has maximum freedom for change.

Ex post refers to the situation after the event. The importance is that options may not be limited and change costly. For example, having entered a market the decision to leave may involved *exit costs*.

Excess demand the amount by which quantity demanded exceeds quantity supplied at the existing market price; negative *excess supply*.

Excess supply the amount by which quantity supplied exceeds quantity demanded at the existing market price; negative *excess demand*.

Exclusive dealing a *vertical restraint* whereby a seller of an *intermediate product* imposes the condition that a purchaser does not purchase substitute products from its rivals.

Exit barriers see *exit costs*.

Exit costs the costs incurred by a firm in leaving a market. These may include commitments to the workforce in terms of severance pay, to customers in terms of after-sales service and the cost of disposing of or scrapping fixed assets. See also *sunk costs*.

Exogenous a variable or factor that exists outside the control of an organization but exerts an influence on its activities.

Expense preference model a model of managerial behaviour most closely associated with Oliver Williamson, whereby managers are assumed to obtain *utility* from the power to exercise discretion over company expenditure.

Experience goods goods and services whose quality can only be accurately assessed after consumption. See also *search goods* and *credence goods*.

Explicit collusion a situation where firms explicitly agree to act as a single entity by co-operating in the setting of a strategic variable. Unless the firms are very small, such arrangements will not be tolerated by the competition authorities where they reduce competition. See also *tacit collusion*.

Extensive form game also called a *game tree*, is a graphical representation of a sequential game. Usually involving two players, it provides information as to the pay-offs to individual players according to each player's response to the other's previous move. The game is solved by *backward induction*.

External economies arise from sources outside of the firm, e.g. a pool of skilled labour but contribute to lower unit production costs.

External effects see *externality*.

Externality a cost (or benefit) arising from a private transaction or activity that is incurred (or received) by a third party but not felt directly by the parties to the transaction or instigators of the activity. Examples include the negative externality of the costs of pollution and the positive externality of an efficient transport system.

Factor markets markets where factor services (inputs) are bought and sold.

Factor services the services of *factors of production*: land, labour and capital.

Factors of production resources used to produce goods and services, frequently divided into the basic physical categories of land, labour and capital. Now more frequently referred to as *productive resources* and include intangible factors such as routines and systems. The *entrepreneur*, although strictly a special category of labour, is frequently defined as a separate factor.

Financial capital the funds used to finance a firm, including both equity capital and debt. Also called money capital.

Firm a productive organization whose role is to produce goods or services which are normally sold for a price. However in an economic sense, a civil service department is a firm. The defining characteristic is the co-ordination of resources to provide an output which may be tangible (e.g. cars) or intangible (e.g. advice).

Firm-specific human capital consists of skills and knowledge that are of direct value to an individual firm and of less value generally see *human capital*.

First-degree price discrimination the practice of charging individual consumers their *reservation price*.

First-mover advantage the advantage that accrues to a firm that reacts first to a market opportunity and thereby establishes a dominant position in either the price charged or the quantity produced. See also *Stackelberg's model*.

Fisher's separation theorem the proposition that a decision maker who is able to borrow and lend at the same rate of interest can base investment decisions solely on estimates of future cash flows and interest rates without regard to preferences regarding consumption.

Five Forces Model a model put forward by Michael Porter to strategically analyse the *business environment*. It shows that in order to achieve competitive advantage not only the behaviour of rivals, but also suppliers, customers, new products and new entrants must be taken into account.

Fixed capital refers to the buildings, plant and machines that a firm must have access to in order to undertake production.

Fixed costs costs that are fixed for the production period and therefore do not change with the level of output. Frequently referred to as the cost of fixed capital, but in practice includes all overhead costs, e.g. administration. Another approach views fixed costs as being unavoidable costs for the production period.

Fixed factors inputs of which the amount available in the short run is fixed.

Fixed investment expenditure on those capital goods that are physical – plant, machinery and buildings – and which are, as the name implies, fixtures belonging to the firm.

Fordism a description of production systems that employ assembly line techniques. With a governing hierarchy the firm's resources are controlled and co-ordinated so as to increase efficiency and lower unit costs.

Fordist model see *Fordism.*

Forward integration describes the situation when a firm vertically integrates *downstream.* See *vertical integration.*

Franchise fee a payment (generally annual) paid by a franchisee to a franchisor that entitles the franchisee to some privilege. In the case of a firm it may be the right to purchase an intermediate product at a low price, e.g. *marginal cost.* See also *two-part tariff.*

Franchising where a firm (the franchisee) owns and runs a business using the franchisor's brand name.

Free market economy an economy in which the spending and production decisions of individuals and firms (as distinct from the central authorities) exert the major influence over the allocation of resources. See also *capitalist system.*

Free-rider an individual who consumes a good or service without paying for it. Free-riders are a problem because in a market system their existence will result in a less-than-optimal quantity of the good or service being produced.

Free trade is the absence of all tariff barriers and distortions – be they quotas, subsidies or standards – to the free flow of goods between countries.

Fringe competitors defined as the small-scale producers who, in total, account for a minority share of a particular industry's output. In a differentiated market such firms would supply *niche markets* and in commodity markets each firm would be a *price taker.* See also *dominant firm.*

Full-cost pricing refers to the situation where, instead of equating marginal revenue with marginal cost, firms set prices equal to average cost at normal capacity output plus a conventional mark-up.

Full-line forcing a *vertical restraint* whereby a seller forces a buyer to carry the seller's full range of products.

Function loosely, an expression of a relationship between two or more variables. Precisely, Y is a function of the variables $X_1, ..., X_n$ if, with every set of values of the variables $X_1, ..., X_n$ there is associated a unique value of the variable Y.

Gains from trade advantages realized as a result of specialization made possible by trade.

Game theory a branch of mathematics that is concerned with how rational individuals make decisions when they are mutually interdependent. The theory is increasingly applied to various branches of economics and, in particular, the behaviour of *oligopolists.* Game theory is divided into two branches: *non co-operative* and *co-operative* game theory. In non-cooperative game theory the unit of analysis is the individual player, who is deemed to act alone in self-interest and be concerned to do as well as possible, subject to the behaviour of other participants. If the players achieve this objective it is described as a *Nash equilibrium*. In co-operative game theory the unit of analysis is the group or coalition who enter into enforceable contractual relationships and the focus of analysis is the agreement between the participants and the terms of their contractual relationship.

Game tree a graphical representation of an *extensive form game* consisting of nodes joined by sets of vertices. Nodes are points where players must choose an action. Starting at the initial or root node, every set of vertices from this point through the tree eventually arrives at a terminal node representing the pay-offs to each player.

General purpose human capital see *human capital*.

Gibrat's law formally the law of proportionate growth, which states that the size of firms and their rates of growth are statistically independent, i.e. starting out, a group of equal-sized firms will grow at different rates therefore over time displaying very different sizes.

Giffen good an inferior good where consumption falls as the price is reduced resulting in a positively sloped demand curve.

Gini-coefficient a measure of inequality. In industrial economies it is used to indicate the inequality of market shares. If all firms in an industry had an identical market share the gini-coefficient would equal zero. The extreme inequality would be represented by a gini-coefficient of unity. See also the *Lorenz curve*.

Globalization a word that has come to represent a number of forces that are bringing about the integration of the world's economies. Key globalization forces are multilateral trade agreements, liberalized capital markets and information and communication technologies.

Goal congruence describes a situation where all members of a firm, or groups of firms in an alliance or joint venture, are focused on achieving the same objective(s).

Going wage rate the rate of pay within a firm, locality or country, for a particular job that would be set by unfettered market forces.

Goods tangible products, such as cars or shoes.

Goods markets markets where goods and services are bought and sold.

Governance approach the modern description of the *transaction costs* approach to the firm, whereby firms exist when the transaction costs of using the market outweigh the costs of using a governing, authoritarian organizational hierarchy to co-ordinate productive resources, i.e. a firm.

Government in economics, all public agencies, government bodies and other organizations that belong to, or owe their existence to, the government. Sometimes (more accurately) called the central authorities.

Gross return on capital the market value of output minus all non-capital costs, split into depreciation, pure return, risk premium and pure profit; typically expressed as a percentage of the capital stock.

Gross revenue the cash generated by a business before any deductions. See also *revenue*.

Growth describes how a firm changes its size from one period to the next. A positive rate of growth means that the firm is getting steadily larger. A firm's size is normally measured by the volume of its sales, so growth measures the annual percentage increase in the volume of sales. Most firms do not grow smoothly; empiricism suggests their sales follow a *random walk*.

Growth–Share Matrix a chart created by the Boston Consulting Group in the 1970s to help corporations analyse their business units or product lines and decide where to allocate financial resources.

Hawk–Dove Game a game which demonstrates that aggressive behaviour (an aggressive strategy) does not always deliver the best outcome to the participants.

Hazard rate refers to the *tournament model* of *innovation* where there is deemed to be an inverse relationship between a firm's expenditure on *research and development* and the risk that a rival's innovation will usurp the firm's competitive position.

Herfindahl index a measure of *seller concentration*, whereby each firm's (percentage) market share is squared and the sum of these squared values yields the Herfindahl index. The closer the index to unity, the greater the degree of concentration.

Hidden actions a conflict of self-interests between a principal and agent, whereby the agent will seek privately to take actions that are of benefit to the agent and a cost to the principal. See also *principal–agent problem*.

Hidden characteristics an example of *asymmetric information* where a principal cannot distinguish between products or people with respect to a particular attribute, e.g. a quality or skill. See *principal–agent problem*.

Hog cycles a term used to characterize cycles of over- and under-production because of the time lags in the production process. For example, high prices for pork today lead many farmers to start breeding pigs; when the pigs mature there will be an increased supply of pork, which will drive down its price; so fewer farmers will breed pigs and the price will rise again – starting the cycle over again.

Hold-up a problem arising from the *transaction costs* associated with *asset specificity* whereby a supplier will not invest for fear of the buyer engaging in *opportunistic behaviour*.

Homogeneous product a product that, in the eyes of purchasers, is identical in every respect – quality, location – to the products being offered for sale by other firms in the industry.

Horizontal agreements arise when firms operating at the same level in the supply chain enter into agreements or concerted practices. The EU Commission will apply the *rule of reason* when determining whether the agreement is likely to reduce competition or deliver benefits, e.g. the sharing of risk or distribution costs, the pooling of knowledge or the more rapid *diffusion* of an invention.

Horizontal boundary refers to the size of a firm in terms of its volume or value of output. For a specialist firm, its horizontal boundary will be determined by the scale of production. For a *diversified firm*, horizontal scale will be determined by both the number of markets in which the firm operates and the scale of production in each market.

Horizontal merger union or *merger* of firms at the same stage of production in the supply chain.

Horizontally differentiated the ranking of products within a *market* or *product space* that absorb the same quantity and quality of resources in their production and hence the basis of their differentiation is design, packaging and branding. See also *differentiated product*.

Human capital the capitalized value of the acquired skills and knowledge arising from investments in people. Usually refers to value derived from expenditures on education, training, and health improvements.

Human resource management refers to the management of a firm's workforce so as to maintain and improve the value to the firm of its *human capital*.

Hyper-rationality the propensity and ability to search for the optimal decision, which implies zero search costs.

Imperfect competition strictly refers to any industry or market where the conditions necessary for *perfect competition* are not satisfied. The imperfection may arise from the industry's structure or information asymmetries. Industries characterized by *monopoly, oligopoly, monopsony* and *oligopsony* are examples of imperfect competition, as is *monopolistic competition*.

Imperfect information describes a situation where an economic agent knows the set of actions the agents they are dealing with can take, but does not know for certain what specific action the agents will take. In *game theory*, players rationalize the likely behaviour of other players.

Implicit contract an informal understanding between economic agents – a buyer and seller or an employee and manager – based on a trusting relationship and with no legal remedy if one side defaults.

Imputed costs the costs of using inputs already owned by the firm, measured by the earnings they could have received in their best alternative employment.

Incidence in tax theory, where the burden of a tax finally falls.

Income constraint refers to the limits, set by a consumer's income, on the set of baskets of goods that can be consumed. See *budget line*.

Income effect effect on quantity demanded of a change in real income, relative prices held constant.

Income elastic describes the situation where the percentage change in quantity demanded exceeds the percentage change in income that brought it about. See *income elasticity of demand*.

Income elasticity of demand the responsiveness of quantity demanded to a change in the incomes of consumers. Defined as the percentage change in quantity demanded divided by the percentage change in income.

Income inelastic describes the situation where the percentage change in quantity demanded is smaller than the percentage change in income. See *income elasticity of demand*.

Incomplete contracts contracts drawn up under *bounded rationality* that are unable to allow for all possible contingencies.

Incomplete information arises in cases of *asymmetric information* where one economic agent has private information that is not available to the agents they are dealing with. In *game theory*, players faced with incomplete information cope by attaching probabilities to the nature of the private information, e.g. whether a rival's production costs are high or low.

Increasing returns to scale see *economies of scale*.

Incremental costs increase in costs associated with a small but discrete change in output.

Indifference curve a line or curve showing alternative bundles of products from which an individual consumer obtains identical levels of *utility*. Consequently, the individual is said to be indifferent as to which bundle to consume.

Indifference map a consumer's set of *indifference curves*. See *preference map*.

Indivisible from the perspective of economics, a resource, say a machine, that cannot be used at low levels of production without loss of efficiency.

Industrial clusters a graphical grouping of firms involving some in direct competition, but also including suppliers and customers, i.e. the clusters include forward and backward linkages. Such clusters are deemed to impart a number of benefits to those involved, including the sharing of information.

Industry group is a classification system whereby industries are generally represented by two-, three- or four- digit codes. The two-digit code is the broadest category group and the three- and four-digit codes represent successively narrower industry groups.

Industrial organization a development of *neo-classical economics* whose focus is the behaviour of firms and the industries in which they compete.

Industrial policies a range of policies designed, in principle, to improve the productive and competitive performance of individual firms and industries. Frequently governments under the guise of industrial policies attempt to protect and support ailing industries. See also *competition policies*.

Industry a group of firms that sell a well-defined product or closely related set of products.

Industry structure the characteristics of an industry that are tied to the ownership of productive resources, and are manifested in aspects such as the number of sellers or buyers, the extent of differentiated products, diversification and vertical integration. The four basic industry structures are perfect competition, monopolistic competition, oligopoly and monopoly.

Inelastic (demand) describes the situation where following a change in price, the percentage change in quantity (demanded) is less than the percentage change in price (elasticity is less than 1 in absolute terms).

Inferior good a commodity with a negative income elasticity, i.e. its demand diminishes when income increases.

Influencing costs a concept introduced by Paul Milgrom, which relates to the increasing cost of efficiently managing an organization whose growth is based on bringing more activities under the control of a single management.

Information and communication technology the *technology* required to process and disseminate information. It embraces computers, computer software and telecommunications.

Infrastructure the basic facilities (particularly transportation and communication systems) on which commerce depends.

Innovation the conversion of new knowledge – an invention – into a commercial opportunity.

Inputs the materials and factor services used in the process of production.

Interest the amount each year paid on a loan, usually expressed as a percentage (e.g. 5 per cent) or as a proportion (e.g. 0.05) of the principal loan.

Intermediate products all goods and services involved in a vertical exchange as inputs into a downstream stage of production.

Internal economies economies that arise from sources within the firm, e.g. learning.

Internalizing an externality an action that makes an *externality* enter into the firm's own calculations of its private costs and benefits, e.g. taxing the price of an environmentally harmful input.

Internal labour market a career system within an organization in which, subject to satisfactory performance, individuals have career paths and consequently senior posts are generally filled by internal promotions.

Internal labour market essentially the province of long-term employment relationships where the firm has limited points for entry and relies on internal promotion and career paths to fill senior positions.

Internal rate of return the discount rate that makes the *net present value* of the returns on a specific investment project equal to zero. It is a measure of the yield on an investment project.

Intermediate markets see *intermediate products*.

Intermediate products are sold by one firm to another firm and normally they are not finished goods, but require further stages of production. Generally, they are the basis of exchange between two vertical stages in a *supply chain* and will frequently involve large volumes.

Intertemporal decision a decision that runs over more than one time period. For example, an investment requires a decision today and a pay-off in future time periods.

Invention the discovery of new knowledge it may be a new production process or a new product.

Inventories see *stocks*.

Investment an intertemporal decision whereby resources are devoted to producing or purchasing an asset, e.g. a machine, that then provides a flow of services over a future period.

Investment expenditure see *investment*.

Invisible hand the *deus ex machina* proposed by Adam Smith to summarize the self-seeking proclivities of the business world that confers benefits on society as a whole.

Isocost line lines drawn on a diagram that have the property that each point on the line represents an equal level of costs.

Isoprofit curves lines drawn on a diagram that have the characteristic that each line represents a fixed level of profits.

Isoquant a curve representing a technologically determined *production function*. Points on the curve show the different combinations of inputs that deliver precisely the same level of output.

Joint-stock company a firm regarded in law as having an identity of its own. Its owners hold shares with limited liability for the company's debts. Called a corporation in North America and now in Europe; more often called simply a company, limited company or PLC in the UK.

Joint venture an agreement by two or more firms to jointly invest in a stand-alone enterprise for the purpose of achieving joint goals.

Keynesian refers to a school of economic theories based on the ideas of John Maynard Keynes, whereby governments take responsibility for maintaining aggregate demand – by means of fiscal and monetary policy – at a sufficiently high level to avoid unemployment

Kinked demand curve a graphical explanation of the frequent observation that oligopolists do not compete on price. The demand curve is kinked to represent the fact that if an oligopolist lowers its price its rivals will normally follow to protect market share – hence the gain in sales will be small, i.e. the demand curve is relatively steep. However, if the oligopolist raises its price, its rivals may not follow, resulting in a significant loss of market share, i.e. the demand curve is relatively flat.

Knowledge-based theory of the firm a view of the firm as being a unique but incomplete collection of the skills and knowledge of its workers. The existence of firms is justified by the activities that co-ordinate the application of these skills to production. See also *competence approach to the firm*.

Kondratiev wave named after the Soviet economist Nikolai Kondratiev who observed cycles of economic activity running from depression to boom and back into recession over a 50–60 year cycle.

Labour all productive human resources, both mental and physical, inherited and acquired.

Labour productivity total output divided by the labour used producing it, i.e. output per unit of labour.

Land the free gifts of nature, such as land, forests, minerals and so on. Sometimes called natural resources.

Lateral merger see *horizontal merger*.

Law of diminishing returns see *diminishing returns*.

Law of one price states that within a geographic space, at any point in time, a product is sold for the same price subject only to transportation costs. The law implies that a market can be defined as the economic space wherein prices differ only by transportation costs.

Lean production model a production system that is based on trusting, long-term relationships with suppliers. Once suppliers can be trusted to do what they say, then the purchasing firm can reduce its inventories and hence lower its production costs.

Learning by doing the idea that a firm achieves additional economies in production as a result of its workforce developing lower-cost co-operative routines and improved cognitive skills as a result of the experience gained from cumulative production. See also the *learning curve*.

Learning curve the graphical representation of learning by doing. The scope for learning effects will vary from industry to industry. The learning curve tends to be steeper in complex industries, e.g. aeroplane manufacture.

Lerner index is the firm's profit margin. The index is constructed to demonstrate that a firm's maximum profit margin is equal to the inverse of its price elasticity of demand. The more competitive a market, the larger the price elasticity of demand and therefore the smaller the profit margin.

Life cycle hypothesis a theory which states that demand goes through four distinct stages during the lifetime of a product: birth, growth, maturity and eventually decline. These stages are deemed to have implications for the prices charged and production costs. See *product life cycle*.

Limit price a pricing strategy available to a dominant firm whereby the market price is held at a sufficiently low level to prevent a potential entrant earning a normal profit after entry.

Limit pricing model see *limit price*.

Limit pricing strategy see *limit price*.

Lisbon Strategy a strategy, agreed by the EU's political leaders in March 2000, to achieve, within a decade, the most competitive and dynamic knowledge-based economy in the world, capable of sustainable growth, with more and better jobs and greater social cohesion.

Living standards the quality of life for individuals. At its most basic, the volume of goods and services they can afford to consume, but also includes less tangible attributes such as political freedoms, safety and minimum pollution.

Long run in microeconomics, a period of time over which all production inputs may be varied but the basic technology of production is unchanged.

Long-run average cost curve an envelope curve showing the least-cost method of producing increasing levels of output – where costs incorporate a *normal profit* – when all inputs can be varied, but subject to a fixed technology.

Lorenz curve a graphical representation of the *gini-coefficient*.

M-form an organizational structure defined by Oliver Williamson in which *business units* or divisions are given autonomy in the way they achieve the objectives set for them by corporate headquarters. See also *multi-divisional firm*.

Macroeconomics the study of the behaviour of the economic system as a whole. Key areas of study include: economic growth, unemployment, inflation, trade performance and the distribution of income.

Management school the name given to a school of economic thought that originated in the 1930s with the purpose of examining the behaviour of firms once ownership and management control were separated. See also *principal–agent problem*.

Managerial theories an approach to understanding the behaviour of professional managers who run companies on behalf of their owners, i.e. the *shareholders*. These theories have in common the idea that professional managers seek to pursue their own goals, subject to any influences or constraints imposed by the owners. Closely allied to this approach is *principle–agent theory*.

Marginal cost the change in total production costs resulting from a small change in the level of output. Once an increasing level of output has reached the point where *diminishing returns* take effect, so the marginal costs of higher levels of production rise continuously. That is, rising marginal costs are the counterpart of falling *marginal productivity*.

Marginal cost of labour the cost to a firm of hiring one more unit of labour. If the firm is a large employer of labour, the effect of hiring more workers could be a general rise in its wage rates.

Marginal cost pricing method of pricing where price is set equal to marginal cost.

Marginal efficiency of capital measures the net cash flow arising from a marginal addition to the firm's capital stock as a percentage of the cost of the addition to the capital stock.

Marginal product the change in a firm's total volume of output resulting from employing one more (or one less) unit of a variable input. Also called the marginal physical product.

Marginal product of labour the addition to a firm's output from employing one more unit of labour.

Marginal productivity see *marginal product*.

Marginal rate of substitution measures, when moving along an indifference curve, the amount of consumption of one product that must be forgone to precisely offset the gain in utility from consuming more of another product.

Marginal rate of time preference measures how much consumption must be received in the future if the loss of utility from forgoing a unit of consumption today is precisely offset.

Marginal revenue the incremental change in total revenue resulting from a small change in the number of units of output sold per period of time or a small change in the price charged.

Marginal revenue product the addition to a firm's revenue resulting from the sale of the *marginal product* of a factor input, e.g. labour. If the firm has monopoly power, an increase in output may reduce the selling price – hence the relevance of the marginal revenue.

Marginal utility the change in total utility resulting from a small change in the number of units consumed.

Market a generic term for the forums in which buyers and sellers negotiate the exchange of goods or services.

Market clearing price the price at which the total units being offered for sale exactly equals the total demand. See *equilibrium price*.

Market clearing wage the wage rate at which the total numbers offering themselves for work exactly equals the total demand.

Market demand curve records the sum of all the individual demands at different market prices. As the demand curves of individuals are generally downward sloping, so too will be the market demand curve. Movements up and down the market demand curve therefore represent changes in aggregate consumption arising from a change in price, *ceteris paribus*.

Market economy an economy in which employment, production, and consumption decisions are made by individuals and firms acting as free agents and interacting through voluntary sale and purchase of goods and services in a range of different market environments.

Market failure any market outcome that is inferior to the best possible outcome achievable for society as a whole.

Market response demand curve the relevant demand curve when all sellers in a market change their prices in the same direction. See also *ceteris paribus* demand curve.

Market segments an identifiable sub-market of a *market* generally for *differentiated products* based on an identifiable consumer need and consisting of those goods or services that are perceived by consumers as close *substitutes* or *near neighbours*. See also *product space* and *strategic group*.

Market structure see *industry structure*.

Marketing mix the blend of product, place, promotion and pricing strategies designed to achieve the seller's strategic goals.

Materials primary goods – coal, oil, electricity – and semi-manufactured goods purchased by firms as inputs to their production processes.

Matrix organization combines a functional structure with a product, or more correctly in this case, a project structure. Decision making is centred on the project and teams are drawn from functional areas according to the nature and size of the project.

Mature market a market that has come to the end of its growth phase and now displays little or zero growth. See also *product life cycle*.

Mergers and acquisitions when two or more formerly independent firms unite. See *horizontal*, *vertical* and *conglomerate mergers*.

Merit goods goods of which the government decides that more should be produced than people would choose to consume left to themselves.

Microeconomics the study of the behaviour of individual elements within the economic system. That is, the behaviour of individuals, groups, firms and markets in the consumption, production and distribution of goods and services.

Minimax is a solution method in *game theory* whereby a player, not knowing for certain rivals' strategies, adopts the strategy that will deliver for certain at least a minimum pay-off and this pay-off is the best (the maximum) of the minimum pay-offs to all possible strategies.

Minimum Efficient Scale the scale of output at which the long-run average cost curve reaches a minimum; the lowest level of output per period that will achieve the lowest unit costs of production.

Mixed bundling a pricing strategy whereby two or more products can either be sold separately or together in a bundle. See also *bundling*.

Mixed economy an economy in which some decisions about the allocation of resources are made by firms and households and some by the central authorities.

Mixed strategy in a 'game' lacking a *saddle point*, a player must keep an opponent guessing by randomly selecting differing strategies.

Money income the cash value of income available for spending in a given period, e.g. one week.

Monopolist see *monopoly*.

Monopolistic competition a market structure credited to Edward Chamberlin in which there are many sellers and freedom of entry and exit, but in which each firm sells a *differentiated product*, giving it some control over the price it charges.

Monopoly a market structure where a single seller, a *monopolist*, is the sole supplier of a product with no close substitutes.

Monopsonist a sole purchaser of a particular product or type of labour. In this position the firm can use its power to lower the price or wage.

Monopsony see *monopsonist*.

Moral hazard risk inherent in *opportunistic behaviour* arising after a contractual arrangement has been undertaken, e.g. an employee may decide to take shirk after having obtained a long-term employment contract.

Multidimensional scaling a data analysis technique that displays distance-like data in a geometrical picture. The distance between each pair of variables reflects the amount of dissimilarity between the pairs.

Multi-divisional firm an organizational structure based on product or geographic divisions, each with their own functional 'silos', e.g. production or marketing. This structural form is suited to a large diversified firm where the head office then audits the performance of the separate divisions.

Nash equilibrium an equilibrium associated with game theory, but having direct relevance to an oligopoly, whereby all firms (players) are doing the best they can given that their rivals are also doing the best they can.

Nationalization the act of taking productive assets in to state ownership.

Natural monopoly an industry whose market demand is sufficient to allow only one firm to produce at its minimum efficient scale.

Near neighbour products in a market consisting of *differentiated products*, reflects the fact that for individuals some products will be closer substitutes than others. These will have a high *cross-price elasticity of demand* and are known as near neighbours.

Neo-classical approach see *neo-classical economies*.

Neo-classical economics a body of economic theories that demonstrate how the ideal of *perfect competition* brings about the socially efficient allocation of a scarce resource. Its models are based on marginal analysis, e.g. *marginal cost* and *marginal revenue*, that enable refutable hypotheses to be constructed and real-world predictions empirically tested. See also *neo-classical paradigm*.

Neo-classical paradigm the grouping of economic theories that rest on three assumptions: people are rational in their preferences; individuals maximize utility and firms maximize profits; and people act on the basis of *perfect information* and are endowed with *hyper-rationality*.

Net investment gross investment minus replacement investment. New capital that represents net additions to the capital stock.

Net present value the future annual stream of *revenue* less *variable production costs* generated by an investment – the cash flow – converted into current values and from which the investment costs are deducted. See also *present value*.

Net revenue essentially, the cash retained by the firm when variable production costs, e.g. labour and materials, are subtracted from sales revenue.

Network externality exists when the value of consuming a product depends on the behaviour of others. For example a network may increase in value as more people join the network, e.g. a mobile phone network or in the case of a *Veblen good* value will decline.

Network organization describes a grouping of separate, independent firms with a common objective.

Networked firms economies of scale and scope that arise from relationships with other firms and result in the value of a firm's output being higher than it otherwise would be. For example, the value of a PC is enhanced by the software that other firms produce.

Nexus of contracts from a business perspective, the idea that firms are a collection of contracts between different parties – primarily shareholders, directors, employees, suppliers and customers.

Niche markets a small *market segment* that constitutes a viable market for a specialist product or a narrowly defined group of products.

Non-cooperative refers to the behaviour of firms that act independently in their own interest.

Non-cooperative equilibrium an equilibrium reached by firms who have calculated and acted upon their own best interests without resort to co-operating or colluding with competitors.

Non-cooperative game theory see *game theory*.

Non-linear pricing a generic term describing pricing schemes with the common feature that the average price paid per unit declines as the volume consumed rises. See also *second-degree price discrimination*.

Non-renewable or exhaustible resources any productive resource that is available as a fixed stock that cannot be replaced once it is used, such as oil.

Non-strategic behaviour behaviour that takes no account of the reactions of others, as when a firm is operating under *perfect competition*.

Normal form game a matrix representation of a simultaneous game for two players. The rows represent one player's strategies and the columns represent the other player's strategies and each cell the pay-offs to each player. Such games are solved by the concept of *Nash equilibrium*.

Normal good a commodity whose demand increases when income increases.

Normal profit this is defined as the notional cost of capital invested in a business which is deemed to comprise three elements the *opportunity cost* of the funds used to purchase the capital; the amount of depreciation; and an appropriate risk premium. The opportunity cost of the funds used depends on the alternatives available. The normal profit might be viewed as the minimum necessary to induce an investor to invest. If *ex post* the return does not equal the sum of these elements, then the *entrepreneur* will not be induced to undertake the investment again, but will deploy available funds elsewhere.

Oligopolist a firm operating in an oligopoly.

Oligopoly a market structure when output is supplied by a small number of firms. In this situation, the price each firm receives for its products and its share of the market depend to a large degree on the behaviour of its rivals. Thus, the performance of oligopolist firms is interdependent and the nature of the rivalry that this interdependence gives rise to is better captured by *game theory*.

Oligopsonist refers to an individual firm within an *oligopsony*.

Oligopsony an industry characterized by a small number of firms that purchase a particular product or type of labour. See also *monopsonist*.

Open access resource a resource that is owned by no one and may be used by anyone.

Opportunistic behaviour the seeking with guile of advantage in an exchange transaction by withholding private information or not fulfilling promises.

Opportunity cost the cost of using a resource for a given purpose, measured by the benefit that might have been generated by using the resource for its best alternative use. For example, the opportunity cost of investing €1,000 in a business is the return the €1,000 could have earned in an alternative use, e.g. on deposit in a bank.

Organizational architecture a framework that identifies three critical organizational characteristics the assignment of decision rights; the systems and routines that monitor and measure performance; and the motivation and reward systems that encourage efficiency. In short, a firm's organizational architecture determines the culture and pattern of relationships amongst its members; it is responsible for *the way the firm gets things done*.

Organizational coherence the ability of a firm as it grows large and engages in *diversification* to keep its workforce focused on common goals, to encourage new thinking and ideas without sacrificing efficiency.

Organizational culture the collective personality which distinguishes individuals within one organization from those in another.

Organizational form the way in which a firm is structured so as to improve information flow and decision making. In essence, it determines what information needs to be communicated within the organization and to what extent decisions are decentralized. See also *M-form*, *unitary form* and *matrix organization*.

Organizational slack a concept similar to *X-inefficiency*, except that management is prepared to countenance a degree of inefficiency until some event, e.g. a fall in profits, prompts action.

Organizational strategy the matching of a firm's internal structure with its external business environment.

Outputs the goods and services that result from the process of production.

Outsource an arrangement whereby one company provides services to another.

Pareto-efficiency a situation in which it is impossible, by reallocating production or consumption activities, to make at least one person better off without making at least one person worse off.

Partnership Alliance the voluntary agreement of two or more firms to work closely together to achieve specific goals. Such alliances work best when there is a high degree of trust between the partners.

Patent the granting of exclusive *property rights* to the inventor of a new product or process for a period of years. The opportunity to earn an *economic rent* from the monopoly that a patent confers is therefore an incentive to engage in R&D activity. This increases the effort put into the search for new knowledge.

Patent licence is a method of allowing a patent holder to control an orderly diffusion of the new knowledge.

Payback period the time it takes to recoup the cost of an investment.

Perfect competition an industry structure in which all firms are *price takers*. This can only be achieved if the industry consists of a large number of small firms where even the largest firms account for a very small fraction of total output – a so-called *atomistic industry*. Each firm must produce an *homogenous product* and there must be freedom of entry into, and exit from, the industry.

Perfect information as regards economics, an agent when making a decision, e.g. to buy, has complete knowledge of the prices and the value of all alternatives on offer.

Piece rates refer to incentive payments whereby earnings are directly related to effort.

Pigovian tax an expenditure tax levied to discourage the consumption of a product with a significant, negative *externality*.

Predation the act or practice of engaging in predatory behaviour. See also *predatory pricing*.

Predatory pricing the policy of deeply cutting prices so that the price cutter is incurring a loss with the intention of, first, driving one or more competitors out of business and, second, of raising prices once competition has been eliminated.

Pre-emption an action by a firm with the strategic purpose of denying new entrants or rivals the opportunity to earn economic rents, for example the practice of holding *sleeping patents*. See also *strategic barriers to entry*.

Preference map a representation of all the bundles of goods and services that an individual would consumer at varying relative prices and money incomes. The preference map is represented graphically with a set of *indifference curves*.

Present value the value now of a sum to be received in the future. The future value is converted to current values by deflating future values using an appropriate discount rate.

Price controls anything that influences prices by laws rather than by market forces, e.g. minimum wage.

Price differentiation reflects the charging of different prices to different customers to reflect differences in the cost of supply, e.g. transport costs.

Price discrimination the act by a single firm of selling the same product, at therefore an identical marginal cost, at different prices to different buyers at the same point of sale. See also *first-degree price discrimination*, *second-degree price discrimination* and *third-degree price discrimination*.

Price elasticity of demand the percentage change in quantity demanded divided by the percentage change in price that brought it about. Often called elasticity of demand, it is the key indicator of the impact of a change in price on the firm's revenue.

Price elasticity of supply the percentage change in quantity supplied divided by the percentage change in price that brought it about. Often called elasticity of supply, it is a concept that only has relevance in a perfect market.

Price index a statistical measure of the average level of some group of prices relative to some basic period.

Price leadership a strategy employed by a *dominant firm* or a *collective dominance* whereby they act like a monopolist and set the profit-maximizing price having subtracted the supply of *fringe firms*. The fringe firms adopt this price and it becomes the market price.

Price system an economic system in which prices play a key role in determining the allocation of resources and the distribution of the national product.

Price taker a firm whose homogenous output is such a small fraction of the industry's output that no matter how it alters its level of production and sales it cannot affect the price of the product it sells.

Price war reflects a state of intense competitive rivalry whereby competitors seek to capture market share by successively lowering their prices resulting in a general loss of profits.

Primary line injury a legal term that refers to the damage a policy of *price discrimination* does to competitors.

Primary products unprocessed or partially processed goods which become *intermediate products*. They include agricultural commodities like grain and raw materials like iron ore and crude oil.

Principal–agent problem arises in a relationship where one party (the principal) contracts with another (the agent) to act on his or her behalf. This raises a potential problem arising from the impossibility of writing a *complete contract* that will induce agents to act solely in their principal's best interests. The problem is solved by devising a process that aligns the agent's self-interest with that of the principal's.

Principle–agent see *principle–agent problem.*

Principle component analysis is a cluster analysis tool designed to capture the variance in a dataset by reducing to two dimensions the dimensionality of the data to summarize the most important relationships, whilst simultaneously filtering out noise.

Principle of substitution the idea that methods of production will change if relative prices of inputs change, with relatively more of the cheaper input and relatively less of the more expensive input being used.

Prisoners' Dilemma a famous example of a 'game' whereby the inability of the players to communicate and trust each other leads to an outcome (*Nash equilibrium*) that is sub-optimal for both players. The game is relevant for understanding the incentive for oligopolists to collude in order to increase profits.

Private sector that part of the economy in which the organizations that produce goods and services are owned by private agents such as households and firms.

Producer any agent that makes goods or services.

Producers' surplus the difference between total revenue and total cost. See *economic rent.*

Product differentiation see *differentiated products.*

Product homogeneity see *homogenous product.*

Product life cycle refers to the succession of stages a product goes through from its development and launch, through growth to maturity and eventual decline. See *life cycle hypothesis.*

Product space a theoretical space within which *differentiated products* can be placed so as to show in what dimensions products are differentiated from each other. In two dimensions, products are assigned according to the degree to which they are *vertically differentiated* and *horizontally differentiated.*

Production the process of making goods and services by combining and co-ordinating *factors of production* in a manner determined by the prevailing *technology.*

Production function a functional relationship between inputs and outputs that is determined by technology. It shows the maximum output that can be produced by each and every combination of inputs.

Production-possibility frontier a function that shows the alternative maximum combinations of output that can be attained if all the productive resources available to a firm are used efficiently; it is the boundary between attainable and unattainable output combinations.

Productive efficiency the co-ordination and motivation of a firm's *resources* within a given production technology such that a given level of output is produced at the lowest attainable cost given the prices of the resources.

Productive resource a tangible or intangible resource used in the process of *production*. See also *factors of production*.

Productivity output per unit of input employed; most frequently applied to *labour productivity*. The productivity of any input, e.g. labour, is in part dependent on the productivity of other inputs, e.g. capital. Hence, the only comprehensive measure of productivity is *total factor productivity* calculated by dividing output by a weighting of all inputs used.

Products general term referring to most goods and services. Products that involve little processing, i.e. primary products, are known as *commodities*.

Profit in ordinary usage, the difference between the *revenue* generated by an output and the total cash cost of producing the output: so-called accounting profit. More formally in *microeconomics*, profits emerge as the excess of total revenue over the *opportunity cost* of producing the output. Opportunity cost includes the *cost of capital*, which is frequently described as *normal profit*. Hence, economic profit is often referred to as *super-normal profit* or *economic rent*.

Profit margin formally the ratio of earnings with respect to revenue, i.e. the proportion of the value of sales a company has left after paying all expences.

Profit-maximizing output The level of output that maximizes a firm's profits achieved when *marginal revenue* equals *marginal cost*.

Profit rate formally the ratio of profits generated with respect to the capital invested in the business.

Progressive tax a tax that takes a larger percentage of people's income the larger their income is. The opposite would be a *regressive tax*.

Property rights the right within reason to determine the use to which a *productive resource* will be put.

Proportionality postulate this is associated with Tjalling Koopmans, who argued that *economies of scale* are impossible unless there is *indivisibility* or *lumpiness* in one or more of the productive resources.

Public good a product or resource that possess two key properties once produced, they do not exhibit *scarcity* from an individual point of view – additional people can consume it without diminishing anyone else's consumption; and, it is impossible to prevent people from gaining access to the good. A radio programme is a good example of a public good.

Public sector that portion of the economy in which production is owned and operated by the government or bodies created by it, such as the nationalized industries.

Purchasing power the amount of goods and services that an income will purchase at ruling prices.

Pure bundling a pricing strategy whereby two or more products can only be purchased together in a bundle. See also *bundling*.

Pure monopoly see *monopoly*.

Quantity fixing a strategy more applicable to a commodity industry, whereby a *dominant firm* or a *collective dominance* control the quantity supplied. See also *Stackelberg's model*.

Quantity forcing a *vertical restraint* whereby a seller of an *intermediate product* imposes the condition that a buyer must purchase a minimum quantity.

Quasi-rent an *ex post* situation where revenue exceeds total opportunity cost. For example, if entering a market involves investment that is a *sunk cost*, then *ex post* the firm's opportunity cost of the investment capital is zero. Providing the market price remains above unit variable costs, the firm will earn a (quasi) rent, by virtue of its capital costs being zero.

Random walk a stochastic process whereby each successive step in the process can move in a random, and hence unpredictable, direction.

Rate of time preference refers to an individual's valuation of future events and the rate of interest they must receive in order to forego consumption today.

Rational behaviour the foundation of the neo-classical approach to individual choice; namely, individuals are assumed to act in their own self-interest, and to do so by having sufficient knowledge of the pay-off from alternative outcomes and be in a position to choose the outcome with the highest return.

Reaction function a function showing the response of a firm operating under *imperfect competition*, e.g.an oligopolist, to actual or conjectural change in a strategic variable by their rivals. The strategic variable may be the level of output, prices or expenditure on factors such as advertising or R&D. See the *Cournot model.*

Real incomes the amount of goods and services a given level of disposable income will purchase.

Real price the change in the price of a good or service relative to prices generally.

Real wage the purchasing power of the money wage normally estimated by deflating the money wage by a price index.

Recoupment fallacy the false notion that a firm operating in more than one market, and profit maximizing in each, can engage in *predation* in one of the markets and recoup the lost profits by raising prices in the other markets.

Research and development systematic study directed towards the discovery and use of new knowledge.

Regression analysis a statistical technique for estimating the relationship between a (dependent) variable and one or more (explanatory) variables. The technique can be used to measure the statistical significance of the relationship or to predict values of the dependent variable.

Regulation a rule or law designed to control or govern some aspect of the behaviour of individuals or firms.

Regulatory capture a situation where an industry standard is set by the firms operating in the industry who have a vested interest in minimizing the effects.

Related diversification describes a situation where a firm diversifies into the production of a product that is closely related to its existing set of outputs. See also *diversification.*

Relative price any price expressed as a ratio of another price.

Relational contract a contract whereby the parties set out the framework of a relationship rather than specific actions in the event of contingencies. A relational contract is a response to *bounded rationality*.

Renewable resources productive resources that can be replaced as they are used up, as with physical capital; distinguished from non-renewable resources, which are available in a fixed stock that can be depleted but not replaced.

Repeated game represents a strategic game that is played more than once. This raises the possibility of punishment for cheating and hence the outcome of the game.

Replacement effect a phrase associated with Kenneth Arrow, whereby a successful *invention* could have the effect of rendering obsolete the *competitive advantage* of a firm or group of firms.

Reputation is a valuable intangible asset that embodies a positive social evaluation by society towards an individual, a group or an organization.

Reputational externality exists where an individual's or a firm's *reputation* depends on the actions or behaviour of a third party, e.g. a manufacturer's reputation is vulnerable to the behaviour of retailers who sell its products.

Resale price maintenance a *vertical restraint* whereby the seller of an *intermediate product* specifies the minimum or maximum price the buyer (normally a retailer) may sell at.

Reservation outlay see *reservation price*.

Reservation price without evidence of some value-adding differentiation, the maximum price an individual consumer is prepared to pay for a particular product. From a seller's perspective, the minimum price at which they are prepared to sell.

Reservation wage the wage that an individual must be paid before they are prepared to take up a particular employment.

Residual claimant is entitled to whatever remains once all revenues have been collected, all costs paid and all debts discharged.

Residual decision rights see *residual rights of control*.

Residual demand curve the market share that is left to a firm or group of firms, at all feasible prices, after allowing for the sales of a rival or group of rival firms.

Residual rights of control refers to the owner of an asset's rights to make decisions concerning the asset's use.

Resource allocation the allocation of the economy's scarce resources among alternative uses.

Resource-based an approach to the firm identified with Edith Penrose, now more commonly known as the *competence approach* to the firm.

Resources refer to both tangible and intangible factors that are utilized in the process of production. Tangible physical resources would include factors such as the number of employees, the stocks of machines, buildings and materials purchased from other firms. Intangible resources would include factors such as the skills and experience of its employees, and intellectual capital including its *organizational architecture*. See also *factors of production*.

Restrictive agreement a strategic agreement between two or more firms not to compete with each other in a particular market or to frustrate the attempts of other firms to compete in the market.

Retention ratio formally the ratio of profits retained in the business with respect to total profits after tax.

Revenue for any good or service it is the product of price and volume sold. Just how changes in the price influence the revenue generated depends on the *price elasticity of demand*.

Risk averse describes an individual, or group, that prefers a certain outcome, rather than take the risk on an outcome that could be higher or lower.

Risk neutral refers to an individual who is indifferent between certain and uncertain outcomes.

Risk premium the return on capital that is necessary to compensate owners of capital for the risk associated with a specific investment; usually expressed as a premium over the risk-free rate of interest.

Rivalry describes the behaviour of firms in the process of competition. Normally associated with market structures where the firm has a degree of market power, i.e. some control over the prices they can charge.

Rule of reason an approach to the enforcement of competition policy where, in deciding a particular case, the authorities must establish a *prima facie* showing that the agreement or restraint produces tangible anti-competitive effects.

Saddle point describes a *Nash equilibrium* in a 'game' lacking dominant strategies. A rational player will attempt to maximize the best of the minimum pay-offs and thereby be assured that the pay-off is no worse than expected. A saddle point reflects this situation as its minimum point in the horizontal plane is also its maximum point in the vertical plane.

Sales revenue maximization this model is associated with Baumol, who on the basis of causal empiricism thought that managers were more concerned with maximizing sales revenue than profits, in part because sales are more controllable than profits.

Satisficing behaviour a consequence of *bounded rationality*, it refers to choosing the first alternative that achieves a satisfactory level of performance, e.g. profit, rather than searching for the very highest level achievable.

Scarce refers to the fact that, with the exception of flow resources such as sunlight, wind and water power, all resources are finite. Consequently, the production generated by employing resources is also finite and generally employing a resource in one use precludes, or at least limits, its simultaneous use elsewhere. See also *choices*.

Search goods goods whose quality can be accurately and relatively cheaply assessed by inspection before purchase. See also *experience goods* and *credence goods*.

Second-degree price discrimination the practice by a supplier, with market power, of dividing its output into tranches and charging consumers a different price for each tranche.

Seller concentration a measure of the extent to which an industry's total production is concentrated under the control of a small number of firms. Popular measures of seller concentration are the *concentration ratio* and the *Herfindahl index*.

Service provision a *vertical restraint* whereby a buyer of an *intermediate product* is required by the seller to provide a specific supporting service.

Set-up costs the cost assembling and making ready a production process.

Shareholders individuals – people or firms – that legally own a joint-stock company. Shareholders are granted special privileges depending on the type of stock, including: the right to vote on elections to the board of *directors*, the right to share in distribution of the company's income and the right to a share of the company's assets if it is wound up.

Shirking describes the deliberate actions of employees to avoid making the effort expected by their employers.

Short run in microeconomics, the period of time over which some inputs in the production process, such as capital, are fixed.

Short-run average total costs total costs – the sum of variable and fixed costs – divided by the total quantity produced. Frequently referred to as unit costs.

Short-run equilibrium generally, equilibrium subject to some inputs or prices being held constant over the time period being considered; while in the long run these will be allowed to adjust.

Short-run supply curve a curve showing the relation between quantity supplied and price when one or more input is fixed. A concept that can satisfactorily only be applied under perfect competition. An industry supply curve is the horizontal sum of marginal cost curves (above the level of average variable costs) of all firms in an industry at a point in time, but excluding any response of newly entering firms.

Shut-down price the price that is equal to a firm's average variable cost, below which it should cease production.

Side-payments payments that are made to individuals or groups to induce particular behaviour and/or outcomes.

Signalling the manipulation by individuals or firms of attributes or activities in order to convey information. The resulting actions and behaviour are intended to reveal strengths, and likely courses of actions to other economic agents, e.g. customers, competitors and potential employees.

Single European Act came in to effect in 1987, thereby enabling the legislators to put in place the necessary legislation to allow the *single market* to be launched in 1993.

Single Market generally refers to the Common Market that came into effect in the EU on 1 January 1993. It allows for the free movement of all factors of production – goods, services, capital and labour – between member states with the purpose of encouraging competition and integration. The

EU single market embraces the European Economic Area countries of Iceland, Liechtenstein and Norway and is an ongoing process, whereby legislation and regulation are used to ensure the free movement of all *factors of production*.

Sleeping patent a patent secured by a firm, but not currently used. Many of these patents serve as a strategic device and should be viewed as an element in the *pre-emption effect* of the patent system.

Social cost private costs plus *externalities*. The true cost to society as a whole of an activity in terms of other potential outputs forgone.

Social efficiency describes a situation where market forces have been augmented, where appropriate, by government intervention to bring about an efficient allocation of resources that takes account of any *externality* and *public good*.

Sole trader non-incorporated business operated by a single owner. Modern UK terminology for a *single proprietorship*.

Spatial differentiation describes how products can be differentiated on the basis of the location where they are sold. See also *differentiated product*.

Specialization refers to a situation where economic activity is devoted to a specific outcome. The economic activity could be at the firm level, at a team or individual level.

Specialization of labour the organization of production by which individual workers specialize in the production of certain goods or services.

Specific human capital includes skills and knowledge that are valuable only in the context of a particular firm. See also *human capital*.

Specific tax a tax expressed as so much per unit, independent of its price. Also called a per-unit tax.

Spot markets are where goods are exchanged in the current period without any commitment to a future transaction.

SSNIP a Small but Significant Non-Transitory Increase in Prices is a method of determining a market. Effectively it starts with a small market and asks whether, *ceteris paribus*, a hypothetical monopolist or cartel could sustain a price increase of 5 per cent for at least one year. If sufficient numbers of consumers are likely to switch to alternative products as to make the price increase unprofitable, then the firm or cartel lacks the power to raise price. The relevant market is therefore expanded by including the next closest substitute and the process is repeated until the point is reached where a hypothetical cartel or monopolist could profitably impose a 5 per cent price increase. The range of products or the geographic area so defined constitutes the relevant market. The European Commission has formally adopted the SSNIP to define markets.

Stackelberg equilibrium see *Stackelberg's model*.

Stackelberg model a quantity-adjusting model of oligopolistic behaviour very similar in approach to the Cournot model, but in this case one firm is the leader or '*first mover*' who does not adjust quantity in response to rivals' output decisions. Hence, only rivals react to the leader's level of output in achieving an equilibrium. See also the *Sylos postulate*.

Stakeholders The different groups that have an interest in the quality, governance and operations of a firm, including not only *shareholders* and employees but also suppliers, customers and the local community. See also *corporate social responsibility*.

Standard deviation a measure of the dispersion of a variable around its population's mean.

State aids intervention by governments to support and sometimes to protect firms and industries. State aids are a key element of *industrial policies* and range from indirect support in the form of advice and information, to large-scale protection or in the extreme government control of a firm or industry.

Stocks accumulation of inputs and outputs held by firms to facilitate a smooth flow of production in spite of variations in delivery of inputs and sales of outputs. Sometimes called inventories.

Strategic alliances a partnership between firms whereby capabilities and assets are combined to achieve specific joint goals. The purpose is to leverage the strengths of the partners and to achieve, over a period of time, strategic objectives that would be more expensive and carry a higher probability of failure if attempted by one firm.

Strategic barrier to entry reflects actions by incumbent firms that raise the pre- and post-entry costs for potential competitors contemplating entering an industry. See also *limit price*.

Strategic behaviour behaviour that takes into account the actual or anticipated reactions of others to one's own actions, as when a firm makes decisions that take account of rival firms' expected reactions in oligopolistic markets.

Strategic conflict an approach to understanding *strategic behaviour* associated with Carl Shapiro that analyses the *oligopoly* behaviour using the tools of *game theory*.

Strategic group a group comprising firms that actively compete to sell a particular good or service or very close *substitutes*. The firms may not all be from the same industry, e.g. hot water bottles compete with electric blankets.

Strategic management an academic discipline that is primarily concerned with the way a firm formulates its strategic objectives; allocates or develops appropriate resources to achieve these objectives and reacts to the responses of rivals and customers to the implementation of strategy.

Strategy no one agreed definition, but might broadly be defined as the decisions that marshal a firm's resources to meet its goals.

Strategy formulation the process of deciding what *strategy* to adopt, involving the identification of opportunities and threats arising in the firm's *business environment*.

Structural barrier a *barrier to entry* resulting from a natural cost advantage accruing to incumbent firms.

Structure–conduct–performance a paradigm generally associated with Joseph Bain, which postulates that *industry structure* influences the behaviour of incumbents, which in turn impacts on the profitability of firms operating in the industry.

Sub-game perfect Nash equilibrium in dynamic games, an equilibrium must not involve incredible threats or promises. An equilibrium therefore requires that in each period – or sub-game – a Nash equilibrium is arrived at by only considering credible courses of action.

Subadditive an expression reflecting a situation where the join production of two or more products results in total costs rising by a smaller proportion. See also *economies of scope*.

Substitutes two goods are substitutes if customers are prepared to switch between the two goods. Consequently, the quantity demanded of one is *positively related* to the price of the other.

Sunk costs costs that, once incurred, can never be recovered. Examples are expenditure on: an advertising campaign; a highly specialized machine; and a unique customer. Funds used to investigate a market are a sunk cost, as are expenditures on training and education. Once such costs have been incurred they should not influence future allocation decisions since they do not affect incremental (marginal) costs in the future.

Supergames a multistage game that is repeated over an infinite number of periods.

Super-normal profit see *economic rent*.

Supply the whole relation between the quantity supplied of some commodity and its own price.

Supply chain the stages involved in converting *primary products* into finished products. For example, the food chain starts with the fertilizer and seed industries, moves on to the agricultural industry, then the food processors, and finally to the wholesalers and retailers.

Supply curve the graphical representation of the relation between the quantity of some product that firms wish to make and sell per period of time and the price of that product, *ceteris paribus*.

Supply function a functional relation between the quantity supplied and all the variables that influence it.

Supply side a phrase that represents a focus on the conditions that determine the prices, quantities, qualities and efficiencies of what is produced.

Sustained competitive advantage an economic rent-creating strategy that competitors find impossible to duplicate.

Sylos postulate the assumption that firms contemplating entry into a market will hold the view that incumbent firms will maintain their current level of output post entry.

Tacit collusion a situation in which a small group of firms, in response to the recognition of the influence each has on the others, choose to act like one entity in terms of a strategic variable, e.g. output, price, expenditure on advertising or R&D, but without any explicit agreement to achieve the co-operative outcome. See also *explicit collusion*.

Tacit knowledge is knowledge that cannot be articulated and is succinctly explained with Polanyi's phrase, we know more than we can tell. Within a firm, a team may work very effectively together, but would be unable to explain exactly how or why.

Takeover when one firm buys another firm.

Tapered integration describes a situation where a firm produces a proportion of one of its inputs (via vertical integration) and also sources a proportion from the market.

Tax wedge the difference between what employers pay out for each employee and the amount of that money that ends up in the employee's pocket.

Team production a perspective on the firm put forward by Armen Alchian and Harold Demsetz, whereby essentially the nature of the firm is that output is the joint product of several workers and cannot be attributed accurately to individuals.

Technical progress a phrase that summarizes the process of developing new higher-value products and new more efficient production processes.

Technological change see *technical progress*.

Technology from an economic perspective, an encompassing term dealing with the knowledge of production, distribution and sales. The term embraces tools, plants and machines, as well as techniques, materials and processes.

Territorial restrictions a *vertical restraint* whereby a seller assigns buyers exclusive territories for the onward sale of their products.

The Council of the European Union (EU) forms, along with the European Parliament, the legislative arm of the EU. It contains ministers of the governments of each of the member states.

Third-degree price discrimination the practice of dividing consumers into two or more groups and charging consumers in each group the profit-maximizing price.

Time series data a sequence of data points spread successively over a period of time and spaced apart at uniform time intervals.

Tobin's q a ratio arising from dividing the *marginal efficiency of investment* by the cost of a marginal unit of capital. If the ratio is greater than unity, then the firm has scope for future profitable investment. The explanation for a ratio in excess of unity is that installation costs require that the firm spread its investment over a number of periods.

Total factor productivity the ratio of the output of a firm, industry or economy with respect to all the factors of production used.

Tournament model refers to an approach that views *research and development* as a race with winners and losers.

Transaction costs the costs, first identified by Ronald Coase, incurred in carrying out a market exchange transaction. Specifically, the phrase refers to the *ex ante* costs in terms of time and effort spent in establishing whether the market price of a good or service represents a fair value and minimizing exposure to *opportunistic behaviour* in the event of unforeseen events. Key transaction costs are the costs of searching for information, the costs of bargaining and the costs of contracting, as well as the costs of enforcement.

Treaty of Rome the founding treaty of the European Community.

Trigger strategy a strategy involving initially a co-operative stance but, on observing an opponent cheating, the stance is changed to a strategy designed to punish the cheating firm. A trigger strategy is employed in the repeated *Prisoners' Dilemma* game.

Total factor productivity a measure of the increase in output that is due to combining the separate factor inputs efficiently. For example, increasing the capital per worker will, *ceteris paribus*, reduce capital productivity but it may increase total factor productivity if it leads to a more efficient balance of capital and labour.

Trademarks a word, symbol, slogan, or design which identifies and distinguishes the goods or services of one party from those of another. A trademark identifies the source of a product or service that indicates certain standards of quality inherent in the product or service.

Transformation curve a graphical device mapping a relationship between how much is received in the future for giving up one unit of consumption today.

Two-part tariff a pricing strategy whereby a firm (with monopoly power) earns a rent by charging customers a fixed fee (a tariff) for being allowed to enter the market and then charging a price equal to marginal cost for each unit sold.

Tying a *vertical restraint* whereby the sale of an *intermediate product* is conditional on the buyer also purchasing complementary products from the seller.

Unit cost the cost of producing a single item of output and calculated by dividing total costs by the number of units produced. See also *average variable costs* and *average fixed costs*.

Unit elasticity an elasticity with a numerical measure of 1, indicating that the percentage change in quantity is equal to the percentage change in price (so that total expenditure remains constant).

Unitary form an organizational structure involving functional 'silos', e.g. marketing or production, reporting to a head office. This type of structure is suited to a one-product, specialist firm.

Unrelated diversification describes a situation where a firm diversifies into the production of a new product that is unconnected in terms of market or production techniques with its existing set of products. See also *diversification*.

Upstream refers to a movement from any point in a *supply chain* towards the primary producers.

Utility the satisfaction that a consumer receives from the consumption of goods and services.

Utility function a functional relationship between the *utility* an individual obtains from consumption and the set of variables that determine the level and pattern of consumption, e.g. the individual's income, tastes, status and security.

Value added the value of a firm's output minus the value of the inputs that it purchases from other firms.

Value chain see *supply chain*.

Value net a network of firms that includes rivals, suppliers, customers and complementors. The benefits are similar to those of *industrial clusters*, though the concept is widened by including *complementors*.

Variable any well-defined input to or output from the process of production. Much economic analysis is concerned with estimating how changes in one variable influence another. .See also *factors of production* and *outputs*.

Variable factors production inputs whose amount can be varied within the production period, i.e. the *short run*.

Variable production costs costs that vary directly with changes in the level of production per period. Obvious examples are material and energy costs. Also if increasing output demands more hours of labour at a cost per hour then labour is also a variable cost.

Veblen good a product that is desired because its high cost demonstrates conspicuous consumption. The higher the price, the richer must be the consumer, who obtains utility from the knowledge that observers are aware of the wealth. A Veblen good results in an upward-sloping demand curve.

Venture a newly established firm that has yet to generate a revenue.

Versioning The deliberate creation of different qualities in order to facilitate *price discrimination*.

Vertical agreements arise when firms operating at successive stages in the supply chain enter into agreements or concerted practices. The EU Commission will apply the *rule of reason* when determining whether the agreement is likely to reduce competition or deliver benefits, e.g. the sharing of risk or distribution costs, the pooling of knowledge or the more rapid *diffusion* of an invention.

Vertical boundary refers to the size of the firm in terms of the number of technologically separable intermediate production stages undertaken within the firm.

Vertical integration the combining within one firm of more than one stage in the production process. If the firm integrates with one of its suppliers, e.g. a car body plant acquires or merges with a steel mill, this is *upstream* or *backward integration*. If a firm acquires or merges with one of its customers, e.g. a retail chain, this is *downstream* or *forward integration*.

Vertical merger union or *merger* of firms at different stages in a supply chain.

Vertical relationships a generic term for all exchange relationships short of *vertical integration* between firms in a supply chain, ranging from spot market transactions to *joint ventures*.

Vertical restraints contractual limitations placed on downstream distributors or retailers by manufacturers or wholesalers with the intention of controlling, to varying degrees, the prices charged, quantities sold or markets secured.

Vertical scale refers to the size of a firm in terms of the stages of production it undertakes. Oil companies typically have a large vertical scale as they drill oil from the ground, refine it and retail its derivative. See also *vertical integration*.

Vertically differentiated the ranking of products within a *market* or *product space* according to the volume of resources absorbed in their production. The more resources absorbed, the greater the product's total costs. See also *differentiated product*.

Voluntary restraint agreements no longer legal for members of the World Trade Organization, these are bilateral, and sometimes secret, agreements stipulating that low-cost exporters 'voluntarily' restrict exports to countries where their goods are threatening industry and employment, and thus forestall official protective action on the part of the importing country.

Wealth effects refers to the influence of wealth on the choices made by individuals. For example, a poor person might be reluctant to take the financial risks that a rich person would welcome.

Winner's curse the observation that the winner of an auction, e.g. a takeover bid or any competitive tendering process, often pays too much for the target. The winner is the highest bidder and thus all other bidders and the previous owner of the assets placed a lower value on the target.

Working capital refers to stocks of materials, work in progress, stocks of finished goods and funds available in the firm's bank account.

X-inefficiency failure to use resources efficiently within the firm so that unit costs are higher than they need be. In effect, the firm is producing above the minimum cost curve and is therefore inside its production-possibility frontier.

Zero-sum game describes a 'game' where the gain to one participant is exactly matched by a loss to another participant. For example, if the pay-off is an increase in market share, a rival would lose precisely an equivalent share.

Index

A

Abbey National, 164
accounting, 74, 109, 119
acquisitions
  defined, 534
  diversified growth, 116, 160–3, 165
  dominant firms, 327
  dynamic processes, 99
  encouragement of, 25
  enhancement of efficiency, 82
  market power, 256
  predatory pricing, 350
  research and development, 507
  see also horizontal mergers; mergers; vertical mergers
Adams, W., 387, 389
Advanta, 264
adverse selection, 37
  defined, 511
  efficiency wages, 231
  employee appointments, 231, 232
  intermediate products, 71
  quality products, 406
  risks of, 75, 231
  transaction costs, 38, 75, 87
  vertical relationships, 423, 424
advertising
  as barrier to entry, 266, 443, 470–2, 472, 473
  changing of consumers' preferences, 142, 462–7, 463, 471–2, 473
  credence goods, 464, 465, 473
  defined, 452
  deterrence strategies, 345, 346
  dominant firm markets, 345, 346, 354
  excess of, 138
  exclusive dealing, 424–5
  experience goods, 464, 466, 473
  firm growth, 186
  game theory, 21, 465–6, 466, 469–70, 469
  growth of demand, 21, 141, 159
  imperfect information, 399, 401
  incomplete information, 453, 458, 459, 464
  as information source, 21, 354, 399, 458–62, 464–5, 471–2, 473
  and market prices, 472
  market structure, 467–72, 468, 473
  monopolistic competition, 252, 443, 468, 470
  monopolists, 453, 455–6, 467, 468
  oligopolies, 443, 468–9, 470
  optimal, 452–7, 455, 457
  predation strategies, 354
  product differentiation, 266, 442–3
  reduction of uncertainty, 138
  rivalry, 21, 256
  as strategic behaviour, 266
  as a sunk cost, 266, 328, 424–5, 443, 465, 470
  welfare effects of, 478–9
advertising intensity, 453–6, 460, 461, 466, 467–72, 468
  defined, 511
  Dorfman-Steiner condition, 455–6
aftermarkets, 419, 426, 432, 433
  defined, 511
agency costs, 74
  defined, 511
  effect of ICT, 87
  innovation and invention, 501–2
  Jensen and Meckling model, 204–6
  principal-agent theory, 191–2
  vertical integration, 79–80, 82, 86, 87, 93
agency problem, 190–1
agency theory see principal-agent theory
agency workers, 215
agents see management
agglomeration, 111–12, 275–6, 277
  defined, 511
aggregate demand, 80
aggregate demand curve, 377, 417
Air France, 380
Airbus, 20, 313
aircraft industry, 313
airline market, 7, 8–9, 364, 380–1
Akerlof, G., 406
Alchemy Partners, 199
Alchian, A., 18, 49, 50, 104, 177, 225, 231
Alken-Maes, 294
Alliance & Leicester, 163
alliances, 88, 89–92, 99, 312
  control of key inputs, 345
  defined, 511
  innovation, 481, 503, 506
  network organizations, 183
  outsourcing, 46, 94
  virtual boundaries, 127–9, 131
Allianz and Generali, 164
allocative efficiency, 4–5, 26
  defined, 511–12
  game theory, 14, 22, 23
  organizational architecture, 60
  perfect competition, 249
  price discrimination, 380
  pricing strategies, 22, 23
  profits, 5, 6

society's demand for, 28
specialization, 119
and total costs, 16–19
total revenue, 21–3
transaction costs, 49
vertical integration, 64, 80
see also deadweight welfare loss
allocative inefficiency, 214, 325, 366, 497
American Management Association, 196
Amgen, 153
AMOCO, 123
Ampex Corporation, 487
Andersen, E., 407
animal testing, 17
Antena 3, 143
anti-competitive practices, 26
  advertising's potential, 453
  dominant firms, 355, 356
  mergers, 161, 163
  price discrimination, 390, 391
  vertical restraints, 399, 400, 429, 430, 431, 433
  see also Article 81
AOL Time Warner, 85
Apple, 46
Aquabase, 160
arbitrage, 366, 377, 378, 383, 384, 393
  defined, 512
Areeda, Phillip, 355, 356
Arrow, Kenneth, 71, 456, 488, 489, 497, 499
Arsenal FC, 467
Article 81, 25, 27, 253
  block exemptions, 26, 311, 430–1, 514
  collusion, 284, 288, 307, 311, 312–13
  horizontal agreements, 392, 505
  monopolies, 26
  vertical agreements, 505
  vertical restraints, 399, 429, 430–1
Asda, 260, 405
assembly lines, learning by doing, 45, 104, 105, 288
asset specialization, 78
asset specificity, 78, 266, 267, 503
  defined, 512
  diversification, 120
  as exit barrier, 328
  governance approach, 79–82, 84, 114, 119, 503
  partnership alliances, 91
  vertical integration, 79–82, 81, 87–8
assets, ownership of, 72, 100, 177, 190, 410

AstraZeneca plc, 160
asymmetric information, 398
  advertising, 458, 464
  agency costs, 191
  complete contracts, 174
  consumer's choice, 442
  contractual relationships, 37
  defined, 512
  employee appointments, 232
  employee motivation, 225, 231
  employee performance measurement, 210
  employment contracts, 222
  entrepreneurs, 36–7
  game theory, 13
  governance approach, 47, 235
  hidden characteristics, 37
  and ICT, 87, 88
  internal labour markets, 235
  managerial slack, 191
  nature of a firm, 36–7
  transaction costs, 49, 57, 87
  and uncertainty, 36
  vertical integration, 65, 71–4, 84, 87
  vertical relationships, 413, 417
  vertical restraints, 420, 433
  see also adverse selection
atomistic industry, 213, 251, 467
  defined, 512
  see also perfect competition
attributes, 9
  defined, 512
  informational advertising, 21, 453, 458–63
  intermediate products, 71
  Lancaster's model, 447–8, 473
  product differentiation, 445–6, 447–8, 447, 450
  product quality, 464
  search qualities, 407
  vertical relationships, 413
auction houses, 418–19
Audi, 138–9, 428
Austria, car price differentials, 368
Austrian school, 272, 482
  see also Schumpeter, Joseph
authority control hierarchy, 18, 19, 36
  development of new knowledge, 85
  economies of scope, 84
  and governance structure, 47–50, 57
  key element of organizational architecture, 32, 39–42
  vertical integration, 64, 72, 93
average cost of labour, 219, 242

average costs *see* long-run average
cost curve (LRAC);
short-run average cost curve
average fixed costs, 138
defined, 512
average product
defined, 512
see also labour productivity;
productivity
average production costs, 106, 340,
374, 378, 393
average total costs, 173, 348
defined, 512
average variable costs, 138, 356
defined, 512
Aviko, 264
avoidable costs, 356
defined, 512

B

backward induction
defined, 512
deterrence strategies, 343
dominant firm markets, 333,
352, 353
extensive form game, 23
paradox of, 304
predatory pricing, 352, 353
principal-agent game, 193
repeated games, 303–4
backward integration, 82, 413
defined, 512
Bain, George, 217
Bain, Joseph, 254, 265, 266, 280,
327, 340, 341
Bakken, Earl, 276
bandwagon effect, 451, *451*
defined, 513
Bang & Olufsen, 425
banking sector, 44, 163–4, 197
bargaining situation
between groups, 188
customer power, 271
defined, 513
entrepreneurs, 148
and increasing scale, 102
market characteristic, 48
market costs of, 49
relational employment contracts,
49
vertical relationships, 415, 417
wages, 221, 222, 244–5
barometric price leadership, 325, 338
defined, 513
barriers to entry
advertising, 266, 443, 470–2,
472, 473
defined, 513
dominant firms, 326–9
economies of scale, 265–6
exclusive dealing, 425
industrial organization
economics, 6

market structure, 250, 265–8,
270, 271
price discrimination, 391–3
price-setting models, 298
product differentiation, 450
sunk costs, 266, 267
technology, 265–6
vertical restraints, 425, 429, 431,
433
see also blockaded entry
Barroso, Jose Manuel, 20
barter, defined, 513
BASF AG, 306
basing point pricing, 385–7, *386*
defined, 513
BATNAs, 244
battle of the sexes, defined, 513
Baumol, W.
contestability, 266, 327
firm growth and profitability, 157
minimum profit constraint, 155
predatory pricing, 356
sales revenue maximization
model, 136–8, *137*, 139, 140,
153, 159, 185
scale effects, 102
Bayes' rule, 328–9, *329*
defined, 513
BBC, 462
Beath, J., 495
Becker, G., 466
behavioural theories, 187–9, 196,
200, 502
defined, 513
Beiker, M., 163
Belgium
beer market, 294
car price differentials, 367, 368
Berlin Wall, fall of, 12
Bertrand competition, 499
Bertrand, J., 294
Bertrand model, 252, 273, 294–7,
298, 300, 322–3, 343
defined, 513
Bertrand paradox, 295
defined, 513
Bertrand-Nash equilibrium, 296,
296, 297, 449
BETAMAX, 487
BEUC, 367
bilateral monopolies, 220–1, *220*,
414–15, *414*
defined, 513
biotechnology sector, 56–7, 151,
152–3
black market, defined, 514
Blair, Tony, 20
block exemptions, 26, 311, 430–1,
432
defined, 514
block pricing, 372
see also second-degree price
discrimination
blockaded entry, 266, 340
defined, 514

Blundell, R., 491
BMW, 199, 224
Body Shop, 17
Boeing, 46, 313, 324
Bonanno, G., 427
Borenstein, S., 382
Bork, R., 392
Boston Consulting Group (BCG),
106, *106*, 118
bounded rationality, 398
collaborative ventures, 128, 131
competency approach, 57, 59,
61, 123–4
complete contracts, 38, 77, 174
of consumers, 442, 458
contractual relationships, 38, 49,
174
defined, 514
demand for labour, 217
diversification, 118–19, 123–4
employee performance
measurement, 210
employment contracts, 222, 223,
237
entrepreneurs, 37
game theory, 13, 304
governance approach, 47, 49, 57,
59, 60, 189
innovation, 484, 485
oligopolies, 304
partnership alliances, 90
satisficing behaviour, 188, 200
transaction costs, 38, 57, 60, 74,
75, 78
vertical integration, 74, 75, 78,
84
vertical relationships, 415
Bovine Spongiform Encephalopathy
(BSE), 412
Bowley, Arthur, 300
Boyer, Herbert, 153
BP, 20, 122–3, 286
brand asset specificity, 78
brand image, 346, 464, 466
see also image advertising
brand loyalty, 346, 453, 471
BBC, 462
brand preferences, 382
brand reputation, 78, 82, 429, 456
brand variety, 346
Brandenburger, Anthony, 21, 278,
517
branding, 254
brands, 53, 252, 408
defined, 514
inter-brand competition, 425,
427, 429, 431, 433, 453
intra-brand competition, 421,
425, 427, 429, 430, 431, 453
Branson, Richard, 5, 7, 8–9, 149
break-even price, 3
defined, 514
Brickley, J., 18, 41
British Aerospace, 199

British Airways (BA), 7, 380, 381
British Coal, 220–1
British Sugar, 393
BSE, 412
budget constraints, 204, 205, 206
defined, 514
budget line, 463
defined, 514
Buick division, 42
building societies, 108, 164
bundling, 364, 387–90, *388*, 398,
426
defined, 514
Burstein, M., 430
business environment, 4–5, 9–12
adverse fluctuations, 237
attempts to influence, 118–19
changes in, 40, 54, 504
collaborative ventures, 128
defined, 514
distinct layers, 5, 10, *11*
diversified growth, 165
dynamic capabilities school, 54,
274, 484
evolutionary approach, 273–4
incentive schemes, 193–5, 201
learning by doing, 107
management need to
understand, 135
organizational architecture, 4, 7,
18–19, *19*, 21
profit equation, 5–7
as random variable, 193, 195
strategic business decisions, 179,
180
vertical integration, 93
see also Five Forces Model;
market structures; shocks
business organizations *see* firms
business strategy, 4, 64
defined, 514
and economic concepts, 6
game theory, 13, 306
M-form (multi-divisional)
organization, 182
price-setting, 295
related diversification, 116
business unit, 41, 64, 116, 182, 200,
250, 274, 504
defined, 514
buyers
imperfect information, 398
moral hazard, 37, 38
SCP paradigm, 254
search costs, 384
vertical integration, 72, 76
see also adverse selection;
asymmetric information; Five
Forces Model; incomplete
contracts; intermediate
products; partnership alliances;
price discrimination;
reservation prices; vertical
relationships; vertical restraints

C

Caballero, R., 143
Cadbury Schweppes, 88, 196
Cadillac division, 42
Canal Plus, 85
Canalt, 143
Cantwell, J., 485
capabilities
    collaborative ventures, 127
    defined, 514
    diversified growth, 145
    dominant firms, 327
    embedded in tacit knowledge, 162
    Five Forces Model, 273
    governance approach, 47
    and growth of firms, 146, 147
    horizontal boundaries, 100, 120,
        124, 125, 128
    influences on, 33
    joint ventures, 89
    lowering of costs, 33
    management knowledge of, 179
    uniqueness of, 148, 156, 164
    vertical integration, 85, 90, 93
    see also competency approach;
        core competencies;
    dynamic capabilities
capital, 28, 80
    defined, 514–15
    opportunity cost of, 341, 350, 358
    and productivity, 233
    property rights over, 17
    sources of, 44–5
    start-ups, 151
    technological advances, 44
    see also fixed capital
capital costs, 101–2, 110, 265
    hold-up, 79
    influence of sunk costs, 328
    joint ventures, 89
    vertical integration, 68–9, 70, 74
capital deepening, defined, 515
capital depreciation, 68
capital goods, defined, 515
capital investment, 35, 350, 374, 429
capital markets, 25, 118–19, 191–2,
    266–7, 351
capital stock, 110, 142, 155, 500
    defined, 515
capital widening, defined, 515
capital–labour ratio, 35, 155, 176
capitalism, 5, 28, 198, 506
    defined, 515
car price differentials, 367–9
car sector see motor vehicle sector
career paths, 210, 234
Carlsberg, Sir Bryan, 357
cartels, 269, 307–8, 314, 324–5
    defined, 515
CASA, 313
cash cow products, 106
cash flow
    diversification game, 125–6

growth of firms, 152
new market entrants, 450
residual claims, 190
small firms, 265
unrelated diversification, 117–18,
    117
variability of, 117
casual workers, 215
CE mark, 47
Celltech, 56–7
Centaur Grain Ltd., 195
Central and Eastern European
    Countries (CEEC), 12, 20, 253
centrally planned economies, 12
Centre for Economic Policy Research
    (CEPR), 368
CEO, 177, 178, 181, 183, 185, 186,
    191, 192
ceteris paribus demand curve, 404,
    448
    defined, 515
chain store paradox game, 351,
    352–3
Chamberlin, E.
    differentiated products, 255
    excess capacity, 404
    free entry assumption, 450
    monopolistic competition, 9,
        404, 404, 405, 432, 444, 445,
        448, 449, 472
chance node, 345
    defined, 515
Chandler, A., 182, 261
change in demand, 52, 77, 217, 300
    defined, 515
Chartered Institute of Personnel
    Development, 237
Cheltenham & Gloucester, 163
Chevrolet division, 42
Choi, Y., 152
choices, 16, 17
    defined, 515
Christie's auction house, 418–19
Christopher, M., 442
CJD, 412–13
Clark, Kenneth, 24
classical economics, 11, 144
    defined, 515
cluster analysis, 262
    defined, 515
clusters see industrial clusters
co-operation, 28–9
    capturing value, 21
    competency approach, 235
    defined, 517
    dominant firm markets, 337
    innovation, 493, 507
    joint ventures, 89
    learning by doing, 105
    partnership alliances, 89–90
    Prisoners' Dilemma, 14–15
    restrictive agreements, 26
    vertical integration, 65, 77, 84, 88
    see also collaborative ventures;

collusion
co-operative agreements, 26–7
co-operative equilibrium, 91
co-operative game theory, 6, 13, 21
co-operatives, 88
    defined, 517
co-opetition, 21
    defined, 517
coal industry, 220–1
Coase, Ronald, 18, 28, 65
    role of employees, 49
    transaction costs, 36, 38, 47, 55,
        60, 64
Coca-Cola Company, 86, 88, 354, 456
Cockburn, I., 496
Cohen, W., 502, 505
collaborative ventures, 4, 127–9,
    131, 284
    R&D activity, 482, 504–6, 507
    see also alliances; co-operation;
        joint ventures
collective dominance, 254, 266,
    324–5, 341
    defined, 515
    see also dominant firms
collusion, 15–16, 254, 256
    advertising, 457
    Article 81, 284, 288, 307, 311,
        312–13
    competition policies, 25
    defined, 516
    dominant firm markets, 337,
        341, 343
    game theory, 252, 266, 302–6
    kinked demand curve model,
        273, 298–300
    oligopolies, 13, 15, 284, 285, 288,
        292–3, 296–7, 298–300,
        301–6, 314, 427
    price leadership, 337
    repeated games, 302–5
    strategic conflict approach, 273
    vertical restraints, 429, 431, 433
    see also cartels; explicit collusion;
        price fixing; tacit collusion
collusive tendering, 269
Comanor, W., 453, 470
commodities, 21, 255, 385
    defined, 516
commodity markets, 21
Common Agricultural Policy (CAP),
    501
common market, 284, 311
    defined, 516
    see also single market
communism, collapse of, 12
company accounts, 6, 19
company reports, 196
Compagnie Générale des Eaux, 85
Compaq, 92
comparative statics, 483
    defined, 516
competency approach, 56, 57–8,
    59–60, 484

behavioural theories, 189
bounded rationality, 57, 59, 61,
    123–4
collaborative ventures, 128, 129
commitment and trust, 189,
    235–6
competitive advantage, 52–5, 60,
    61, 145, 235, 273, 280
    defined, 516
diversification, 119–21, 121, 122,
    124–5, 128, 129
firm-specific human capital, 235
growth of firms, 145–7, 164
heterogeneity, 52–5, 57, 61, 120,
    121, 129, 273, 503
horizontal boundaries, 100,
    119–21, 122, 124–5, 128, 129
imperfect information, 59, 61,
    123–4
innovation and invention, 503–4
knowledge-based resources, 32,
    52–6, 57, 60, 61, 83–5, 121,
    122, 147, 273
partnership alliances, 90
reputation, 235
vertical integration, 65–6, 83–5
vertical restraints, 432
    see also core competencies;
        dynamic capabilities
competition, 250–3
    defined, 516
    as force for greater efficiency, 128
    global nature of, 10
    influence of government policies,
        9–10
    inter-brand, 425, 427, 429, 431,
        433, 453
    intra-brand, 421, 425, 427, 429,
        430, 431, 453
    restrictive agreements, 26
    Schumpeter on, 480–1
    structure of the market, 7
    see also anti-competitive
        practices; duopolies;
        imperfect competition;
        monopolies/monopolists;
        monopolistic competition;
        monopsonists;
        oligopolies/oligopolists;
        perfect competition
competition authorities
    defining of market, 262
    dominant firms, 327, 338
    mergers, 128, 161, 162, 350
    oligopoly power, 302
    predatory pricing, 355–6, 391,
        392
    price discrimination, 367
    price leadership, 338
    resale price maintenance, 421,
        431
    tacit co-operation, 285
    vertical restraints, 419, 429,
        430–2, 433

Competition Commission (CC), 69, 259–60, 338
competition policies, 5, 9, 11, 268–9
    alternative approaches, 27
    Article 82, 25, 27–8, 83, 253, 311, 326, 334, 347, 392, 393
    block exemptions, 26, 311, 430–1, 432, 514
    defined, 516
    European Union, 10, 16, 25–8, 27, 252, 253, 308–13, 314, 324, 325
    oligopolies, 285, 308–13
    price discrimination, 391–3
    vertical restraints, 429–32
    see also rule of reason
competitive advantage, 4, 251, 480–1
    Austrian school, 272
    collaborative ventures, 128, 131
    competency approach, 52–5, 60, 61, 145, 235, 273, 280
    core competencies, 274, 280
    defined, 516
    diversification, 123, 125
    economies of scale, 339
    employees as source of, 210
    firm's internal organization, 31–2, 39
    Five Forces Model, 269–74
    governance structure, 47, 49, 52, 54, 60
    horizontal boundaries, 100, 123, 125
    importance of quality, 47
    innovation, 482–7, 486, 506–7
    key structures, 250
    knowledge-based resources, 52–5
    learning as source of, 85, 235
    monopolistic competition, 252
    neo-classical paradigm, 57, 60
    and reputation, 236
    and Schumpeter, 482–3, 486, 487
    strategic behaviour of firms, 269–74
    vertical integration, 71
complementarity, decision-making, 179, 180
complementary goods, 276, 388, 426, 430
    defined, 516
complementary innovation, 498
complementors, 278–9, 280
    defined, 516
complete contracts, 197
    asymmetric information, 174
    bounded rationality, 38, 77, 174
    defined, 516
    employment, 48, 174, 222
    transaction costs, 74, 77
    vertical relationships, 72, 74, 77, 414
complex monopolies, 260
computer software sector, 149, 330, 390–1, 492

concentration ratio, 257–8, 266, 468, 470
    defined, 516
concerted practices, 26, 284, 505
confusion marketing, 387
conglomerate mergers, 160, 162, 165
    defined, 517
conglomerates, 116, 123, 182, 196, 264
    defined, 516
conjectural variations, 300–1, 302, 404
    advertising, 457, 468, 469
    defined, 517
    innovation, 494
    product differentiation, 445, 448–9, 449
Conner, K., 85
conspicuous consumption, 451, 452
    defined, 517
constant prices, 101, 142, 154, 155, 377
    defined, 517
constant returns to scale, 102, 103, 120, 488
    defined, 517
constrained optimization, 33, 34, 60
    defined, 517
consultant group reports, 162
consultants, 507
    market exchange contracts, 48
consumer behaviour, 142, 463
consumer goods, 346, 413, 414, 446, 454
consumer needs, 21, 142, 278, 442, 450
consumer preferences, 21
    advertising's attempts to change, 142, 462–7, 463, 471–2, 473
    for brands, 382
    imperfect information, 399, 403–4, 443
    informational advertising, 460, 461–2
    product differentiation, 442, 443, 444–51, 472–3
consumer relationship marketing (CRM), 442
    defined, 517
consumers
    changing tastes, 463–4
    customer turnover, 454, 460
    decision-making, 171
    diversity of tastes, 446
    information available to, 9, 46, 382, 398–9, 400–5, 437–8, 458–62
    preference map, 463
    price sensitivity, 363, 366
    search costs, 366, 398, 400, 402, 403, 405, 406–7, 420, 424, 432, 454, 459
    utility-maximization, 60, 171
    willingness to pay, 446

    see also adverse selection
consumers' surplus
    bundling, 387, 390
    defined, 517
    patents, 498
    predatory pricing, 349
    price discrimination, 369, 371, 374, 375, 390, 393
    uniform pricing, 382
    versioning, 384
    vertical restraints, 433
contestability, 266–8, 267, 270, 327, 350, 403
    defined, 517
contractual relationships, 13
    asymmetric information, 37, 174, 222
    bounded rationality, 38, 49, 174
    governance approach, 48–50, 48, 57, 60
    for labour services, 48–50
    market exchange, 48–9
    opportunistic behaviour, 49, 77, 222
    reputational externalities, 420
    transaction costs, 49
    vertical relationships, 413–14, 415, 420, 421
    see also complete contracts; employment contracts; implicit contracts; incomplete contracts; relational contracts; vertical restraints
control loss, 93, 181, 182
    defined, 517
conventional behaviour, 151
Coombs, R., 504
copyright, 497
    defined, 518
core competencies, 54, 55
    competitive advantage, 274, 280
    defined, 518
    growth of firms, 145–6, 147, 164
    learning, 59
    mergers, 162
    Microsoft, 148–9
    strategic behaviour, 249–50
    vertical integration, 83, 84
Cornerstone-Hanson Building Materials America, 184
corporate social responsibility, 197, 201
    defined, 518
corporate strategy, 4, 100
    coherence of diversifies firm's evolution, 123
    defined, 518
    M-form (multi-divisional) organization, 182
    unrelated diversification, 116
corporation, 4, 10, 181
    defined, 518
correlation coefficient, 118
    defined, 518

cost benefit analysis
    agglomeration, 112
    complementary goods, 388
    defined, 518
    intermediate products, 80
    multi-plant operations, 116
cost of capital
    defined, 518
    dominant firm markets, 341, 358
    growth of firms, 159
    innovation risks, 265
    price discrimination, 392
    sunk costs, 328
cost-efficiency frontier, 172–3
cost-minimization, 3, 81
    defined, 518
    monitoring costs, 231
    neo-classical paradigm, 33–4, 60, 100, 172–3
    transaction costs, 83, 91
    vertical integration, 70, 85
Costin, Mike, 75
costs, 5–7
    vertical integration, 68–9, 69
    see also agency costs; fixed costs; long-run average cost curve (LRAC); marginal costs; short-run average cost curve; total costs; transaction costs; unit production costs; variable costs
Cosworth Engineering, 75
cottage workers, 43
Council of the European Union, 311
    defined, 548
Cournot, Augustin, 289
Cournot duopoly model, 292, 456–7
Cournot model, 252, 273, 298, 300, 301, 343, 491
    defined, 518
Cournot-Nash equilibrium, 382, 417–18
    advertising, 457
    defined, 518
    dynamic models, 301, 303–4
    price-setting models, 294
    quantity setting models, 290–1, 290, 292, 293
Court of First Instance, 311
covariance, 118
    defined, 518
creative destruction, 144, 146, 481, 483, 488, 506
    defined, 518
credence goods
    advertising, 464, 465, 473
    defined, 518
    pricing quality, 406, 407, 408, 411, 432, 461
    vertical restraints, 420
credit terms, 376
Cremer, J., 223
Crick, Francis, 152
cross-price elasticity of demand, 262, 326

advertising, 462, 463
defined, 518
price discrimination, 379–80
price-setting models, 296
product differentiation, 445, 446, 447, 448
see also price elasticity of demand
culture see organizational culture
customer turnover, 454, 460
customers
bargaining power of, 271
Five Forces Model, 271, 280
interaction with, 7
knowledge of, 4
market contracts, 48
needs of, 21
opportunistic behaviour, 78
stakeholder capitalism, 197, 201
treatment of, 197
welfare of, 11
see also adverse selection; consumers; downstream; vertical integration; vertical relationships
Creutzfeldt-Jakob disease, 412–13
Cyert, R., 188, 189, 502

D
Daily Express, 357
Daily Mail, 357
Daimler-Chrysler, 20
dairy farming, 69, 88
Danone, 294
Darby, M., 406, 407, 461
Darling, Alistair, 372
Dasgupta, P., 489–90, 491, 492, 494, 495
deadweight welfare loss, 369, 370, 372, 380, 498
defined, 519
decision control rights, 190, 191, 200
defined, 525
see also extensive form game
decision management rights, 172, 190, 200
defined, 519
decision-making
assignment of rights, 178–81
centralization of, 178, 179, 180, 200
complexity within firms, 171
decentralization of, 162, 178–9, 180, 200
delegation of, 6, 42
Fordist versus post-Fordist, 46
information flows, 179–80, 185, 200
multiplicity of groups, 188, 200
nature of, 171
operational, 179–80
organizational architecture, 40–2, 171, 178–81, 180
strategic, 179–80

see also authority control hierarchy; game theory
decreasing returns to scale see diseconomies of scale
dedicated asset specificity, 78
deep pocket model, 345, 348–51, 354, 492
defined, 519
defence industry, 274–5
Dell Computer Corporation, 46, 47–8, 92–3
Dell, Michael, 47–8, 92
demand
bandwagon effect, 451, 451
changes in, 52, 77, 217, 300
defined, 519
determination of market size, 9
Five Forces Model, 271, 280
influence on firm growth, 139–43, 140, 154, 157, 159
influence of government policies, 9–10
unrelated diversification, 117–19
see also cross-price elasticity of demand; price elasticity of demand
demand curve
consumer preferences, 460
defined, 519
dominant firm markets, 324, 331, 335
downward sloping, 137, 139, 252, 291, 295, 324, 365, 366, 393, 405, 432, 445, 454, 472
duopolies, 287, 307
firm growth, 140
imperfect information, 400, 401, 401, 402, 404, 405
labour market, 216
price discrimination, 365, 366, 370, 371, 374, 375, 379, 380, 393
price leadership, 335
price-setting models, 295, 296
product differentiation, 445
quantity setting models, 289, 291
sales-maximization model, 137, 140
total revenue, 168–9
upward sloping, 451
Veblen effect, 451
vertical relationships, 414, 416, 417
vertical restraints, 422
see also aggregate demand curve; ceteris paribus demand curve; inverse demand curve; kinked demand curve; market demand curve; market response demand curve; residual demand curve
demand function, 455
defined, 519
democracies, 10
demonstration facilities, 423, 424

Demsetz, H., 18, 49, 50, 177, 225, 231, 266
Denmark, 279
car price differentials, 367, 368
Dennison, S., 28
Department of Trade and Industry (DTI), 176
deregulation, 310
derived demand, 216
defined, 519
deterrence strategies, 141, 325, 339–47, 357, 363
defined, 519
see also entry deterrence; predatory pricing
Deutsche Airbus Gmbh, 313
differentiated companies, 264
differentiated products
advertising, 266, 442–3
attributes, 445–6, 447–8, 450
Austrian school, 272
competitive performance of, 181
conjectural variations, 445, 448–9, 449
consumers' preferences, 442, 443, 444–51, 472–3
contestable markets, 327
cross-price elasticity of demand, 445, 446, 447, 448
defined, 519
deterrence strategies, 346
dominant firm markets, 346
Five Forces Model, 271
market boundaries, 255
oligopolies, 252, 295–6, 298–9
patent breadth, 499
patent licences, 499
price discrimination, 381–7, 393
sales revenue maximization, 138
as structural barrier, 266
sunk costs, 266, 449, 450
and technology, 483
see also Bertrand model
diffusion, 482, 497–500, 500, 506, 507
defined, 519
digital technology, 46, 143, 256
diminishing marginal utility, 448
defined, 519
diminishing rate of technical substitution, defined, 519
diminishing returns
advertising, 460
analytics of monopoly, 319
Baumol's model, 137
defined, 519–20
diversification, 156
labour market, 216, 241
price leadership, 335
price-setting models, 294
pricing with imperfect information, 402
R&D expenditure, 491, 498
directors, 171, 177, 184, 185, 190, 191

defined, 520
discount coupons, 377, 390
discounted cash flow, defined, 520
discounts, 307, 346, 364, 471, 495
European Court of Justice, 393
price discrimination, 377, 381
pricing quality, 410, 412
primary line injury, 392
supermarket sector, 376
vertical restraints, 423, 424, 427
discretionary expenditure, 186, 204–6
discretionary investment, 186
diseconomies of scale, 101, 102, 103
defined, 520
disequilibrium, 144, 159
defined, 520
disposable income, 171, 365, 377, 380, 443
defined, 520
disruption costs, 110
diversification
bounded rationality, 118–19, 123–4
coherence, 122–4, 124, 125, 127, 147
competency approach, 119–21, 121, 122, 124–5, 128, 129
defined, 520
demand as incentive for, 139–43, 140, 154, 157, 159
economies of scale, 116, 119, 120, 124–5, 266
economies of scope, 116, 119, 120, 121, 124–5, 139, 153–4, 181
extensive form game, 125–6, 125
horizontal boundaries, 100, 101, 116–29, 139, 145, 181–2
knowledge, 119, 120, 121, 125
learning, 120, 123, 124, 125, 131
management discretion, 186–7
managerial model of growth, 153–9
measurement of, 116
patent licences, 499
R&D expenditure, 502
related, 116
resource requirements, 153–4
steady-state rate of growth, 154, 156
structure-conduct-performance (SCP) paradigm, 254
and uncertainty, 124–6
unrelated, 116–21, 124, 127, 131
Virgin, 7
virtual boundaries, 127–9, 129, 131
see also acquisitions; conglomerates; mergers; organizational coherence
diversification index (DI), 116
diversified growth, 139–43, 140, 144–8, 149, 153–9, 186–7
see also acquisitions; mergers
dividends, 16, 155, 158, 159, 198

division of labour
  defined, 520
  productivity gains, 34, 36, 43
  Smith on, 43, 66, 143, 482
  unitary (U) form of organization, 181
Dixit, A., 444
dog products, 106
dominant firms
  advertising, 345, 346, 354
  anti-competitive practices, 355, 356
  backward induction, 333, 352, 353
  barriers to entry, 326–9
  collusion, 337, 341, 343
  concept of dominance, 326–9
  defined, 520
  demand curve, 324, 331, 335
  deterrence strategies, 325, 339–47, 357
  economic rent, 44, 336, 340, 348, 349–51
  game theory, 328, 333–4, 337–8, 342–3, 342, 344–5
  limit pricing model, 339–45, 346, 355, 357, 358
  non-cooperative behaviour, 325, 331, 333, 341, 343
  predation strategies, 325, 347–54
  predatory pricing, 347–54, 349, 355–6, 357–8, 391, 392
  price leadership, 325, 335–8, 335, 336, 339, 342–3, 358
  profit-maximization, 325, 330, 331–2, 335, 336, 339, 341, 343
  quantity fixing, 289, 325, 330–4
  strategic behaviour, 324–58
  sunk costs, 327–8, 343, 350, 351
  unit costs, 327, 328–9, 337, 340, 344, 345–6, 348–9, 355
dominant strategy, 22, 91, 293, 297, 343
  defined, 520
Dorfman, R., 455, 491
Dorfman-Steiner condition, 455–6
  defined, 520
Dorrell, Stephen, 412
dot.com boom, 20, 458
double marginalization, 415, 419, 421, 425, 433
  defined, 520
downsizing, 65, 196
downstream
  clusters, 277
  defined, 520
  dominant firms, 354
  Five Forces Model, 271
  price discrimination, 391
  strategic behaviour, 250
  technological advances, 271
  vertical integration, 65, 66, 67, 68, 70, 71, 72, 82, 84, 86

vertical relationships, 413, 414–17, 433
vertical restraints, 420, 421, 424, 425
  see also franchising
Doyle, P., 460
drastic innovation, 488, 489, 497–8, 499
  defined, 521
Duckworth, Keith, 75
Dulux, 160
duopolies, 252, 287–8
  advertising, 456–7
  collusion, 307, 307
  defined, 521
  incentive to innovate, 493–5, 498
  price discrimination, 385, 386
  product differentiation, 449
  quantity setting models, 288–9
  see also Cournot duopoly model
durable goods, 454
dynamic capabilities, 54, 59, 179, 273–4, 484
  defined, 521
  see also core competencies
dynamic efficiency, 480, 481, 487, 506
  defined, 521
dynamic games, 328
  defined, 521
dynamic models
  Baumol's model, 138
  oligopolies, 285, 298–302, 305
  Shapiro's model, 408–10

E

Eastern Europe see Central and Eastern European Countries (CEEC)
Eastman-Kodak, 324
EasyJet, 364, 380–1
econometric studies, 142
economic liberalization, 10, 310
  defined, 521
economic models, 5, 482
  defined, 521
Economic and Monetary Union (EMU), 368
economic organizations see firms
economic profits or losses, defined, 521
economic rent
  Baumol model, 137
  competency approach, 52–3
  contestable markets, 327
  defined, 521
  dominant firm markets, 44, 336, 340, 348, 349–51
  governance approach, 44, 47, 50
  incentive to innovate, 488–9
  innovation, 483, 506–7
  knowledge-based resources, 52–3
  neo-classical paradigm, 251, 327

patent breadth, 499
predatory pricing, 348, 349–51
price discrimination, 370, 371, 375
pricing with imperfect information, 402, 404
product differentiation, 449
reputation for quality products, 411
strategic management, 251
supply of labour, 213–14
vertical relationships, 415, 416
economies of massed reserves, 102
  defined, 521
economies of scale, 23, 308, 502
  as barrier to entry, 265–6
  BSG Growth-Share Matrix, 106
  co-operatives, 88
  collaborative ventures, 127
  competitive advantage, 339
  defined, 521
  diversification, 116, 119, 120, 124–5, 266
  dominant firms, 325, 327, 337, 339
  and economies of scope, 114–15, 266
  franchising, 88
  horizontal boundaries, 100, 101–3, 105, 106, 107–8, 109, 110, 111, 112, 113, 124–5, 130
  mergers, 161
  monopolies, 26
  multi-plant economies, 109, 110, 111, 112
  neo-classical paradigm, 100, 144
  product differentiation, 444
  quantity fixing, 325
  R&D activity, 501
  unit costs, 101–3, 110
  vertical integration, 80, 81
  vertical restraints, 426, 429
  see also proportionality postulate
economies of scope, 502
  bundling, 388
  collaborative ventures, 127, 128, 131
  core competencies, 145, 164
  defined, 521–2
  diversification, 116, 119, 120, 121, 124–5, 139, 153–4, 181
  dominant firms, 327
  and economies of scale, 114–15, 266
  horizontal boundaries, 101, 112–16, 119, 120, 121, 124–5, 130
  innovation, 496
  mergers, 161
  neo-classical paradigm, 144
  strategic decision-making, 179
  vertical integration, 80, 84
  vertical restraints, 426, 429
effective impediments, 340, 341

efficiency
  impact of competition, 128
  imperfect monitoring, 172–6
  lack of motivation, 172–6
  and learning, 173
  separation of ownership and control, 171
  see also allocative efficiency; dynamic efficiency; productive efficiency; productivity
efficiency frontier, 172–3
efficiency wages, 105, 229–31, 229, 234, 238
  defined, 522
efficient capital market, 89, 267
  defined, 522
elasticity, 102
  defined, 522
  see also cross-price elasticity of demand; price elasticity of demand
electricity generation industry, 83
Eli Lilly, 153
empiricism, 11, 12
  advertising as barrier to entry, 471
  advertising intensity, 468
  advertising and prices, 472
  advertising quality, 466
  collaboration, 127
  diversification, 122
  firm size and R&D activity, 502
  firm's changes in operations, 143
  growth of firms, 164
  inefficiencies, 200
  innovative intensity, 491
  labour market, 211–12, 217
  Leibenstein's studies, 173, 175
  patent licences, 500
  patents, 499
  post-merger effects, 162
  product differentiation, 444
  SCP postulates, 269, 280
  stability of start-ups, 152
  tacit collusion in oligopolies, 304
employees, 209–40
  adverse selection, 231, 232
  career paths, 210
  development of, 210
  efficiency of, 209
  hierarchy contracts, 48–50
  incentive schemes, 209–10, 225–31, 237–8
  leisure-income trade-off, 211–13, 212
  measurement of performance, 209–10, 227–31, 228, 232, 237–8
  motivation, 209–10, 222, 223, 224–32, 227, 232, 237–8
  neo-classical paradigm, 211–17, 222, 233, 235, 237
  performance rewards, 6, 209–10, 225–6, 233

recruitment of, 232–6
rent seeking, 234
as a resource, 16
retention of, 210, 232–6
risk aversion, 214, 226, 229, 237, 238
as source of competitive advantage, 210
stakeholder capitalism, 197, 201
training, 233–4
see also agency costs; efficiency wages; human capital; human resource management (HRM); wage rates
employment contracts, 48–50, 177–8, 200, 222–5, 237
endogenous change, 152, 305
endogenous factors, 139, 143
defined, 522
The Energy Group, 184
English Food and Farming Partnership (EFFP), 195
entrepreneurial bias, 152
entrepreneurs, 34
asymmetric information, 36–7
Austrian school, 272
bounded rationality, 37
contingencies, 37–8
defined, 522
EU policies, 136, 150–1
factories of industrial revolution, 43, 44
growth of firms, 134, 146–8, 149–52, 164, 265
hidden action, 37
horizontal boundaries, 100
incomplete information, 36–7
invention-innovation process, 148, 150, 482
knowledge, 149, *150*
manager's role as, 135
moral hazard, 37, *38*
neo-classical paradigm, 36, 60, 149–50, 170, 174–5
productive opportunities, 59, 147–8, 149, 152, 164, 265
entry barriers *see* barriers to entry
entry deterrence, 125, 265, 266, 268, 388
environmental damage, 10
Epogen, 153
equilibrium
defined, 522
diversified growth, 146
dynamic models, 299, 300
game theory, 273
neo-classical paradigm, 144, 149
oligopolies, 288, 289–93, 294–7, *296*
price-setting models, 294, 295, *296*
pricing with imperfect information, 402–3, 404
pricing quality, 408
product differentiation, 448–9

quantity setting models, 288, 289, 290, 291, 292
see also Bertrand-Nash equilibrium; Nash equilibrium; non-cooperative equilibrium; Stackelberg-Nash equilibrium; sub-game perfect Nash equilibrium
Ericsson, 126, 129
Estonia, car price differentials, 369
ethical considerations, 17
European Commission
block exemptions, 26, 311, 430–1, 432, 514
car price differentials, 367–9
Coca-Coal Company, 354
defined, 522
entrepreneurship, 136, 150–1
Eurotunnel price fixing, 297–8
exclusive agreements, 429
genetically modified (GM) crops, 501
innovation, 432
joint ventures, 129–30
mergers, 162–3, 262, 326
motor vehicle sector, 428, 431–2
price discrimination, 392–3
resale price maintenance, 421, 431
small and medium-sized enterprises (SMEs), 20, 150–1, 431, 502
soda ash market, 334
software market, 390–1, 492
telecommunications sector, 347
vertical mergers, 86
vertical restraints, 399, 419, 429, 430–2, 433
European Competition Network (ECN), 253, 313
European Court of Justice, 311, 326, 391–2, 429, 467
European Economic Area (EEA), 25, 391, 392
European Monetary Union (EMU), 161
European Patent Office, 497
European Strategic Programme for Research and Development (ESPRIT), 310
European Union, 5
Article 37, 311
Article 82, 25, 27–8, 83, 253, 311, 326, 334, 347, 392, 393
Article 86, 83, 311
Articles 87-89, 311
casual workers, 215
clusters, 279
competition policy, 10, 16, 25–8, 27, 252, 253, 308–13, 314, 324, 325
defence industry, 275
dominant firms, 324, 326
effect of globalization, 10
ice cream market, 429
industry classification, 255, *255*

merger boom, 161
Merger Regulation, 162
mergers in retail markets, 405–6
new CEEC members, 12, 20, 253
patents, 497
price discrimination, 367, 391, 392
quality directives, 47
resale price maintenance, 421, 431
Single European Act (1987), 161, 309–10
single market, 26, 104, 115, 253, 263
SSNIP, 262–3
state aids, 310–11
see also Article 81; Lisbon strategy
Eurostat, 256
Eurotunnel, 6, 297–8
evolutionary theory, 54, 146, 159, 273–4, 432, 483
defined, 522
ex ante, 78, 79, 232, 300, 342, 343, 344
defined, 523
ex post
asset specificity, 78
competitive capabilities, 55
contractual relationships, 77, 78, 222
defined, 523
dominant firms, 328, 331, 339, 342, 343, 344, 345
innovations, 481
sunk assets, 328, 339
Sweezy's model, 300
excess demand, defined, 523
excess supply, defined, 523
exclusive dealing, 421, 424–5, 428, 429, 432
defined, 523
exhaustible resources, defined, 536
exit barriers, 267, 270, 328
defined, 523
exit costs, 266, 267, 327, 348
defined, 523
exogenous change, 250, 306
exogenous demand forces, 157, 159
exogenous factors, 143, 159, 266, 268, 270
exogenous variable, 482
defined, 523
expectancy theory, 232
expense preference model, 186, *187*, 200
defined, 523
experience goods
advertising, 464, 466, 473
defined, 523
pricing quality, 406, 407, 408, 411, 461
vertical restraints, 420
explicit collusion, 5, 254, 301, 307, 431, 457
defined, 523
see also cartels

extensive form game, 23, *23*
contract to supply game, 71–2
defined, 523
deterrence strategies, 343
diversification, 125–6, *125*
labour contracting, 48
market share, 141
opportunistic behaviour, 76–7, *76*
Prisoners' Dilemma, 296
see also backward induction
external economies, 130
defined, 523
external environment *see* business environment
externalities, 197, 199
agglomeration, 111
defined, 523
horizontal, 424, 425, 433
internalizing of, 530
positive, 111
reputational, 420, 424

F

factor markets, 144, 270
defined, 523
factor services, defined, 524
factors of production, 31, 486
defined, 524
neo-classical paradigm, 34
see also capital; entrepreneurs; labour; land factory production, development of, 43, 44
Fama, E., 190
farming industry, 69, 195, 501
Farrell, J., 161
fashion industry, 73, 451
fast food sector, 288
Felipe, Crown Prince of Spain, 73
Figuier, Louis, 297
financial capital, 351
defined, 524
financial incentives *see* incentive schemes
financial integration, 88, 128
financial rating, 114
financial services sector, 108, 161, 163–4, 171
finished products, 453
Finland, car price differentials, 368, 369
firm-specific human capital *see* specific human capital
firms
collective goals, 3, 4, 7
defined, 3, 31, 524
historical development, 43–6, *45*
history and experience, 58
integrated approach, 57–60, *58*, *59*
limits to size of, 53
objectives, 185–9, 200
strategic approach, 31–63

see also allocative efficiency;
business environment;
competency approach;
dominant firms; governance
approach; growth; neo-
classical paradigm;
organizational architecture;
productive efficiency
first-degree price discrimination,
367, 369–72, *369*
defined, 524
first-mover advantage, 6, 124, 306,
331–4, 457, 483
defined, 524
fiscal policies, 9–10
Fisher, F., 285
Fisher's separation theorem, defined,
524
Five Forces Model, 9, 269–74, 275,
280
defined, 524
fixed capital, 113, 114, 138, 392, 492
defined, 524
fixed costs, 80, 110, 113, 349, 370,
490
defined, 524
see also average fixed costs
fixed factors, defined, 524
fixed investment, defined, 524
flexibility, 46, 49, 119, 502
alliances, 127
employees, 45
encouragement of, 40
evolutionary approach, 54
joint ventures, 127
multi-plant operations, 109
organizational architecture, 7
product innovation, 484
flexible production systems, 45
flexible working, 196
focused companies, 263–4
Fokker-VFM, 313
Food and Drug Administration, 408
food processing value chain, 66–9
food retail sector, 259–60, 271
food safety, 408, 411–12, 501
Food Standards Agency, 408, 413
foot and mouth disease, 195
football merchandising, 467
footwear cluster, 277, *277*
Ford, Henry, 43, 180
Ford Motor Company, 42, 43, 75,
123, 180, 199, 252, 253
Fordism, 44, *46*
defined, 524
forward integration, 346
defined, 524
see also downstream
Foss, N., 120
foundation hospitals, 24
France
car price differentials, 367, 368
competition policy, 310, 311
labour productivity, 176
mergers, 162

wine industry, 452
franchise fee, 415–17, 419, 422
defined, 525
franchising, 82, 88
defined, 525
reputational externalities, 420
vertical restraints, 426
free market economy, 32, 481, 485
defined, 525
free-rider problem, 237, 423–4, 425,
433, 456, 470
defined, 525
teams, 231, 340
free trade, 10, 25
defined, 525
Freeman, C., 502
Friedman, Milton, 175
Friesland Dairy Foods, 264
fringe competitors, 324, 328–9
defined, 525
deterrence strategies, 339–47, 357
predatory pricing, 347–54, *349*,
355–6, 357–8, 391, 392
price leadership, 335–8, 342–3,
358
quantity fixing, 330–4
Fudenberg, D., 351
full-cost pricing, defined, 525
full-line forcing, 421, 426, 429–30
defined, 525
function, defined, 525
fundholding GPs, 24
Furse, M., 308

G

gains from trade, defined, 525
Gallini, N., 499
game theory, 6, 9, 13–15
advertising, 21, 465–6, *466*,
469–70, *469*
allocative efficiency, 14, 22, 23
assumption of rationality, 285
bounded rationality, 13, 304
capturing value, 21–3
collusion, 252, 266, 302–6
defined, 525
deterrence strategies, 342–3
dominant firm markets, 328,
333–4, 337–8, 342–3, *342*,
344–5
imperfect information, 13, 15,
22, 304, 305
incentive to innovate, 493–4, *494*
incomplete information, 304, 305
oligopolies, 285, 288, *288*,
302–6, 314
productive efficiency, 14, 22, 23
reputation and quality, 410–11,
411
strategic behaviour of firms, 5,
249, 273, 274, 280, 302–6
strategic conflict approach, 273
tacit collusion, 266, 273, 280,
302, 304–5, 306

trust, 90–1, *90*, *235*, 236
two-period game, 302–4, *303*
vertical relationships, 415–16, *416*
wage bargaining, 221, 244–5
see also backward induction;
extensive form game; Nash
equilibrium; normal form
game; repeated games
game tree, 37
defined, 525
see also extensive form game
GAP, 73
Garnsey, E., 151, 152
Gates, Bill, 149, 150
GEC, 126
General Motors, 31, 42–3, 107, 180,
252, 253
general purpose human capital, 233–4
Genetech, 153
genetically modified (GM) crops, 501
geographic markets, 260
geography
advertising intensity, 454
price discrimination, 365, 384–7
Germany
car price differentials, 367, 368,
369
ice cream market, 429
industrial organization, 44
labour productivity, 176
limited liability companies, 170
Geroski, P., 142, 265, 471, 484, 491,
497
Ghoshal, S., 146
Gibrat, R., 264
Gibrat's law, 264–5
defined, 526
Giffen good, defined, 526
Gilbert, R., 497, 499
gini-coefficient, 258–9
defined, 526
Glazer, Malcolm, 189–90
Global Competitiveness Report, 279
global financial markets, 25, 46
global markets, 46, 198
globalization, 10, 87, 233, 256, 280,
306
defined, 526
GM crops, 501
goal congruence, 42, 146, 152, 162,
192, 195, 234
defined, 526
going wage, 211, 213, 214, 215–16,
217
defined, 526
in imperfect markets, 218–19
Goldberg, V., 78
goods, 3, 16, 31, 407
defined, 526
evaluation continuum, 407, *407*
see also complementary goods;
consumer goods; credence
goods; differentiated
products; experience goods;
homogeneous products;
intermediate products; search
goods

goods markets, 413, 446
defined, 526
goodwill trust, 90
Google, 391
governance approach, *50*, 59–61, 484
asset specificity, 79–82, 84, 114,
119, 503
asymmetric information, 47, 235
behavioural theories, 189
bounded rationality, 47, 49, 57,
59, 60, 189
competitive advantage, 47, 49,
52, 54, 60
contractual relationships, 48–50,
48, 57, 60
defined, 526
economic rent, 44, 47, 50
growth of firms, 145, 164
horizontal boundaries, 100, 114
imperfect information, 47, 59
incentive schemes, 49–50, 57,
60, 235
incomplete contracts, 100, 114
opportunistic behaviour, 60, 189,
235
organizational architecture, 32,
47–50, 52, 57–8, 145
outsource, 87
partnership alliances, 90
specialization, 119
technical progress, 503
transaction costs, 32, 47–50, 100
vertical integration, 65, 79–82,
84, 85, 86, 87
vertical restraints, 432
governing hierarchies *see* authority
control hierarchy
government
defined, 526
influence on competition, 9–10
state aids, 25, 268–9
see also competition policies;
industrial policies
GPs, 24
Grabowski, H., 471
Greece
car price differentials, 367, 368
electricity generation, 83
Green, Charlie, 39
Green, Philip, 149
Greenbury, Sir Richard, 51
Gregory, A., 162
gross return on capital, defined, 526
gross revenue, 140, 455, 469
defined, 526
Grossman, G., 460
Grossman, S., 72, 177
growth
competency approach, 145–7,
164
defined, 526
entrepreneurs, 134, 146–8,
149–52, 164, 265
firm's rate of, 134
governance approach, 145, 164

influence of demand, 139–43, *140*, 154, 157, 159
managerial model of, 153–9, 186
organizational architecture, 144–8, 265
organizational coherence, 144, 145, 146, 147, *147*, 156, 164
profitability, 134, 138, 153, 155–9
sales revenue maximization, 136–8, 153
start-up firms, 151
and supply, 143–8, 155, 157–8
within strategic groups, 265
see also acquisitions; diversified growth; mergers
Growth-Share Matrix, 106, 118
defined, 526
guarantees, 412
Guinness, 196

H

haggling, 370
Haji-Ioannou, Stelios, 149, 380
Hakansson, H., 432
Halifax, 163, 164
Hamel, G., 54
Hanson, 55, 116, 160, 184
Hanson Brick, 184
Hanson, Lord, 184
Hanson Pacific, 184
Hanson Quarry Products Europe, 184
Hanson Trust, 184
Harisson, I., 110
Hart, O., 72, 177
Harvard Business School, 86
Hawk-Dove game, defined, 527
Hawker Siddeley Aviation, 313
hazard rate, 494
defined, 527
Heineken, 263
Henderson, Bruce, 106
Henderson, R., 496
Hennes and Mauritz, 73
Hereward milling wheat, 195
Herfindahl index, 258
defined, 527
Herfindahl-Hirschman index (HHI), 258, 291
heterogeneity
of assets, 84
neo-classical paradigm, 60
organizational architecture, 19, 39, 40, 47, 49, 52–3, 503
skills and routines, 236
heterogeneous capabilities, 61, 120, 121, 123, 305, 327, 503
heterogeneous knowledge, 84, 85, 88
competency approach, 53, 54, 55, 57, 61, 129
heterogeneous resources
competency approach, 52–5, 57, 61, 120, 121, 129, 273, 503
competitive advantage, 52, 53, 54, 61, 145, 235, 273, 503

diversified growth, 146, 148
horizontal expansion, 123
hidden actions, 37, 38, 222, 224, 225
defined, 527
hidden characteristics, 37, 38
defined, 527
hierarchies *see* authority control hierarchy
Hoffmann La Roche & Co, 306, 393
hog cycles, defined, 527
hold-up, 78, 79, 81, 128
defined, 527
hollowed-out firms, 46, 94
Holmstrom, B., 179, 226
homogeneous products
advertising, 453
defined, 527
duopolies, 287–9
neo-classical paradigm, 55, 251, 255
oligopolistic markets, 252, 291, 294, 295
predatory pricing, 348
price discrimination, 364, 365, 384, 385, 398, 446
pricing with imperfect competition, 400, 401–2, 403
Honda, 88, 224
Hoover, 252
horizontal agreements, 392, 505
defined, 527
horizontal boundaries, 64, 99–133, 308
capabilities, 100, 120, 124, 125, 128
competency approach, 100, 119–21, 122, 124–5, 128, 129
competitive advantage, 100, 123, 125
defined, 527
diversification, 100, 101, 116–29, 139, 145, 181–2
economies of scale, 100, 101–3, 105, 106, 107–8, 109, 110, 111, 112, 113, 124–5, 130
economies of scope, 101, 112–16, 119, 120, 121, 124–5, 130
entrepreneurs, 100
governance approach, 100, 114
knowledge, 114, 119, 120, 121, 125, 128–9, 130
learning, 114, 120, 123, 124, 125, 128–9, 131
learning by doing, 104–8, *107*, 130
location, 100, 111–12
long-run average cost curve (LRAC), 102–3, *103*, 106, 107–8, 110, 112
minimum efficient scale (MES), 103, 104, 106, 110, 112, 130
multi-plant economies, 109–12, *111*, 116, 130
neo-classical paradigm, 100

organizational coherence, 122–4, *124*, 125, 127
production costs, 100
rent seeking, 100
U-form organizations, 181–2
and uncertainty, 124–5
unit costs, 100, 101–8, 110–12, 124–5, 127
vertical restraints, 430
virtual boundaries, 127–9, *129*, 131
horizontal differentiation, 446, 450
defined, 527
horizontal externalities, 424, 425, 433
horizontal mergers, 160, 161–2, 165
defined, 527
horizontal scales, measurement of, 99
HP, 92
HSBC, 20
human asset specificity, 78
human capital, 55, 102, 107, 123, 209–11, 233–5, 238, 481
defined, 527
human resource management (HRM), 18, 210, 233, 234, 235
as core competence, 145
defined, 528
diversification, 109, 119
vertical integration, 74
human resources *see* employees
Huntley and Palmer, 262
hyper-rationality
consumers' preferences, 444
demand for labour, 211, 216, 237
neo-classical paradigm, 33, 34, 36, 49, 57, 60, 172, 200, 398, 485
supply of labour, 214–15, 237
hypothesis testing, 59

I

IBM, 47–8, 92, 123, 149, 324, 499
ice cream market, 429
ICI, 160, 170, 196, 224, 236, 334
image advertising, 142, 462–7, *463*, 471–2, 473
imperfect competition, 6, 21, 249, 284
capital markets, 118–19
defined, 528
economies of scope, 113–14
innovation, 492, 507
labour market, 218–21, *219*
price discrimination, 365
pricing, 400–5
profit-maximization, 355
vertical restraints, 427, 433
see also
monopolies/monopolists; monopolistic competition; monopsonists; oligopolies/oligopolists; reaction function
imperfect information, 36, 191, 398

about dominant firms, 328
advertising, 399, 401
cartels, 307
competency approach, 59, 61, 123–4
conjectural variations, 300, 301
consumer preferences, 399, 403–4, 443
decision-making, 180
defined, 528
demand curve, 400, 401, *401*, 402, 404, 405
diversification, 123–4
employee motivation, 225
employment, 222
game theory, 13, 15, 22, 304, 305
generation of transaction costs, 49
governance approach, 47, 59
learning, 125
management, 172
oligopolies, 288, 300, 301, 304, 305
price discrimination, 393
price distribution, 398–9, 400–5, 432
price elasticity of demand, 400, 401, *401*, 403, 404, 405
product quality, 406–12
and reputation, 408
resale price maintenance, 424
transaction costs, 87
trust normal form game, 90–1
vertical integration, 65, 71–4, 87
vertical relationships, 413, 416
vertical restraints, 420, 424
Imperial Tobacco, 170, 184
implicit contracts, 200
defined, 528
employment, 178, 210, 223, 236, 237
partnership alliances, 90
Toyota, 91
imputed costs, defined, 528
incentive schemes
creation of, 178, 179
employee motivations, 209–10, 225–31, 237–8
governance approach, 49–50, 57, 60, 235
organizational architecture, 18, *19*, 41, 42
and risk, 192–5, 201, 227, 229, 230–1, 238
for senior management, 171, 192–5, 201
see also efficiency wages
income *see* disposable income; real incomes
income constraints, 171, 446
defined, 528
income effect, 365, 370, 443
defined, 528
income elasticity, 262, 377
defined, 528
income inelastic, defined, 528

income-leisure trade-off, 211–13, *212*
incomplete contracts
  and agency costs, 192
  asset specificity, 114
  bounded rationality, 38
  defined, 528
  employment, 210
  governance approach, 100, 114
  opportunistic behaviour, 77
  organizational architecture, 179
  principal–agent theory, 192
  vertical relationships, 72, 77
  see also employment contracts
incomplete information, 191
  about dominant firms, 328–9
  advertising, 453, 458, 459, 464
  consumers' preferences, 442, 443
  decision-making, 180
  defined, 528
  demand for labour, 217
  dominant firm markets, 351, 353, *353*
  employment, 222, 228
  entrepreneurs, 36–7
  game theory, 304, 305
  innovations, 484, 500
  learning, 125
  limit pricing model, 344–5, *344*
  management, 172
  nature of a firm, 36–7
  oligopolies, 304, 305
  predatory pricing, 351, 353, *353*
  product differentiation, 445
  and uncertainty, 36
  vertical integration, 65, 66
increasing returns to scale, 101, 102, 104, 125, 295
  defined, 528
  see also economies of scale
incremental costs, defined, 528
The Independent, 357
indifference curves, 206, 212, 227, 229, 448, 463
  defined, 528
indifference map, 205, 212, 227
  defined, 529
Inditex, 73
indivisibilities, 101, 102, 113–14, 120, 130, 501
  defined, 529
induced invention, 484
industrial advertising, 453–4
industrial clusters, 111, 275–9, *276*, *277*, 280
  defined, 529
  value net concept, 278–9, *278*, 280
industrial economics, 269
industrial organization economics, 6, 11–12
  defined, 529
industrial policies, 9, 11, 25
  defined, 529

European Union, 162, 308–13
  nomenclature of, 309, *309*
  oligopolies, 285, 308–13, 314
  state aids, 25
  UK defence industry, 274–5
industrial relations, 221–2
industrial revolution, 43, 44, 181, 277
industry, defined, 529
industry classification, 255, *255*, 256, 262
industry groups, 9, 255, 256–9, 260–3, 265, 267–8
  defined, 529
  Five Forces Model, 270
industry standards, development of, 26
industry structure, 108, 109, 161, 267
  defined, 529
  and R&D intensity, 491
  see also Five Forces Model; monopolies/monopolists; monopolistic competition; oligopolies/oligopolists; perfect competition; structure-conduct-performance (SCP) paradigm
inefficiency *see* allocative inefficiency; X-inefficiency
inelastic demand, 296, 319, 451
  defined, 529
inferior goods, 465
  defined, 529
Interbrew, 294
inflation, 26, 211, 312
  influence of government policies, 9–10
influencing costs, 174, 179, 225
  defined, 529
information
  about dominant firms, 328
  governance approach, 47
  as key element of organizational architecture, 40–1, 47
  as strategic variable, 305
  see also asymmetric information; imperfect information; incomplete information; perfect information; private information
information and communication technology (ICT), 151, 502
  defined, 529
  EU policies, 310
  growth of, 10, 54, 87, 93–4, 196
  investment in, 87
  mergers, 161
  reduction of information asymmetrics, 87, 88
  vertical relationships, 87, 93–4
information costs, 179
information, lack of *see* uncertainty
infrastructure, 44, 111, 275–6
  defined, 529
infrastructure policies, 25
innovation

Austrian school, 272
clusters, 277
competitive advantage, 482–7, *486*, 506–7
decision-making, 179
defined, 529
diffusion, 482, 497–500, *500*, 506, 507
entrepreneurs, 148, 150, 482
growth of firms, 265
inter-organizational, 88
learning as source of, 85
market structures, 488–92, *488*, 495
motor vehicle sector, 432
organizational form, 503, 505, *505*
organising for, 501–6
strategic behaviour, 492–6
vertical integration, 85
vertical restraints, 432
see also complementary innovation; drastic innovation; process innovation; product innovation
innovative profits, 485, 502
inputs, 11, 66–70, 345
  defined, 529
  neo-classical firm, 34, 36
intellectual capital, 235
intellectual property, 52, 58
interdependence, 9, 13, 14, 314
  between products, 262
  oligopolies/oligopolists, 285, 286–8, *286*
  oligopolist markets, 7, 308
  strategic conflict approach, 273
  see also game theory
interest, 265, 351
  defined, 529
Intermarché, 405
intermediate markets, 384, 413–17, 433
intermediate products, 399
  advertising, 453
  buyer's demand for, 384
  defined, 530
  joint ventures, 89
  overseas sourcing of, 87
  partnership alliances, 91
  tapered integration, 86
  transaction costs, 74, 76
  vertical integration, 65–7, 71–2, 80–2, 86, 93
  vertical relationships, 400, 413, 414, 415, 416, 417, 433
  vertical restraints, 346–7, 419, 420, 422, 426, 433
internal economies, 40, 53, 84, 135
  defined, 530
internal labour markets, 211, 234–5, 238
  defined, 530
internal rate of return, defined, 530

International Standard Industrial Classification (ISIC), 255, 256
International Standards Organization (ISO), 47
internationalization, 263–4
internet
  price discrimination, 387
  vertical relationships, 91
internet boom, 151
internet marketing, 457–8
intertemporal decisions, defined, 530
invention, 482, 484, 506
  defined, 530
inverse demand curve, 289, 320, 414, 422, 488
inverted-U hypothesis, 468, 470
investment, 16, 55, 155
  by banking sector, 45
  by multinationals, 87
  defined, 530
  dominant firms, 327–8, 346
  as strategic variable, 305
  see also capital investment; net investment
invisible hand, 36
  defined, 530
Ireland, 279
  car price differentials, 367, 368
isocost line, 33, *33*, 486
  defined, 530
isoprofit curves, 292–3, *293*, 332, 333, 495
  defined, 530
isoquant diagram, 33–4, 172–4, 486–7
  defined, 530
Italy, car price differentials, 367, 368

J
Japan
  corporate core competencies, 54, 55
  partnership alliances, 90
  production models, 45
Jensen, M., 190–1, 204–6
Jensen, R., 500
Jobs, Steve, 150
joint production, 113, 117
joint stock companies, 44, 170
  defined, 530
joint ventures, 89, 99, 127–30
  application orientation, 506
  bounded rationality, 131
  competitive advantage, 481
  defined, 88, 531
  European Commission policies, 312
  outsourcing, 46, 94
  pro-competitive effects, 27
  transaction costs, 131
Just-in-Time systems, 45
JVC (Victor Corporation of Japan), 487

K

Kaizen system, 45
Kaldor, N., 453
Kanban systems, 45
Karni, E., 406, 407, 461
Katz, M., 382, 384, 486, 489
Kay, J., 18
Kessides, N., 471
Keynesian policies, 308, 310
    defined, 531
Khanna, T., 118
Kihlstrom, R., 465, 466
kinked demand curve, 273,
    298–300, *299*, *300*, 401
    defined, 531
Kirin, 153
Klein, B., 78
Klein, P., 78
Klemperer, P., 498, 499
Klepper, S., 505
Knight, Frank, 149
knowledge, 28
    accumulation of, 6, 7, 19, 108,
        128, 496, 503
    as an intangible resource, 16,
        114, 127, 130, 161
    collaborative ventures, 128, 131
    competency approach, 32, 52–6,
        57, 60, 61, 83–5, 121, 122, 273
    diversification, 119, 120, 121,
        125
    dominant firm markets, 343
    entrepreneurship, 149, *150*
    horizontal boundaries, 114, 119,
        120, 121, 125, 128–9, 130
    as key element of organizational
        architecture, 40–1, 123
    Marshall on, 482
    neo-classical paradigm, 179
    reuse of, 114
    vertical integration, 82, 83–5
    see also diffusion; heterogeneous
        knowledge; human capital;
        innovation; invention; learning
        by doing; proprietary
        knowledge; tacit knowledge
knowledge spillovers, 278, 499
knowledge-based economies, 20
knowledge-based resources
    competency approach, 32, 52–6,
        57, 60, 61, 121, 122, 147, 273
    defined, 531
    evolutionary firm, 54
    growth of firms, 148
    and integrated approach, 58
known value items, 338
Kodak, 499
Koehler, Georges, 153
Kondratiev wave, 151
Koopermans, T., 101
KPMG, 162
Krattenmaher, T., 356
Kreditbank, 44
Krugman, P., 277

kyoroku gaisha, 90
Kyoto Protocol, 83

L

LA Dodgers, 189
labour, 17, 28, 80
    average cost of, 219, 242
    clusters, 277
    defined, 531
    demand for, 215–17, *216*, 237
    imperfect markets, 218–21, *219*
    supply of, 211–14, *213*, *214*, 237
    see also capital-labour ratio;
        division of labour; employees;
        internal labour markets
labour productivity
    defined, 531
    differences in, 176–7
    as efficiency measure, 173
    knowledge acquisition, 104
    random events, 230
    see also learning by doing
Lancaster, Kelvin, 447–8, 473
land, 16
    defined, 531
Land Rover, 199
Langlois, R., 120, 146
Langnese-Iglo, 429
lateral mergers *see* horizontal
    mergers
law of diminishing returns *see*
    diminishing returns
Law of One Price, 400
    defined, 531
law of proportionate growth, 264
Leach, D., 187
leader-follower model, 331–4, 335
Leahy, J., 187
lean manufacturing techniques, 35
lean production model, 45
    defined, 531
learning
    collaborative ventures, 128
    competency approach, 53, 54, 61
    competitive advantage, 85, 235
    as core capability, 59
    creating a culture of, 105
    diversification, 120, 123, 124,
        125, 131
    dynamic capability model, 54
    economies of scope, 114
    and efficiency, 173
    encouragement of, 40
    evolutionary firm, 54
    facilitation of, 53
    horizontal boundaries, 114, 120,
        123, 124, 125, 128–9, 131
    industrial organization
        economics, 6
    organizational architecture, 123
    vertical integration, 80, 81, 84,
        85
learning by doing, 53, 339, 346
    defined, 531

horizontal boundaries, 104–8,
    107, 130
    new growth ventures, 151
learning curve, 105, *105*, 106, 107–8
    defined, 531
Leblanc process, 334
legal commitments, as exit barrier,
    328
legal statutes, 40, *41*
legislative environment, 271, 280
Leibenstein, Harvey, 173, 174, 175
leisure-income trade-off, 211–13, *212*
Lenscrafters, 472
Lerner index of market power, 319
    defined, 531
leverage, 159
Levi Strauss, 430
Levin, R., 502
Levinthal, D., 107, 273
licensing agreements, 506
life cycle hypothesis, 272
    defined, 531
life cycle theories of firms, 143, 164
Lillehei, Dr C.W., 276
limit price, 339–45, *339*, 346, 355,
    357, 358, 471
    defined, 532
    incomplete information, 344–5,
        344
limited liability company, 44, 89, 170
linear (third-degree) pricing, 367,
    377–80, *379*
    defined, 548
Lisbon strategy, 20, 136, 150–1,
    279, 431, 509
    defined, 532
listing fees, 376
living standards, 28, 223
    defined, 532
    and R&D, 480, 485, *485*, 506
Lloyds TSB, 163
location, horizontal boundaries, 100,
    111–12
Lockheed Tristar, 313
long-run, 102, 103, 104, 134, 138,
    488
    defined, 532
long-run average cost curve (LRAC)
    defined, 532
    dominant firms, 340
    horizontal boundaries, 102–3,
        103, 106, 107–8, 110, 112
    incentive to innovate, 488, 489
    monopolistic competition, 404
    mutual independence, 287
long-run average costs, 454
long-term contracts, 88
Lorenz curve, 258–9, *259*
    defined, 532
loss-leader argument, 424
Lotus Cars, 75
Low Pay Commission (LPC), 217–18
loyalty retailers, 393
Lufthansa, 380

lumpiness, 101, 113, 130
Lundström, A., 151
Luxembourg, car price differentials,
    367, 368

M

M-form (multi-divisional)
    organization, 182, *182*, 183–4,
    200, 503
    defined, 532
Maastricht Treaty, 310
McAfee, R., 389
McDonald's, 88
Machlup, F., 18
McKinsey and Company, 35, 458
macroeconomic shocks, 161
macroeconomics, 11, 16, 31
    defined, 532
    see also Keynesian policies
Madhok, A., 125, 127
management
    ascendancy of the professional,
        44
    career concerns, 179
    as co-ordinators, 135
    discretionary behaviour, 136,
        171, 186–7, 190, 196, 201
    external vision, 135
    firm's reputation for fairness,
        178, 223–4, 237
    incentive schemes, 171, 192–5,
        201
    incomplete/imperfect
        information, 172
    influences on, *198*, 199
    model of firm growth, 153–9, 186
    motives, 185–6
    neo-classical paradigm, 33, 35
    non-profit maximizing behaviour,
        185–9, 200
    objectives, 185–9, 200
    opportunistic behaviour, 192, 229
    Penrosian view of, 134
    risk aversion, 138, 158, 192–3, 195
    sales revenue maximization,
        136–8, 153
    separation from ownership,
        170–1, 190–1, 201
    and shareholders, 35, 156, 185,
        190, 191, 192, 201, 204
    see also decision management
        rights; entrepreneurs;
        principal-agent theory
management costs, 172–6
management hierarchy, 28, 60, 99,
    135, 152, 171, 182
management resources
    competitive advantage, 53
    as critical, 134
    quality of, 3
management school, 170–1
    defined, 532
managerial ability, 54, 114, 154
managerial efficiency, 156, 158

managerial moral hazard, 191
managerial slack, 186, 191
managerial specificity, 328
managerial talent, 35
managerial theories, 186–7, 200
    defined, 532
Manchester United, 189–90, 467
March, J., 107, 188, 189, 502
Marconi plc, 126
margin support payments, 376
marginal cost curve, 307, 330, 348,
    370, 378
marginal cost of labour, 220, 242
    defined, 532
marginal cost pricing, 267, 372
    defined, 532
marginal costs
    advertising, 454, 455, 461
    analytics of monopoly, 319
    Bertrand model, 322
    defined, 532
    dominant firm markets, 331,
        335, 336, 348, 349, 355, 356
    Five Forces Model, 271
    oligopolies, 289, 291–2, 294–5,
        300, 301, 305, 321
    predatory pricing, 348, 349, 355,
        356
    price discrimination, 365, 370,
        371, 372, 374, 376, 378, 379,
        383–4, 385, 386, 387, 393
    price-setting models, 294–5
    process innovation, 488
    proprietary knowledge, 121
    quantity setting models, 289,
        291, 292
    vertical integration, 70, 71
    vertical relationships, 414, 415,
        416, 417
    vertical restraints, 422
marginal efficiency of capital,
    defined, 532
marginal product, defined, 533
marginal product of labour, 216,
    241–3
    defined, 533
marginal production costs, 340, 385,
    408, 416, 417
marginal rate of substitution, 448
    defined, 533
marginal rate of time preference,
    defined, 533
marginal revenue, 169, 241, 491
    advertising, 455
    analytics of monopoly, 319
    Bertrand model, 322
    defined, 533
    oligopolies, 289, 291, 299–300,
        320
    predatory pricing, 349, 355
    price discrimination, 377–8, 384,
        385
    price leadership, 336
    quantity setting models, 289,
        291

vertical integration, 71
vertical relationships, 417
marginal revenue curve, 299–300,
    307
    dominant firm markets, 331, 336
    price discrimination, 370, 379
    vertical relationships, 414
marginal revenue product (MRP),
    216, 241–3
    defined, 533
marginal utility, 211, 448
    defined, 533
market clearing price, 289, 320
    defined, 533
market clearing wage, 214, 215,
    219–20
    defined, 533
market demand curve, 287, 289,
    307, 320, 331, 335, 340
    defined, 533
market economies, 12, 28–9, 32,
    481, 485
    defined, 533
market failure, 118, 327, 425, 430,
    433
    defined, 533
market penetration costs, 470, 471
market research, 21
market response demand curve, 404
    defined, 533
market saturation, 140–1
market segments, 9, 410, 448
    defined, 533
    motor vehicle sector, 42–3
    price discrimination, 377–9, 382,
        383, 384
    Virgin, 7
market size
    determined by demand, 9
    deterrence strategies, 343
    dominant firm markets, 340, 343
    for labour, 213
    price discrimination, 393
market structures, 249–83, 481
    advertising, 467–72, 473
    incentive to innovate, 488–92,
        488, 495
    industry versus strategic groups,
        260–3
    seller concentration, 250, 256–9,
        268, 271
    strategic behaviours, 264–8
    structure-conduct-performance
        (SCP) paradigm, 254–5, 254,
        256, 265, 268, 268, 269–70,
        280
    see also imperfect competition;
        monopolies/monopolists;
        monopolistic competition;
        oligopolies/oligopolists;
        perfect competition
marketing
    bundling, 387, 390
    consumer relationship marketing
        (CRM), 442

defined, 442, 452
    diversification, 109, 119
    economies of scope, 113
    essence of, 21
    goal of, 188
    knowledge spillovers, 278
    need to be effective, 4
    partnership alliances, 91
    price discrimination, 364, 390
    product heterogeneity, 443
    product innovation, 501
    sales maximization, 138
    vertical integration, 74
    see also advertising
marketing campaigns, 84, 451
marketing expenditure, 139–40,
    141–2, 156, 159, 186
marketing mix, 452
    defined, 534
marketing techniques, 84
markets
    boundaries, 255, 260–3
    defined, 9, 533
    volatility, 9
Marks and Spencer, 51, 52, 55, 91,
    224, 236–7
Marlboro cigarettes, 462–3
Marris, Robin
    growth model, 139, 154, 156,
        157, 158, 159, 186
    managerial incentives, 185
Mars group, 429
Marshall, Alfred, 275, 276, 277, 482
Martens, 294
Marx, Karl, 144
Mason, Edward, 9, 254
mass-production see Fordism
materials, 17, 28, 66, 80, 84, 114
    defined, 534
Mathewson, G., 430
matrix organizations, 182–4, 183, 200
    defined, 534
mature markets, 139–41, 272
    defined, 534
Meckling, W., 190–1, 204–6
merchandising, 467
merger boom, 161
mergers, 99, 160–3, 165
    as alternative to predation, 350
    competition authorities, 128,
        161, 162, 350
    defined, 534
    diversification, 116
    dominant firms, 327
    encouragement of, 25
    European Commission, 162–3,
        262, 326
    market power, 256
    retail markets, 405–6
    UK financial services sector, 108
    see also conglomerate mergers;
        horizontal mergers; vertical
        mergers
merit goods, defined, 534
Messier, Jean-Marie, 85, 86

Metcalfe, J., 504
Metro AG, 405
MG Rover, 199
microeconomics, 11, 59, 211, 254,
    269
    defined, 534
Microsoft, 31, 130, 148–9, 198, 330,
    390–1, 492
Midland Electricity, 196
Milgrom, P., 48, 174, 197, 225, 233,
    461
Milk Link, 69
Milk Marque, 69
Millennium Chemicals, 184
Milstein, Cesar, 153
Mini brand, 224
minimax strategy, 469
    defined, 534
minimum efficient scale (MES)
    as barrier to entry, 265
    collaborative ventures, 127
    defined, 534
    horizontal boundaries, 103, 104,
        106, 110, 112, 130
    mature markets, 141
    multi-product firms, 115, 115, 179
    pricing with imperfect
        information, 403
minimum profit constraint, 155
Ministry of Agriculture, Fisheries and
    Food, 413
Minneapolis medical devices cluster,
    276–7
Mitsubishi, 46
mixed bundling, 388, 389–90, 390
    defined, 534
mixed economy, defined, 534
mixed strategy, defined, 534
mobile telephone sector, 21, 270–1,
    347
Moir, L., 197
molecular biology, 152–3
monetary policies, 9–10
money income, defined, 534
money wage, 204, 211–13
monitoring costs, 206
    employees, 231, 235, 236, 238,
        420
    vertical integration, 79, 82, 86
monitoring systems
    demands on management time,
        120
    employee motivation, 225,
        227–31, 228, 232, 237–8
    expense of, 225
    impact on efficiency, 172–6
    importance of, 225
    setting up of, 178
    transaction costs of, 423, 426
    see also performance monitoring
monopolies/monopolists, 9, 21
    advertising, 453, 455–6, 467, 468
    analytics of, 318–19
    defence of, 26
    defined, 534

first-degree price discrimination, 369–72

food retail sector, 259–60

incentive to innovate, 488–9, 497–8, 507

labour market, 218–19, *219*

neo-classical paradigm, 144, 249, 251, 254, 284

price discrimination, 366

profit maximization, 364

second-degree price discrimination, 373–6

third-degree price discrimination, 377–80

vertical integration, 82

vertical relationships, 414–17, 439–41

see also bilateral monopolies

monopolistic competition, 249, 251

advertising, 252, 443, 468, 470

Chamberlin's model, 9, 404–5, 404, 432, 444, 445, 448, 449, 472

defined, 534

price discrimination, 382

price quality, 408–9

monopoly profits, 349–50

monopsonists, 217–18, 219–20, *219*, 242–3, 414–17, 439–41

defined, 535

see also bilateral monopolies

Montgomery, C., 123

Monti, Mario, 253

moral hazard

defined, 535

employee motivation, 225, 237

incentive schemes, 195

influencing costs, 174

intermediate products, 71, 75

management, 191

principal-agent theory, 191, 195

product quality, 411, 412

reputational externalities, 420

transaction costs, 37, *38*, 87

vertical relationships, 413, 414, 415, 417

vertical restraints, 420

Moran, P., 146

Morgenstern, Oskar, 9, 13

Morrison, Sir Ken, 122

Morrison's, 122

motivations, 6

employees, 209–10, 222, 223, 224–32, *227*, *232*, 237–8

impact on efficiency, 172–6

management, 185–6

motor vehicle sector, 42–3, 199, 288, 428, 431–2

Motorola, 130

multi-divisional firms, 182, *182*

defined, 535

multi-plant economies, 109–12, *111*, 116, 130

multi-product firms, 112–16, 130–1

see also diversification; economies of scope; horizontal boundaries

multidimensional scaling, 262

defined, 535

multilateral trade agreements, 10

Multinational Enterprises (MNEs), 115

Murdoch, Rupert, 357

Murfin, A., 471

Murphy, K., 466

N

Nabisco, 262

NACE classification scheme, 255, *255*, 256, 262

Nalebuff, Barry, 21, 278, 517

Nash equilibrium, 22–3, 221, 298

advertising as a game, 466, 470

defined, 535

employee relations, 236

price-setting models, 294–5, 296

quantity setting models, 291

R&D as a game, 493, 494

trust normal form game, 91

vertical relationships, 416

see also Cournot-Nash equilibrium

Nash formulas, 245

Nash, John, 22, 291

National Coal Board, 220–1

National Health Service (NHS), 24

national minimum wage, 217–18, 220

National Union of Miners, 220–1

nationalization, 308

defined, 535

natural monopolies, 308

defined, 535

NatWest, 196

near neighbour products, 446, 447, 448–50, 453, 462, 473

defined, 535

Nelson, P., 406, 461, 464, 465, 466

Nelson, R.

cycles of innovation, 485

entrepreneurial bias, 152

evolutionary approach, 54, 146, 159, 274, 432, 483

innovation, 484

organizational architecture, 123

routines and processes, 53, 123, 504

steady-state models, 159

neo-classical economics, 6, 144, 249, 250, 482

defined, 535

neo-classical paradigm, 43–4, 59

advertising, 453, 458, 467

competition, 250–1

competitive advantage, 57, 60

consumer's preferences, 444

cost-minimization, 33–4, 60, 100, 172–3

defined, 535

demand for labour, 215–17, *216*, 237

economic rent, 251, 327

economies of scale, 100, 144

economies of scope, 144

employees, 211–17, 222, 233, 235, 237

entrepreneurship, 36, 60, 149–50, 170, 174–5

equilibrium, 144, 149

firm growth, 144

homogeneous products, 55, 251, 255

horizontal boundaries, 100

hyper-rationality, 33, 34, 36, 49, 57, 60, 172, 200, 398, 485

identical knowledge, 55

innovation, 483

inventions, 484

labour market, 211–17, 222, 233, 235, 237

Law of One Price, 400

management, 33, 35

market structures, 249, 250–1

monopolies, 144, 249, 251, 254, 284

multi-product firms, 100

new knowledge, 179

oligopolies, 251–2

perfect competition, 31, 34, 249, 251, 254, 284

perfect information, 33, 34, 36, 43, 49, 57, 60, 149, 172, 200, 398

profit-maximization, 32–5, 60, 170, 174–6, 200

specialization, 119

supply of labour, 211–14, *213*, 237

transaction costs, 114

utility-maximization, 32–5, 60

neo-liberal economics, 20

Nerlove, M., 456

Nestlé, 20, 264

Net Book Agreement, 424

net governance cost (NGC), 80, 81–2

net investment, 155, 164

defined, 535

net present value, 450, 465, 493

defined, 535

net production costs (NPC), 80–2, 87

net revenue, 370, 455, 469

defined, 535

Netherlands

agrifood sector, 263–4

car price differentials, 367, 368

clusters, 279

competition policies, 269

Netscape, 198

network externalities, 451

defined, 536

network organizations, 183–4

network strategy, 4

networked firms, 277, 278–9

defined, 536

new classical economics, 310

new ventures, 151–2, 179

Newberg, D., 497

News International, 357

newspaper industry, 357

nexus of contracts, 18, 36, 49, 177, 190, 200

defined, 536

NHS Trusts, 24

niche markets, 55, 265, 271

defined, 536

Nimrod project, 275

Nissan, 224

no-milking condition, 409

Nokia, 20, 126, 129

non-cooperative behaviour, 284–5, 302–4

advertising, 457

defined, 536

dominant firm markets, 325, 331, 333, 341, 343

duopolies, 288

innovation, 493, 494, 504, 505, 507

price-setting models, 294–7, *297*

quantity setting models, 288–93, 298, 301, 302–5

Stackelberg's model, 331, 343

see also backward induction; Cournot model; Cournot-Nash equilibrium; Nash equilibrium

non-cooperative equilibrium, 91, 292, 296, 457, 494

defined, 536

non-cooperative game theory, 13, 22–3

non-linear (second degree) pricing, 367, 373–6, *373*, *374*

defined, 536

non-pecuniary income *see* discretionary expenditure

non-profit maximization, 159, 172, 177, 185–9, 200

see also sales revenue maximization

non-renewable resources, defined, 536

non-strategic behaviour, defined, 536

non-uniform prices, 364, 366

Nooteboom, Bart, 88, 128

Nordhaus, W., 498

normal form game, 22–3, *22*, 293, 415–16, 493–4

defined, 536

trust, 90–1, *90*

normal goods, defined, 536

normal profits, 137, 140, 291, 294, 295, 340, 492

defined, 536

North American Industrial Classification System (NAICS), 255, 256

Northampton, 277, *277*
Northern Rock, 163
not-for-profit organizations, 3, 5
Novartis, 20

O

Oakland division, 42
OECD, 176, 256
Office of Fair Trading, 357
Oi, W., 373
Oldsmobile division, 42
oligopolies/oligopolists, 249, 326, 404
  advertising, 443, 468–9, 470
  airline market, 7
  analytics of, 320–1
  Baumol's model, 136–7
  bounded rationality, 304
  collusion, 13, 15, 284, 285, 288,
    292–3, 296–7, 298–300,
    301–6, 314, 427
  competition policies, 285, 308–13
  defined, 284, 536
  differentiated products, 252,
    295–6, 298–9
  dynamic models, 285, 298–302,
    305
  equilibrium, 288, 289–93, 294–7,
    296
  game theory, 285, 288, *288*,
    302–6, 314
  homogeneous products, 252,
    291, 294, 295
  imperfect information, 288, 300,
    301, 304, 305
  incentive to innovate, 489–91
  incomplete information, 304, 305
  industrial policies, 285, 308–13,
    314
  kinked demand curve, 273,
    298–300, *299*, *300*
  marginal costs, 289, 291–2,
    294–5, 300, 301, 305, 321
  marginal revenue, 289, 291,
    299–300, 320
  mutual independence, 285,
    286–8, *286*
  neo-classical paradigm, 251–2
  opportunistic behaviour, 13
  price discrimination, 382, 385
  price rigidities, 299–300
  price-setting models, 288,
    294–7, *297*, 298, 305
  profit maximization, 321, 364
  quantity setting models, 288–93,
    298, 301, 302–5
  rationality, 287–8, 289
  strategic behaviour, 284–314
  strategic conflict approach, 273
  strategic innovation behaviour,
    492–6
  uncertainty, 298–302
  vertical relationships, 417–18
  see also Bertrand model; cartels;
    conjectural variations;

Cournot model; duopolies;
    Nash equilibrium
oligopsonists, 417
  defined, 536
oligopsony, defined, 537
one-stop shopping, 260
open access resource, defined, 537
Open University, 462
opportunistic behaviour, 38, 399
  advertising, 465
  asset specificity, 78, 114
  collaborative ventures, 127, 128,
    131
  contractual relationships, 49, 77,
    222
  customers, 78
  defined, 537
  employee motivation, 225, 229,
    237
  employment contracts, 222
  extensive form game, 76–7
  governance approach, 60, 189,
    235
  incomplete contracts, 77
  internal labour markets, 235
  monopolists, 251
  oligopolies, 13
  partnership alliances, 90
  repeated games, 302–4
  senior management, 192, 229
  and transaction costs, *38*, 74,
    75–7, 78
  trust normal form game, 90–1,
    90
  unitary (U) form of organization,
    182
  vertical integration, 74, 75–7, 78
  vertical relationships, 414, 423,
    425
  see also moral hazard
opportunity costs, 17, 18, 454
  competency approach, 53
  consumer choices, 454
  decentralization, 179
  defined, 537
  dominant firm markets, 328,
    341, 350, 358
  incentive to innovate, 488
  labour market, 211, 213, 227
  neo-classical paradigm, 34
  price discrimination, 366
  trust normal form game, 91
  vertical restraints, 425
optician services, 472
Oracle, 198
Ordover, J., 354, 356
organic growth, 65, 99, 162
organizational architecture, 4,
    18–19, *19*, 21, 28, 35, 134
  aligning of goals, 40, 177–84, 200
  change over time, 178
  co-ordination of effort, 177–84,
    200
  competency approach, 57–8, 146

creative destruction, 481
decision rights, 178–81, *180*
decision-making process, 40–2,
    171
  defined, 537
  diseconomies of scale, 103
  distinct human elements of, 177,
    185, 200
  efficiency of mergers, 82
  employee motivation, 225
  and employees, 209
  essence of, 178
  evolution of, 41
  flexibility, 7
  governance approach, 32, 47–50,
    52, 57–8, 145
  growth of firms, 144–8, 265
  heterogeneity, 19, 39, 40, 47, 49,
    52–3, 503
  hierarchical control, 32, 39–42
  historical perspective, 43–6
  horizontal boundaries, 103
  incentive schemes, 18, 41, 42
  incomplete contracts, 179
  influence on technical progress,
    501–6
  information as key element of,
    40–1, 47
  integrated approach, 57–8
  key elements of, 40–1, 123
  knowledge as key element of,
    40–1, 123
  learning, 123
  performance, 42, 185
  as potential core competence, 146
  productive and allocative
    efficiencies, 60
  routines, 40, 41, 123
  sub-groups, 41
  uniqueness of, 41, 178
  vertical integration, 82
  Virgin, 7
organizational change, 43–6, 148, 482
organizational coherence
  decision-making, 179, 180, 200
  defined, 537
  growth of firms, 144, 145, 146,
    147, *147*, 156, 164
  horizontal boundaries, 122–4,
    124, 125, 127
  managerial discretion, 190
  managerial resources, 134
  mergers, 162
organizational costs *see* agency costs
organizational culture, 18
  based on organizational
    architecture, 210
  defined, 537
  and growth of firms, 265
  mergers, 162, 163
  roles of, 223–4
  uniqueness of, 41
organizational form, 181–4, 185,
    200, 265

defined, 537
evolutionary approach, 273–4
  and innovation, 503, 505, *505*
  legal status, 40
  as part of creative process, 484
  vertical integration, 93
organizational goals
  behavioural theories, 188–9, 200,
    502
  employee motivation, 225
  organizational architecture, 40,
    177–84, 200
organizational hierarchies *see*
    authority control hierarchy
organizational integration, 128
organizational routines *see* routines
organizational slack, 174, 185, 189,
    200, 268, 345
  defined, 537
organizational strategy, 17
  defined, 537
  organizational architecture, 4, 7,
    18–19, *19*, 21
organizations, 3
  see also firms; not-for-profit
    organizations
Ortiz Rocasolano, Letizia, 73
outputs, 31
  defined, 537
  neo-classical firm, 34, 36
  possible range of, 16–17
  specialization in, 119
outsource, 46, 65, 86–8, *87*, 94
  defined, 537
ownership
  objectives, 185
  principal-agent theory, 190–5,
    201
  as residual claimant, 190
  residual decision rights, 190
  right of possession, 190
  separation from management
    control, 170–1, 190–1, 201
Oxfam, 31

P

Palepu, K., 118
Paludrine, 160
Pan Am, 7
Panzar, J., 112
parallel imports, 367–9
parallel pricing, 338
Paraquat, 160
Pareto-efficiency, defined, 537
partnership alliances, 66, 88, 89–92,
    481
  defined, 537
  see also alliances
patent licences, 489, 499, 500, 507
  defined, 538
patents, 481, 484, 489, 496,
    497–500, 506–7
  costs of, 20
  defined, 537

dominant firms, 327
  and Penrose, 53
path dependencies, 58, 494, 503
  competitive advantage, 482
  growth of firms, 146, 148
  horizontal boundaries, 123–4, 127
  organizational architecture, 40
  and Schumpeter, 482, 483
payback period, 494
  defined, 538
PC software sector, 149, 330, 390–1, 492
Penrose, Edith
  characteristics of firms, 53
  competency approach, 53, 119–20, 484
  definition of firm, 53
  growth of firms, 53, 134, 135, 144, 145, 483, 504
  resource-based theory, 53, 84, 119–20, 143, 145, 156
People Express, 7
Pepall, L., 383, 466
perfect competition, 6, 21, 405
  defined, 538
  demand for labour, 215, 216
  intensity of rivalry, 252–3
  neo-classical paradigm, 31, 34, 249, 251, 254, 284
  profit-maximization, 355
  supply of labour, 214–15
  vertical relationships, 420
  see also efficient capital market
perfect information, 197
  buyers lack of, 398
  consumers' preferences, 444
  defined, 538
  demand for labour, 211, 216, 217, 237
  inventions, 484
  neo-classical paradigm, 33, 34, 36, 43, 49, 57, 60, 149, 172, 200, 398
  supply of labour, 211, 214–15, 237
  X-inefficiency, 174
perfect price discrimination (first-degree), 367, 369–72, 369
  defined, 524
performance evaluation, 18, 19
  employees, 209–10, 227–31, 228, 232, 237–8
  organizational architecture, 42, 185
  teams, 174, 225, 229
performance monitoring, 42, 58, 103, 109, 179, 180, 182, 200
Perloff, J., 445
personalized services, 370
Perspex, 160
persuasive advertising, 142, 462–7, 463, 471–2, 473
Peters, T., 123
Pfizer, 57
pharmaceutical companies, 153, 306, 367, 427, 496

Philips, 487
Philips, L., 365, 383, 384, 386, 387
Phoenix Venture Holdings Group, 199, 224
physical asset specificity, 78
Pickering, F., 162
piece-work schemes, 227, 238
Pigou, A., 7, 367
Pigovian tax, defined, 538
Pilkington, 196
Pischetsrieder, Bernd, 139
pollution, 197
Porter, Michael
  clusters, 276
  competitive advantage, 480, 483
  Five Forces Model, 9, 269–74, 270, 275, 280
  technical progress, 483
Portugal, car price differentials, 367, 368
positive externalities, 111, 112, 451
post-entry costs, 266, 443
post-Fordism, 46
post-sale services, 424, 442, 452
Prahalad, C., 54, 85
pre-emption, 6
  defined, 538
pre-emptive effect, 497–8
pre-sale services, 423, 424, 430, 433
predation strategies, 325, 354
  defined, 538
predatory pricing, 347–54, 349, 357–8
  competition law, 355–6, 391, 392
  defined, 538
preference map, 212, 448, 463
  defined, 538
present value, 204, 489
  defined, 538
  diversification, 125–6
  dominant firm markets, 337–8, 339, 341, 342, 343, 344, 345, 350, 352, 358
  dynamic behaviour, 303, 304
  firm's rate of growth, 159
  innovation, 493, 498
  pricing quality, 409
  see also net present value
price controls, defined, 538
price differentiation, 365, 391, 392
price discrimination, 363–87
  competition policies, 391–3
  consumers' surplus, 369, 371, 374, 375, 390, 393
  defined, 365, 538
  demand curve, 365, 366, 370, 371, 374, 375, 379, 380, 393
  differentiated products, 381–7, 393
  first-degree, 367, 369–72, 369
  freight absorption, 385, 386
  homogeneous products, 364, 365, 384, 385, 398, 446
  information perspective, 382
  marginal costs, 365, 370, 371, 372, 374, 376, 378, 379, 383–4, 385, 386, 387, 393

marginal revenue, 377–8, 384, 385
  market segments, 377–9, 382, 383, 384
  marketing mix, 452
  profit-maximization, 363–4, 370, 374, 377–9, 384
  reservation prices, 366, 367, 369, 370–1, 374, 382, 393
  search costs, 366, 384, 393
  second-degree, 367, 373–6, 373, 374
  spatially differentiated products, 365, 384–7, 446–7
  third-degree, 367, 377–80, 379
  transaction costs, 366, 371, 376
  two-part tariffs, 371–2, 375–6, 375, 393
  vertical integration, 354
  vertical restraints, 422, 430
  see also bundling
price distribution, imperfect information, 398–9, 400–5, 432
price elasticity of demand, 169, 287
  advertising, 455, 456, 461, 462, 468
  analytics of monopoly, 319
  analytics of oligopoly, 321
  consumer preferences, 460
  defined, 538
  dominant firm markets, 340
  imperfect information, 400, 401, 401, 403, 404, 405
  incentive to innovate, 491
  price discrimination, 378–80
  price-setting models, 296
  quantity setting models, 291
  R&D expenditure, 490, 491
  Sweezy's model, 300
  Veblen goods, 451
  vertical integration, 71
  vertical restraints, 430
  see also cross-price elasticity of demand
price elasticity of supply, defined, 538
price fixing, 269, 284, 285, 297, 312
price index, 368
  defined, 538
price leadership, 325, 335–8, 335, 336, 339, 342–3, 358
  defined, 539
  see also barometric price leadership
price rigidities, 298, 299–300
price system, 430
  defined, 539
price takers, 21, 69, 218, 251, 335
  defined, 539
price wars, 22, 23, 328, 345, 350–1, 356, 427
  see also predatory pricing
price-setting models
  oligopolies, 288, 294–7, 297, 298, 305

  see also Bertrand model
prices
  and advertising expenditure, 472
  informational advertising, 458–62
pricing quality, 365, 383–4, 406–12, 409, 432–3, 461
pricing strategies, 4
  capturing value, 21–3
  imperfect information, 398–9, 400–5, 432
  mature markets, 140–1
  vertical relationships, 413–18, 439–41
  see also basing point pricing; bundling; predatory pricing; price discrimination; price leadership; price-setting models; resale price maintenance
primary line injury, 392–3
  defined, 539
primary products, 66, 70
  defined, 539
principal-agent game, 192, 193
principal-agent theory, 190–5, 201, 209–10, 484
  defined, 539
  motivation, 209–10, 222, 223, 224–32, 227, 232, 237–8
  vertical relationships, 413–14
  vertical restraints, 399, 420–6
  see also agency costs; employment contracts
principals see ownership; shareholders
principle component analysis, 262
  defined, 539
principle of substitution, defined, 539
Prisoners' Dilemma, 14–15, 14, 293, 293, 296–7, 304, 427
  defined, 539
private information
  dominant firms, 328, 345
  employee appointments, 232, 233
  employment contracts, 222
  high-cost rivals, 305
  joint ventures, 89
  rational raiders, 191
  vertical integration, 70–4, 89
  vertical relationships, 417
private sector, 309, 310, 485
  defined, 539
privatization, 88, 220, 310
problem child products, 106
process innovation, 265, 488–9, 500
  distinction from product innovation, 495
  effects of transaction costs, 503
  licensing, 499
  patents, 497
  and Schumpeter, 272
  secrecy of, 491–2, 497
Procion, 160

Proctor and Gamble, 252
producer-processors, 88
producers
  defined, 539
  limited influence on price, 21
  specialist, 66
producers' surplus, 393
  defined, 539
product development, 21, 138, 449, 452, 454
product differentiation *see* differentiated products
product homogeneity *see* homogeneous products
product innovation, 265, 484, 491, 501
  coherence and complementarity, 179
  distinction from process innovation, 495–6
  as non-price predation, 354
  as part of marketing, 452
  and Schumpeter, 272
product life cycle, 106, 140, 154, 272, *272*, 465
  defined, 539
product line diversification, 116
product space, 142, 261, 495
  advertising, 452, 458–9, 460, 461–2
  defined, 540
  differentiated products, 445–7, *445*, 449–51, 472–3
product varieties, 346, 403–4, 443, 444, 445
production, 31
  defined, 540
  Fordist versus post-Fordist, *46*
production cost curve, 140
production costs *see* unit production costs
production function, 32–5, 36, 52, 55, 134
  defined, 540
production routines *see* routines
production stages *see* vertical integration
production systems, historical perspective, 43–6
production-possibility curve, 150
production-possibility frontier (PPF), 17–18, *17*, 22
  defined, 540
productive efficiency, 3–5, 26
  defined, 540
  game theory, 14, 22, 23
  organizational architecture, 60
  perfect competition, 249
  pricing strategies, 22, 23
  profits, 5, 6
  society's demand for, 28
  specialization, 119
  and total costs, 16–19
  total revenue, 21–3
  transaction costs, 49
  vertical integration, 64, 78, 80

productive inefficiency, 497
productive opportunities
  competency approach, 145, 164
  entrepreneurial skill, 59, 147–8, 149, 152, 164, 265
  growth of firms, 144, 145, 147–8, 152, 265
  mergers, 163
  Penrose on, 144
  shareholder information, 192
productive resources, 16, 17
  allocation of, 32, 36, 49, 171
  alternative uses, 145
  co-ordination and motivation, 151, 174
  competency approach, 32
  defined, 540
  economies of scale, 101
  rate of growth, 155
  transaction cost theory, 49
  see also factors of production; property rights
productivity
  boost from specialization, 43
  defined, 540
  as efficiency measure, 173
  factories of industrial revolution, 43
  gains from division of labour, 34, 36, 43
  human capital, 233
  manufacturing sector, 35
  motivation, 18
  neo-classical paradigm, 233
products
  defined, 3, 540
  see also complementary goods; consumer goods; credence goods; differentiated products; experience goods; homogeneous products; intermediate products; search goods
professional services, 370
profit
  allocative/productive efficiency, 5, 6
  defined, 540
  differences between firms, 6
  as firm's collective goal, 3, 4, 5–7
  from innovation, 485, 502
  as means of financing growth, 134, 138, 153, 155–9
  related to incentive schemes, 192–5, 201
  see also monopoly profits; normal profits
profit constraints, 138, 155, 186
profit margin, 157, 460, 461, 471, 490
  defined, 540
profit rate, 6, 141, 156–7, 158, 161, 162
  defined, 540
profit-maximization
  advertising, 455–6
  analytics of monopoly, 319

demand for labour, 216, 237
dominant firm markets, 325, 330, 331–2, 335, 336, 339, 341, 343
imperfect competition, 355
imperfect labour markets, 219–21
implications of, 174–6
monopolists, 364
neo-classical paradigm, 32–5, 60, 170, 174–6, 200
oligopolists, 321, 364
owner-managed factories, 44, 170, 174–5
perfect competition, 355
price discrimination, 363–4, 370, 374, 377–9, 384
versus growth-maximization, 141, 159
versus sales maximization, 136–8
vertical relationships, 414, 415
vertical restraints, 422
and X-inefficiencies, 174
see also non-profit maximization
profit-maximizing output, 307, 491
  defined, 540
  dominant firm markets, 331, 336, 340
  monopolists, 379
  monopsonists, 414
  neo-classical paradigm, 34
  quantity setting models, 289, 290, 292, 301
  vertical relationships, 414, 417
progressive tax, defined, 540
promotion, 141, 424
property rights, 16, 17, 31, 171, 197 209
  defined, 540
  and entrepreneurs, 149
  organizational architecture, 18
  patents, 497, 498
  quality of products, 408
  relational contracts, 49–50
  vertical integration, 65, 66, 72, 82
  see also patents
proportionality postulate, 101
  defined, 541
proprietary knowledge, 114, 121
Psion, 129
public companies, 185, 198
  overriding goal, 196
  principal-agent theory, 190, 191, 192
  residual risk, 190, 191
  rise of, 44
  shareholder value, 21
public good, 113, 120–1, 130, 146, 424, 425, 497
  defined, 541
Public Power Corporation (PPC), 83
public sector, 222, 485
  defined, 541
publicly owned firms, 170, 171, 308
purchased input-gross margin ratio, 69–70

purchasing power, 212
  defined, 541
pure bundling, 388, 389
  defined, 541

Q
quality
  advertising, 461, 464–6, 473
  importance of, 47
  pricing, 365, 383–4, 406–12, *409*, 432–3, 461
  and reputation, 408–11, *411*, 416, 422–3, 432–3
  resale price maintenance, 422–3
  unit costs, 422, 432, 464, 466
  see also vertical differentiation
quantity discounts, 364, 393
quantity fixing, 289, 325, 330–4
  defined, 541
quantity forcing, 421, 426, 429–30
  defined, 541
quantity setting models, oligopolies, 288–93, 298, 301, 302–5
quasi-monopolies, 70, 483
quasi-public resources, 113–14
quasi-rents, 78, 79, 114, 214, 229–30, 350, 450
  defined, 541

R
Radner, R., 231
random events, 7, 226, 230
random shocks, 142, 154, 173
  see also shocks
random walk, 142, 154, 164, 265, 484
  defined, 541
rate of time preference, 341
  defined, 541
rational behaviour
  decision-makers, 13
  defined, 541
  game theory, 285
  oligopolists, 287–8, 289
  predatory pricing, 352
  see also bounded rationality; hyper-rationality
reaction function
  advertising, 457
  defined, 541
  dominant firm markets, 332
  innovation, 494, 495, *495*
  price-setting models, 295–6, 298, 323
  product differentiation, 449
  quantity setting models, 289–90, 292, 293, 298
real incomes, 139, 157, 212
  defined, 541
real prices, 485
  defined, 541
real wage, 211–13
  defined, 541
record retailing industry, 8
recoupment fallacy, 348

defined, 542
recruitment policies, 232–6
Reed, Mr., 467
regression analysis, 262
  defined, 542
regulation, 308
  defined, 542
regulatory capture, defined, 542
regulatory commitments, as exit
  barrier, 328
regulatory environment, 20
regulatory uncertainty, 313
Reinganum, J., 499, 500
related diversification, 116
  defined, 542
relational contracts, 48–50, 177–8,
  200, 210, 222–3, 237
  defined, 542
relative price
  advertising, 455, 461, 463
  defined, 542
  neo-classical paradigm, 32–3, 34
  oligopolists, 295
  price discrimination, 382
  price-setting models, 295
  pricing with imperfect
    information, 403
  substitute products, 262
  technical progress, 487
religious considerations, 17
renewable resources, 92
  defined, 542
rent seeking, 61, 506
  employees, 234
  horizontal boundaries, 100
  innovation, 485
rent-earning capacity, 93, 124–5,
  127, 484
repeat purchases, 410, 420, 461,
  465, 466
repeated games, 76, 89, 178, 236,
  302–5, 337–8, 410–11, 416
  defined, 542
replacement effect, 489
  defined, 542
representative firm concept, 57
reputation
  competency approach, 235
  defined, 542
  dominant firms, 337
  for fairness, 178, 223–4, 237
  fear of loss of, 191
  game theory, 6, 15, 410–11, *411*
  importance of, 236
  as indicator of quality, 408–11,
    416, 422–3, 432–3
  as strategic behaviour, 273
  see also brand reputation
reputation signalling model, 348,
  351–4, 355
reputational externalities, 420, 424
  defined, 542
resale price maintenance, 421–4, *422*,
  426–7, 429, 430, 431, 433
  defined, 542

research clubs, 506
research and development, 256
  competitive advantage, 482, 484,
    485, 486
  defined, 542
  firm size, 501–2, 507
  game theory, 493–4, *494*
  incentive to invest in, 488–94
  influence of market structures,
    488–92, *488*, 495
  inter-firm co-operation, 504–6
  living standards, 480, 485, *485*,
    506
  organizing for, 501–6
  strategic expenditure, 492–6
  substitute product risks, 271
reservation outlay, 374
reservation prices
  bundling, 388–90
  defined, 542
  price discrimination, 366, 367,
    369, 370–1, 374, 382, 393
  pricing with imperfect
    information, 402, 404
reservation wage, 213–14
  defined, 543
residual claimants, 190, 204
residual demand curve, 307, 331,
  331, 336, 340
  defined, 543
residual rights of control, defined, 543
residual risk, 190, 191
resource allocation, 190, 430
  defined, 543
resource-based approach, 6,
  119–20, 145, 164
  defined, 543
  see also competency approach;
    Penrose, Edith
resources
  competency approach, 32, 52–6,
    57, 60, 61, 273
  defined, 543
  efficient utilization of, 16–19,
    32–4
  as finite, 16–17
  and integrated approach, 58
  quality of, 3
  scarcity of, 16, 17, 28
  see also allocative efficiency;
    factors of production;
    heterogeneous resources;
    knowledge-based resources;
    productive efficiency;
    productive resources;
    property rights
restrictive agreements, 26, 430–1
  defined, 543
retention ratio, 155–6, 158, 159
  defined, 543
revenue, 5–7
  defined, 543
  see also gross revenue; marginal
    revenue; net revenue; sales
    revenue maximization; total
    revenue

revenue flow, 16, 389
reward systems
  creation of, 178
  demands on management time,
    120
  employee motivation, 6, 209–10,
    225–6, 233
  as key element of organizational
    architecture, 19, 41, 42
  and relational employment
    contracts, 49–50
  see also incentive schemes
Rewe AG, 405
Rey, P., 427
Richardson, George, 52
Riordan, M., 465, 466
rising star products, 106
risk
  adverse selection, 75, 231
  dominant firm markets, 327–8
  and incentive schemes, 192–5,
    201, 227, 229, 230–1, 238
  and innovation, 265
  managerial attitudes, 158
  of market entry, 266, 429
  and multi-plant economies, 109
  pricing strategies, 22
  principal-agent theory, 192, *194*
  unrelated diversification, 117–18
  and vertical integration, 75–6
  see also residual risk
risk aversion, 207–8
  defined, 543
  employees, 214, 226, 229, 237,
    238
  management, 138, 158, 192–3,
    195
risk neutrality, 193, 195, 208
  defined, 543
risk premium, 265, 328, 351
  defined, 543
risk taking, 40, 502
rivalry, 250–3
  advertising, 21, 256
  clusters, 111, 275–9, 280
  contestability, 266–8, *267*, 270,
    327, 350, 403
  defined, 325, 543
  deterrence strategies, 325,
    339–47, 357
  Five Forces Model, 269–72, 275
  incentive to innovate, 483
  interaction with rivals, 7
  knowledge of rivals, 4
  perfect competition, 252–3
  predation strategies, 325
  private information, 305
  seller concentration, 256, 257–8
  strategic behaviour, 10–11
  strategic conflict approach, 273
  strategic versus industry groups,
    260–1
  structure-conduct-performance
    (SCP) paradigm, 254, 269–70

  see also collusion; competitive
    advantage; conjectural
    variations; dominant firms;
    game theory; oligopolies;
    opportunistic behaviour;
    predatory pricing
Rizzo, J., 471, 472
road pricing, 372–3
Roberts, J., 48, 197, 233, 461
Robertson, Dennis, 28
Robertson, P., 120
Robinson-Pateman Act, 392
Rockefeller, John D., 348
rollback *see* backward induction
Rolls-Royce, 313
Rose, Stuart, 236–7
Ross, D., 102, 109, 251, 269, 348,
  352, 495
routines, 6
  competency approach, 52, 53,
    54, 61
  demands on management time,
    120
  development of, 236
  dynamic capability model, 54
  evolutionary firm, 54
  heterogeneity of, 236
  integrated approach, 58
  as key element of organizational
    architecture, 40, *41*, 123
  as knowledge-based resource, 52
  learning by doing, 104, 105
  Nelson and Winter on, 53, 123,
    504
  as productive resource, 34, 524
  as quasi-public resource, 114
Rover Car Company, 88, 199, 224
Royal Society for the Arts, 196
RTVE, 143
rule of reason, 26–7, 128, 312, 314,
  400, 431, 433
  defined, 543
Rumelt, R., 123, 146, 273
Ryanair, 380

S

saddle point, defined, 543
Safeway supermarket, 122, 260
Saffil, 160
Sainsbury, 260
Sako, M., 90
sales revenue maximization, 136–8,
  137, 139, 140, 153, 185
  defined, 544
Salop, J., 234
Salop, S., 345, 356, 445, 446
SAP, 20
satisficing behaviour, 188–9, 200, 201
  defined, 544
scale monopolies, 259–60, 326
scarcity, 16, 17, 28
  defined, 544
Scheffman, D., 345

Scherer, F.
  innovation, 491–2, 495, 498
  market structures, 251
  multi-plant economies, 109
  patents, 499
  predatory pricing, 348
  rivalry, 352
  scale effects, 102
  SCP paradigm, 269
Schmalensee, R., 11, 372, 453, 455, 461, 465
Schöller, 429
Schumpeter, Joseph
  competency approach, 53
  competitive advantage, 482–3, 486, 487
  creative destruction, 144, 146, 481, 483, 488, 506
  dynamic efficiency, 487, 506
  entrepreneurs, 146–7, 148, 150
  firm size and R&D activity, 502
  growth of firms, 144, 146–7
  innovation, 148, 150, 272, 432, 482–3, 488
  investment in R&D, 488
  period of calm, 486
  technical progress, 480–1, 482–3, 486, 487, 503, 506–7
Scottish Widows Life Assurance, 163
Seagram's Universal, 85, 86
search goods, 406–7, 461, 464, 466, 473
  defined, 544
second-degree price discrimination, 367, 373–6, 373, 374
  defined, 544
secret agreements, 26
seller concentration, 250, 256–9, 268, 271
  defined, 544
sellers
  market structures, 251
  moral hazard, 37, 38
  SCP paradigm, 254
  see also adverse selection; asymmetric information; Five Forces Model; incomplete contracts; intermediate products; partnership alliances; vertical relationships; vertical restraints
Selten, Reinhard, 352
service provision, 421, 423–4
  defined, 544
set-up costs, 116, 127, 444
  defined, 544
The Sex Pistols, 8
Shaffer, G., 426
Shapiro, C.
  advertising, 460
  dynamic models of strategic interaction, 305
  employees, 230
  game theory, 13

incentive for innovation, 489
mergers, 161
no-milking condition, 409
patent breadth, 499
profit incentive, 486
quality rent dynamic model, 408, 409
strategic conflict approach, 273
versioning, 384
share prices, 151, 159, 196, 198
shareholder value, 3, 21, 162, 198
shareholders
  defined, 544
  dividend payments, 16, 155, 158, 159, 198
  expectations and objectives, 158, 185
  financial institutions, 171
  incentive schemes, 195
  investments, 16
  as key to better firm performance, 196
  mergers, 160, 162
  non-profit maximization, 186
  as *primus inter pares*, 199, 201
  principal-agent theory, 190, 191, 192, 204
  sales maximization model, 136, 137, 138
  and senior managers, 35, 156, 185, 190, 191, 192, 201, 204
  and stakeholders, 196–7
  see also ownership
Sharp, B., 426
Shelanski, H., 78
Shell, 224, 286
Shepard, A., 415
Sherman Act, 26
shirking, 225, 227–30, 231
  defined, 544
shocks, 7, 119, 128
  collapse of Soviet Union, 10
  innovation success, 265
  learning by doing, 107
  merger booms, 161
  multi-plant economies, 109
  random, 142, 154, 173
  Schumpeter on, 481
short-run, 36
  defined, 544
short-run average cost curve, 144, 173, 348, 374–5, 402, 402, 404, 471
short-run average costs, 346, 402
  defined, 544
short-run average total cost curve, 173, 348
short-run average variable cost, 356
short-run disruption costs, 110
short-run equilibrium, 336, 403, 487
  defined, 544
short-run profits, 137, 138, 325, 358
short-run supply curve, 335
  defined, 544
shut-down price, defined, 545

side payments, 188, 307, 314
  defined, 545
Siemens, 20
signalling
  defined, 545
  dominant firm markets, 328, 333, 343, 345, 346
  game theory, 280
  imperfect competition, 293, 297, 303, 305, 314
  of quality, 410, 433, 464, 465, 466, 473
  see also reputation signalling model
Silicon Valley, 276
Simon, Herbert, 6, 37, 55, 187–8
Simpson, Lord, 126
Single European Act (1987), 161, 309–10
  defined, 545
single market, 26, 104, 115, 312
  defined, 545
Slade, M., 415
sleeping patents, 498
  defined, 545
Sloan, Alfred, 42, 43, 180
small and medium-sized enterprises (SMEs)
  cash flow crisis, 152
  entrepreneurial flair, 150–1
  European Union, 20, 150–1, 431, 502
  Five Forces Model, 271
  industry groups, 257
Smith, Adam, 43, 66, 143–4, 149, 482
snob goods, 451, 452
social costs, 308, 498
  defined, 545
social efficiency, 197, 499
  defined, 545
Social Market Foundation, 372
social responsibility, 197, 201
soda ash market, 334
software sector, 149, 330, 390–1, 492
sole trader, 35
  defined, 545
Solvay, Ernest, 334
Solvay Group, 334
Somerfield, 260
Sony, 31, 46, 487
Sotheby's auction house, 418–19
Southwest Airlines, 380
Soviet Union, collapse of, 10, 12
Spain
  car price differentials, 367, 368
  digital technology, 143
spare capacity, 113–14, 127, 154, 346
spatial organizational form, 277–8
spatially differentiated products, 365, 384–7, 446–7, 446
  defined, 545
specialization
  abilities of a specialized resource, 119

boost to productivity, 43
clusters, 278
defined, 545
heterogeneous nature of, 120
learning by doing, 105, 107
multi-plant economies, 116
neo-classical paradigm, 43, 60
organizational architecture, 42
unitary (U) form of organization, 181
unrelated diversification, 119–20
see also asset specialization; division of labour
specialization of labour, defined, 545
specific human capital, 211, 233–4, 233, 235, 238
  defined, 545
specific tax, defined, 545
Spengler, J., 415
spontaneous invention, 484
sport merchandising, 467
spot market transactions, 65, 74, 86, 88, 89, 399, 414, 419
  defined, 545
SSNIP (Small but Significant Non-Transitory Increase in Prices), 262–3
  defined, 546
Stackelberg-Nash equilibrium, 332, 332, 457
Stackelberg's model, 331–4, 333, 335, 343
  defined, 546
stakeholder pensions, 163–4
stakeholders, 196–9, 201
  defined, 546
standard deviation, 117–18, 390
  defined, 546
Standard Oil Company, 348
start-up period, 105, 151, 152, 181
state aids, 25, 310–11, 312
  defined, 546
state-owned enterprises, 310
states of nature, 329, 345
statistical techniques, 262, 269
steady-state growth, 139, 140, 154, 156
steady-state methodology, 159
Steiner, P., 455, 491
Stevenson, L., 151
Stewart, M., 220
Stigler, G., 149–50, 365, 383, 459, 460
Stiglitz, J., 230, 400, 427, 444, 489–90, 491, 492, 494, 495
stock market valuation theory, 159
stock markets, 119, 151, 161, 165
stocks, 102, 154, 188
  defined, 546
Storey, D., 152
Stowe School, 8
strategic alliances, 88, 89, 127, 506
  defined, 546
  see also alliances
strategic barriers, 265, 266–8, 328, 444, 471, 473

defined, 546
strategic behaviour, 249–50
    defined, 546
    dominant firms, 324–58
    Five Forces Model, 9, 269–74, *270*, 275, 280
    game theory, 5, 249, 273, 274, 280, 302–6
    influence on market structure, 264–8
    oligopolies, 284–314
strategic conflict, 65, 273
    defined, 546
strategic environment *see* business environment
strategic groups, 260–3, *261*, 445, 446
    defined, 546
    Five Forces Model, 270–1
strategic innovation behaviour, 492–6
strategic interaction, 23, 250, 273
    advertising, 443, 456
    capturing of value, 274
    co-operative behaviour, 21
    influences on, 9
    kinked demand curve, 300
    Porter's framework, 280
    predatory pricing, 355
    R&D activity, 489, 497
    SCP paradigm, 280
strategic management, 251
    defined, 547
strategy
    defined, 547
    see also business strategy; corporate strategy; network strategy
strategy formulation, 17, 32, 84, 93, 269
    defined, 547
strikes, 221–2
structural barriers, 265, 266
    defined, 547
structure-conduct-performance (SCP) paradigm, 254–5, *254*, 256, 268, *268*, 280
    advertising, 463
    barriers to entry, 265, 270
    defined, 547
    Five Forces Model, 269–70, 271, 272
    industrial economics school, 269
    neo-classical paradigm, 265
Student magazine, 7, 8
sub-contractors, 43, 65, 90
sub-game perfect Nash equilibrium, 304, 333–4
    defined, 547
subadditive, 113
    defined, 547
subsidiaries, 45, 65, 86, 115, 499
substitute products, 262–3, 270–1, 280, 326
    defined, 547
    see also near neighbour products

succession planning, 236–7
Sud-Aviation, 313
Sudarsanam, S., 162
Sun Microsystems, 130
sunk costs
    advertising, 266, 328, 424–5, 443, 465, 470
    asset specificity, 78
    concentration ratio, 470
    defined, 547
    deterrence strategies, 343
    dominant firm markets, 327–8, 343, 350, 351
    as endogenous, 266
    as entry barrier, 266, 267
    investment as, 55
    predatory pricing, 350
    product differentiation, 266, 449, 450
    quantity setting models, 288, 298
    R&D expenditure, 497
    relative costs, 267
    risks of entry, 266
    vertical restraints, 420, 427
    see also contestability
super-normal profit *see* economic rent
super-rationality *see* hyper-rationality
supergames, 304–5, 306
supermarket sector, 259–60, 271, 338, 376, 405–6
suppliers
    asymmetric information, 36–7
    clusters, 277
    Five Forces Model, 271, 280
    Fordist versus post-Fordist, 46
    hidden action, 37
    incomplete information, 36–7
    interaction with, 7
    lean production model, 45
    market contracts, 48
    stakeholder capitalism, 197, 201
    vertical integration, 86
    see also upstream
supply
    defined, 547
    and growth, 143–8, 155, 157–8
    of labour, 211–14, *213*, *214*, 237
    quantity setting models, 288–93
    unrelated diversification, 119
supply chains *see* value (supply) chains
supply curve, 307, 335, 336
    defined, 547
    for labour, 212, 213, 215, 219, 234, 242, 243
supply function, defined, 547
supply side, 5
    defined, 547
    growth of firms, 143, 155, 157
    industry classification schemes, 256
    policy focus, 309

product differentiation, 444
    R&D motivation, 486
    unrelated diversification, 119
sustained competitive advantage, 4, 52, 54, 60
    defined, 547
Sutherland, Peter, 312
Sutton, J., 266, 450, 468, 470
Swanson, Robert, 153
Sweden, car price differentials, 367, 368
Sweezy, P., 273, 298, 299, 300
Sylos postulate, 340, 343, 344
    defined, 548
Sylos-Labini, P., 339
Symbian, 129–30

T
tacit collusion, 256, 308
    advertising, 457
    Article 81, 284, 307, 311
    defined, 548
    dominant firm markets, 337, 341, 343
    dynamic models, 301
    game theory, 266, 273, 280, 302, 304–5, 306
    oligopolies, 284, 293, 296–7, 298–300, 302, 304–5, 306, 314, 427
    price leadership, 337
    Sweezy's model, 298–300
    vertical restraints, 431
tacit information, 41
tacit knowledge
    clusters, 278
    competency approach, 32, 53, 55
    core capabilities embedded in, 162
    defined, 548
    difficulty of replicating, 41
    difficulty of sharing, 114, 162
    diversification, 119, 120, 121
    firm-specific human capital, 233
    human asset specificity, 78
    in invention and innovation, 506
    mergers, 162, 506
    teams, 114, 162
    and vertical integration, 82, 84–5
takeovers, 174
    defined, 548
    hostile, 160, 198
    threat of, 158, 191, 196, 198
Tallman, S., 125
Tampa Bay Buccaneers, 189, 190
tapered integration, 86
    defined, 548
tax wedge, defined, 548
taxation rates, 10
team production, 33, 36, 105, 210, 224, 231
    defined, 548
teams, 49, 238
    BMW, 224
    free-rider problem, 231, 340

information on performance of, 174, 225, 229
    learning process, 105, 123
    matrix organizations, 183
    specialization, 231
    stakeholder capitalism, 197
    tacit knowledge, 114, 162
    valuation of, 231
technical progress, 480
    competition policies, 26
    competitive advantage, 482–7, *486*, 506–7
    defined, 548
    dominant firm markets, 327, 343–4
    as exogenous change, 306
    Five Forces Model, 271, 280
    historical perspective, 44
    market characteristic, 9
    organizational architecture, 501–6
technological diversity, 504
technological economies, 70, 76
technology
    as barrier to entry, 265–6
    defined, 548
Teece, D., 54, 120, 146, 265, 274, 484
Tele 5, 143
telecommunications sector, 126, 270–1, 347, 376
Telser, L., 424, 453
territorial restrictions, 421, 425–6, 427, 429
    defined, 548
Tesco, 260, 405
Tetra Pack II, 392
Thatcherism, 184
Theory of Games and Economic Behaviour, 13
The Theory of the Growth of the Firm (Penrose), 134
third-degree price discrimination, 367, 377–80, *379*
    defined, 548
third-party endorsements, 412
Thorn EMI, 9
time, price discrimination, 365
time series data, 262
    defined, 548
The Times, 357
Tirole, J., 351, 412, 445, 498
Tobin's q, defined, 548
total cost curve, 137, 173, 348
total costs
    Baumol model, 137
    economies of scale, 102, 103
    economies of scope, 113
    and efficiency, 16–19
    labour market, 216, 220, 242, 243
    product differentiation, 449
    profit equation, 6
    profit-maximization, 364
    sales maximization, 138
    see also average total costs; marginal costs; short-run average total cost curve

total factor productivity, 487
  defined, 549
Total Oil Company, 86
Total Quality Management (TQM), 47
total revenue, 168–9, 241–3
  analytics of monopoly, 318
  Baumol model, 137
  bundling, 389
  defined, 22
  and efficiency, 21–3
  price discrimination, 371, 377
  profit equation, 6
  profit-maximization, 364
  quantity-setting models, 289, 322
tournament model, 494
  defined, 549
Towers, John, 199
Toyota, 45, 91, 224
TQM (Total Quality Management), 47
trade barriers, 46, 87, 93, 306, 308, 502
trade policies, 10, 271
trade unions, 214, 218, 221–2
trademarks, 467, 497
  defined, 549
transaction costs, 6, 32, 36–9
  adverse selection, 38, 75, 87
  asset specificity, 78
  asymmetric information, 49, 57, 87
  bounded rationality, 38, 57, 60, 74, 75, 78
  Coasian perspective, 36, 38, 47, 55, 60, 64
  collaborative ventures, 128, 131
  complete contracts, 74, 77
  of contract agreements, 49
  cost-minimization, 83, 91
  defined, 549
  dominant firm markets, 328
  efficiency wages, 231
  employment contracts, 223
  governance approach, 32, 47–50, 100
  imperfect information, 87
  information acquisition, 459
  innovation, 503
  intermediate products, 74, 76
  monitoring systems, 423, 426
  moral hazard, 38, 87
  multi-product firms, 114, 120, 130
  neo-classical paradigm, 114
  opportunistic behaviour, 38, 74, 75–7, 78
  partnership alliances, 90
  price discrimination, 366, 371, 376
  of resale, 366
  trust normal form game, 91
  unitary (U) form of organization, 181, 182
  vertical integration, 74–8, 76, 77, 79–80, 82, 93

vertical relationships, 414, 415
vertical restraints, 420, 423, 426, 432, 433
transformation curve, defined, 549
transnational corporations, 10, 181
transport costs, 109–10, 111, 112, 130, 366, 367, 384–7
transport developments, 44
Treaty of Rome, 252, 308, 309
  Article 82, 25, 27–8, 83, 253, 311, 326, 334, 347, 392, 393
  defined, 549
  see also Article 81
trigger strategy, 337, 337
  defined, 549
trust, 45, 432, 504
  clusters, 280
  competency approach, 189, 235–6
  consumer's level of, 443, 450
  credence goods, 422
  game theory, 90–1, 90, 235, 236
  horizontal boundaries, 128
  importance of, 77, 235–6, 238
  partnership alliances, 89–90, 90
  pricing quality, 407, 410
  Prisoners' Dilemma, 14–15
  stakeholder capitalism, 197, 199
  value of, 223
Tucker, Albert, 14
Turner, Donald, 355, 356
two-part tariffs
  defined, 549
  innovations, 489
  price discrimination, 371–2, 375–6, 375, 393
  vertical relationships, 415–17
  vertical restraints, 71, 419, 424, 427
tying, 421, 426, 429–30
  defined, 549

U

uncertainty, 13, 57
  asymmetric information, 36
  diversification, 124–6
  governance approach, 59–60
  horizontal boundaries, 124–5
  incomplete information, 36
  influence on firms, 47, 58
  and innovation, 23, 265, 492
  key characteristic of business life, 49
  oligopolies, 298–302
  organizational architecture, 58
  transaction costs, 60
  use of advertising, 138
  vertical integration, 65, 69–74, 75–6, 78
  volatile markets, 9
  see also game theory; regulatory uncertainty
unemployment, 191, 214, 230
Unilever, 123, 160, 170, 252, 264
Unipart, 196

Unison, 218
unit elasticity, defined, 549
unit production costs, 252
  agglomeration, 111–12
  asset specificity, 78
  Austrian school, 272
  bundling, 388
  Chamberlin's model, 404, 432
  constrained optimization, 33, 34, 60
  defined, 549
  dominant firm markets, 327, 328–9, 337, 340, 344, 345–6, 348–9, 355
  economies of scope, 112
  and efficiency, 16–19, 163
  Five Forces Model, 270, 271, 272
  horizontal boundaries, 100, 101–8, 110–12, 124–5, 127
  impact of learning on, 104–8
  impact of price setting, 22
  incentives to innovation, 488
  mergers, 163
  minimization of, 3, 33–4, 100, 172–3, 172
  neo-classical paradigm, 100
  oligopolies, 291–2
  predatory pricing, 348–9, 355
  price discrimination, 374, 375, 384
  pricing quality, 408, 411
  process innovation, 265
  and quality, 422, 432, 464, 466
  Sweezy's model, 299
  vertical integration, 74, 80–1
  vertical restraints, 429
  see also average production costs; economies of scale; marginal production costs; net production costs (NPC)
unitary (U) form of organization, 181–2, 181, 200
  defined, 549
United Kingdom
  car price differentials, 367, 368, 369
  industrial clusters, 276, 277
  labour productivity, 173, 176–7
  motor vehicle sector, 199
  power of shareholders, 196
United Nations, 10, 255, 256
United States
  antitrust law, 312
  corporate core competencies, 54, 55
  entrepreneurship, 136
  industry classification, 255
  labour productivity, 173, 176
  limited liability companies, 170
  merger boom, 161
  power of shareholders, 196
  price discrimination, 391, 392
  vertical restraints, 419, 429
  see also Fordism
United States Steel (USS), 343

unrelated diversification, 116–21, 124, 127, 131
  defined, 549
upstream
  clusters, 277
  defined, 550
  dominant firms, 346
  Five Forces Model, 271
  strategic behaviour, 250
  technological advances, 271
  vertical integration, 65, 66, 67, 68, 70, 71, 76, 82, 84, 346, 384
  vertical relationships, 413, 414–17, 433
  vertical restraints, 419, 420–7, 429–30, 433
utility
  advertising, 463, 465, 466
  consumers, 409, 447, 450, 451, 466
  defined, 550
  entrepreneurs, 170
  management, 186, 187, 200
  principal-agent theory, 193–4
  supply of labour, 211, 212, 223, 227, 230, 236, 245
  see also marginal utility
utility functions, 185, 186, 188, 207–8
  defined, 550
utility-maximization, 185, 200
  consumer decision-making, 171, 448
  management, 175, 186, 190, 204, 205
  neo-classical paradigm, 32–5, 60, 175
  supply of labour, 211

V

value
  capturing of, 21–3, 28–9, 274
  maximization of, 5–6
value added, 53, 64, 88, 209, 218, 424, 481, 483
  defined, 550
value creation, 4, 16–19, 21, 47
  competency approach, 52–3, 124–5
  knowledge-based resources, 52–3
value net concept, 278–9, 278, 280
  defined, 550
value (supply) chains, 66, 67, 263, 413, 414, 433
  defined, 547
  Five Forces Model, 271, 483
  vertical integration, 64–5, 66–8, 74, 83, 84–5, 86
variable costs, 71, 102, 490
  defined, 550
  dominant firms, 349
  economies of scope, 113
  hold up, 79
  sales-maximization model, 138

vertical relationships, 414
see also average variable costs
variable factors, defined, 550
variables, 3, 142
  business environment as, 193
  defined, 550
  dominant firms, 345
  firm's internal organization, 39
  investment as, 305
  knowledge accumulation as, 108
  new knowledge as, 482
  quality as, 406
  quantity as, 294
Varian, H., 372, 384
vCJD, 412–13
VCRs (video cassette recorders), 487
Veblen goods, 450–1, *451*, 466
  defined, 550
Veblen, Thorstein, 450–1
ventures, 151–2
  defined, 550
Vernon, J., 471
versioning, 384, *384*
  defined, 550
vertical agreements, 399, 431
  defined, 550
vertical boundary, 64–5, 68, *68*
  defined, 550
vertical differentiation, 445–6,
    450–1, 461, 472, 495
  defined, 551
vertical expansion, 65, 68–9, 84
vertical formation, 65
vertical integration, 64–86, 93–4,
    399, 414, 503
  agency costs, 79–80, 82, 86, 87,
    93
  alternatives to, 86–92, *89*
  asset specificity, 79–82, *81*, 87–8
  asymmetric information, 65,
    71–4, 84, 87
  bounded rationality, 74, 75, 78,
    84
  capabilities, 85, 90, 93
  capital costs, 68–9, 70, 74
  co-operation, 65, 77, 84, 88
  competency approach, 65–6,
    83–5
  and costs, 68–9, *69*
  defined, 66, 550
  deterrence strategies, 345, 346
  dominant firms, 354
  Dutch agrifood sector, 264
  Five Forces Model, 271
  governance approach, 65, 79–82,
    84, 85, 86, 87
  imperfect information, 65, 71–4,
    87
  intermediate products, 65–7,
    71–2, 80–2, 86, 93

learning, 80, 81, 84, 85
marginal costs, 70, 71
monitoring costs, 79, 82, 86
opportunistic behaviour, 74,
    75–7, 78
predation strategies, 354
private information, 70–4, 89
property rights, 65, 66, 72, 82
structure-conduct-performance
    (SCP) paradigm, 254
transaction costs, 74–8, *76*, 77,
    79–80, 82, 93
and uncertainty, 65, 69–74,
    75–6, 78
unit production costs, 74, 80–1
vertical mergers, 65, 84, 86
  defined, 550
  Vivendi, 85–6
vertical relationships, 86–92, *89*,
    271, 439–41
  adverse selection, 423, 424
  complete contracts, 72, 74, 77,
    414
  contract to supply game, *72*
  contractual relationships,
    413–14, 415, 420, 421
  defined, 551
  game theory, 415–16, *416*
  incomplete contracts, 72, 77
  intermediate products, 400, 413,
    414, 415, 416, 417, 433
  marginal costs, 414, 415, 416,
    417
  pricing, 413–18, *414*, *416*, 417,
    418
vertical restraints, 82, 354, 399–400,
    414, 419–27
  anti-competitive practices, 399,
    400, 429, 430, 431, 433
  asymmetric information, 420,
    433
  barriers to entry, 425, 429, 431,
    433
  collusion, 429, 431, 433
  competition authorities, 419,
    429, 430–2, 433
  competition policy, 429–32
  defined, 551
  European Commission, 399, 419,
    429, 430–2, 433
  imperfect competition, 427, 433
  intermediate products, 346–7,
    419, 420, 422, 426, 433
  transaction costs, 420, 423, 426,
    432, 433
  two-part tariffs, 71, 419, 424,
    427
  see also aftermarkets
vertical scale, defined, 551
Vezzoso, S., 432

VHS (Video Home System), 487
Vickers, J., 427
Victor Corporation of Japan (JVC),
    487
video cassette recorders (VCRs), 487
Video Home System (VHS), 487
Viner, J., 102
Virgin, 5
Virgin Atlantic, 8–9
Virgin brand, 7–9
Virgin Cola, 9
Virgin Direct Financial Services, 9
Virgin Music Group, 9
Virgin Records, 8
Virgin trains, 9
virtual boundaries, 127–9, *129*, 131
virtual integration, Dell, 92–3
Vision Express, 472
vitamin supplements, 306
Vivendi, 85–6
Vodafone, 20
volatile markets, 9
Volkswagen, 20, 139
voluntary restraint agreements
    (VRA), 309
  defined, 551
von Neumann, John, 9, 13
Vroom, V., 232

W

wage bargaining, 220–1, 222, 244–5
wage rates
  demand for labour, 215–17, *216*,
    237
  imperfect markets, 218–21, *219*
  national minimum, 217–18, 220
  supply of labour, 211–14, *213*,
    214, 237
wages *see* efficiency wages; going
    wage; money wage; real wage
Wal-Mart, 272, 405
Warburtons, 195
warranties, 412
washing powder market, 252
waste, avoidance of, 3, 7, 19, 35
Waterman, R., 123
Watson, James, 152
wealth effects, 142, 451
  defined, 551
The Wealth of Nations (Smith), 482
web-site marketing, 457–8
Weinstock, Lord, 126
welfare system, 10
welfare-based capitalism, 20
Wernerfelt, B., 123
Williamson, J., 10
Williamson, Oliver, 57
  asset specificity, 78, 80

discretionary spending, 204
expense preference model, 186,
    187, 200
  governance approach, 47, 49, 65
  M-form (multi-divisional)
    organization, 182
  minimum profit constraint, 155
  transaction costs, 503
  unitary (U) form of organization,
    181
Willig, R., 11, 112, 356
Wilson, T., 453, 470
wine industry, 452
winner's curse, defined, 551
Winter, R., 430
Winter, S.
  cycles of innovation, 485
  entrepreneurial bias, 152
  evolutionary approach, 54, 146,
    159, 274, 432, 483
  innovation, 484
  locus of creation, 53
  organizational architecture, 123
  routines and processes, 53, 123,
    504
  steady-state models, 159
wireless information systems,
    129–30
Woolwich, 163
workforce *see* employees
working capital, defined, 551
World Economic Forum, 279
World Health Organization (WHO),
    413
World Trade Organization (WTO), 5,
    10

X

X-inefficiency, 173–4, *173*, 175, 185,
    200
  contestable markets, 268
  defined, 551
  dominant firm markets, 335, 345
  tapered integration, 86
xerography, 499

Y

Yahoo, 391
Yellen, J., 387, 389

Z

Zara, 73
Zeckhauser, R., 471, 472
Zeithaml, V., 407
Zeneca, 160
zero growth, 139, 157
zero-sum game, 21, 141, 220, 493
  defined, 551